Methods for Effective Teaching

Sixth Edition

Methods for Effective Teaching

MEETING THE NEEDS OF ALL STUDENTS

Paul R. Burden
Kansas State University

David M. Byrd
University of Rhode Island

PEARSON

Boston • Columbus • Indianapolis • New York • San Francisco • Upper Saddle River
Amsterdam • Cape Town • Dubai • London • Madrid • Milan • Munich • Paris • Montreal • Toronto
Delhi • Mexico City • São Paulo • Sydney • Hong Kong • Seoul • Singapore • Taipei • Tokyo

Vice President/Editorial Director: Jeffery W. Johnston
Senior Acquisitions Editor: Kelly Villella Canton
Editorial Assistant: Annalea Manalili
Executive Marketing Manager: Darcy Betts
Production Editor: Paula Carroll
Editorial Production Service: Electronic Publishing Services Inc.
Manufacturing Buyer: Megan Cochran
Electronic Composition: Jouve
Interior Design: Electronic Publishing Services Inc.
Photo Researcher: Annie Fuller
Cover Designer: Diane Lorenzo

Credits and acknowledgments borrowed from other sources and reproduced, with permission, in this textbook appear on the appropriate page within text or below.

pp. xx–xxi, 5, 29, 59, 97 , 129, 158, 174, 195, 229, 257, 287, 315, 339: Council of Chief State School Officers. (2011, April). *Interstate Teacher Assessment and Support Consortium (InTASC) Model Core Teaching Standards: A resource for state dialogue.* Washington, DC: Author. The InTASC Model Core Teaching Standards were developed by the Council of Chief State School Officers and member states. Copies may be downloaded from the council's website at www.ccsso.org/intasc.

Many of the designations by manufacturers and sellers to distinguish their products are claimed as trademarks. Where those designations appear in this book, and the publisher was aware of a trademark claim, the designations have been printed in initial caps or all caps.

Library of Congress Cataloging in Publication Data

Burden, Paul R.
  Methods for effective teaching : meeting the needs of all students / Paul R. Burden, David M. Byrd.—6th ed.
    p.   cm.
  Includes bibliographical references and index.
  ISBN-13: 978-0-13-269816-0 (pbk.)
  ISBN-10: 0-13-269816-1 (pbk.)
1. Teaching.   2. Effective teaching.   I. Byrd, David M.   II. Title.
  LB1025.3.B87   2013
  371.102—dc23
                                                                    2011036987

10   9   8   7   6   5   4   3   2   1

ISBN-10: 0-13-269816-1
ISBN-13: 978-0-13-269816-0

Paul R. Burden is an assistant dean and professor in the College of Education at Kansas State University, Manhattan, where he has supervised student teachers and taught courses on teaching methods, classroom management and discipline, foundations of education, and instructional leadership. Previously, he was a middle-level science teacher in Buffalo, New York, and later earned his doctoral degree at Ohio State University. He has received the College of Education's Outstanding Undergraduate Teaching Award at Kansas State University and the Distinguished Service award from the National Staff Development Council.

His publications include *Classroom Management: Creating a Successful K–12 Learning Community* (2013, John Wiley & Sons), *Countdown to the First Day of School* (2006, National Education Association), *Powerful Classroom Management Strategies: Motivating Students to Learn* (2000, Corwin Press), as well as *Establishing Career Ladders in Teaching* (1987, Charles C Thomas). He served for 11 years as the editor of the *Journal of Staff Development*, a quarterly journal sponsored by the National Staff Development Council, and he has presented over 70 papers at regional and national educational conferences in addition to authoring 15 articles and four book chapters.

Married with three children, Dr. Burden enjoys traveling with his family and working on genealogy. He can be contacted at Kansas State University, 18 Bluemont Hall, Manhattan, Kansas 66506; (785) 532-5595; burden@ksu.edu.

David M. Byrd is director of the School of Education at the University of Rhode Island. He is a graduate of the doctoral program in teacher education at Syracuse University. Prior to coming to Rhode Island, he was an associate professor at Southern Illinois University. He has a long-term professional and research interest in programs for beginning teachers and teacher professional development.

Dr. Byrd has authored and co-authored over 30 articles, books, and chapters. He has served as co-editor of the Association of Teacher Educators' *Teacher Education Yearbook* series (2000–2006). Yearbook titles that he edited include *Preparing Tomorrow's Teachers: The Field Experience, Research on the Education of Our Nation's Teachers, Research on Career Long Teacher Education, Research on Professional Development Schools,* and *Research on Effective Models for Teacher Education.* He has served as chairperson of the Research Committee for the Association of Teacher Educators and on the journal board for *Action in Teacher Education.* Dr. Byrd can be contacted at the University of Rhode Island, 706 Chafee Hall, Kingston, Rhode Island 02881; (401) 874-5484; dbyrd@uri.edu.

BRIEF CONTENTS

CONTENTS

PART III SELECTING INSTRUCTIONAL STRATEGIES

6 STUDENT-CENTERED INSTRUCTIONAL STRATEGIES 145

7 STRATEGIES THAT PROMOTE UNDERSTANDING, THINKING, AND ENGAGEMENT 169

PART IV MANAGING INSTRUCTION AND THE CLASSROOM

8 MANAGING LESSON DELIVERY 193

12 GRADING SYSTEMS, MARKING, AND REPORTING 311

PART VI WORKING WITH OTHERS

13 COLLABORATING WITH COLLEAGUES AND FAMILIES 333

The sixth edition of *Methods for Effective Teaching* provides research-based coverage of general teaching methods while emphasizing contemporary topics such as culturally responsive teaching, differentiated instruction, and data-driven decision making. The numerous features, tables, and lists of recommendations ensure that the text is reader friendly and practically oriented. Its unique content includes strategies to promote student understanding, differentiate instruction, manage lesson delivery, apply motivational techniques for instruction and assessment, and work with colleagues and parents. In addition, thorough coverage of classroom management and discipline is provided, along with ways to create a positive learning environment.

 ## Intended Audience

This book is designed primarily as the core textbook for courses in K–12 general teaching methods, secondary/middle teaching methods, or elementary school teaching methods. The content is applicable for teachers at all levels—elementary, middle level, and high school. Additionally, it may be used as a supplementary book for other teaching methods courses. This book is also appropriate for courses and staff development programs for in-service teachers and as a handbook for teacher reference due to its comprehensive coverage of current classroom issues and practical teaching applications.

 ## New to This Edition

There are a number of significant changes in this sixth edition:

- Moved the information on diverse learners earlier in the book (in Chapter 2).
- Restructured and updated Chapter 2, Knowing Your Students.
- Restructured and updated Chapter 3, Fundamentals of Planning.
- Completed a major revision of Chapter 4, Lesson and Unit Planning.
- Restructured Chapter 5, Teacher-Centered Strategies, with an expanded description of explicit instruction.
- Restructured the sections on discipline interventions and the three-step response plan (in Chapter 10).
- New sections in several chapters:
  - Developmental differences by age (in Chapter 2)
  - Sexual orientation (in Chapter 2)
  - Anti-bias educational environment (in Chapter 2)
  - Getting to know your students (in Chapter 2)
  - Contextual factors to guide planning (in Chapter 2)
  - Curriculum considerations in planning (in Chapter 3)
  - Common core curriculum (in Chapter 3)
  - 21st Century Skills (in Chapter 3)
  - Planning for the response to intervention (RTI) (in Chapter 3)
  - A continuum of instructional approaches (in Chapter 5)
  - The gradual release of responsibility (in Chapter 5)

- Problem-based strategies (in Chapter 6)
- Helping students become better thinkers (in Chapter 7)
- Strategies that promote student engagement (in Chapter 7)
- Bullying (in Chapter 10)
- Data-driven decision making (in Chapter 11)
- Adapting assessments for students with special needs (in Chapter 11)
- Standardized achievement tests (in Chapter 11)
- Working collaboratively with colleagues (in Chapter 13)
- Collaboration skills (in Chapter 13)

- Updated the section on the teacher as a reflective decision maker (in Chapter 1).
- Updated the section on struggling learners (in Chapter 2).
- Updated the section on brain-compatible learning (in Chapter 2).
- Included 35 new teacher statements in the Voices from the Classroom feature, many of them from urban districts, with a balance of elementary and middle/high school teachers.
- Added 15 more What Would You Decide? features throughout the book to engage the reader in decision making about the chapter content.
- Provided a list of technology resources at the end of each chapter.
- Revised the Sample Standards tables in each chapter reflecting the new InTASC standards.
- Changed the titles of six chapters to reflect the new and updated content

 # Special Features

To maintain the reader's interest and to accommodate different learning styles and instructional settings, *Methods for Effective Teaching* contains a variety of pedagogical features.

- **Standards Tables.** Four tables of professional standards can be found on pages xx–xxiv. These tables feature references to the chapters in this book that address each part of the standards.
- **Objectives.** Each chapter begins with a list of objectives that identify expected reader outcomes.
- **Chapter Outline.** Each chapter begins with a graphic organizer displaying chapter headings and subheadings to provide an advance organizer for the reader.
- **Voices from the Classroom.** These features are included in each chapter to provide descriptions of ways that actual elementary, middle school, and high school teachers deal with particular topics addressed in the chapter. These teachers come from all parts of the country and different community sizes. There are over 50 Voices from the Classroom features, evenly balanced among elementary and middle/high school levels, including many from urban districts.
- **Sample Standards.** Each chapter has a Sample Standards feature that lists representative performances, essential knowledge, and critical dispositions from InTASC standards that relate to the chapter in an effort to direct the reader's attention to important content and characteristics.
- **Classroom Case Studies.** Each chapter includes a case study describing a situation that a teacher may need to confront. Two or three questions following each case study require the reader to reflect on and apply chapter concepts.

- **What Would You Decide?** Several features are placed in each chapter to consider the application of the content. Each feature includes several sentences describing a classroom situation related to an issue in the chapter followed by a few questions asking the reader to make decisions about the application of the concepts.

- **Key Terms.** A list of key terms at the end of each chapter draws the reader's attention to significant terms. Each term is highlighted in the text.

- **Major Concepts.** At the end of each chapter, a list of major concepts serves as a summary of the significant chapter ideas.

- **Discussion/Reflective Questions.** Questions at the end of each chapter promote discussion and reflection in a classroom or seminar in which a number of people are considering the chapter's content.

- **Suggested Activities.** These activities are listed at the end of each chapter both for clinical (on-campus) settings and for field (school-based) settings to enable the reader to investigate and apply issues addressed.

- **Further Reading.** An annotated list of recommended readings at the end of each chapter suggests readings for further enrichment.

- **Technology Resources.** An annotated list of useful technology resources at the end of each chapter suggests web links for further enrichment.

- **References.** References cited in the chapters to document the research base of the content are all listed at the end of the book.

 # Relating This Book to Standards

A variety of professional standards are listed, correlated to the book, and referenced throughout. Standards are used to guide the development of new teachers, help in-service teachers improve their performance, and assess both teacher preparation and teacher performance. Many teacher education programs are designed around the Interstate New Teacher Assessment and Support Consortium (InTASC) standards. Those standards were updated in 2011, so states using those standards will likely adjust their standards accordingly. Many states require a passing score on the Principles of Learning and Teaching test (Praxis II) before granting a teaching license. The Praxis III standards (which are consistent with Danielson's Framework for Teaching domains) and the National Board for Professional Teaching Standards (NBPTS) are used to assess and improve the teaching of in-service teachers. A brief description of these standards is provided here, and tables of these standards can be found on pages xx–xxiv.

InTASC Standards

The Interstate New Teacher Assessment and Support Consortium (INTASC) was formed as a consortium of state education agencies and national educational organizations dedicated to the reform of the preparation, licensing, and ongoing professional development of teachers. Created in 1987, INTASC's primary constituency is state education agencies responsible for teacher licensing, program approval, and professional development. Its work is guided by one basic premise: *An effective teacher must be able to integrate content knowledge with the specific strengths and needs of students to ensure that all students learn and perform at high levels.* With the 2011 updating of the standards, they removed the word *new* from their title and made a lowercase *n* in the acronym (now it is InTASC). More information can be found at the organization's website: http://www.ccsso.org/projects/Interstate_New_Teacher_Assessment_and_Support_Consortium.

Praxis Series

The Praxis Series is a set of tests developed and disseminated by the Educational Testing Service (ETS) for assessing skills and knowledge of each stage of a beginning teacher's career, from entry into teacher education to actual classroom performance. More information about the Praxis Series can be found at http://ets.org/praxis/index.html.

There are three parts of the Praxis Series:

■ **Praxis I: Pre-Professional Skills Tests (PPST).** These academic skills tests are designed to be taken early in a student's college career to measure reading, writing, and mathematics skills.

■ **Praxis II: Subject Assessments.** There are several assessments available in the Praxis II series, and they measure a teacher candidate's knowledge of the subjects he or she will teach, as well as general and subject-specific pedagogical skills and knowledge. One of these assessments is the Principles of Learning and Teaching (PLT) test, which many states require teachers to pass for their licensure.

■ **Praxis III: Classroom Performance Assessments.** These assessments are conducted for beginning teachers in classroom settings. Assessment of teaching practice is through direct observation of classroom practice, a review of documentation prepared by the teacher, and semistructured interviews. The framework for knowledge and skills for these assessments consists of 19 assessment criteria organized within four categories: planning and preparation, the classroom environment, instruction, and professional responsibilities. Charlotte Danielson's (2007) *Enhancing Professional Practice: A Framework for Teaching* is based on the categories of the Praxis III Classroom Performance Assessments.

Methods for Effective Teaching is not intended to address the preprofessional skills of reading, writing, and mathematics in Praxis I. However, it is designed to address the Praxis II test on Principles of Learning and Teaching and the Praxis III classroom performance criteria areas.

NBPTS

The National Board for Professional Teaching Standards (NBPTS) has established standards for highly accomplished teaching, based on five core propositions. NBPTS has a national voluntary system of certifying teachers who meet the standards in their teaching performance. Teachers meeting all of the standards are certified National Board Certified Teachers. More information about the NBPTS standards can be found on their website: http://www.nbpts.org.

 # Supplements

Instructor's Manual/Test Bank and PowerPoint Slides

An instructor's manual to accompany this textbook has been developed by the authors to guide teacher educators on using this book for their courses. This manual includes multiple-choice, true–false, short-answer, and essay/discussion questions for each chapter. It also includes a sample course syllabus that is aligned to this book and teaching suggestions to introduce content for each major section of each chapter. Additionally, about 20 PowerPoint slides are provided for each chapter.

The instructor's manual/test bank may be downloaded in PDF from the Instructor Resource Center at the Pearson Higher Education website (http://www.pearsonhighered.com). Your local Pearson sales representative can help you set up a password for the Instructor Resource Center.

MyEducationLab™

Proven to **engage students**, provide **trusted content**, and **improve results**, Pearson MyLabs have helped over 8 million registered students reach true understanding in their courses. **MyEducationLab** engages students with real-life teaching situations through dynamic videos, case studies and student artifacts. Student progress is assessed, and a personalized study plan is created based on the student's unique results. Automatic grading and reporting keeps educators informed to quickly address gaps and improve student performance. All of the activities and exercises in MyEducationLab are built around essential learning outcomes for teachers and are mapped to professional teaching standards.

In *Preparing Teachers for a Changing World*, Linda Darling-Hammond and her colleagues point out that grounding teacher education in real classrooms—among real teachers and students and among actual examples of students' and teachers' work—is an important, and perhaps even an essential, part of training teachers for the complexities of teaching in today's classrooms.

In the MyEducationLab for this course you will find the following features and resources.

Study Plan Specific to Your Text

MyEducationLab gives students the opportunity to test themselves on key concepts and skills, track their own progress through the course, and access personalized Study Plan activities.

The customized Study Plan—with enriching activities—is generated based on students' results of a pretest. Study Plans tag incorrect questions from the pretest to the appropriate textbook learning outcome, helping students focus on the topics they need help with. Personalized Study Plan activities may include eBook reading assignments, and review, practice and enrichment activities.

After students complete the enrichment activities, they take a posttest to see the concepts they've mastered or the areas where they may need extra help.

MyEducationLab then reports the Study Plan results to the instructor. Based on these reports, the instructor can adapt course material to suit the needs of individual students or the entire class.

Connection to National Standards

Now it is easier than ever to see how coursework is connected to national standards. Each topic, activity and exercise on MyEducationLab lists intended learning outcomes connected to the InTASC Model Core Teaching Standards.

Assignments and Activities

Designed to enhance your understanding of concepts covered in class, these assignable exercises show concepts in action (through videos, cases, and/or student and teacher artifacts). They help you deepen content knowledge and synthesize and apply concepts and strategies you read about in the book. (Correct answers for these assignments are available to the instructor only.)

Building Teaching Skills and Dispositions

These unique learning units help users practice and strengthen skills that are essential to effective teaching. After presenting the steps involved in a core teaching process, you are given an opportunity to practice applying this skill via videos, student and teacher artifacts, and/or case studies of authentic classrooms. Providing multiple opportunities to practice a single teaching concept, each activity encourages a deeper understanding and application of concepts, as well as the use of critical thinking skills. After practice, students take a quiz that is reported to the instructor gradebook.

Course Resources

The Course Resources section of MyEducationLab is designed to help you put together an effective lesson plan, prepare for and begin your career, navigate your first year of teaching, and understand key educational standards, policies, and laws.

It includes the following:

- The **Lesson Plan Builder** is an effective and easy-to-use tool that you can use to create, update, and share quality lesson plans. The software also makes it easy to integrate state content standards into any lesson plan.

- The **Preparing a Portfolio** module provides guidelines for creating a high-quality teaching portfolio.

- **Beginning Your Career** offers tips, advice, and other valuable information on:

  - *Resume Writing and Interviewing:* Includes expert advice on how to write impressive resumes and prepare for job interviews.

  - *Your First Year of Teaching:* Provides practical tips to set up a first classroom, manage student behavior, and more easily organize for instruction and assessment.

  - *Law and Public Policies:* Details specific directives and requirements you need to understand under the No Child Left Behind Act and the Individuals with Disabilities Education Improvement Act of 2004.

Certification and Licensure

The Certification and Licensure section is designed to help you pass your licensure exam by giving you access to state test requirements, overviews of what tests cover, and sample test items.

The Certification and Licensure section includes the following:

- **State Certification Test Requirements:** Here, you can click on a state and will then be taken to a list of state certification tests.

- **Licensure Exams:** You can click on the exams you need to take to find:

  - Basic information about each test

  - Descriptions of what is covered on each test

  - Sample test questions with explanations of correct answers

- **National Evaluation Series™** by Pearson: Here, students can see the tests in the NES, learn what is covered on each exam, and access sample test items with descriptions and rationales of correct answers. You can also purchase interactive online tutorials developed by Pearson Evaluation Systems and the Pearson Teacher Education and Development group.

- **ETS Online Praxis Tutorials:** Here you can purchase interactive online tutorials developed by ETS and by the Pearson Teacher Education and Development group. Tutorials are available for the Praxis I exams and for select Praxis II exams.

Visit www.myeducationlab.com for a demonstration of this exciting new online teaching resource.

 # Acknowledgments

Many people provided support and guidance as we prepared this book. A very special acknowledgment goes to our spouses: Jennie Burden and Mary Byrd. Their support kept our spirits up when deadlines were pressing, and their understanding during our absences while preparing the content enabled us to complete the project.

We also appreciate the help from the staff at Pearson who provided editorial guidance, facilitated the preparation of the manuscript, and coordinated the production.

A number of classroom teachers provided descriptions of their professional practice, which are included in the Voices from the Classroom features. Their experiences help illustrate the issues and bring life to the content.

At Kansas State University, Sandi Faulconer provided valuable assistance in preparing several tables and the permissions log. Tom Vontz, Diane DeNoon, and Cyndi Danner-Kuhn shared materials and provided useful suggestions to guide the revision. Finally, we would like to extend our gratitude to the following reviewers who provided constructive feedback for this edition: Lisa A. Hazlett, The University of South Dakota; John Kambutu, University of Wyoming/Casper College Center; Alan Markowitz, The College of St. Elizabeth; Kimberly Rombach, State University of New York at Cortland; Frances van Tassell, University of North Texas.

Paul R. Burden
David M. Byrd

InTASC Model Core Teaching Standards

The following table indicates how the 2011 Interstate Teacher Assessment and Support Consortium (InTASC) model core teaching standards are addressed in this book.

STANDARDS	CHAPTER COVERAGE
THE LEARNER AND LEARNING	
1. Learner Development Understands how learners grow and develop, recognizing that patterns of learning and development vary individually within and across the cognitive, linguistic, social, emotional, and physical areas, and designs and implements developmentally appropriate and challenging learning experiences.	2–7
2. Learning Differences Uses understanding of individual differences and diverse cultures and communities to ensure inclusive learning environments that enable each learner to meet high standards.	2–7
3. Learning Environments Works with others to create environments that support individual and collaborative learning, and that encourage positive social interaction, active engagement in learning, and self-motivation.	7–10
CONTENT KNOWLEDGE	
4. Content Knowledge Understands the central concepts, tools of inquiry, and structures of the discipline(s) he or she teaches and creates learning experiences that make these aspects of the discipline accessible and meaningful for learners to ensure mastery of the content.	3
5. Application of Content Understands how to connect concepts and use differing perspectives to engage learners in critical thinking, creativity, and collaborative problem solving related to authentic local and global issues.	4–7
INSTRUCTIONAL PRACTICE	
6. Assessment Understands and uses multiple methods of assessment to engage learners in their own growth, to monitor learner progress, and to guide the teacher's and learner's decision making.	2, 11–12
7. Planning for Instruction Plans instruction that supports every student in meeting rigorous learning goals by drawing on knowledge of content areas, curriculum, cross-disciplinary skills, and pedagogy, as well as knowledge of learners and the community context.	3–7
8. Instructional Strategies Understands and uses a variety of instructional strategies to encourage learners to develop deep understanding of content areas and their connections, and to build skills to apply knowledge in meaningful ways.	5–7

STANDARDS	CHAPTER COVERAGE
THE LEARNER AND LEARNING	
PROFESSIONAL RESPONSIBILITY	
9. **Professional Learning and Ethical Practice** Engages in ongoing professional learning and uses evidence to continually evaluate his/her practice, particularly the effects of his/her choices and actions on others (Learners, Families, Other Professionals, And The Community), and adapts practice to meet the needs of each learner.	1
10. **Leadership and Collaboration** Seeks appropriate leadership roles and opportunities to take responsibility for student learning, to collaborate with learners, families, colleagues, other school professionals, and community members to ensure learner growth, and to advance the profession.	13

Source: Council of Chief State School Officers. (2011, April). *Interstate Teacher Assessment and Support Consortium (InTASC) Model Core Teaching Standards: A resource for state dialogue.* Washington, DC: Author. The InTASC Model Core Teaching Standards were developed by the Council of Chief State School Officers and member states. Copies may be downloaded from the council's website at www.ccsso.org/intasc.

Praxis II:
Standards for Principles of Learning and Teaching

The following table indicates how the Praxis II standards for the Principles of Learning and Teaching are addressed in this book.

STANDARDS	CHAPTER COVERAGE
1. **Students as Learners**	
Student development and the learning process	2, 3
Students as diverse learners	2
Student motivation and the learning environment	2, 8–10
2. **Instruction and Assessment**	
Instructional strategies	2, 5–7
Planning instruction	3–4
Assessment strategies	11–12
3. **Communication Techniques**	
Basic, effective verbal and nonverbal communication techniques	2, 8-9
Effect of cultural and gender differences on communications in the classroom	2, 7
Types of communications and interactions that can stimulate discussion in different ways for particular purposes	5–7
4. **Profession and Community**	
The reflective practitioner	1
The larger community	13

Source: Reprinted by permission of Educational Testing Service, the copyright owner. Permission to reprint the Praxis II materials does not constitute review or endorsement by Educational Testing Service of this publication as a whole or of any other testing information it may contain.

Framework for Teaching

The following table indicates how the domains of the framework are addressed in this book. This framework for teaching is based on the categories of the Praxis III Classroom Performance Assessments.

DOMAINS	CHAPTER COVERAGE
1. Planning and Preparation	
Demonstrating knowledge of content and pedagogy	**5–7**
Demonstrating knowledge of students	**2**
Selecting instructional goals	**4**
Demonstrating knowledge of resources	**3–4**
Designing coherent instruction	**3–4**
Designing student assessments	**11–12**
2. The Classroom Environment	
Creating with students	**9**
Establishing a culture for learning	**2, 9**
Managing classroom procedures	**9**
Managing student behavior	**10**
Organizing physical space	**9**
3. Instruction	
Communicating clearly and accurately	**8**
Using questioning and discussion techniques	**5**
Engaging students in learning	**2, 7**
Using assessments in instruction	**2, 11–12**
Demonstrating flexibility and responsiveness	**2, 5–7**
4. Professional Responsibilities	
Reflecting on teaching	**1**
Maintaining accurate records	**8–9, 12**
Communicating with families	**13**
Participating in a professional community	**13**
Growing and developing professionally	**1**
Showing professionalism	**1**

Source: From *Enhancing professional practice: A framework for teaching* (2nd ed.), by Charlotte Danielson, 2007. Alexandria, VA: Association for Supervision and Curriculum Development. Reprinted with permission.

NBPTS Core Propositions

The following table indicates how the National Board for Professional Teaching Standards (NBPTS) core propositions are addressed in this book.

PROPOSITIONS	CHAPTER COVERAGE
1. Teachers are committed to students and their learning.	2, 5–7
■ Teachers are dedicated to making knowledge accessible to all students. They believe all students can learn.	
■ Teachers treat students equitably. They recognize the individual differences that distinguish their students from one another and they take account for these differences in their practice.	
■ Teachers understand how students develop and learn.	
■ Teachers respect the cultural and family differences students bring to their classroom.	
■ Teachers are concerned with their students' self-concept, their motivation, and the effects of learning on peer relationships.	
■ Teachers are also concerned with the development of character and civic responsibility.	
2. Teachers know the subjects they teach and how to teach those subjects to students.	2–7
■ Teachers have mastery over the subject(s) they teach. They have a deep understanding of the history, structure, and real-world applications of the subject.	
■ Teachers have skill and experience in teaching it, and they are very familiar with the skills gaps and preconceptions students may bring to the subject.	
■ Teachers are able to use diverse instructional strategies to teach for understanding.	
3. Teachers are responsible for managing and monitoring student learning.	7–12
■ Teachers deliver effective instruction. They move fluently through a range of instructional techniques, keeping students motivated, engaged, and focused.	
■ Teachers know how to engage students to ensure a disciplined learning environment, and how to organize instruction to meet instructional goals.	
■ Teachers know how to assess the progress of individual students as well as the class as a whole.	
■ Teachers use multiple methods for measuring student growth and understanding, and they can clearly explain student performance to parents.	
4. Teachers think systematically about their practice and learn from experience.	1, 13
■ Teachers model what it means to be an educated person—they read, they question, they create, and they are willing to try new things.	
■ Teachers are familiar with learning theories and instructional strategies and stay abreast of current issues in American education.	
■ Teachers critically examine their practice on a regular basis to deepen knowledge, expand their repertoire of skills, and incorporate new findings into their practice.	

PROPOSITIONS	CHAPTER COVERAGE
5. Teachers are members of learning communities.	**1, 13**

- Teachers collaborate with others to improve student learning.
- Teachers are leaders and actively know how to seek and build partnerships with community groups and businesses.
- Teachers work with other professionals on instructional policy, curriculum development, and staff development.
- Teachers can evaluate school progress and the allocation of resources in order to meet state and local education objectives.
- Teachers know how to work collaboratively with parents to engage them productively in the work of the school.

Source: Reprinted with permission from the National Board for Professional Teaching Standards, *What Teachers Should Know and Be Able to Do,* http://www.nbpts.org. All rights reserved.

The Teacher as a Decision Maker

1

THIS CHAPTER PROVIDES INFORMATION THAT WILL HELP YOU TO

1. Describe the basic teaching functions and the key characteristics of effective teachers.

2. Recognize the professional teaching standards and understand the purposes they serve.

3. Formulate a plan to use reflection to enhance teacher decision making.

4. Describe ways that instruction of English language learners can be enhanced in all classrooms.

Your journey to become a teacher continues. You want to be an effective teacher, but what are the characteristics of effective teachers? What do they need to know and do? To a large extent, effective teaching involves making good decisions to help students learn.

Even before instruction takes place, teachers think about and make decisions concerning content, instructional strategies, the use of instructional materials and technology, delivery techniques, classroom management and discipline, assessment of student learning, and a host of other related issues. During instruction, teachers must implement these decisions as they interact with students in a dynamic way.

Decision making involves giving consideration to a matter, identifying the desired end result, determining the options to get to the end result, and then selecting the most suitable option to achieve the desired purpose. Teacher decisions about the issues just mentioned ultimately will influence student learning.

To examine teacher decision making and its relationship to teaching methods, the discussion in this chapter centers on four questions: What is effective teaching? What are the standards used to guide the professional development of teachers? How can a teacher be a reflective decision maker? How can instruction of English language learners (ELLs) be enhanced in all classrooms?

Effective Teaching

What are teachers' responsibilities, and what makes teachers effective in meeting these responsibilities? To answer these questions, it is useful to examine the basic teaching functions, essential teacher characteristics, and expectations for effectiveness.

DECISIONS ABOUT BASIC TEACHING FUNCTIONS

Teachers make countless decisions all day long in an effort to promote student learning. When you break the decisions down, they fall into three categories: planning, implementing, and assessing. Some decisions are made at the desk when preparing lesson or unit plans, designing an instructional activity, or grading papers. Other decisions are made on the spot during the dynamic interactions with students when delivering a lesson. Let's briefly examine these three basic teaching functions. Each will be considered in more detail in later chapters.

Planning. Planning involves teacher decisions about student needs, the most appropriate goals and objectives, the content to be taught, instructional strategies, lesson delivery techniques, instructional media, classroom climate, and student assessment. These decisions are made before actual instruction takes place. The goal of planning is to ensure student learning. Planning occurs when teachers are alone and have time to reflect and consider issues such as short-range and long-range plans, student progress, time available, and instructional materials. Planning helps arrange the appropriate flow and sequence of instructional content and events. Planning is considered in more detail in Chapters 3 and 4.

Implementing. **Implementing** involves the actual enactment of the instructional plans concerning lesson delivery and assessment. Implementation occurs when interacting with students. Teaching skills that support implementation include presenting and explaining, questioning, listening, monitoring, giving feedback, and demonstrating. Additional skills are needed to monitor student behavior, enforce rules and procedures, use instructional technology, exhibit caring and respect, and create a positive learning environment.

As you can see, a multitude of skills are required for implementation of the instructional plans, and teachers make decisions constantly during the delivery of instruction to enact those plans and to promote student learning. Several chapters in this book relate to implementation, including topics such as differentiating instruction for diverse learners, instructional strategies, motivating students, strategies to promote student understanding, managing lesson delivery, and classroom management and discipline.

Assessing. **Assessing** involves determining the level of student learning. Actually, many aspects of assessment are determined during the planning phase when instructional goals and content are identified. The means to measure student learning include paper-and-pencil tests, portfolios, work samples, projects, reports, journals, models, presentations, demonstrations, and various other types of product and performance assessments. Once assessment data has been gathered, the information is recorded and judgments are made. Assessment is considered in more detail in Chapters 11 and 12.

Teacher decisions about planning, implementing, and assessing matter a great deal. As attempts are made to improve schools and increase student achievement, one constant has remained: Teachers are the most important factor in improving schools. Attempts to reform or improve education depend on the knowledge, skills, and commitment of teachers. This point is made emphatically by Darling-Hammond and Baratz-Snowden (2007) in "A Good Teacher in Every Classroom: Preparing the Highly Qualified Teachers Our Children Deserve." Teachers need to know how to implement new practices concerning the basic teaching functions, but they must also take ownership or the innovation will not succeed.

ESSENTIAL TEACHER CHARACTERISTICS

When you reflect about the most effective teachers you have had, you may think about their warmth and caring, their creative instructional strategies, their strong command of the content, or their unique presentation skills. When examining effective teachers, the essential teacher characteristics fall into three categories: knowledge, skills, and dispositions. Let's briefly examine each of these. The descriptions provided here are closely tied to the definitions of those terms provided by the National Council for Accreditation of Teacher Education (2008).

Knowledge. Effective teachers must know the facts about the content they are teaching. That is vital, but it is not sufficient. Teachers also must have at least three other types of knowledge.

First, they must have professional knowledge related to teaching in general. This includes information about the historical, economic, sociological, philosophical, and psychological understanding of schooling and education. It also includes knowledge about learning, diversity, technology, professional ethics, legal and policy issues, pedagogy, and the roles and responsibilities of the profession of teaching.

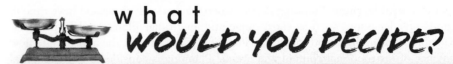

DEMONSTRATING YOUR EFFECTIVE TEACHING

Teachers need to have the necessary knowledge, skills, and dispositions to be effective in the classroom. Throughout your teacher preparation program, you will learn and acquire many of these characteristics. Imagine that you are teaching a lesson in your first year of teaching.

1. How would it be evident in your lesson that you have the necessary knowledge, skills, and dispositions to be an effective teacher? What would the students observe in your teaching to identify these qualities?

2. What could you do during your teacher preparation program to acquire these qualities?

Second, teachers must have pedagogical knowledge, which includes the general concepts, theories, and research about effective teaching, regardless of the content area. Thus, it involves general teaching methods.

Finally, teachers must have pedagogical content knowledge. This involves teaching methods that are unique to a particular subject or the application of certain strategies in a manner particular to a subject. For example, there may be some unique ways to teach map reading skills in a social studies class. This also involves a thorough understanding of the content to teach it in multiple ways, drawing on the cultural backgrounds and prior knowledge and experiences of the students.

Thus, teachers must possess rich knowledge about the content, foundational information about teaching and learning, information about teaching methods in general, and information about teaching techniques unique to particular subjects.

Skills. Teachers also must possess the necessary skills to use their knowledge effectively in the four areas just described to ensure that all students are learning. Teachers must be able to apply these skills as they plan, implement, and assess in diverse teaching settings. In listings of professional standards, the term *performances* is sometimes used instead of the term *skills*.

Dispositions. Teachers also must have appropriate dispositions to promote learning for all students. **Dispositions** include the necessary values, commitments, and professional ethics that influence teacher behaviors. Dispositions are guided by beliefs and attitudes related to values such as caring, fairness, honesty, responsibility, and social justice. Dispositions are affective, thus in the mind of teachers. But dispositions show up in teacher behaviors. For example, a teacher might be willing to use a variety of instructional strategies to promote learning for all students. This disposition could be evidenced by written plans indicating the use of cooperative learning groups, demonstrations, and a role-playing activity and by the actual use of those approaches when instruction took place.

When making decisions, you must have the necessary knowledge, skills, and dispositions to help promote learning for all students. Research has shown that teacher expertise is one of the most important factors that influences student growth and achievement. There is interest in the educational community to develop criteria for the knowledge, skills, and dispositions that teachers need to promote student achievement.

As a prospective teacher, it is important that you identify these essential teacher characteristics (knowledge, skills, dispositions) when you examine the main teaching functions

sample STANDARDS

DECISION MAKING AND REFLECTION

There are 10 InTASC standards (see pagse xx–xxi), and each standard in the original document includes a list of performances, essential knowledge, and critical dispositions to indicate more clearly what is intended in the standard.

Since this chapter deals with decision making and reflection, some representative statements from InTASC Standard #9, Professional Learning and Ethical Practice, are listed here concerning topics in this chapter.

PERFORMANCES

■ The teacher engages in ongoing learning opportunities to develop knowledge and skills in order to provide all learners with engaging curriculum and learning experiences based on local and state standards.

■ The teacher engages in meaningful and appropriate professional learning experiences aligned with his/her own needs and the needs of the learners, school, and system.

ESSENTIAL KNOWLEDGE

■ The teacher understands and knows how to use a variety of self-assessment and problem-solving strategies to analyze and reflect on his/her practice and to plan for adaptations/adjustments.

■ The teacher knows how to build and implement a plan for professional growth directly aligned with his/her needs as a growing professional using feedback from teacher evaluations and observations, data on learner performance, and school and systemwide priorities.

CRITICAL DISPOSITIONS

■ The teacher sees him-/herself as a learner, continuously seeking opportunities to draw upon current education policy and research as sources of analysis and reflection to improve practice.

■ The teacher understands the expectations of the profession including codes of ethics, professional standards of practice, and relevant law and policy.

of planning, implementing, and assessing. As the teaching functions are discussed in this book, several chapters have a boxed feature to indicate the knowledge, skills, and dispositions related to the chapter topic using the descriptions provided in the InTASC standards. For example, Chapter 3 on planning will include a box of information about representative knowledge, skills, and dispositions related to planning.

EXPECTATIONS FOR EFFECTIVENESS

Over the years, there have been calls to improve the quality of teaching, the quality and substance of the K–12 curriculum, and the performance of students on standardized tests. School districts and teachers always feel some degree of pressure from the local school district, the state and federal governments, professional organizations, legislators, and the public in general. Occasionally, there are major education reports with information about student performance, and then there are new calls for improving teacher education and the quality of teaching. Effective teaching is expected.

Measures of Effectiveness. Various approaches have been used to indicate the quality of teaching and its influence on student learning. One approach has been to examine student achievement test scores over a three-year time period in a so-called value-added comparison. This value-added concept compares the performance of a student against that same student's performance at an earlier time. The difference in the two assessments is taken as a measure of student learning growth, which can also be conceptualized as the value added by the instructional effectiveness of the teacher. Students' average annual rates of improvement are then used to estimate how much value a teacher has contributed to student achievement (Crane, 2002; Teaching Commission, 2004).

A second approach to determining the quality of teaching has involved the study of teacher test scores and their relationship to the achievement of their students. A series of studies correlated teachers' basic skills tests and college entrance exams with the scores of their students on standardized tests. These studies have found that high-scoring teachers are more likely to elicit significant gains in student achievement than their lower-scoring counterparts (Ferguson, 1998).

A third approach to determining the quality of teaching has involved the review of the content knowledge of teachers. A teacher's deep understanding of the content he or she teaches has a positive influence on student achievement. This appears especially true for science and mathematics teachers. In a review of research, Michael Allen, program director for the Education Commission of the States (ECS) Teaching Quality Policy Center, found support for the necessity of teachers being knowledgeable in their subjects and on how best to teach a particular subject (Allen, 2003).

In addition, teaching experience appears to have an influence on student achievement. Teachers with less teaching experience typically produce smaller learning gains in their students compared with more seasoned teachers (Murnane & Steele, 2007). However, most of those studies have also discovered that the benefits of experience level off after the first five or so years of teaching.

No Child Left Behind. While education is often considered a local and state matter, the federal government in the last decade has increased its involvement in how teachers are prepared and certified. This was undertaken through the "highly qualified" teacher provisions of the **No Child Left Behind Act** (NCLB, 2002). There are several provisions of this act.

1. *Highly qualified teachers.* To be deemed highly qualified, teachers must have a bachelor's degree, have full state certification or licensure, and prove that they know each subject they teach.

2. *State requirements.* NCLB requires that states (a) measure the extent to which all students have highly qualified teachers, particularly minority and disadvantaged students; (b) adopt goals and plans to ensure that all teachers are highly qualified; and (c) publicly report plans and progress in meeting teacher quality goals.

3. *Demonstration of competency.* Teachers (in middle and high schools) must prove that they know the subject they teach with (a) a major in the subject they teach, (b) credits equivalent to a major in the subject, (c) passage of a state-developed test, (d) meeting state standards for evaluation, (e) an advanced certification from the state, or (f) a graduate degree.

4. *State standards of evaluation.* NCLB allows states to develop a way for current teachers to demonstrate subject-matter competency and meet highly qualified teacher requirements. These standards must be high, objective, and uniform throughout the state. Proof may consist of a combination of teaching experience, professional development, and knowledge in the subject garnered over time in the profession.

Standards for Teachers

Each state identifies the licensure requirements for teachers. The states do not arbitrarily select criteria—they often rely on standards proposed by professional educational agencies. The following standards are among those commonly used by states: (a) InTASC standards, (b) Principles of Learning and Teaching (PLT), (c) a Framework for Teaching, and (d) National Board for Professional Teaching Standards (NBPTS). Each of these standards is outlined in detail on pages xx–xxiv of this book.

A state may use one of the standards, such as the InTASC standards, and then adapt them somewhat to serve as the basis for the teacher licensure requirements. Once a state establishes its teacher licensure requirements, these become the standards that colleges use to design their teacher education programs. Consequently, you may see that your teacher education program includes many of the topics listed in the standards. Let's examine these four sets of standards.

INTASC STANDARDS

Sponsored by the Council of Chief State School Officers, the Interstate New Teacher Assessment and Support Consortium (INTASC) asked a committee of teachers, teacher educators, and state agency officials to prepare a set of standards for competent beginning teachers. Its 1992 report on model standards served as a guide for states as they determined their own teacher licensure requirements. Many states found those standards appropriate and enacted state licensure requirements that were identical or very similar to the INTASC standards.

The InTASC standards were revised in 2011. The new standards are no longer intended only for beginning teachers, but as professional practice standards. To reflect this emphasis, InTASC removed "New" from its name (and made the *N* a lower-case letter), renaming itself the Interstate Teacher Assessment and Support Consortium (InTASC). The new **InTASC Model Core Teaching Standards** (Council of Chief State School Officers, 2011) reflect many contemporary goals of education. The model core teaching standards outline what teachers should know and be able to do to ensure every K–12 student reaches the goal of being ready to enter college or the workforce in today's world. The standards outline the common principles and foundations of teaching practice that cut across all subject areas and grade levels and that are necessary to improve student achievement.

As shown on the table of standards on pages xx–xxi, there are 10 InTASC standards in four areas: (1) the learner and learning—learner development, learning differences, and learning environments; (2) content knowledge—content knowledge and application of content; (3) instructional practice—assessment, planning for instruction, and instructional strategies; and (4) professional responsibility—professional learning and ethical practice and leadership and collaboration. For each standard, InTASC outlines the performances, essential knowledge, and critical dispositions for teachers. The identification of the dispositions makes the InTASC standards unique when comparing them to standards identified by other agencies.

PRINCIPLES OF LEARNING AND TEACHING

The Educational Testing Service (ETS) prepared several Praxis II tests to measure the knowledge of specific subjects that K–12 educators will teach, as well as general and subject-specific teaching skills and knowledge. The three Praxis II tests include Subject Assessments, Principles of Learning and Teaching, and Tests and Teaching Foundations Tests.

The **Principles of Learning and Teaching (PLT)** test assesses general pedagogical knowledge concerning (a) students as learners, (b) instruction and assessment, (c) communication techniques, and (d) profession and community. These topics are outlined in more detail in the PLT standards list on page xxi of this book. Many states require applicants for teaching licenses to take the PLT and report a passing score before granting the teaching license. Because of this, colleges with teacher education programs often give a great deal of attention to the content of the PLT and incorporate the necessary topics into their teacher education programs.

FRAMEWORK FOR TEACHING

The Educational Testing Service (ETS) developed the Pathwise Series of Professional Development programs as a research-based approach to advance professional learning and practice for school leaders and teachers. Charlotte Danielson (2007) worked with ETS to prepare and validate the criteria for this program and then, based on the ETS program criteria, she proposed a framework for teaching in her book *Enhancing Professional Practice: A Framework for Teaching*.

Framework for Teaching is divided into four domains and provides a useful organizer for examining the important responsibilities of teachers. In her book, Danielson provides rubrics for each item to assess the level of teacher performance. The rubric descriptors for unsatisfactory, basic, proficient, and distinguished provide clarity for the meaning of each item. A detailed outline of Danielson's Framework for Teaching is displayed on page xxii of this book.

Many teacher education programs give a great deal of attention to the Framework for Teaching because of its strong research support. As a result, these colleges have incorporated the domains into their teacher education programs. Here is a brief review of the four domains in Danielson's Framework for Teaching.

Domain 1: Planning and Preparation. Planning provides a structure for how content is organized during the process of planning for instruction. Key concepts within this domain are (a) demonstrating knowledge of content and pedagogy, (b) demonstrating knowledge of students, (c) selecting instructional goals, (d) demonstrating a knowledge of resources, (e) designing coherent instruction, and (f) designing student assessments.

Domain 2: Classroom Environment. The classroom environment is more than just the physical space of a classroom. It encompasses the interactions between the teacher and students, as well as the expectations for learning and achievement and the expectations and norms for learning and behavior. Positive classroom environments are associated with a range of important outcomes for students related to motivation, achievement, and safety. Key concepts in this domain are (a) creating an environment of respect and rapport, (b) establishing a culture that promotes learning, (c) managing classroom procedures, (d) managing student behavior, and (e) organizing physical space.

Domain 3: Instruction. Instruction is the central focus of the teaching–learning act. It is where the teacher and the student move through an instructional sequence. Key concepts within this domain are (a) communicating with students, (b) using questioning and discussion techniques, (c) engaging students in learning, (d) using assessments in instruction, and (e) demonstrating flexibility and responsiveness.

Domain 4: Professional Responsibilities. Professional responsibilities focus on those dispositions and skills that the teacher uses not only to be effective in the present but also to ensure future success as a professional. Central to this domain is the ability to reflect accurately on the planning process and the implementation of instruction and then to think deeply about how to improve the teaching–learning process for students. Key concepts within this domain are (a) reflecting on teaching, (b) maintaining accurate records, (c) communicating with families, (d) participating in a professional community, (e) growing and developing professionally, and (f) showing professionalism.

NATIONAL BOARD FOR PROFESSIONAL TEACHING STANDARDS

The **National Board for Professional Teaching Standards (NBPTS)** was initiated in 1987 to establish "high and rigorous" standards for the teaching profession, create a voluntary system to certify accomplished teaching, create professional development opportunities, and increase the status of the teaching profession in America. The board's work is guided by five core propositions that articulate what accomplished teachers should know and be able to do (NBPTS, 2005). These core propositions are used as a foundation to assess teaching in a variety of subjects and for teachers working with students at all grade levels.

Details for the five core propositions are outlined on pages xxiii–xxiv. Briefly stated, the NBPTS core propositions are as follows:

1. Teachers are committed to students and their learning.
2. Teachers know the subjects they teach and how to teach those subjects to students.
3. Teachers are responsible for managing and monitoring student learning.
4. Teachers think systematically about their practice and learn from experience.
5. Teachers are members of learning communities.

These five core propositions describe the knowledge, skills, and dispositions that characterize accomplished teaching. Because of the recognized importance of these criteria, many teacher education programs incorporate features of the five core propositions in their programs.

Experienced teachers choosing to be nationally board certified must prepare portfolios and include a videotape of their teaching, provide samples of student learning products, and provide analyses and reflection on their professional practice. A central goal of the NBPTS assessment process is to improve teacher performance through the collection of evidence of teaching excellence. After completion of the portfolio, teachers travel to an assessment center where they answer questions related to the subject area in which they teach. This rigorous process is voluntary. Some school districts provide a financial bonus for teachers who become certified through this process.

The Teacher as a Reflective Decision Maker

When teachers examine and reflect on their teaching, it opens a door to personal and professional development. The ultimate goal, of course, is to promote student learning, and teacher reflection is one way to achieve that goal. In this section, we examine reflection from several perspectives, aspects of instructional decision making, reflection as part of a constructivist way to teaching, and tools for becoming more reflective.

REFLECTION

To learn requires that a person reflect on past practice. As a consequence, reflection about one's experiences is a cornerstone of professional competence (York-Barr, Sommers, Ghere, & Montie, 2006). **Reflection** can be defined as a way of thinking about educational matters that involves the ability to make rational choices and to assume responsibility for those choices. Reflection requires that teachers be introspective, open-minded, and willing to accept responsibility for decisions and actions. Reflection facilitates learning and continued professional growth, and it is an important factor in the ability of teachers to be effective throughout their careers (Steffy, Wolfe, Pasch, & Enz, 2000). Educators can reflect on many things, such as their dispositions, objectives, teaching strategies, and the effect each of these factors have on student achievement.

As reflective practitioners, teachers need to be willing to analyze their own traits and behaviors in relation to the events that take place in the classroom. Teachers, therefore, need to observe and attempt to make sense of situations by checking their insights against prior experience. Information they receive from their students can also be helpful.

Some schools arrange for two or more teachers to meet to address issues and reflect on their practice. **Reflective practice** is a problem-solving strategy by which individuals or groups can work to improve practice by reviewing routines and the procedures and other aspects of the instructional environment. To engage in reflective practice requires an environment of support. It requires an organizational climate that encourages open communication, critical dialogue, risk taking, and collaboration (Osterman & Kottkamp, 2004).

We next examine the relationship between effective teaching and reflection, reflection in the professional standards, approaches to reflection, characteristics of reflective teachers, and benefits of reflection.

Effective Teaching and Reflection. There is a relationship between effective teaching and reflection. An effective teacher draws on education and experience to make decisions about what to teach, how to teach, and how to provide an atmosphere that supports student learning (Cooper, J. M., 2011; Jensen & Kiley, 2005). Thus, effective teachers reflect on and examine their own teaching and the success of their students. Each of these skills is essential to an effective teacher who is focused on students' achievement and meeting intended learning outcomes. The relationship of these topics is displayed in Figure 1.1.

1. *What to teach.* Effective teachers have a strong command of the subject matter they are assigned to teach. In addition, they have the ability to make decisions about the selection of materials and examples used to introduce the subject matter to their students.

2. *How to teach.* Effective teachers have a large collection of teaching strategies that they can draw on to maximize student achievement. Expert teachers recognize that they need to use a variety of methods and strategies to meet the varied learning needs of their students and to capture and maintain student interest and motivation. This is especially important when teachers realize that the strategy they are using has not led to success for all students and that a different strategy needs to be employed.

3. *How to provide an atmosphere that supports student learning.* Knowing the content and knowing about instructional strategies are not sufficient to promote student learning. Effective teachers also must create the necessary classroom conditions to enable student learning; they must create a positive learning community.

Reflection in the Professional Standards. Reflection by teachers to improve their practice is included in the NBPTS and InTASC standards. Core Proposition 4 of the NBPTS states that "teachers think systematically about their practice and learn from experience." With this standard, teachers critically examine their practice on a regular basis to deepen knowledge, expand their repertoire of skills, and incorporate new findings into their practice. When reflecting on how a lesson went, teachers answer two reflective questions: (1) What would I do differently and (2) what are my next steps to improve my teaching and student learning?

FIGURE 1.1

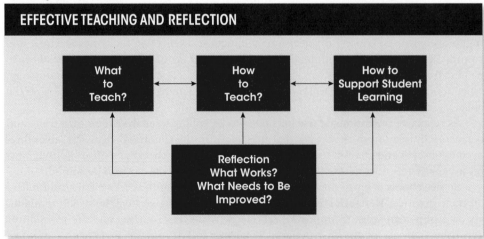

EFFECTIVE TEACHING AND REFLECTION

What to Teach? ↔ How to Teach? ↔ How to Support Student Learning

Reflection
What Works?
What Needs to Be
Improved?

The InTASC standards also offer a vision for teacher reflection. Standard #9, Professional Learning and Ethical Practice, is especially relevant to being a reflective teacher. This standard calls for teachers to engage in ongoing professional learning and use evidence to continually evaluate their practice and adapt their practice to meet the needs of each learner. Representative statements from Standard #9 for performances, essential knowledge, and critical dispositions are displayed in the Sample Standards table in this chapter on page 5.

The InTASC standards are also embraced by the National Council for Accreditation of Teacher Education (2008). The council asserts that teacher candidates should be able to work with students, families, and communities to reflect the dispositions of professional educators as delineated in professional, state, and institutional standards.

Approaches for Reflection. Three commonly used approaches that teachers use as a basis for reflection are (1) classroom observations by supervisors and peers, (2) digital tapes of their teaching, and (3) document analysis. Reviewing a digital tape of one's teaching, for example, can bring focus and clarity to what worked and what did not. Building on what worked can make a real difference for students. Along with the digital tapes, analyzing related documents facilitates reflection. Examples of documents that may be collected and analyzed include daily lesson plans, long-term plans, samples of student work, instructional materials, and assessment instruments. All of these pieces of evidence can be evaluated against specific criteria related to instructional behaviors, classroom management, and teacher expectations for their students' performance.

The following six activities also can provide a focus for reflection:

1. Classroom visitations to a master teacher's classroom to view a lesson being taught, along with an opportunity to reflect and debrief.

2. Reading an article on a new strategy and discussing it with colleagues in a study group.

3. Reviewing sample lesson plans and adapting them for your classroom.

4. Co-planning and co-teaching lessons with a coach or knowledgeable peer.

5. Planning with colleagues to implement new practices, such as students' exhibits of their work.

6. Digital taping a lesson and requesting collegial review and feedback.

Learning takes place when teachers reflect on their own practice and when they are formally evaluated. Learning also happens for supervisors and peers who serve as mentors or evaluators of teachers during this reflective process (Darling-Hammond, 2010).

Characteristics of Reflective Teachers. Reflective teachers share characteristics that enable them to grow and improve as they learn from experience. Teachers make decisions both big and small issues, such as how to organize students in groups, how to motivate students and promote positive behaviors, and how to focus students on the tasks and assess their learning.

Reflective teachers exhibit the following qualities:

- *Have a disposition toward reflection*. They have a good sense of when they need to think deeply about their teaching. They are purposeful and committed to improving their craft.

- *Ask questions and are curious*. They have inquisitive minds. Reflective thinking in teaching is associated with the work of Dewey (1933, 1938) who suggested that reflection begins with a dilemma. Effective teachers suspend making conclusions about a dilemma in order to gather information, study the problem, gain new knowledge, and come to a sound decision. This deliberate contemplation brings about new learning.

- *Seek deep understanding of the issues*. Reflective thought is the opposite of superficial thinking, which is thinking that lacks evidence, is based on false beliefs or assumptions,

from the **VOICES** *Classroom*

SUE GARVER, third-grade teacher, Riley, Kansas

REFLECTIONS ON MY INSTRUCTIONAL PLANS

I find myself constantly evaluating what I do in my classroom on a daily and yearly basis. There are several things that I do on a regular basis that help me be more reflective in my teaching. First, I meet with other teachers during our breaks or after school to compare ways we teach a subject and share new ideas. This is a time when I reflect on the methods I currently use to present a subject and on ways that I could improve my teaching methods.

Second, I take a few minutes at the end of each day to evaluate the lessons I taught that day. I write my reflective comments in my plan book next to the plans for each lesson. These notes address the success

of the lesson, what I did right in the lesson, what could be done to better meet the needs of individuals, and anything else that might be helpful next time I teach that lesson. I keep those lesson plans close by when planning for the following year.

Third, reflecting upon my teaching makes it easier for me to set goals for myself. I have found that I can set goals easily when I make these reflective notes during the school year and when I take time at the end of the school year to reflect on my teaching. Being a reflective person has allowed me to grow and improve in my teaching.

or mindlessly conforms to custom or authority (Valli, 1997). The experience of teaching and the events that transpire in classrooms have value. When reflected on, these experiences can shape the future for both teachers and their students. Reflective teachers seek deep understanding of all issues related to curriculum and instruction.

■ *Take responsibility for their teaching decisions.* Reflective teachers accept the consequences of their decisions. They seek out better solutions for challenges or problems.

■ *Are purposeful and committed to improving their craft.* Reflective teachers are not satisfied with the status quo. They want to continually improve themselves and their teaching.

Benefits of Reflection. The primary benefit of reflection is that it helps teachers improve their ability to teach and meet the needs of the students in their classes. A recent study of preservice teachers found that higher levels of reflection by the teachers were related to higher final student teacher evaluations (Pultorak & Barnes, 2009). Novice teachers also report that they value and benefit from reflecting on teaching (Cruickshank et al., 2009).

There are many benefits for teachers who reflect on their practice. Reflective teaching can enhance your learning about teaching, increase your ability to analyze and understand classroom events, help you to establish an inviting and thoughtful environment, help you to become self-monitoring, and promote personal and professional development (Cruickshank et al., 2009).

Minott (2007) points out that reflective teaching leads to a number of positive effects for teachers, including the development of the following:

■ Self-directed critical thinking inquiry skills

■ Contextualized knowledge about teaching and learning that can be applied in similar situations (e.g., when to change instructional strategies or lesson pacing)

■ Willingness to question, take risks in learning, and try new strategies and ideas

- Higher-order thinking skills and the ability to reflect on one's own learning process
- Both cognitive (e.g., knowing how to ask questions that help students engage and think deeply) and affective skills (e.g., valuing students as individuals capable of learning)
- Increased ability to react, respond, assess, and revise while teaching
- Ability to implement new activities and approaches on the spot
- Improved self-awareness and knowledge
- Improved coping strategies (e.g., the ability to redirect student inappropriate behaviors rather than with a response that will escalate the situation).

See Figure 1.2 for a sample teacher reflection written after viewing a recorded lesson.

ASPECTS OF INSTRUCTIONAL DECISION MAKING

The classroom teaching environment is complex and multifaceted, and dealing with complex problem situations is a dominant element in the life of a teacher. The complex life of teachers can be better understood by considering the relationship of teachers' decision making and the conditions and purposes they are trying to address in the classroom. Four aspects of decision making in the teaching environment are considered here.

First, teachers make decisions when planning, implementing, and assessing instruction and when creating proper conditions for a positive learning environment. Each step involves multifaceted classroom conditions and student characteristics. When planning for instruction, for example, teachers must decide on goals and objectives, needs assessments, appropriate instructional strategies, materials and technology, and evaluation of student performance. Numerous factors must be considered when making decisions about each step.

Second, teachers make moment-by-moment decisions to adjust their plans to fit the continually changing and uncertain conditions found in classrooms. Teachers learn to make these adjustments through the knowledge they have gained within the context of their classrooms, the interactive nature of their thinking, and their speculations about how these adjustments will affect the classroom environment.

Third, teachers make decisions to achieve varied academic, social, and behavioral goals. For instance, a teacher might make decisions about monitoring student behavior while working with a single small group of students. At the same time, the teacher might have expectations for students' social and academic performance. Thus, the teacher must consider these varied goals and decide on ways to plan and implement the goals simultaneously.

Fourth, teachers make decisions to interact with students in a variety of ways in a complex environment. For example, teachers do a number of things to monitor and respond to students' off-task behavior. Effective teachers have a high degree of **withitness,** which is their ability to be aware of what is happening in the classroom and to communicate that awareness to the students through their actions (Kounin, 1970). Decisions related to withitness are continually made by teachers.

REFLECTION AND A CONSTRUCTIVIST APPROACH TO TEACHING

A related concept to teacher decision making and reflection is constructivist theory. **Constructivist theory** holds that individuals construct meaning and understanding through their prior knowledge and then apply this knowledge in new current situations. In a constructivist classroom, the teacher searches for students' understandings of concepts

FIGURE 1.2

A SAMPLE TEACHER REFLECTION

The Scenario

Ms. P, a third-year eighth-grade science teacher, wrote the following reflection after viewing her recorded lesson on the effectiveness of common stomach antacids. Students were required to test the initial pH of a solution representing stomach acid, and then attempt to counteract the "heartburn" by adding doses of various liquids and tablet antacids. She digitally recorded the lesson and asked her school principal to observe the lesson and provide feedback.

The Teacher's Reflection

After viewing myself in front of the classroom, I noticed several things about my methods, technique, and delivery of instruction. For example, I think of myself as being quite mobile in the classroom, visiting with students in small groups during independent work and circulating around the room when I am engaging the whole class in instruction. I feel this helps my classroom management and keeps students more on task and engaged in the lesson. In the video, however, I was not as mobile as I typically think I am.

I also noticed that I tend to repeat myself frequently. I always considered this to be a positive aspect of my teaching, as I am sure that most students benefit from repeated instruction. My principal's feedback suggested that I rephrase information and present it in multiple ways. This way, I am still providing the information repeatedly, but in such a way that a wider range of students will be able to access the material.

Before viewing this video I prided myself on being on top of the students and keeping their attention focused for the entire length of the class. My opinion of my strengths has changed since viewing my lesson. Throughout the video, I noticed students who were totally uninterested, making faces behind my back, and uneager to take risks when answering questions. I was surprised to notice that even when they were involved in hands-on activities, some students were as uninterested as they were during direct instruction.

I know that I need to increase my students' interest and motivation during instruction, but at this point I am unsure how to proceed. That's the area I want to focus on. I need to think about that and look at the research literature.

Follow-Up Questions for the Reader

What steps can Ms. P take to improve her teaching? What strategies could she utilize to maximize student interest?

How can constructive criticism from colleagues help teachers improve their practice?

What value can digitally recording lessons contribute to helping teachers reflect on their practice?

Comments Concerning the Teacher's Reflection

By digitally recording her lesson and asking the principal to observe and provide feedback, Ms. P was open to gaining new insights about her teaching and expressed interest in reflecting on her experiences in the lesson. The recording and the principal's feedback provided information that she might not otherwise have had.

Ms. P next wanted to focus on increasing student interest and motivation. She spoke to peers and researched this topic. She found one particularly useful article on the topic and decided to apply motivational concepts and strategies recommended in that article (Pintrich, 2003). The first motivational concept was *supporting the students' belief that they can succeed*. If students believe they are able to do well, they are likely to be motivated in terms of effort and persistence. Confident students will also be more cognitively engaged in thinking and learning. To apply this motivational concept, Ms. P provided opportunities for students to build skills and master the course material, and she also provided clear and accurate feedback to students on their performance. She designed tasks that challenge students but also offered the support they need to be successful.

In a later laboratory experience, students conducted a survey of the school grounds and developed appropriate classification keys to group plants and animals by shared characteristics. After the project was finished, a student mentioned that the assignment was hard but she learned a lot. Ms. P was pleased and saw this as a sign that she was providing a supportive but rigorous classroom atmosphere.

The second motivational concept was for students to *practice self-control and choice* during activities and for the teacher to *develop relationships with her students and to promote the development of a community of learners who support each other*. Ms. P began emphasizing the importance of previous lessons and their link to the current and future lessons; students then connected more readily with the material. She also stressed that students need to work hard every day and that effort, planning, and self-control lead to classroom success. She worked to build an atmosphere where students felt responsible for their

FIGURE 1.2 (continued)

A SAMPLE TEACHER REFLECTION

learning and rejected the perception that they are "helpless learners" with no control over their engagement or achievement.

While doing this, Ms. P worked to build personal relations with her students. She did this through a series of routines, including moving around the room and engaging students on a personal level during independent work time. Her engagement had an academic focus (e.g., feedback and correctives) but also provided an opportunity for her to show students that she values them as individuals and that she cares about their personal and educational success. She also wanted to take more opportunities to praise students and refer to their work products or behaviors: "Ella you were a great scribe today for your group," or "Aiden your hypothesis and research design in today's activity was very well thought out."

The third motivational concept was recognizing that *goals motivate and direct student success.*

Ms. P continues to have her students work in cooperative groups for laboratory activities but now incorporates practices into the labs that her students follow, such as students agreeing to take on a specific responsibility (e.g., organizer, timekeeper, recorder), agreeing to work together on a common activity, and everyone taking responsibility for supporting the learning of everyone in the group.

As Ms. P continues to ask questions about how she teaches and what she expects from students, she continues to use reflection and research to improve her teaching, her classroom climate, and her students' mastery and deep understandings of science. It is not unusual for Ms. P to feel that while she is perceived as being effective, she is not satisfied. However, she plans to continue to engage in reflection about her teaching and to expand her repertoire of teaching skills. She is modeling being a reflective teacher.

and then structures learning opportunities for students to refine or revise these understandings by posing contradictions, presenting new information, asking questions, encouraging research, and/or engaging students in inquiries designed to challenge current concepts.

In a constructivist classroom, there are five overarching principles: (1) Teachers seek and value their students' points of view, (2) classroom activities challenge students' suppositions, (3) teachers pose problems of emerging relevance, (4) teachers build lessons around primary concepts and "big" ideas, and (5) teachers assess student learning in the context of daily teaching. As you can see, a tremendous amount of teacher decision making and reflection is needed to establish and maintain a constructivist classroom in an effort to meet the academic needs of the students when using this instructional approach.

Students should be challenged by the activities and stimulated by questions from both the teacher and themselves. A key feature of this model is that students are encouraged to actively seek understanding and knowledge by relating new investigations to previous understandings (Gagnon & Collay, 2006; Marlowe & Page, 2005).

Teachers who reflect on their own practice employ a constructivist perspective. They constantly review significant events that take place in the classroom and try to clarify and improve their understanding of teaching and learning. In a study of beginning teachers (McCombs, 2003), the teachers reported that the process of reflection and self-assessment helped them identify areas for improvement and assisted them in implementing practices to be more effective in reaching students. As you read this text, you will encounter many concepts related to teaching, and you will have the opportunity to reflect on how these concepts can help you become a better teacher and help your students become better learners.

TOOLS FOR BECOMING MORE REFLECTIVE

Teachers can improve their ability to reflect on practice by using a variety of methods. Your willingness to use these techniques can promote your professional growth.

TEACHER AS A REFLECTIVE PRACTITIONER

After the last class of each day, I take a moment to reflect on my daily plans. I usually put an asterisk (*) on each activity that hit a major Core Standard in a positive, productive way. I place a minus sign (–) on any area that I think needs more attention. Taking the time each day to reflect on my teaching forces me to change the lesson plan to best meet the needs of my students. I don't treat my lesson plans as pristine documents to archive for the next year. Instead, I write notes on them and scribble in the margins to guide my revision for the next time I teach the lesson.

1. *Portfolio development.* The development of portfolios in which teachers collect and organize materials and artifacts such as lesson plans, videotapes of lessons with self-critiques, and examples of analysis of students' work is fast becoming the norm in teacher preparation and professional licensure. Purposefully collecting and analyzing sets of artifacts demonstrate the ability to reflect on important indicators of success.

Many of the current portfolio review processes share common features with National Board Certification. Using the InTASC standards, a number of states including California, Colorado, Connecticut, and Oregon have begun requiring a portfolio as the basis for granting an initial teacher license or for beginning teachers as part of a mentoring and induction process. The Council for the Accreditation of Educator Preparation (CAEP), the national organization that accredits college and university teacher education programs, also uses a performance-based model of assessments to provide evidence that teachers meet teaching standards.

The portfolio process calls for you to document your plans and instructional strategies within a unit of instruction; videotape a lesson and analyze your teaching; provide students with an assessment; and evaluate whether students met objectives and if not, how you will move students to higher levels of learning. The reflection section calls for careful thought on what worked and what did not, along with an analysis and description of how you would change or improve your unit and lessons in the future.

2. *Journaling.* It has long been known that writing can help to clarify your thoughts and enhance your ability to think about your classroom and improve your teaching. A dialogue journal (Cruickshank et al., 2009) takes the journaling process and makes it interactive. A conversation about teaching can provide you with feedback on your analyses of your teaching and your next steps to improve your teaching or classroom procedures.

Advances in technology have made sharing journals and receiving feedback electronically fast and easily implemented. Social networking software has also expanded the number of people who can respond to a posted reflection. As the audience for a reflection is expanded, it becomes important that your journal entry include enough information about the event you are reflecting on to be helpful. These steps of journal writing are also valuable to ensure you reflect fully (Hole & McEntee, 1999):

1. *What happened?* A brief description of the incident or event central to your reflection.

2. *Why did it happen?* Why do you think this event, student behavior, or situation occurred?

3. *What could I have done differently?* What strategy could you use in the future to be a more effective teacher?

4. *What might it mean for student learning?* Think about what this classroom event or incident might mean and what might you change in the future to improve student learning.

3. *Action Research.* **Action research** is systematic inquiry by teachers with the purpose of improving their practice (Levin & Rock, 2003). It often is done collaboratively by a group of colleagues who are searching for solutions to the everyday problems they face. These real problems frequently center on improving curriculum, instruction, student achievement, or other issues related to school improvement. Many school districts use action research as a powerful professional development strategy for teachers. Teachers work alongside colleagues in their buildings to collect and analyze data to gain insights into their question, take action based on what they learn in the process, and share their learning with others so the entire education community can benefit (Dana, 2009; Ferrance, 2000).

Action research projects may focus on one teacher's classroom or on broader, schoolwide concerns. In a single classroom, a teacher may conduct an action research project concerning questioning techniques, the effects of a certain teaching strategy, the effects of the use of technology, or other curriculum and instruction topics. Action research projects also may focus on school improvement efforts such as assessing the impact of efforts with low-performing students, exploring alternatives to suspension as a disciplinary consequence, determining the effects of a newly implemented inclusion model for students with special needs, or other schoolwide issues.

Data collected in action research often includes measures of student achievement such as standardized test scores, grades, and dropout rates. Each of these measures can have significant implications for deciding if a program or strategy is effective. Action research also focuses on *why* certain program results were achieved, not just what was achieved. Therefore, many forms of data are collected and analyzed, including faculty and student interviews, student work samples, reflective journals, surveys, and other measures.

4. *Student Journal Writing.* Just as teachers can gain greater understanding from reflecting through journal writing, so can their students. Student journal writing can serve a number of goals (e.g., recording events or notes, personal reflections on experiences, or developing questions for future study). For our purposes, we are focusing on journals in which students construct knowledge or demonstrate understanding of what they learned and how it relates to class goals and objectives.

Journal writing can become an important tool for student learning when they are asked to write about what they learned. It promotes students' critical thinking and serves as a record of students' ability to focus on critical aspects of their education. It also reinforces the importance of writing across the curriculum and serves as a record of student thought. Journal writing helps students unpack how and what they learned and encourages students to take ownership of their learning (Boud, 2001).

Reflective journal writing has advantages for both students and teachers (Spaulding & Wilson, 2002). For students, journal writing serves as a permanent record of thoughts and experiences, establishes and supports a relationship with the teacher, provides a safe outlet for frustrations and concerns, and aids students' ability to reflect about important class objectives. For the teacher, reflective journal writing serves as a window into student thinking and learning, establishes and maintains a relationship with the student, and can also serve as a dialog between teacher and student to enhance learning for both (e.g., Bolin, 1990). Reflective journal writing provides an opportunity for both teachers and students to assess and learn.

Increasing Student Diversity

Students in your classroom will vary in many ways. This **diversity** may be in ethnicity, race, socioeconomic status, gender, exceptionalities, language, religion, sexual orientation, and even geographical area (National Council for Accreditation of Teacher Education,

2008). Many of these characteristics will be examined in Chapter 2. Of course, this diversity has always been evident in U.S. classrooms.

There are two areas of diversity that demand special attention—students with disabilities and English language learners. The Individuals with Disabilities Education Act (IDEA) addresses educators' responsibilities concerning students with disabilities. Disabilities include visual, hearing, speech, or physical impairments; emotional or behavioral disorders; intellectual disabilities; autism; and other classifications. The number of students identified as disabled has increased over the years, and regular classroom teachers have a responsibility to work with these students.

The number of English language learners, however, has increased even more. Over the past 25 years, the characteristics of the U.S. population have changed, and consequently, the characteristics of the K–12 student population also have changed. The most apparent changes in schools are the increasing number of students from ethnic and racial minority groups and the significant increase in the number of students whose first language is not English. Consider the following facts about the current U.S. student population (most from Kober, 2006, unless noted otherwise):

- Children of color account for 4 out of 10 public school students—a proportion that is expected to increase in coming years (57 percent white, 19 percent Latino, 16 percent African American, 4 percent Asian/Pacific Islander, 3 percent other).

- Children of color make up the majority of public school enrollments in six states and many districts.

- Hispanics, African Americans, and Asians combined make up the majority of the population in 48 of the 100 largest U.S. cities (Macionis, 2011).

- About one in five school-age children is a child of immigrants.

- English language learners—students whose first language is not English and who are learning English—account for 1 in every 10 public school students.

CLASSROOM CASE STUDY

IMPROVING TEACHING THROUGH REFLECTION

Joel Escher is an experienced seventh-grade language arts teacher. After attending a professional development session on reflective teaching, he decided to videotape himself during some of his classes to better understand how to involve more of his students in whole-group discussions.

After watching the videotaped sessions of his recent classes, Mr. Escher noticed that he was neglecting some of his students during class discussions because he tended to stand on one side of the room. Since his posture was directed to only half of his class, he did not notice students outside his field of vision who were raising their hands but not called on to participate in the discussion.

In addition, Mr. Escher recognized that he didn't give students much time to formulate a response after he asked a question. On the videotape, several students appeared to be considering his question, but he called on another student before more students could formulate a response. To resolve this problem, Mr. Escher decided that he would write key questions on the board prior to class and then give students a couple of minutes prior to class discussions to jot down some ideas to share with the whole group.

FOCUS QUESTIONS

1. If Mr. Escher did not have access to video equipment, how else could he have learned why his whole-group discussions were unsuccessful?

2. Reflecting on your own classroom experiences, what recommendations can you make for conducting successful whole-class discussions?

- More than one third of public school students are from low-income families.
- Almost 14 percent of public school students receive special services because they have a disability. Three fourths of these students with disabilities were educated in regular classrooms with other children for a significant part of the school day.

MORE ENGLISH LANGUAGE LEARNERS

As just noted, **English language learners (ELLs)** are students whose first language is not English and who need help learning to speak, read, and write in English. Due to immigration and the higher levels of ethnic diversity in the U.S. student population, it is not surprising that the number of ELLs has also increased significantly in the past 15 to 20 years. There are many different types of ELLs, ranging from students who are very educated to those with limited schooling, from children of professional families to children of migrant workers, from recent arrivals to the United States to those born here. In addition to functioning in two languages, ELLs also navigate two cultures.

According to statistics compiled by the National Clearinghouse for English Language Acquisition (NCELA, 2011), the number of ELLs has increased by 51 percent from 1999 to 2009, totaling more than 5.3 million students, or almost 11 percent of the student population. The largest numbers of ELLs are in seven states: California, Arizona, Texas, Florida, Illinois, North Carolina, and New York. There are almost 1.5 million ELLs in California schools, representing almost 24% of the student enrollment (California Department of Education, 2011). From 1999 to 2009, high rates of growth in ELL enrollments have taken place in many Southern and Midwestern states (NCELA, 2011). Even small cities and rural areas are now home to immigrant families and their children.

Currently, over 400 different languages are spoken in the United States, with the most common language groups being Spanish (representing over 79 percent of all ELLs), Vietnamese, Hmong, Chinese, and Korean (NCELA, 2004, 2005, 2008).

You should expect to have students in your classroom who are learning English, and you should be prepared to meet their learning needs. In a national study, most new teachers ranked reducing class size and preparing teachers to adapt or vary their instruction to meet the needs of a diverse classroom as the top ways to improve teaching (Public Agenda, 2008).

CHALLENGES OF ENGLISH LANGUAGE LEARNERS

Imagine what it would be like to have limited knowledge of English when attending school. It would be difficult to understand the teacher and the other students, and it would affect your ability to understand teacher directions, participate in the instructional activities, and complete classroom assessments. Your overall school performance would be affected. In fact, ELLs often experience challenges in school, as indicated by the following facts:

- A dramatic, lingering divide in achievement exists between white students and those from culturally and linguistically diverse groups on state and national measures of achievement (California Dept. of Education, 2004; Grigg, Daane, Jin, & Campbell, 2002; Kindler, 2002).
- ELLs have some of the highest dropout rates and are more frequently placed in lower-ability groups and academic tracks than language-majority students (Ruiz-de-Velasco & Fix, 2000; Steinberg & Almeida, 2004).
- Only 10 percent of young adults who speak English at home fail to complete high school, but the percentage is three times higher (31 percent) for young adult ELLs (NCES, 2005).

TEACHING ENGLISH LANGUAGE LEARNERS IN ALL CLASSROOMS

Because of the large number of ELLs in schools today, *all* teachers are teachers of English. There are four major instructional models for serving ELLs, characterized by the degree to

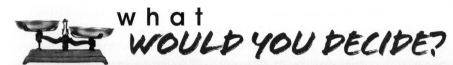

HOW YOU ADDRESS STUDENT DIVERSITY

You will likely have students with many different characteristics in your first year of teaching. Student diversity is evident in many ways, such as by language, disability, or cognitive ability. Some types of diversity are easily recognized or noticed, other types are less obvious. Nevertheless, effective teachers need to promote learning by all of their students.

1. In what ways are you similar to other students in your current college class? In what ways are you different?

2. What challenges do you envision when you address the diversity of students in your first year of teaching? What can you do during your teacher preparation program to minimize these challenges?

which they incorporate a student's native language and the approach they take to delivering academic content (Rothenberg & Fisher, 2007): (1) instructional methods using the native language, (2) instructional methods using the native language as support, (3) instructional methods using English as a second language (ESL), and (4) content-based or sheltered instruction.

The last approach, sheltered instruction, has been widely used in the United States. **Sheltered instruction** is an approach to teaching content to ELLs in strategic ways that make subject-matter concepts comprehensible while promoting the students' English language development. There are two well-known sheltered instruction programs: the cognitive academic language learning approach (CALLA) and the sheltered instruction observation protocol (SIOP).

CALLA is a program that integrates content-area instruction with language development activities and explicit instruction in learning strategies (Chamot, 2009). It helps ELLs become active learners who focus on concepts and meanings, rather than language forms. CALLA teachers develop five-phase lesson plans that include preparation, presentation, practice, evaluation, and expansion. This approach has been used successfully by many teachers in sheltered classes, but some teachers have found the planning to be difficult. In addition, ELLs with low levels of English proficiency and limited background knowledge still struggle to learn grade-appropriate content in English (Freeman & Freeman, 2007). Of the sheltered instruction programs, the SIOP model is widely adopted and is emphasized here.

THE SIOP MODEL

One of the best researched and most highly developed models to teach ELLs is the **sheltered instruction observation protocol (SIOP) model** (Echevarria, Vogt, & Short, 2008). The SIOP model was originally a lesson plan observation protocol, but it has evolved to an effective lesson planning and delivery system. It is a way to plan and teach content in a way that is understandable for ELLs and that also promotes their English language development. With increasing student diversity in language, meeting the needs of ELLs can be facilitated by the SIOP model because it provides more flexibility in the design and delivery of instruction.

The SIOP model may be used as a lesson planning guide for sheltered content lessons, and it embeds features of high-quality instruction into its design. The model is not an add-on responsibility for teachers but rather a planning framework that ensures effective practices are implemented to benefit all learners (Echevarria et al., 2008). The SIOP model has eight components and 30 features, as displayed in Figure 1.3. Other than the lesson preparation component being first, there is no particular hierarchy or order to the eight

SIOP components. The components and features of the SIOP model are interrelated and integrated into each lesson.

Even students who are not struggling readers or English learners will benefit when a teacher plans and delivers instruction using the SIOP model (Echevarria et al., 2008). Mainstream teachers at all grade levels can effectively use the SIOP model to benefit all learners in their classrooms. Because of this, various components of the SIOP model will be more fully described in other chapters in this book. For example, information in the SIOP model concerning lesson delivery will be discussed in Chapter 8, Managing Lesson Delivery. Other topics will be considered in the appropriate chapters to provide guidance in using the SIOP model components to meet the needs of all learners.

FIGURE 1.3

COMPONENTS OF THE SIOP MODEL

Lesson Preparation

- Clearly define, display, and review content objectives with the students.
- Clearly define, display, and review language objectives with the students.
- Select content concepts that are appropriate for age and educational background of the students.
- Use supplementary materials to a high degree, making the lesson clear and meaningful.
- Adapt content to all levels of student proficiency.
- Provide meaningful activities that integrate lesson concepts with language practice opportunities.

Building Background

- Explicitly link concepts to students' background experiences.
- Make explicit links between past learning and new concepts.
- Emphasize key vocabulary.

Comprehensible Input

- Speak appropriately for students' proficiency levels.
- Provide clear explanations of academic tasks.
- Use a variety of techniques to make content concepts clear.

Strategies

- Provide ample opportunities for students to use learning strategies.
- Consistently use scaffolding techniques to assist and support student understanding.
- Use a variety of questions or tasks that promote higher-order thinking skills.

Interaction

- Provide frequent opportunities for interaction and discussion.

- Group students to support language and content objectives of the lesson.
- Consistently provide sufficient wait time for student responses.
- Give ample opportunities for students to clarify key concepts in their first language.

Practice/Application

- Supply hands-on materials for students to practice using new content knowledge.
- Provide activities for students to apply content and language knowledge.
- Integrate all language skills into each lesson.

Lesson Delivery

- Clearly support content objectives by lesson delivery.
- Clearly support language objectives by lesson delivery.
- Engage students during 90–100 percent of the lesson.
- Appropriately pace the lesson to the students' ability levels.

Review and Assessment

- Provide comprehensive review of key vocabulary.
- Supply comprehensive review of key content concepts.
- Provide regular feedback to students on their output.
- Conduct assessments of student comprehension and learning of all lesson objectives throughout the lesson.

Source: Adapted from Echevarria, J., Vogt, M., & Short, D. J. (2008). *Making content comprehensible for English learners: The SIOP model.* Boston: Allyn & Bacon.

Key Terms

Action research
Assessing
Constructivist theory
Decision making
Dispositions
Diversity
English language learners
(ELLs)

Framework for Teaching
Implementing
Interstate Teacher Assess-
ment and Support
Consortium (InTASC)
National Board for Pro-
fessional Teaching
Standards (NBPTS)

No Child Left Behind Act
Planning
Principles of Learning and
Teaching (PLT)
Reflection
Reflective practice
Sheltered instruction

Sheltered instruction
observation protocol
(SIOP) model
Withitness

Major Concepts

1. Teachers make decisions concerning three basic teaching functions: planning, implementing, and assessing.

2. Essential teacher characteristics fall into three categories: knowledge, skills, and dispositions.

3. Teachers are expected to be effective, and many surveys, reports, and state and federal guidelines address ways for them to achieve this.

4. Professional teaching standards are used to guide the selection of state teaching licensure requirements and the development of teacher education programs at colleges and universities.

5. Teaching is centrally the act of decision making. Teachers plan and act through the process of thought and reflection.

6. Reflection can be defined as a way of thinking about educational matters that involves the ability to make rational choices and to assume responsibility for those choices.

7. The strategies in the SIOP model can be used to reach English language learners in all classrooms.

Discussion/Reflective Questions

1. Which is the most important teaching function: planning, implementing, or assessing? Why?

2. Give some examples of dispositions related to teaching. Why are dispositions important?

3. How might teacher reflection help teachers improve their practice?

4. What are some of the strengths of the SIOP model?

Suggested Activities

FOR CLINICAL SETTINGS

1. Select a significant event from a class you have attended on campus during the last three weeks. Reflect on what worked well in that class using one of the teacher standard tables discussed in this chapter. (The standard tables with the complete list of items and subitems are displayed in this book just before Chapter 1.)

2. Teach a brief lesson to a small group of peers. Write and reflect about a significant event that took place during your lesson. Consider how you could improve the lesson if you were to teach it again.

3. Imagine that you will be teaching a lesson on your state's history to eighth graders. Identify ways that you might apply at least five aspects of the SIOP model (see Figure 1.3) in that lesson.

FOR FIELD EXPERIENCES

1. Talk with several teachers to see how they have continued their professional development since beginning to teach (e.g., staff development programs, graduate courses). Show them the Framework for Teaching table (just before Chapter 1) and ask them to identify and discuss the areas where they have improved.

2. Ask several teachers to discuss how they think about their teaching and then decide to make improvements. Do they have a regular process for this? What suggestions do they have for your reflective process?

3. Ask several teachers to describe how they teach English language learners in their classroom.

Further Reading

Carr, J. F., Fauske, J. R., & Rushton, S. (2008). *Teaching and leading from the inside out: A model for reflection, exploration, and action.* Thousand Oaks, CA: Corwin Press.

Explains reflective practice and offers practical strategies to integrate reflective practice into daily work.

Echevarria, J. J., Vogt, M. J., & Short, D. J. (2008). *Making content comprehensible for English learners: The SIOP model* (3rd ed.). Boston: Allyn & Bacon.

Provides details about each SIOP component, rubric rating forms on SIOP use, lesson plan formats, and guidelines for use.

Taggart, G. L., & Wilson, A. P. (2005). *Promoting reflective thinking in teachers: Fifty action strategies* (2nd ed.). Thousand Oaks, CA: Corwin Press.

A thorough presentation of strategies for instilling reflective practices in educators. The tasks and tools provided were specifically designed to help teachers become critical thinkers.

York-Barr, J., Sommers, W. A., Ghere, G. S., & Montie, J. (2006). *Reflective practice to improve schools: An action guide for educators* (2nd ed.). Thousand Oaks, CA: Corwin Press.

A very useful guide that provides a framework for reflective thinking and acting. Offers examples of strategies to guide individuals, small groups, or schoolwide reflection.

Technology Resources

PRINCIPLES OF LEARNING AND TEACHING

http://www.ets.org/Media/Tests/PRAXIS/pdf/0524.pdf

This is the official website describing the PLT test. A detailed outline for each of the six content categories is provided.

WORDPRESS

http://wordpress.com/

This is one of the more popular blogging platforms that can be used for reflective practice. This free service also gives access to plenty of tools such as spell-check, an integrated statistics tracker, and spam protection. A hosted WordPress has many more options and features than the free version. A good place to have a hosted (i.e., paid) WordPress blog is DynamicsDS (http://dynamicsds.com/w/).

BLOGGER

http://www.blogger.com

Blogger is a Google application that offers lots of tools for easy blogging. You will need a Google account, but it also works well with all the other Google tools.

WRIGHT'S ROOM

http://shelleywright.wordpress.com/

Is an actual blog by a high school teacher, and is a fine example of reflective blogging and information sharing.

MyEducationLab™

Go to the **MyEducationLab** (www.myeducationlab.com) for General Methods and familiarize yourself with the content:

- Topically organized Assignments and Activities, tied to learning outcomes for the course, that can help you more deeply understand course content
- Topically organized Building Teaching Skills and Dispositions learning units allow you to apply and develop understanding of teaching methods.
- A chapter-specific pretest that assesses your understanding of the content offers hints and feedback for

each question and generates a study plan including links to Review, Practice, and Enrichment activities that will enhance your understanding of the concepts. A Study Plan posttest with hints and feedback ensures you understood concepts from the chapter after having completed the enrichment activities.

A Correlation Guide may be downloaded by instructors to show how MyEducationLab content aligns to this book.

Knowing Your Students

2

THIS CHAPTER PROVIDES INFORMATION THAT WILL HELP YOU TO

1. Describe multiple ways in which diversity is exhibited in students.

2. Select ways to create an inclusive, multicultural classroom.

3. Apply various ways to differentiate instruction.

4. Differentiate instruction based on the principles of the universal design for learning.

5. Select ways to know your students.

6. Prepare a contextual factors classroom analysis.

© iStockphoto

Just think about the diversity apparent in a typical urban classroom. There may be a wide range of student cognitive and physical abilities. Students may have different degrees of English proficiency, and some may have a disabling condition such as a hearing disorder. A wide range of ethnic characteristics may be evident, and various socioeconomic levels are likely to be represented. The students may prefer to learn in different ways, such as in pairs, in small groups, or independently. Some may prefer written work; others may learn best when performing an activity.

These examples are just a few of the human and environmental variables that create a wide range of individual differences and needs in classrooms. Individual differences need to be taken into account when instructional methods and procedures are selected. What are the sources of student diversity? How can our understanding of these student characteristics help teachers to create an inclusive, multicultural classroom? How can you differentiate your instruction to meet the learning needs of all students? These issues are explored in this chapter.

Implications for Diverse Classrooms

Students who are in the classroom affect classroom management and instruction. Schools in the United States are very diverse with students from different economic, cultural, ethnic, and linguistic backgrounds. In addition, you may find that your classroom has students with a range of ability or achievement levels, groups of students with skills below grade level, and students with special needs. All of these factors contribute to the diversity in your classroom.

For you and your students to be successful, you may need to make adjustments in instructional and management practices to meet the needs of different groups in your class. For example, you may find a wide variety of academic abilities in your classroom and consequently need to vary your curriculum, instruction, and assessments. You also may have several students whose primary language is not English, and similar adjustments may need to be enacted. Your job is to enhance student learning, and adjustments based on student characteristics will be necessary.

Your understanding of your students will likely influence your decisions about ways that you will organize the physical environment, manage student behavior, create a supportive learning environment, facilitate instruction, and promote safety and wellness. To be an effective classroom manager in a diverse classroom, you should make a commitment to do these things:

- Get to know all of your students.
- Create an inclusive classroom by making instructional and management modifications based on an understanding of your students.
- Create a classroom environment that promotes positive behavior and enhances student learning.

Sources of Student Diversity

Individual differences abound, and adapting instruction to student differences is one of the most challenging aspects of teaching. The first step in planning to address the diversity of students is to recognize those differences. This section explores differences in development by age; differences in cognitive, affective, and physical areas; differences due to gender, sexual orientation, ethnicity, learning style, language, or creative potential; differences due to exceptionalities and at-risk characteristics; and other types of differences (Gollnick & Chinn, 2009). In the classroom, students rarely fall cleanly into one category or another and may exhibit characteristics from several categories.

DEVELOPMENTAL DIFFERENCES BY AGE

Any elementary teacher can tell you that kindergarten students are profoundly different from sixth-grade students, and those differences need to be taken into account when planning and teaching. Similarly, any middle level or secondary teacher can tell you that eighth-graders are quite different from seniors.

Students at the grade level you teach will be of a certain age and will possess certain developmental characteristics of that age. Those characteristics must be taken into account when planning and delivering instruction. Part of your review of contextual factors in your classroom, examined later in this chapter, includes careful identification of the characteristics of the students in your class.

It is beyond the scope of this book to review developmental characteristics of students at various age levels. However, it is important to alert prospective teachers that those developmental characteristics must be taken into account when planning for instruction. College courses in human development examine characteristics of children as they grow older. Educational psychology courses also consider various theories of development. Recall some of those developmental concepts, such as: (1) Jean Piaget's four stages of cognitive development, (2) Eric Erikson's eight stages of psychosocial development, (3) Lawrence Kohlberg's three levels and six stages of moral reasoning, and (4) additional perspectives on the development of language, memory, and physical and emotional development.

Seek out resources that provide information about the developmental characteristics of children at the age of the grade level you teach. One such resource is *Yardsticks: Children in the Classroom, Ages 4–14* by Chip Wood (2007). In a separate chapter for each age, Wood describes the social, physical, and cognitive characteristics of children of that age. Dig out your educational psychology books (e.g., Ormrod, 2011) to find useful reviews of developmental characteristics by age. All of these are useful resources to help you understand developmental characteristics by age and to take those characteristics into account when planning and delivering instruction.

COGNITIVE AREA

Cognitive activity includes information processing, problem solving, using mental strategies for tasks, and continuous learning. Children in a classroom will differ in their cognitive abilities to perform these tasks. Thus, there may be a range of low-academic-ability to high-academic-ability students in a classroom. **Intelligence** involves the capacity to apprehend facts and their relations and to reason about them; it is an indicator of cognitive ability.

Howard Gardner (1983, 1995, 1999) believes that all people have multiple intelligences. He has identified eight independent intelligences: linguistic, musical, logical–mathematical, spatial, bodily kinesthetic, naturalistic, interpersonal, and intrapersonal. According to this theory, a person may be gifted in any one of the intelligences without being exceptional in the others. Gardner proposes more adjustment of curriculum and instruction to individuals' combinations of aptitudes. Do not expect each student to have the same interests and abilities or to learn in the same ways.

The work of Gardner and other cognitive psychologists provides ideas for teachers when selecting instructional techniques and differentiating instruction. When considering the cognitive differences of your students, you should do the following:

1. Expect students to be different.
2. Spend the time and effort to look for potential.
3. Realize that student needs are not only in deficit areas. Development of potential is a need, too.
4. Be familiar with past records of achievement.
5. Be aware of previous experiences that have shaped a student's way of thinking.
6. Challenge students with varied assignments, and note the results.
7. Use a variety of ways of grading and evaluating.
8. Keep changing the conditions for learning to bring out hidden potential.
9. Challenge students occasionally beyond what is expected.
10. Look for something unique that each can do.

There are many useful resource guides for addressing the diversity of students by applying the multiple intelligences to lesson activities (e.g., Campbell, B., 2008; Campbell, Campbell, & Dickinson, 2004; Fogarty & Stoehr, 2008; Lazear, 2003).

Struggling Learners. A student who is considered a **struggling learner** cannot learn at an average rate from the instructional resources, texts, workbooks, and materials that are designated for the majority of students in the classroom. This student often has a limited attention span and deficiencies in basic skills such as reading, writing, and mathematics. He or she needs frequent feedback, corrective instruction, special instructional pacing, instructional variety, and perhaps modified materials (Educational Research Service, 2004). Resources are available for supporting struggling readers in the secondary grades (McEwan, 2007).

In *How to Support Struggling Students*, Jackson and Lambert (2010) state that effective support is ongoing, proactive, targeted, accelerative (rather than remedial), learning focused, and managed by the teacher as an advocate. They suggest strategies to support struggling students at certain points of instruction:

■ Before instruction: Activate and create background knowledge, prepare students with advance organizers, and help students pre-learn key vocabulary.

■ During instruction: Select "red flags" to identify when a student's struggle to learn has become destructive, and link the red flags to interventions that quickly get struggling students back on course.

■ After instruction: Provide meaningful remediation for the few students who do not achieve mastery even with acceleration and intervention.

In *Teaching Boys Who Struggle in School*, Kathleen Cleveland (2011) examines what causes boys to struggle in school and offers recommendations. She suggests (1) replacing an underachieving boy's negative attitudes about learning; (2) reconnecting each boy with school, with learning, and with a belief in himself as a competent learner; (3) rebuilding learning skills that lead to success in school and life; and (4) reducing the need for unproductive and distracting behaviors as a means of self-protection.

For the struggling learners in your class, you should (1) frequently vary your instructional technique; (2) develop lessons around students' interests, needs, and experiences; (3) provide for an encouraging, supportive environment; (4) use cooperative learning and peer tutors for students needing remediation; (5) provide study aids; (6) teach content in small sequential steps with frequent checks for comprehension; (7) use individualized materials and individualized instruction whenever possible; (8) use audio and visual materials for instruction; and (9) take steps to develop each student's self-concept (e.g., assign a task where the student can showcase a particular skill).

DIFFERENTIATING INSTRUCTION FOR DIVERSE LEARNERS

There are 10 InTASC standards (see pages xx–xxi), and each standard in the original document includes a list of performances, essential knowledge, and critical dispositions to indicate more clearly what is intended in the standard.

Since this chapter deals with differentiating instruction for diverse learners, some representative statements from InTASC Standard #2 on Learning Differences, Standard #3 on Learning Environments, and Standard #6 on Assessment are listed here concerning topics in this chapter.

PERFORMANCES

■ The teacher designs, adapts, and delivers instruction to address each student's diverse learning strengths and needs, and creates opportunities for students to demonstrate their learning in different ways. (InTASC #2)

■ The teacher uses a variety of methods to engage learners in evaluating the learning environment and collaborates with learners to make appropriate adjustments. (InTASC #3)

■ The teacher effectively uses multiple and appropriate types of assessment data to identify each student's learning needs and to develop differentiated learning experiences. (InTASC #6)

ESSENTIAL KNOWLEDGE

■ The teacher knows about second-language acquisition processes and knows how to incorporate instructional strategies and resources to support language acquisition. (InTASC #2)

■ The teacher understands how learner diversity can affect communication and knows how to communicate effectively in differing environments. (InTASC #3)

■ The teacher understands how to prepare learners for assessments and how to make accommodations in assessments and testing conditions, especially for learners with disabilities and language learning needs. (InTASC #6)

CRITICAL DISPOSITIONS

■ The teacher respects learners as individuals with differing personal and family backgrounds and various skills, abilities, perspectives, talents, and interests. (InTASC #2)

■ The teacher is a thoughtful and responsive listener and observer. (InTASC #3)

■ The teacher is committed to the ethical use of various assessments and assessment data to identify learner strengths and needs to promote learner growth. (InTASC #6)

Gifted or Talented Learners. Gifted or talented learners are those with above-average abilities, and they need special instructional consideration. Unfortunately, some teachers do not challenge high-ability students, and these students just "mark time" in school. Unchallenged, they may develop poor attention and study habits, form negative attitudes toward school and learning, and waste academic learning time. Many resources for teaching gifted students are available (e.g., Karnes & Stephens, 2008; Smutny & von Fremd, 2009).

For these students, you should (1) not require that they repeat material they already have mastered; (2) present instruction at a flexible pace, allowing those who are able to progress at a productive rate; (3) condense the curriculum by removing unneeded assignments to make time for extending activities; (4) encourage students to be self-directing and self-evaluating in their work; (5) use grading procedures that do not discourage students from intellectual risk taking or penalize them for choosing complex learning activities; (6) provide resources beyond basal textbooks; (7) provide horizontal and vertical curriculum enrichment; (8) encourage supplementary reading and writing; and (9) encourage the development of hobbies and interests.

AFFECTIVE AREA

Education in the **affective area** focuses on feelings and attitudes. Emotional growth is not easy to facilitate, but sometimes the feelings students have about their skills or a particular subject are at least as important as the information they learn (Slavin, 2012).

Self-esteem, time management, confidence, and self-direction are typical affective education goals.

Though affective goals have played a secondary role to cognitive goals in school, they should be given an important place when planning and carrying out instruction. Love of learning, confidence in learning, and cooperative attitudes are important objectives that teachers should have for students. You may find a range of affective characteristics exhibited in the classroom, from low to high self-esteem, confidence, cooperation, self-direction, and the like.

PHYSICAL AREA

Perhaps the best place to observe the wide range of physical differences among students is the hallway of any junior high or middle school. Tall and short, skinny and heavy, muscular and frail, dark and fair, active and quiet describe just a few of the extremes one can see there.

Physical (psychomotor) differences among students have sometimes been overlooked by teachers who are not involved in physical education (Woolfolk, 2010). **Psychomotor skills** involve gross motor skills and fine motor skills, such as dribbling a basketball and drawing a fine line. These skills are integral parts of most learning activities. Indeed, psychomotor and affective objectives often overlap.

Physical demands on learning are obvious in the areas of handwriting, industrial arts, sewing, typing, art, and driver education. However, they must not be minimized in less obvious areas such as science labs, computer classes, speech and drama, and music. Vision and hearing deficiencies also contribute to individual differences. You should recognize the importance of physical skills to the total learning program and explore the possibilities for including psychomotor development activities in classroom objectives.

LEARNING STYLES

A **learning style** is an individual's preferences for the conditions of the learning process that can affect his or her learning (Woolfolk, 2010), including where, when, and how learning takes place, and with what materials. These styles may play an integral role in determining how the student perceives the learning environment and responds to it. Therefore, knowledge about learning styles can allow teachers to provide options in the classroom that can enhance students' learning.

Theories and research studies about learning styles are tentative and ongoing, but several promising areas of instructional assistance have emerged. These include cognitive style, brain-compatible learning, and sensory modalities. Students' learning styles can be addressed by using differentiated instructional techniques (Gregory, 2005).

Cognitive Style. Cognitive style should be considered in planning. **Cognitive style** refers to the way people process information and use strategies in responding to tasks. Conceptual tempo and field dependence/field independence are two categories of cognitive style that educators may consider when planning instruction.

First, **conceptual tempo** deals with students being impulsive or reflective when selecting from two or more alternatives. For example, impulsive students look at alternatives only briefly and select one quickly. They may make many errors because they do not take time to consider all the alternatives. However, not all cognitively impulsive students are fast *and* inaccurate. On the other hand, reflective students deliberate among the alternatives and respond more slowly.

Second, **field dependence/field independence** deals with the extent to which individuals can overcome the effects of distracting background elements (the field) when trying to differentiate among relevant aspects of a particular situation. You can expect field-dependent students to be more people oriented, to work best in groups, and to prefer subjects such as history and literature. Field-independent students would prefer science, problem-solving tasks, and instructional approaches requiring little social interaction (Slavin, 2012). Field-dependent students respond more to verbal praise and extrinsic

VOICES
from the Classroom

EDIE GUERRA, middle school science teacher, Las Vegas, Nevada

STUDENT INVENTORY SHEETS ABOUT LEARNING STYLES

At the beginning of the year, I give my students a "Student Inventory Sheet." There are nine sections, each focusing on a different learning style—visual, logical/mathematical, visual/spatial, bodily/kinesthetic, musical, interpersonal, intrapersonal, and naturalistic. I do this is to see how my students learn best, and then I tailor my lessons to their preferred learning styles.

By knowing my students' learning styles, I am able to develop lessons that appeal to their interests. I want my students to be highly engaged in their learning. By altering and adapting to their preferred styles, I have more student buy-in for basic grade-level concepts. I think of it as adding the bells and whistles to an otherwise dry curriculum.

URBAN EDUCATION

motivation, while field-independent students tend to pursue their own goals and respond best to intrinsic motivation.

Brain-Compatible Learning. In *How the Brain Learns,* David Sousa (2011) examines how the brain processes information and how teachers can promote student memory, retention, and learning. He supports the use of many instructional approaches, and recommends a fairly explicit type of lesson delivery.

In *Designing Brain-Compatible Learning,* Gregory and Parry (2006) review the cognitive research and pedagogical theory of learning in relation to the brain. Many of the suggestions are consistent with those about differentiating instruction reviewed later in this chapter. Among the strategies they review and endorse are: (1) creating classroom climates that support thinking, (2) activating prior knowledge, (3) using advance organizers, (4) implementing cooperative group learning, (5) providing direct teaching of thinking, (6) using higher-order questioning, (7) promoting creative problem solving, (8) using strategies for advancing concept development (e.g., concept attainment and concept development strategies), (9) teaching metacognition (e.g., students learning to examine and monitor how they think), and (10) using advance organizers.

Brain hemisphericity is another aspect of student preferences for learning environments. The two halves of the brain appear to serve different functions, even though they are connected by a complex network that orchestrates their teamwork (Sousa, 2011). Each side is dominant in certain respects. Left-brain-dominant people tend to be more analytical in their orientation, being generally logical, concrete, and sequential. Right-brain-dominant people tend to be more visually and spatially oriented and more holistic in their thinking.

Teacher presentations focusing on left-hemisphere activity include lecture, discussion, giving verbal clues, explaining rules, and asking yes–no and either–or questions in content areas. Useful materials include texts, word lists, workbook exercises, readings, and drill tapes. To develop left-hemisphere functions, teachers should (1) introduce and teach some material in the linear mode, (2) sequence the learning for meaning and retention, (3) conduct question-and-answer periods, (4) emphasize the meanings of words and sentences, and (5) increase student proficiency with information-processing skills such as note taking, memorization, and recall.

Teacher presentations featuring right-hemisphere activity involve demonstration, experiences, open-ended questions, nonverbal clues, manipulations, and divergent thinking activity. Useful materials for these activities include flashcards, maps, films, drawings, and manipulatives. To develop right-hemisphere functions, teachers should (1) encourage intuitive thinking and "guesstimating," (2) allow for testing of ideas and principles, (3) introduce some material in the visual/spatial mode, (4) use some nonsequential modes for instruction, and (5) integrate techniques from art, music, and physical education into social science, science, and language arts disciplines.

Sensory Modality. Sensory modality is a third factor in students' preferences for a learning environment. A **sensory modality** is a system of interacting with the environment through one or more of the basic senses: sight, hearing, touch, smell, and taste. The most important sensory modalities for teachers are the visual, auditory, and kinesthetic modes. Information to be learned is first received through one of the senses. The information either is forgotten after a few seconds or, after initial processing, is placed in short-term or long-term memory. Learning may be enhanced when the information is received through a preferred sensory modality. Use a variety of instructional approaches that enable the students to receive the content through one or more of the basic senses.

GENDER

There are obviously differences between males and females, and some of those differences influence students' performance at school. Researchers have found that females generally are more extroverted, anxious, and trusting; are less assertive; and have slightly lower self-esteem than males of the same age and background. Females' verbal and motor skills also tend to develop faster than those of males (Berk, 2010, 2012; Sadker & Silber, 2007).

Gender differences are caused by a combination of genetics and environment. These differences are examined in *Boys and Girls Learn Differently* (Gurian & Henley, 2010), which includes discussions concerning elementary, middle, and high school classrooms. Concerns about boys' performance in school are examined in sources such as *The Minds of Boys* (Gurian & Stevens, 2007) and *Teaching the Male Brain* (James, 2007).

In a study by Auwarter and Aruguete (2008), teachers' perceptions and expectations for students were shaped by students' gender and socioeconomic status (SES). Teachers rated high-SES boys more favorably than low-SES boys but low-SES girls more favorably than high-SES girls. Teachers perceived that low-SES students have less promising futures than do high-SES students. Findings suggest that teachers are likely to develop negative attitudes toward low-SES students in general but especially boys. The study did not find that all teachers have these preconceived attitudes but suggests that teachers should be cautious about holding differing expectations for students based on gender or SES.

There are also gender differences in career preparation and career choice. Teachers should keep both boys and girls academically motivated, especially in science, technology, engineering, and math areas, where gender-based differences in career choices still exist. To address this, you take the following actions (Tsui, 2007):

- Provide students with a mix of successful male and female role models.
- Make sure that girls take an active part in math and science classes, especially given boys' tendency to be more assertive in such settings.
- Use more hands-on experiments and group activities and less teaching by telling and lecturing.
- Allow students to investigate real-world problems, both large and small.
- Encourage students to see that academic achievement is more a product of effort than of natural ability.
- Help parents recognize the importance of having gender-neutral expectations for their children's education.

from the VOICES Classroom

PATRICIA SMITH, sixth-grade teacher, Monroe Township, New Jersey

KNOWING YOUR STUDENTS' LEARNING STYLES

At the beginning of each school year, I have my students identify their own particular learning styles with the use of checklists, questionnaires, and other tools I have collected. When we discuss the results, my students realize that they have their own unique learning style and that every other student in the room does as well.

We then consider how to use this information to help them be successful. We discuss various study skills that work well for their learning style. For example, we know that many of the boys identify themselves as kinesthetic learners, so I suggest making flashcards as a study aid. We also discuss how having choices in the way they demonstrate what they have learned allows them to use their learning style strengths. For instance, they might choose to write and present a song for a book report project, or create an illustrated storyboard.

For me, the benefit of this process is having the students accept themselves and each other as unique, and it helps me select content, strategies, and assessments that better meet their learning needs.

What can you do to prevent gender inequity in your classroom? First, be aware that you may have stereotypical attitudes that influence the ways you interact with boys and girls. Research indicates that teachers interact with boys more often and ask them more questions; boys are also more likely to ask questions and volunteer comments about ideas being discussed in class (Good & Brophy, 2008). These patterns can lead to girls being less involved in learning activities and ultimately having lower achievement.

You can make your classroom more gender friendly for all students by following these guidelines: (1) incorporate movement in instruction, (2) make learning visual, (3) give students choice and control, (4) provide opportunities for social interaction, (5) find ways to make learning real, (6) blend art and music into the curriculum, (7) connect with your students, (8) promote character development for the benefit of the individuals and the classroom environment, and (9) encourage equal participation (Gurian, Stevens, & King, 2008; James, 2007).

SEXUAL ORIENTATION

It is estimated that 5 to 10 percent of the population is lesbian, gay, bisexual, or transgender (LGBT) (Ost & Gates, 2004). As adults, LGBT individuals face discrimination in housing, employment, and social institutions. Society's prejudices and discriminatory policies result in many gays and lesbians hiding their sexual orientation. Early indicators of sexual orientation may show up in students in the elementary grades.

During adolescence, about 8 percent of boys and 6 percent of girls report engaging in some same-sex-activity or feeling strong attractions to same-sex individuals (Steinberg, 2011). Most models describing the development of an identity as gay, lesbian, or bisexual follow these stages (Yarhouse, 2001):

- Feeling different: Beginning around age 6, the child may be less interested in the activities of other children who are the same sex. Some children may find this troubling and fear being "found out." Others do not experience these anxieties.

- Feeling confused: In adolescence, students may be confused, upset, lonely, or unsure what to do if they feel attractions for someone of the same sex.

- Acceptance: As young adults, many of these young people sort through sexual orientation issues and identify themselves as gay, lesbian, or bisexual. They may or may not make their sexual orientation public, but may share the information with a few friends.

Loneliness and isolation are experienced by many gay and lesbian youth. If gays and lesbians openly acknowledge their sexual orientation or appear to be LGBT, they are likely to be harassed or bullied by peers. Sixty-four percent of LGBT students fear for their safety in schools. They feel more comfortable and safer in a school when faculty and staff are supportive, gay-straight alliance or similar clubs exist, and a comprehensive policy on harassment is enforced (Ost & Gates, 2004).

Teachers need to reach out to help students who are struggling with sexual identity and to address harassment and bullying. First, listen to the students to allow them to vent or to express what is going on in their lives. Second, affirm to them that they are not alone and that others are dealing with the same issues. Third, refer the students to someone who is trained to deal with the issues. Fourth, address any verbal or physical harassment or bullying related to sexual orientation. Finally, follow up to be sure students' situations have improved and whether there is anything further you may be able to do. In addition to interacting with students who are addressing these issues, teachers may need to interact with parents who are gay or lesbian.

LANGUAGE

Some students come from homes where English is not the primary language or is not spoken at all. They may have limited proficiency in English. In descending order, Spanish, French, German, Italian, and Chinese are the top five languages other than English spoken at home. This fact has bearing on teachers' decisions about management and work.

There are four major instructional models for serving English language learners (ELLs) (Rothenberg & Fisher, 2007), each varying in the degree to which it incorporates a student's first language and the approach it takes in delivering academic content:

1. Instructional methods using the student's first language (which are transitional programs)
2. Instructional methods using the first language as support
3. Instructional methods using English as a second language
4. Content-based instruction or sheltered instructional methods

Presently, one in nine students in U.S. public schools, or over 5 million students, have limited English proficiency. This is an increase of 150 percent over the last decade. Some estimates claim that by 2025, one in four public K–12 students will come from a home where a language other than English is spoken (NCELA, 2005, 2006). Many students will have limited English proficiency when they begin school, and some will remain less than completely fluent for years (Goldenberg, 2008).

As an educator, it is increasingly likely that you will have ELLs in your classes. To help address the learning needs of ELLs, apply the following principles:

1. *Instruction in the primary language aids achievement*. Academic instruction in a student's home language should be part of the educational program of an ELL when possible. The National Literacy Panel conducted a meta-analysis of experimental studies and concluded that teaching reading skills in the first language is modestly more effective in terms of second-language achievement than immersing children in English (August & Shanahan, 2006).

2. *Good instruction for ELLs is similar to good instruction for other English-speaking students*. Primary-language instruction is often not feasible for various reasons, including the fact that over 400 different languages are spoken in the United States (NCELA, 2008). The best evidence researchers have suggests that ELLs learn in much the same way as other students and that good instruction for students in general tends to be good instruction for ELLs in particular. Thus, ELLs benefit from (a) clear goals and objectives, (b) well-designed instructional routines, (c) active engagement and participation, (d) informative feedback, (e) opportunities to practice and apply new learning and transfer it to new situations, (f) periodic review and practice, (g) opportunities to interact with other students, and (h) frequent assessments, with reteaching as needed (Marzano, 2007).

3. *ELLs require instructional accommodations.* While general principles of effective instruction should be the basis for instructing ELLs, these students need certain accommodations. The National Literacy Panel found that the impact of instructional interventions is weaker for English learners than it is for English speakers, suggesting that additional supports or accommodations are needed for ELLs to derive as much benefit from effective instructional practices. These additional supports or accommodations include the following:

- Using the primary language strategically
- Providing predictable, clear, and consistent instructions, expectations, and routines
- Offering extended explanations and additional opportunities for practice
- Providing redundant information, such as visual cues and physical gestures
- Focusing on the similarities/differences between English and the native language
- Building on students' knowledge and skills in the native language
- Identifying and clarifying difficult words and passages
- Consolidating text knowledge through summarization
- Providing extra practice in reading words, sentences, and stories
- Providing opportunities to have students work in pairs or small groups with tutors
- Discriminating and manipulating the sounds of the language (phonemic awareness)
- Decoding words (phonics)
- Targeting vocabulary and checking comprehension frequently
- Paraphrasing students' remarks and encouraging expansion

CLASSROOM CASE STUDY

ADJUSTMENTS FOR ENGLISH LANGUAGE LEARNERS

Jason Kulpinski teaches high school history in an urban school in which 25 percent of the students are Hispanic and many are English language learners. To introduce his classes to some of the major events and themes of U.S. history, Mr. Kulpinski uses short texts: texts that can be read in one sitting and that combine both words and pictures to tell a story. He has found that all the students in his classes have benefited from reading the short texts.

The short texts provide ELLs with background knowledge on the content they will learn in the course. Without this background, many students would have no prior knowledge as a reference point for learning new content in the unit. With a design that incorporates both words and pictures providing context clues, the short texts help struggling readers and English language learners to negotiate meaning from the material.

Mr. Kulpinski has seen many of his hesitant readers grow in confidence after they have read several short texts and have been able to comprehend the content. Class discussions also have been enhanced by the use of short texts.

FOCUS QUESTIONS

1. How does Mr. Kulpinski's strategy of using short texts help him to teach diverse learners?

2. How do all learners in the classroom benefit from this strategy?

Instruction in English language development and opportunities to extend oral English skills are critical for ELLs. Every lesson should target both course content and English language development. Students must make rapid progress in their oral English skills if they are to enter the educational mainstream and derive maximum benefit from classroom instruction delivered in English. To do so, they must have a supportive learning environment (Goldenberg, 2008; Slavin, Cheung, Groff, & Lake, 2004).

CULTURAL DIVERSITY

Cultural diversity is reflected in the wide variety of values, beliefs, attitudes, and rules that define regional, ethnic, religious, and other culture groups. Minority populations wish their cultures to be recognized as unique and preserved for their children. The message from all cultural groups to schools is clear: Make sure that each student from every cultural group succeeds in school.

Culturally responsive teaching is instruction that acknowledges cultural diversity (Gay, 2000, 2005). It attempts to accomplish this goal in three ways: (1) accepting and valuing cultural differences, (2) accommodating different cultural interaction patterns, and (3) building on students' cultural backgrounds. Culturally responsive teachers use the best of what is known about good teaching, including strategies such as the following (Irvine & Armento, 2001):

- Connecting students' prior knowledge and cultural experiences with new concepts by constructing and designing relevant cultural metaphors and images
- Understanding students' cultural knowledge and experiences and selecting appropriate instructional materials
- Helping students find meaning and purpose in what is to be learned
- Using interactive teaching strategies
- Allowing students to participate in planning
- Using familiar speech and events
- Helping learners construct meaning by organizing, elaborating, and representing knowledge in their own way
- Using primary sources of data and manipulative materials

In a culturally responsive classroom, the student's culture is seen as a source of strength on which to rely, not as a problem to be overcome or as something to be overlooked (Ladson-Billings, 2009). Teachers can weave a range of cultural perspectives throughout the curriculum to make education more relevant for students who see their cultures recognized. In doing so, teachers need to be aware of a variety of cultural experiences to understand how different students may learn best (Moje, Collazo, Carillo, & Marx, 2001). Learning about the various cultures is important. Resources such as *Through Ebony Eyes* (Thompson, G. L., 2004) and *Up Where We Belong* (Thompson, G. L., 2007) provide information about helping African American and Latino students in school.

Each cultural group teaches its members certain lessons about living. Differences exist among cultures in the way members conduct interpersonal relationships, use time, use body language, cooperate with group members, and accept directions from authority figures. You need to treat each student as an individual first, because that student is the product of many influences. Many resources are available concerning cultural diversity (e.g., Banks, 2006; Gollnick & Chinn, 2009). As you consider individual differences produced by cultural diversity, you should do the following:

1. Examine your own values and beliefs for evidences of bias and stereotyping.
2. Regard students as individuals first, with membership in a culture group as only one factor in understanding individuals.
3. Learn something about students' family and community relationships.

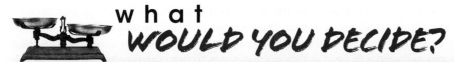

what
WOULD YOU DECIDE?

YOUR CULTURE IS DIFFERENT

Many classrooms have students from a variety of ethnic and cultural backgrounds. It is possible that you will feel disconnected from your students because you have a different ethnicity or different cultural background from your students.

1. What can you do so that you and your students feel comfortable with one another?

2. What can you do so that the different backgrounds do not contribute to misunderstandings and off-task behavior?

4. Consider nonstandard English and native languages as basic languages for students from culturally diverse populations to support gradual but necessary instruction in the majority language.

5. Allow students to work in cross-cultural teams and facilitate cooperation while noting qualities and talents that emerge.

6. Infuse the curriculum with regular emphasis on other cultures, rather than providing just one unit a year or a few isolated and stereotyped activities.

EXCEPTIONALITIES

Exceptional students include those who need special help and resources to reach their full potential. Exceptionalities include both disabilities and giftedness.

More than 10 percent of students in the United States are identified as having disabling conditions that justify placement in a special education program (Turnbull & Turnbull, 2010). This figure increases to 15 percent when gifted children are counted as special education students. Categories for special education services include learning disabilities, speech or language impairment, mental retardation, emotional or behavioral disabilities, other health impairments, multiple disabilities, hearing impairment, orthopedic impairment, visual impairment, deafness or blindness, traumatic brain injury, and autism spectrum disorder.

The Individuals with Disabilities Education Act (IDEA) committed the United States to a policy of mainstreaming students who have handicapping conditions by placing them in the least restrictive environment in which they can function successfully while having their special needs met. The degree to which they are treated differently is to be minimized. The **least restrictive environment** means that students with special needs are placed in special settings only if necessary and only for as long as necessary; the regular classroom is the preferred least restrictive placement.

Teachers often make accommodations and modifications to their teaching to meet the learning needs of students with exceptionalities (Haager & Klingner, 2005). An **accommodation** is an adjustment in the curriculum, instruction, learning tasks, assessments, or materials to make learning more accessible to students. For example, a student might have an adapted test with fewer test items. The student may also have the same test but take it orally in a one-on-one situation with the teacher, or he or she might be given extra time to take a test. Different materials might be used to teach the same content, or additional practice or various instructional approaches may be used. In any case, accommodation is *not* a watering down or change in the content or a change in expected learner outcomes.

A **modification** is a change in the standard learning expectations so that they are realistic and individually appropriate. The curriculum or instruction is altered as needed. Modifications are used for students for whom all possible accommodations have been considered and who still need additional measures to help them progress. For example, students with skill deficits in reading or math may need modifications in assignments or the level of the content and reading materials, or they may need an alternative assessment or test.

STUDENTS AT RISK

Other environmental and personal influences may converge to place a student at risk. **Students at risk** are children and adolescents who are not able to acquire and/or use the skills necessary to develop their potential and become productive members of society. Conditions at home, support from the community, and personal and cultural background all affect students' attitudes, behaviors, and propensity to profit from school experiences. Students potentially at risk include children who face adverse conditions beyond their control, those who do not speak English as a first language, talented but unchallenged students, those with special problems, and many others. At-risk students often have academic difficulties and thus may be low achievers.

Students at risk, especially those who eventually drop out, typically have some or all of the following characteristics (Ormrod, 2011): (1) a history of academic failure, (2) older age in comparison with classmates, (3) emotional and behavioral problems, (4) frequent interaction with low-achieving peers, (5) lack of psychological attachment to school, and (6) increasing disinvolvement with school.

Here are some general strategies to support students at risk (Ormrod, 2011):

- Identify students at risk as early as possible.
- Create a warm, supportive school and classroom atmosphere.
- Communicate high expectations for academic success.
- Provide extra academic support.
- Show students that they are the ones who have made success possible.
- Encourage and facilitate identification with school.

SOCIOECONOMIC STATUS

Socioeconomic status (SES) is a measure of a family's relative position in a community, determined by a combination of parents' income, occupation, and level of education. There are many relationships between SES and school performance (Woolfolk, 2010). SES is linked to intelligence, achievement test scores, grades, truancy, and dropout and suspension rates.

Students' school performance is correlated with their socioeconomic status: higher-SES students tend to have high academic achievement, and lower-SES students tend to be at greater risk for dropping out of school (Books, 2004; Lee & Bowen, 2006; Ormrod, 2011). As students from lower-SES families move through the grade levels, they fall further and further behind their higher-SES peers. Students from higher-SES families, however, may face pressure from their parents to achieve at a high level, which can lead to anxiety and depression.

To better address the learning needs of students living in poverty, some educators seek to understand the characteristics of the students and their culture and then make appropriate decisions about curriculum and instruction. In *A Framework for Understanding Poverty*, Ruby Payne (2005, 2008) strongly advocates seeking this understanding. However, others have been critical of this approach as stereotyping students living in poverty (e.g., Bomer, Dworin, May, & Semingson, 2008; Gorski, 2008).

Taking these factors into account, you should (1) capitalize on students' interests; (2) make course content meaningful to the students and discuss the practical value of the material; (3) give clear and specific directions; (4) arrange to have each student experience some success; (5) be sure that expectations for work are realistic; and (6) include a variety of instructional approaches, such as provisions for movement and group work. Additional useful resources include *Teaching with Poverty in Mind* by Eric Jensen (2009) and *Why Culture Counts: Teaching Children of Poverty* by Donna Tileston and Sandra Darling (2008).

Creating an Inclusive, Multicultural Classroom

Understanding the sources of student diversity is not enough. You must use this information as the basis for many classroom decisions when creating a positive learning environment, selecting a responsive curriculum, determining instructional strategies, and providing assistance. A number of useful resources offer guidance about these issues, including *Culturally Proficient Instruction* (Robins, Lindsey, Lindsey, & Terrell, 2011), *Building Culturally Responsive Classrooms* (Gaitan, 2006), and *How to Teach Students Who Don't Look Like You* (Davis, 2006).

CREATE A SUPPORTIVE, CARING ENVIRONMENT

How students feel about the classroom can make a big difference in how they participate. Your attitude toward students and the curriculum can influence these student feelings. To create a supportive, caring environment, you should translate your attitude into the following actions:

1. *Celebrate diversity.* Student diversity exists in many ways, as reviewed earlier in this chapter. Students do not want to be criticized because they have some characteristic that is different from others. Through your actions, recognize that each student contributes to the rich variety of ideas and actions in the classroom. Show that you appreciate and value the diversity that is reflected in the students in the classroom. In turn, students will feel appreciated, rather than different, and this will make them feel more comfortable in the classroom.

2. *Have high expectations for students and believe that all students can succeed.* Teachers sometimes consider certain sources of student diversity—cognitive ability, language, disabilities, socioeconomic status, for example—as having a negative effect on student performance. Thus, teachers may lower expectations and adjust the content and activities accordingly. However, this is a disservice to the students when they are not given the opportunity to address meaningful and challenging content and to develop their knowledge and skills. It is important to hold high expectations for all students and to believe that all students can succeed. Students appreciate the challenge and will find the classroom more stimulating and worthwhile as compared to a classroom with lowered expectations.

3. *Encourage all students.* Students who perform well academically often receive words of praise, reinforcement, and encouragement from teachers. There may be many students in a classroom who do not perform at the highest academic levels, but they would appreciate hearing encouraging statements as well. Encouraging words and guiding suggestions will help all students to feel that they are being supported in their efforts.

4. *Respond to all students enthusiastically.* When students see that their teacher is welcoming and enthusiastic about each student, they feel more comfortable in the classroom and more willing to participate fully. Warm greetings when students enter the classroom, conversations with individual students, and positive reactions when students contribute to classroom discussion are just a few ways that enthusiasm might be expressed. The main thing is that each student needs to feel valued and that each sees this through enthusiastic teacher responses.

5. *Show students that you care about them.* When students know that you care for them and that you are looking out for them, it makes all the difference in the world. Students then feel valued, regardless of their characteristics, and are more likely to actively participate in the classroom. Even when a teacher needs to deal with a student concerning a problem, the student recognizes that the teacher's actions are well intentioned.

6. *Create an anti-bias educational environment.* Sometimes when students interact with others who are different from them, they may talk or act in ways that express disapproval. Teachers need to take steps to overcome this bias. In an anti-bias classroom, teachers intervene with immediate actions and follow-up activities to counter the cumulative, hurtful effects of these messages. In an anti-bias classroom, children learn to be proud of themselves and of their families, to respect human differences, to recognize bias, and to speak up for what is right (Derman-Sparks & Edwards, 2010). Anti-bias teachers are committed to the principles that every child deserves to develop to his or her fullest potential. Derman-Sparks and Edwards (2010) identified four goals of anti-bias education:

1. Each child will demonstrate self-awareness, confidence, family pride, and positive social identities.
2. Each child will express comfort and joy with human diversity; accurate language for human differences; and deep, caring human connections.
3. Each child will increasingly recognize unfairness, have language to describe unfairness, and understand that unfairness hurts.
4. Each child will demonstrate empowerment and the skills to act, with others or alone, against prejudice and/or discriminatory actions.

OFFER A RESPONSIVE CURRICULUM

Students feel that they are valued when the curriculum is fair and relevant and when the content and curriculum materials reflect the diversity of learners in the classroom.

1. *Use a fair and relevant curriculum.* Teachers can make decisions to ensure that the curriculum is inclusive, relevant, and free of bias. Using the district-approved curriculum guide as a starting point, teachers can select appropriate instructional content to demonstrate that their students are valued as people and that they offer a challenging, culturally relevant curriculum. This content may involve integrating subject areas from diverse traditions, and the content may even arise out of students' own questions so that they can construct their own meaning.

2. *Consider differentiating curriculum materials.* Curriculum materials must also reflect the diversity of learners in the classroom. Books and other instructional materials should be free of bias, and they should provide the voices and perspectives of diverse people.

Once appropriate curriculum materials have been selected, teachers may allow students options in the use of these materials. Learning activity packets, task cards, and learning contracts are examples of **differentiated materials** that address individual differences by providing curriculum options. Learning centers, for example, include differentiated materials with several kinds and levels of goals and activities. Centers, packets, and cards can be made for a particular student's needs and then stored until another student has need of them. When prepared properly, these materials accommodate different rates of learning and different cognitive styles.

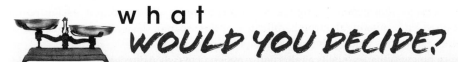

what
WOULD YOU DECIDE?

DIFFERENTIATED MATERIALS

Various types of materials can be used to meet the instructional objectives of a lesson and meet the learning interests of the students. Let's say that you are planning to teach a lesson on soil erosion.

1. How might you vary your instructional materials to accommodate students' individual differences?

2. How can you relate this topic to students' lives and make it interesting?

3. How might students' individual differences affect your planning decisions?

VARY INSTRUCTION

To meet the needs of diverse students, instruction cannot be one-dimensional. A variety of instructional approaches are needed to challenge all students and to meet their instructional needs. Several ways to vary your instruction are highlighted here.

1. *Challenge students' thinking and abilities.* Students have various learning styles, and they may learn best with their preferred learning style. However, should teachers always try to match student preferences and instructional methods? Probably not.

You should (a) start where the learner is (i.e., in concert with the pupil's level of development), (b) then begin to mismatch (i.e., use a different approach than what the student prefers) by shifting to a slightly more complex level of teaching to help the student to develop in many areas, and (c) have faith that students have an intrinsic drive to learn. These practices complement the recommendations of Lev Vygotsky, Lawrence Kohlberg, and others to nudge students beyond comfort zones of learning into just enough cognitive dissonance to facilitate growth.

2. *Group students for instruction.* Grouping makes differentiation of instruction more efficient and practical. When each group is challenged and stimulated appropriately, students are motivated to work harder. Differentiated materials can be used more easily. On the other hand, labeling can be stigmatizing if grouping is based on variables such as ability or achievement. Grouping too much and changing groups too infrequently can obstruct student integration and cooperation.

With the proper planning, structure, and supervision, grouping is a useful way to provide for individual differences. When using grouping arrangements, you should follow these guidelines:

- Make liberal use of activities that mix group members frequently.

- Adjust the pace and level of work for each group to maximize achievement. Avoid having expectations that are too low for low groups. Students tend to live up or down to teachers' expectations.

- Provide opportunities for gifted students to work with peers of their own level by arranging cross-age, between-school, or community-based experiences.

- Form groups with care, giving attention to culture and gender.

- Structure the experience and supervise the students' actions.

- Prepare students with the necessary skills for being effective group members, such as listening, helping, cooperating, and seeking assistance.

3. *Consider differentiated assignments.* **Alternative** or **differentiated assignments** can be provided by altering the length, difficulty, or time span of the assignment. Alternative assignments generally require alternative evaluation procedures.

Enrichment activities qualify as alternative assignments when directed toward an individual student's needs. There are three types of enrichment activities. First, relevant enrichment provides experiences that address the student's strengths, interests, or deficit areas. Second, cultural enrichment might be pleasurable and productive for the student even if not particularly relevant to his or her needs. An example would be an interdisciplinary study or a global-awareness topic. Third, irrelevant enrichment might provide extra activity in a content area without really addressing student needs.

4. *Consider individualized study.* **Individualized study** can be implemented through learning contracts or independent studies as a means to address individual needs. Such plans are most effective when developed by the student with your assistance. Individualized study facilitates mastery of both content and processes. Not only can the student master a subject, but he or she can also master goal setting, time management, use of resources, self-direction, and self-assessment of achievement. Independent study is ideal for accommodating student learning styles. Individual ability is nurtured, and students often learn more than the project requires.

Independent study encourages creativity and develops problem-solving skills. It can be used in any school setting and all curricular areas. Most important, this method of learning approximates the way that the student should continue to learn when no longer a student in school.

This method requires varied, plentiful resources, and it may not provide enough social interaction. The student may spend too long on the study, and parents may complain that nothing is being accomplished.

When considering individualized study, you should do the following:

- Include the student in all phases of planning, studying, and evaluating.
- Encourage the student to ask higher-order questions (analysis, synthesis, evaluation) as study goals.
- Encourage the student to develop a product as an outcome of the study.
- Provide the student with an opportunity to share the product with an interested audience.
- Emphasize learner responsibility and accountability.

5. *Provide opportunities for students to try different types of activities.* Although certain class activities and instructional strategies may seem well suited for a particular student, it is important to involve the student in many different types of activities to challenge the student and the student's thinking and understanding.

6. *Use authentic and fair assessment strategies.* Some students demonstrate their learning better through certain types of assessment. Since there are many types of students in classrooms, a variety of methods for evaluating student learning should be used. Using a variety of approaches—such as written or oral tests, reports or projects, interviews, portfolios, writing samples, and observations—will circumvent bias. In addition, evaluation of student learning should be at several levels: recall, comprehension, application, analysis, synthesis, and evaluation.

PROVIDE ASSISTANCE WHEN NEEDED

Many classrooms include students who can benefit from special assistance in their learning. In an inclusive, multicultural classroom, these students must not be overlooked, because they may not advance in their learning without such assistance.

1. *Provide special individualized assistance to all students.* Teachers often provide individualized assistance to students who have difficulty learning. This assistance can make a big difference in helping students to overcome hurdles and can lead to better understanding. However, other students can benefit from this type of assistance as well. By providing assistance to all types of diverse learners, teachers express their interest in students, provide support for student learning, and have the opportunity to challenge students in new ways.

2. *Work with students with special needs.* As a first step, teachers need to know district policies concerning students with special needs and what their responsibilities are for referrals, screening, and the preparation of individualized educational plans (IEPs). Learning materials and activities can be prepared commensurate with the abilities of students with special needs. Positive expectations for student performance are a means to promote student learning.

Differentiating Instruction

Differentiated instruction is a principle-guided method to approach teaching and learning in which the teacher adjusts the learning environment, curriculum, assessment, and instruction to meet the needs of all learners (Tomlinson & Imbeau, 2010). **Differentiation** is classroom practice with a balanced emphasis on individual students and course content.

With differentiation, a teacher actively plans a variety of ways for students to learn the content and to express their learning, taking into account the range of learner characteristics. The teacher adjusts the nature of the content and assessments rather than just adding more. Differentiated instruction is rooted in assessment to determine the learner's needs in relation to the unit goals. Thus, differentiation is consistent with data-driven decision making. Differentiated instruction provides multiple approaches to content, process, and product. It is student centered, and it includes a blend of whole-class, small-group, and individual instruction (Tomlinson, 2005b).

How might teachers differentiate their instruction? As Figure 2.1 indicates, differentiation can take place when planning, grouping students, using instructional activities and materials, identifying assignments, and determining which assessments to use. The discussion of the vehicles of differentiation is organized in three areas: the curriculum, student characteristics, and instructional strategies.

ELEMENTS OF THE CURRICULUM
THAT CAN BE DIFFERENTIATED

The curriculum can be differentiated in three ways: (1) the content—the curriculum and the materials and approaches used for students to learn the content, (2) the process—the instructional activities or approaches used to help students to learn the curriculum, and (3) the products—the assessment vehicles through which students demonstrate what they have learned (Tomlinson & Imbeau, 2010).

Content. Content includes the knowledge, skills, and attitudes related to a subject and the materials and mechanisms through which learning is accomplished. In practice, many districts have curriculum guides outlining objectives and content that are expected for all students at a particular grade level or subject area. So there may not be much variation in the content to be taught, but differentiation in the materials could be used in instruction (Gregory & Chapman, 2006).

Some ways that a teacher might differentiate access to the content include the following (Tomlinson, 2005a, 2005b; Tomlinson & Allan, 2000):

- Use texts or novels at more than one reading level.
- Present instruction through both whole-to-part and part-to-whole approaches.
- Use texts, computer programs, videos, and other media to convey key concepts to varied learners.

FIGURE 2.1

WHAT A DIFFERENTIATED CLASSROOM LOOKS LIKE

Planning should:

- Be based on understanding student characteristics and needs

- Be based on ongoing, diagnostic assessments to make instruction more responsive to students

- Be based on an understanding of student readiness, interest, and learning profiles

- Include students working with the teacher to establish whole-class and individual learning goals

Grouping of students should:

- Include many types of groupings (whole class, small group, independent)

- Allow for flexible groups

Instructional activities should:

- Permit multiple approaches to the content, activities, and products demonstrating student learning

- Guide students in making interest-based learning choices

- Permit many learning profile options

- Use time flexibly based on student needs

- Permit students to share multiple perspectives on ideas and events

- Encourage students to be more self-reliant learners

- Support students helping other students and the teacher to solve problems

- Foster the students' responsibility for their own learning

Materials should:

- Be many and varied, including instructional technology

Assignments should:

- Vary in content, based on student need

- Vary in difficulty, based on student readiness

- Allow for choice based on student interests and strengths

- Vary in time allotted

- Contain directions that are clear and direct enough for students to understand

- Provide a mechanism for students to get help when the teacher is busy with other students

Assessments should:

- Be used to guide initial planning

- Be conducted throughout instruction of a unit to guide teacher decisions when making adjustments for the students

- Be conducted in multiple ways

- Define excellence in large measure as individual growth from a starting point

- Focus on teaching the concepts and principles, rather than on all the minute facts about the subject.

- Have advanced students work on special, in-depth projects, while the other students work on the general lessons.

- Use varied texts and resource materials.

- When reteaching is necessary, alter the content and delivery based on student readiness, interests, or learning profile.

- Provide various types of support for learning, such as using study buddies, note-taking organizers, and highlighted printed materials.

Process. **Process** includes the instructional activities or approaches used to help students learn the curriculum. Process is how students come to make sense of and understand the key facts, concepts, generalizations, and skills of a subject. An effective activity involves students using an essential skill to understand an essential idea, and the activity is clearly focused on the learning goal.

Some ways that a teacher might differentiate process or activities include the following (Tomlinson, 2005b; Wormeli, 2007):

- Provide options at differing levels of difficulty or options based on differing student interests.
- Give students choices about how they express what they learn in a project (e.g., create a newspaper article report or display key issues in some type of graphic organizer).
- Differ the amounts of teacher and student support for a task.

Products. **Products** are the vehicles through which students demonstrate what they have learned. Products can also be differentiated, and they may include actual physical products (e.g., portfolios, reports, diagrams, or paper-and-pencil tests) that students prepare, as well as student performances designed to demonstrate a particular skill. Performance-based assessment, including student products and performances, is discussed more thoroughly in Chapter 11. A good product causes students to rethink what they have learned, apply what they can do, extend their understanding and skill, and become involved in both critical and creative thinking.

Examples of ways to differentiate products include the following:

- Allow students to help design products around essential learning goals.
- Provide product assignments of varying degrees of difficulty to match student readiness.
- Use a wide variety of assessments.
- Work with students to develop rubrics that allow for demonstration of both whole-class and individual goals.
- Provide or encourage the use of varied types of resources in preparing products.

from the VOICES Classroom

STEFFANIE OGG, high school teacher, St. Paul, Minnesota

LET YOUR STUDENTS SELECT THE TEST FORMAT

One way that I accommodate various student learning styles is to offer students a choice of test formats. I usually offer my tests in three formats: multiple choice, short essay (or fill-in-the-blank), and matching questions. The student can then select the test format that he or she prefers. The test questions are similar, but the way that the student needs to respond to the questions addresses various ways that students learn and retain information.

I knew that this was a good idea when I heard the students say, "I want to do the matching test; that is a breeze." But another student will say the same thing about one of the other test formats.

At first, creating different versions of a test may be more work for the teacher, but it is worth it when you have greater student success. In fact, some textbook companies provide computer programs with premade tests in different formats.

I also provide students with a little orientation about how to take different types of tests. This includes teaching a simple testing strategy and giving a few practice problems. The results have been great.

URBAN EDUCATION

Particular attention often needs to be paid to struggling learners so they have challenging products to create and the support systems that lead to success. Here are some suggestions (Tomlinson, 2005a):

- Be sure product assignments for learners require them to apply and extend essential understandings and skills for the unit or other product span.
- Use product formats that allow students to express themselves in ways other than written language alone.
- Give product assignments in smaller increments, allowing students to complete one portion of a product before introducing another.
- Think about putting directions on audio- or videotape so students can revisit explanations as needed.
- Prepare or help students to prepare time lines for product work so that tasks seem manageable and comfortably structured.
- Provide miniworkshops on particular skills, such as note taking, conducting interviews, and various study skills.
- Provide templates or organizers that guide students through each step of doing research.
- With challenging tasks, help to set up groups so that students can work together.
- Help students to analyze sample products from prior years so that they develop an awareness of what is expected.
- Provide time, materials, and partnerships at school for students who do not have resources and support at home for project completion.
- When students speak a primary language other than English, be sure that they have access to information in their first language.

Advanced learners need to be stretched in their learning as they prepare products. To do so, here are some suggestions (Tomlinson, 2005a):

- Structure product assignments for advanced learners so that they move forward in a number of ways.
- Consider having advanced learners study the key issues or questions across time periods, disciplines, or cultures.
- As much as possible, include advanced-level research and information.
- Let each advanced learner help you to develop criteria for expert-level content and production.

STUDENT CHARACTERISTICS THAT TEACHERS CAN DIFFERENTIATE

Students vary in at least three ways that make modifying instruction a wise strategy for teachers. Students differ (1) in their readiness to work with a particular idea or skill at a given time, (2) in the topics that they find interesting, and (3) in learning profiles that may be shaped by gender, culture, learning style, or intelligence preference (Tomlinson & Imbeau, 2010).

Readiness. Readiness is a student's entry point into a particular content or skill. To differentiate in response to student readiness, teachers can construct tasks or provide learning choices at different levels of difficulty.

Some general strategies to adjust for readiness include these:

- Adjust the degree of difficulty of a task to provide an appropriate level of challenge.
- Make the task more or less familiar based on the proficiency of the learner's experiences or skills for the task.
- Add or remove teacher or peer coaching, use of manipulatives, or presence or absence of models for a task. This varies the degree of structure and support being provided.

- Vary direct instruction by small-group need.

When planning lessons, consider the various dimensions of the content and the learning tasks as they relate to readiness. For example, simple concepts should be taught before students are ready for complex concepts.

Students with less-developed readiness may need the following (Tomlinson, 2005b):

- Someone to help them to identify and make up gaps in their learning so they can move ahead
- More opportunities for direct instruction or practice
- Activities or products that are more structured or concrete, with fewer steps, closer to their own experiences, and calling on simpler reading skills
- A more deliberate pace of learning

Advanced students may need these opportunities (Tomlinson, 2005b):

- Ability to skip practice with previously mastered skills and understandings
- Activities and products that are quite complex, open ended, abstract, and multifaceted, drawing on advanced reading materials
- A brisk pace of work or perhaps a slower pace to allow for greater depth of exploration of a topic

Interest. **Interest** refers to a student's affinity, curiosity, or passion for a particular topic or skill. To differentiate in response to student interest, a teacher aligns key skills and material for understanding from a curriculum segment with topics or pursuits that intrigue students. Some ways to differentiate in response to student interest include the following:

- Provide broad access to a wide variety of materials and technology.
- Give students a choice of tasks and products, including student-designed options.
- Provide a variety of avenues for student exploration of a topic or expression of learning.
- Encourage investigation or application of key concepts and principles in student interest areas.

Learning Profiles. The term **learning profile** refers to the ways in which we learn best as individuals. It may be shaped by intelligence preferences, gender, culture, or learning style (Tomlinson & Imbeau, 2010). Integrating issues related to learning styles and multiple intelligences provides additional guidance for ways to differentiate instruction (Silver, Strong, & Perini, 2000).

Some ways that teachers can differentiate in response to student learning profiles include the following:

- Create a learning environment with flexible spaces and learning options.
- Present information through auditory, visual, and kinesthetic modes.
- Encourage students to explore information and ideas through auditory, visual, and kinesthetic modes.
- Allow students to work alone or with peers.
- Ensure a choice of competitive, cooperative, and independent experiences.

DIFFERENTIATING WITH THE UNIVERSAL DESIGN FOR LEARNING

Teachers at any grade level can use the **universal design for learning (UDL)** to meet the needs of all students by adapting the curriculum and delivery of instruction. UDL is an instructional approach that helps meet the challenge of diversity by suggesting flexible instructional materials, techniques, and strategies which empower educators to meet students' varied needs (Center for Applied Special Technology, 2011; Council for Exceptional Children, 2005). Version 2.0 of the UDL Guidelines was released in 2011. To create the flexible design and delivery of instruction in UDL, teachers must provide multiple means of representation, expression, and engagement.

Provide Multiple Means of Representation. Teachers should provide multiple means of representation to give learners various ways of acquiring information and knowledge. Students differ in the ways they perceive and comprehend information presented to them. For example, students with learning disabilities or language or cultural differences may require different ways of approaching content.

There is no single means of representation that is optimal for all students. Providing options in representation is essential, and can be facilitated with the following strategies:

1. *Provide options for perception.* To be effective in diverse classrooms, curricula must be presented in ways that are perceptible to all students. To reduce barriers to learning, teachers can (a) provide the same information through different sensory modalities (e.g., vision, hearing, or touch) and (b) provide information in a format that will allow for adjustability by the student (e.g., text that can be enlarged, sounds that can be amplified). For example, when the same information is presented in both speech and text, the complementary representations enhance comprehension for most students. To facilitate the perception of content, teachers can (a) offer ways to customize the display of information, (b) offer alternatives for auditory information, and (c) offer alternatives for visual information.

2. *Provide options for language, mathematical expressions, and symbols.* Students vary in their facility with different forms of representation, both linguistic and nonlinguistic. A graph that illustrates the variables between two concepts may be helpful to one student but puzzling to another. Similarly, vocabulary may clarify concepts to one student but not another. Inequities arise when information is presented to all students through one approach. Provide alternative representations for accessibility, clarity, and comprehensibility for all students. To vary the use of language and symbols, provide options that (a) clarify vocabulary and symbols, (b) clarify syntax and structure, (c) support decoding text, mathematical notations, and symbols, (d) promote understanding across languages, and (e) illustrate through multiple media.

3. *Provide options for comprehension.* In addition to perceiving the information, students need to use information-processing skills, such as integrating new information with prior knowledge, using strategic categorization, and practicing active memorization. Since students differ in information-processing skills, teachers can provide cognitive "ramps" that will help all students gain access to the information. To facilitate comprehension, use options that (a) activate or supply background knowledge, (b) highlight patterns, critical features, big ideas, and relationships, (c) guide information processing, visualization, and manipulation, and (d) maximize transfer and generalization.

Provide Multiple Means of Action and Expression. Teachers should also provide multiple means of **expression** to provide learners with alternatives for demonstrating what they know. Students differ in the ways they can navigate a learning environment and express what they know. For example, students with attention-deficit disorder or those who have language barriers may approach learning tasks and demonstrate mastery very differently. Some may be able to express themselves in writing but not in oral speech, and vice versa.

There is no single means of expression that will be optimal for all students. Again, providing options for expression is essential and include the following:

1. *Provide options for physical action.* A textbook or workbook in a print format provides limited means of navigation or physical interaction (e.g., turning the pages, writing in a workbook). Navigating and interacting in limited ways may be a barrier for some students, such as those who are physically disabled, blind, or have other disorders. Teachers can (a) vary the methods for response and navigation, and (b) optimize access to tools and assistive technologies.

2. *Provide options for expression and communication.* There is no medium of expression that is equally suited for all students. Also, there are some types of media that may be poorly suited for some kinds of expression and for some kinds of students. A student with dyslexia, for example, might excel at storytelling in conversation but have a difficult time writing the story. Alternative approaches to expression should be used. Teachers can (a) use multiple media for communication, (b) use multiple tools for construction and composition, and (c) build fluencies with graduated levels of support for practice and performance.

3. *Provide options for executive functions.* Higher-level brain functioning permits people to overcome impulsive, short-term reactions to their environment and instead set long-term goals, plan effective strategies for reaching those goals, monitor their progress, and modify strategies as needed. The UDL approach involves efforts to expand these executive functions by scaffolding lower-level skills to promote higher levels of development. Provide options that (a) guide effective goal setting, (b) support planning and strategy development, (c) facilitate managing information and resources, and (d) enhance capacity for monitoring progress.

Provide Multiple Means of Engagement. Teachers should provide multiple means of **engagement** to tap learners' interests, offer appropriate challenges, and increase motivation. Students differ markedly in the ways in which they can be engaged or motivated to learn. Some students are highly engaged by spontaneity and novelty, while other students are not affected by these aspects.

No single means of representation will be optimal to engage students in learning. Providing multiple options for engagement is essential:

1. *Provide options for recruiting interest.* Students do not learn information that does not attract their attention or engage their understanding. Also, students differ significantly in what attracts their attention and engages their interest. Provide options that (a) optimize individual choice and autonomy, (b) optimize relevance, value, and authenticity, and (c) minimize threats and distractions.

2. *Provide options for sustaining effort and persistence.* Many kinds of learning require sustained attention and effort. However, students differ considerably in their ability to self-regulate due to their initial motivation, their capacity and skills for self-regulation, their susceptibility to interference, and other reasons. Provide options that (a) heighten the importance of goals and objectives, (b) vary demands and resources to optimize challenge, (c) foster collaboration and communication, and (d) increase mastery-oriented feedback.

3. *Provide options for self-regulation.* The ability to **self-regulate**—to modulate one's emotional reactions to increase effectiveness at coping and engaging with the environment—is a critical aspect of human development. Students benefit from self-regulation. It can be promoted by providing alternatives to support learners with very different aptitudes and prior experiences in learning how to regulate themselves. Provide options for self-regulation that (a) promote expectations and beliefs that optimize motivation, (b) facilitate personal coping skills and strategies, and (c) develop self-assessment and reflection.

Getting to Know Your Students

The more information teachers have about their students, the better able they are to meet students' needs and support student learning. With a better understanding of their students, teachers can be more effective in their selection of instructional strategies, their adjustments for individual differences, and their interactions with the students and their families.

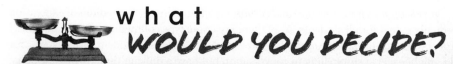

SUSTAINING EFFORT AND PERSISTENCE IN UDL

Strategies with the universal design for learning (UDL) are intended to meet the needs of all students by adapting the curriculum and delivery of instruction. Look at the suggestions described in this section of the chapter for providing options to sustain effort and persistence. Then select one topic in your grade level or subject area that you might teach over a three-day period.

1. Identify what you would write in your lesson plans to indicate the ways you would provide options to sustain student effort and persistence (e.g., have small-group discussion for a certain activity).

2. What are the benefits for students when you provide these options to sustain effort and persistence?

TYPES OF INFORMATION

Several types of information would be useful for teachers to achieve these purposes. Teachers would benefit from information about each student concerning:

1. *Academic abilities, needs, and interests.* Is the student a gifted or a struggling learner? What is the student's reading level? What is the student's performance on achievement tests? What are the student's strengths and weaknesses in relation to the academic work? What are the student's academic interests?

2. *Special needs, learning problems, or disabilities.* Are there any emotional or physical disabilities? Does the student have a learning disability of any kind? What accommodations or modifications are needed? Are there any health problems?

3. *Personal qualities related to diversity.* What is the student's preferred learning style? Is the student a second language learner? How does the student's culture or socioeconomic status influence behavior or learning? Are there any gender or sexuality issues that might influence the student? Is the student considered at-risk for any reason?

4. *The student's life and interests.* What are the student's interests? How does the family and community influence the student? What does the student like to do in spare time? What are the student's ambitions?

5. *Problematic or atypical parent custodial arrangements.* Many family arrangements and conditions exist, and it is useful for teachers to know which family member to contact, along with any other special considerations. One parent may have custody of a child with conditions to limit contact with the other parent. The student may be living with grandparents or other relatives. The student may have a parent away from the home, due to military obligations, prison, or other reasons. The student may have gay or lesbian parents.

SOURCES OF INFORMATION

Some information about your students can be obtained from existing records, such as the student's cumulative record. Much information can be obtained directly from the students and their families. While there are many ways you can obtain information about the students in your class, here are some commonly used sources:

Cumulative Records. The school office will have a cumulative record folder for each student. That folder includes personal information, home and family data, school attendance records, scores on standardized achievement tests, year-end grades for all previous years of schooling, and other teachers' anecdotal comments. Other types of additional information may be included, such as which family member to contact (or not to contact). Collectively, the cumulative record provides considerable information.

Using Student Questionnaires. Asking students to fill out a questionnaire can provide much insight into their actions, interests, and skills. Include questions that provide information helpful to you as you (1) select curricular content, instructional activities, and strategies; (2) determine your way of interacting with the students in the class; (3) identify how to address the diversity of learners in the class; (4) address any challenges, problems, or disabilities the students may have; and (5) try to get to know each student to enable their successful learning. Some open-ended questions can yield useful information (e.g., It helps me learn when . . . , or, What I appreciate about my family is . . .).

Using Family Questionnaires and Contacts. Information from families about their own children also can provide great insight into the qualities and needs of the students in your class. A brief questionnaire may be prepared for parents at the start of the school year. Items may include asking how parents describe their children, what makes their children special, what their children do at home, their children's strengths and weaknesses, and parents' hopes for their children during the school year. In addition, teachers may see some parents at back-to-school night or at parent–teacher conferences.

Observing and Interacting with Students. Arrange for icebreaker activities for students to get to know each other at the start of the school year. Much information about each student can be learned simply by watching students interact during these icebreakers. Informal observation and interaction with students also provide opportunities to learn more about each student.

USING THE INFORMATION

To know how to use the information you gather, think about the reasons you wanted that information in the first place—to be more effective in your selection of instructional strategies, adjustments for individual differences, and interactions with the students and their families. Gathering information is not sufficient. You must read, review, and mentally process the information to guide the decisions you will make in the classroom.

It may be useful to first summarize the information you have on each student, and perhaps on the class as a whole. Whether you have a class of 22 fifth-grade students or 143 high school students in several classes makes a big difference in how you might summarize the information. Some teachers may read through the information about each student from the various sources reviewed earlier and then simply make mental notations. Other teachers may want to summarize results of each question on a student questionnaire, for example, to get a picture of the entire class. Still other teachers may have a card for each student, with key information listed on the card. For certain types of information (e.g., the preferred type of learning approaches or styles), it may be helpful to make a list of students so that you pay proper attention to the students on that issue.

Contextual Factors to Guide Planning

Teachers must know their students before they can effectively plan instruction. The sources of diversity reviewed earlier in this chapter are among the student characteristics that need to be taken into account. But there are more factors to consider in the planning process.

Many teacher education programs require their students to prepare a teacher work sample at some point in the program, often during student teaching. Various names may be used for the teacher work sample, such as the student teaching portfolio, comprehensive unit plan, or other variations. The required sections also may vary somewhat.

A **teacher work sample** is a report describing how the student has planned, taught, and assessed a multiday instructional unit, and it includes several specific sections. The Renaissance Teacher Work Sample Consortium (2011) is a group of organizations that developed guidelines for the teacher work sample and endorsed and supported its use in member universities. The work of this consortium was well received, and their guidelines for teacher work samples have been used by other universities.

Teacher work samples have seven sections: contextual factors, learning goals, the assessment plan, the design for instruction, instructional decision making, analysis of student learning, and reflection and self-evaluation. The section on **contextual factors** includes information the teacher uses about the teaching–learning context and students' individual differences to set learning goals and plan instruction and assessment. The written report on contextual factors includes a discussion of the relevant factors and how they affect the teaching and learning process. The discussion also identifies any supports and challenges that affect instruction and student learning. Considering the contextual factors is the critical first step in the planning process.

The contextual factors discussion is organized in the following four categories, with pertinent information needed in each category (Renaissance Teacher Work Sample Consortium, 2011):

1. *Community, district, and school factors*. Address geographic location, community and school population, socioeconomic profile, and race/ethnicity. Address stability of the community, political climate, community support for education, and other environmental factors.

2. *Classroom factors*. Address physical features, availability of technology equipment and resources, and the extent of parental involvement. Address other relevant factors such as classroom rules and routines, grouping patterns, scheduling, and classroom arrangement.

3. *Student characteristics*. Address student characteristics to consider in designing instruction and assessing learning. Include factors such as age, gender, race/ethnicity, special needs, achievement/development levels, culture, language, interests, learning styles/modalities, or students' skill levels. Address students' skills and prior learning that may influence the development of learning goals, instruction, and assessment.

4. *Instructional implications*. Address contextual characteristics of the community, classroom, and students that have implications for instructional planning and assessment.

Preparing a report on contextual factors enables teachers to gather much pertinent information and apply that information to the planning process. As noted above, one part of the contextual factors section includes information on the characteristics of students and the corresponding implications for making accommodations and modifications to instruction. Figure 2.2 displays a sample reporting format for student characteristics in the class.

FIGURE 2.2

CONTEXTUAL FACTORS—STUDENT CHARACTERISTICS IN A CLASS

CLASSROOM DESCRIPTION

_____Grade level

_____Age range of students

_____Percentage of students receiving free or reduced lunch

CONTEXTUAL FACTORS

Indicate the number of students from your class for each item. On a separate paper, describe how you will provide student learning adaptations to meet your students' needs for each category.

Gender

_____Females

_____Males

Ethnicity

_____White

_____Black or African American

_____Hispanic of any race

_____Asian

_____American Indian or Alaskan Native

_____Native Hawaiian or Pacific Islander

_____Two or more races

_____Race or ethnicity unknown

Language Proficiency

_____Fluent in English

_____English language learner

Academic Proficiency

_____Below grade level

_____Above grade level

Special Needs

_____Specific learning disability

_____Visually impaired

_____Hearing impaired

_____Speech/language impaired

_____Physically impaired

_____Deaf/blind

_____Other health impaired

_____Traumatic brain injury

_____Multiple disabilities

_____Emotional or behavioral disorders (EBD)

_____Autism

_____Intellectual disabilities

_____Gifted or talented

_____Developmentally delayed

_____Other (specify)

DEVELOPMENTAL CHARACTERISTICS OF YOUR STUDENTS

Look at your class as a whole. For each type of development listed below, on a separate paper describe: (1) specific characteristics of that type of development, and (2) specific implications for instruction in your class.

- Cognitive development (e.g., cognitive abilities, learning needs, readiness)
- Physical development (e.g., developmental level, size, energy)
- Emotional development (e.g., self-concept, security and structure)
- Social development (e.g., socializing, peer influence, working preferences)

Key Terms

Accommodation	Cultural diversity	Gifted or talented learners	Psychomotor skills
Advanced learners	Culturally responsive	Individualized study	Readiness
Affective area	teaching	Intelligence	Self-regulate
Alternative or differenti-	Differentiated	Interest	Sensory modality
ated assignments	materials	Learning profile	Socioeconomic status
Brain hemisphericity	Differentiation	Learning style	(SES)
Cognitive activity	Engagement	Least restrictive	Struggling learner
Cognitive style	Exceptional students	environment	Students at risk
Conceptual tempo	Expression	Modification	Teacher work sample
Content	Field dependence/	Process	Universal design for
Contextual factors	independence	Products	learning (UDL)

Major Concepts

1. Individual differences need to be taken into account when instructional methods are selected and procedures are determined.

2. Diversity can be due to influences of learning style, creative potential, gender, language, cultural diversity, disabilities, conditions placing the student at risk, and socioeconomic factors.

3. Information about the sources of student diversity can be used as the basis for classroom decisions to create a supportive, caring learning environment.

4. A variety of instructional approaches is needed to challenge all students and to meet their instructional needs.

5. Differentiation is simply attending to the learning needs of a particular student or group of students, rather than the more typical pattern of teaching the class as though all individuals in it were basically alike.

6. Teachers can adapt one or more of the curricular elements (the content, the learning process, and the products students prepare) based on student characteristics (readiness, interests, and learning profiles) at any point in a lesson or unit using a range of instructional and management strategies.

7. Universal design for learning (UDL) is a way to adapt a curriculum and the delivery of instruction to meet the needs of all learners.

8. In an effort to get to know students, teachers can select the types of information they need, identify the sources for that information, and then use that information to be more effective in their selection of instructional strategies, their adjustments for individual differences, and their interactions with the students and their families.

9. Preparing a report on contextual factors enables teachers to gather and organize much pertinent information and apply that information to the planning process.

Discussion/Reflective Questions

1. What types of student diversity were evident in classrooms in your own K–12 schooling experience? In what ways did your teachers take these student characteristics into account in the selection of content and the use of instructional approaches?

2. Are you enthusiastic or skeptical about the relevance of learning style theory and brain hemisphere research for classroom instruction? Why?

3. What are some challenges that you might experience in dealing with students who have limited English proficiency? What could you do to overcome these challenges to promote student learning?

4. What challenges might teachers face when trying to differentiate the curriculum and the techniques of delivering the content?

5. What is the value of preparing a contextual factors report for the class that you will be teaching?

Suggested Activities

FOR CLINICAL SETTINGS

1. Make a list of 10 or more questions that you would like to ask an effective teacher about addressing the diversity of students in the classroom.

2. Examine a unit from a textbook you might use, and identify ways that you might differentiate elements of the curriculum.

3. Make a list of several ways that you could provide accommodations when students take a test.

FOR FIELD EXPERIENCES

1. Using the categories of differences addressed in this chapter as a guide, ask several teachers to describe individual differences that they notice in their students. How do the teachers take these differences into account?

2. Ask several teachers how they vary instruction to better meet the needs of their students.

3. For one classroom, prepare a contextual factors report describing the characteristics of the students and the ways that student learning adaptations might be made to address the diversity of learners.

Further Reading

Center for Applied Special Technology. (2011). *Universal design for learning guidelines version 2.0.* Wakefield, MA: Author. Retrieved May 28, 2011, from http://www.udlcenter.org/aboutudl/udlguidelines

Describes the three principles of universal design and provides examples to apply them in teaching.

Gollnick, D. M., & Chinn, P. C. (2009). *Multicultural education in a pluralistic society* (8th ed.). Boston: Allyn & Bacon.

Examines differences in students based on class, ethnicity and race, gender, exceptionality, religion, language, and age. Considers ways that education can be multicultural.

Gregory, G. H., & Chapman, C. (2006). *Differentiated instructional strategies: One size doesn't fit all* (2nd ed.). Thousand Oaks, CA: Corwin Press.

Provides reasons for and examples of various ways to differentiate. Considers learner characteristics, assessment techniques, grouping, instructional strategies, and curricular approaches.

Tomlinson, C. A. (2005). *How to differentiate instruction in mixed-ability classrooms* (2nd ed.). Upper Saddle River, NJ: Pearson/Prentice-Hall.

Describes ways that teachers can differentiate content, process, and product according to a student's readiness, interests, and learning profile.

Tomlinson, C. A., & Imbeau, M. B. (2010). *Leading and managing a differentiated classroom.* Alexandria, VA: Association for Supervision and Curriculum Development.

Provides reasons and background for differentiating classrooms. Offers specific ideas for managing a differentiated classroom with the learning environment, routines, and other suggestions.

Technology Resources

TIPS ON SUPPORTING ALL STUDENTS: EQUITY AND DIVERSITY

http://www.nctm.org/resources/content
.aspx?id=15863

Offers guidelines for classroom teachers in addressing student diversity and providing equitable opportunities for all students.

PRINCIPLES FOR CULTURALLY RESPONSIVE TEACHING

http://www.alliance.brown.edu/tdl/tl-strategies/
crt-principles.shtml

Describes seven characteristics of culturally responsive teaching.

KIDBLOG

http://kidblog.org

This site is designed for elementary and middle school teachers who want to provide students with their own, unique blog. Kidblog's simple, yet powerful tools allow students to publish posts and participate in discussions within a secure classroom blogging community. Teachers maintain complete control over student blogs.

DIFFERENTIATING INSTRUCTION

http://www.learnerslink.com/curriculum.htm

This site provides links to numerous websites concerning many aspects of differentiating instruction and related topics.

MyEducationLab™

Go to the **MyEducationLab** (www.myeducationlab.com) for General Methods and familiarize yourself with the content:

- Topically organized Assignments and Activities, tied to learning outcomes for the course, that can help you more deeply understand course content
- Topically organized Building Teaching Skills and Dispositions learning units allow you to apply and develop understanding of teaching methods.
- A chapter-specific pretest that assesses your understanding of the content offers hints and feedback for

each question and generates a study plan including links to Review, Practice, and Enrichment activities that will enhance your understanding of the concepts. A Study Plan posttest with hints and feedback ensures you understood concepts from the chapter after having completed the enrichment activities.

A Correlation Guide may be downloaded by instructors to show how MyEducationLab content aligns to this book.

The Fundamentals of Planning

3

THIS CHAPTER PROVIDES INFORMATION THAT WILL HELP YOU TO

1. Describe the reasons for instructional planning.

2. Describe the relationship of curriculum standards to instructional planning.

3. Apply backward design when planning courses, terms, units, weeks, and lessons.

4. Apply the linear-rational approach to instructional planning.

5. Identify additional resources that can be used when planning.

Planning for instruction is a critical element in the instructional process. Carefully designed, comprehensive plans will have a positive effect on student learning. To help you to understand and be prepared to plan for instruction, this chapter will examine the planning process, curriculum considerations, types of teacher plans, the linear-rational approach to planning, and related planning issues.

What Is Planning?

Planning for instruction refers to decisions that are made about organizing, implementing, and evaluating instruction. Planning is one of the most important tasks that teachers undertake. It allows teachers to deeply reflect about the subject matter and the content they teach.

When making planning decisions, you also need to consider who is to do what, when and in what order instructional events will occur, where the events will take place, the amount of instructional time to be used, and resources and materials to be used. Planning decisions also deal with issues such as content to be covered, instructional strategies, lesson delivery behaviors, instructional media, classroom management, classroom climate, and student evaluation.

The goal of planning is to ensure student learning. Planning, therefore, helps teachers create, arrange, and organize instructional events which facilitate that learning. Planning helps to arrange the appropriate flow and sequence of instructional events and also to manage time and events. The amount of time spent on planning varies greatly among individual teachers. It is influenced by factors such as pupil needs, the complexity of the teaching assignment, facilities and equipment, and the experience of the teacher.

To more fully understand instructional planning, it is useful to consider the reasons for planning and many factors that are considered while planning.

REASONS FOR PLANNING

When looking at the entire school year, planning is needed for the year, each term, each unit, each week, and each lesson. School districts typically require written weekly plans, and the school principal often reviews the plans of beginning teachers. Plans for the year, term, and units are not commonly reviewed by the principal. There are a number of reasons to prepare thorough plans for all of these time frames, with some plans written in detail and some not so thoroughly written (Freiberg & Driscoll, 2005).

Planning can help you to do the following:

- Gain a sense of direction, and through this, a feeling of confidence and security. Planning can help you stay on course and reduce your anxiety about instruction.

- Organize, sequence, and become familiar with course content.

- Collect and prepare related instructional materials, and plan to use various types of instructional media. This planning will help when ordering instructional supplies.

There are 10 InTASC standards (see pages xx–xxi), and each standard in the original document includes a list of performances, essential knowledge, and critical dispositions to indicate more clearly what is intended in the standard.

Since this chapter deals with planning and curriculum, some representative statements from InTASC Standard #4, Content Knowledge, and Standard #7, Planning for Instruction, are listed here concerning topics in this chapter.

PERFORMANCES

■ The teacher creates opportunities for students to learn, practice, and master academic language in their content.

■ The teacher evaluates plans in relation to short- and long-range goals and systematically adjusts plans to meet each student's learning needs and enhance learning.

ESSENTIAL KNOWLEDGE

■ The teacher has a deep knowledge of student content standards and learning progressions in the discipline(s) she or he teaches.

■ The teacher knows when and how to adjust plans based on assessment information and learner responses.

CRITICAL DISPOSITIONS

■ The teacher realizes that content knowledge is not a fixed body of facts but is complex, culturally situated, and ever evolving. The teacher keeps abreast of new ideas and understandings in the field.

■ The teacher takes professional responsibility to use short- and long-term planning as a means of ensuring student learning.

■ Use a variety of instructional strategies and activities over time.

■ Prepare to interact with students during instruction. This may include preparing a list of important questions or guidelines for a cooperative group activity.

■ Incorporate techniques to motivate students to learn in each lesson.

■ Take into account individual differences and the diversity of students when selecting objectives, content, strategies, materials, and requirements.

■ Arrange for appropriate requirements and evaluation of student performance.

■ Become a reflective decision maker about curriculum and instruction.

■ Provide substitute teachers and members of a teaching team with a specific plan to follow if you are absent.

■ Show other members of a teaching team what you are doing and how you are doing it.

■ Satisfy administrative requirements. Teachers are often required to turn in their weekly plans for review by their principal.

■ Use written plans as resources for future planning.

FACTORS CONSIDERED IN PLANNING

When making plans for instruction, you will need to take into account factors related to your beliefs about teaching and the role of teachers, the instructional activities, your own personal and professional characteristics, and your reflections on your practice. Taken together, these factors will affect the decisions that you make about your instructional plans.

Factors Related to Instructional Activities. Instructional activities are the basic means through which teachers interact to present concepts and skills to students. There are a number of factors which you may consider when you plan any given instructional activity.

1. *Content.* **Content** refers to the knowledge, skill, rule, concept, or creative process that you wish students to learn. Students are expected to achieve school district goals stated in curriculum guides, and you select content related to the goals. While you have some autonomy, you are expected to teach and deal with content that is consistent with the district-approved goals.

Planning for content varies with the level of instruction, whether it be an advanced course, general content, or remedial material. Also, the nature of the content may affect your planning decisions. For example, you might plan and teach in different ways for mathematics, reading, laboratory-related content, and social studies. Thus, what is taught determines to a great extent how you might plan and teach your lessons.

2. *Materials.* **Materials** are the tangible written, physical, or visual stimuli that are used in instruction. Textbooks, workbooks, computers, software, and websites are some materials that you might use.

The availability of these materials influences your planning decisions. For example, when planning a lesson in which the students will paint with watercolors, an art teacher would need to be sure that certain materials are available. If the materials are not available, the teacher would need to make alternative plans. Teachers also need to consider how closely matched the materials are to the instructional objectives. For example, when considering using a DVD or a web-based field trip in a lesson, you would need to check to see if the nature and level of the content is suitable.

3. *Instructional strategies.* Selecting a variety of instructional strategies used to teach content is a central planning decision for teachers. You might use presentations, demonstrations, questions, recitations, practice, and drills, or you could use discussions, panels and debates, or small groups. You might also select inquiry and discovery approaches through the use of gaming, role playing and simulation, laboratory work, or computer-assisted instruction.

4. *Teacher behaviors.* Teachers do a number of things during a lesson to conduct the lesson and to help engage students in learning activities. You need to make plans to state expectations, provide a set induction, maintain a group focus, provide smooth transitions, clearly present lesson content, provide closure and a summary, and handle other aspects of conducting a lesson.

5. *Structure of the lesson.* Structure refers to actions that take place at certain points in the class period or the lesson presentation, and you need to plan that structure in advance. For example, at the start of the class period you may provide directions, pass out materials, or direct students to new locations. As the lesson proceeds, students might be reading, discussing, writing, or participating in a particular instructional strategy. At the end of the class, students may return to their seats, clean up, or collect materials. When delivering lesson content, you might use a certain sequence of actions reflecting a certain approach to instruction.

6. *Learning environment.* When planning for instructional activities, consider the type of learning environment you would like to create. While many factors need to be taken into account, several issues warrant special attention. First, you need to plan for and establish an effective classroom management system that deals with issues such as instituting classroom rules and procedures, reinforcing desired behaviors, holding students academically accountable, and creating a positive classroom climate. Second, you need to establish a plan of dealing with misbehavior. Third, you need to plan for ways to provide for individual differences. Fourth, you need to plan for ways to motivate students to learn. All of these issues affect the learning environment, and you need to plan for effective ways to address them.

7. *Students.* When planning for instructional activities, consider characteristics of the particular students you have in your classroom. Take into account students' motivational needs, academic needs, cultural backgrounds, and physical and psychological needs. Furthermore, consider how students will be grouped for instruction (i.e., whole group, small group, independent work), and consider which particular students will be in groups. As you plan, take into account the ability levels of the students and the ways in which students might be

grouped to achieve instructional objectives. In addition, consider the number of students who are involved in the instructional activities.

8. *Duration of the lesson.* Make plans for the time that is available or allocated. Instructional activities tend to last from 10 to 60 minutes. In a kindergarten class, 10 minutes of an activity may be the limit of student concentration and attention. Class lengths in primary and intermediate elementary grades are commonly up to the discretion of the teacher, but they often last no longer than 20 to 30 minutes. Classes in middle schools, junior high schools, and high schools commonly have predetermined lengths, ranging from 45 to 60 minutes or as much as 90 minutes in a block schedule. Within the time available, teachers need to use a variety of activities and resources to achieve lesson objectives and maintain student motivation. You need to be a good time manager to ensure that students have the opportunity to achieve the goals of the lesson during this time period.

9. *Location of the lesson.* When planning for instructional activities, consider where the lesson will take place. The location of an activity may change based on the need for (a) space to work on a set of materials (e.g., a computer station or a learning center); (b) additional new references, materials, or experiences (e.g., the library, a field trip); or (c) a different social structure (e.g., a debate, a play, or any activity in which students work together).

Teacher Characteristics. Planning decisions about instructional activities and instructional routines are affected by the characteristics of the teachers themselves:

1. The amount of teaching experience you have influences planning decisions. Previous experiences provide you with a more complete mental image of lessons and thus your initial lessons need less adjustment.

2. Your philosophy of teaching and learning will have an effect on planning decisions.

3. Your knowledge of content also affects planning decisions. Teachers who know their content usually can plan more varied and flexible lessons because they can readily use and arrange information.

4. Your organizational style affects planning decisions. This style is reflected by your need for structure, planning routine, and style of solving problems.

5. Expectations that you set for your classes, for student learning, and for your own teaching also influence your planning and lesson images.

6. General feelings of security and control about teaching play an influential role in the planning process. When you feel secure in all dimensions of teaching, teaching plans tend to be less rigid. When teachers are not so secure, they tend to be more structured and plan in greater detail.

In summary, your characteristics serve as a filter through which instructional activities and routines are considered.

Curriculum Considerations When Planning

The curriculum is the content that is taught in school settings. School districts prepare curriculum guides that describe the content for each subject at each grade level. When planning for your classroom, it is important to use district curriculum guides, but also to be aware of current curriculum standards and new influences on the curriculum such as the Common Core State Standards and curriculum recommendations related to the 21st Century Skills.

CLASSROOM CASE STUDY

GOOD LESSON PLAN, POOR RESULTS

Carla Ramirez, a third-grade teacher, has some concerns about her ability to carry out her lesson plans as the first half of the year is coming to a close. At the beginning of the school year, Ms. Ramirez asked her students to fill out a questionnaire regarding their interests and the types of activities they like. She planned to use the student responses to come up with ideas for her lessons to meet students' interests and to engage them in the learning process.

Since the majority of her students indicated that they enjoy cooking and/or baking with adults, Ms. Ramirez decided to incorporate recipes and food measurements in her math lesson today on fractions. She also made a note of all of the resources she would need and made sure the materials were gathered and available for the lesson. Prior to teaching the lesson, she wrote a detailed lesson plan, including a list of anticipated student questions and corresponding responses.

During instruction, Ms. Ramirez found that most of the students answered her questions with ease. While she anticipated that a number of concepts in the lesson would be challenging for the students, many students appeared to have previous experience with these topics and grasped them effortlessly. Ms. Ramirez continued with her lesson as planned, but she became anxious when a group of students who completed the activity early became talkative and distracting.

FOCUS QUESTIONS

1. What were the strengths of Ms. Ramirez's planning process? Her weaknesses?

2. What would you suggest that she do to improve her lessons in the second half of the year?

CURRICULUM STANDARDS

It is useful to have some background information about curriculum when you are planning for instruction. Information is provided here about national and state learning standards, state and local curriculum frameworks, and the translation of curriculum standards into classroom instruction.

National and State Learning Standards. In the United States, education is primarily a state and local responsibility. States and communities develop curricula and determine requirements for enrollment and graduation. The financial infrastructure for the support of K–12 education reflects the primary role that local and state financing play. Of the more than $1 trillion being spent nationwide on education in 2010–2011, the vast majority comes from state and local sources. At the elementary and secondary level, about 89 percent of all monies comes from nonfederal sources.

Therefore, the federal contribution to elementary and secondary education is about 11 percent, which includes funds for the Department of Education, the Department of Health and Human Services' Head Start program, and the Department of Agriculture's School Lunch program. Most federal funds are in Title I programs which are directed to improve learning for students at risk of educational failure, such as low-achieving children in our nation's highest-poverty schools, children with disabilities, Alaska Native and American Indian children, children who are neglected or delinquent, and young children and their families who are in need of family literacy services.

While the federal role in education remains small, an interesting trend has begun in which several groups are engaging in the development of standards for nationwide application. For example, the Council of Chief State School Officers (CCSSO), which represents the commissioners and state school superintendents across the United States, has recently supported the development of the revised Interstate Teacher Assessment and Support Consortium (InTASC) standards that serve as model core teaching standards for what teachers should know and be able to do to in order to meet the needs of students. In addition, the Common Core State Standards and curriculum standards identified by professional organizations are influencing curriculum.

Curriculum Influence from InTASC. The InTASC standards outline principles for teaching and provide a model for effective teaching and learning (CCSSO, 2011). InTASC Standards 4 and 5 are centrally focused on the fact that teachers must know the content they teach and also be able to make that content engaging for your students. See the wording of these two InTASC standards on page xx of this book.

To plan effectively, teachers must have a deep understanding of the content they teach and be able to utilize their content knowledge to access information, apply knowledge in real-world settings, and ensure students' mastery of content. Teachers must use multiple means of communication, including electronic media and information technology, to bring appropriate content to learners. They must also combine critical thinking, problem solving, creativity, and strong communication skills to assist learners in solving problems and gaining new insights concerning this content.

The InTASC teaching standards describe what *teachers* should know and be able to do to ensure their students reach meaningful learning goals in relation to curriculum. Cross-disciplinary skills (e.g., communication, collaboration, critical thinking, and the use of technology) can be found throughout the teaching standards because of their importance for learners. Additionally, the teaching standards stress that teachers build literacy and thinking skills across the curriculum, as well as help learners address multiple perspectives in exploring ideas and solving problems. The teaching standards also address interdisciplinary themes (e.g., financial literacy, civic literacy) and the teacher's ability to design learning experiences that draw upon multiple disciplines.

Curriculum Influence from the Common Core State Standards. A state-led effort to establish a shared set of clear educational standards resulted in the Common Core State Standards (discussed later in this chapter). Those standards define the knowledge and skills students should have within their K–12 education so that they will graduate from high school able to succeed in college and the workforce. Although the federal government has not put forth a set of officially recognized national standards, currently over 40 states have adopted the Common Core State Standards for student learning. If this trend continues among the remaining states, American education may soon have a set of national standards by default.

Curriculum Influence from Professional Organizations. Several professional education organizations, often referred to as professional societies, have volunteered to take on the challenge of creating curriculum standards or guidelines to be used on a national level, including the following:

- National Council of Teachers of Mathematics
- National Council of Teachers of English
- National Academies of Science
- National Council for the Social Studies
- National Center for History in the Schools
- National Geographic Society
- National Council on Economic Education
- Center for Civic Education
- Consortium of National Arts Education Associations
- International Society for Technology in Education (ISTE)

Professional societies such as the National Council of Teachers of Mathematics, National Council of Teachers of English, and the National Council for the Social Studies have worked to develop a codified set of standards. The goal of their efforts is to improve student learning in the subjects they represent. These societies use the expertise of their members from K–12 and higher education to identify what it means to be "educated" in the fields they represent. The curriculum standards prepared by these professional societies have influenced the selection of curriculum at the state and national levels. The curriculum standards from these professional societies are generally available from their society's website.

State and Local Curriculum Frameworks.

Historically, curriculum frameworks have differed from state to state but have had influences similar to the standards movement described in the section above. A **curriculum framework** is an organized plan or set of standards that defines the content to be learned in terms of clear, definable standards for what students should know and be able to do. The purpose of state curriculum frameworks is to provide guidelines for local school districts to prepare their K–12 curriculum.

The state curriculum framework is useful in that it provides: (1) a structure from which a standards-based district, school, and classroom curriculum can be developed, organized, implemented, and assessed; (2) the basis for the development of a comprehensive state, local, and classroom assessment system; and (3) an explicit map of what is to be included in statewide assessments of student learning. The curriculum framework shows teachers what students are expected to know and be able to do at any specific grade level, and it helps them identify building blocks to student skills and knowledge that can be helpful in providing remediation or extra help to students.

Since standards differ from state to state, the wording in the curriculum frameworks varies in the depth and breadth of the content being addressed and in how clearly the standards are stated. Standards that are not clearly or specifically written are open to wide interpretation by teachers and curriculum specialists. Without a common understanding of what students should learn by grade level, there might be much variation from one teacher to the next in how the standards are interpreted and applied in the classroom.

A Sample State Curriculum Framework.

A brief description from the *Mathematics Framework for California Public Schools* (California Department of Education, 2006) is provided here to give you an idea of what is included in a state curriculum framework. Only part of the framework is presented here. To access the complete K–12 mathematics framework, visit the department's website at http://www.cde.ca.gov/ci/ma/cf. That site is worth exploring with many useful sections, including guiding principles of an effective math program, content standards, grade-level considerations, instructional strategies, assessment, and use of technology. You can begin to reflect on how you will plan instruction based on a curriculum framework.

Right at the start, the mathematics framework states that the purpose of the framework is to guide the curriculum development and the instruction that teachers provide in their efforts to ensure that all students meet or exceed the mathematics standards. The framework provides a context for implementing the standards in the form of guidelines for the design of curricula, instructional materials, instructional practices, and staff development.

For illustration purposes, we will look at the elementary mathematics standards in grade 4 in the California framework. The general description at the start states: "By the end of grade four, students understand large numbers and addition, subtraction, multiplication, and division of whole numbers. They describe and compare simple fractions and decimals. They understand the properties of, and the relationships between, plane geometric figures. They also can collect, represent, and analyze data to answer questions."

The mathematics content standards in California for grade 4 (and all K–7 grades) are organized by the grade level and presented in five strands: (1) number sense; (2) algebra and functions; (3) measurement and geometry; (4) statistics, data analysis, and probability; and (5) mathematical reasoning. Each strand has several subdivisions, which are the standards. For fourth-grade mathematics, here is the number sense strand along with the four standards related to that strand. In the California mathematics framework, sample content and problems are provided for each strand.

Number Sense (Grade 4)

1. Students understand the place value of whole numbers and decimals to two decimal places and how whole numbers and decimals relate to simple fractions.

2. Students extend their use and understanding of whole numbers to the addition and subtraction of simple decimals.

3. Students solve problems involving addition, subtraction, multiplication, and division of whole numbers and understand the relationships among the operations.

4. Students know how to factor small whole numbers.

Translating Curriculum Standards into Classroom Instruction. While familiarizing yourself with the important issues concerning the role of standards in education, you may be wondering how those state standards translate into your classroom teaching. Figure 3.1 illustrates the relationship between the framework set forth in a state curriculum

FIGURE 3.1

CURRICULUM PLANNING: FROM STATE LEVEL TO THE CLASSROOM

State Curriculum Framework

- Provides philosophy that guides curriculum implementation
- Sets forth essential content to be taught, grade by grade
- Demonstrates increasing complexity of material within content
- Notes modifications of curriculum to meet needs of special populations such as students with learning disabilities, English language learners, or at-risk students

District Curriculum Guides

- Provides content goals aligned with state curriculum framework
- Describes appropriate teaching activities
- Provides outlines for unit plans and a sequence of topics

Teacher's Unit and Lesson Plans

- Describes how curriculum goals are implemented in daily classroom environment
- Identifies topics to be covered, materials needed, and activities to be completed
- Clearly describes the basis and process for assessment
- Notes accommodations and modifications to support students with special needs

Teacher's Grade Book

- Records objectives mastered
- Identifies areas to be retaught
- Provides indicators of progress in student learning
- Informs student retention and promotion decisions

and a living, breathing classroom. The curriculum content flows from the state framework through district levels to ultimately inform teacher instruction.

While the state framework sets forth goals for what students should know and be able to do, teachers have an active role to play in translating those content goals into the classroom. Teachers are responsible for considering their individual students' needs, capabilities, and developmental levels when planning and implementing instruction. The reflective process described in Chapter 1 is again at work when teachers carry out the objectives described at the state level in a way that is both accessible and challenging for their students.

COMMON CORE CURRICULUM

The **Common Core State Standards** initiative is a state-led effort coordinated by the National Governors Association Center for Best Practices (NGA Center) and the Council of Chief State School Officers (CCSSO). The curriculum standards were developed in collaboration with teachers, school administrators, and education experts to provide a clear and consistent framework to prepare students for college and the workforce. The standards underwent a series of drafts and revisions, incorporating input from state departments of education, teachers' unions, curriculum content associations, and the general public.

The standards provide teachers and parents with a common understanding of what students are expected to learn. Consistent standards will provide appropriate benchmarks for all students, regardless of where they live. The standards define the knowledge and skills students should have within their K–12 education so that they will graduate from high school being able to succeed in college courses and in workforce training programs. The standards (Common Core, 2011):

- Are aligned with college and work expectations
- Are clear, understandable, and consistent
- Include rigorous content and application of knowledge through high-order skills
- Build on strengths and lessons of current state standards
- Are informed by other top-performing countries, so that all students are prepared to succeed in our global economy and society
- Are evidence-based

The federal government was not involved in the development of the standards. Individual states choose whether to adopt these standards, and over 40 states have adopted the Common Core Standards.

The Common Core State Standards are available for (1) mathematics, K–12, and (2) English-language arts and literacy in history/social studies, science, and technical subjects for grades K–12. These subject areas were chosen for the Common Core State Standards because these two subjects provide the foundational knowledge and skills for other subject areas. The Common Core Standards are aligned with college and work expectations and are internationally benchmarked. The complete listing of the Common Core Standards can be found on the Common Core webpage at http://www.corestandards.org. Rather than summarizing some information from these standards, we encourage you to go to the Common Core website and examine the actual standards and all of the related material.

The Common Core State Standards will *not* keep local teachers from deciding what or how to teach. The standards are a clear set of shared goals and expectations for what knowledge and skills will help students succeed. However, local teachers, principals, superintendents, and others will decide how the standards are to be met. Teachers will continue to devise lesson plans and tailor instruction to their students. Teachers' professional judgment and decision making is important in translating the standards into the classroom. The Common Core State Standards differ from previous standards in math and English-language arts in a variety of ways and have the following implications for the classroom teacher:

The Common Core State Standards

- Fewer, focused standards in each subject
- More depth for each standard
- Teach for understanding
- Teach with more higher-level objectives

Instruction

- More focus on main ideas (rather than simply getting the answer correct)
- More project-based and real-life learning
- More inquiry
- More on the application of the content
- More student-centered instructional approaches

Classroom Assessments

- More performance-based assessments
- More short answer and constructed response questions

The states that have adopted the Common Core Standards will have curriculum and instruction that is consistent with the standards. Once instruction takes place, assessment soon follows. There are two multistate consortia that are developing an assessment system based on the Common Core State Standards. One of these consortia—the SMARTER Balanced Assessment Consortium (SBAC)—is a collection of more than 30 states that have been working collaboratively to develop this assessment system.

Common Core for Mathematics. The mathematics standards are designed to stress conceptual understanding and organizing principles, such as place value. The mathematics standards define what students should know and be able to do. The standards are grade specific and provide descriptions of the mathematical knowledge needed for college and career readiness. The Common Core State Standards that focus on mathematical practice describe the capabilities that students need to develop. These practices rest on important processes that support success in mathematics. They include students mastering the National Council for Teachers of Mathematics (NCTM) process standards of problem solving, reasoning and proof, communication, representation, and connections.

Common Core for English-Language Arts. The standards set requirements for English-language arts (ELA) and literacy in history/social studies, science, and technical subjects. The standards address reading, writing, speaking and listening, language, and media and technology. Literacy standards for grade 6 and above were designed to ensure that teachers of English-language arts, history/social studies, science, and technical subjects can use their expertise to help students meet the particular challenges of reading, writing, speaking, listening, and language in their content areas. The 6–12 literacy standards in history/social studies, science, and technical subjects do not replace content standards but rather promote literacy in each of the content areas.

21st CENTURY SKILLS

The term **21st Century Skills** is generally used to refer to certain core competencies such as collaboration, digital literacy, critical thinking, and problem solving. Advocates of these skills believe schools need to integrate them into today's curriculum so that students succeed in today's competitive world as citizens and workers.

The Partnership for 21st Century Skills (P21) has emerged as a major advocacy group for education, and its mission is to infuse 21st Century Skills and content into education. It advocates for the integration of essential skills like critical thinking, problem solving, and communication and collaboration into the teaching of core academic subjects such as English, reading or language arts, world languages, arts, mathematics, economics, science, geography, history, government, and civics.

In addition to the core subjects, P21 believes that schools must also promote understanding of academic content at much higher levels by weaving 21st century interdisciplinary themes into core subjects. These themes include (1) global awareness; (2) financial, economic, business, and entrepreneurial literacy; (3) civic literacy; (4) health literacy; and (5) environmental literacy (Partnership, 2009).

When instruction of the subjects takes place, P21 advocates incorporating student outcomes in three important skills most in demand in the 21st century (Partnership, 2009; Trilling & Fadel, 2009):

Learning and Innovation Skills

- Creativity and innovation
- Critical thinking and problem solving
- Communication and collaboration

Information, Media, and Technology Skills

- Information literacy
- Media literacy
- Information, communications, and technology (ITC) literacy

Life and Career Skills

- Flexibility and adaptability
- Initiative and self-direction

VOICES from the Classroom

LISA ZEBLEY, first-grade teacher, Virginia Beach, Virginia

21st CENTURY SKILLS

Our school division has embraced 21st Century Skills this school year. Many skills are being embedded into our curriculum, and we are encouraged to plan activities to incorporate these skills into lessons and units when appropriate. I have found that my first-graders are taking advantage of these opportunities and becoming great thinkers.

For example, they have the chance to analyze and evaluate the rules and expectations in our classroom, generate new uses of our curriculum content for everyday things, and identify problems and solutions with math exemplars. I've also allowed them to collaborate more on group projects and share the work instead of just doing individual work. We are also taking on small projects around the school to help make them more socially responsible.

What they are learning from each other is invaluable. It's never too early to begin to prepare them for what will be expected of them as 21st century workers and citizens.

URBAN EDUCATION

- Social and cross-cultural skills
- Productivity and accountability
- Leadership and responsibility

The Partnership for 21st Century Skills encourages schools, districts, and states to infuse the 21st Century Skills and content into education and provides tools and resources to help facilitate and drive change. P21 maintains that the 21st century standards, assessments, curriculum, instruction, professional development, and learning environments must be aligned to produce a support system that produces 21st century outcomes for students.

For states that adopt the 21st Century Skills, the following strategies can be used to create a successful statewide 21st Century Skills initiative to address these support structure issues (Partnership, 2006):

- *High-profile leadership*: State leaders such as the governor, chief state school officer, legislators, educators, business leaders, and influential citizens must advocate for 21st century learning.

- *Broad consensus and shared vision*: States should create an active coalition of business, education, nonprofit and community organizations, and parents to develop consensus and a shared vision on the 21st Century Skills they value for their children.

- *Ongoing professional development*: States should support administrators and teachers with ongoing professional development in 21st Century Skills.

- *Standards and curriculum aligned with 21st Century Skills*: Fully integrate 21st Century Skills into the entire curriculum.

- *21st century assessments*: Create modern assessments that measure 21st Century Skills, such as critical thinking, problem-solving, communications skills, and information and communication technology (ICT) literacy.

- *Effective communications strategy*: Engage everyone, from state-level officials to front-line educators, parents, and students in the vision of 21st century learning.

- *Aggressive implementation strategy*: Showcase existing models of success and reach to potential partners such as business, community nonprofits, colleges, and universities.

To learn more about the P21 Framework for 21st Century Learning, go to the Partnership's website at http://www.p21.org.

Types of Teacher Plans

Comprehensive planning is needed for effective teaching at all grade levels. When making plans for instruction, teachers typically think of the big picture first—the entire course. Then, their planning is broken down into successively smaller subparts—into each marking term, each unit, each week, and finally each lesson. See Figure 3.2 for an illustration showing plans of different duration.

Plans for an entire course are more general than plans for each particular lesson. But course plans serve as a framework for term plans, just as term plans serve as a framework for unit plans. Thus, you will likely refer to earlier general plans as you proceed to more specific plans for each unit, week, and lesson. Teacher plans are more specific at the unit and daily levels, and teachers tend to deviate less from unit and daily plans than from course or term plans.

FIGURE 3.2

PLANS OF DIFFERENT DURATIONS

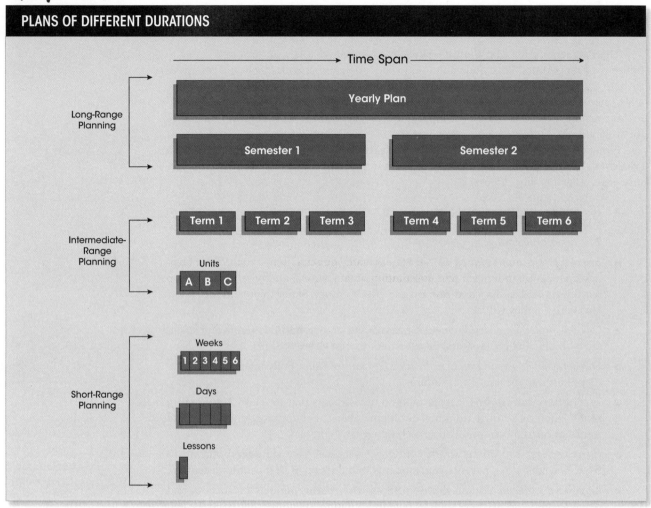

BACKWARD MAPPING

Backward mapping, which is sometimes referred to as *backward design*, is a planning tool that prompts you to begin planning by asking the following questions: What intended learning outcomes or goals do you have for your students? How will students demonstrate their achievement or understanding of these learning outcomes?

Asking what students are going to learn at the start of planning ensures that your lessons will be directly related to what you want your students to know and be able to do. You have worked backward, in effect, to design instructional activities that focus on learning outcomes. Therefore, what students should ultimately take from instruction drives planning, rather than occurring as an afterthought (Wiggins & McTighe, 2006).

Two educators known for their expertise in differentiated instruction and backward design, Tomlinson and McTighe (2006), have noted that "deliberate use of backward design for planning courses, units, and individual lessons results in more clearly defined goals, more appropriate assessments, and more purposeful teaching."

The following steps illustrate the process of planning using the concept of backward mapping:

1. Select and then analyze the outcome or standard to be achieved.

2. Design or select an assessment through which students can demonstrate mastery of the standards; determine the required performance level, if it is not already given.

3. Identify what students must know and be able to do to perform well on the assessment.

4. Plan and deliver instructional activities that include direct instruction and teacher–student interaction. This process helps all students gain the knowledge and skills identified in the standards.

5. Provide all students with adequate opportunities to learn and practice the necessary skills and knowledge.

6. Assess students and examine their results to plan further instruction or individual support, if needed. If appropriate, give a grade or other feedback.

In *Understanding by Design*, Wiggins and McTighe (2006) provide a template that teachers can use to guide their decision making when planning backwards. Their first stage addresses *desired results*, including statements about established goals, essential questions, and understanding about what students will understand, will know, and will be able to do. The second stage addresses *assessment evidence*, and prompts the teacher to identify specific assessments to be used during the unit. The third stage addresses the *learning plan*, which includes a listing of the major learning activities and lessons.

Backward mapping starts with your expected result: What do your students need to know to meet the performance expectation? If you want your students to do a culminating activity, such as using a PowerPoint presentation to outline the similarities and differences between *West Side Story* and *Romeo and Juliet*, then they will need to know many things. For example, they will need to know how to use PowerPoint, how to collaborate on a project, and what certain vocabulary words mean. They will also need to have a working knowledge of textual analysis, character traits, dialect recognition, and reading skills/strategies specific to drama and dialogue. Each of these areas of knowledge will be part of both assessments and instructional activities. By identifying where and how each assessment will occur and how students will receive feedback, then remediating as necessary, you can assist students to successfully meet the instructional goal.

COURSE PLANNING

A **course** is a complete sequence of instruction that includes a major division of the subject matter. Courses in middle schools, junior high schools, and high schools vary in length. Some courses, such as required courses in English, social studies, and

VOICES from the Classroom

ROB COHEN, middle school language arts teacher, Franklin Lakes, New Jersey

WORKING BACKWARD WHEN PLANNING

For the first few years of my teaching, I found there often was a big gap between what I intended to do in my classroom and the things that actually happened. When planning day by day and week by week, I sometimes overlooked the final end-of-the-year goals that I wanted my students to achieve.

Finally, I changed my planning approach to first look at what I wanted my students to achieve by the end of the year. It then became more obvious what the intermediate steps should be to help lead up to the final goals. I could then more easily select the sequence of projects, novels, or other activities that would help lead to the end-of-the-year goals. By working backward when planning, I have been more effective in my long-range planning and in building the connections between the various units. I view this planning as a type of narrative that unfolds across a school year but that is constructed in a deliberate way knowing from the beginning where you want to go.

mathematics, may run the entire school year. Other courses are completed within a semester, a trimester, or a quarter.

Course planning involves organizing and scheduling the content to be taught during the time allotted for the course, whether that time is for a year, semester, trimester, or quarter. School districts break up the school year in various ways and have the courses completed within these time frames. When the school year is broken up into two parts, each part is called a *semester*. When the school year is broken up into three parts, each part is called a *trimester*. When the school year is broken up into four parts, each part is called a *quarter*.

Reasons for Course Planning. There are several reasons for planning for an entire course:

- To become familiar with the content to be taught
- To determine the sequence in which the content will be taught
- To incorporate any changes in materials, textbooks, or content that may have been made since the last time you taught a particular topic
- To develop a rough schedule of when various topics will be taught during the course
- To make additions, deletions, and adaptations to the curriculum, taking into account your own particular circumstances and the needs of your students

Resources and Factors for Course Planning. Several resources can be useful when preparing course plans. If available, the curriculum guide for the course may include objectives, an outline of content, and a proposed timetable for the amount of time to spend on each unit. The textbook for the course and the accompanying teacher's edition, if one is available, provide information about goals and content. The school calendar also needs to be taken into account when planning for the course because it indicates the vacation days, holidays, and other days that school is not in session as well as the grading-term weeks and other special events.

If you have taught the course before, the unit file folders that you have prepared are commonly full of useful information and materials that can aid in course planning. These unit file folders often include lecture notes, handouts, worksheets, quizzes, tests, lists of guest speakers, and other resources used in previous years. Teachers usually keep a unit file folder for each unit they teach for the course. Thus, the folders can be a rich resource when planning for a course.

Steps in Course Planning. There are several steps to course planning that can lead to useful results (e.g., Kellough & Carjuzaa, 2009):

1. Determine the course goals (to indicate what you plan for students to learn from the course) and the principal supporting objectives.
2. Decide on course content that is related to the course goals. This includes selecting the topics to be studied, arranging them into an appropriate sequence, and deciding how much emphasis to place on each topic.
3. Decide how much time to spend on each topic.
4. After considering the goals and topics you selected, determine your approach in the course, including basic strategies, major assignments, texts, and so on. A course syllabus is one of the products of this step.
5. Make plans to order special supplies, books, computer software, and other materials and also to arrange for special speakers or for collaborative planning when conducting term, unit, or weekly planning.
6. Determine procedures for evaluating student attainment of course objectives.

The Products of Course Planning. Course planning commonly takes the form of a general outline of content with specific ideas noted within the outline concerning course content, methods, and evaluation. Other accompanying materials are also produced as a result of course planning. You could keep these materials in separate notebooks for each course or subject area that you teach. When you prepare your plans for the term, unit, and week, you will likely need to refer to these materials:

1. *A list of course goals.* Using the steps in course planning as a guide, a list of course goals would be the first product you would prepare. You may determine these goals after careful review and consideration of the goals that are in the curriculum guide, the teacher's edition of the textbook, state department of education guidelines, and other sources.

2. *An outline of course content.* For many teachers, this outline is a listing of the various units within a course and the chapter numbers and titles within each unit. This outline of units, in fact, may be the same as what is in the textbook that you use, or you might decide to change the sequence of the units.

3. *Notations for time to be spent on each unit.* Using that content outline as a base, you indicate how much time you plan to spend on each particular unit. For example, you could make notations in your outline that the first unit, consisting of four chapters, will be covered from the start of the school year to the middle of October. Similar notations would be made for each unit.

4. *A course syllabus.* This is the printed material that you will give your students concerning general information about the course, the course description, materials required, instructional approaches and activities to be used, course requirements and evaluation procedures, policies on various issues, and an outline of course content. It is especially important that you decide about course requirements and evaluation procedures before the course begins and include detailed information about these issues in the syllabus so students are well informed.

5. *Notes about ordering supplies and other instructional resources.* You may immediately need to order special supplies, books, computer software, or other materials, or you might make notes to yourself to order these items at a later point in the course. Similarly, you might need to arrange for special speakers or for collaborative planning at that time, or you could make notes to yourself to do this closer to the time the unit will actually be conducted.

TERM PLANNING

A **term** is the amount of time the school district designates for the length of a marking period (typically 8 to 10 weeks) for report cards. **Term planning** involves the preparation of more detailed outlines of the content to be covered within a marking period or term. They are elaborations of course-planning outlines and indicate which units will be covered during that term. Term plans help you arrange for handling specific issues related to the curriculum and instruction of each unit; they will be useful resources when preparing your unit plans.

Term plans are commonly broken down into weeks, with an outline indicating instructional activities and materials to be included each week. The balance of content, goals, and time are important considerations when preparing term plans. Curriculum guides may include a recommended number of weeks to cover each part of the content outline. This is very helpful, especially for beginning teachers, when making decisions about the pace of content coverage.

UNIT PLANNING

A **unit** is a major subdivision of a course involving planned instruction about some central theme, topic, issue, or problem for a period of several days to a maximum of three weeks. Essentially, **unit planning** involves developing a sequence of daily plans that addresses the

from the *VOICES* Classroom

PETER ERIKSSON, high school literature and composition teacher, Buffalo Grove, Illinois (a suburb of Chicago)

PLANNING WITH THE END GOALS IN MIND

I like to begin planning my units with the end goals in mind. Since our curriculum is increasingly skills driven, I usually start with the district goals and their corresponding skills that I plan to teach. I then consider the textbook, resource materials, and the unit's summative assessment as well as the ways my students will practice and execute the skills. Designing my unit backward from the skills and summative assessment provides me with concrete goals on which to base the rest of my unit. One thing needs to lead back to another. No lesson is isolated.

In my sophomore World Literature and Composition class, I teach visual reading, synthesizing ideas, comprehending main ideas, and oral communication while reading excerpts from *The Odyssey*. I plan the unit based on the summative assessment, which is a speech that aligns these skills in one project. With a rubric that outlines skills at the beginning of the unit, I am able to provide my students with the long-term goals and the main concepts ahead of time. Thus by planning backward, from the goals and skills all the way back to the unit's introduction, I keep my students aligned from the start.

topic of the unit in a cohesive way. Unit planning is considered by many teachers to be the most important phase of planning.

Unit plans have more detail than term plans and are often linked directly to major themes or concepts within the curriculum (e.g., exploration in social studies, fractions in mathematics, poetry in English, nutrition in science). A unit plan should provide increased organization and ensure that the material presented is accurate, thorough, and comprehensive.

Reasons for Unit Planning. There are several reasons for unit planning. First, planning for units allows you to organize and sequence a related body of material into a series of lesson plans. Next, unit planning allows you to decide on the specific activities that you will use to teach the content. Finally, unit planning helps you gather and make the materials that are necessary for the various activities throughout the unit.

Teachers usually begin planning their units several weeks before they intend to teach them. In this way, you have sufficient time to develop your plans and take any needed actions resulting from your plans prior to the first lesson of the unit. For example, you may need to schedule a field trip, arrange for a guest speaker, develop a cooperative learning activity, or prepare handouts some time in advance of the first lesson.

More information is provided in Chapter 4 concerning resources and factors in unit planning, steps in unit planning, the products of unit planning, and strategies leading to successful implementation of unit plans.

WEEKLY PLANNING

Weekly planning involves laying out the week's activities within the framework of the daily schedule throughout the week. While the degree of detail that teachers write in weekly plans varies, weekly plans for each class period may include a list of the instructional objectives, the instructional activities, resources and materials (e.g., the page numbers in the textbook, the title of the DVD), and student assignments. Many school districts require beginning teachers to submit weekly lesson plans to the principal for review, sometimes several days before instruction is to begin.

Consider student performance during the preceding weeks as you identify content to be covered and determine the pace of instruction. Identify what you expect students to complete and how you will evaluate student progress. Interruptions and any special events (e.g., field trips, assemblies, holidays) should be noted in the weekly plans. The completeness of the plans and mesh of activities with goals are important considerations in weekly plans.

Using a Plan Book for Weekly Plans. A **plan book** is used to display weekly plans in a brief way, commonly on a two-page grid format. In commercially prepared plan books, the days of the week are often labeled on the top of the grid and the class period or subject area is labeled on the left of the grid. Consequently, there is only about a $1\frac{1}{2}$- by $1\frac{1}{2}$-inch box to write the planning notes for each class period to be taught in that week. A sample plan book format for weekly plans is displayed in Figure 3.3. This sample format indicates the plans in the order of the class periods for each day throughout the week.

School districts often provide teachers with commercially prepared plan books to display their weekly plans. Due to the limited amount of space in the boxes of the plan books,

FIGURE 3.3

SAMPLE PLAN BOOK FORMAT FOR WEEKLY PLANS: VERSION A

PERIOD SUBJECT GRADE	MONDAY	TUESDAY	WEDNESDAY	THURSDAY	FRIDAY

TEACHER_____ ROOM NUMBER_____ WEEK OF_____

you might prefer to develop your own format in a separate notebook. Regardless of the format that you use, it is important to prepare the weekly plans and write them in a plan book for your own use, for review by your school administrator, and for use by a substitute teacher in case you are absent.

It is possible that you will teach several subjects and need to prepare plans for each subject. For example, you might have two classes of algebra, two classes of geometry, and one class of trigonometry. If you use the format shown in Figure 3.4, you will need one page of that format for each subject area that you teach. You may prefer this format because it provides more space for your plans as compared to the format shown in Figure 3.3. Additional weekly plan templates can be found with an Internet search.

DAILY PLANNING

A **lesson** is a subdivision of a unit, usually taught in a single class period or, on occasion, two or three successive periods. **Daily planning** involves preparing notes about objectives, materials, activities, evaluation, and other information for a lesson for a particular day but

FIGURE 3.4

SAMPLE PLAN BOOK FORMAT FOR WEEKLY PLANS: VERSION B

TEACHER_____ CLASS PERIOD(S)_____

WEEK OF_____ GRADE LEVEL AND COURSE TITLE_____

ROOM NUMBER_____ UNIT TOPIC_____

DAY	DATE	OBJECTIVES	PROCEDURES	MATERIALS	ASSIGNMENT	COMMENTS
MONDAY						
TUESDAY						
WEDNESDAY						
THURSDAY						
FRIDAY						

in more detail than in the weekly plan. Several useful resources provide additional guidance when preparing lesson plans (Price & Nelson, 2011; Schoenfeldt & Salsbury, 2009; Serdyukov & Ryan, 2008; Skowron, 2006).

Reasons for Daily Planning. There are a number of reasons for planning, and many of these reasons apply specifically to preparing written daily lesson plans. Written daily plans help you clarify the instructional objectives of a particular lesson, precisely identify the content, determine the instructional activities and the specific means about how the activities will be conducted, and arrange for appropriate evaluation of student learning.

Written daily plans give you a sense of direction and a feeling of confidence and security about what you are doing. They help you organize, sequence, and familiarize yourself with a lesson's content. The preparation of the plans also sparks your preparation or collection of the necessary instructional materials needed for the lesson.

To be able to plan effective lessons takes practice in the skills and knowledge necessary to structure lessons that are standards based, motivational, and built on students' prior knowledge and skills. Numerous sample lessons are available on the Web—some of them of excellent quality. However, individual isolated lessons that are not tied to the flow and structure of your instructional goals and objectives will add little to student understanding and skill building. Therefore, it is imperative that you gain the skills to develop your own lessons.

There is no single best format for a lesson plan, but the best plans incorporate many of the aspects listed in the following examples. Keep in mind that a good lesson plan is a way of communicating a pathway for student learning. Good lessons communicate; poor lessons do not. Lesson plans also help organize content, materials, teaching strategies, and assessment activities. As time goes on you will get better at the art and skill of planning based in large part on the feedback you receive from students, parents, and colleagues.

More information about lesson planning is provided in Chapter 4 concerning the learning domains, components of a daily lesson plan, instructional objectives, and characteristics of good lesson planning. Daily lesson plan templates can be found with an Internet search.

The Linear-Rational Approach to Planning

The type of planning taught most often in teacher education programs is a sequential process based on clear goals and objectives. The **linear-rational** **approach** to instructional planning involves sequential decisions about the (1) formulation of goals, (2) specification of objectives, (3) assessment of student needs relative to the stated goals and objectives, (4) selection of strategies and learning activities linked to the objectives, and (5) evaluation of student performance (see Figure 3.5).

It is a logical and organized way to plan for instruction. With this model, you build on the knowledge gained from each step. Insights gained in one step lead to changes in other steps. In this way, objectives, methods, and evaluation are logically linked and given consideration in the initial planning. For example, you must think about evaluation even when making decisions about objectives, activities, content, and sequence.

The rational model is sometimes referred to as *instructional design* or the *systems approach* to planning. It requires the analysis of the components of planning in a logical order with an orderly but flexible sequence. Each of the five steps in the linear-rational model for instructional planning is discussed in the following sections.

FIGURE 3.5

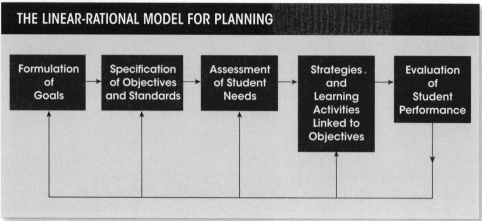

THE LINEAR-RATIONAL MODEL FOR PLANNING

Formulation of Goals → Specification of Objectives and Standards → Assessment of Student Needs → Strategies and Learning Activities Linked to Objectives → Evaluation of Student Performance

FORMULATION OF AIMS AND GOALS

The first step of the linear-rational model of instructional planning involves the formulation of goals. Educational goals are the broad statements of purpose that educators use to provide a direction for the courses they plan. The purposes of education are stated at a number of levels: national, state, school district, subject, grade level, unit plan, or lesson plan. The terms *aims, goals,* and *objectives* are commonly used to identify the educational purposes at each of these levels.

Aims. The term *aim* refers to broad statements about the intent of education. Aims are often written by national or state panels, commissions, or policy-making groups. **Aims** express a philosophy of education and concepts about the social role of schools and the needs of children. They guide our schools and give educators direction.

The terms *philosophy, aims,* or *goals* are often used interchangeably in reference to any statement associated with the broad purposes of education. As a rule, statements of philosophy and aims are the most abstract and general statements of the purposes of education. Furthermore, statements of philosophy are often written in paragraph form, with short statements of aims following them to further clarify and delineate the educational mission.

Historically, the aims of education have changed very little. For example, the "Seven Cardinal Principles of Secondary Education," written by the Commission on the Reorganization of Secondary Education in 1918, include many beliefs found in current statements of educational philosophy, aims, or goals. The seven principles include (1) health, (2) command of the fundamental processes, (3) worthy home membership, (4) vocation, (5) citizenship, (6) worthy use of leisure time, and (7) ethical character.

Goals. Educators need to translate general aims into statements that will describe what schools are expected to accomplish. These translations of aims into more specific, subject-related terms are called **goals**.

Goals are more definite than aims. Goals are nonbehavioral and provide direction for educators, but they do not specify achievement levels. Goals are often written by professional associations and state and local educational agencies to serve as guidelines for school and curriculum guides for what all students should accomplish over their entire school career. General school goals are then written by school district personnel in more specific terms for each subject area in curriculum guides.

Subject-specific educational goals are written as a bridge to even more explicit learning objectives. Luckily, the task of translating general school goals to subject-area goals is not placed solely on the shoulders of the individual teacher. Most school districts have curriculum guides that the district prepares, adopts, and makes available for teachers to use. These curriculum guides are based on goals selected by the district.

Curriculum guides commonly include subject-specific course goals, a fairly detailed outline of curricular content, and recommended instructional activities and materials. Curriculum guides are prepared by teachers in a district and are formally adopted by the school board. The guides ensure that the goals have proper coverage at appropriate grade levels. Teachers are expected to use these curriculum guides in their planning.

SPECIFICATION OF OBJECTIVES

When preparing unit plans, teachers commonly look at the subject-specific course goals and curriculum content in the curriculum guide for their subject. **Subject-specific course goals** are more precise translations of district goals and are stated in curriculum guides. Subject-specific course goals can be translated and broken down into more explicit educational objectives used in unit or weekly plans (Gronlund & Brookhart, 2009).

Educational objectives are statements of what is hoped that students will achieve through instruction, are narrower in scope than subject-specific goals, and are commonly used in units. For example, a subject-specific course goal concerning increasing student literacy might lead to a more narrow and specific educational objective about students writing a well-organized business letter. To write educational objectives for a unit, look at the subject-specific course goals that are printed in the curriculum guide and break those goals down into several more specific objectives. You then use the unit's educational objectives as the basis for writing your daily instructional objectives.

Instructional objectives are written for daily lesson plans and are stated in terms that indicate what is to be observed and measured. Information about writing instructional objectives is addressed in Chapter 4.

In summary, aims are translated into general school goals, which in turn are translated into subject-specific course goals. These course goals are in the curriculum guides that are made available to teachers. You use the course goals in the curriculum guide to identify educational objectives for your unit plans and weekly plans. When you prepare daily lesson plans, you translate the unit's educational objectives into instructional objectives. As displayed in Figure 3.6, general aims undergo a series of translations and ultimately result in a number of specific instructional objectives used in daily lesson plans.

ASSESSMENT OF STUDENT NEEDS

The next step in the linear-rational model of planning is **needs assessment** or **diagnosis**. Diagnosis means looking at a situation to fully understand it and to find clues for deciding what to do. Successful diagnosis reveals (1) the students' aptitudes, aspirations, backgrounds, problems, and needs; (2) the level of learning your students have reached; and (3) where your students are weak and strong.

This information will help you make a number of planning decisions about both curriculum and instruction. With this information, you will be able to capitalize on students' strengths and intrinsic motivation and to help correct their deficiencies. This information also can serve as the basis for placing students in appropriate groups and for adjusting assignments; this is especially useful when assigning students to groups, such as those for cooperative learning. Information obtained through diagnosis also helps you make decisions about curricular material to be covered. Areas of need can vary widely within the same classroom and therefore you need to be aware of both the general needs of your students and the specific needs of individual students.

The process of diagnosis involves seeing what the situation is and what should be done next. The steps of diagnosis are to (1) assess the situation; (2) determine if there is any difficulty; (3) if there is any difficulty, identify what it is, determine its cause, and search for factors in the situation that would help you to make your teaching more effective and eliminate the difficulty and its cause; (4) make a final estimate of the situation in view of the information obtained in the earlier steps; and (5) make decisions based on your final estimate of the situation.

FIGURE 3.6

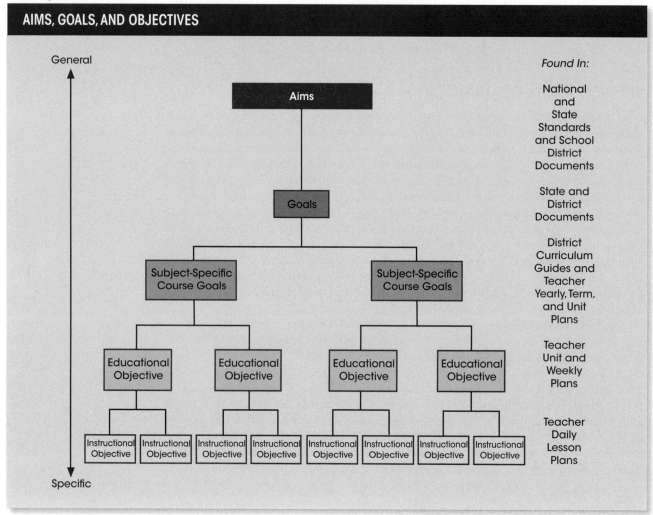

AIMS, GOALS, AND OBJECTIVES

Information for needs assessment or diagnosis comes from a variety of sources. A number of printed records are available, such as the cumulative record folder kept for each student, test results, anecdotal records, and even reports of physical exams. Indirect contacts also provide information. These include contacts with parents, other teachers who have had involvement with the student, the guidance counselor, and others. Direct contacts with the students also provide very useful information. This can be done through personal observations, through student autobiographies or questionnaires, or through diagnostic, formative, or summative tests.

STRATEGIES AND LEARNING ACTIVITIES

In the linear-rational model to instructional planning, teachers formulate goals, specify objectives, and assess students' needs before selecting strategies and learning activities. After carefully selecting the precise performance objectives in different levels of the learning domains, you need to select strategies and learning activities that will help students achieve those objectives.

There are many instructional strategies that teachers can select to achieve the instructional objectives for a particular lesson. These include presentations, demonstrations, practice and drills, reviews, group and discussion methods, inquiry approaches,

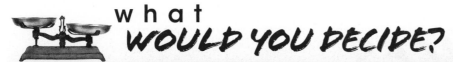

ASSESSING STUDENTS' PRIOR KNOWLEDGE

Before selecting specific content and instructional activities for a unit, it is useful to find out what students already know about the content in the unit.

1. If you were teaching about the electoral process in the state and federal governments, how would you assess your students' current knowledge?

2. What are some alternative assessment approaches that would bring novelty and variety to the class?

discovery learning and problem solving, role playing, community involvement, and other approaches.

Here, it is useful to consider an important aspect in the delivery of the content and the choice of instructional strategies—planning for the sequence of instructional tasks. Sequencing has two basic purposes (Orlich, Harder, Callahan, Trevison, Brown, & Miller, 2013). First, it can be used to isolate knowledge (a fact, concept, generalization, or principle) so that students can understand the unique characteristics of the selected information or to isolate a thinking process so that students can master the process under varying conditions. This makes learning more manageable. Second, sequencing can be used to relate the knowledge or process being taught to the larger organized body of knowledge. This makes learning more meaningful. A sequence is process related in that it establishes a schedule for learning the various parts of the related content.

There are several principles that apply to all kinds of sequencing (Orlich et al., 2013):

1. Start with a simple step. Structure the presentation so the students can easily identify content. It is helpful to provide numerous examples.

2. Proceed to the concrete. This means that you should illustrate the objective or content with materials, models, simulations, or artifacts.

3. Plan to structure a lesson or learning sequence so that it becomes more complex. This means that you might introduce additional variables, generate new sets of criteria, or establish relationships between the content of the lessons and other content.

4. You may introduce abstractions in which students are asked to generalize, predict, or explain information generated.

EVALUATION OF STUDENT PERFORMANCE

The last step in the linear-rational model of instructional planning involves evaluating student performance. You need to make decisions about evaluating student performance *before instruction occurs,* and thus it should be considered when making planning decisions.

While details about establishing a framework for evaluation will be covered in Chapter 11, it is useful to examine aspects of evaluation that need to be addressed when planning for instruction. The reasons for evaluation must first be determined. A classroom test, for instance, can serve a variety of purposes such as judging student mastery, measuring growth over time, ranking students, and diagnosing difficulties. Different purposes lend themselves to various evaluation measures. Evaluation measures include tests, observations, discussions, interviews, work samples, experience summaries, rating instruments, questionnaires, and other approaches.

VOICES
from the Classroom

SANDRA CLARK, middle school mathematics teacher, Pueblo, Colorado

PREPARING LONG-RANGE PLANS

As a lead mathematics teacher in the district for the past three years, I have helped develop and update curriculum guides. Through that process, I realized more than ever before that I should use the district curriculum guide when preparing my long-range plans.

I now print monthly calendars and then write down important concepts on a daily, weekly, and monthly basis, and I use that calendar as an organizer when planning units and lessons. I intersperse the state testing preparation activities on the calendar, and add in dates for reporting grades for each grading period. This long-range planning calendar has also helped me get photocopies of instructional materials ready on time.

URBAN EDUCATION

Course content that is to be evaluated must be specified, and general objectives (learning objectives at the unit level of planning) must be identified. Then performance objectives need to be prepared in the cognitive, affective, and psychomotor domains. A table of specifications must then be created with the content and objectives placed within a grid. All these steps for evaluation need to be done before instruction occurs. Therefore, you need to plan for the evaluation of student performance when you are preparing your instructional plans.

Additional Planning Considerations

In addition to the fundamentals of planning already discussed, there are a few other issues that you should consider as you plan for your instruction.

RESOURCES FOR PLANNING

Teachers can consult a number of resources when they begin planning for the school year and for each unit and lesson. Many of these resources relate to the **curriculum**, which is the content to be taught. Resources are also available concerning how you go about instruction and how you might take into account related issues such as meeting diverse student needs, guiding student study, using instructional media, and evaluating student learning. Resources commonly used by K–12 teachers include the following:

1. *Curriculum guides.* A **curriculum guide** is a document that identifies the objectives and content for a given subject at a given grade level. Not all districts make curriculum guides available. But for those that do, the curriculum guides are approved by the local school board, and teachers are expected to help students master that material during the school year.

Curriculum guides commonly include subject-specific course goals, a fairly detailed outline of curricular content, recommended instructional activities, an annotated bibliography, and other instructional resources. Curriculum guides are often revised every few years, and teachers in the district who teach in the subject area of the curriculum guide usually have an opportunity to serve on revision committees.

2. *Curriculum bulletins or materials published by the state department of education or by professional organizations.* The state department of education in each state may have additional curricular materials available such as curriculum bulletins, suggested curriculum guides for the various subject areas, and related materials concerning the content. Contact your state department of education to inquire about materials that might be available in the subject area that you teach.

Many professional organizations prepare materials that relate to the middle school level and secondary curriculum. These materials may include resource books on the particular subject matter but also may include thorough descriptions of objectives, outcomes, and content for the various grade levels. The National Council of Teachers of Mathematics (NCTM, 2000), for example, has prepared comprehensive documents that outline and describe standards for K–12 mathematics instruction. These are significant resources for teachers of mathematics. In varying degrees, professional organizations in the other subject areas have similar resources available about curriculum and instruction.

3. *The teacher's edition of the textbook being used or instructor's manuals.* Most textbook companies provide a teacher's edition for each textbook that is used by students. The teacher's edition often includes chapter objectives, suggested activities and resources, suggested time frames for each chapter, lists of vocabulary words, suggested questions, and other guides. It may also include lists of suggested test questions, technology resources, and other resources.

4. *Other textbooks for the course.* In addition to the textbook that you use for your course, there probably are several textbooks for that course available from other companies. Even though the material might be slightly different, these books and their accompanying teacher's editions can be a good source of additional information. You might be able to use suggested activities, resources, or test questions listed in the teacher's edition, or you might be able to use photocopies of certain tables or figures.

5. *Professional journals and publications.* Most fields have professional organizations that produce subject-related journals, books, monographs, videotapes, and other resource materials for curriculum and instruction of that discipline. These organizations include the National Council of Teachers of English, the National Council for the Social Studies, the National Association of Biology Teachers, the Home Economics Education Association, and the National Art Education Association.

6. *Web-based resources.* Abundant resources are available on the Internet. Conducting a search on a topic will lead to many sources of information and materials that can assist you in instruction.

7. *Other sources.* Additional resources may be obtained from a variety of sources. Many public and private agencies have prepared materials that are suitable for middle level and secondary instruction. For example, the National Dairy Council can be contacted about nutrition-related content and instructional materials and resources. Similarly, many state and national governmental agencies distribute useful materials. The extension departments of many public universities provide materials on request. Museums may have some curricular materials, and resources may be available from many community agencies. Parents and other teachers should not be overlooked as resources for additional information about curriculum and instruction.

TEACHER–STUDENT PLANNING

Teacher–student planning means that the teacher does not make all the decisions about the curriculum and instruction and that students are involved in some degree in the planning and decision making. The amount of freedom that you give students in cooperative planning will depend on many things, such as student maturity, student ability levels, the subject area, your educational philosophy, and the students' previous experience with cooperative planning. Teacher–student planning may not be suitable for every teacher or every subject area.

There are several ways that students might be involved in this cooperative planning. One way is to present alternative plans to the students and allow them to select the plans they prefer. For example, you might give students the choice of several activities related to the unit objectives and let students select which activities will be used. Second, you might let students, individually or as a whole class, select their goals from a list of behavioral objectives. Third, you could propose a plan of action and then ask students for their suggestions and approval. It is best to start by giving students limited choices and to have successful experiences with those choices before moving to approaches involving more student freedom.

TEAM PLANNING

Teachers in some schools plan together, but that does not necessarily mean that they also are involved in team teaching. **Team planning** occurs when two or more teachers collaboratively prepare instructional plans. Planning procedures that a group of teachers use are often similar to the steps you might take when planning alone. The success of teams can be enhanced through the use of team-building activities and clarification of team roles and procedures. Time to plan and the authority to make changes are issues related to team collaboration.

There are two ways that team planning may occur. First, all teachers who teach the same course may get together to plan cooperatively. For example, all teachers of algebra may meet on a regular basis to plan a common curriculum for the students going through that course. These teachers may agree to a common set of course objectives, activities, and outcomes. They may even meet on a weekly basis to share ideas about weekly and daily lesson plans. This type of team planning for the same course occurs most often at the junior and high school levels where there may be several teachers teaching a given course.

Second, teachers from several different subject areas may meet to arrange for **interdisciplinary planning**, which involves planning and coordinating instructional activities and assignments for each subject area represented by the teachers. Thus, an interdisciplinary team may consist of the teachers of social studies, mathematics, English or language arts, science, and perhaps teachers in other subject areas. The team may meet several times a week. This type of planning is more common at the middle level where there may be blocked courses involving investigation of an issue from the perspective of several subject areas.

There are several advantages of team planning. First, groups can help complement the talents of each team member. Each person has strengths and weaknesses, and ideas coming from others in the group may help cover the weakness of an individual member.

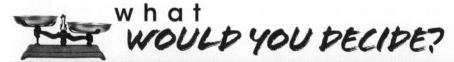

what WOULD YOU DECIDE?

INVOLVING YOUR STUDENTS IN PLANNING

Some teachers like to involve their students in planning in varying degrees. They may involve students in the selection of content, instructional strategies, and even assessments.

1. What might be the benefits of involving students in planning? The disadvantages?

2. If you were to involve your students in planning, what type of background information and guidance might you need to provide to help ensure a successful process and useful suggestions?

For example, one teacher on the team may not be very familiar with the computer software available for the unit under discussion. Collectively, other team members may be able to provide this information that the teacher would not have had. Second, team planning can help teachers address the interdisciplinary nature of the content they teach. Further, team planning can enhance classroom management. Teams may plan common rules and procedures that are consistently implemented and enforced by all team members. Finally, teams can help establish collegiality among teachers, which provides support and encouragement for all team members.

PREPARING A SYLLABUS

A **syllabus** is a written statement about the content, procedures, and requirements of a particular course. A course syllabus serves the following purposes (Kellough & Kellough, 2008):

- States requirements, rules, expectations, and other policies and thus helps eliminate misconceptions about the course
- Serves as a plan to be followed by the teacher and the students
- Helps students feel at ease by providing an understanding of what is expected of them
- Helps students organize, conceptualize, and synthesize their learning experiences
- Serves as documentation about the course for those outside the classroom (e.g., the principal, parents, other teachers)
- Serves as a resource for members of a planning team (In fact, team members should have a copy of each other's syllabus.)

Many teachers prepare a course syllabus before the school year begins and thoroughly discuss it with their students on the opening day of school. Syllabi are more commonly shared with students at the middle and high school levels. A course syllabus typically has the following information (e.g., Kellough & Kellough, 2008):

- *General information about the course.* List the teacher's name, course title, class period, beginning and ending times, and room number. This may include times when you are available for a conference, and perhaps your phone number.
- *Course description.* Describe the course, and mention how students will profit from it. This may also include a list of course goals and expected outcomes.
- *Materials required.* Mention the textbook, notebook, or other supplies needed by the student. Indicate what is provided by the school and what the student should provide. Mention what should be brought to class each day.
- *Instructional approaches and activities.* Indicate the type of instructional approaches you plan to use during the course, and also mention any special events or activities that are planned (e.g., field trips, experiments, guest speakers, special projects).
- *Course requirements and evaluation procedures.* Indicate the means of evaluating student learning: tests, quizzes, homework, projects, group work, work samples, and so on. Indicate the point value or relative weight for each of these items when the report card grade is determined.
- *Policies on various issues.* Include your policy on late homework or papers, tardiness, absenteeism, extra credit, makeup work, plagiarism, rules for classroom behavior, procedures for completing work, procedures for various classroom tasks, and others.
- *A course outline of content.* Provide an outline of the content to be covered in the course. This should include some headings to reveal some details about the course.

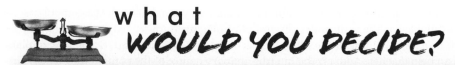

what WOULD YOU DECIDE?

DEVELOPING A SYLLABUS

A course syllabus includes much useful information for the students concerning course content, procedures, and requirements.

1. Would you want your students to participate in the preparation of your course syllabus? Why or why not?

2. Would the grade level or the subject of the course that you teach make a difference in your decision about student involvement?

3. How might you accommodate student learning style differences as you develop your syllabus?

PLANNING FOR THE RESPONSE TO INTERVENTION (RTI)

Response to intervention (RTI), as referenced in the Individuals with Disabilities Improvement Act of 2004, was conceived as a method to ensure that students receive early intervention and assistance before falling too far behind their peers. RTI requires that these students receive supplementary support, guided by regularly gathered assessment data, referred to as progress monitoring. When planning for instruction, teachers need to take into account the needs of all their students, and struggling students require extra attention and assistance. Thus, all levels of planning need to take these students into account as RTI is applied.

RTI requires that all teachers at all levels (K–12) assess students systematically and provide levels of support for students who need assistance (Allington, 2009; Howard, 2009). Most RTI models include three levels, or tiers (Fisher & Frey, 2010b); see Figure 3.7.

FIGURE 3.7

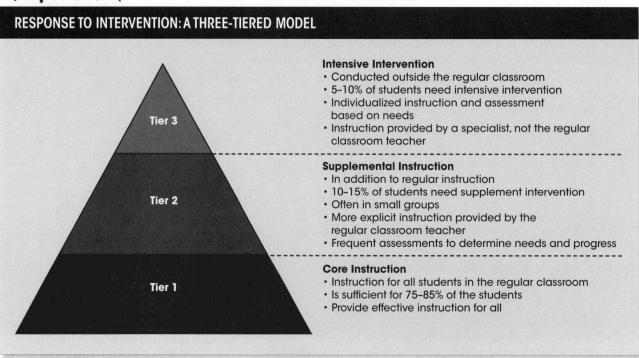

RESPONSE TO INTERVENTION: A THREE-TIERED MODEL

Tier 3

Intensive Intervention
- Conducted outside the regular classroom
- 5–10% of students need intensive intervention
- Individualized instruction and assessment based on needs
- Instruction provided by a specialist, not the regular classroom teacher

Tier 2

Supplemental Instruction
- In addition to regular instruction
- 10–15% of students need supplement intervention
- Often in small groups
- More explicit instruction provided by the regular classroom teacher
- Frequent assessments to determine needs and progress

Tier 1

Core Instruction
- Instruction for all students in the regular classroom
- Is sufficient for 75–85% of the students
- Provide effective instruction for all

■ *Tier 1: Core instruction.* This is regular classroom instruction, and it involves assessing, instructing, and diagnosing learning difficulties. The focus is on quality teaching and implementing systems to determine which students respond to this instruction and which students do not. Approximately 75 to 85 percent of students should make sufficient progress through core instruction alone.

■ *Tier 2: Supplemental phase.* This phase can occur either in the regular classroom or as an adjunct to the classroom. In this phase, teachers begin to monitor how students respond to various interventions that are put in place to provide them with assistance. In Tier 2, students receive instruction in addition to that received in Tier 1, and assessment occurs more frequently in order to determine responsiveness and to plan subsequent interventions. This intervention often takes the form of additional small-group instruction, which complements the core instruction. About 10 to 15 percent of students at one time or another need supplemental interventions. These interventions may last up to 20 weeks, and more frequent assessments take place during this time. The regular classroom teacher typically provides this intervention, sometimes with guidance and support from other educators in the building.

■ *Tier 3: Intensive intervention.* Some students do not benefit from the supplemental interventions in Tier 2 and will benefit from even more intensive interventions. Five to 10 percent of students will require this level of intensive intervention. Students in Tier 3 often receive instruction on a one-to-one basis from a curriculum specialist, learning coach, speech-language pathologist, or related intervention specialists. The regular classroom teacher typically does not provide this intervention.

PLANNING TO USE ACADEMIC TIME WISELY

When considering how to use academic time wisely, it is first useful to examine the time that actually is available for instruction. Students are in school for several hours a day, yet much of that time is used for lunch, getting to and from classes, and homeroom or

from the VOICES Classroom

MARGARET PRICE, first-grade teacher, West Bloomfield, Michigan

USING RESPONSE TO INTERVENTION (RTI)

After administering district assessments, the data are analyzed and used to plan and implement interventions for those children who are not meeting the district standards. Based on the data, two children from my first-grade classroom were significantly below our district standard in reading.

With our response to intervention (RTI) arrangements, Tier 1 intervention consisted of having these students meet with me five days a week for an individual 10-minute guided reading lesson. I would also individually conference with them either in reading or writing at least three days a week. In addition, they would have the lesson repeated another two times a week with one of our bilingual paraeducators.

Although the student needs were different, the lesson format is similar for each child. The lessons consist of reading or guided writing, working with the alphabetic principle (word study), and learning concepts about print. At the end of a six-week period, the students are assessed again to determine how much growth they have made. A determination is then made to continue the intervention or to alter it for more acceleration.

announcements. Of the allocated class time, some time is used for announcements, collecting or distributing papers and supplies, transitions between activities, and other noninstructional events. Thus, the actual academic time is less than the allocated time.

Some students may be daydreaming or be off task, so the time spent in learning is less than the allocated time. The time students are actually paying attention and are engaged in action is called **time-on-task**. **Academic learning time** refers to the amount of time a student engages in learning tasks that yield fairly high rates of success. What really counts is for students to be successful during that allocated time. As you can see, the amount of engaged time is much less than the time students are in school.

To illustrate this, consider a 45-minute class. Within this allocated time, 5 minutes may be spent on taking attendance and making announcements, 5 minutes on describing an activity and giving directions, and 5 minutes for cleanup and preparation to finish the class. That leaves 30 minutes of actual academic time, but students may not even be fully engaged during all that time. Furthermore, their engagement during this time may not be entirely fruitful.

The amount of time students are engaged in learning academic content is positively related to their achievement in that content area. A student who is continually off task will not achieve as well as one who remains on task. Students often are off task in rather obvious ways, such as getting out of their seats, reading notes or materials, or talking to other students. Off-task behavior can often manifest itself in daydreaming or other forms of mental or emotional disengagement that may be difficult to detect.

To engage students in the learning process, you could (1) elicit the desired behavior; (2) provide opportunities for feedback in a nonevaluative atmosphere; (3) use group and individual activities as motivational aids when necessary; (4) use meaningful verbal praise; and (5) monitor seatwork and check it (Borich, 2011). You can begin and end lessons precisely on time, reduce transition time between tasks and activities in a lesson, and minimize waste time in an effort to maximize time-on-task and student engagement. The time available for instruction increases when you (1) follow schedules; (2) begin and end activities on time; (3) facilitate transitions from activity to activity; and (4) assign scheduled activities first priority rather than engaging in spontaneous alternative activities.

Effective classroom management and scheduling can lead to increased learning and a reduction of discipline problems. Good and Brophy (2008) indicate that time-on-task is important, but the task itself must be relevant, appropriate, lead to a reasonably successful outcome (such as designing the difficulty of the assignment to enable the student to have at least 80 percent of the problems correct), and be followed by timely feedback. Instructional time should be allocated in relation to the importance of the academic task.

Key Terms

Academic learning time	Curriculum guide	Linear-rational approach to planning	Teacher–student planning
Aims	Diagnosis	Materials	Team planning
Backward mapping	Daily planning	Needs assessment	Term
Content	Educational objectives	Plan book	Term planning
Common Core State Standards	Goals	Planning for instruction	Time-on-task
Course	Instructional objectives	Response to Intervention	21st Century Skills
Course planning	Interdisciplinary planning	Subject-specific course goals	Unit
Curriculum	Lesson	Syllabus	Unit planning
Curriculum framework			Weekly planning

Major Concepts

1. Planning for instruction refers to decisions teachers make about organizing, implementing, and evaluating instruction.

2. Curriculum design, curriculum standards, and the common core curriculum all influence the planning process.

3. Planning is needed for the school year, each term, each unit, each week, and each lesson. Backward planning with the end in mind helps teachers make decisions when planning back to unit and lessons.

4. The linear-rational model of instructional planning emphasizes planning in a linear sequence when formulating goals, specifying objectives, assessing student needs, developing strategies and learning activities, and evaluating student performance.

5. Aims are translated into general school goals, which are translated into subject-specific course goals. These course goals are in curriculum guides and are used by teachers when they translate the course goals into more specific educational objectives. These, in turn, are translated by teachers into instructional objectives for daily lesson plans.

6. Additional considerations for planning include resources for planning, teacher–student planning, team planning, preparing a syllabus, and planning to use academic time wisely.

Discussion/Reflective Questions

1. Select one class session you recently experienced. Identify and discuss factors that the instructor might have taken into account when planning the lesson.

2. What are some positive consequences for using the Common Core State Standards?

3. Why is the preparation of a series of daily lesson plans not sufficient when planning for an entire course?

4. What is the reasoning for the backward design approach to planning?

5. What are the merits of using the linear-rational model for instructional planning by beginning teachers?

6. What might be the merits and disadvantages of involving your students in instructional planning? What factors might affect your decision about involving students in planning?

Suggested Activities

FOR CLINICAL SETTINGS

1. Select a course you are now taking and consider how content was sequenced in several class sessions. Consider why content was sequenced in that way. Describe alternative ways to successfully sequence the content.

2. List possible merits and disadvantages for the linear-rational model to instructional planning.

3. Search the Web for the Common Core State Standards (corestandards.org) and examine the standards for English language arts and for mathematics. What conclusions do you have about the nature of the standards? About using these standards nationwide (since more than 40 states have adopted them)?

FOR FIELD EXPERIENCES

1. Examine several curriculum guides that are produced by a school district. Look at the goals, objectives, content outline, recommended activities, instructional materials, and other features of the curriculum guides.

2. Ask several teachers how they planned for instruction during their first year of teaching. Ask them to describe how their approach to planning has changed as they became more experienced. How do they plan now?

3. If there are teachers in your school who are team planning, ask one or more of them to discuss the planning procedures they use and to identify the strengths of this process as well as any problems with it.

Further Reading

Burke, J. (2010). *What's the big idea? Question-driven units to motivate reading, writing, and thinking.* Portsmouth, NH: Heinemann.

Discusses the value of questions when planning and designing curriculum and instruction. Applies the concepts by endorsing the use of big, vital questions in units to promote spirited inquiry, natural curiosity, and meaningful conversations.

Carter, L. (2007). *Total instructional alignment: From standards to student success.* Bloomington, IN: Solution Tree.

A concise book discussing the value of aligning the total instruction system—aligning the standards, the curriculum, instruction, and assessments to promote student success.

Martin-Kniep, G., & Picone-Zocchia, J. (2009). *Changing the way you teach: Improving the way students learn.* Alexandria, VA: Association for Supervision and Curriculum Development.

Considers what factors support effective teaching. Examines the curriculum, assessment, and instruction as the vehicles for ways to improve student learning.

Morrison, G. R., Ross, S. M., Kemp, J. E., & Kalman, H. (2010). *Designing effective instruction* (6th ed.). New York: John Wiley & Sons.

Designed for prospective educators, this book presents a 10-element model of instructional design. Includes real-life examples to reinforce concepts.

Technology Resources

COMMON CORE STATE STANDARDS

http://www.corestandards.org

This is the official website. Includes background information and all of the standards for mathematics and English/language arts.

PARTNERSHIP FOR 21st CENTURY SKILLS

http://www.p21.org

This is the official website of the national organization that advocates for 21st century readiness for every student. Has links showing the framework for the skills and other related information.

WORKING BACKWARDS LESSON PLANS

http://www.lessonplanet.com/search?keywords=working+backwards&media=lesson

This at the Lesson Planet website, which is a paid service with abundant resources for lesson plans in many subject areas and grade levels, worksheets, articles, and state standards.

RESPONSE TO INTERVENTION

http://nichcy.org/schools-administrators/rti

Much information on what RTI is, its essential elements, RTI models, and other related topics. Has many links to other useful resources.

MyEducationLab™

Go to the **MyEducationLab** (www.myeducationlab.com) for General Methods and familiarize yourself with the content:

- Topically organized Assignments and Activities, tied to learning outcomes for the course, that can help you more deeply understand course content
- Topically organized Building Teaching Skills and Dispositions learning units allow you to apply and develop understanding of teaching methods.
- A chapter-specific pretest that assesses your understanding of the content offers hints and feedback for

each question and generates a study plan including links to Review, Practice, and Enrichment activities that will enhance your understanding of the concepts. A Study Plan posttest with hints and feedback ensures you understood concepts from the chapter after having completed the enrichment activities.

A Correlation Guide may be downloaded by instructors to show how MyEducationLab content aligns to this book.

If you wanted to have a family reunion with relatives coming from three states for a reunion weekend at a local resort, you would need to think through all of the arrangements, make a lot of decisions, and then take steps to enact your plans so that the reunion was successful. A successful family reunion doesn't just happen, it requires a lot of thought and preparation.

Similarly, good instruction doesn't just happen. Much thoughtful planning must take place even before the students walk through the classroom door. At the foundation of a successful lesson is effective planning of lessons and unit. This chapter reviews many critical aspects of good planning, including information about setting goals and objectives, identifying objectives within the learning domains, planning lessons, planning units, and applying the SIOP model to planning.

Setting Goals and Objectives

An **instructional objective** is a statement of intended learning outcomes of the instruction. Instructional objectives serve several purposes, they: (1) provide a focus for instruction, (2) provide guidelines for learning, (3) provide targets for formative and summative assessments, (4) convey instructional intent to others, and (5) provide for evaluation of instruction (Gronlund & Brookhart, 2009, p. 8). Teachers must convert content standards into general educational objectives at the unit level and more specific instructional objectives for individual lessons. Teachers also must determine which type of instructional objective to prepare—behavioral objectives or descriptive objectives.

CONVERTING STANDARDS INTO OBJECTIVES

As discussed in Chapter 3, broad aims of education are translated into more specific goals in state and district curricular documents, which in turn are translated into subject-specific course goals in a school district's curriculum guides. Teachers then translate course goals from the curriculum guides into educational objectives when planning units. Teachers finally break down a unit's educational objectives into a number of specific instructional objectives used in daily lessons.

In many states, the state department of education has identified a set of curricular standards for the districts of that state. **Standards** are statements that describe the subject matter students should know and perform at each grade level. These standards are often stated in broad terms (as goals), but then each standard is broken down into many more specific indicators (similar to subject-specific course goals or even educational objectives in units). These broad goals and indicators are often used by districts in their curriculum guides. When determining their subject content standards, state departments of education have been influenced by professional organizations in the content fields. For example, the National Council of Teachers of Mathematics prepared K–12 mathematics standards that can be used as a guide when states develop their own content standards.

More recently, over 40 states have adopted the Common Core State Standards, which are replacing the existing curriculum standards in those states. Consequently, it is wise to become familiar with the common core standards and to know how to convert those standards into instructional objectives used in individual lessons. The curriculum standards for a state can typically be obtained from the state's department of education.

Regardless of the type and source of standard, teachers need to be able to examine a subject-specific course goal and break it down into several, more specific educational objectives at the unit level. Then teachers must be able to further break down the unit's educational objectives into the instructional objectives used in daily lessons.

TYPES OF INSTRUCTIONAL OBJECTIVES

There are several ways to write instructional objectives, and they fall into two categories— behavioral objectives and descriptive objectives.

Behavioral Objectives. Robert Mager (1997) argues that for instructional objectives to be meaningful, they must clearly communicate a teacher's instructional intent and be very specific. Objectives written in Mager's format became known as **behavioral objectives**, which state what is to be learned in language that specifies student actions, testing conditions, and performance criterion. Behavioral objectives have three parts:

1. Action—This is the student action or behavior that will provide evidence of learning.
2. Conditions—This is set of conditions or circumstances under which learning will take place.
3. Criterion—This is the standard or performance level defined as acceptable when assessment takes place.

For example, "Write an essay describing the process of selection of members of the House of Representative (*action*), incorporating the five major steps central to the election process (*criterion*) listed in the textbook (*condition*)."

VOICES
from the Classroom

DANIELLE RAMAGE, third-grade teacher, Ocala, Florida

USING FORMATIVE ASSESSMENTS TO GUIDE PLANNING

Each year, the students in third grade take a benchmark assessment to see which benchmarks they have mastered and which they still need to master. I use this assessment data to form guided reading groups according to the skills that still need to be mastered.

I can look at assessment data for a particular language arts benchmark, for example, and see which students have not mastered it. I then can form a group with these students so that I can remediate them in a small-group setting. The rest of the class will be working at another literacy center at this time.

When writing behavioral objectives, it is recommended you use precise words that are not open to many interpretations. Precise words include *identify*, *list*, and *compare*. Less precise words include to *know*, *understand*, or *appreciate*. Well-written behavioral objectives give students a clear and specific idea of what is expected of them.

Descriptive Objectives. **Descriptive objectives** indicate what the students are to learn without using language that specifies observable behavior; they state the student performance and the product of learning. Descriptive objectives are often adequate when you share your instructional intent with students. There are various approaches to writing descriptive objectives, including those of Gronlund and Brookhart, Marzano and colleagues, and Anderson and Krathwohl.

Gronlund and Brookhart (2009) maintain that objectives can be written first in more general terms, with appropriate specifics added later for clarification. Unlike the strict behaviorists, they are more willing to use words such as *understand* and *appreciate* with this approach, particularly at the unit level. Even though these words are open to a range of interpretation, Gronlund and Brookhart believe these words communicate more clearly the educational intent of teachers. Broad educational objectives at the unit level may be broken down into two or three subobjectives that are more specific for individual lessons.

In *Classroom Instruction That Works*, Marzano, Pickering, and Pollock (2005) provided three generalizations on setting objectives based on their meta-analysis of research studies in this area. Their work provides support for descriptive, more general instructional objectives. Here are their research-based generalizations:

1. *Instructional goals narrow what students focus on.* At first, this may seem desirable, but setting an overly specific goal can have the unintended consequence of focusing students' attention so narrowly that they ignore other related information.

2. *Instructional goals should not be too specific.* Their review of the research indicated that behavioral objective formats did not lead to results as high as instructional objectives written in more general formats. Behavioral objectives may simply be too specific.

3. *Students should be encouraged to personalize the teacher's goals.* Students should be encouraged to adapt the goals to their personal needs and desires.

Marzano (2011) identified two effective approaches to writing and using instructional objectives. First, have students translate the instructional objective in their own words. This clarifies for students what the teacher expects them to know or be able to do. By paraphrasing and restating the objective, students translate the objective into specific actions. Second, teachers could write each objective at multiple levels. The first one would be written at the target level. Two other objectives could then be written, one that's simpler and one that's more complex. These three versions of objectives provide students with a scaffold for different levels of understanding.

Another set of educators support using descriptive objectives, but with some requirements. Anderson and Krathwohl (2001) revised Bloom's Taxonomy of Educational Objectives (1956), which is described later in this chapter. Anderson and Krathwohl argue that traditional, behavioral objectives focus on content and skills of instruction and have ignored student thinking and decision making. Consequently, they identified a standard format for instructional objectives that requires only a verb and a noun. The verb describes the cognitive process and the noun describes the knowledge students are supposed to acquire. Using their guidelines, here are some examples:

- The student will learn to distinguish (verb for cognitive process) fact from fiction (noun for knowledge).

- The student will learn to classify (verb for cognitive process) different types of objectives (noun for knowledge).

- The student will be able to distinguish (verb for cognitive process) dominant from subordinate ideas in poetry (noun for knowledge).

Which Approach to Use? Behavioral objectives or descriptive objectives—each has merits and disadvantages. The approach teachers use may be influenced by school-wide policies, but there likely is considerable flexibility in a teacher's selection of the type of instructional objectives to be written. Instructional objectives are supposed to communicate a teacher's intent for a lesson and aid in assessing student learning. Research reviewed here, and common sense, indicate that some middle ground may be suitable between the strict adherence to behavioral objectives and the high levels of abstraction in some descriptive objectives. The approach by Gronlund and Brookhart (2009) may be the best approach since it provides for description, yet is flexible enough to allow for needed adjustments.

WRITING INSTRUCTIONAL OBJECTIVES

Since there are differences between behavioral objectives and descriptive objectives, there are also differences in the way they are written.

Writing Behavioral Objectives. As suggested by Mager (1997), each behavioral objective should include (1) an **action statement** identifying the action that the teacher expects students to perform, (2) a **conditions statement** identifying the conditions under which the action occurs, and (3) a **criterion statement** identifying the criteria or level of performance expected of students.

Here's another example: "After practicing the concept during class in small work groups (*condition*), the students will underline the key information needed to solve each of 10 word problems (*action*) with 80 percent accuracy (*criterion*)." It is useful to examine each part of the performance objective in more detail in the sections that follow.

Action Statements. The action statement is always stated in terms of what students are expected to know or do. This central action or performance by students is observable by

PLANNING

There are 10 InTASC standards (see pages xx–xxi), and each standard in the original document includes a list of performances, essential knowledge, and critical dispositions to indicate more clearly what is intended in the standard.

Since this chapter deals with planning, some representative statements from InTASC Standard #7, Planning for Instruction, are listed here concerning topics in this chapter.

PERFORMANCES

■ The teacher plans how to achieve each student's learning goals, choosing appropriate strategies and accommodations, resources, and materials to differentiate instruction for individuals and groups of learners.

■ The teacher develops appropriate sequencing of learning experiences and provides multiples ways to demonstrate knowledge and skill.

ESSENTIAL KNOWLEDGE

■ The teacher understands learning theory, human development, cultural diversity, and individual differences and how these impact ongoing planning.

■ The teacher understands the strengths and needs of individual learners and how to plan instruction that is responsive to those strengths and needs.

CRITICAL DISPOSITIONS

■ The teacher respects learners' diverse strengths and needs and is committed to using this information to plan effective instruction.

■ The teacher believes that plans must always be open to adjustment and revision based on learner needs and changing circumstances.

the teacher. Through observation or assessment of the performance, the teacher knows whether students have learned the content or skill under study. The action verb describes the behavior you will observe as the students successfully complete the learning task.

Behavioral objectives are intended to give students clear statements about what they are to do or complete in the learning situation. Specific words open to limited interpretations are desired (e.g., to *write, recite, identify, differentiate, contrast, list,* or *compare*). For example, it is very appropriate to have student appreciation of literature as an instructional goal, but that is an abstract goal. Thus, you should write performance objectives in observable terms, rather than with abstract terms open to many interpretations. Action verbs need to be selected that are specific and that clarify what is expected of students.

Conditions Statements. Condition statements indicate the circumstances under which the students are to perform the task or assignment given to them by the teacher. These conditions or circumstances may include (1) materials given to students (e.g., with a calculator, without using the text), (2) time limits for the completion of the task (e.g., in 15 minutes, in a two-week period of time), and (3) the location for the task to be performed (e.g., at the student's desk, in small groups, in the library).

For example, if students are asked to list the states that border their own state, it matters a great deal whether they can use a map to answer the question or if they are expected to respond from memory. In another example, you might ask, "What rights does the First Amendment to the Constitution of the United States of America give to the citizens of this country?" It is important for students to know if they should turn to the Bill of Rights in their textbooks or if they are to respond from memory, and the performance objective should be written accordingly.

Criterion Statements. The third component of a behavioral objective is the standard by which students' successful completion of the objective is measured. This level, sometimes referred to as the *standard of performance*, sets the level of acceptable performance for the objective. Some examples of criterion statements include the following:

- Five out of five parts of the definition
- 80 percent of the given problems will be answered correctly
- Write a topic sentence and at least three supporting sentences
- With 90 percent accuracy

While this level of performance is often thought of as the minimum level of acceptable performance, you may want your students to master a given objective at a higher

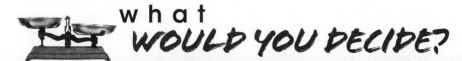

what WOULD YOU DECIDE?

WRITING BEHAVIORAL OBJECTIVES

Lesson plan objectives can be written in behavioral or descriptive terms. Behavioral objectives include the criterion or standard by which students' completion of the objective will be measured. Some topics or subjects may lend themselves to behavioral objectives.

1. If you were a physical education teacher and the lesson concerned effective passing in basketball, what kind of criterion statements would be appropriate in a behavioral objective?

2. How might you take into account the various levels of students' experiences in basketball and overall physical coordination?

rate than simply a grade of D. You may identify a necessary level of proficiency to enable students to proceed to the next lesson or unit.

Writing Descriptive Objectives. As noted earlier, there are various types of descriptive objectives, and the authors endorsing each type have their own particular guidelines. For the purpose of this introduction to writing descriptive objectives, the following guidelines are offered, with some of the guidelines coming from Gronlund and Brookhart (2009), Marzano et al. (2005), and Anderson and Krathwohl (2001).

Descriptive objectives should:

- Include a verb and a statement of the intended learning outcome
- Begin with an action verb that specifies observable student performance (Do not begin each with "The student is able to . . .)
- Describe student performance rather than teacher actions
- Be stated in terms of the learning outcome rather than the learning product or process
- Include only one intended learning outcome for each instructional objective
- Be clear, easy to understand, and unambiguous
- Be developmentally appropriate for the age and background of the learners
- Be relevant to the curriculum standards
- Promote learning across the learning domains and the various levels of the learning domains (addressed in the next section)

Examples include:

- Describes the function of each part of the circulatory system.
- Identifies the parts of the microscope.
- Distinguishes between probable and improbable economic forecasts.
- Differentiates between facts and inferences.

Objectives Within the Learning Domains

When preparing instructional objectives, it is helpful to refer to some frame of reference that clarifies the various types of learning outcomes to consider. One way of translating goals into instructional objectives is to categorize the desired outcomes into a classification system. A **taxonomy** is a system that classifies items and shows relationships among them.

One taxonomy that has been a useful tool for making decisions about instructional objectives and for assessing learner outcomes is Benjamin Bloom's Taxonomy of Educational Objectives. This taxonomy was originally developed by Bloom and colleagues (Bloom, 1956). It was recently revised by some of Bloom's students (Anderson & Krathwohl, 2001) and renamed a Taxonomy for Learning, Teaching, and Assessing. Bloom's taxonomy has three domains (or categories) of educational outcomes:

1. **Cognitive domain**—development of intellectual abilities and skills
2. **Affective domain**—development of attitudes, beliefs, and values
3. **Psychomotor domain**—coordination of physical movements and performance

The categories and subcategories in each of the three domains are arranged in hierarchical order, from the simplest outcomes to the most complex. The originators of the taxonomy developed a complete classification system for the cognitive and affective domains but did not complete the psychomotor domain system as scheduled. Other individuals, not connected with the original taxonomy, developed classification systems for the psychomotor domain (Harrow, 1972; Simpson, 1972).

The taxonomy can be helpful when you (1) get ideas for types of objectives to consider, ranging from simple to complex, (2) arrange the objectives in terms of complexity, and (3) check the completeness of the final set of objectives (Gronlund & Brookhart, 2009). The taxonomy is arranged in order of complexity, not difficulty. Thus, higher-order learning outcomes such as thinking and reasoning can be taught at any grade level.

Selection of a learning outcome in a particular level of the cognitive domain, for example, will influence your selection of content and assessments related to that learning outcome. If students are expected to describe the reasons for Columbus's voyage, then more than dates and a calendar of events need to be presented to help identify the reasons. Also, the test over this material should be in line with the instructional objective and content covered (i.e., test questions should deal with the reasons for the voyage if the objectives and content were about reasons for the voyage). In short, a taxonomy allows the cross-checking of objectives, instructional processes, and evaluation instruments to ensure that content is taught, practiced by students, and evaluated at the same level of complexity.

COGNITIVE DOMAIN

Bloom's revised cognitive taxonomy is two-dimensional (Anderson & Krathwohl, 2001)—the knowledge dimension and the cognitive process dimension. The **knowledge dimension** describes different types of knowledge and organizes knowledge into four categories: factual knowledge, conceptual knowledge, procedural knowledge, and metacognitive knowledge. These categories lie along a continuum from very concrete knowledge (factual) to more abstract (metacognition).

The **cognitive process dimension** contains six categories: remember, understand, apply, analyze, evaluate, and create (see Table 4.1). These are also along a continuum of increasing cognitive complexity, from lower-order thinking to higher-order thinking.

Higher-level objectives

Lower-level objectives

Level 6: Creating

Level 5: Evaluating

Level 4: Analyzing

Level 3: Applying

Level 2: Understanding

Level 1: Remembering

The column in Table 4.1 for alternative names for the categories provides examples of verbs that can be used when writing instructional objectives in the cognitive domain. That table also provides an example for the wording of an instructional objective at each level and sublevel in the cognitive domain.

AFFECTIVE DOMAIN

The taxonomy for the affective domain deals with students' attitudes, values, and emotions. While schools focus heavily on the cognitive domain, students' attitudes about learning and the content are equally important to their long-term success in school. To aid the task of classification of these attitudes, values, and emotions related to schooling, the affective taxonomy was developed by Krathwohl, Bloom, and Masia (1964).

Using the structure set up by Krathwohl and colleagues, the affective taxonomy has five levels. Descriptions of each level are presented along with sample descriptive objectives for each.

TABLE 4.1

The Cognitive Process Dimension of the Cognitive Domain

CATEGORIES & COGNITIVE PROCESSES	ALTERNATIVE NAMES	DEFINITION AND EXAMPLES
1. Remember—Retrieve relevant knowledge from long-term memory		
1.1 Recognizing	Identifying	Locating knowledge in long-term memory that is consistent with presented material (e.g. Recognize the dates of important events in U.S. history)
1.2 Recalling	Retrieving	Retrieving relevant knowledge from long-term memory (e.g., Recall the dates of important events in U.S. history)
2. Understand—Construct meaning from instructional messages, including oral, written, and graphic communication.		
2.1 Interpreting	Clarifying, paraphrasing, representing, translating	Changing from one form of representation (e.g., numerical) to another (e.g., verbal) (e.g., Paraphrase important speeches and documents)
2.2 Exemplifying	Illustrating, instantiating	Finding a specific example or illustration of a concept or principle (e.g., Give examples of various artistic painting styles)
2.3 Classifying	Categorizing, subsuming	Determining that something belongs to a category (e.g., Classify observed or described cases of mental disorders)
2.4 Summarizing	Abstracting, generalizing	Abstracting a general theme or major point(s) (e.g., Write a short summary of the event portrayed on a videotape)
2.5 Inferring	Concluding, extrapolating, interpolating, predicting	Drawing a logical conclusion from presented information (e.g., In learning a foreign language, infer grammatical principles from examples)
2.6 Comparing	Contrasting, mapping, matching	Detecting correspondences between two ideas, objects, and the like (e.g., Compare historical events to contemporary situations)
2.7 Explaining	Constructing models	Constructing a cause-and-effect model of a system (e.g., Explain the cause of important 18th Century events in France)
3. Apply—Carry out or use a procedure in a given situation		
3.1 Executing	Carrying out	Applying a procedure to a familiar task (e.g., Divide one whole number by another whole number, both with multiple digits)
3.2 Implementing	Using	Applying a procedure to an unfamiliar task (e.g., Use Newton's Second Law in situations in which it is appropriate)
4. Analyze—Break material into its constituent parts and determine how the parts relate to one another and to an overall structure or purpose		
4.1 Differentiating	Discriminating, distinguishing, focusing, selecting	Distinguishing relevant from irrelevant parts, or important from unimportant parts of presented material (e.g., Distinguish between relevant and irrelevant numbers in a mathematical word problem)

TABLE 4.1 (continued)

The Cognitive Process Dimension of the Cognitive Domain

CATEGORIES & COGNTIVE PROCESSES	ALTERNATIVE NAMES	DEFINITION AND EXAMPLES
4.2 Organizing	Finding coherence, intergrating, outlining, parsing, structuring	Determining how elements fit or function within a structure (e.g., Structure evidence in a historical description into evidence for and against a particular historical explanation)
4.3 Attributing	Deconstructing	Determine a point of view, bias, values, or intent underlying presented material (e.g., Determine the point of view of the author of an essay in terms of his or her political perspective)
5. Evaluate—Make judgments based on criteria and standards		
5.1 Checking	Coordinating, detecting, monitoring, testing	Detecting inconsistencies or fallacies within a process or product; determining whether a process or product has internal consistency; detecting the effectiveness of a procedure as it is being implemented (e.g., Determine if a scientist's conclusions follow from observed data)
5.2 Critiquing	Judging	Detecting inconsistencies between a product and external criteria, determining whether a product has external consistency; detecting the appropriateness of a procedure for a given problem (e.g., Judge which of two methods is the best way to solve a given problem)
6. Create—Put elements together to form a coherent or functional whole; reorganize elements into a new pattern or structure		
6.1 Generating	Hypothesizing	Coming up with alternative hypotheses based on criteria (e.g., Generate hypotheses to account for an observed phenomenon)
6.2 Planning	Designing	Devising a procedure for accomplishing some task (e.g., Plan a research paper on a glven historical topic)
6.3 Producing	Constructing	Inventing a product (e.g., Build habitats for a specific purpose)

Source: Anderson, Lorin W., & Krathwohl, David R. (Eds.) (2001). *A taxonomy for learning, teaching, and assessing: A revision of Bloom's taxonomy of educational objectives.* Boston: Pearson/Allyn & Bacon. (pp. 67–68). Reprinted by permission of Pearson.

1. *Receiving.* The student is aware of or attending to something in the environment. At this level, students are expected to listen and be attentive. Sample verbs used in instructional objectives include: *attend, be aware, hear, listen, look,* and *notice.* Examples of objectives for this level of the affective domain include:

- The student pays close attention to directions for an activity.
- The student shows awareness of the importance of fire safety practices.
- The student listens closely to classroom presentations.

2. *Responding.* The student displays some new behavior as a result of experience and responds to the experience. Objectives at this level require the student to comply with given directions by attending or reacting to certain stimuli. Students are expected to obey, participate, or respond willingly when asked or directed to do something. Sample verbs used in instructional objectives include: *comply, discuss, follow, obey, participate, practice,* and *volunteer*. Examples of objectives for this level of the affective domain include:

- The student completes assigned homework.
- The student volunteers for special tasks.
- The student finds pleasure in reading.

3. *Valuing.* The student displays definite involvement or commitment toward some experience. Students are expected to demonstrate a preference or display a high degree of certainty and conviction. Sample verbs used here include: *act, argue, convince, debate, display, express,* and *prefer*. Examples of objectives at this level include:

- The student recognizes the value of freedom of speech.
- The student expresses an appreciation for the role of science in everyday life.
- The student shows concern for language by trying to speak and write precisely.

4. *Organization.* The student has integrated a new value into his or her general set of values and given it its proper place in a priority system. Students are expected to organize their likes and preferences into a value system and then decide which ones will be dominant. Sample verbs used here include: *balance, compare, decide, define, formulate, select,* and *systematize*. Examples of objectives at this level include:

- The student forms judgments about proper behavior in school.
- The student decides what values are most important to him or her.
- The student forms a judgment about his or her life work based on abilities, interests, and beliefs.

5. *Characterization.* The student acts consistently according to his or her values. The student has acquired the behaviors at all previous levels and also has integrated his or her values into a system representing a complete philosophy that does not allow contradictory expressions. Sample verbs used here include: *avoid, display, exhibit, internalize, manage, resist,* and *resolve*. Examples of objectives at this level include:

- The student regularly cooperates in class and group activities.
- The student tries to solve problems objectively.
- The student works independently and diligently.

what **WOULD YOU DECIDE?**

THE AFFECTIVE DOMAIN

Many lesson objectives deal with content in the cognitive domain. Yet you may want a lesson to address your students' attitudes, values, and emotions in the affective domain. For example, you might have a lesson on safe and appropriate use of the Internet, and one lesson objective might address your students making a commitment to these safe practices.

1. How might you teach the lesson with the end goal of students making a commitment to safe Internet use?

2. What are the challenges that teachers might experience when teaching lessons with objectives in the affective domain dealing with attitudes, values, and emotions?

PSYCHOMOTOR DOMAIN

The psychomotor domain is primarily concerned with the development of movement and coordination, ranging from reflex to creative movement. This domain receives vastly different levels of interest depending on the subject area being taught. The psychomotor domain is especially important in physical education, vocational education, music education, and early childhood education.

In physical education, students may be expected to learn to throw, catch, swim various strokes, or hit a golf ball. All these tasks require psychomotor skills, as do learning to write or use word processing, playing a musical instrument, drilling a hole, or sketching a picture. Cognitive and affective goals are also present in each of these examples.

Although a number of authors have attempted to clarify the elements of the psychomotor domain, Harrow (1972) has presented perhaps the most comprehensive system or classification, and her classification system is described here. It has several levels ranging from simple reflex movements to highly complex integrated movement. Descriptions of each level are presented along with sample objectives for each.

1. *Reflex movements.* Student actions can occur involuntarily in response to some stimulus. Sample verbs used in objectives include *blinks* and *ducks*. Examples of objectives at this level include:

- The student will blink when something comes at his or her face.
- The student will contract a muscle.

2. *Fundamental movements.* The student has innate movement patterns that are built on reflex movements. Sample verbs include: *walk, run, jump, push, pull, reach,* and *crawl.* Examples of objectives at this level include:

- The student will run a 100-yard dash.
- The student will perform push-ups.

3. *Perceptual abilities.* The student can translate stimuli received through the senses into appropriate desired movements. Objectives may include kinesthetic, visual, auditory, tactile, and coordination abilities. Sample verbs include: *distinguish, discriminate,* and *coordinate.* Examples of objectives at this level include:

- The student will distinguish distant and close sounds.
- The student will distinguish smooth and rough surfaces.

4. *Physical abilities.* The student has developed basic movements that are essential to the development of more highly skilled movements. The student meets the demands of complex sustained movement. The verb *express* can be used for this level (i.e., expresses endurance, strength, flexibility, agility, or dexterity). Examples of objectives at this level include:

- The student will be able to run four laps around the playing field without stopping.
- The student will be able to complete 10 sit-ups.

5. *Skilled movements.* The student has developed more complex movements requiring a certain degree of efficiency. The student performs skillfully in games, sports, dances, and the arts. Sample verbs include: *serve, dance, play,* and *draw.* Examples of objectives at this level include:

- The student will be able to accurately serve a volleyball.
- The student will be able to play the piano.

6. *Nondiscursive communication.* The student has the ability to communicate through bodily movement. The student demonstrates expressive and interpretive movements through posture, gestures, facial expressions and creative movements. Sample verbs include: *move*, *dance*, *express*, and *gesture*. Examples of objectives at this level include:

- The student will act a part in a play.
- The student will create interpretative dance steps to music.

Planning Lessons

When planning effective lessons, it is important to recognize the three main parts of an effective lesson, to be aware of the value of using lesson plan formats when writing lesson plans, to know the sections of a generic lesson plan format, and to be aware of additional guidelines when lesson planning.

PARTS OF AN EFFECTIVE LESSON

Take into account the three parts of an effective lesson as you make planning decisions about the content and sequence of events within the lesson. Many planning experts recommend that each lesson have introductory, developmental, and closing activities:

1. *Introductory activities*. **Introductory activities** are designed to introduce the content to the students, capture student attention and interest, and set the stage for the developmental activities that follow. It is important to have activities at the start of the lesson to capture the interest of the students as a means to motivate them to learn that particular content. Introductory activities serve these purposes. Relating a lesson to aspects of students' lives, reviewing key points from previous lessons and stating the objectives and their purpose, and finding out what prior knowledge students retain are the types of activities often used at the beginning of a lesson (Serdyukov & Ryan, 2008).

This introductory overview of a lesson helps students understand what they will be studying, how the lesson is related to previous lessons, and how the lesson fits into the larger framework of the course content. This brief introduction about the lesson's objectives and about your expectations of the students is very important. Telling students in advance what they are going to learn, what the key points will be, and what the students should know by the end of the lesson has been positively related to student achievement.

2. *Developmental activities*. **Developmental activities** address the content and are the vehicles for student learning. As discussed in Chapters 5 and 6, there are many instructional strategies to use, including lectures, questions, practice, group and discussion methods, and inquiry and discovery approaches. Furthermore, there are various ways to group the students for instruction, including whole-group instruction, small-group instruction, and independent work.

The instructional strategies selected must help students be successful in meeting the instructional objectives for the lesson. It is often helpful to plan for the sequential use of several different types of instructional strategies during a lesson to add instructional variety, to take into account students' attention spans, and to accommodate students' different learning styles.

For example, a lesson in a 10th-grade literature class might begin with a brief lecture about the parts of a short story. Next, the class may view a DVD about short stories and then work in pairs to analyze and identify the parts of a particular short story they recently read as a class assignment. The class might end with a whole-class discussion about these issues and perhaps a listing on the board of the key concepts. This lesson has four major segments with each part requiring a different type of activity and student role in the activity.

3. *Closing activities.* **Closing activities** are designed to summarize the lesson's content and to allow the students time to prepare to leave the classroom. Effective teachers plan to stop the developmental part of the lesson a few minutes before the end of the class period to provide sufficient time for the content closing and the procedural closing of a lesson.

The **content closing** of a lesson includes a summary of the main points in the lesson. This helps reinforce the content that was covered in the lesson and helps students see how the content fits with the context of the other information in the unit and the course. The **procedural closing** of a lesson involves actions that help students get ready to move on to the next subject or class at the appropriate time. Students might use the time during the procedural closing to write down the homework assignment, put away materials and supplies, turn in papers, and get ready leave the classroom.

Some additional considerations in managing lesson delivery are addressed in Chapter 8.

LESSON PLAN FORMATS

Throughout your teacher education program but especially during student teaching, you will be expected to prepare a detailed lesson plan for each lesson that you teach. The main purpose of this activity is to ensure that you have a clear representation of how you expect the lesson to progress. A daily lesson plan defines the purposes and activities for a class session. This plan can be invaluable as you reflect on the success of the lesson relative to both student performance and your ability to implement a plan successfully.

As a beginning teacher, it is wise to continue writing lesson plans. As you become more experienced, you may find that you do not have to write such detailed descriptions of your lesson plans. Many districts require beginning teachers to submit their weekly or daily lesson plans to the building principal for review prior to instruction, such as submitting the plans each Friday for the lessons planned for the following week.

When preparing lesson plans, it is useful to use a **lesson plan format**, which is a lesson plan template that has a separate section to record all of the types of standard information you need in a lesson plan. There may be a section for the curriculum standards being addressed in the lesson, the specific instructional objectives for the lesson, the materials and technology needed for the lesson, a description about how you will introduce the lesson objectives and content, and other possible parts. It is helpful to clearly indicate what happens at the beginning of the lesson for the introductory activities, during the middle of the lesson for the developmental activities, and at the end of the lesson for the closing activities.

However, no single lesson plan format is used by all teachers, nor is there a list of universally accepted components of a lesson plan. As a result, you need to decide on the

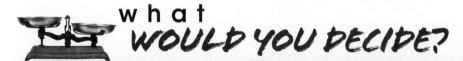

what
WOULD YOU DECIDE?

PARTS OF AN EFFECTIVE LESSON

An effective lesson should have a beginning, a middle, and an end. This includes introductory activities, developmental activities, and closing activities.

1. Why would this lesson structure be helpful for students?

2. What are the disadvantages for students if these components are not there?

type of information that you would like to include in your lesson plans and then display this information in a format that suits your needs and preferences.

Your selection of a lesson plan format may be influenced by the subject you are teaching, the type of instructional approach you intend to use in the lesson, or other factors. There also are web-based resources showing many alternatives in lesson plan formats.

Some subject areas have preferred lesson plan formats, which might thus influence your selection of the lesson plan format. For example, the 5-E instructional model is recommended by many science educators (e.g., Bass, Contant, & Carin, 2009). The 5-E model was developed by the Biological Sciences Curriculum Study (1989) group, and it builds on the learning cycle model. This model of instruction consists of five teaching phases during a lesson: engage, explore, explain, elaborate, and evaluate. If planning a science lesson, you might design your lesson plan format to include these five elements. At the beginning of the lesson, you would engage the learners. During the middle of the lesson, you would explore, explain, and elaborate. At the end of the lesson, you would evaluate.

Other subject areas may have preferred lesson plan formats. Similarly, the instructional strategy that you use in a lesson may influence your selection of a lesson plan format. When using the small-group learning strategy, for example, students need to be prepared for the tasks, guided during the small-group work, and debriefed upon completion. A lesson plan format could be created to indicate these sections of the lesson.

One generic lesson plan format is recommended here for beginning teachers (see Figure 4.1). This lesson plan format includes sections that are recommended by many educators, and it can be readily adapted to accommodate many subject areas and instructional approaches.

As a beginning teacher, you may use the generic lesson plan format displayed in Figure 4.1, or you may use one that you adapt for your own purposes. Guidelines for information needed in each part of the lesson plan format are provided in Figure 4.1.

It is helpful to create a master lesson plan format on your computer so you can simply copy the file and type in the detailed information about the lesson that you are working on. In this way, you have a computer file for each lesson, making it easier to read, print, and modify the next time you teach the lesson. It is helpful to keep lessons filed or organized by unit topic.

Beginning teachers generally benefit from writing down detailed, well-organized lesson plans and from the experience of conducting these lessons. As you become more experienced, you may be able to write your plans in less detail, knowing that in your mind you have made decisions about some parts that are not written in detail.

SECTIONS OF A LESSON PLAN FORMAT

A description of each section of the generic lesson plan format from Figure 4.1 is provided here. You may want to add some sections or modify these components in some way.

Identifying Course Information. Certain information about the course, subject, and lesson is needed at the top of each lesson plan. This information can include the name of the teacher, the course title, the grade level, the room number, the name of the unit, the topic of that particular lesson, the date of the lesson, and the length of the lesson in minutes. Certainly, you will know this information, but anyone else reading your lesson plans will need it. Substitute teachers, for example, will need that information in order to use the appropriate lesson plan that you briefly described in your weekly plans. Your principal or members of your planning team also will also need to see that information on the plan sheet.

FIGURE 4.1

A GENERIC LESSON PLAN FORMAT WITH GUIDELINES

Your Name: Grade Level:
Lesson Title: Date Taught:
Subject: Length of Lesson (minutes):

STANDARDS:
Write out the Curriculum Standards, Benchmarks, and Indicators that the lesson will address.
Choose 1 or 2 indicators to focus the lesson.

OBJECTIVES:
Write 1–3 clear, age-appropriate, measurable, standards-based objectives that are aligned to indicators.

MATERIALS:
List all the materials required for teaching this lesson. Cite resources (e.g., textbook and page numbers, websites) when applicable. Attach supporting documents (student handouts, examples, etc.) if they are available. Indicate how technology is used in planning and enhancing instruction.

POSSIBLE QUESTIONS:
Write 4–5 interesting, engaging, open-ended, and meaningful questions you might ask during the lesson. Questions must relate to the lesson objectives and the associated content.

BEGINNING OF THE LESSON:
Describe how you will capture and focus student interest.
Indicate how you will help students understand why it is important that they learn this.
You may include daily and/or weekly review in this lesson segment.
Plan for about 3–6 minutes for this part of the lesson.

MIDDLE OF THE LESSON:
Identify and describe the events of the lesson. In doing so, give consideration to:
- Aligning the content and activities with the lesson objectives.
- Using a variety of instructional strategies to meet the needs of all students.

ENDING OF THE LESSON:
Describe what you and the students will do to close the lesson.
Indicate how you will ask students to demonstrate their knowledge or skills in some new way and allow you to assess student achievement of the lesson objectives.

Standards. Each lesson should be designed to address one or more curriculum standard. The standard's number, title, and description can be included in this section of the lesson plan format. You will likely be citing curriculum standards for your grade level and subject area that are from your state's department of education. Some states have several indicators under each standard, so you would refer to the standard and the indicator that your lesson addresses. The Common Core State Standards have been adopted by over 40 states, so the standards that you cite may be from the common core.

Objectives for the Lesson. Each lesson will have one or more instructional objectives. Recall that an *objective* is a statement of the intended learning outcomes. Objectives commonly describe what students will be able to do when instruction has been completed. Follow the guidelines described earlier for writing behavioral or descriptive objectives. In this section of the lesson plan, you may list one to three objectives.

Materials. Your lesson plan should include a listing of materials you will need during instruction of that lesson, including items such as textbooks, additional resource books, handouts, DVDs, computer equipment, maps, pictures, posters, globes, charts, supplies, laboratory equipment, bulletin boards, and other items. Before making final decisions in your lesson plan, check to be sure the items that you are thinking about will be available on the day and time of the class. For example, you might want to have a demonstration with a computer and a program related to your subject area, but the computer might already be reserved for the day that you were planning the lesson.

Possible Questions. It is helpful to write four or five interesting and engaging questions that you might ask during the lesson. Questions must relate to the lesson objectives and the associated content. This helps you identify essential questions about important content before the lesson, thus avoiding overlooking a key issue when the lesson is being conducted. These questions also enable you to focus on the critical issues related to the curriculum standard.

Beginning of the Lesson. This is where you describe how you will capture and focus student interest and attention on the lesson objectives. For science 5-E lessons, for example, you would put your engage activities here. Set induction activities, described later, would be placed in this part of the lesson plan format. Typically only 3–5 minutes is reserved for these opening activities. Daily and weekly reviews are often included at the beginning of a lesson.

Middle of the Lesson. This is the body of the lesson when you conduct developmental activities. Most of the time for the lesson is reserved for the middle of the lesson, and it often is helpful to indicate an approximate amount of time to be taken for each lesson segment. Identify and describe the instructional strategies you will use in the lesson. Select age-appropriate strategies, and align the content and activities to the lesson objectives.

When you select instructional activities, you should consider many factors such as student characteristics, the nature of the instructional activities themselves, the instructional setting and physical environment, the complexity of the task, the degree of student engagement, the amount of time required, and other factors.

When deciding how to sequence the activities, you should consider two guidelines. First, your activities should lead students from simple to complex and from concrete to abstract. Second, in general, students should not be asked to do something new and difficult for the first time on their own.

There are a number of ways to group students for instruction (see Chapter 8). Briefly, you might choose whole-group instruction, small-group instruction (including cooperative learning and peer tutoring), or independent work. You will have to decide what type of grouping best helps students meet the objectives of the lesson. Your decision could be affected by your desire to vary your instructional delivery over time.

At some point, you need to evaluate whether your students have achieved the goals of the unit and the objectives of each lesson. However, you do not have to give a test or quiz in each class period. Instead, you may formally evaluate your students periodically. It is important, however, to check for student understanding in each lesson as you proceed through it.

Your evaluation during a lesson might simply include checking for comprehension by questions or activities in which the students are quizzed about the content of the lesson.

Student responses will give you important feedback about student mastery of the content and will help you decide whether to continue with your lesson plan or perhaps reteach some part of the lesson that students had difficulty with.

Ending of the Lesson. Closing activities are designed to provide a summary of the lesson's content and to allow the students time to prepare to leave the classroom. Stop the lesson with sufficient time to handle these closing responsibilities. As noted earlier, there is the content closing in which a summary of main points can be highlighted and a procedural closing in which students put things away and prepare to move to the next subject or to prepare to leave the classroom.

Other Possible Parts in the Lesson Format. The items discussed so far are common elements of a lesson plan. Depending on your needs and preferences, you might also want to include a section in your lesson plan format for some of the following seven items:

1. *Rationale for the lesson.* Some teachers prefer to include the rationale for why the lesson is important. In this way, you can identify and clarify the value of the lesson and convey this rationale to the students.

2. *An outline of the subject matter.* Some teachers prefer to attach an outline of the subject matter to be covered in the lesson to the lesson plan sheet. In this way, all important information is together.

3. *A list of key points.* Sometimes there is a key point that you want to emphasize in a lesson. By having a spot on your lesson plan sheet, you are able to clarify that point for yourself and then convey it to students during the lesson.

4. *The assignment of homework or other requirements.* You may prefer to include a spot in your lesson plan sheet to list any assignment given to students.

5. *A timetable.* Some lesson plan sheets include a column on one side for you to indicate the approximate amount of time each activity will take. As an alternative,

VOICES from the Classroom

JOANN SNOOK, high school English/language arts teacher, Allentown, New Jersey

FOCUSING ON ESSENTIAL QUESTIONS

When planning, it is very helpful to identify a few essential questions that help structure the lesson and focus students on important content and issues. During instruction, it is equally important for students to be aware of those essential or overarching questions at all times.

Since I think students tend to remember what they see often, I display the essential questions in my room in various ways. I often post the essential questions in large print on a bulletin board or on large paper placed on a classroom wall. I also keep Post-it Notes available

in the room at all times. As we move through the unit and as students learn material relevant to the essential questions, they can use the Post-it Notes to display their ideas and new learning on the essential questions bulletin board.

We end up with an "Aha! Board" that is an area of constant attention showing the essential questions and related content. This board helps keep the students and me on target, and helps the students see relationships and participate in new discoveries related to the essential questions.

you might simply indicate this estimate of the number of minutes next to the activity description in the plan.

6. *Special notes or reminders.* You may have special announcements that you want to make to students on a particular day, such as information about special projects, reminders about an upcoming due date for a project, additional information about an assignment, or other information.

7. *Evaluation of the lesson.* This space is reserved for you to make notes about the lesson after instruction has taken place. For example, one activity might have required more time than you originally planned or would have worked better with fewer students in each group. Or you could make notes about the quality of a DVD you used. In this way, you will have a written record about your experiences with the lesson. When you begin your planning for the next time you teach this lesson, you can read these notes and comments and make any needed changes to improve it.

ADDITIONAL LESSON PLANNING ISSUES

Teachers need to consider how detailed they need to make their lesson plans, to be prepared to make ongoing changes to the lesson plan during actual instruction, and to consider some tips for daily planning.

How Detailed? The degree of detail that teachers include in daily lesson plans varies considerably. Experienced teachers prepare their weekly plans in a plan book and may not prepare any additional, detailed plans for each particular lesson. Therefore, an experienced teacher may write the objective(s) that he or she wants students to achieve, the content standard that students will be working on, and some short notations about activities and materials. From these short notes, the experienced teacher knows exactly how to conduct the lesson.

A novice teacher, however, may need to write out an explicit step-by-step lesson plan just to be sure that everything is considered and planned in an appropriate manner. As mentioned previously, the building principal may also require beginning teachers to submit their written plans, and a simple outline is usually not sufficient. The practice of preparing detailed lesson plans and experiencing the actual instruction of those plans will help build and reinforce a teacher's planning skills. Over time, teachers realize that they have the knowledge and skill to conduct their lessons with lesson plans that are not as explicit as what they used in their teacher preparation program or during their early years of teaching.

Making Ongoing Changes. Be prepared to make ongoing changes to your lesson plans. You may have three classes of world history and prepare only one daily lesson to be used for each class. Yet no two classes are the same; each has its own characteristics that will likely affect how you actually go about instruction. In one class, for example, you might have some students who have traveled to a country that you are covering in the lesson, and you might want to draw on these particular students during the lesson. Another class may work better with cooperative learning activities. Consequently, even before instruction begins, you may modify your daily lesson somewhat after taking into account the unique characteristics of each class.

In another case during actual instruction, you might find that the lesson is not working out in the way that you had planned. Students may have difficulty grasping the concepts, they may have little interest in the topic, or participation may not be what you expected. For these and other reasons, you might find that you need to alter the lesson during instruction. You might decide to alter the approach of an activity to have students work in pairs instead of individually, or you might shorten one activity and add in something entirely different. If things do not work as you had planned, you should change the type of activity or the manner of delivery in some way. Therefore, when preparing your initial lesson plans, consider how you might alter your lessons on the spot.

CLASSROOM CASE STUDY

IMPROVING LESSON PLANNING

Terrell Green is an eighth-grade science teacher who has been teaching for two years. While he knows his content well, his lesson plans still lack organization. To spark intrigue and interest in his students, he likes hands-on and fun activities. Last year, Mr. Green's students worked in teams to create pop rockets with effervescing antacid tablets. To increase student interest, he added incentives by rewarding the team whose rocket flew the highest. However, he did not bring enough effervescing antacid tablets for one class, putting them a day behind. Also, his lessons took longer than he expected, and his closing activities were rushed and poorly executed. His students began side conversations when they realized that Mr. Green wasn't going to have enough time to finish the lesson. Further, students were not required to submit lab reports and were graded only on class participation. This left students wondering about the main goals of the assignment and did not provide them with closure.

Mr. Green has revisited his lesson plans and is having trouble finding the problem. He has a good mental image of his lesson plans and briefly outlines his objectives and developmental activities on paper. He puts little consideration into the circumstances under which his students will perform activities, however. He is looking for some guidance.

FOCUS QUESTIONS

1. What factors contributed to the problems in the science lesson?

2. What specific suggestions do you have for Mr. Green to improve his lesson planning and to increase the effectiveness of the lessons?

3. How might Mr. Green put more emphasis and accountability on students' assessment of their own learning?

Tips for Daily Planning. As you become more experienced at daily planning, you will automatically take into account a number of factors as you design each lesson. As a starting point, here are 10 tips to help you prepare your daily lesson plans:

1. Use a template for your lesson plan format, and organize your lesson plans on your computer.

2. Select a regular day and time to prepare your weekly and daily plans.

3. Seek help from other teachers when planning; they can be a rich source of ideas and support.

4. Have the lesson's objectives tie in directly to the unit and course goals.

5. Be sure that each instructional activity addresses a lesson objective.

6. Plan for a variety of instructional activities within each lesson as well as varied use of instructional media.

7. Build motivational strategies into the lesson.

8. Arrange for a suitable amount of time for each instructional activity.

9. Provide extended practice activities to ensure students have opportunities for independent practice and skill building.

10. Have some additional backup plans if something unexpected happens, such as equipment not working.

Planning Units

Unit planning involves developing a sequence of daily plans that addresses the topic of the unit in a cohesive way. In *Understanding by Design*, Wiggins and McTighe (2006) suggest that unit plans be developed around essential questions. **Essential questions** address the big ideas or fundamental concepts that we want student to think about and learn during the span of the unit. By posing questions, students and teacher are able to focus their attention on content that will help answer the questions. Therefore, essential questions provide a focus for the unit. In *What's the Big Idea?* Jim Burke (2010) provides guidance and examples for using essential questions in units to motive students and promote thinking.

To effectively plan units, teachers should be aware of resources and factors in unit planning, know the steps in unit planning, be able to prepare the components of a unit plan, and use strategies to lead to successful unit planning.

RESOURCES AND FACTORS IN UNIT PLANNING

When planning a unit, you will likely use some of the same materials used in course planning, such as unit file folders, the curriculum guide, the textbook, and the calendar. At this point, you need to give special attention to planning and selecting instructional resources. You might need to order or schedule certain supplies or guest speakers, or you might need to prepare various instructional materials. You also will need to consider issues such as differentiating instruction, meeting the needs of diverse learners, integrating technology into instruction, and using assessment data to guide instructional planning. In addition, you will likely need to take into account your previous experiences with the unit, student interest, and other issues when planning a unit.

THE COMPONENTS OF A UNIT PLAN

While unit plans can have many components, the following items are frequently included in unit plans.

- *Overview*—This includes descriptive information such as the grade level, the course being taught, the title of the unit, and the length (in days) of the unit.

- *Rationale*—This includes a description of what you will be teaching and what it is that students will be learning. The rationale also can include a description of how this unit fits into the existing curriculum. This rationale can help connect the unit content to the course as a whole. Also, sharing the rationale for the unit with students enables them to see the importance of the material in their lives.

- *Course Goals*—As shown in Figure 3.6, subject-specific course goals are typically included in district curriculum guides. Identify the course goals that relate to the unit, and include them in your unit plan.

- *Educational Objectives and Essential Questions*—Also shown in Figure 3.6, course goals are translated into educational objectives used in the unit plan. Look at the course goals you identified in the previous step that relate to this unit, and then translate them to educational objectives that are specific to the unit you are planning. In addition, select several essential questions that address the big ideas or fundamental concepts in the unit. These essential questions also can be shared with the students when instruction begins.

- *Outline of Content*—Include an outline of content that students will learn from the unit. This is not a list of activities, but rather an outline of the subject matter to be learned. The content outline is often referred to as the *scope of the content* since it identifies the breadth and depth of the content to be addressed. Outlining the content helps you clarify the subject matter and provides organization to the unit. It helps you consider the most appropriate order of the content and examine the interrelationships among the content.

- *A Calendar That Sequences the Daily Lessons*—The unit calendar gives an overview of the sequence of the lessons over a certain time frame, such as 10 days. There are three types of lessons to consider in this sequence (Kellough & Carjuzaa, 2009). First, there should be some **introductory lessons** that identify the reasons for studying this unit, provide for pre-assessment and diagnostic activities, set the tone for the lessons to follow, and generally motivate the students. Second, there should be **developmental lessons** that build the learning that makes up the unit objectives and content. Many instructional strategies can be used, including presentations, questions, practice, group and discussion methods, and inquiry and discovery methods (see Chapters 5 and 6). Finally, there should be **culminating lessons** that tie together what has been learned in the developmental lessons. These may include review lessons, student reports, and some type of student evaluation such as a test.

- *Daily Lesson Plans*—In daily lesson plans, the unit's educational goals are translated into more specific instructional objectives for individual lessons. Follow the guidelines discussed earlier for preparing daily lesson plans.

- *Assessments and Evaluations*—Various types of assessment can be used, such as assessing students' prior knowledge before instruction, assessment during instruction to check for understanding, and summative assessment at the end. Plans for the various types of assessment need to be determined and then built into the daily lesson plans. Student learning can be assessed in a variety of ways including tests, observation tools, work samples, logs, portfolios, and other approaches.

- *Materials and Resources*—List the materials and resources needed for the unit, and then gather and prepare the materials. Materials to be prepared for students may include handouts, study guides, bibliographies, project guideline sheets, books and resource materials for the students, and various supplies and equipment. In addition, you may need to gather and organize materials for yourself that will help you prepare for instruction or that you will use during instruction. These include notes, resources, texts, posters, maps, computer programs, or other items. Materials needed on specific days of the unit should be stated in the daily lesson plans.

VOICES from the Classroom

KEVIN MABIE, high school English teacher, Chesterfield, Missouri

FORMATIVE ASSESSMENT FOCUSING ON STANDARDS

The best decision I have ever made as a teacher was shifting to a standards-based grading system. To do so, I first identified the knowledge and skills that students are expected to learn, and then I determined how to measure them. In my class, students are responsible for mastering 10 skills each semester, and they are given a rubric indicating several levels of proficiency for each skill. Students are expected to demonstrate consistent mastery of each skill before the semester is over; if they can do so, they will receive a grade of A.

I begin each semester by giving my students a variety of diagnostic assessments to determine where they fall on the rubric for each of the 10 skills. For example, I may assign an essay that tests six of the skills, and then assess the other skills by having my students respond

to a reading. After I have recorded an initial score for each student for each skill in my grade book, the teaching begins. Students understand that this grade book score represents their ability level rather than a score for an assignment. I use the next 4–6 weeks working with students on their weaknesses.

If the entire class is weak on a particular skill, I work with the whole group and then give them a formative assessment to measure improvement. In other cases, I have several small groups, each working on a different skill. In that case, I rotate to each group to provide guidance and assistance. After I have had ample time to work with the students on their skills, I give them a new authentic assessment and see if their ability levels have changed.

STRATEGIES LEADING TO SUCCESSFUL IMPLEMENTATION OF UNIT PLANS

It is one thing to successfully plan a unit by choosing objectives or standards, selecting content and materials, and sequencing lessons. Yet it is another thing to actually incorporate learning strategies that help students to learn (Marzano, Pickering, & Pollack, 2005). Some strategies that can be used to successfully implement your unit plans include the following:

- Set clear learning goals for students, and let them personalize and record their own learning goals.

- Provide students with corrective feedback and the criteria used in grading to help them to assess their own progress. Ask students to reflect on their own learning, effort, and achievement. Celebrate meaningful progress.

- Provide an environment in which students are expected to articulate what they know about topics in the unit. Help students to link the information that they know to the new information that they will be learning. Have students keep notes on what they are learning.

- Vary instructional strategies and have students work both individually and as members of collaborative groups.

- Assign homework that allows students to practice, review, and apply what they have learned. Then provide feedback on their performance.

- Involve students in long-term projects.

- Ask students to represent what they have learned in paragraph form and by drawing figures, comparison charts, and outlines.

- Provide clear assessment of student progress concerning the learning objectives and standards and have students compare these assessments to their own self-assessments using the same rubric or criteria. Ask students what they have learned about the content and themselves as learners.

Applying the SIOP Model to Planning

Meeting the needs of English language learners (ELLs) can be facilitated by using the SIOP model to provide more flexibility in the design and delivery of instruction. As outlined in Chapter 1, there are eight components of the model, and two components relate to planning: lesson preparation and building background (Echevarria, Vogt, & Short, 2008). While these strategies were originally designed for use with ELLs, they are also helpful in meeting the needs of all learners in the classroom.

The excellent information from Echevarria, Vogt, and Short (2008) serves as the organizer for much of the content in this section.

LESSON PREPARATION

When planning lessons, teachers should consider factors such as content and language objectives, depth of content, supplementary materials, adaptations for the learners, and instructional activities that promote understanding of the content and also promote language development. Take the following six factors into account as you make your planning decisions:

1. *Clearly define, display, and review content objectives with the students.* Content objectives should be written in terms of what the students will learn or do, be stated simply, and be tied to specific grade-level content. It also is important to write the objectives on the board and to state them orally. It may be necessary to limit content objectives to only one or two per class period to reduce the complexity of the learning task.

2. *Clearly define, display, and review language objectives with the students.* Language objectives should also be written on the board and stated orally. Recognize that acquiring a new language is a process, so sequence the objectives to give students an opportunity first to explore and then to practice before demonstrating mastery of an objective. Language objectives, for example, may relate to vocabulary, listening, reading comprehension, the writing process, spelling, and grammar, even while teaching a social studies lesson.

3. *Select content concepts that are appropriate for the age and educational background of the students.* When planning lessons, consider students' first language, second-language proficiency, and reading ability, along with the cultural and age appropriateness of the sec-ond-language materials and the difficulty level of the materials to be read. You may need to find reading materials that will provide the scaffolding students need to understand the content concepts. If students do not have much prior knowledge about the subject, you can provide a small-group minilesson that precedes the regular whole-class lesson. In some cases, you may also need to provide extensive background building.

4. *Use supplementary materials to a high degree, making the lesson clear and meaning-ful.* Information that is embedded in context allows ELLs to understand and complete more cognitively demanding tasks. You should use many supplementary materials that support the core curriculum and contextualize learning. Plan for supplementary materials that will enhance meaning and clarify confusing concepts, making lessons more relevant. Examples of supplementary materials include hands-on manipulatives, real-life objects, pictures and photographs, graphs, maps, bulletin board displays, audiovisual materials, and demonstrations.

5. *Adapt content to all levels of student proficiency.* Make the text and other resource materials accessible for all students, adapting them so the content concepts are left intact. Be cautious about selecting reading materials suited to earlier grades; students may object to them, and the necessary content may not be included. Instead, adapt content through the use of graphic organizers, outlines (with some spots empty, to be filled in by the student), various study guides designed for learners of varied reading ability, highlighted texts, taped texts, jigsaw reading, and marginal notes.

6. *Provide meaningful activities that integrate lesson concepts with language practice opportunities for reading, writing, listening, and/or speaking.* Students are more success-ful when they are able to make connections between what they already know and what they are learning by relating classroom experiences to their own lives. These meaningful experiences represent a reality for the student, since they mirror what actually occurs in the learner's world. Authentic, meaningful experiences are especially important for ELLs because they are learning to attach labels and terms to things already familiar to them. Ex-amples of meaningful activities include interviews, letter writing, simulations, and models.

BUILDING BACKGROUND

When planning lessons, take into account the students' background experiences, prior knowledge, and vocabulary level to design effective lessons that enable learning. Informa-tion about these factors will influence your planning decisions concerning content and delivery of instruction:

1. *Explicitly link concepts to students' background experiences.* A student's knowledge of the world provides a basis for understanding, learning, and remembering facts and ideas. This prior knowledge helps the student organize and learn new related information. When students have limited prior knowledge, three instructional interventions may be used:

CLAUDIA ARGUELLO COCA, fifth-grade teacher, Las Cruces, New Mexico

ADDRESSING LANGUAGE OBJECTIVES IN SIOP LESSON PREPARATION

A huge concept in SIOP is incorporating language objectives into our daily plans for all core subject areas. When I am teaching an essential core standard, which will usually take place over five to seven days, I embed language objectives into my teaching. The content objective will stay the same over the course of the instruction, what changes is the language objective.

It is very important for students to have the opportunity to develop language in various ways. In my classroom, language is purposefully planned, scaffolded, and measured. During the first days of a lesson, the language objective for drawing conclusions, as an example, would be to identify one fact that they read. The next day we would use that fact, drawing on previous learning, and add a schema connection

(something that the student has experienced or knows about). Following this lesson the student would then be expected to use both a fact and schema, leading to a conclusion.

To assist students in this process, I use sentence frames to help them verbalize their thinking in complete sentences so that their thinking is more concise and focused. By the end of this instructional period, the students are able to identify, discuss, write, and create examples of drawing conclusions. The powerful aspect of language objectives is that they are measurable, and thus I can assess the student learning immediately and make adjustments as needed.

- Teach vocabulary as a prereading step. In a SIOP lesson, teachers select words that are critical for understanding the text or the material and provide a variety of ways for students to learn, remember, and use those words. In this way, students develop a core vocabulary over time.

- Provide meaningful experiences for students. Connect students' prior knowledge and experiences to new content through authentic experiences.

- Introduce a conceptual framework that will enable students to develop appropriate background information. This can be accomplished through teaching techniques such as graphic organizers and chapter previews.

2. *Explicitly make links between past learning and new concepts.* Build a bridge from previous lessons to the new content; students do not automatically make these connections. Learning is enhanced when new information is integrated with material, vocabulary, and concepts students already know. This connection to previous lessons can be accomplished by referring to outlines, charts, maps, timelines, and graphic organizers or by asking questions such as "How does this idea relate to what we learned in the last chapter?"

3. *Emphasize key vocabulary.* Vocabulary development is strongly related to academic achievement for all learners, but it is especially critical for English language learners. Systematic and comprehensive vocabulary development is necessary, and it should be included as a priority in planning lessons. Vocabulary related to lesson content should be introduced, written, repeated, and highlighted for students to see and use.

Key Terms

Action statement
Affective domain
Behavioral objectives
Closing activities
Cognitive domain
Cognitive process
    dimension

Conditions statement
Content closing
Criterion statement
Culminating lessons
Descriptive objectives
Developmental
    activities

Developmental
    lessons
Essential questions
Instructional objective
Introductory activities
Introductory
    lessons

Knowledge
    dimension
Lesson plan format
Procedural closing
Psychomotor domain
Standards
Taxonomy

Major Concepts

1. The planning process helps you organize the curriculum and address complex classroom variables and also provides you with a sense of direction and a feeling of confidence and security.

2. Daily planning involves preparing notes about objectives, materials, activities, evaluation, and other information for a lesson for a particular day but in more detail than in the weekly plan.

3. Behavioral objectives include (a) an action statement identifying the action that the teacher expects students to perform; (b) a conditions statement identifying the conditions under which the action occurs; and (c) a criterion statement identifying the criteria or level of performance expected of students. Descriptive objectives are more general, include a noun and a verb, but do not indicate the criterion for student performance.

4. Learning objectives can be written in three learning domains: (a) cognitive, which refers to mental or intellectual thinking skills; (b) affective, which classi-

fies student attitudes toward learning; and (c) psychomotor, which involves physical movement and related skills.

5. When planning for instructional activities and procedures, select introductory, developmental, and closing activities within the lesson.

6. Lesson plan formats enable recording of essential information about the lesson, including items such as the curriculum standard for the lesson, objectives, materials, essential questions, and actions at the beginning, middle, and end of a lesson.

7. Unit planning involves developing a sequence of daily plans that addresses the topic of the unit in a cohesive way. To effectively plan units, teachers should be aware of resources and factors in unit planning, know the steps in unit planning, be able to prepare the products of unit planning, and use strategies to lead to successful unit planning.

8. The SIOP model can be used when planning to meet the needs of English language learners.

Discussion/Reflective Questions

1. Explain why it is a good thing to use both general educational objectives at the unit level and specific instructional objectives for individual lessons. What is the function of each, and how do they complement each other?

2. Should all objectives that you write be at the upper three levels of the cognitive domain? Why or why not?

3. What is the rationale for novice teachers to prepare detailed lesson plans?

4. What are the benefits and problems with using a generic lesson plan form?

5. What are the benefits of unit planning? What might be some consequences if you did not conduct unit planning?

6. How do all students benefit from use of the SIOP model in planning?

Suggested Activities

FOR CLINICAL SETTINGS

1. Obtain a textbook for a course that you might teach. Select a unit within the text, and outline the introductory, developmental, and culminating lessons that you would include in the unit.

2. Write at least three behavioral objectives and three descriptive objectives concerning content in this chapter representing different levels of the cognitive domain.

3. After considering the information in the generic lesson plan format provided in this chapter, consider any changes that you would want and design a lesson plan format for your use.

FOR FIELD EXPERIENCES

1. Examine the curriculum guide for one course, and compare it to the textbook that is used. In what ways would the curriculum guide help you in your planning of units and lesson?

2. Ask several teachers to look at their weekly plans. Ask the teachers to describe how they prepared those weekly plans and to identify factors they took into account when planning.

3. Ask several teachers about ways they plan to meet the needs of English language learners.

Further Reading

Gronlund, N. E., & Brookhart, S. M. (2009). *Gronlund's writing instructional objectives* (8th ed.). Upper Saddle River, NJ: Pearson/Prentice-Hall.

A thorough, practical guide that examines how to prepare instructional objectives in each learning domain. Considers performance objectives. Includes many examples and summary charts.

Price, K. M., & Nelson, K. L. (2011). *Planning effective instruction: Diversity responsive methods and management* (4th ed.). Belmont, CA: Thomson Wadsworth.

Provides a thorough review about planning what to teach and how to teach, preparing the plans, selecting strategies, and arranging the classroom environment.

Roberts, P. L., & Kellough, R. D. (2008). *A guide for developing interdisciplinary thematic units* (4th ed.). Upper Saddle River, NJ: Pearson/Prentice Hall.

Addresses how interdisciplinary thematic units fit in the curriculum, ways to get started, and ways to arrange for all the parts such as objectives, plans, and assessments.

Technology Resources

HOW TO WRITE A LESSON PLAN OBJECTIVE

http://www.ehow.com/how_4888533_write-lesson-plan-objective.html

Offers instructions along with links to other related issues.

BLOOM'S TAXONOMY FROM A DIGITAL PERSPECTIVE

http://edorigami.wikispaces.com/Bloom%27s+Digital+Taxonomy

This is an educator's suggestion to adapt Bloom's Revised Taxonomy with digital applications for students. Includes useful charts, descriptions, and examples.

DAILY LESSON PLAN TEMPLATES

http://www.lessonplans4teachers.com/daily_lesson-plan_templates.php

Includes sample lesson plan templates. This site also has links to lesson plans, rubrics, worksheets, and teacher tools.

THE SIOP INSTITUTE LESSON PLAN TEMPLATES

http://www.siopinstitute.net/classroom.html

Includes sample lesson plan templates that incorporate the components of the SIOP model.

MyEducationLab™

Go to the **MyEducationLab** (*www.myeducationlab.com*) for General Methods and familiarize yourself with the content:

- Topically organized Assignments and Activities, tied to learning outcomes for the course, that can help you more deeply understand course content
- Topically organized Building Teaching Skills and Dispositions learning units allow you to apply and develop understanding of teaching methods.
- A chapter-specific pretest that assesses your understanding of the content offers hints and feedback for each question and generates a study plan including links to Review, Practice, and Enrichment activities that will enhance your understanding of the concepts. A Study Plan posttest with hints and feedback ensures you understood concepts from the chapter after having completed the enrichment activities.

A Correlation Guide may be downloaded by instructors to show how MyEducationLab content aligns to this book.

Teacher-Centered Instructional Strategies

5

THIS CHAPTER PROVIDES INFORMATION THAT WILL HELP YOU TO

1. Describe the continuum of instructional approaches.

2. Distinguish the features of each teaching model in the continuum of approaches.

3. Identify the main characteristics of direct instruction.

4. Apply the components of direct and explicit instruction into lesson plans.

5. Utilize guidelines for the effective use of presentations, demonstrations, questions, and recitations.

6. Apply effective techniques when using practice, drills, reviews, guided practice, and homework.

With necessary background information about student characteristics, planning, and differentiating instruction, you are now ready to select the instructional strategies you will use in your lessons. You have a choice of many strategies that fall on a continuum ranging from teacher-centered instructional strategies to student-centered instructional strategies. An overview of that continuum is provided at the start of this chapter. Characteristics and components of the direct instruction model are then discussed, followed by descriptions of many instructional approaches used in direct instruction.

A Continuum of Instructional Approaches

Here you are, starting to plan a new unit in your science class, and you just can't imagine how your students will learn all that information about the human circulatory system. Essentially, you need to select instructional strategies for each lesson that will be the vehicles for students to learn the material.

An **instructional strategy** is a method for delivering instruction that is intended to help students achieve the learning objective. Strategies range from being very explicit and teacher directed to being less explicit and student centered. This section considers a continuum of instructional approaches from various perspectives: (1) teacher-centered to student-centered approaches, (2) direct to indirect approaches, and (3) the gradual release of responsibility model. In addition, the issue of using deductive and inductive instructional strategies is considered.

TEACHER-CENTERED TO STUDENT-CENTERED APPROACHES

As you plan for instruction, consider instructional strategies that are most suited to help achieve the objectives of the lessons. A wide range of possible strategies exists. Some strategies are teacher directed, such as lectures, recitations, questions, and practice. Others are more interactive, such as various group and discussion methods. Still other strategies are more student directed; these often emphasize inquiry and discovery.

Predominant instructional strategies are displayed in Figure 5.1 within four categories on a continuum ranging from teacher-centered, more explicit methods to student-centered, less explicit methods. They are as follows:

- **Direct instructional approaches** are those in which teachers tell the students the concept or skill to be learned and then lead students through most of the instructional activities designed to bring about student learning. Direct instructional approaches include direct instruction, presentations, demonstrations, questions, recitations, practice and drills, reviews, and guided practice and homework.

FIGURE 5.1

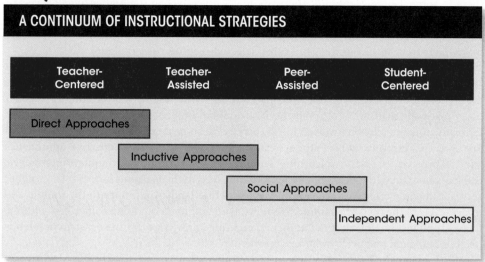

A CONTINUUM OF INSTRUCTIONAL STRATEGIES

Teacher- Centered	Teacher- Assisted	Peer- Assisted	Student- Centered

Direct Approaches

Inductive Approaches

Social Approaches

Independent Approaches

- **Inductive instructional approaches** are those that involve some type of exploratory activity that helps lead students to discover a concept or generalization. Teachers employ several strategies to help students attain the concepts. Inductive approaches include concept attainment strategies, inquiry lessons, and projects, reports, and problems.

- **Social instructional approaches** have students working together in various ways to gather, process, and learn information or skills. The teacher acts as a facilitator, rather than the information giver. Social approaches include discussions, cooperative learning, panels and debates, role playing, simulations, and games.

- **Independent instructional approaches** allow students to pursue content independently with less teacher direction than other lessons. Students sometimes are permitted to pursue their own interests. Independent approaches include learning centers, contracts, and independent work.

When deciding on a particular teaching strategy for a lesson, weigh the advantages and disadvantages of the various strategies along with the objectives of the intended lesson. Effective teachers use many different strategies throughout a unit and the school year as a means to differentiate their instruction and be more responsive to student needs.

DIRECT AND INDIRECT INSTRUCTIONAL APPROACHES

A range of instructional approaches can be placed on a continuum from teacher-centered to student-centered. Another way to look at that continuum is to classify the instructional approaches as being direct or indirect.

Direct Instructional Approaches. Teacher-centered instructional strategies are sometimes referred to as **direct instruction**. With direct instruction, the teacher typically selects the instructional objectives, the corresponding content, and the instructional strategies that will be used in the lessons. The teacher structures the learning environment and is primarily the conveyer of information in teacher-directed instructional activities (e.g., presentations, demonstrations, recitations, drill and practice). Students generally are not involved in the selection of objectives, content, or instructional strategies. Students have a relatively passive role in the process, often responding to teacher-specified directions to achieve the learning outcomes. Direct instruction lends itself more to the lower level of the revised Bloom's taxonomy (Anderson & Krathwohl, 2001), with emphasis on knowing and remembering the facts, understanding the facts, and applying them to some degree. Generally, there are fewer objectives in the higher-higher levels of Bloom's taxonomy in direct instruction, partly because students are not expected to be very active in the learning process or in constructing their own learning. Assessments are more likely to be tests, quizzes, and other selected-response assessments.

Indirect Instructional Approaches. Student-centered instructional strategies are sometimes referred to as **indirect instruction**. With indirect instruction, the teacher often takes the lead in identifying the instructional objectives and corresponding content, but students may be involved in this process to some degree. Instructional strategies are used that actively involve students through cooperative and interactive approaches such as projects, cooperative learning, problem-based learning, and inquiry approaches. Students interact with peers and are actively involved in the learning process. The teacher serves as a guide and a resource. Indirect instruction lends itself more to the middle and upper levels of the revised Bloom's taxonomy, with emphasis on doing something with the facts—applying, analyzing, evaluating and creating knowledge. Indirect instruction lends itself to authentic and performance assessments.

However, when selecting instructional strategies, it is not an either–or decision. It is not either a teacher-centered, direct instructional strategy or a student-centered, indirect instructional strategy. As noted in Figure 5.1, there are different degrees along the continuum—teacher-centered, teacher-assisted, peer-assisted, and student-centered.

Teachers sometimes like to start with teacher-centered approaches since they can control the classroom conditions and environment. When teachers see they have control and students are learning with these approaches, they next try instructional approaches in which they give more responsibility to the students with peer-assisted and student-centered instructional approaches. This leads to our next section on the gradual release of responsibility to students.

THE GRADUAL RELEASE OF RESPONSIBILITY MODEL

In *Better Learning Through Structured Teaching*, Fisher and Frey (2008) present a model for the gradual release of responsibility to students when selecting and using the instructional strategies. First proposed by Pearson and Gallagher (1983), the gradual release of responsibility model of instruction suggests that the cognitive work should shift slowly and intentionally from teacher-as-model, to joint responsibility between teacher and student, to independent practice and application by the learner.

The model provides a structure for teachers to move from assuming "all the responsibility for performing a task . . . to a situation in which the students assume all of the responsibility" (Duke & Pearson, 2002, p. 211). This gradual release may occur over one day, a week, a month, or a year. Over time, students assume more responsibility for the task, moving from participants in the modeled lessons, to apprentices in guided instruction, to collaborators with their peers, and finally, to independent performers (see Figure 5.2).

The gradual release of responsibility model is built on several theories. These include (1) Piaget's (1952) work on cognitive structures and schema; (2) Vygotsky's (1962, 1978) work on zones of proximal development; (3) Bandura's (1965, 1977) work on attention, retention, reproduction, and motivation; and (4) Wood, Bruner, and Ross's (1976) work on scaffolded instruction. Taken together, these theories suggest that learning occurs through interactions with others, and when these interactions are intentional specific learning occurs.

The framework proposed by Fisher and Frey (2008) for implementing the gradual release of responsibility has the following components:

- *Focus lessons*—Teachers establish a lesson's purpose and then model their thinking to illustrate for students how to approach the new learning. Focus lessons include modeling and direct explanation of the skills, strategies, or tasks being taught. This is followed by teacher-led metacognitive awareness lessons that show students when and how to use new learning, as well as to evaluate the success

FIGURE 5.2

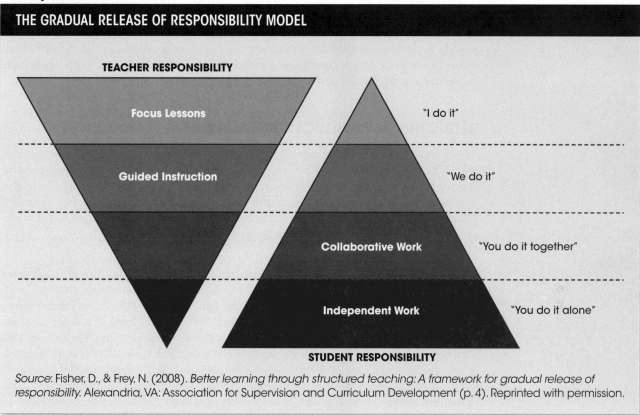

THE GRADUAL RELEASE OF RESPONSIBILITY MODEL

TEACHER RESPONSIBILITY

Focus Lessons — "I do it"

Guided Instruction — "We do it"

Collaborative Work — "You do it together"

Independent Work — "You do it alone"

STUDENT RESPONSIBILITY

Source: Fisher, D., & Frey, N. (2008). *Better learning through structured teaching: A framework for gradual release of responsibility.* Alexandria, VA: Association for Supervision and Curriculum Development (p. 4). Reprinted with permission.

of the approach they have selected. Then teachers use think-alouds in which they describe how they make decisions, implement skills, active problem-solving procedures, and evaluate whether success has been achieved.

■ *Guided instruction*—Teachers strategically use questions and assessment-informed prompts, cues, direct explanations, and modeling to guide students to increasingly complex thinking and facilitate students' increased responsibility for task completion. Students are typically grouped with other learners who are similarly performing, based on assessment data. The groupings change frequently due to ongoing formative assessments. The guided instruction phase facilitates differentiated instruction by content, process, and product because the small group sizes allow for much higher levels of customization (Fisher & Frey, 2010a).

■ *Collaborative work*—Teachers design and supervise tasks that enable students to be in productive groups to consolidate their thinking and understanding, and that require students to generate individual products that can provide formative assessment information (Fisher & Frey, 2009). There is individual and group responsibility for small-group, collaborative work. In most cases, the groupings should be heterogeneous.

■ *Independent Work*—Teachers design and supervise tasks that require students to apply information they have been taught to create new and authentic products. Students demonstrate their expanding competence. Independent learning tasks need to provide students with opportunities to apply what they have learned and to become increasingly self-directed and engaged. Independent work is not just a pile of worksheets or rote memorization. Effective strategies for effective independent learning tasks include independent learning centers, sustained silent reading and independent reading, writing to prompts, and conferring with the teacher or other adult to discuss progress, ask questions, obtain feedback, and plan next steps for independent assignments (Fisher & Frey, 2008).

The gradual release of responsibility model may take some time to learn. However, it complements other research-based programs such as differentiated instruction (Tomlinson, 2005a) and backward planning (Wiggins & McTighe, 2006). Students will also need to be prepared for using some of the instructional strategies. In particular, it is useful to provide instruction on the various routines and procedures used in guided instruction, collaborative work, and independent work so students will know what to do when these instructional practices are employed.

DEDUCTIVE AND INDUCTIVE STRATEGIES

A continuum of instructional approaches from three different perspectives was just presented, ranging from teacher-centered, direct approaches to student-centered, indirect approaches in which students assume more responsibility for their learning. Deductive and inductive instructional strategies can be used within the continuum just reviewed. While not representing a continuum themselves, these strategies lend themselves to use at various points on the continuum presented earlier.

Deductive Strategies. Think of deductive strategies as being direct. **Deductive strategies** involve deductive reasoning in which the teacher starts with a known principle or concept followed by examples of the concept. For example, a teacher using a deductive approach might give students the following definition of a topic sentence (the main concept): "A topic sentence is usually the first sentence in a paragraph. This sentence provides the reader with a sense of the writer's purpose. The rest of the paragraph contains specific details related to this purpose." With the deductive approach, the teacher next might give students some sample paragraphs and highlight the topic sentence to illustrate the concept (examples are provided). Students then could be given sample paragraphs that do not have a topic sentence, and be asked to write a topic sentence for each paragraph. The teacher could then review these sentences and give feedback on the students' performance.

The strengths of the deductive strategy are the directness and specific focus of the teaching strategy and the tight linkage between the teacher's examples and the task required of students. Deductive strategies are more direct and straightforward and lend themselves to direct instructional approaches.

Inductive Strategies. Think of inductive strategies as being indirect. **Inductive strategies** involve inductive reasoning where the lesson begins with examples, and the students examine the examples in an effort to identify the main principle or concept. For example, a teacher using an inductive approach might give students sample paragraphs with the topic sentences underlined (provide examples). With this strategy, the teacher would not tell students at the start that they are studying topic sentences, nor would the teacher provide a definition of a topic sentence. Instead, students would study the paragraphs and answer questions posed by the teacher. For example, the teacher might ask, "What do the underlined sentences in these paragraphs have in common?" And after receiving a series of answers, the teacher might ask a second question: "Can anyone provide a name for the underlined sentences?" From these two questions, many ideas could be generated. Student thinking is engaged throughout this process. Ultimately, the concept of topic sentences would be identified through this inductive, indirect process. This inductive approach is indirect, but it can be very effective because students interact with the content to make meaning.

Sometimes, you may want to have fairly direct presentation of the content and thus would use deductive teaching approaches. Other times, you may want to start out with examples and then lead to the main concept through the use of inductive approaches.

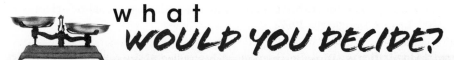

DEDUCTIVE AND INDUCTIVE STRATEGIES

Deductive strategies start with a known concept followed by examples of that concept. Inductive strategies start with the examples and then follow with students trying to determine the concept or principle based on the examples.

1. What are the advantages of each of these strategies?
2. Select one topic from the grade level or subject you will be teaching. Identify how you could teach that topic with a deductive strategy. Also identify how you could teach it instead with an inductive strategy.

The Direct Instruction Model

Direct instruction involves teacher-led instructional strategies. This section examines the characteristics of direct instruction and the components of direct and explicit instruction lessons.

CHARACTERISTICS OF DIRECT INSTRUCTION

Direct instruction involves instructional approaches in which the teacher structures lessons in a straightforward, sequential manner focusing on mastery of knowledge and skills that can be taught in a step-by-step manner. The teacher is clearly in control of the content or skill to be learned and the pace and rhythm of the lesson. The direct teaching format calls for teacher-led and teacher-assisted instruction involving presentations, demonstrations, questions and answers, review and practice, and feedback and correction of student errors.

Generally, direct instruction allows a teacher to introduce new skills or concepts in a relatively short period of time. Direct instructional strategies are academically focused, with the teacher clearly stating the goals for the lesson to the students. The teacher closely monitors student understanding and provides feedback to students on their performance. A direct instruction lesson requires careful orchestration by the teacher and the creation of a learning environment that is businesslike and task-oriented. Direct instruction focuses mainly on academic learning tasks and aims at keeping students actively engaged.

Direct instruction has four key components:

1. Clear determination and articulation of goals
2. Teacher-directed instruction
3. Careful monitoring of students' outcomes
4. Consistent use of effective classroom organization and management methods

Direct instruction is effective because it is based on behavioralistic learning principles, such as obtaining students' attention, reinforcing correct responses, providing corrective feedback, and practicing correct responses. It also tends to increase the academic learning time, or the amount of instructional time during which students are attending to the task and performing at a high success rate.

Many studies have found that students learn basic skills more rapidly when they receive a greater portion of their instruction directly from the teacher. It is particularly effective in working with low achievers and students with exceptionalities (Flores & Kaylor, 2007; Leno & Dougherty, 2007).

Uses and Limitations. Direct instruction can be applied to any subject, but it is most appropriate for performance-oriented subjects such as reading, writing, mathematics, grammar, music, and physical education, and the skill components of science and history (e.g., reading a map, using a time line, using lab equipment). Younger children and slower learners can benefit from direct instruction. It also can help students of all ages and abilities during the first stages of learning new information or material that is difficult to learn.

Direct instruction is not intended to achieve social learning outcomes or higher-order thinking. Opponents of direct instruction note that this instruction is too teacher centered and puts too much emphasis on teacher talk. Critics also argue that the model is limited to teaching basic skills and low-level information, while not being as useful when teaching higher-level objectives. Some critics disagree with the behavioral theory underlying direct instruction and do not support the view that students are empty vessels to absorb information rather than active learners who can construct their own knowledge.

Degrees of Direct Instruction. There are different degrees of direct instruction. Some approaches are more structured than others. First, the teacher-directed approach is the most structured in which the teacher transmits information to students in the most direct way possible. This often takes the form of a structured presentation, with explanations, examples, opportunities for practice and feedback, and checking for understanding. The teacher-directed approach is typically fairly scripted and sequential, and peer-assisted and student-centered instruction would not be very evident. Some forms of this instruction may involve creating homogeneous learning groups to focus on specific knowledge and skills that must be mastered. There is little opportunity for student input or variation.

Second, a less direct approach is called explicit instruction (Rosenshine, 1987, 1995). **Explicit instruction** calls for the teacher to gain student attention, present new material, reinforce correct responses, provide feedback to students on their progress, and increase the amount of time that students spend actively engaged in learning course content. Its objective is to teach skills and help students to master a body of knowledge. It is teacher-led instruction, with some involvement by students. Ten general principles apply when developing an explicit instruction lesson (Rosenshine, 1987, p. 76):

1. Begin a lesson with a short statement of goals.
2. Begin a lesson with a short review of previous prerequisite learning.
3. Present new material in small steps, with student practice after each step.
4. Give clear and detailed instructions and explanations.
5. Provide a high level of active practice for all students.
6. Ask many questions, check for student understanding, and obtain responses from all students.
7. Guide students during initial practice.
8. Provide systematic feedback and corrections.
9. Provide explicit instruction and practice for seatwork exercises, and when necessary, monitor students during seatwork.
10. Continue practice until students are independent and confident.

More recently, Goeke (2009) and Hollingsworth and Ybarra (2009) have described an explicit instruction approach with even more flexibility and more student involvement than Rosenshine's version. Their instruction is still teacher led, but with greater emphasis on teacher–student interaction. It also involves teacher-assisted instruction, peer-assisted instruction, and student-centered instruction (see Figure 5.1). This more flexible version of explicit instruction serves as the basis for the components of direct and explicit instruction lessons in the next section.

There are 10 InTASC standards (see pages xx–xxi), and each standard in the original document includes a list of performances, essential knowledge, and critical dispositions to indicate more clearly what is intended in the standard.

Since this chapter deals with instructional strategies, some representative statements from InTASC Standard #2, Learner Differences, and Standard #8, Instructional Strategies, are listed here concerning topics in this chapter.

PERFORMANCES

■ The teacher designs instruction to build on learners' prior knowledge and experiences, allowing learners to accelerate as they demonstrate their understandings. (InTASC # 2)

■ The teacher asks questions to stimulate discussion that serves different purposes, for example, probing for learning understanding, helping learners articulate their ideas and thinking processes, stimulating curiosity, and helping learners to question. (InTASC # 8)

ESSENTIAL KNOWLEDGE

■ The teacher understands and identifies differences in approaches to learning and performance and knows how to design instruction that uses each learner's strengths to promote growth. (InTASC #2)

■ The teacher knows how to apply a range of developmentally, culturally, and linguistically appropriate instructional strategies to achieve learning goals. (InTASC #8)

CRITICAL PERFORMANCES

■ The teacher values diverse languages and dialects and seeks to integrate them into his/her instructional practice to engage students in learning. (InTASC #2)

■ The teacher values flexibility and reciprocity in the teaching process as necessary for adapting instruction to learner responses, ideas, and needs. (InTASC #8)

COMPONENTS OF DIRECT AND EXPLICIT INSTRUCTION LESSONS

Depending on the degree of directed instruction desired, there are various ways to organize lessons. Based on studies of explicit teaching, for example, Rosenshine (1987) identified six teaching functions that are part of a lesson design: (1) daily review, (2) presenting new material, (3) conducting guided practice, (4) providing feedback and correctives, (5) conducting independent practice, and (6) providing weekly and monthly reviews.

A particular lesson framework for direct and explicit instruction lessons is proposed here. The content on explicit instruction from Goeke (2009) serves as the foundation for much of the information in this section. Material from Hollingsworth and Ybarra (2009) and Rosenshine (1987) is also incorporated. The components of explicit instruction lessons are described here in the sequence they should be arranged in the lesson.

1. *Provide set induction*. **Set induction** is the initial activity of a lesson that is used to gain students' attention, inform students of the lesson objectives, and describe the lesson to students. It is intended to create a mental "set" in students so that they are in a receptive frame of mind for the lesson. Set induction is also referred to by various authors as pre-instructional set, anticipatory set, and advance organizer. There are three parts to set induction (Goeke, 2009).

First, *gain students' attention for the lesson*. This is done at the beginning of the lesson, focuses students' attention and interest on the learning about to take place, and is brief (a few seconds to two minutes). It can be a focusing statement, a standard signal, or a question that elicits curiosity.

Second, *inform students of the learning objectives for the coming lesson*. The objectives should be stated in terms of what the students will be able to do at the end of the lesson (e.g., At the end of today's lesson, you will be able to distinguish between facts and opinions from examples of political reporting). Stating the objectives provides a focus that results in more effective, goal-directed teaching and learning.

Third, *describe the lesson to the students*. Students need explicit details about the activities and evaluation that will be required for them to successfully achieve the objective. Describe the activities or procedures to be used in the lesson, what they will be able to do at the end of the lesson, and why it is important for them to reach these lesson objectives. This information prepares students for instruction, increases the efficiency of their learning, and can serve as a means of motivation.

2. *Prepare students for the knowledge base*. Effectiveness of teaching depends partly on the teacher's presentation and partly on students' prior knowledge and active thought processes during learning. Thus, teachers need to cognitively prepare students for the lesson. There are three parts to preparing students for the knowledge base (Goeke, 2009).

First, *activate students' prior knowledge*. What students already know about a topic is their prior knowledge. Teachers can ask students to identify and share what they already know about a given subject so they can actively link relevant background knowledge with the lesson goals. This can be done in various ways such as a K-W-L chart (What I **K**now; What I **W**ant to Know; What I've **L**earned), a questionnaire, and charts and diagrams. Activating prior knowledge is done before the current topic is taught. It reveals students' knowledge, and facilitates comprehension and learning. It may take from 2 to 10 minutes at the start of a new unit or topic of study, but not necessarily in each lesson.

Second, *provide daily reviews of previously learned knowledge and skills*. Before beginning a lesson, conduct a brief review of previously achieved, related learning. This facilitates the storage of information in long-term memory, helps connect old learning to new, and indicates when reteaching is necessary. This review may take 2–10 minutes. In addition, Rosenshine (1987) suggested reviewing the previous week's work every Monday and the previous month's work every fourth Monday.

Third, *preteach new vocabulary*. Briefly preteaching new vocabulary can set students up for success by fostering fluency and prevent them from faltering over unknown words or terms during reading or instruction (Marzano & Pickering, 2005). This part of the lesson may take 2–10 minutes. For reading in the text, preview words that appear most frequently or that students will not be able to figure out given their current skill level. For a lesson, preview vocabulary that will be used during the class session.

3. *Provide instruction of new material*. Teacher-directed strategies are usually employed when providing new instruction. To do so, teachers may select some of the instructional strategies reviewed later in this chapter, such as presentations, demonstrations, and questioning. Student learning is promoted when teachers reveal their thinking process concerning the content being presented. Through this cognitive modeling, teachers verbalize their own thoughts or "think aloud" so the students hear how they process the information. Modeling the thinking process is helpful for cognitive skills such as reading strategies, math problem solving, editing and revising written work,

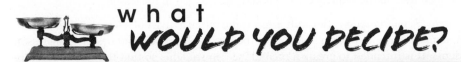

what WOULD YOU DECIDE?

CONDUCTING A DAILY REVIEW

Let's say that you are teaching an art lesson concerning painting styles (e.g., impressionistic, modern). As part of your daily review, you want to know if the students can identify the names of the various styles, representative painters, and characteristics of each style that you have covered in the previous three class sessions.

1. What strategies might you use to conduct your daily review in this case?

2. How might you incorporate the use of technology into the daily review?

and even solving social dilemmas (Goeke, 2009). For example, teachers may physically perform a task while verbally guiding oneself, describe each individual step of a process and its importance, make predictions, and even verbalize confusing points.

4. *Provide guided practice.* Guided practice helps students transfer information from working memory into long-term memory. After instruction of new material, teachers can arrange for guided practice with practice with peers, group problem solving, or teacher-directed individual guided practice. A worksheet at the beginning of an activity is not guided practice. Guided practice is most effective following a presentation or cognitive modeling of an initial concept. It also is directly linked to the learning objectives of the lesson, enables active participation, and promotes student self-direction. The teacher provides cues and support during guided practice, and this is considered a teacher-assisted approach.

5. *Provide independent practice.* Once students have completed enough guided practice to facilitate independent performance, it is time to check students' understanding and then reinforce individual proficiency with the new skill, concept, or strategy (Goeke, 2009). Sometimes this check for understanding will result in the need for more guided practice.

Independent practice is self-directed; students work independently with little or no teacher interaction. For younger students, independent practice may be group or individual work done in class. For middle and secondary students, independent practice is often in the form of homework.

Independent practice is not always written and can be conducted through various means of expression. Independent practice activities may be skill based (e.g., worksheets, games, or drills) or application based (e.g., essays, PowerPoint presentations, oral presentation, diorama). Skill-based independent practice promotes mastery, while application-based independent practice often promotes generalizations to meaningful, real-life settings. It is useful to use a variety of approaches.

6. *Provide closure to the lesson.* **Closure** refers to actions that are designed to bring a lesson presentation to an appropriate and satisfying conclusion (Shostak, 2011). Closure has several purposes. First, it helps organize student learning, and promote memory and recall. Second, it helps reinforce important points from the lesson. Third, it helps students reflect on their learning. Fourth, it is an opportunity for the teacher to gauge student understanding and to determine whether there are any remaining misunderstandings.

from the **VOICES** Classroom

LAUREN KRAFT, high school literature and composition teacher, Buffalo Grove, Illinois

USING STUDENT RESPONSE SYSTEMS FOR QUICK FORMATIVE ASSESSMENT

My school recently ordered a number of classroom performance systems (CPS) that teachers have used for a variety of formative assessments, from vocabulary to math problems. The system allows teachers to make a PowerPoint with a set of questions that can be displayed as a quiz. Each student picks up a response pad, which looks like a remote control, and inputs his or her answer to the displayed question. The teacher can quickly see a tally of the correct answers.

The CPS is helpful when conducting formative assessments, but also works well when reviewing content.

Students who take pretests retain information longer. Also, the students are highly engaged and even somewhat competitive with the system, resulting in higher scores on summative assessments.

We've also developed a low-tech way to quickly assess student performance with the use of dry-erase paddles. When I ask a question, students respond by holding up the paddle with their answer on it. We often use the paddles for grammar work. Students can work in groups or alone, and the exercise can take the form of a game or competition. The kinesthetic aspect improves student engagement and helps teachers quickly assess learning.

Instructional Approaches for Direct Instruction

When using teacher-led instructional approaches, several instructional strategies are common including presentations, demonstrations, questioning, recitations, practice and drills, reviews, guided practice, and homework. These same strategies may be used by teachers in various ways when using teacher-assisted, peer-assisted, and student-centered approaches.

PRESENTATIONS

A **presentation** is an informative talk that a more knowledgeable person makes to less knowledgeable persons. There may be little or no student participation by questioning or discussion. Presentations can be used to disseminate information in a short time, to explain difficult ideas, to stimulate student desire to learn, to present information in a certain way or adapt it to a particular group, or to introduce or explain learning tasks.

Presentations should not be used when (1) objectives other than knowledge acquisition are sought; (2) the information is complex, abstract, or detailed; (3) learner involvement is important; higher cognitive learning is sought; or (4) students are below average in ability. Presentations often do not actively engage students in learning or permit passive learning and generally do not give the teacher opportunities to check student understanding. You should thoroughly plan and prepare presentations, know the content like an expert, limit the length of the presentation to the tolerance levels of the particular age group, present in a way that is interesting to students, provide appropriate levels of structure and sequence, maintain flexibility, provide organizers, use the presentation in combination with other methods, use instructional media and materials, summarize the content, and provide follow-up activities.

Good and Brophy (2008) suggest that the attention span of students needs to be taken into consideration when preparing a presentation. Certainly, the age and maturity level of the students need to be taken into account. Few students can sustain their interest when a teacher talks for over 20 minutes. After presenting for a short time, you could add variety by asking a series of questions that would be the focus of large-group or small-group discussions. Then you could return to the presentation. It is useful to alternate class time with various presentation techniques that require active involvement by students. Some teachers minimize presentations and use more interactive discussion; they often teach by asking questions.

Based on a review of the research, Rosenshine and Stevens (1986) describe several useful guidelines for delivering clear presentations: (1) clearly state goals and main points, (2) provide step-by-step presentations, (3) use specific and concrete procedures, and (4) check for students' understanding. In addition, teaching behaviors such as clarity, enthusiasm, and smooth transitions are all necessary for the presentation if the students are to be motivated and learn the material. Some teachers like to provide students with a note-taking outline to help students to follow the lecture and fill in selected information.

Also take these guidelines into account as you plan for and conduct presentations (Rosenshine, 1987; Rosenshine & Stevens, 1986):

1. Present the lesson objectives to the students.
2. Use an advance organizer to introduce the topic and capture the students' interest.
3. Present the information in an organized, step-by-step manner.
4. Give step-by-step directions.
5. Organize material so that one point can be mastered before the next point needs to be introduced.

6. Focus on one thought at a time, completing one point and checking for under-standing before proceeding to the next.

7. Expect student interaction in the form of questions and comments.

8. Move from general ideas to specific ideas.

9. Use a graphic organizer (see Figure 5.3) or other aids to promote learning.

10. Use good explanations and examples.

11. Encourage students to reflect on and apply what they have learned.

12. Check for student understanding.

DEMONSTRATIONS

A demonstration is similar to a lecture in its direct communication of information from teacher to students. A **demonstration** involves a visual presentation to examine processes, information, and ideas. The demonstration allows students to see the teacher as an active learner and a model. It allows for students to observe real things and how they work.

There may be pure demonstrations, demonstrations with commentary, or partici-pative demonstrations with students. In many cases, a teacher demonstrates a certain action or activity prior to having the students perform the activity individually, such

FIGURE 5.3

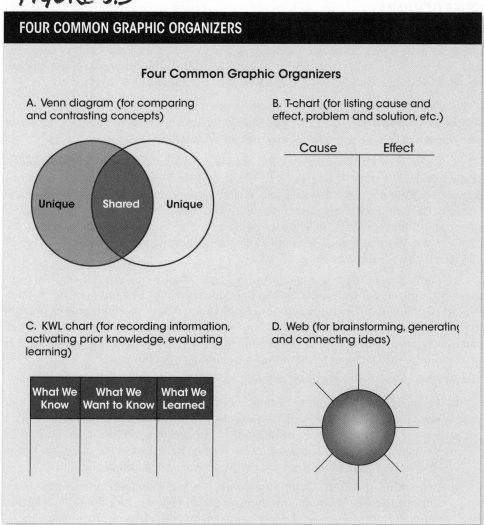

FOUR COMMON GRAPHIC ORGANIZERS

Four Common Graphic Organizers

A. Venn diagram (for comparing and contrasting concepts)

B. T-chart (for listing cause and effect, problem and solution, etc.)

Cause   Effect

Unique   Shared   Unique

C. KWL chart (for recording information, activating prior knowledge, evaluating learning)

D. Web (for brainstorming, generating and connecting ideas)

What We Know	What We Want to Know	What We Learned

as the teacher locating certain points on a map before students are asked to do so. For many students, this teacher demonstration provides a model of the actions and establishes expectations. Demonstrations can be used to illustrate points or procedures efficiently, stimulate interest in a particular topic, provide a model for teaching specific skills, and provide a change of pace.

To carry out effective demonstrations, follow these guidelines:

1. Carefully plan the demonstration.

2. Break down complex procedures into separate components that can be adequately demonstrated.

3. Practice the demonstration.

4. Develop an outline to guide the demonstration.

5. Make sure that everyone can see the demonstration.

6. Introduce the demonstration to focus attention.

7. Describe the procedure at the same time that you demonstrate it. Repeat as needed.

8. Ask and encourage questions.

9. Permit students to practice the procedure if they are expected to use the procedure.

10. Provide individual corrective feedback.

11. Plan a follow-up to the demonstration

QUESTIONING

Questioning is a critical instructional tool, but there are many facets to successful questioning. Guidance about questioning falls into two categories: the kinds of questions and questioning techniques. Useful guidelines for improving classroom questions are provided by Morgan and Saxton (2006) and Walsh and Sattes (2005, 2011).

Kinds of Questions. When using questions, consider the level of question, the use of convergent and divergent questions, and the type of question:

1. *Questions for the learning domains.* Most questions focus on the cognitive domain, as discussed in Chapter 4. Questions can be developed for each level of the cognitive domain (see Table 4.1): remembering, understanding, applying, analyzing, evaluating, and creating. The first three levels generally require low-level questions because they emphasize primarily the recall and moderate use of the information. The upper three levels of the cognitive domain require high-level questions that go beyond memory and partial recall; they deal with abstract and complex thinking.

2. *Convergent and divergent questions.* Two types of answers might be required from questions. **Convergent questions** tend to have one correct or best answer (e.g., What is the capital of Illinois? Who is the author of *Moby Dick*?). These questions may be phrased to require either low- or high-level thinking. **Divergent questions** are often open ended and usually have many appropriate but different answers (e.g., Why is it important that we continue to explore space? What would be a good title for this story?).

3. *Types of questions.* There are different types of questions for different purposes:

■ **Focusing questions** are used to focus students' attention on the day's lesson or on material being discussed. They may be used to determine what students have learned, to motivate and arouse students, to generate interest at the start of or during a lesson, or to check for understanding during or at the close of a lesson (Moore, 2011). You may need to prompt students when asking questions.

■ **Prompting questions** include hints and clues to aid students in answering questions or to assist them in correcting an initial response. A prompting question is usually a rewording of the original question with clues or hints included.

■ **Probing questions** may be needed when a student does not answer a question completely. In this case, you may stay with the same student by asking one or more probing questions that are intended to seek clarification and to provide guidance to more complete answers (e.g., What do you mean by that? Could you explain that more fully? What are your reasons for that?).

Questioning Techniques.
To be effective, teachers don't just walk into a classroom and ask questions. They need to give careful consideration to formulate questions, present questions, prompt student responses, assess and use questions, and encourage student questions (Walsh & Sattes, 2005). Guidelines presented here represent a synthesis of suggestions from Morgan and Saxton (2006), Walsh and Sattes (2005, 2011), and other sources.

Formulating Questions.
Consider the following guidelines when formulating questions.

Plan key questions in advance to provide lesson structure and direction. Write questions into lesson plans, at least one question for each objective, especially higher-level questions necessary to guide discussions. During the lesson, ask spontaneous questions based on student responses.

Ask questions at various levels of the cognitive domain. Use knowledge-level questions to determine basic understandings and diagnose potential for higher-level thinking. Higher-level questions provide students opportunities to use knowledge and engage in critical and creative thinking.

Phrase questions clearly and specifically. Avoid vague or ambiguous questions such as "What did we learn yesterday?" or "What about the heroine of the story?" Ask single questions; avoid run-on questions that lead to student confusion and frustration. Clarity increases the probability of accurate responses.

Adapt questions to student ability level. This enhances understanding and reduces anxiety. For heterogeneous classes, phrase questions in natural, simple language, adjusting vocabulary and sentence structure to students' language and conceptual levels.

Ask questions that relate to students' own lives or similar situations. Students will find learning more meaningful when it can be related to their own lives and interests. Useful questions might include "Have you ever felt this way?" or "Do you believe it is right to . . . ?"

Vary the types of questions being asked. Questions might be convergent (leading to a single correct answer: "What is the capital of Florida?") or divergent (there may be a number of possible answers: "What are the consequences of sex role stereotyping in K–12 textbooks?").

Presenting Questions and Prompting Student Responses.
Consider the following guidelines when presenting questions during the class session.

Ask questions logically and sequentially. Avoid random questions lacking clear focus and intent. Consider students' intellectual ability, prior understanding of content, topic, and lesson objective(s). Asking questions in a planned sequence will enhance student thinking and learning, particularly during discussions.

Ask the question before calling on a particular student. Asking the question before calling on someone allows all students more time to consider the question and a possible answer, creates greater interest, and increases attentive behavior. If one student is named before asking the question, others may not pay attention to what follows because they realize they will not have to perform.

Use random selection when calling on students. Calling on students in a prearranged format often leads to boredom and disruptive behavior for those who have already answered a question. Calling on students at random helps to keep them more attentive. Teachers tend to call on higher-achieving students rather than their lower-achieving peers. However, you should call on students at all achievement levels. In addition, it is important to create an environment that encourages success for everyone. You will want to ask the lower-achieving students questions that allow them to be successful.

Encourage wide student participation by calling on many students. Distribute questions to involve the majority of students in learning activities. For example, call on nonvolunteers, using discretion regarding the difficulty level of questions. Be alert for reticent students' verbal and nonverbal cues, such as perplexed looks or partially raised hands. Encourage student-to-student interaction. Use circular or semicircular seating to create an environment conducive to participation, particularly during discussions.

Use variety and unpredictability in asking questions and calling on students. Students should know that they might be called on at any time, regardless of what has gone on before. You need to be cautious about using predictable patterns, such as calling only on students who raise their hands, always calling on someone in the first row first (or another particular area), taking questions in the same order as in the textbook, and not questioning a student again after he or she has answered one question.

Wait at least three to five seconds after asking a question before calling on a student. This gives students time to think about the question and their possible response. After asking a question, the average teacher waits for less than one second before calling on a student or answering the question himself or herself. This short amount of time may be fine when posing a lower-order question that deals with recall. However, one second or even three seconds do not provide students with enough time to reflect on a complex question and formulate an appropriate answer.

While five seconds does not seem like a long time, research indicates that many possible benefits can be gained from waiting that amount of time. Increasing your wait time to five seconds can result in an increase in the length of students' responses, the number of unsolicited but appropriate responses, students' confidence, the number of students' questions, lower-achieving students' contributions, the variety of students' responses, and also increased evidence to support answers.

Do not consistently repeat student answers. Teachers do this for a variety of reasons, but most commonly it is done to make sure that all students hear the answer. Although the motive for this behavior is meant to be positive, it often results in students believing that they do not need to listen to their fellow students' answers and that the individual answering the question does not need to speak loudly.

Have students respond to classmates' answers. It is important that all students attend to their classmates' responses to the teacher's questions. This can be accomplished by occasionally asking other students to comment on another's answer. After one student finishes giving reasons for the United States to maintain membership in the United Nations, for example, you might ask others if they agree with that answer or if they might elaborate on these reasons. This strategy not only results in increased attentiveness but also encourages additional student–student interaction.

Assessing and Using Questions. Consider the following guidelines when assessing and using questions in class sessions.

Follow-up on student responses. Develop a response repertoire that encourages students to clarify initial responses, expand their responses, lift thought to higher levels, and support a point of view or opinion. For example, "How would you clarify that further?" or "Can you defend your position?"

Provide appropriate feedback to students. Consider whether to give praise and feedback about positive answers. Decide whether to give students a chance to correct their own wrong answer. Be sure that you leave the questioning with students understanding the correct answer.

Expand and use correct responses. Consider expanding on correct answers, perhaps referring to past and future lesson content. This also might provide the opportunity to redirect questions to encourage students to think of alternative correct answers.

Encouraging Student Questions. Consider the following guidelines when trying to encourage student questions during class sessions.

Teach students how to generate good questions. Talk about the type of questions you ask and about the different cognitive levels of questions. Provide opportunities to practice asking questions with teacher and peer feedback.

from the VOICES Classroom

SUSAN BOSCO, fourth-grade teacher, East Greenwich, Rhode Island

USING WAIT TIME WHEN QUESTIONING

I made the decision to practice wait time during a social studies lesson. *Wait time* is the amount of time that a teacher waits between asking a question and calling on students. I realize that I have not always practiced enough wait time. Therefore, I asked some higher-order questions and waited a while before calling on students. Wondrous things happened!

In a review of a unit entitled "The Northeastern States," by my asking complex questions and waiting for responses, I had students talking to each other about the questions. Also, a greater number of students were willing to answer questions. By waiting for a longer time after asking my questions, students were able to think about the material more completely, and I had better answers and more involvement by students.

Encourage student questions. This promotes active participation. Student questions at higher cognitive levels stimulate higher levels of thought, essential for inquiry. Give students opportunities to formulate questions and carry out follow-up investigations of interest.

Encourage students to ask questions when they need help in understanding content. Create a risk-free environment where not knowing and making mistakes are viewed as part of learning. Make it acceptable for students to ask questions any time they need help understanding an issue.

RECITATIONS

A **recitation** involves a teacher asking students a series of relatively short answer questions to determine if they remember or understand previously covered content. There are three main purposes of a well-orchestrated recitation (Walsh & Sattes, 2005): (1) to ensure that all students know whether a given answer is right or wrong; (2) to ensure that all students are aware of the most complete, appropriate, and correct response to each question; and (3) to help students connect new knowledge to prior learning and experiences and help move it into long-term memory.

You might use recitations as a means to diagnose student progress. The typical interaction pattern is teacher question, student response, and teacher reaction. Questions often ask who, what, where, and when. Questions posed in recitation are usually low-level questions, asking students to remember or recall facts, provide definitions, or demonstrate comprehension. Recitation questions rarely engage students in thinking deeply about an issue. Recitation is highly structured, with the teacher clearly in control of directing the learning. It is important to direct questions to both volunteering and nonvolunteering students.

Teachers usually ask known information questions during recitations. Thus, you ask questions to find out if the student knows the answer, not to get information. Recitation is frequently used in middle and secondary schools. It has flexible uses because it can be tailored to the amount of time and the number of students. The most common uses of recitation are in review, introduction of new material, checking answers, practice, and checking understanding of materials and ideas.

Recitation questions might be posed for the following purposes (Walsh & Sattes, 2005):

- To review before a test
- To see if students have read or understood a passage

- To check on completion and/or comprehension of homework
- To assess what students know about a topic—either before, during, or after instruction
- To cue students to important content
- To get students to talk
- To provide opportunities for drill and practice

PRACTICE AND DRILLS

Practice involves going over material just learned. Practice is intended to consolidate, clarify, and emphasize what the student has already learned. Practice sessions are more meaningful when spread out over time (not just the day before a test), when conducted in context, when whole issues are examined rather than parts, and when used in different activities.

Drills involve repeating information on a particular topic until it is firmly established in the students' minds. It is used for learning that needs to be habitualized or to be retained a long time (e.g., multiplication tables). Many teachers find that drills work best at a certain point in the lesson, such as at the beginning of class.

Practice and drills involve repetition that is intended to help students to better understand and recall information. They are useful in developing speed and accuracy in the recall of facts, generalizations, and concepts. They could be used, for example, when learning certain information, such as dates and events in history, chemical symbols, or translations in foreign language. Practice and drills aid the long-term retention of facts.

REVIEWS

A **review** is an opportunity for students to look at a topic another time. A review differs from practice and drill in that it does not require drill techniques. It does involve reteaching and is intended to reinforce previously learned material and to sometimes give new meaning to the material. Reviews can be in the form of summaries at the ends of lessons, units, or terms; quiz games; outlines; discussions; questioning sessions; and other approaches.

VOICES from the Classroom

STACI WILLIAMS, middle school reading teacher, Mesquite, Texas

REVIEWING IN A UNIQUE WAY

Air Ball Review is an instructional strategy that is great when you want to get every student in your class involved in a lesson. A small beach ball is used that has discussion questions on it or topics that will be discussed in class. The ball must be kept in the air while music is playing. When the music stops, the student holding the ball must either answer a question on the ball or give input on the lesson.

Air Ball Review gets the class moving. It turns a boring lesson or review session into one of excitement.

Students have a great time while learning or reviewing at the same time. The best part is that it allows for them to get out of their seat, move around, and work together as a team. This type of review may not be suitable for every class, and the guidelines for these review sessions can be easily adjusted to better fit the circumstances in other classrooms.

URBAN EDUCATION

A daily review at the start of a class will help you to determine if your students have the necessary prerequisite knowledge or skills for the lesson. Weekly and monthly reviews help to check student understanding, ensure that the necessary prior skills are adequately learned, and also check on the teacher's pace.

GUIDED PRACTICE AND HOMEWORK

Another teacher-directed instructional approach involves techniques through which students use and practice the knowledge and skills being addressed in class. The use of guided practice in class and through homework are the two most common techniques.

Guided Practice. Although teachers commonly use seatwork for guided practice, there are additional approaches such as teacher-led practice and student cooperative practice.

Seatwork. **Seatwork** involves students working on in-class assignments, often independently. Students in grades 1 through 7 spend more time working alone on seatwork than on any other activity; approximately 50 to 75 percent of their time involves seatwork (Rosenshine & Stevens, 1986). Therefore, it is important to learn how to maintain student engagement during seatwork.

Successful independent practice requires both adequate preparation of students and effective teacher management of the activity. In addition to the guidelines described previously for identifying and introducing assignments, the following suggestions from the research are ways to improve student engagement during seatwork (Rosenshine & Stevens, 1986, p. 388):

1. Circulate around the classroom during seatwork, actively explaining, observing, asking questions, and giving feedback.

2. Have brief contacts with individual students (i.e., 30 seconds or less).

3. For difficult material in whole-class instruction, have a number of segments of instruction and seatwork during a single class period.

4. Arrange seats to facilitate monitoring of students (i.e., face both small-group and independently working students).

5. Establish a routine to use during seatwork activity that prescribes what students will do, how they will get help, and what they will do when they have completed the exercises.

Teacher-Led Practice. **Teacher-led practice** often takes the form of repetition drills and question-and-answer sessions. Drill is the intensive repetition of content to ensure swift, accurate responses. It is intended to establish associations that are available without "thinking through" each time that the associations are needed. Drill is useful for skill learning and intellectual skills; it is not effective on complex principles and appreciations.

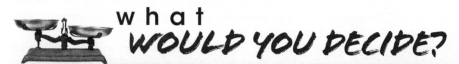

what WOULD YOU DECIDE?

SEATWORK

You often plan time at the end of math class for students to work independently on problems while you monitor the students and provide assistance.

1. What routines would you establish for students during this seatwork?

2. How might you use peer tutoring as part of this seatwork time?

Student Cooperative Practice. Another type of in-class supervised study is **student cooperative practice**, in which students help each other during seatwork. In some cases, the students in the groups prepare a common product, such as an answer to a drill sheet, and in other situations the students study cooperatively to prepare for competition that takes place after the seatwork.

Homework.

Homework is study that students do when they are not under the direct supervision of their teachers, such as study at home, in the library, or in study hall. Homework does not include in-school guided study; home study courses delivered through the mail, television, or on audio- or videotape; or extracurricular activities such as sports teams and clubs (Cooper, H. M., 2007).

There are four types of homework assignments: (1) practice, to help students to master specific skills and to reinforce material presented in class; (2) preparation, to prepare students for upcoming lessons; (3) extension, to go beyond the information obtained in the classroom and to transfer new skills and ideas to new situations; and (4) creative, to offer students the opportunity to think critically and engage in problem-solving activities.

Use the following guidelines as you make decisions about homework for your students (Alleman, et al., 2010; Cooper, H. M., 2007; Vatterott, 2009):

1. *Recognize that homework serves different purposes at different grade levels.* For younger students, homework should be used to foster positive attitudes toward school and better academic-related behaviors and character traits, not to measurably improve subject-matter achievement. As students grow older, the function of homework should change toward facilitating the acquisition of knowledge in specific topics.

2. *Assign a mixture of mandatory and voluntary homework.* Some homework should be mandatory at each grade level. A mixture of mandatory and voluntary assignments may be most beneficial to students. Voluntary assignments are probably most helpful for producing intrinsic motivation.

3. *Use homework to address topics previously covered, those covered on the day of the assignment, and those yet to be covered.* In this way, students are reinforced for topics previously covered, address topics covered on the day of the assignment, and became familiar with topics soon to be covered.

4. *Focus homework on simple skills and material or on the integration of skills already possessed by the student.* Do not use homework to teach complex knowledge and skills. Also be sure that the assignments and directions are very clear since students will be working on the homework independently.

5. *Select an appropriate amount of homework for the grade level.* While much will depend on the individual community, teacher, and student, general guidelines can be offered. After reviewing research on homework, Cooper (2007) has made recommendations for the frequency and duration of assignments. Grades 1 to 3 may have one to three mandatory assignments each week, each lasting no more than 15 minutes. Each week, grades 4 to 6 may have two to four mandatory assignments; grades 7 to 9, three to five; and grades 10 to 12, four to five. At all grade levels, additional voluntary assignments may be presented at the discretion of the teacher.

It is important to note that these time recommendations represent the total of all assignments from all subject areas at a given grade level. For example, each teacher of a ninth-grade subject should not assign three to five homework assignments of 45 to 75 minutes each week; instead, all the subject areas combined can come up to this time recommendation.

6. *Select a process for providing feedback and grading homework.* Different strategies for providing feedback differ little in their influence. Cooper (2007) suggests that the practice of grading homework be kept to a minimum, especially if the purpose of homework is to foster positive attitudes toward the subject matter (as in the lower grades). He proposes that the purpose of homework should be to diagnose individual learning problems and

CLASSROOM CASE STUDY

QUESTIONING STRATEGIES

Teachers use questioning in the classroom for a variety of instructional purposes. In Abby Lebowitz's high school social studies class, questioning is used to promote students' critical-thinking and problem-solving skills. In a discussion on global warming, the two sample interactions listed below between Ms. Lebowitz and her students illustrate different degrees of effectiveness when using questions.

SAMPLE 1

Ms. Lebowitz: Global warming is such a huge issue. As a concerned citizen, what are some things I can do to be more environmentally conscious?

Joshua raises his hand immediately.

Ms. Lebowitz: Joshua, what do you have in mind?

Joshua: Well, you could start by buying a more fuel-efficient car.

Ms. Lebowitz: I could buy a more fuel-efficient car. Yes. That is a good idea.

Joshua: You can also decrease the amount of time you spend driving by carpooling or taking a bus.

Ms. Lebowitz: Yes. Carpooling and taking a bus are both great examples. Morgan, what else can I do?

Morgan: Um . . .

Ms. Lebowitz: Can anyone help Morgan out?

Chris: You can use energy-saving light bulbs—

Maria (interrupting): —I don't think those things make any big difference.

Ms. Lebowitz: You don't think the energy-saving bulbs make a difference?

Maria: Nope.

Maria rolls her eyes.

SAMPLE 2

Ms. Lebowitz: Global warming is such a huge issue. As a concerned citizen, what are some things I can do to be more environmentally conscious?

Three students raise their hands right away. Ms. Lebowitz waits until half of the students show they are ready to respond.

Ms. Lebowitz: Joshua, what do you have in mind?

Joshua: Well, you could start by buying a more fuel-efficient car.

Ms. Lebowitz: Yes. That is a good idea, but what if I can't afford to buy a new car?

Ms. Lebowitz looks around the classroom to see who else has his or her hand raised. She calls on Kaya.

Kaya: You can decrease the amount of time you spend driving by carpooling or taking a bus.

Ms. Lebowitz: Those are both great examples, Kaya. Does anyone have anything to add?

Chris raises his hand. Ms. Lebowitz makes eye contact with him and nods.

Chris: You can use energy-saving light bulbs—

Maria (interrupting): —I don't think those things make any big difference.

Ms. Lebowitz: Maria, I am glad that you want to contribute, but please let Chris finish his thought. You will have time to respond when he is finished.

FOCUS QUESTIONS

1. Which dialogue sample illustrates better questioning techniques? Why?

2. How can you prepare yourself for effective questioning in lessons that you will teach?

provide feedback, rather than to test students. You should collect homework, check it for completeness, and give intermittent instructional feedback.

7. *Do not use homework as punishment.* Using homework as punishment conveys an inappropriate message about the value of academic work. If a student misbehaves and punishment is needed, nonacademic consequences should be selected.

8. *Clearly communicate your homework policy to students.* Students need to know the procedures and policy for homework. The importance of doing homework must be carefully explained. Students' motivation to do homework is enhanced when they recognize its value and its place in the academic program.

9. *Show students ways to overcome distractions.* The most prominent disturbances for students studying and doing homework at home are the phone, television, family members, and the radio. You can provide guidance for ways to minimize, overcome, or respond to these distractions. These include selecting a quiet study place and using a regular study time.

10. *Teach homework skills to students.* Students can improve homework skills by establishing appropriate places and times for studying, previewing the material, focusing attention, reading carefully and thinking about the concepts covered, casting what is learned in different forms, self-testing, and taking notes effectively.

Key Terms

Closure	Explicit instruction	Instructional	Seatwork
Convergent questions	Focusing questions	strategy	Set induction
Deductive strategies	Homework	Practice	Social instructional
Demonstration	Independent instructional	Presentation	approaches
Direct instructional	approaches	Probing questions	Student cooperative
approaches	Indirect instruction	Prompting questions	practice
Direct instruction	Inductive instructional	Questioning	Teacher-led practice
Divergent questions	approaches	Recitation	
Drill	Inductive strategies	Review	

Major Concepts

1. An instructional strategy is a method for delivering instruction that is intended to help students to achieve a learning objective. Strategies range from being very explicit and teacher directed to being less explicit and student centered.

2. A continuum of instructional approaches can be used to display (1) teacher-centered to student-centered approaches, (2) direct to indirect approaches, and (3) the gradual release of responsibility model.

3. Deductive strategies involve deductive reasoning in which the teacher starts with a known principle or concept followed by examples of the concept. Inductive strategies involve inductive reasoning in which the lesson begins with examples, and then students examine the examples in an effort to identify the main principle or concept.

4. Direct instruction involves instructional approaches in which the teacher structures lessons in a straight-

forward, sequential manner focusing on mastery of knowledge and skills that can be taught in a step-by-step manner. Some direct instruction approaches are more structured and teacher led than others.

5. Explicit instruction is a version of direct instruction that is not exclusively teacher centered and includes teacher-assisted, peer-assisted, and student-centered approaches.

6. There are several components of explicit instruction lessons that must be used and sequenced in a particular way in the lesson.

7. When using teacher-led instructional approaches, several instructional strategies are commonly used including presentations, demonstrations, questioning, recitations, practice and drills, reviews, guided practice, and homework. These same strategies may be incorporated by teachers in various ways when using teacher-assisted, peer-assisted, and student-centered approaches.

Discussion/Reflective Questions

1. What are the merits of using direct, teacher-centered instructional strategies, such as lectures, demonstrations, practice, and reviews? What are some disadvantages?

2. What are the strengths of the Gradual Release of Responsibility Model?

3. In a direct/explicit instruction lesson, how can the step early in the lesson on "preparing students for the knowledge base" (review all three parts) help enable student learning?

4. Why might some teachers prefer a direct approach to instruction? Why might some teachers prefer approaches that are more student centered?

5. From the teacher's perspective, what are some of the challenges of dealing with homework?

Suggested Activities

FOR CLINICAL SETTINGS

1. Select a unit topic and prepare a two-week unit plan that includes several types of direct, teacher-centered strategies throughout the unit. Be sure to include all key components of direct instruction lessons.

2. Prepare a description of how you will use seatwork as part of your instructional approach. What types of tasks will you include in seatwork? How often will you require it? Will every item be assessed, and how? What weight will homework carry in the report card grade?

FOR FIELD EXPERIENCES

1. Talk to several teachers to explore how they make presentations. Ask them to offer you guidelines for planning and delivering effective presentations.

2. Talk to several teachers to explore how they use questions during instruction. Ask them for recommendations for the effective use of questions.

Further Reading

Cooper, H. M. (2007). *The battle over homework: Common ground for administrators, teachers, and parents* (3rd ed.). Thousand Oaks, CA: Corwin Press.

Provides useful guidance about the purposes and types of homework assignments. Research evidence is reviewed.

Fisher, D., & Frey, N. (2008). *Better learning through structured teaching: A framework for gradual release of responsibility*. Alexandria, VA: Association for Supervision and Curriculum Development.

Discusses specific ways to implement the four parts of the gradual release of responsibility model.

Goeke, J. L. (2009). *Explicit instruction: A framework for meaningful direct instruction*. Upper Saddle River, NJ: Pearson/Merrill.

Discusses the need for and characteristics of explicit instruction. Provides many specific guidelines for each component in the explicit instruction lesson.

Hollingsworth, J., & Ybarra, S. (2009). *Explicit direct instruction: The power of the well-crafted, well-taught lesson*. Thousand Oaks, CA: Corwin Press.

Discusses all aspects of direct/explicit instruction with reasoning and examples.

Walsh, J. A., & Sattes, B. D. (2005). *Quality questioning: A research-based practice to engage every learner*. Thousand Oaks, CA: Corwin Press.

Provides very detailed and useful guidance when formulating and using questions to promote student thinking.

Technology Resources

GRADUAL RELEASE OF RESPONSIBILITY

http://www.literacyleader.com/?q=node/477

This website includes figures to illustrate the gradual release of responsibility. It has been used in literacy education, but can be applied to any subject and any grade level.

WHAT IS DIRECT INSTRUCTION?

http://www.teach-nology.com/teachers/methods/models/direct

Provides descriptions and Web links to additional resources illustrating this instructional approach.

DEDUCTIVE AND INDUCTIVE REASONING

http://www.socialresearchmethods.net/kb/dedind.php

This site clarifies the difference between these two types of reasoning with illustrations and descriptions.

MyEducationLab™

Go to the **MyEducationLab** (www.myeducationlab.com) for General Methods and familiarize yourself with the content:

- Topically organized Assignments and Activities, tied to learning outcomes for the course, that can help you more deeply understand course content
- Topically organized Building Teaching Skills and Dispositions learning units allow you to apply and develop understanding of teaching methods.
- A chapter-specific pretest that assesses your understanding of the content offers hints and feedback for

each question and generates a study plan including links to Review, Practice, and Enrichment activities that will enhance your understanding of the concepts. A Study Plan posttest with hints and feedback ensures you understood concepts from the chapter after having completed the enrichment activities.

A Correlation Guide may be downloaded by instructors to show how MyEducationLab content aligns to this book.

Student-Centered Instructional Strategies

THIS CHAPTER PROVIDES INFORMATION THAT WILL HELP YOU TO

1. Design lessons that involve inquiry instructional approaches, such as concept attainment, inquiry and discovery lessons, problem-based strategies, and projects and reports.

2. Design lessons during which students work cooperatively in groups.

3. Identify ways to effectively use discussions, panels, debates, and other social instructional approaches.

4. Determine ways to have students learn through independent means with learning centers, contracts, and other approaches.

SELECTING STUDENT-CENTERED STRATEGIES

INQUIRY APPROACHES

CONCEPT ATTAINMENT APPROACHES

INQUIRY AND DISCOVERY LEARNING

PROBLEM-BASED STRATEGIES

PROJECTS, REPORTS, AND PROBLEMS

SOCIAL APPROACHES

DISCUSSIONS

COOPERATIVE LEARNING

PANELS AND DEBATES

ROLE PLAYING, SIMULATIONS, AND GAMES

INDEPENDENT APPROACHES

LEARNING CENTERS OR STATIONS

INDEPENDENT WORK AND LEARNING CONTRACTS

As you consider your students' abilities, interests, and needs, you will want to differentiate your instruction. One way to differentiate is by your selection of instructional approaches. There is a continuum of instructional approaches to use. At times, you may want to use some of the more direct, teacher-centered instructional approaches discussed in Chapter 5. At other times, you will want to use some strategies that are less direct and more student-centered. A number of these indirect instructional strategies are discussed in this chapter, including inductive approaches, social approaches, and independent approaches.

Selecting Student-Centered Strategies

Instructional methods are of two types: those that actively involve students in shaping their own learning and those where learning is directed by the teacher. Table 6.1 provides a comparison of both teacher-centered and student-centered approaches. Many of the student-centered methods referred to in the table are discussed in more detail in this chapter. Teacher-centered approaches tend to have students learn by reading for understanding or listening to the teacher.

Inquiry, discovery, and problem-solving approaches allow students to become involved in the process of discovery and enable students to collect data and test hypotheses. As such, these approaches are inductive in nature. Teachers guide students as they discover new meanings, practice the skills, and undergo the experiences that shape learning. Generally, inquiry, discovery, and problem solving approaches are student-centered and less explicit than direct teaching approaches.

Indirect, student-centered instruction (Arends, 2012; Moore, 2011):

- is based in cognitive and constructivist learning theories
- helps teachers involve students in planning of activities, encourage and accept student ideas, and establish criteria for student learning while providing them with autonomy and choice
- engages students in active roles and encourages cooperation and collaboration with peers
- balances teacher and student intellectual output
- is generally loosely structured and characterized by a democratic and investigative process
- couples well with authentic performance assessment

Whether you choose to use a student-centered or a teacher-centered method, one of the most important things to keep in mind is that the method should be well matched with your goal. If you want to have students become active citizens, you can have them

TABLE 6.1

Student-Centered and Teacher-Centered Strategies

METHOD	INTENT AND UNIQUE FEATURES
Student-Centered Methods	
Cooperative Learning	Students work together to perform specific tasks in small mixed-ability groups with shared responsibility for learning.
Debate	Competitive discussion of topic between individuals or teams of students.
Differentiated Instruction	Students engage in different pathways to learning designed to meet their needs and abilities.
Discovery	Students take an active role in their learning process by answering a series of questions or solving problems designed to introduce a concept or skill.
Discussion	Students are active in processing information, defining problems, understanding different points of view.
Independent Study	Student works with teacher to define a topic or concept for an individualized plan of study.
Inquiry	Students explore course content and learn to ask questions, make discoveries, or solve problems.
Panel	Students present and/or discuss information on important topics.
Role Playing	Students act out roles or situations followed by a debriefing to define what they have learned.
Simulations/Games	Students engage by becoming directly involved in mock events or conflict.
Teacher-Centered Methods	
Demonstration	Teacher exhibits or displays an experiment, process, or skill to the class and discusses concepts embedded in lesson.
Lecture	Teacher-directed lesson with teacher verbalizing for a majority of the class time with questions often asked and answered.
Modeling	Teacher clearly describes the skill or concept often in multisensory manner (tactile, visual, auditory, kinesthetic) and thinks aloud during modeling.
Socratic	Teacher uses questions to draw out student thinking and analysis.

read about the three branches of government, or you can have them investigate individual issues that affect their lives and the lives of their family and have them write a one-page policy brief to their legislators, major, governor, or school board (Arends, 2012; Moore, 2011).

Not all methodologies work equally well for all students at all times but variation in methodologies can be a big help in maintaining student interest and engagement. One important concept regardless of the methodology you choose is for you as the teacher monitor the learning of students; they need feedback on their performance.

Inquiry Approaches

Inductive instructional approaches often begin with exploratory activities and then lead to students discovering a concept or generalization. There are various ways to use inductive approaches; some have a higher degree of teacher-directed activity, and others have students more actively involved in planning and designing their instructional activities. Some of the more common inductive instructional approaches are (1) concept attainment strategies, (2) inquiry and discovery learning, (3) problem-based strategies, and (4) projects, reports, and problems.

CONCEPT ATTAINMENT APPROACHES

Concepts serve as the building blocks for student higher-level thinking. In general, concepts are main ideas used to help us to categorize and differentiate information. Therefore, when you ask students to place things together or to classify them, you are asking students to use concepts. Robert Gagné (1985) believes being able to label or classify things demonstrates an understanding of concepts and that combinations of concepts can be joined together into rules. He takes this a step further to say that the understanding of concepts and rules is what allows students to problem solve.

According to Jensen and Kiley (2005), three types of concepts are incorporated into the concept attainment model. First, *conjunctive concepts* address steady, unchanging content. For instance, the sun always rises in the east and sets in the west. Second, *disjunctive concepts* take alternate forms of the topic being considered. For example, the form of government may be democratic, aristocratic, or theocratic. Third, *relational concepts* describe the relationship between two or more concepts. When discussing the concept of driving, for example, the relationship between the driver, the mode of transportation, and the environment needs to be considered. It's essential that teachers correctly categorize these concepts because understanding the concept type shapes the way the concepts are processed and learned. Consequently, it should also influence teachers' organizational behaviors regarding methods of instruction implementation and instructional strategy choice.

Concepts are central to the curriculum in every classroom. Table 6.2 lists a number of common concepts that students are asked to understand in various content areas. As demonstrated in the table, concepts can be simple, such as *verb,* or difficult, such as *evolution.* Many strategies designed to help students understand concepts call for students to identify similarities and differences. This can be accomplished through a number of research-based methods.

Concept attainment is an instructional strategy in which students are provided both examples and nonexamples of a concept. For instance, you might list a series of words containing some examples of, or attributes of, the concept that you want students to recognize. Table 6.3 shows a list of words, and each word is followed by a yes or a no. The yes answers form the concept under study. Can you guess the concept?

TABLE 6.2

Typical Curricular Concepts

LANGUAGE ARTS	SCIENCE	SOCIAL STUDIES	MATHEMATICS
Summarize	Technology	Cities	Congruent
Metaphor	Density	Democracy	Fractions
Perspective	Energy	NATO	Patterns
Verb	Motion	Terrorism	Equations
Audience	Evolution	Representative	Estimate
Context	Ecosystems	Manifest destiny	Predict
Theme	Diversity	Power	Triangle
Grammar	Genes	Distribution of wealth	Area
Essay	Cells	Culture	Volume
Point of view	Climate	Citizenship	Relationship

Based on the work of Bruner (1966), Joyce and Weil (2009) suggest that the following process be used for indirect concept learning:

1. You prepare labeled examples.
2. Students compare attributes of positive and negative examples.
3. Students put forward possible concepts.
4. Students provide a definition based on the essential attributes of the concept. From the attributes listed in Table 6.3, for example, students might define a *democracy* as follows: "A country with a government that has been elected freely and equally by all its citizens."
5. Add examples, and call on students to indicate a yes or no descriptor for each label.
6. You confirm student hypotheses, name the concept, and have students come up with a common definition.
7. Students generate examples.
8. Students describe their thought processes and discuss the role of hypotheses and attributes.

TABLE 6.3

Concept Lesson

Elections	Yes	Volume	No
Snowstorms	No	Closure	No
Right to Vote	Yes	Majority decision making	Yes
Osmosis	No	Freedom	Yes
Participation	Yes		

A variation of this approach would involve your providing students with a list of examples of countries that practice democracy in the first column and countries that do not in the second column. Concept-based lessons can take either a direct or indirect form. In using the indirect form, you would not label the columns as democratic or totalitarian countries, rather, you would let students reflect on what similarities the words share and have the students respond with concepts that they feel join the examples together.

Concept learning activities can take a number of other forms. Some of the most productive concept attainment approaches are based on a rich line of research (Marzano, Pickering, & Pollock, 2005) in four key areas: comparisons, classifications, metaphors, and analogies.

Comparisons. Comparing involves identifying similarities and differences between concepts. Students can only compare if they have deep understanding of the topics or concepts they are comparing. Comparing is a complex process that students need to practice to use skillfully (Marzano, Norford, Paynter, Pickering, & Gaddy, 2005). A key to success with this teaching strategy is to provide models of comparisons for students.

For example, Figure 6.1 uses a Venn diagram to provide a comparison of life before and after creation of the U.S. Constitution. A **Venn diagram** is a type of graphic organizer or visual tool that can be used to visually represent concepts you want to compare. Similarities are listed in the intersection between the circles, and differences are listed in the areas of the circles that do not intersect. Therefore, similarities in life between colonists before the U.S. Constitution was ratified and after include open immigration patterns, freedom of religion, the collection of taxes, and ownership of private property.

FIGURE 6.1

VENN DIAGRAM EXPLAINING LIFE BEFORE AND AFTER CREATION OF THE U.S. CONSTITUTION

Life before the U.S. Constitution

- Colonies have local governments that fall under British monarchy.
- No branches of government.
- No checks and balances in government.
- Bill of Rights was not established.
- No national bank.
- No establishment of judicial review.
- No national armed forces.

- People could immigrate to the United States from any country.
- Freedom of religion was respected.
- Taxes were collected.
- People owned private property.

Life after the U.S. Constitution

- Formation of a democratic form of government whereby colonies became states in a Union.
- Three government branches established.
- Guarantee of certain inalienable rights for citizens.
- Established national armed forces.
- System of checks and balances created.

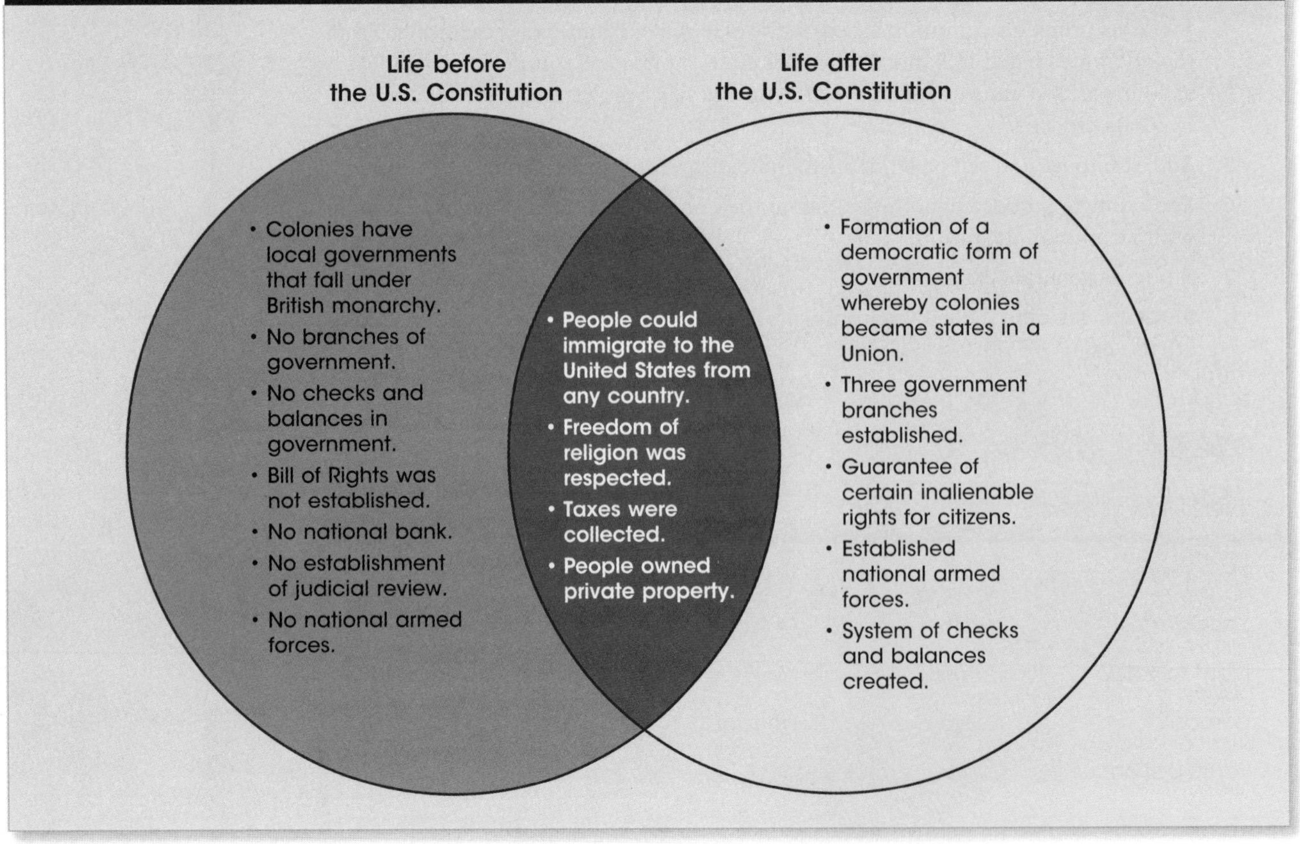

Venn diagrams and other graphic organizers can be used in two ways: (1) *indirectly* by asking students to create the diagrams and fill in the information and (2) more *directly* when you as the teacher develop the diagram. If you choose the indirect approach and have students create their own diagrams, it is helpful to start with content that is familiar to them. Once familiar with the process, students can then move to unfamiliar or more challenging material.

The feedback you give to students on the diagrams they create is very important. You can comment on important characteristics that are being compared, on the accurate iden- tification of similarities and differences, and on student explanations for their decisions. Be cautious, however, about students waiting to hear the ideas from you or the other students. You can increase the probability of student involvement in these ways:

1. Give students sufficient time to think and reflect about the issue before asking for responses.

2. Ask for completed work from all students.

3. Have students work in small cooperative groups.

Another method that can be used to represent similarities and differences is a simple matrix. For example, you could have students who are investigating various expeditions throughout history fill out a matrix for the concept of *exploration*. A basic start would be for them to fill in a matrix that compares various explorers based on key concepts, such as personal information, goals for exploration, resources, and accomplishments. Table 6.4 presents a matrix for comparing Neil Armstrong, the first human to walk on the moon, and Richard Byrd, a polar explorer. A matrix allows you to design lessons so that your students respond to set categories of information.

Classifications. **Classifying** is the grouping of ideas or concepts into categories or groups based on similar characteristics. A useful method for showing the organizational structure of major concepts is by creating concept webs or maps. The Iroquois League of Nations before 1492, for example, could be organized into a web to illustrate the key concepts that represented these native peoples' way of life. A web representing the economy, housing, and social structures of the Iroquois League of Nations is shown in Figure 6.2.

TABLE 6.4

Comparison Matrix Exploration			
COMPARISON (Similarities and Differences)	**CONCEPT TO COMPARE: EXPLORERS**		**CHARACTERISTICS FOR COMPARISON**
	Neil Armstrong	*Richard Byrd*	
Similarities			Personal information
Differences			
Similarities			Goals for exploration
Differences			
Similarities			Resources
Differences			
Similarities			Accomplishments
Differences			

FIGURE 6.2

CONCEPT WEB FOR THE IROQUOIS LEAGUE OF NATIONS

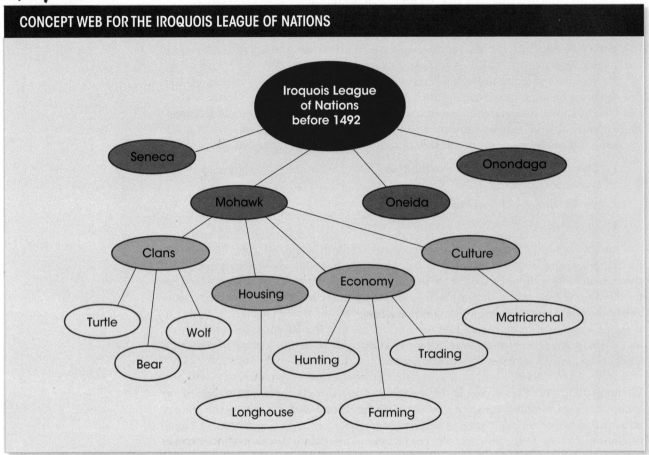

Through organized representation, students can link concepts they already know to new concepts being considered. Students either can be given a web to work with, or they can be asked to produce their own.

Metaphors. A **metaphor** is a figure of speech, often used in poetry, to make an implicit comparison or connection between two unlike things (e.g., He was a rock through all this; She is a pillar in the community; I have a song in my heart). Upon examination, however, the two seemingly unrelated things share a relationship on an abstract level. For example, a rock is literally solid and hard to break; on an abstract level, someone is strong and resilient in a difficult situation; and, therefore, on a literal level, some people appear to remain unmoved and stay tough during hard times.

Beyond their role as a figure of speech, metaphors can be used as instructional strategies to help your students to understand abstract patterns and convey the meaning of complex concepts or ideas in simpler terms. To prepare your students for identifying metaphors, you can warm them up with a discussion of a familiar topic, such as being moody. First, ask students to volunteer words that relate to being moody and record the words so everyone can see. Then, state another concept, such as a thunderstorm. Next, relate traits of a thunderstorm that line up with the traits the students identified for being moody. Thunderstorms may be loud and then quiet, or they may be bright and then dark.

Similar metaphors can be identified with other concepts. A chameleon changes colors with changes in conditions, and moods may change in a similar way. A thermometer records hot and cold temperatures, and moods may be hot and cold. The roll of dice is unpredictable, and moods may be the same way. Practicing the use of metaphors is helpful, and students will be more prepared when you want to identify metaphors with the content in the curriculum.

Another way to use metaphors in the classroom is to ask students to take the topic that you are studying, talk about it in literal terms, and then create a metaphor, or an abstract method of discussing it. For example, in science, you can ask students to create a metaphor for the role that arteries and veins play in the circulatory system. The students could use streets and highways to explain how blood moves through the body. In geology, students could say that Earth's crust is a cake to explain the various layers in its crust.

Analogies. An **analogy** is a comparison between two similar things and can be used to explain something or to make it easier to understand. Analogies are often represented by asking students to identify pairs of concepts. When students can fill in the appropriate word, they demonstrate comprehension of the concept that they are studying.

Analogies are represented in the following relationship: A is related to B in the same way that C is related to D. Consider these examples:

Galaxy is to Star as Beach is to	(Sand)
Deciduous is to Maple as Evergreen is to	(Pine)
Blood is to Vein as Water is to	(Pipe)
Shakespeare is to Hamlet as J. K. Rowling is to	(Harry Potter)

INQUIRY AND DISCOVERY LEARNING

Inquiry and discovery approaches involve students in the process of discovery by enabling them to collect data and test hypotheses. As such, these approaches are inductive in nature. Teachers guide students as they discover new meanings, practice the skills, and undergo the experiences that will shape their learning. Generally, inquiry and discovery approaches are student centered and less explicit than direct-teaching approaches. Several common inquiry and discovery approaches are considered here.

Inquiry is an open-ended and creative way of seeking knowledge. One of the strengths of this approach is that both the lesson content and the process of investigation are taught at the same time. The steps of inquiry essentially follow John Dewey's (1933) model of reflective thinking. The common steps include the following: (1) identify and clarify a problem; (2) form hypotheses; (3) collect data; (4) analyze and interpret the data to test the hypotheses; and (5) draw conclusions.

Dewey, along with Jean Piaget and Lev Vygotsky, was instrumental in developing a major concept central to understanding the power of inquiry learning. This concept is referred to as *constructivism*. Through studies of how children think and develop, Piaget confirmed that children strive to construct understandings of the world in which they live. Vygotsky held that individuals develop intellectually when they confront new and puzzling events that they try to understand by linking this new knowledge to knowledge that they already possess in an effort to create new meanings.

Therefore, a **constructivist approach** involves students in constructing meaning out of information that they have been exposed to through active engagement and investigation. Constructivism promotes (1) the student point of view, (2) teacher–student interaction, (3) questioning to encourage student thought, and (4) the importance of nurturing student reflection and thought, rather than a primary focus on a single correct answer or product. Useful resources are available, such as *Creating and Sustaining the Constructivist Classroom* (Marlowe & Page, 2005) and *Constructivist Learning Design* (Gagnon & Collay, 2006).

A constructivist approach provides students with the opportunity to investigate concepts and assists students in understanding new information by providing an environment of student-based discussion and investigation. You should ensure that your students are challenged by the instructional activities and stimulated by their own questions and the questions that you also might offer. Encourage your students to actively seek understanding and knowledge and to use prior knowledge to help them to understand new material.

STUDENTS AS ACTIVE PARTICIPANTS IN INQUIRY

Teacher-oriented, passive-student approaches to instruction are outdated. Especially in the middle school, we cannot effectively conduct our classes as if students were sponges who sit passively and absorb attentively. I base my approaches on the philosophy that the teacher is a coach of students. Thus, I view the student as having an active role in learning, and I serve as a guide in the pursuit of knowledge. This approach to instruction makes all gained knowledge more valuable, well learned, and better retained.

For students to care, the knowledge must be provocative, valuable, and reality based. Therefore, instruction should have much problem solving, research, and cooperative investigations. This doesn't mean that we eliminate standard lectures or guided practice. In fact, guided practice becomes essential to reinforce learning of useful knowledge. Overall, I have included a variety of instructional approaches in my teaching to help students to learn things that are important to them.

URBAN EDUCATION

Several approaches to inquiry may be used. **Guided inquiry** involves the teacher providing the data and then questioning the students in order to help them arrive inductively at an answer, conclusion, generalization, or solution. **Unguided inquiry**, or open-ended inquiry, has students take more responsibility for examining data, objects, or events; these investigations are commonly done individually. Guided and unguided inquiry approaches may involve discussion and question sessions, guided or controlled discussions, projects, and research projects.

PROBLEM-BASED STRATEGIES

In problem-based learning, students learn by doing, not by listening to you teach or being asked to read and memorize. As you begin to think about a problem-based assignment, carefully consider what your outcome is for student learning. What knowledge, skills, or attitudes do you want them to take away from your lesson and how will your strategy choice and assessment strategies promote student interest, motivation, and achievement?

For example, when you have students working on different tasks, your active engagement with them is crucial. You need to gather data on student progress throughout the project. You do this by asking questions, observing group interaction, giving formative tests, and reviewing work to date. This type of just-in-time feedback can make all the difference between a student staying focused and productive or becoming isolated and lost (Eggen & Kauchak, 2010).

The learning process can be greatly enhanced by using reflective practices and online communication through wikis, blogs, Google docs, and other social network tools that allow students to form communities for discussion, learning, and collaboration. Students can post their reflections, answer questions posed by the teacher or peers, and post reports of progress and drafts of projects—all of which can be reviewed, commented on, and edited by the community.

Active learning is at the center of project teamwork. Collaborative learning strategies that include group responsibility for each member's learning, project timelines, and providing an audience for student final products can be extremely motivating. Audiences can include community experts, family, peers, and online participants through digital storytelling or podcasts (Arends, 2012; Edutopia, n.d.).

There are different degrees of teacher direction with problem-based learning. You can have teacher-directed inquiry, teacher-student shared inquiry, student-directed inquiry, and even multidisciplinary approaches (Barell, 2007).

Let's look in detail at the characteristics of a problem-based project or lesson. A problem-based lesson typically consists of these five components:

1. *Students are presented with a problem* that is socially important and personally meaningful to them. The problem should be authentic, one that stimulates and motivates the students by having them seek solutions to meaningful problems that exist in the world. Problems often have an interdisciplinary focus that encourages students to investigate and apply many subjects—science, math, economics, government. A cooperative learning approach, in which students work in pairs or small groups, is often used in an inquiry problem-solving lesson.

2. *Students describe what is creating the problem* or the barriers barring its solution.

3. *Students identify solutions* for overcoming constraints and hypothesize which solution is likely to work. Students should feel free to brainstorm regarding the hypotheses. At this point, there is no right answer, so no hypotheses should be rejected. All hypotheses should be recorded either within individual student groups or as a whole class on the board.

4. *Students gather data and try solutions* to solve the problem. During this stage, the students, not the teacher, should do the thinking.

5. *Students analyze the data,* compare the results to the earlier generated hypotheses, and decide if they want to test another solution or hypothesis. Students construct exhibits or reports that present their solutions. These could take many forms, from an experiment in science to a mock debate in social studies (Arends, 2012; Marzano, Pickering, & Pollock, 2005).

Problem solving involves the application of knowledge and skills to achieve certain goals. There are several components for problem-solving skills (Slavin, 2012). First, means-ends analysis is a problem-solving technique that encourages identifying the goals (the ends) of a problem, the current situation, and what needs to be done (the means) to reduce the difference between the two conditions. Second, creative problem solving involves cases for which the answers are not very clear or straightforward.

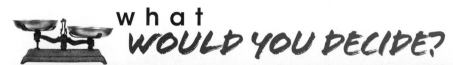

A DISCOVERY LEARNING ACTIVITY

In your science class, you want the students to participate in a discovery learning activity concerning the characteristics of various rocks and minerals. You haven't had your students do an activity like this before.

1. What preparations would you need to make to ensure the success of this activity?

2. How might your preparations be different if you were to have the students work independently as compared to working in small groups?

3. How might you include the students in your preparations?

PROJECTS, REPORTS, AND PROBLEMS

Project-based lessons flow naturally in a problem-solving environment. Students often work either independently or cooperatively on projects related to the objectives of the unit being covered. A **project** is an activity that involves investigation about the facts of a particular issue and the reporting of these facts in various ways. Projects include research reports, surveys, or case studies that have a particular purpose or objective. Projects provide students with the opportunity to work somewhat independently from the teacher, have positive academic experiences with their peers, develop independent learning skills, become especially knowledgeable in one area of the subject matter, and develop skill in reporting this knowledge.

VOICES from the Classroom

WENDY WHITTEN-LAVERY, third-grade teacher, Ocala, Florida

INTERACTION FOCUSING ON ESSENTIAL QUESTIONS

I have used many social approaches to engage students in the learning process, but I realized that group discussions and role playing alone didn't give me enough immediate feedback on all of my students' comprehension. I decided to use a graphic organizer to help me take cooperative learning to the next level. It is a piece of chart paper with a circle drawn in the middle and the rest divided into fourths.

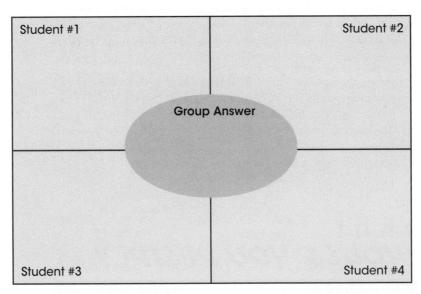

When students in groups of four are asked to answer an essential question (a higher-order thinking question), they quickly jot their response on the chart paper. Each student writes his or her answer in a different corner of the paper. Then students are asked to discuss their individual answers with the group with the goal of coming up with a single answer for the group.

While students are discussing, I go around and check individual answers. I have one-on-one conversations with students who need more probing to get to the correct response. After approximately two minutes, I direct the groups to put their group answer in the circle in the middle of the paper. I call on a student to share the group's response with the rest of the class.

At the end of the week, students are asked to individually write their answers to essential questions. This gives me the chance to again see who needs more one-on-one instruction before the assessments are given. This is a proactive approach in promoting students' understanding.

The degree of teacher direction can vary with projects. For a given unit, you may ask all students to prepare a report on one particular topic, or you may offer a choice of several topics. You may ask students to work independently or in small groups, or you could let each student select the grouping that he or she would prefer. It is often helpful to provide written guidelines and time lines for the outlines, drafts, and completed projects. Criteria for evaluation of the project should be clearly stated.

After receiving initial guidelines, students decide on the tasks to be done, such as conducting library research or interviewing, and then collect the information in a cohesive way to report their findings and conclusions that they have drawn. Provide sufficient class time over a number of days to enable students to plan their actions, gather the information, and organize and prepare their report. After providing the initial project guidelines, your role will be to assist, advise, and facilitate student learning.

Social Approaches

Another indirect, student-oriented approach to instruction involves **social instructional approaches**, which permit students to interact with each other in various ways to help each other learn. Some common social approaches include discussions; cooperative learning; panels and debates; and role playing, simulations, and games.

DISCUSSIONS

A group discussion is a powerful indirect instructional strategy, since students learn and remember when they participate. No matter what the format of the discussion—whole group, small group, or other types of interaction—students have the opportunity to think out loud about concepts, giving them practice that they can then apply to other concepts. As instructional strategies go, discussions are generally less explicit and less teacher centered than other strategies. The class setting may range from informal to formal, with the teacher having a dominant to nondominant role.

Whole-Class Discussions. A **discussion** is a conversation among several people who have a particular purpose or objective. A **whole-class discussion** involves all students in the class in discussing a topic with guidance from the teacher. When conducting a whole-class discussion, you must be able to clearly focus the discussion, keep it on track by refocusing, and encourage all participants to listen carefully to all points of view.

Teachers often direct whole-class discussions. Whole-class discussions may go astray when the class drifts from the main objectives of the discussion. Thus, prior to the discussion, it is important to plan key questions to be used so that the discussion is more likely to remain focused on the objectives. Useful resources are available for leading student-centered discussions (Hale & City, 2006).

Before beginning a whole-class discussion, make sure that students have an adequate knowledge base about the subject. A discussion cannot take place if students do not know much about the topic. Sometimes a discussion can be used before instruction as a means to generate interest, but the information must still be presented to students at some point.

Take the following guidelines into account when planning and implementing effective discussions (e.g., Borich, 2011; Jacobsen, Eggen, & Kauchak, 2009). These eight guidelines apply to whole-class and small-group discussions, as well as to panels and debates.

1. *Consider the goals of the discussion.* The goals of the lesson should structure the discussion. If the objective is to focus on cognitive development, then questions dealing with concepts and ideas are appropriate. If the discussion is to focus on the affective domain, then questions dealing with values and personal experiences are appropriate.

2. *Consider the experience and development of the students.* Younger and/or inexperienced students may need more direction during the discussion. The directions and questions may need to be more explicit, and the discussion itself may need to be shorter than it might be with an older group of students. As students become more mature and gain experience in discussions, they can take on more direction themselves.

3. *Study the issues.* Be familiar with the issues and/or material to be discussed during the lesson. This may appear too obvious to mention, but too often, teachers have not prepared themselves by learning about all the various issues surrounding a topic and thereby allow the discussion to drift during presentation.

4. *Orient the students to the objective of the discussion.* Explaining the objectives of the discussion to the students provides a road map for them and gives students a better idea of what to expect during the lesson.

5. *Provide a supportive classroom environment.* If a classroom discussion is to be successful, students must believe that they can contribute to the discussion without fear of embarrassment or ridicule. The effective teacher creates an environment where all ideas are welcome and where students give and receive constructive criticism in a supportive climate.

6. *Provide new or more accurate information when it is necessary.* At times, it may be necessary for you to contribute information to the discussion. This allows the discussion to remain focused on the objectives.

7. *Review, summarize, or weave opinions and facts into a meaningful relationship.* At times, restate the major themes emerging from the discussion in order to provide a needed structure to the lesson. This permits the students to see how ideas are interrelated.

8. *Use humor.* Some discussions can cause tension within the class. Depending on the topic, students may not always agree with the opinions of their classmates. Students may say something, without realizing it, that offends another student. You can reduce any tension in the classroom by interspersing humor into the discussion.

INSTRUCTIONAL STRATEGIES

There are 10 InTASC standards (see pages xx–xxi), and each standard in the original document includes a list of performances, essential knowledge, and critical dispositions to indicate more clearly what is intended in the standard.

Since this chapter deals with instructional strategies, some representative statements from InTASC Standard #3, Learning Environments, and Standard #8, Instructional Strategies, are listed here concerning topics in this chapter.

PERFORMANCES

■ The teacher develops learning experiences that engage learners in collaborative and self-directed learning and that extend learner interaction with ideas and people locally and globally. (InTASC #3)

■ The teacher varies his/her role in the instructional process (e.g., instructor, facilitator, coach, audience) in relation to the content and purposes of instruction and the needs of learners. (InTASC #8)

ESSENTIAL KNOWLEDGE

■ The teacher knows when and how to use appropriate strategies to differentiate instruction and engage all learners in complex thinking and meaningful tasks. (InTASC #8)

■ The teacher knows how to use a wide variety of resources, including human and technological, to engage students in learning. (InTASC #8)

CRITICAL DISPOSITIONS

■ The teacher is committed to supporting learners as they participate in decision making, engage in exploration and invention, work collaboratively and independently, and engage in purposeful learning. (InTASC #3)

■ The teacher values the variety of ways people communicate and encourages learners to develop and use multiple forms of communication. (InTASC #8)

Small-Group Discussions. **Small-group discussions** can meet the goal of increased student participation by allowing more students to become involved in the discussion. Groups of four to five students are most appropriate for small-group work. In addition to promoting higher-level thinking skills, small-group discussions help to promote the development of communication skills, leadership ability, debate, and compromise.

Students involved in small-group discussions often get off task easily. Careful organization can help these discussions to run more smoothly. There are at least four things that you can do to effectively conduct small-group discussions:

1. Carefully monitor the activity by moving around the room and checking with each group to make sure it remains focused on the discussion's objectives.

2. Make sure that students have enough background knowledge to effectively contribute to the discussion. Thus, small-group discussions should follow a lesson focusing on content and should build on topics previously developed.

3. Plan for relatively short discussions. If you see that the students are interested and are on task, the discussion can be allowed to continue. If a time limit is specified at the beginning of the lesson, the students are encouraged to remain on task.

4. Give students precise directions for the activity. If the students realize specifically what they are to do during the discussion, they are more than likely to remain on task. At the conclusion of the small-group activity, each group should report its results to the class. This can be accomplished by a written report or by having a representative from the group give an oral report to the class.

COOPERATIVE LEARNING

Cooperative learning involves students working together in small, mixed-ability learning teams to address specific instructional tasks, thus aiding and supporting each other during the learning process. It is a popular instructional approach. The teacher presents the group with a problem to solve or task to perform. Students in the group then work among themselves, help one another, praise and criticize one another's contributions, and often receive a group performance score (Gillies, 2007; Jolliffe, 2007).

For example, you might divide the class into cooperative groups of four and assign each group to prepare a report on a different country in South America. Within each group, students agree to take on various responsibilities: leader–organizer, recorder of discussions, timekeeper, or other needed roles. Each group also decides on strategies to divide up the work—for example, who will be responsible for (a) collecting information, (b) organizing the information collected from various group members, (c) preparing the report, and (d) presenting the report to the class as a PowerPoint presentation. You would serve as a resource for the students in each group.

Collaborative learning generally occurs in three different ways:

1. Students have specific responsibilities within a larger group task or project.

2. Students work together on a common project or task.

3. Students take responsibility for all group members' learning.

Research indicates that cooperative learning approaches lead to higher academic achievement than strategies that call for students to complete similar tasks as individuals or to compete against each other (Marzano, Pickering, & Pollock, 2005). In addition, cooperative learning has been shown to have a positive effect on student attitudes. Students in cooperative learning groups have (a) better interpersonal relationships and (b) more positive attitudes toward subjects studied and the overall classroom experience (Johnson & Johnson, 1999).

Cooperative learning works best with heterogeneous groupings of students. Having students work in groups generally has a positive effect on their achievement when compared to their work as individuals. However, the findings become more complex when comparing the achievement of low-ability students who worked in homogeneous groups to that of low-ability students who were grouped heterogeneously. Low-ability students actually perform significantly worse when placed in homogeneous groups (Lou, et al., 1996).

Through cooperative learning, students understand that they are responsible not only for their own learning but also for the learning of their team members. Cooperative learning approaches are often used to supplement other instructional practices. Research conducted by Lou and colleagues (1996) reported that cooperative learning works best when used in a weekly, systematic fashion.

Johnson and Johnson (1999) point out that each lesson in cooperative learning should include five basic elements:

1. *Positive interdependence*—students must feel they are responsible for their own learning and other members of the group.

2. *Face-to-face interaction*—students work in groups of three to five and, therefore, have the opportunity to explain what they are learning to each other.

3. *Individual accountability*—each student must be held accountable for mastery of the assigned work.

4. *Interpersonal and small-group skills*—each student must be taught to communicate effectively, maintain respect among group members, and work together to resolve conflicts.

5. *Group processing*—groups must be assessed to see how well they are working together and how they can improve.

Cooperative learning is represented in three different styles: informal groups, formal groups, and base groups (Johnson & Johnson, 1999).

CLASSROOM CASE STUDY

USING COOPERATIVE LEARNING

Eric Johansson is a third-grade teacher who uses literature circles when his students read *Charlotte's Web*, by E. B. White. *Literature circles* are groups made up of four to six students in which students work together to discuss a piece of literature. While in literature circles, students may read the novel aloud to each other and/or respond to questions about it. Mr. Johansson believes that working in literature circles is a productive way for his students to gain a firmer grasp of a piece of literature by learning from each other.

After getting to know his students, Mr. Johansson formed several heterogeneous groups based on students' reading and cognitive abilities coupled with their individual learning styles, personality traits, and interests. Thus, Mr. Johansson created well-balanced, five-member groups that provide opportunities for students to learn from one another's differences while utilizing one another's strengths.

Each group must summarize five key plot developments in *Charlotte's Web*, and each student is responsible for summarizing one key plot development. The students then combine their work to create a brief plotline of the entire story. Students must interact with each other to ensure the main plot points are covered. When finished, groups will have the opportunity to share their summaries with the entire class.

FOCUS QUESTIONS

1. Based on this example, what are some of the positive factors associated with cooperative learning?

2. What factors would you consider when selecting which students to place in each group?

3. How would you use this strategy to enhance your teaching?

Informal Groups. **Informal groups** are short term, often accomplished by asking students to "turn to a neighbor," and used to clarify information, focus students on objectives, or bring about closure on a topic. These groups usually take place after lectures or other direct-teaching strategies. There are numerous types of informal groupings, but a feature central to all informal groups is that students are encouraged to actively participate and stay engaged by sharing their solutions with others.

All activities start with the teacher asking students a question or giving them a problem to work on. During *think–pair–share*, students initially work independently but then move to pairs to discuss their answers. To conclude, you would call on students to report. In a *round-robin* activity, you place students in groups of three or four and have them share their answers with others in their group.

Formal Groups. **Formal groups** are carefully designed so that a heterogeneous mix of students works together on specific learning tasks. Several common types of cooperative learning techniques are described in this section. Robert Slavin and his associates developed the first four; these rely on student team-learning methods, which include team rewards, individual accountability, and equal opportunities for success (Slavin, 1995).

1. *Student teams–achievement divisions* (STAD) involves four-member learning teams that are mixed in performance level, gender, and ethnicity. After the teacher presents a lesson, students work within their teams to make sure that all members have mastered the lesson. Students then individually take a quiz, and their scores are based on the degree to which they meet or exceed their earlier performances. These points are then totaled to form team scores. Teams that meet certain criteria may earn certificates or other awards. If students want their team to earn rewards, they must help their teammates to learn the material. Individual accountability is maintained since the quiz is taken without the help of teammates. Because team scores are based on each student's improvement, there is equal opportunity for all students to be successful.

2. *Teams–games–tournaments* (TGT) uses the same teacher presentations and teamwork as in STAD. In TGT, however, students demonstrate individual subject mastery by playing academic games. Students play these games in weekly tournaments in which they compete with members of other teams who have similar past records in the subject. The competition takes place with three students at each tournament table. Since the tables include students of similar ability (i.e., high-achieving students are at the same table), all students have the opportunity to be successful. High-performing teams earn certificates or other team-based awards. Individual accountability is maintained during competition since teammates cannot help each other.

3. *Team accelerated instruction* (TAI) is a combination of individualized instruction and team learning. With TAI, students again work in heterogeneous teams, but each student studies individualized academic materials. Teammates check each other's work from answer sheets. Team scores are based on both the average number and the accuracy of units completed by team members each week.

4. *Jigsaw* involves six-member teams working on academic material that has been broken down into sections. Each team member reads his or her section. Then members of different teams who have studied the same sections meet in "expert groups" to discuss their section. Next the students return to their teams and take turns teaching their teammates about their sections. Since the only way students can learn about sections other than their own is to carefully listen to their teammates, they are motivated to support and show interest in each other's work.

5. *Learning together* is a cooperative approach in which students are organized into teams that include a cross section of ability levels (Johnson & Johnson, 1999). Each team is given a task or project to complete, and each team member works on a part of the project that is compatible with his or her own interests and abilities. The intent is to maximize strengths of individual students to get a better overall group effect. Each team is responsible for gathering the information and materials needed to complete its assigned task or project.

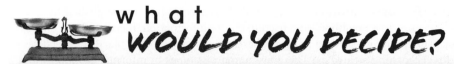

what WOULD YOU DECIDE?

COOPERATIVE LEARNING GROUPS

Before starting cooperative learning groups, it is important to show students how to work together as a supportive group. You should provide clear written directions and opportunities for students to receive feedback on their academic performance and the group's success in working together.

1. What additional orientation or training will enable students to work effectively in cooperative learning groups?

2. How might this orientation be different for second-graders as compared to 10th-graders?

3. How might you accommodate the different knowledge and skills of the students in their roles within the groups?

Final assessment is based on the quality of the team's performance. Each student on the team receives the same grade. This encourages students to pool their talents so each student makes the greatest possible contribution to the effort.

Base Groups. **Base groups** are long-term, heterogeneous groups that stay together across tasks throughout the year. Base groups provide student-to-student support and a sense of routine in the classroom. Students in these groups build long-term relationships and a support system that encourages academic progress.

In elementary schools, base groups might meet in the morning and again at the end of the day. Morning tasks might include taking a lunch count, making sure everyone in the group has completed the homework, getting materials ready for the day, and catching up on outside activities. Afternoon meetings would allow groups to make sure that everyone has the correct homework assignment, share insights into the assignments and tasks, and focus on a question that brings closure to the day's activities.

After working with various students in cooperative learning groups, you will gain a sense of how to get the most out of all participants, how much time is needed for groups to complete their work, and how to transition to other activities. You should move around the room as groups work so that you can assess learning and plan follow-up activities.

PANELS AND DEBATES

Panels, symposiums, task forces, and debates all involve a group of students becoming informed about a particular topic, presenting information to the class, and interacting in discussion. Each approach has unique characteristics. Panels and debates are designed to help students to understand several points of view related to a topic or issue. They combine prepared activities and statements with the give and take of discussions. They are useful in large-class activities when more informal whole-class or small-group discussions are not feasible.

A **panel** is a fairly informal setting in which four to six participants with a chairperson discuss a topic among themselves while the rest of the class listens. Later, there is give and take with the class. Each participant makes an opening statement. A round table is an informal version of a panel.

A **symposium** is very similar to a panel, but it involves a more formal presentation of information by each panel member. A **task force** is also like a panel, but it involves thorough investigation of a particular problem prior to the presentation to the rest of the

ANN HARLAND, middle school English teacher, Las Vegas, Nevada

ENGAGING STUDENTS FOR HIGHER-ORDER THINKING

I use a social, interactive instructional strategy that teaches empathy, cause and effect, research skills, and persuasive techniques. In small groups, students are asked to bring awareness and give a voice to an animal which cannot speak for itself. The groups that I use are the lions, elephants, and monkeys. I combine articles, books, websites, and a nonfiction book for each group to use during their campaigns.

Students have to research their animal and decide what issue they need to bring awareness to (e.g., animal testing, circuses, zoos, poaching, entertainment). Students persuade the class to join their cause through a campaign and a PowerPoint presentation. Also, the

students discuss, pose questions, thoughts, and connections through Edmodo, which is a safe social networking site.

After the campaigns the students create a website on their own, incorporating information they have learned through the campaigns. Here they also post their thoughts, feelings, and reflections about the project. This strategy engages students in nonfiction text and promotes higher-level thinking. This project incorporates all levels of depth of knowledge.

URBAN EDUCATION

class about the problem investigated. A **debate** is a formal discussion approach consisting of set speeches by participants of two opposing teams and a rebuttal by each participant. Panels and debates are conducted for the benefit of the whole class, which becomes involved through question-and-answer sessions upon the panel's completion.

ROLE PLAYING, SIMULATIONS, AND GAMES

Role playing is a student-directed activity in which students act out or dramatize a particular situation, circumstance, or idea. The teacher structures and facilitates the role playing and conducts the follow-up discussion. The majority of the class will be involved in observing and analyzing the enactments. Role playing can be successfully used at both the middle and secondary levels.

Role playing is particularly useful in helping students to understand the perspectives and feelings of other people concerning a variety of personal and social issues. In addition, role playing can be used to clarify and demonstrate attitudes and concepts, plan and test solutions to problems, help students to prepare for a real situation, and deepen understanding of social situations.

Joyce and Weil (2009) suggest a nine-step process to maximize students' role-playing performance and learning:

1. *Warm up the group.* The warm-up centers on introducing students to the problem and making sure that they comprehend the problem. Next you provide examples of the problem. These examples can come from a variety of sources, including classroom situations (e.g., how to deal with situations that students often face with peers, such as use of cigarettes, alcohol, or drugs or a friend asking to copy homework) or historical problems without an ending or resolution disclosed. Examples can also come from students' life experiences, films, texts, newspapers, or other source materials. The final phase of the warm-up is for you to ask students questions to make sure that they understand the problem and that they are ready to start predicting various scenarios and outcomes: "What would you do in this situation?" "What are some possible ways this story could end?"

2. *Select the participants.* In this phase, you and your students describe the various characters or roles: What are they like? How do events affect different characters in different ways? How might a specific character act? What would they do and say? Students must want to play a particular role. As the teacher, you should ensure that students are well matched to their roles and understand the complexities these roles bring.

3. *Set the stage.* Ask students to outline the scene and set aside a place for the action to take place.

4. *Prepare the observers.* Several students without roles should be asked to act as observers. They should analyze the enactment relative to its realism, logical sequence of effects, and whether the actors covered the full range of their characters' likely feelings and perceptions.

5. *Enact.* The players start to role play, responding to the situation and to each other as realistically as possible. This first enactment should be kept short, and you should stop it when the major points have been made and the purpose of the enactment is clear. You can ask other students to provide a second enactment to fully investigate the issue.

6. *Discuss and evaluate.* You focus the discussion on what motivated the actors and what would be likely to occur should the scene continue. Alternative scenarios should be investigated.

7. *Reenact.* Reenactments can take place to ensure that students have opportunities to bring in new interpretations. Reenactments and discussion should alternate freely. Cause and effect should be investigated. For example, how does a change in one player's interpretation change the behavior of other players?

8. *Discuss and evaluate.* Repeat this step as needed.

9. *Share experiences and generalize.* As the teacher, you should help students to clarify their perceptions and relate the experience to other real-life problems or historical situations.

Simulations are exercises that place students in situations that model a real-life environment. They require students to assume roles, make decisions, and face consequences. The goal of the simulated experience is for students to understand the important factors and how to behave in real situations. Students will also benefit by seeing how others behave in real situations. Although the roles for the students in the simulation are clearly defined, student responses are impromptu.

Games are designed to involve students in competition as the primary means to achieve a learning goal. Games can be used to teach a wide variety of skills, including problem solving and decision making. Of course, you need to select a game to fit the desired objectives. An instructional game has rules, a structure for playing the game, and a method for determining the winners and losers. You structure the setting, facilitate conducting the game, and supervise the students. Educational games can be useful in an interdisciplinary thematic unit.

Independent Approaches

Independent instructional approaches are those in which students work by themselves on some project or at a learning center or learning station in the classroom. The teacher may be involved in some way in the identification and design of the particular instructional tasks. However, there is often considerable latitude for students with independent instructional approaches.

INDIRECT INSTRUCTION THROUGH SCIENCE CENTERS

I have found that allowing students to explore freely through learning centers is one of the most effective ways to facilitate understanding of science. All the materials for their explorations are placed on the tables. Depending on the complexity of the topic, either instructions or guiding questions are provided. During this time, I walk around the room and ask the students questions such as: Why did you chose to solve the problem this way? Is it working? What might you do differently? What have you discovered?

Beginning a topic of study this way builds background and allows the students to develop a point of reference for class discussions. Giving students a problem to solve without telling them how to solve it encourages students to think critically and to become problem solvers. Centers are not meant to replace formal labs, but they can provide that spark of curiosity and wonder which motivates students to know more about a subject.

URBAN EDUCATION

LEARNING CENTERS OR STATIONS

A **learning center** is a designated place within the room where a student goes to pursue either required or optional activities on a given topic. It is a self-contained environment that includes all materials that students will need. Learning centers or learning stations are used to provide enrichment and reinforcement opportunities for students. Learning centers can be used to motivate students and provide a variety of instructional activities designed to meet the various ability levels and learning styles of the students.

Teachers often design and prepare a number of instructional tasks that the student can perform while in the learning center. These tasks typically accommodate a range of academic abilities and a variety of student interests. Students usually are not required to complete all tasks at a center, but may select the ones that they prefer based on their ability, interests, or other factors.

INDEPENDENT WORK AND LEARNING CONTRACTS

Independent work refers to any assignment or activity that students complete without the direct involvement of a teacher or other students. For example, students can independently read and complete writing compositions. Cruickshank and colleagues (2009) note that while there are many reasons why teachers incorporate independent work in the classroom, the most appropriate time for students to work independently is when they need to rehearse or practice a particular skill or set of material. For example, elementary school teachers often allow their students time to rehearse words for a spelling test.

Effective independent study should be distinguished from work that some teachers occasionally (and unfortunately) use for convenience. *Busywork* is when students are given a task to do just to keep them occupied so that a teacher can do something else. In contrast to busywork, effective independent work is meant to advance the learner and aid in the learning process, as well as help students to learn by themselves (Cruickshank 2009).

Learning **contracts** provide a structure for a student and teacher to agree on a series of tasks to be completed in a given time frame. Many contracts are designed to allow students to work independently through a body of required content or to carry out an individual project. Most contracts entail specific assignments drawn from the regular curriculum and optional activities either drawn from the curriculum or planned around student interest.

It is not necessary that all students have learning contracts. Contract activities may be pursued during any independent work time, such as when other students are involved in skills instruction, when other assignments have been completed, or at any other time designated by the teacher as being appropriate for independent work.

Key Terms

Analogy
Base groups
Classifying
Comparing
Concept attainment
Constructivist
    approach
Contracts
Cooperative learning

Debate
Discussion
Formal groups
Games
Guided inquiry
Independent
    work
Inductive instructional
    approaches

Informal groups
Inquiry
Learning center
Metaphor
Panel
Problem solving
Project
Role playing
Simulations

Small-group
    discussion
Social instructional
    approaches
Symposium
Task force
Unguided inquiry
Venn diagram
Whole-class discussion

Major Concepts

1. Inductive instructional approaches often begin with exploratory activities and then lead to students discovering a concept or generalization. Some inductive approaches have a higher degree of teacher-directed activity, and others have students more actively involved in planning and designing their instructional activities.

2. Examples of inquiry instructional approaches include concept attainment strategies, inquiry and discovery lessons, problem-based strategies, and projects, reports, and problems.

3. Social instructional approaches are indirect, student-oriented strategies that permit students to interact with each other in various ways to help each other learn.

Some common social approaches include discussions, cooperative learning, panels and debates, and role playing, simulations, and games.

4. Cooperative learning involves students working together in small, mixed-ability learning teams to address specific instructional tasks while aiding and supporting each other during the learning process.

5. Independent instructional approaches are those in which students work by themselves on some project or at a learning center or learning station in the classroom. The teacher may be involved in some way in the identification and design of the particular instructional tasks, but there is often considerable latitude for students in independent instructional approaches.

Discussion/Reflective Questions

1. Why should you be competent in the use of a variety of indirect, student-centered instructional strategies?

2. Why might some teachers prefer more student-centered approaches?

3. What skills does a teacher need to effectively conduct a whole-class discussion?

4. What are the advantages and possible disadvantages of using cooperative learning, inquiry, and concept-based instructional strategies?

5. How might the subject area that you are teaching affect your selection of the instructional strategy to be used in a lesson? How might the age and maturity of the students affect this decision?

Suggested Activities

FOR CLINICAL SETTINGS

1. Select a unit topic and prepare a two-week unit plan that includes inquiry strategies, cooperative learning, discussion methods, and group activities throughout the unit.

2. Explore computer software and other computer-assisted technology that is available. Evaluate this material and determine how you can use it in your instruction.

3. Prepare a list of guidelines and procedures for how you would use cooperative learning groups, problem solving, and independent work in your classroom.

FOR FIELD EXPERIENCES

1. Talk to several teachers to identify the types of student-centered instructional strategies they use in the classroom. Determine why they selected these particular strategies. Ask for recommendations for the effective use of these strategies.

2. Talk to several teachers to explore how they use discussions during instruction. Ask them for recommendations for holding effective discussions.

3. Examine a school's computer equipment, software, and facilities. What procedures are established for teachers and students to use the computers? How do teachers in the school use computers and related technology to assist instruction?

Further Reading

Barell, J. (2007). *Problem-based learning: An inquiry approach* (2nd ed.). Thousand Oaks, CA: Corwin Press.

Provides practical guidance for preparing problem-based inquiry lessons. Thoroughly describes teacher-directed, teacher–student shared, and student-directed inquiry approaches.

Gillies, R. M. (2007). *Cooperative learning: Integrating theory into practice.* Thousand Oaks, CA: Sage.

Discusses key components of cooperative groups, including ways to form groups, assign student roles, promote student thinking and learning, use strategies to promote student discourse, and assess student learning.

Joyce, B., & Weil, M. (2009). *Models of teaching* (8th ed.). Boston: Allyn & Bacon.

Provides an overview of different approaches to instruction, including many indirect, student-centered instructional strategies.

Technology Resources

COOPERATIVE LEARNING INSTRUCTIONAL STRATEGY

http://www.teach-nology.com/currenttrends/cooperative_learning

Describes the cooperative learning strategy and provides links to many other sites for more guidance and depth.

PROJECT-BASED LEARNING

http://en.wikipedia.org/wiki/Project_Based_Learning

Provides information on the purposes of project-based learning, characteristics, student roles, outcomes, and key features, as well as useful external links.

LESSON PLAN RESOURCES

http://teachers.net/lessons

Has 4,500 free lesson plans that you can browse by subject area or grade level. The site also provides links to other useful topics.

MORE LESSON PLAN RESOURCES

http://www.thinkfinity.org/lesson-plans

Provides lesson plans in many subject areas at all grade levels and has links to other useful topics.

MyEducationLab™

Go to the **MyEducationLab** (www.myeducationlab.com) for General Methods and familiarize yourself with the content:

- Topically organized Assignments and Activities, tied to learning outcomes for the course, that can help you more deeply understand course content
- Topically organized Building Teaching Skills and Dispositions learning units allow you to apply and develop understanding of teaching methods.
- A chapter-specific pretest that assesses your understanding of the content offers hints and feedback for

each question and generates a study plan including links to Review, Practice, and Enrichment activities that will enhance your understanding of the concepts. A Study Plan posttest with hints and feedback ensures you understood concepts from the chapter after having completed the enrichment activities.

A Correlation Guide may be downloaded by instructors to show how MyEducationLab content aligns to this book.

Strategies that Promote Understanding, Thinking, and Engagement

7

THIS CHAPTER PROVIDES INFORMATION THAT WILL HELP YOU TO

1. Select and use instructional strategies that have a high probability of enhancing student achievement.

2. Differentiate instruction with strategies that promote student understanding.

3. Use strategies that help students become better thinkers.

4. Apply strategies that promote student engagement.

5. Describe how strategies can be used for English language learners.

Students don't just walk into a classroom, absorb the material, and then perform wonderfully on assessments. Even after careful planning, the decisions and actions of teachers to guide students in actual lessons greatly influence student learning. There are many specific actions that teachers can take to promote student understanding. With the Common Core State Standards, there is increased interest in higher-order thinking skills and engaging students actively in the learning process. In addition, there are certain strategies that can be used when working with English language learners. These issues are explored in this chapter.

Strategies That Promote Student Understanding

Sometimes, it can be frustrating: you try everything possible, yet your students still don't seem to be learning the material. You have tried different types of activities and tasks, different ways to group students to work together, and various types of instructional materials. Yet they just don't seem to get it.

Fortunately, recent research on instruction provides guidance for the use of specific strategies to enhance student understanding. Robert Marzano and colleagues reviewed the results of many research studies on instructional strategies and then applied additional research techniques on the data from those studies to determine how influential the instructional strategies were in enhancing student achievement. In *Classroom Instruction That Works*, Marzano, Pickering, and Pollock (2005) reported the results of that analysis and outlined several very specific instructional strategies that were proven to have a high probability of enhancing student achievement. From that book, Marzano and colleagues prepared a handbook providing very detailed guidance for classroom teachers in the use of these effective strategies (Marzano, Norford, Paynter, Pickering, & Gaddy, 2005). The excellent content in both books serves as the organizer for much of the content in this chapter.

In *Classroom Instruction That Works with English Language Learners*, Hill and Flynn (2006) build on the foundational work of Marzano and colleagues to examine how effective research-based instructional strategies can be used when working with English language learners (ELLs). Specific approaches are suggested, and these ideas are incorporated in this chapter.

Certainly, a number of factors influence student learning, including management techniques and curricular design. However, classroom teachers should consider using the specific strategies presented in this chapter because of their proven effectiveness in positively influencing student achievement. Although these strategies are good tools, you should not expect them to work equally well in all situations.

IDENTIFYING SIMILARITIES AND DIFFERENCES

Student achievement can be enhanced by asking students to identify similarities and differences. There are four common approaches to identify similarities and differences: comparing, classifying, creating metaphors, and creating analogies.

Based on Marzano's review of the research (Marzano, Pickering, & Pollock, 2005), there are some general guidelines for using similarities and differences during instruction:

1. Provide students with explicit guidance in identifying similarities and differences.

2. Ask students to independently identify similarities and differences.

3. Ask students to represent similarities and differences in graphic or symbolic form.

4. Use a variety of ways to examine similarities and differences.

Several common approaches should be used in the classroom when applying any of the approaches to identifying similarities and differences. First, give students a completed model or example of the process to be used. This will help them understand the way that the strategy is being used to examine the content. Second, use familiar content to teach students the steps of the process. Illustrating the process with real-life content relevant to the students will help them understand the process. Third, give students graphic organizers when using the process since visual organizers help students see the relationships among the ideas. Finally, guide students through the process of identifying similarities and differences, and provide some practice sessions. Lessen the support as you repeat activities. Allow for plenty of talk time as students demonstrate verbal abilities before moving them into written forms of distinguishing similarities and differences. Adjustments will need to be made depending on the ELLs' level of language fluency.

Now, let's examine each of the four approaches in a little more detail:

1. Comparing is the process of identifying similarities and differences between or among things or ideas (e.g., Kayla's shirt is red with long sleeves, whereas Clayton's shirt is green with short sleeves). The key to an effective comparison is the identification of important characteristics. The characteristics are then used as the basis for which similarities and differences are identified. Teachers should introduce the process of comparing with highly structured tasks. Thus, the teacher identifies the items that are to be compared and the characteristics on which students are to base the comparison (Silver, 2010). As an alternative, students might be asked to identify the items to be compared and the characteristics for the comparisons. Two types of graphic organizers are commonly used for comparisons: Venn diagrams (see Figure 6.1) and comparison matrices.

2. Classifying is the process of grouping things that are alike into categories on the basis of their characteristics (e.g., Louis Armstrong is a jazz artist, and Trisha Yearwood is a country singer). One of the critical elements of classifying is identifying the rules that govern the class or category membership. Just as with comparing, either teachers or students can identify the elements to be classified and the categories into which the elements should be classified.

3. Creating metaphors is the process of identifying a general or basic pattern in a specific topic and then finding another topic that appears to be quite different but has the same general pattern (e.g., give a strong mental image, such as "You are walking on thin ice" or "Her eyes were pools of blue").

4. Creating analogies is the process of identifying relationships between pairs of concepts—in other words, identifying the relationship between relationships (e.g., Buzz is to a bee as chirp is to a bird). An analogy is probably the most complex format for identifying similarities and differences. Analogies can help explain an unfamiliar concept by making a comparison to something we understand—for example, "One is to a trillion as one square foot tile is to a kitchen floor the size of Indiana."

FINDING SIMILARITIES AND DIFFERENCES IN GUIDED READING

I know that identifying similarities and differences is a powerful technique to promote student learning. To use this approach, I asked my third-graders to read two books and compare the literary elements (plot, characters, setting) in each book. I described the two-column note-taking organizer for recording similarities and differences between the two books, and I modeled how to do this before asking the students to continue. With this approach, the students were able to answer 98 percent of the questions correctly, and they could speak deeply about the literary elements.

I asked my students to share their comments about using this strategy, and they were very favorable. Danielle said, "This strategy was awesome because it helped me think." Demaris said, "I like using the note taking of similarities and differences because it helps me understand the book. It gives me a reason to read." Finally, Kallyn said, "The note-taking strategy gave me a focus. I wasn't afraid to mess up. I had courage to read."

SUMMARIZING AND NOTE TAKING

Student achievement also can be enhanced by asking students to summarize content and to take notes to distill information. Summarizing and note taking actually involve complex skills.

Summarizing involves examining information, choosing what is the most important, and then restating it in a brief, synthesized fashion. It involves deciding which information is important, which is trivial, and which is repetitious. It involves deleting some information, rewording some ideas, and reorganizing information. Similarly, **note taking** involves synthesizing material, prioritizing pieces of data, restating some information, and organizing concepts, topics, and details. With appropriate modifications, both summarizing and note taking can be effective strategies for ELLs.

Summarizing. Three generalizations can be made from the research on summarizing. First, to summarize effectively, students must keep some information, delete some information, and substitute some information. Second, to keep, delete, and substitute information effectively, students must analyze the information at a fairly deep level. Third, being aware of the explicit structure of information is an aid to summarizing information. Some useful materials are available on summarization (e.g., Wormeli, 2005).

Summarizing techniques work best for ELLs when the teacher uses comprehensible input, such as visuals and kinesthetic clues, while keeping in mind the appropriate questioning strategies for each stage of language acquisition. Reciprocal teaching is a particularly effective form of summarizing when working with ELLs.

There are several useful approaches to summarizing:

- *Teach students the rule-based summarizing strategy.* Ask the students to follow the steps in this process: (1) delete trivial material that is unnecessary; (2) delete redundant information; (3) substitute superordinate terms for lists (e.g., *cars* for *Honda, Buick, and Ford*); and (4) select a topic sentence or create one. You might demonstrate these steps for your students at the beginning of the school year and then provide opportunities for them to practice and receive feedback so they develop the summarizing skills.

- *Use summary frames.* A **summary frame** is a series of questions asked by the teacher designed to highlight the important elements of specific patterns commonly found in the text. The type of content in texts varies, such as problems and solutions, stories, narrative essays, and definitions. The teacher selects summary questions suited to the type of text being used.

- *Teach students* reciprocal *teaching.* **Reciprocal teaching** is a technique in which one student leader of the class guides the rest of the students in summarizing information. The student leader first summarizes the main ideas and then asks questions for the rest of the students. The student leader then clarifies any confusing points, and finally the students collectively predict what will happen in the next segment of the text.

Note Taking. Four generalizations can be made about the research on note taking. First, verbatim note taking is perhaps the least effective way to take notes. When students are trying to take everything down, they are not engaged in the act of synthesizing information. Second, notes should be considered a work in progress. After students take their initial notes, teachers should encourage students to continually add to the notes and revise them as their understanding of the content deepens and sharpens. This implies that teachers should systematically provide time for students to go back over their notes.

Third, notes should be used as study guides for tests. One of the more practical uses of notes is for test preparation, because they can be a powerful tool for review. Fourth, the more notes taken, the better. Studies show that there is a strong relationship between the amount of information taken in notes and students' achievement on exams.

Note taking works well with ELLs when teachers encourage them to supplement their written notes with visual representations. Combining linguistic and nonlinguistic learning increases the likelihood that knowledge will be stored and retained.

There are several useful approaches to note taking:

- *Teach students a variety of note-taking formats.* Three common types of notes are (1) informal outlines, where ideas are listed and subdivisions and subordinate ideas are indented; (2) webs, where circles of different sizes are drawn and lines connect circles to show relationships; and (3) combination notes, where both informal outlines and webs are used in unison, often side by side on the page.

- *Give students teacher-prepared notes.* Providing students with notes before exposing them to new content is a powerful way to introduce note taking to students. Teacher-made notes give a clear idea of what you think is important, and they also provide a model of how notes might be taken.

- *Remind students to review their notes.* Reviewing their notes before tests is one of the most powerful uses students can make of their notes.

REINFORCING EFFORT AND PROVIDING RECOGNITION

Students' achievement can be enhanced by reinforcing their efforts and by recognizing their accomplishments. While it makes sense to teachers that effort pays off in enhanced achievement, studies show that some students are not aware of the fact that the effort they put into a task has a direct effect on their success relative to the task. Further, students can learn to change their beliefs to have an emphasis on effort.

Reinforcing Effort. Because some students do not recognize the connection between their own effort and achievement, it is important to discuss effort and reinforce their efforts to achieve. Here are two useful approaches to reinforce student effort:

- *Teach students that effort can improve achievement.* Explicitly teach and exemplify the connection between effort and achievement. For example, you might share personal examples of times when you have succeeded after making particular

sample STANDARDS

STRATEGIES TO PROMOTE UNDERSTANDING, THINKING, AND ENGAGEMENT

There are 10 InTASC standards (see pages xx–xxi), and each standard in the original document includes a list of performances, essential knowledge, and critical dispositions to indicate more clearly what is intended in the standard.

Since this chapter deals with instructional strategies to promote student understanding, thinking, and engagement, some representative statements from InTASC Standard #3, Learning Environments; Standard #4, Content Knowledge; Standard #5, Application of Content; and Standard #8, Instructional Strategies are listed here concerning topics in this chapter.

PERFORMANCES

■ The teacher effectively uses multiples representations and explanations that capture key ideas in the discipline, guide learners through learning progressions, and promote each learner's achievement of content standards. (InTASC #4)

■ The teacher engages learners using a range of learning skills and technology tools to access, interpret, evaluate, and apply information. (InTASC #8)

ESSENTIAL KNOWLEDGE

■ The teacher understands the relationship between motivation and engagement and knows how to design learning experiences using strategies that build learner self-direction and ownership of learning. (InTASC #3)

■ The teacher understands the cognitive processes associated with various kinds of learning (e.g., critical and creative thinking, problem framing and problem solving, invention, memorization and recall) and how these processes can be stimulated. (InTASC #8)

CRITICAL DISPOSITIONS

■ The teacher values flexible learning environments that encourage learner exploration, discovery, and expression across content areas. (InTASC #5)

■ The teacher is committed to exploring how the use of new and emerging technologies can support and promote student learning. (InTASC #8)

---

efforts. You also could give examples of well-known athletes, educators, musicians, or social leaders who did not give up and ultimately achieved a great deal. You could ask your students to recall situations in their own lives when their efforts paid off with some important achievement.

■ *Ask students to chart their effort and achievement.* Keeping track of effort and achievement will help students recognize the connection. Students might have a record of their assignments, with columns for the name of the assignment, a rubric score (e.g., 1 to 5) for the effort they put into the assignment, and a rubric score for their achievement in the assignment. In this way, students will see patterns in their effort and achievement. For ELLs, rubrics or rating forms can employ photographs, diagrams, or symbols, rather than words, to indicate the various levels of student effort and achievement.

Providing Recognition. Rewards can be powerful motivators if they are contingent on attaining a stated goal and if they are symbolic. Student achievement can be enhanced by recognizing their accomplishments. Since ELLs are learning both content *and* language, it is important to provide recognition for achievements in both areas.

Here are several guidelines when providing recognition:

■ *Establish a rationale for recognition.* It is a good idea to establish a rationale for the types of recognition you plan to use in your classroom. Explain to students that you will give recognition when they have achieved an identified level of performance. At the same time, students need to understand that if they do not receive recognition, it does not mean that they have failed.

■ *Follow guidelines for effective praise.* Effective praise is delivered contingently, specifies the particulars of the accomplishment, rewards the attainment of a specified level of performance, provides students with information about their competence, and focuses on the student's own task-related behavior.

■ *Use recognition tokens.* In addition to verbal recognition, symbolic tokens, such as stickers and certificates, can be effective tools to recognize the successful completion of specific learning goals. They should be given only when a student achieves a certain performance standard, not for simply completing an activity.

■ *Use the pause, prompt, and praise technique.* This strategy works well when students are having difficulty with a challenging task. When a student experiences a problem, he or she may look to the teacher for help. The teacher *pauses* to give the student time to identify and correct the mistake or use this time to discuss the difficulty. The teacher then *prompts* the student by giving a specific suggestion for improvement. Finally, the teacher *praises* the student when he or she overcomes the difficulty. However, the praise statement should be based on the student's specific achievement and be contingent on the student overcoming the difficulty.

HOMEWORK AND PRACTICE

Homework and practice are commonly used in K–12 classrooms. Both give students opportunities to deepen their understanding of and proficiency with the content they are learning. **Homework** is the study that students do when they are not under the direct supervision of their teachers. **Practice** involves doing something repeatedly in order to acquire or perfect a skill.

Homework. Homework has been a regular topic of debate over the years, with people both supporting and opposing its use. Those opposing homework note it contributes to a corporate-style, competitive culture that overvalues work to the detriment of personal and familial well-being. There are also claims that students of low socioeconomic status are harmed by homework, since their environment often makes it difficult, if not impossible, to complete assignments at home (Kralovec & Buell, 2000). However, other educators and researchers have reported positive academic gains when students complete homework, and they have highlighted the strategies to use homework effectively (Cooper, H. M., 2007; Marzano & Pickering, 2007).

Four generalizations can be made from the research on homework. First, the amount of homework assigned to students should vary from elementary to middle school to high school. Generally, the higher the grade, the more influence homework has on student achievement. Thus, less homework may be assigned in elementary classrooms as compared to middle school and high school. Second, parent involvement in homework should be kept to a minimum. Parents should facilitate homework by providing the proper conditions for student study at home, but it is not advisable to have parents help their children with homework. Third, the purpose of homework should be identified and articulated. Fourth, if homework is used, it should be commented on. When students receive feedback on their work, their understanding and achievement are enhanced.

When working with ELLs, Hill and Flynn (2006) suggest the following strategies to help ensure that homework assignments are understood and accomplished: (1) provide concrete, nonlinguistic examples, such as photographs, objects, outlines, and visual organizers; (2) provide opportunities for students to ask questions and discuss assignments orally; (3) provide native language support; (4) provide peer support; (5) provide modified or additional directions; and (6) provide tips and strategies for learning. In addition to the discussion of homework in Chapter 5, here are several guidelines for using homework:

■ *Establish and communicate a homework policy.* Students and their parents need to understand the purposes of homework, the amount of homework that will be assigned, the consequences for not completing the homework, and the types of parental involvement that are acceptable.

- *Clarify the purpose of homework.* Three possible purposes for assigning homework are to (1) give students opportunities to practice skills, (2) prepare students for a new topic, and (3) elaborate on introduced material. The purposes of homework should be communicated to the students.

- *Ask students to use homework assignment sheets.* Students can use an assignment notebook to keep track of their daily assignments. Assignment sheets are to be included in the notebook. Each assignment has a separate sheet, and students fill in certain information about the assignment: the subject, the due date, a brief description of the assignment, a description of the purpose of the assignment, and a place where they list information or skills they need to have to complete the assignment.

- *Comment on and provide feedback to homework.* Timely and specific feedback on homework can improve student achievement. Teachers do not have enough time to provide extensive feedback on every homework assignment, so make this task practicable by using different methods to comment on homework. For example, you might set up opportunities for students to share their work with each other and offer feedback. Or you might ask students to keep a homework portfolio that you would collect and comment on once a week.

Practice. Two generalizations can be made from the research on practice. First, mastering a skill requires a fair amount of focused practice. Second, while practicing, students should adapt and shape what they have learned. One aspect of shaping and adapting involves pointing out errors and pitfalls that lead to inaccurate understanding. Here are several guidelines for using practice:

- *Determine which skills are worth practicing.* Practice takes a great deal of time and effort, and your students can't practice every skill they encounter. You must distinguish between content students will practice in depth and content they will simply be introduced to.

CLASSROOM CASE STUDY

CHALLENGES WITH HOMEWORK

Paige Hutton, a 10th-grade English teacher, has a student who is struggling with the homework reading assignments. DeShawn is a bright student, a talented athlete in multiple sports, and a gifted musician. However, he has been earning low marks on Ms. Hutton's weekly quizzes on the assigned reading from Zora Neale Hurston's *Their Eyes Were Watching God.*

When talking with DeShawn's track coach, Ms. Hutton learned that DeShawn's aunt and cousins recently moved in with his family, which includes his mother and four brothers and sisters. DeShawn now shares a bedroom with two of his cousins, and he has complained about how crowded his home is now.

Ms. Hutton called DeShawn's mother to confirm the home living conditions and to tell her that DeShawn is talented and bright but struggling with his homework reading assignments. DeShawn's mother was concerned

and asked how she could help her son. First, Ms. Hutton recommended that a consistent time each day be set aside for homework. Second, she suggested that DeShawn find a favorite spot in the house where he can comfortably complete his reading without distraction. Third, she recommended that DeShawn's mother have a brief conversation with DeShawn once a week about the books he is reading. In fact, DeShawn's mother asked for the reading list and said that she might read some of the books along with DeShawn.

FOCUS QUESTIONS

1. What about DeShawn's home situation makes it a challenge to do homework?

2. How does Ms. Hutton help DeShawn's mother facilitate her son's successful study habits? Do you have any additional suggestions?

what WOULD YOU DECIDE?

PROVIDING GUIDANCE DURING PRACTICE

After instruction on a topic, you may want to provide regular opportunities during class for your students to practice with the content. This often occurs in math instruction, where students participate in supervised seatwork to practice working out the math problems. During this seatwork, teachers can provide guidance and corrective feedback to individual students and the entire class to shape a skill or process.

1. How might you draw the attention of the entire class to common problems without embarrassing individual students who are making the errors during seatwork?

2. How might you reinforce effort and provide recognition during this feedback process?

■ *Schedule massed and distributed practice.* At first, practice sessions should be timed close together; this is *massed practice*. Over time, you can gradually space the practice sessions farther apart; this is *distributed practice*. Thus, you might arrange for considerable massed practice in the first week or two of practice on a certain skill. Then, you would space practice out over the next few weeks to be less frequent.

■ *Ask students to chart speed and accuracy.* When developing some skills, the emphasis is on accuracy. With others, however, the emphasis may be on both speed and accuracy. If working on accuracy, student can divide a series of problems into several clusters and then chart the number they solved correctly for each cluster. If working on speed and accuracy, students might create a chart that indicates how many problems they solved correctly in a given period of time.

■ *Help students shape a skill or process.* It is easy for errors to creep into a skill when students are first learning it. Thus, it is important to indicate errors and pitfalls, such as pointing out common mistakes or identifying errors as students make them. Helping students shape a new skill or process also involves illustrating important variations. When teaching division in math, for example, ask students what they might do differently if certain numbers were different. Students learn the rules of division more thoroughly when they can handle variations in the content and problems.

NONLINGUISTIC REPRESENTATIONS

We can store what we know in ways associated with words (linguistic forms) or with images (nonlinguistic forms). There are several types of nonlinguistic representations: graphic organizers, pictures or pictographic representations, mental images, physical models, and kinesthetic representations. Because ELLs cannot rely solely on their linguistic ability to learn and retain knowledge in a new language, nonlinguistic methods of learning and demonstrating their knowledge are particularly important for them.

1. *Create graphic organizers.* Using graphic organizers is likely the most common way to help students generate nonlinguistic representations. **Graphic organizers** combine the linguistic mode, in that they use words and phrases, and the nonlinguistic mode, in that they use symbols and arrows, to represent relationships. Useful resources for graphic organizers are available (e.g., Bellanca, 2007; Drapeau, 2009; McKnight, 2010).

Six common graphic organizer patterns are described here:

- *Descriptive patterns.* Descriptive patterns represent facts about specific persons, places, things, and events. The information does not need to be organized in any particular order.

- *Time–sequence patterns.* Time–sequence patterns organize events in a specific chronological order. For example, a history timeline could be created identifying the key legislation and judicial rulings concerning civil rights.

- *Process/cause–effect patterns.* These patterns organize information into a causal network leading to a specific outcome or into a sequence of steps leading to a specific product. For example, information about the factors that typically lead to the development of a healthy body might be organized as a process/cause–effect pattern.

- *Episode patterns.* These patterns organize information about specific events, including a setting (time and place), specific people, a specific duration, a specific sequence of events, and a particular cause and effect. For example, students might organize information about the Civil Rights Act of 1964 into an episode pattern.

- *Generalization/principle patterns.* These patterns organize information into general statements with supporting examples. For example, a generalization might be "The most popular television shows at this time are crime and legal shows." Then a list of examples can be provided below this generalization.

- *Concept patterns.* Concept patterns organize information around a work or phrase that represents an entire class or category of people, places, things, and events. Concept patterns are the most general of all the graphic organizer patterns. The main characteristics of the concept are included along with examples. A web can be used to graphically display concept patterns (see Figure 7.1 for an example).

FIGURE 7.1

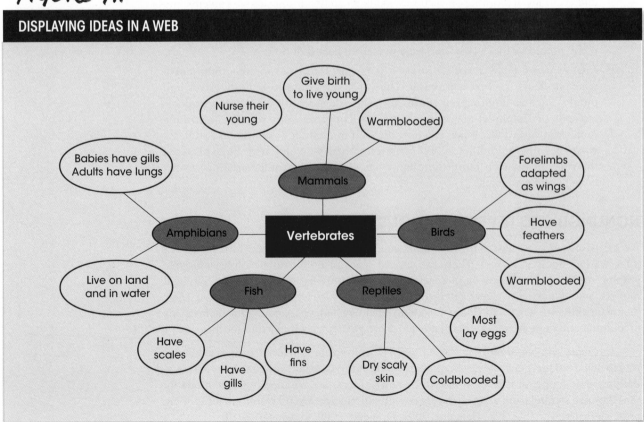

DISPLAYING IDEAS IN A WEB

2. *Draw pictures or pictographs.* Drawing pictures or pictographs (i.e., symbolic pictures) to represent knowledge is an effective way to generate nonlinguistic representations in the minds of students. For example, students might be asked to draw a picture of the parts of the human eye as a means to promote understanding.

3. *Generate mental images.* The most direct way to generate a mental representation is to construct or imagine a mental picture of knowledge you are learning. For example, when reading a story, students might create a mental picture of the physical setting or other key aspects of the story.

4. *Make physical models.* Physical models are concrete representations of the knowledge that is being learned. Manipulatives are often used in math and science to help students learn the concepts. Students also could be asked to make physical models to help them extend their understanding of the concepts.

5. *Engage in kinesthetic activities.* Kinesthetic activities involve physical movement. Physical movement associated with specific knowledge generates a mental image of the knowledge in the mind of the learner. Students could be asked to role-play many processes or events in the classroom. Most students find this an enjoyable way to express their knowledge.

SETTING OBJECTIVES AND PROVIDING FEEDBACK

Setting objectives and providing feedback give students direction and help them think about their own learning. Since ELLs are learning both content and language, they may feel overwhelmed about all the new things they must learn. These concerns tend to subside when they are told what they are going to learn each day, with clear objectives and feedback about their performance.

Setting Objectives. Goal setting is the process of establishing a direction for learning. Three generalizations can be made from the research on goal setting. First, instructional objectives narrow what students focus on. Second, these objectives should not be too specific. Third, students should be encouraged to personalize the teacher's goals.

Here are several guidelines for setting objectives:

- *Set objectives that are not too specific.* Learning goals that are too specific might actually constrain students' learning. When students are engaged in a rich learning experience, they might not attend to all of the learning that could result from the experience if the objective is too narrow or if it focuses too much on a specific skill.

- *Personalize the objectives.* Objectives become powerful learning tools when they give direction to students but also allow them some flexibility to further define their own interests in a topic. Students might be asked to identify their personal learning goals in relation to the topic being considered. In a health unit, for example, a student might want to know more about how kidneys work because he or she has a relative with kidney problems.

- *Communicate the objectives.* Communicating objectives is just as important as designing them. Both short-term and long-term goals need to be clearly visible to students and in language that they can understand. For example, all goals for a grading period can be posted, and goals for a unit can be included in a handout. Consider ways to communicate learning goals to parents as well.

- *Negotiate contracts.* Contracting with students to attain specific goals is a variation on goal setting. Contracts individualize goals for learning so students have some say about what they will work on and the grade they will receive for their work.

Providing Feedback. A common yet powerful strategy to promote student understanding is the teacher providing students with feedback about how well they are doing. This topic has been heavily researched. Four generalizations can be made from the research

VOICES from the Classroom

JENNIFER ADAM, grades 1–2 multiage classroom teacher, West Chicago, Illinois

ESTABLISHING LEARNING TARGETS AND ENABLING STUDENT SELF-ASSESSMENT

The objectives or learning targets in our writing units are based on our quarterly report card expectations, the Core Curriculum Map, and the forms of writing. As I introduce new concepts in writing, I translate my teaching objectives into student-friendly learning targets.

For example, if I am looking for organized, detailed personal narratives, one of the student targets would be "I can write a lead for my narrative. This means I used words that will make my audience want to read my story." Another would be "I added details to my narrative. This means I talked about what I saw, what I heard, and what I felt."

After writing their draft, each student assesses his or her work by using a checklist that is based on our learning targets. In this self-assessment, the student circles words to describe his or her performance in reaching each target. For example, if a student was inconsistent in adding details, he or she would circle "Sometimes." Students are then encouraged to revise their writing based on their self-assessment.

Next, I meet with each student to reflect on and assess the revised piece of writing, and together we score the writing using a rubric. We then use the student's self-assessment and the rubric we scored together to establish a goal for future growth. The student then continues in the writing process by performing additional revisions, editing the work for conventions, and/or publishing the piece.

URBAN EDUCATION

on providing feedback. First, feedback should be corrective in its design. Second, feedback should be timely, delivered soon after the instructional event. Third, feedback should be specific to a criterion. Fourth, students can effectively provide some of their own feedback.

Hill and Flynn (2006) suggest that rubrics offer many benefits when used with ELLs in mainstream classrooms and recommend their use to provide feedback on information, processes, and skills. The use of rubrics helps students better understand expectations, and grading seems less subjective and more comprehensible to them.

Here are several guidelines for providing feedback:

- *Use criterion-referenced feedback and explanations.* When possible, teachers should try to focus their feedback on specific types of knowledge and skill, help students understand how well they are doing as compared to a performance standard, and explain why their work exceeds, meets, or misses the standard. Rubrics are very helpful in providing students with the criteria and the performance expected in relation to the criteria.

- *Use feedback from assessments.* Scores from assessments can provide students with feedback about their learning. Feedback on classroom assessments is most effective if it is given in a timely manner, without much delay after the assessment is conducted. Explanations about what is correct and what is incorrect also enhance the effectiveness of the feedback.

- *Engage students in peer feedback.* Using peer feedback does not mean that students actually grade each other's papers. Instead, the goal is for students to clarify for each other what was correct or incorrect in an assessment. This could be done simply by having a student who answered a question correctly explain the correct answer to another student who answered it incorrectly.

■ *Ask students to self-assess.* Self-assessment can be as simple as asking students to score themselves on an assignment using a rubric or asking them to summarize their progress on learning goals at the end of a grading period. Asking students to give some written response about their learning further encourages reflection on their level of skill and knowledge.

GENERATING AND TESTING HYPOTHESES

The process of generating and testing hypotheses involves the application of knowledge. Two generalizations can be made from the research in this area. First, hypothesis generation and testing can be approached through inductive and deductive approaches. **Inductive approaches** require students first to discover the principles and then to generate the hypotheses. With a **deductive approach**, a teacher would first present the principle and then ask students to generate and test hypotheses based on this principle. When discussing the scale of hardness for rocks and minerals, for example, a teacher might use an inductive approach by giving students various mineral samples and asking them to try scratching the materials to see what conclusions or principles they might draw. However, with the deductive approach, the teacher would first describe the principle and then ask the students to use the mineral sample to test out the principle.

Second, teachers should ask students to explain their hypotheses and their conclusions clearly. This can be done in various ways, such as providing students with templates for reporting their work, providing sentence stems for students to help them articulate their explanations, and providing rubrics so students know the criteria that will be used to evaluate their explanations.

Set aside time for students to verbally explain their hypotheses and conclusions. This will assist in ELLs' verbal language development and will also help them develop academic knowledge.

Teachers can use six types of tasks to engage students in generating and testing hypotheses:

1. *Systems analysis.* Students study many systems across the disciplines, such as ecosystems, weather systems, and systems of government. One way to enhance students' understanding of these systems is to ask them to generate hypotheses that predict what would happen if some aspect of a system were to change. For example, what would happen if there were not a Supreme Court in the United States? Systems analysis involves several steps. First, explain the purpose of the system and the parts and functions of each part. Second, describe how the parts affect each other. Third, identify a part of the system, describe a change, and then hypothesize what would happen because of this change. Finally, test the hypothesis whenever possible.

2. *Problem solving.* Students are often asked to solve structured problems with specific goals and conditions. However, asking students to solve unstructured problems involves generating and testing hypotheses. *Unstructured problems* do not have clearly defined goals or constraints, and there is more than one way to solve the problem. Problem solving involves several steps. Identify the goal you are trying to accomplish, describe the constraints or conditions in reaching the goal, identify different solutions and hypothesize which solution is likely to work, try the solution, and then explain whether the solution was correct.

3. *Historical investigation.* Students engage in historical investigation when they investigate plausible scenarios for events from the past about which there is no general agreement. For example, there has been considerable public debate about whether President George W. Bush had justification to take the United States to war in Iraq. Historical investigation involves several steps. Clearly describe the historical event to be examined. Identify what is known or agreed on and what is not known or about which there is disagreement. Based on the students' understanding about the situation, offer a hypothetical scenario. Finally, seek out and analyze evidence to determine whether the hypothetical scenario is plausible.

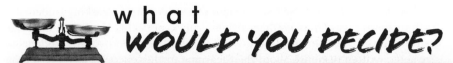

GENERATING AND TESTING HYPOTHESES

Even though generating and testing hypotheses effectively promotes student learning, it is not as commonly used in classrooms as some other approaches.

1. For the grade level or subject area you will be teaching, identify one topic that could be taught in a lesson using this approach of generating and testing hypotheses.

2. Since students may be somewhat unfamiliar with this process, what might you do to prepare your students for the use of this approach?

4. *Invention.* The process of invention involves generating and testing hypotheses. To do so, students must hypothesize what might work, develop an idea, and then conduct tests to determine whether their idea does work. Invention often involves generating and testing multiple hypotheses until one of them proves effective. We need invention in situations when we ask, "Shouldn't there be a better way to . . .?"

5. *Experimental inquiry.* Experimental inquiry involves making observations, generating explanations, making predictions, and testing them. While experimental inquiry is often associated with science classes, it can be effectively used in all subject areas.

6. *Decision making.* Using a structured decision-making framework can help students examine hypothetical situations, especially those requiring them to select what is the most or least of something or what is the best or worst of something. In a literature class, for example, you might ask students to examine the characters in two books read in class and to identify which character best fulfills the civic responsibilities of a good citizen. Students might select various characters. But the results might be different if you identified a structured decision-making framework in which several criteria were identified and a rating system was established for the criteria as students considered the main characters. Using a decision-making process to test their prediction requires students to reflect on and use a broad range of knowledge related to the topic.

CUES, QUESTIONS, AND ADVANCE ORGANIZERS

Cueing and questioning are at the heart of classroom practice. **Cues** are explicit hints concerning what students are about to experience. **Advance organizers** are organizational frameworks that teachers present to students prior to teaching new content to prepare students for what they are about to learn. Taken together, cues, questions, and advance organizers help students understand and make connections to the content.

Cues and Questions. Here are several guidelines for using cues and questions:

- *Focus cues and questions on what is important, not on what is unusual.* Questions designed to help students obtain a deeper understanding of the content will eventually increase their interest in the topic.

- *Use explicit cues.* Cues are more effective when they relate to specific content and purposes.

- *Use higher-level questions because they promote deeper understanding.* Questions that require students to analyze information produce more learning than do questions that simply require students to recall or recognize information.

- *Wait briefly before accepting responses from students to increase the depth of students' answers.* Wait time involves pausing several seconds after asking a question to give students time to think before being called on for an answer. Wait time promotes more student discourse and more student-to-student interaction.

- *Use questions before a learning activity to establish a mental set for the learning experience.* Questions after a learning activity are useful, but they should be supplemented with questions before the learning activity.

Advance Organizers. Advance organizers provide a preview of the content that is to be addressed. They take the surprise out of what is to come, help students retrieve what they already know about a topic, and focus them on the new information. Advance organizers are most useful with information that is not well organized; using an advance organizer helps students recognize the important information and put it in context with related information.

Several types of advance organizers can be used:

- *Use expository advance organizers.* Expository advance organizers are straightforward descriptions of the new content that students will be learning. The descriptions can be written or oral, should focus on the important information, and may include text and pictures. The objectives of the lesson may be stated within this advance organizer. Graphic organizers also can be effectively used as an advance organizer to provide a preview of the lesson.

- *Use narrative advance organizers.* Narrative advance organizers are stories that help the students make personal or real-world connections to the content. For example, teachers may tie in a personal experience, refer to current television shows or movies, or describe a current event in relation to the content to be addressed.

- *Have students skim the textbook as a form of advance organizer.* Skimming allows students to preview important information they will encounter later by noting what stands out in the textbook in headings, subheadings, and highlighted information. Students need to see that these features help outline the main information.

- *Use graphic advance organizers.* By using a graphic organizer, students can become familiar with the information that will be studied along with the relationships among the pieces of information. Graphic organizers give students a visual map of the upcoming information to be studied.

Helping Students Become Better Thinkers

A critical objective of education and one that is increasingly referenced as essential to teacher education is critical thinking and higher-order thinking. You will be expected to be a critical thinker, and you also will be expected to teach students to be better thinkers. The 21st century skills discussed in Chapter 3 also emphasize critical thinking and problem solving skills (Partnership, 2009), and many school districts are adopting those guidelines.

When we consider helping students become better thinkers, we typically want to move students into higher-order thinking. There are different kinds of higher-order thinking, and definitions of higher-order thinking fall into three categories (Brookhart, 2010):

1. *Higher-order thinking as transfer.* The cognitive domain was discussed in Chapter 4, and six levels of Bloom's revised taxonomy were identified: remembering, understanding, applying, analyzing, evaluating, and creating. The lower levels focus on recall, but learning for transfer requires "meaningful learning" (Anderson & Krathwohl, 2001).

Thus, analyzing, evaluating, and creating would involve higher-order thinking. Students transfer their learning to new uses beyond those they were specifically taught.

2. *Higher-order thinking as critical thinking.* **Critical thinking** is often defined as "enhancing students' abilities to think critically and make rational decisions about what to do or what to believe" (Slavin, 2012, p. 242). Critical thinking involves evaluating the accuracy, credibility, and worth of information and the lines of reasoning (Ormrod, 2011). Thinking critically involves six skills—interpretation, analysis, evaluation, inference, explanation, and self-regulation (Facione, 1990).

3. *Higher-order thinking as problem solving.* Problem solving is the nonautomatic decision making required for reaching a goal (Nitko & Brookhart, 2011). This involves processing information, thinking creatively, and coming to a solution.

Let's look at one aspect of critical thinking mentioned above—self-regulation. Self-regulation is the ability to control your learning behaviors and remain aware of where you are in the learning task and be committed to succeeding. Self-regulation includes (1) examining your thinking and academic behaviors, (2) comparing yourself to the standard for high quality work, and (3) using self-administered, productive work habits (e.g., going online to Facebook *after* completing homework). Self-regulated learning takes place when there is deliberate planning and self-monitoring of the mental and emotional processes involved in completing a learning task.

The next time you are in a classroom, consider whether students are self-monitoring. You are likely to see students who are deeply engaged in their own learning and those who are not. When asked during a writing assignment what they are working on, self-regulated students have a good idea about the academic goal and progress they have made toward that goal. For example, on a writing task they can talk about working to include more examples or using metaphors to add interest. Students who are not self-regulated may find themselves surrounded by materials but disengaged from the task at hand (Abrami et al., 2008).

GUIDANCE FROM TEACHING STANDARDS

What should teachers do to promote student thinking? Professional teaching standards provide some guidance for actions that teachers can take in their classrooms to promote student thinking. The InTASC standards, introduced in Chapter 1, are used in over 40 states and provide examples of concepts central to teacher excellence. A major theme embedded in these standards is critical thinking and problem solving (CCSSO, 2011). Thinking skills are prominent in several standards.

Standard 4 on Content Knowledge is directly linked to the building blocks for teaching students to think critically. As the teacher, you are expected to understand the central concepts, tools of inquiry, and structures of the discipline you teach and to create learning experiences that make the discipline accessible and meaningful for your students. Through knowing the content that you will teach, it is expected that you will engage your students in learning experiences that encourage them to question, analyze ideas from diverse perspectives, and apply methods of inquiry and standards of evidence. This enables students to link new concepts to familiar concepts and make connections to past knowledge and experiences. You are expected to recognize learner misconceptions that interfere with learning, and create experiences to build accurate understanding.

For InTASC Standard 5, Application of Content, you are expected to connect concepts and use different perspectives to engage your students in critical thinking, creativity, and collaborative real-world problem solving. For example, these goals are supported if you have your students study the quality of water in their community or state (biology and chemistry) and engage in the policy debate about the issue (social studies). Standard 5 also calls on you to engage learners in questioning and challenging assumptions and approaches in order to foster innovation and problem solving in local and global contexts. You also need to help students generate and evaluate new ideas and novel approaches, seek inventive solutions to problems, and develop original work.

VOICES from the Classroom

RENATA MACKENZIE, high school language arts teacher, Monroe Township, New Jersey

STUDENT REFLECTION FOR BETTER THINKING

Reflection is a key component for helping students to become better thinkers. At the end of a lesson, I ask my students to reflect on the nature of the content they learned, as well as the learning process. They complete this reflection through a written response and then share it with the class.

When first teaching students how to reflect, it is helpful to give them prompts, such as "Today, I learned . . ." and "Next time I will . . . ," in order to stimulate their think-

ing. It forces students to review their notes and the lesson in order to make sense of the material.

As students become better at the process of reflection, I have them include applications to everyday life. By making these connections, students will be more apt to remember the material and utilize it in the future. By teaching students how to reflect and giving them time to incorporate it into their day, it inevitably forces them to become better and more critical thinkers.

InTASC Standard 6 focuses on the assessment of students. The teacher uses varied assessment strategies to engage students in their own growth, to monitor student progress, and to guide the teacher's and learners' decision making.

Each of these standards is directly related to nurturing and assessing your students' ability to think critically as a central skill for successful employment and active citizenship. Critical thinking takes place in each content area (mathematics, science, history, and English language arts) but is also an important concept for active citizenship—the need in a democracy for citizens to be able to analyze political, social, and ethical issues that face society every day (e.g., Is global warming a problem? How do we invigorate the economy? Whom should I vote for?). Critical thinkers are able to recognize misleading statements, identify assumptions, weigh evidence, and come to conclusions.

ENHANCING CRITICAL THINKING

It is not enough to know that students differ in their ability to think critically and make decisions about what to do or what to believe. Effective teaching of critical thinking comes when you create a climate for learning where a student would agree with the statement: "This assignment is hard, but I can do it." It is also important that students believe they can engage in critical thinking because they are prepared to give an answer and can provide evidence and a rationale from the knowledge they have gained.

The following ten critical thinking skills can be useful as you work to help your students become better thinkers (Beyer, 1988; Slavin, 2012):

1. Distinguishing facts from assertions of value without evidence
2. Distinguishing relevant from irrelevant information, claims, or reasons
3. Determining the factual accuracy of a statement
4. Determining the credibility of a source
5. Identifying ambiguous claims or arguments
6. Identifying unstated assumptions
7. Detecting bias

8. Identifying logical fallacies

9. Recognizing logical inconsistencies in a line of reasoning

10. Determining the strength of an argument or claim

This list does not represent sequential tasks but rather is an aid to students as they evaluate information and move toward conclusions.

If your students are to become critical thinkers, they need to have a classroom atmosphere that supports open discussion and the collection and analyses of information. You also have to be willing to create a climate that can change students' learning habits and dispositions.

The ability to think critically varies, but it can be improved through nurturing students in the classroom in the following ways (Abrami et al., 2008; Ormrod, 2011):

1. Teach fewer topics, but in greater depth—the less is more principle.

2. Encourage some intellectual skepticism by urging students to question and challenge ideas and to understand that our knowledge and understanding change over time.

3. Model critical thinking by thinking out loud while analyzing a persuasive argument in a scientific or public policy document.

4. Provide opportunities to practice critical thinking (e.g., flaws in arguments, substituting an opinion for fact).

5. Ask questions that encourage students to think critically. (Does this author have a predisposition? Are the findings valid? Is there information that contradicts the authors? Have you listed the facts you know about this issue? Do the facts support the conclusion?)

6. Have students debate issues from different perspectives.

7. Assist students in building dispositions and habits that support the hard work of thinking critically.

8. Build authentic learning activities to help students hone their critical thinking skills.

Students need support if they are to develop the dispositions, skills, and habits to think critically. Finally, many people believe that the highest purpose of an education is to help students become engaged citizens who can think critically—citizens who are more analytical in their jobs and parents who are more discerning about the complex issues they face in raising a family.

Strategies that Promote Student Engagement

Student engagement has been recognized as a critical aspect of student learning. Despite its importance, engagement is not easily defined. Skinner, Kindermann, Connell, and Wellborn (2009) noted that there is no single, correct definition of engagement. In fact, a variety of terms seem to overlap in meaning and use, including terms such as *motivation, engagement, interest, participation, active learning, involvement, attention,* and *effort.* Barkley (2010) sees student engagement as a blending of a student's motivation to learn with opportunities for active learning. Motivation is viewed as the portal to engagement. For this discussion, **student engagement** is defined as active student involvement on learning tasks that are meaningful, relevant, and motivating to the student.

Csikszentmihalyi (1990, 1997) states that people enter into a "state of flow" when they are completely absorbed in the task at hand, to the point where they lose track of time and are unaware of fatigue or anything else but the activity itself. Flow is optimized when people are confident that they have the requisite skills necessary to be competent in a given task. Thus, teachers need to consider how to support their students' feelings of confidence about the tasks at hand.

Flow experiences in the classroom occur when students are actively involved in challenging tasks that stretch their physical and mental abilities (Brophy, 2010). Newmann (1990) reported that thoughtful tasks were used in classes that challenged students with cognitively complex tasks. Thoughtful tasks:

- Focus on sustained examination of a few topics rather than superficial coverage of many

- Encourage discourse that is characterized by substantive coherence and continuity

- Challenge students to clarify or justify their assertions

- Generate original and innovative ideas

In *The Highly Engaged Classroom*, Marzano, Pickering, and Heflebower (2011) recognize the overlap and interaction between attention and engagement and the related concepts of motivation and involvement. They maintain that teachers should consider using specific engagement strategies in every unit of instruction. Marzano and colleagues organized their suggested strategies to engage students in two categories:

1. *Daily strategies.* These include (1) using effective pacing, (2) demonstrating intensity and enthusiasm, (3) building positive teacher–student and peer relationships, and (4) using effective verbal feedback.

2. *Opportunistic strategies.* Teachers look for opportunities within upcoming lessons where engagement strategies will naturally fit as opposed to trying to make them fit into every lesson. These include (a) incorporating physical movement, (b) using humor, (c) using games and inconsequential competition, (d) initiating friendly controversy, (e) presenting unusual information, (f) questioning to increase response rates, (g) connecting to students' lives, (h) connecting to students' life ambitions, (i) encouraging application of knowledge, (j) tracking and studying progress, (k) providing examples of self-efficacy, and (l) teaching self-efficacy.

From the work of Barkley (2010), Brophy (2010), Csikszentmihalyi (1990, 1997), Newmann (1990), VanDeWeghe (2009), and others, some commonalities emerge for suggestions in addressing student engagement. Teachers should consider the following strategies to promote student engagement in their classrooms.

- *Provide a supportive learning environment.* Provide appropriate conditions in the classroom to promote active, highly engaged learning. Teacher instructional behaviors, curriculum, and instruction all influence the learning environment.

- *Have clear goals that are meaningful and relevant.* Be sure students can articulate the goals themselves so they understand why they are engaging in a learning activity.

- *Provide feedback on student performance.* Feedback should be immediate and relevant. Provide feedback-in-action rather than relying only on summative feedback or assessment.

- *Provide an optimal level of challenge for the students' ability levels.* When challenge exceeds skill, students feel defeated. When skill exceeds challenge, students get bored. The challenge should align with the ability level.

- *Provide opportunities for students to concentrate on tasks.* Consider the tasks and the classroom environment when arranging for sufficient time and conditions for concentration on tasks.

what WOULD YOU DECIDE?

USING SOFTWARE FOR DIAGRAMMING AND OUTLINING IDEAS

Software is available for students to create concept maps, webs, and other graphic organizers using pictures and text to represent concepts and relationships and then to convert those concepts and images easily into an outline format, or vice versa. This helps strengthen students' critical thinking skills, comprehension, and writing skills across the curriculum. *Inspiration* is one such program for grades 6-12, and *Kidspiration* is available for grades K-5 (see http://www.inspiration.com).

1. How might you use this software to apply the strategies discussed in this chapter?
2. What advantages might you experience with the use of this software?
3. What disadvantages or problems might exist?

Applying the SIOP Model to Strategies

Meeting the needs of English language learners can be facilitated by using the SIOP model to provide more flexibility in the design and delivery of instruction. As outlined in Chapter 1, the SIOP model has eight components, and two of them relate to instructional strategies to promote learning: strategies and practice/application (Echevarria, Vogt, & Short, 2008). While these strategies were originally designed for use with ELLs, they are also helpful in meeting the needs of all learners in the classroom. The excellent content from Echevarria, Vogt, and Short (2008) serves as the foundation for much of the information in this section.

STRATEGIES

Teachers need to give careful and deliberate thought to their choice of instructional strategies and the results they hope to achieve. Using a variety of instructional strategies, providing students with support and assistance with the strategies, and using higher-order questions all require much attention prior to instruction.

1. *Provide ample opportunities for students to use learning strategies.* Students need to be actively involved in their learning, and many instructional strategies provide opportunities for active involvement. However, many ELLs have difficulty assuming active roles because they focus their energies on developing language skills. Therefore, teachers should provide many opportunities for learners to use a variety of learning strategies, and the strategies should be taught through explicit instruction, and carefully modeled and supported.

2. *Consistently use scaffolding techniques to assist and support student understanding.* Teachers scaffold instruction when they provide substantial amounts of support and assistance in the earliest stages of teaching a new concept and then gradually decrease the amount of support as the learners acquire experience through multiple practice opportunities.

There are two types of scaffolding. First, verbal scaffolding involves the use of prompts, questioning, and elaboration to facilitate students' movement to higher levels of language proficiency, comprehension, and thinking. This can be done, for example, by paraphrasing a student response to model correct English usage, reinforcing definitions in class discussions or questions, sharing your thinking about an issue, or simply slowing speech and including pauses. Second, procedural scaffolding includes the use of instructional approaches such as partnering or grouping students for reading activities, one-on-one teaching, and small-group instruction.

3. *Use a variety of questions or tasks that promote higher-order thinking skills.* Learning is promoted with higher-order questions that ask students to apply, analyze, and evaluate information. It is important that you carefully plan higher-order questions prior to lesson delivery; it is too difficult to think of them during instruction. Encouraging students to respond with higher levels of thinking requires teachers to consciously plan and incorporate questions at a variety of levels.

PRACTICE/APPLICATION

Teachers need to give students a chance to practice with new material, to demonstrate how well they are learning it, and then to apply that new knowledge in new ways. Practice and application is especially important for ELLs' academic language development. Oral and written practice can be achieved through the use of hands-on materials, activities where students apply content and language knowledge, and activities where all language skills are integrated:

1. *Supply hands-on materials for students to practice using new content knowledge.* While all students benefit from guided practice, English language learners make more rapid progress in mastering content objectives when they have multiple opportunities to practice with hands-on materials and manipulatives. Manipulating materials is important for ELLs because it helps them connect abstract concepts with concrete experiences and thus reduces the language load for students. As a general rule, provide short meaningful amounts of material to be practiced, practice for a short time, schedule several episodes of practice close together, and provide specific feedback.

2. *Provide activities for students to apply content and language knowledge in the classroom.* All students learn best when they are involved in relevant, meaningful application of what they are learning. For students acquiring a new language, the need to apply new information is important because discussing and participating in activities helps make abstract concepts concrete. Application can occur when using graphic organizers, participating in discussions, solving problems in cooperative learning groups, or doing a variety of other meaningful activities. Application must also include opportunities to practice language knowledge in the classroom. Opportunities for social interaction promote language development; these include discussion, reporting information orally and in writing, and working with partners and in small groups.

3. *Integrate all language skills into each lesson.* Reading, writing, listening, and speaking are complex cognitive language processes that are interrelated and integrated. Teachers need to create many opportunities for ELLs to practice and use all four language processes in an integrated way. This can be accomplished by designing varied activities that incorporate reading, promote interactions with others, encourage writing about what has been learned, and provide the chance to listen to peers' ideas.

Key Terms

Advance organizers	Critical thinking	Homework	Reciprocal teaching
Classifying	Cues	Inductive approaches	Student engagement
Comparing	Deductive approaches	Note taking	Summarizing
Creating analogies	Graphic organizers	Practice	Summary frame
Creating metaphors			

Major Concepts

1. There are four common approaches to identifying similarities and differences: comparing, classifying, creating metaphors, and creating analogies.

2. Summarizing content and taking notes both require students to distill information.

3. Homework and practice give students opportunities to deepen their understanding and proficiency with the content they are learning.

4. Nonlinguistic representations use images to represent the content.

5. Setting objectives and providing feedback give students direction and help them think about their own learning.

6. Generating and testing hypotheses can be achieved by inductive or deductive approaches.

7. Cues, questions, and advance organizers help students understand and make connections to the content.

8. Higher-order thinking can be defined in terms of transfer, critical thinking, or problem solving.

9. Student engagement is defined as active student involvement in learning tasks that are meaningful, relevant, and motivating to the student.

10. Instructional strategies can be adapted to meet the needs of English language learners.

Discussion/Reflective Questions

1. From your own school experiences, which of the major strategies presented in this chapter were most helpful in promoting your understanding of the content?

2. What are the benefits of using several approaches when identifying similarities and differences?

3. What are the advantages and disadvantages of occasionally providing students with teacher-made notes?

4. What might be the consequences if teachers do not set objectives and provide student feedback?

5. What have been some effective ways your teachers have used advance organizers to introduce lesson objectives?

Suggested Activities

FOR CLINICAL SETTINGS

1. Examine a chapter from a textbook you might use, and determine ways that you could use similarities and differences for part of the instruction.

2. Prepare a paper describing how you will use homework in a course that you will be teaching.

3. Imagine that you are the person teaching this chapter. Identify three ways you might use advance organizers to introduce the chapter's content to students in the course.

FOR FIELD EXPERIENCES

1. Talk with several teachers to see how they set objectives and provide feedback to their students.

2. Talk with several students about how they summarize and take notes. What insights did you gain from this experience?

3. When considering strategies in the SIOP model, examine a chapter in the textbook being used in an actual course and identify ways that tasks or questions could be used to promote higher-order thinking. Discuss your ideas with a teacher to get feedback and suggestions.

Further Reading

Bellanca, J. (2007). *A guide to graphic organizers* (2nd ed.). Thousand Oaks, CA: Corwin Press.

An excellent resource with examples of numerous types of graphic organizers that can be used in any subject or grade level.

Hill, J. D., & Flynn, K. M.(2006). *Classroom instruction that works with English language learners*. Alexandria, VA: Association for Supervision and Curriculum Development.

Focuses on nine instructional strategies that are effective in promoting achievement when working with English language learners.

Marzano, R. J., Pickering, D. J., & Heflebower, T. (2011). *The highly engaged classroom*. Bloomington, IN: Marzano Research Laboratory, powered by Solution Tree.

Provides many specific strategies for teachers to create an environment conducive for student engagement.

Quate, S., & McDermott, J. (2009). *Clock watchers: Six steps to motivating and engaging disengaged students across the content areas*. Portsmouth, NH: Heinemann.

Provides strategies to engage students in learning.

Walsh, J. A., & Sattes, B. D. (2011). *Thinking through quality questioning: Deepening student engagement*. Thousand Oaks, CA: Corwin Press.

Provides a framework to create questions that promote student thinking. Examines types of questions, how they are used, how they can provide feedback, and how they create a culture for learning.

Technology Resources

WISE MAPPING

http://www.wisemapping.com/c/home.htm

Wise Mapping is a free collaborative mind-mapping tool; it looks like a concept web. The site's editing and sharing functions are fairly easy to use. Each cell created in a mind map can be dragged and moved around without losing any text or text formatting. Users can collaborate on creating a mind map. Mind maps can be shared with others via email or a URL link, or be embedded into your blog or website.

EXPLORATREE

http://www.exploratree.org.uk

Exploratree is a free graphic organizer creation tool. Students can use premade graphic organizer templates (which Exploratree refers to as "thinking guides") or they can create their own templates. The thinking guides can be used online or downloaded and printed. Thinking guides can be created collaboratively, which makes it a good tool for students working in groups.

EXAMPLES OF ACTIVITIES THAT PROMOTE HIGHER-ORDER THINKING

http://teaching.uncc.edu/resources/best-practice-articles/instructional-methods/promoting-higher-thinking

Though this site provides examples in science, math, and social studies, its examples can be extended to most subject areas at all grade levels.

TEN STEPS TO BETTER STUDENT ENGAGEMENT

http://www.edutopia.org/project-learning-teaching-strategies

This site offers useful suggestions for student engagement, and has many links by grade level, teaching strategy, and other categories.

SWEET SEARCH

http://www.sweetsearch.com

This helpful search engine for students has received very favorable reviews. It uses only 35,000 websites, and sorts out the spam or sites that lack academic rigor.

MyEducationLab™

Go to the **MyEducationLab** (www.myeducationlab.com) for General Methods and familiarize yourself with the content:

- Topically organized Assignments and Activities, tied to learning outcomes for the course, that can help you more deeply understand course content
- Topically organized Building Teaching Skills and Dispositions learning units allow you to apply and develop understanding of teaching methods.
- A chapter-specific pretest that assesses your understanding of the content offers hints and feedback for

each question and generates a study plan including links to Review, Practice, and Enrichment activities that will enhance your understanding of the concepts. A Study Plan posttest with hints and feedback ensures you understood concepts from the chapter after having completed the enrichment activities.

A Correlation Guide may be downloaded by instructors to show how MyEducationLab content aligns to this book.

Managing Lesson Delivery

THIS CHAPTER PROVIDES INFORMATION THAT WILL HELP YOU TO

1. Select ways to structure lessons, group students, and hold students academically accountable.

2. Handle administrative and instructional responsibilities at the start of a lesson.

3. Take actions that contribute to effective group management during the middle part of a lesson.

4. Take actions at the end of a lesson to provide for lesson summary and enable students to prepare to leave.

5. Manage seatwork, assignments, records, and paperwork.

6. Guide learning with whole-group instruction.

7. Adjust lesson delivery to enhance instruction for English language learners.

When planning for a vacation trip, you often need to plan ahead. Do you want to stay in one place and relax, or do you want to visit a number of areas? Would you like to schedule several events for each day, or would you like to leave the daily schedule very open? What types of accommodations would you like? To ensure an enjoyable vacation, you need to give these questions attention.

Similarly, you need to give advance thought to the type of classroom that you would like to have. How structured do you want your classroom and lessons? How do you want to group your students for instruction? How will you hold the students academically accountable? How will you handle various aspects of lesson delivery? How will you manage student work? How will you provide for whole-group instruction? How can lesson delivery be enhanced for English language learners (ELLs)? These issues will be explored in this chapter. How you attend to these issues will make a difference in managing instruction and student behavior.

Issues Affecting Lesson Delivery

Preparing daily lesson plans is a vital task for effective classroom management and discipline, because effective, engaging lessons can keep students on task and minimize misbehavior. You need to consider the degree of structure that will occur in each lesson. The grouping planned for the instructional activities will also affect student interaction. Furthermore, students are more likely to stay on task and be engaged in instruction when they know that they will be held academically accountable.

DEGREE OF STRUCTURE IN LESSONS

Many instructional strategies can be used, ranging from teacher-centered, explicit approaches to the presentation of content to student-centered, less explicit approaches. **Teacher-centered approaches** include lectures, demonstrations, questions, recitations, practice and drills, and reviews. **Student-centered approaches** include inquiry approaches, discovery learning and problem solving, role playing and simulation, gaming, laboratory activities, computer-assisted instruction, and learning or activity centers. Various types of grouping and discussion methods may be student or teacher directed, depending on how they are used. Teacher-centered approaches are often more structured than student-centered approaches. As a result, the management issues will vary depending on the approach used.

When deciding on your instructional strategy, you need to weigh the advantages and disadvantages of the various strategies along with the lesson objectives. Effective teachers use several strategies, ranging from teacher-directed to student-directed. The lesson objectives may determine what type of approach is most appropriate. Some content

There are 10 InTASC standards (see pages xx–xxi), and each standard in the original document includes a list of performances, essential knowledge, and critical dispositions to indicate more clearly what is intended in the standard.

Since this chapter deals with lesson delivery, some representative statements from InTASC Standard #6, Assessment, and Standard #8, Instructional Strategies, are listed here concerning topics in this chapter.

PERFORMANCES

■ The teacher engages learners in understanding and identifying quality work and provides them with effective descriptive feedback to guide their progress toward that work. (InTASC #6)

■ The teacher uses appropriate strategies and resources to adapt instruction to the needs of individuals and groups of learners. (InTASC #8)

ESSENTIAL KNOWLEDGE

■ The teacher understands the positive impact of effective descriptive feedback for learners and knows a variety of strategies for communicating this feedback. (InTASC #6)

■ The teacher understands how content and skill development can be supported by media and technology and knows how to evaluate these resources for quality, accuracy, and effectiveness. (InTASC #8)

CRITICAL DISPOSITIONS

■ The teacher is committed to using multiples types of assessment processes to support, verify, and document learning. (InTASC #6)

■ The teacher is committed to deepening awareness and understanding the strengths and needs of diverse learners when planning and adjusting instruction. (InTASC #8)

lends itself to inquiry and discovery techniques, whereas other content may be better handled with direct instruction. Over time, students should be given the opportunity to learn through a variety of instructional strategies.

GROUPING STUDENTS FOR INSTRUCTION

You need to consider the type of student grouping that is most appropriate for the instructional strategies and instructional objectives. Focus on a group as a collection of individuals who learn. Within groups, individual students observe, listen, respond, take turns, and so on. Instructional groups can be large or small. Whole-group instruction, small-group instruction, and independent work are options to consider.

Whole-Group Instruction. In **whole-group instruction**, the entire class is taught as a group. In the large group, you can (1) lecture, demonstrate, and explain a topic; (2) ask and answer a question in front of the entire class; (3) provide the same recitation, practice, and drill exercises for the entire class; (4) work on the same problems; and (5) use the same materials. Although instruction is directed to the whole group, you can still ask specific students to answer questions, monitor specific students as they work on assigned activities, and work with students on an individual basis. Even with whole-group instruction, give consideration to the individual differences of students.

Small-Group Instruction. Sometimes instructional objectives can be better met when students work in small groups; this is **small-group instruction**. Small groups enable students to be more actively engaged in learning, and teachers can better monitor student progress. Groups of four students often work well. In a group of more than six, generally not everyone will actively participate.

Since group work helps develop relationships, it is useful to vary the membership of groups based on gender and ethnicity. Students with disabilities can be placed in groups with nondisabled students to integrate them into the mainstreamed classroom. Though there may be good reasons for planning a homogeneous group for certain activities, educators in general recommend the use of heterogeneous groups (Johnson & Johnson, 1999; Slavin, 2012).

There are three types of groupings: cooperative learning groups, ability grouping, and peer tutoring. An explanation of each follows:

1. *Cooperative learning groups.* **Cooperative learning** refers to a variety of teaching methods in which students work in small groups to help one another to learn academic content (Slavin, 2012). One such approach involves student team learning methods in which there are team goals, and success is achieved if all team members learn the objectives being taught. Other types of cooperative learning groups include group investigations, jigsaw activities, and complex instruction. All these approaches are discussed more fully in Chapter 6.

As you consider ways to differentiate your instruction, remember that cooperative learning groups serve as an important means to provide instructional variety for your students while responding to various learning styles and student learning preferences. These groups also provide the opportunity to differentiate the content and tasks to meet the diversity of student interests and skills.

2. *Ability groups.* **Ability grouping** involves the clustering of students who are judged to be similar in their academic ability into classes for instruction. There are two common types of ability grouping: between-class grouping and within-class grouping.

Between-class grouping involves having separate classes for students of different abilities. When reporting research on between-class ability grouping, Slavin (2012) noted that grouping arrangements made on the basis of standardized test scores are not effective in reducing the range of differences that affect the specific class. In addition, the quality of instruction often is lower in lower-track classes, and students feel stigmatized by their assignments to low tracks. They may become delinquent and truant and may eventually

VOICES
from the Classroom

SARALEE WITTMER, second-grade teacher, Amarillo, Texas

GROUPING STUDENTS FOR INSTRUCTION

Students in my room are arranged in small groups of four students according to ability. I shuffle the mix every four to six weeks. Students get the chance to work with all other students and can sit close to the teacher, at the back of the room, close to the door, and up by the whiteboards.

Students are encouraged to discuss lessons with each other in their groups. It's amazing how much they learn from each other if we will only give them the opportunities. I can tell what the class might not have gotten from my lesson presentations by listening carefully to them when they are in their groups.

GLADIS DIAZ, fifth-grade teacher, Reno, Nevada

When preparing to group my students, I have them complete some cooperative activities so that I can see their skills and personalities. This helps me place them in homogeneous groups and establish the roles for each person in a group. Each group has a leader, a recorder, a go-getter, a speller, and an organizer. I choose the leader who remains in that role throughout the school year. The roles of the others rotate four times during the school year. I meet with the group leaders at least twice a week to discuss their role for the week and to be sure everything is running smoothly.

URBAN EDUCATION

drop out of school. The disadvantages of between-class ability grouping suggest that it be avoided when possible (Oakes, 2005). Instead, you might consider within-class ability grouping for a short time, as well as individualized instruction techniques.

Within-class grouping involves creating subgroups within a class, with each subgroup being fairly homogeneous in terms of ability. A small number is better than a large number of groups. In this way, group assignments can be flexible, role models for low achievers are available, teacher morale is higher, and the stigmatizing effect is minimized (Slavin, 2012). Within one classroom, you may group students for various activities or subjects. For example, middle school and secondary teachers may use ability groups for only part of a class period and whole-group activities or other approaches for the rest of the class time. You may group students to work on selected projects or activities.

3. *Peer tutoring.* **Peer tutoring** involves students teaching students. The two types of peer tutoring are (a) cross-age tutoring, by which older students work with younger students, and (b) peer tutoring, by which students within the same class work together.

There are several advantages of peer tutoring (Johnson & Johnson, 1999): (a) peer tutors are often effective in teaching students who do not respond well to adults; (b) peer tutoring can develop a bond of friendship between the tutor and tutee, which is important for integrating slow learners into the group; (c) peer tutoring allows the teacher to teach a large group of students while giving slow learners the individual attention that they need; (d) tutors benefit by learning to teach; and (e) peer tutoring happens spontaneously under cooperative conditions, so the teacher does not have to organize and manage it in a formal, continuing way.

Independent Work. You might give students opportunities to work on tasks of their own choosing, or you may assign activities that enable students to work alone. This is **independent work**. Good and Brophy (2008) found that one third of elementary teachers attempt to individualize instruction, as do one fifth of secondary teachers.

When assigning independent work, you may involve students in any of a number of instructional strategies. In inquiry and discovery instructional approaches, students learn about the process of discovery by collecting data and testing hypotheses. Teachers guide students as they discover new meanings, practice the skills, and undergo the experiences that will shape their learning. These approaches include computer-assisted instruction, learning centers, learning stations, laboratories, discovery techniques, and others.

HOLDING STUDENTS ACADEMICALLY ACCOUNTABLE

In planning lessons, you must also select procedures to help manage student work. **Academic accountability** means that the students must complete certain activities related to the instructional objectives. Teacher responsibilities for holding students academically accountable are displayed in Figure 8.1, some of which are adapted from Emmer and Evertson (2009), Evertson and Emmer (2009), and Jones and Jones (2010).

Consider the following guidelines when holding students academically accountable:

- *Determine a system of grading* (e.g., letter grades or numerical grades, and measures for nonachievement outcomes). This decision may be made for you by the school district, as reflected in the report card format. Use a variety of evaluation measures (e.g., tests, written or oral reports, homework, ratings, projects) throughout the marking period, and describe the grading system to the students.

- *Make decisions about assignments.* This includes deciding where and how you will post assignments, as well as the requirements and criteria for grading. Students should understand that completed assignments are part of the grading system.

- *Decide on work and completion requirements.* Students need to have guidelines or work requirements for the various assignments. Details about due dates, late work, and missed assignments due to absence should be explained. The relevant procedures will help students understand your expectations for them and should minimize questions on a case-by-case basis.

FIGURE 8.1

HOLDING STUDENTS ACADEMICALLY ACCOUNTABLE

Consider your grade level and subject area as you make decisions on the following issues in an effort to hold students academically accountable.

1. **Grading System**
   a. Select a grading system.
   b. Select types of evaluation measures.
   c. Determine how grades will be assigned.
   d. Address nonachievement outcomes.
   e. Communicate the grading system to students.
   f. Design a grade book.
   g. Report grades and communicate to parents.

2. **Assignments**
   a. Post assignments.
   b. State requirements and grading criteria for assignments.
   c. Make long-term assignments.

3. **Work and Completion Requirements**
   a. Identify work requirements.
      - Use of pencil or pen
      - Headings on papers
      - Writing on the back of the paper
      - Neatness and legibility guidelines
   b. Identify completion requirements.
      - Due dates
      - Late work
      - Incomplete work
      - Missed work
   c. Make provisions for absent students and makeup work.
      - Have an assignment list or folder.
      - Identify a due date.
      - Select a place to pick up and drop off absent assignments.
      - Provide a regular time to assist students with makeup work.

4. **Monitoring Progress and Completion of Assignments**
   a. Determine when and how to monitor in-class assignments.
   b. Determine when and how to monitor longer assignments, projects, and works in progress.
   c. Determine when and how to monitor in-class oral participation and performance.
   d. Determine which activities will receive a grade and which will be used only for formative feedback for the student.
   e. Select the checking procedures that will be used in class.
      - Students exchanging papers
      - Marking and grading papers
      - Turning in papers

5. **Providing Feedback**
   a. Decide what kind of feedback will be provided to students and when it will be provided.
   b. Determine what records students will keep concerning their progress.
   c. Select incentives and rewards.
   d. Record scores in the grade book.
   e. Post selected student work.

■ *Monitor student progress and completion of the assignments.* You may want to use some in-class activities as formative exercises for students but not count performance on these in your grading. The activities may be written, oral, or performance demonstrations. Student progress should be monitored. In many cases, the entire class is at work on the designated activity; this enables you to walk around and observe each student carefully to see how he or she is progressing.

■ *Provide students with feedback about their progress.* Feedback on in-class activities may take the form of statements to the individuals or to the class. Students may exchange papers to evaluate progress on formative exercises. Papers or projects that are to be part of the report card grade should be collected, graded, and returned promptly. In this way, students receive regular feedback about their progress throughout the marking period. Computer programs available for maintaining a grade book can easily generate progress reports for both students and teacher.

Managing Parts of the Lesson

You have finished your planning. You have selected the instructional strategies. You have prepared and gathered the instructional materials. Now it is the day of your lesson. You are all ready to begin, but wait. You also must recognize that you can take certain actions during your instruction that will have an effect on maintaining order in the classroom and on achieving the lesson objectives.

You can use a number of strategies at certain points in a lesson to effectively manage the group, maintain order and control, and fulfill various administrative and academic objectives. If these activities are not handled appropriately, students may be more inclined to be off task and possibly misbehave. As a result, it is important to examine these lesson delivery tasks from the perspective of management and order in the classroom.

BEGINNING OF A LESSON

A successful lesson beginning can greatly contribute to a meaningful learning experience for students. The beginning of a lesson should be designed to capture the students' interest and focus their attention on the learning objectives to be addressed during the lesson. An effective beginning can increase students' ability to focus on the objectives.

Actions you take at the start of a lesson help establish an atmosphere in which students have the "motivation to learn" (Brophy, 2010). **Motivation to learn** draws on the meaningfulness, value, and benefits of the academic task to the learner. For example, math problems may be developed that relate to student interests such as selling products for a youth-group fund-raiser. Thus, the focus is on learning, rather than on merely performing. Often students can be motivated at the beginning of a lesson by emphasizing the purpose of the task or the fact that students will be interested in the task.

Prior to beginning the substance of a lesson, take attendance and get attention. At the beginning of the lesson, your actions include providing daily review, providing a set induction, introducing lesson objectives, distributing and collecting materials, and giving clear, focused directions.

Taking Attendance. Elementary teachers in self-contained classrooms commonly take attendance first thing in the morning, whereas secondary teachers take attendance at the start of each class. Tardiness also must be noted, and teachers need to follow school policies when recording and responding to tardy students. It is helpful not to hold up the beginning of class to take attendance. You should plan an opening activity for students to do while you take attendance. Some teachers have the first daily activity posted on the board for the students to do while attendance is taken. Have a seating chart for each class; a substitute teacher will find this especially useful.

Getting Attention.

Students should understand that they are expected to give full attention to lessons at all times. A lesson should not begin until you gain their full attention. There should be a predictable, standard signal that tells the class "We are now ready to begin the lesson." The type of signal will vary with teacher preferences. For example, you can raise your hand, ring chimes or a bell, stand in a certain location, or make a statement. After giving the signal, pause briefly to allow it to take effect. Then when you have attention, move quickly into the lesson.

There are a number of ways to get attention at the beginning of a lesson. These approaches are designed to secure the students' attention and reduce distractions that might occur at the beginning of a lesson (Jones & Jones, 2010):

1. *Select a cue for getting students' attention.* Students often need a consistent cue to focus their attention. These cues may include a special phrase chosen by the class to indicate that you want immediate attention, or they may include a nonverbal cue such as closing the door at the beginning of class.

2. *Do not begin until everyone is paying attention.* It is important not to begin a lesson until all students are paying attention to the teacher. Teachers who begin lessons without the attention of all their students spend much more time repeating directions. Also, a teacher who begins a lesson in such a fashion is a poor role model, since it indicates that it is all right to talk while others are talking. Teachers sometimes just stand silent, waiting. Students soon get the message.

3. *Remove distractions.* Some students cannot screen out distracting stimuli. You can help remove distractions by closing the door, having the students remove unnecessary materials from the tops of their desks, adjusting the blinds, or taking other appropriate actions.

Providing Daily and Weekly Reviews.

A lesson can start with a brief review of previously covered material, correction of homework, and review of prior knowledge that is relevant to the day's lesson. The purpose of daily review is to determine if the students have obtained the necessary prerequisite knowledge or skills for the lesson. This review may last from three to eight minutes, and the length will vary according to the attention span of the learners and the nature of the content. Daily review is especially useful for teaching material that will be used in subsequent learning. Examples include math facts, math computation and factoring, grammar, chemical equations, and reading sight words.

You can conduct a daily review at the beginning of a lesson to provide additional practice and overlearning for previously learned material and to allow the teacher to provide corrections and reteaching in areas where students are having difficulty. Vary the methods for reviewing material.

Checking homework at the start of class is one form of review. Game formats, such as a trivia game, can be used as a means for review. You can conduct review through discussion, demonstration, questioning, written summaries, short quizzes, individualized approaches, and other methods of instruction. During reviews, students might answer questions at the whiteboard, in small groups, or as a whole class. Some additional techniques include asking questions about concepts or skills taught in the previous lesson, having students meet in small groups of two to four to review homework, and having students prepare questions about previous lessons or homework and ask them of each other or the teacher can ask them of the class.

In addition to daily review, the learning of new material is also enhanced by weekly and monthly reviews. Weekly reviews could occur each Monday, and monthly reviews every fourth Monday. These reviews provide additional checks by the teacher for student understanding, ensure that the necessary prior skills are adequately learned, and also check on the teacher's pace.

from the VOICES Classroom

CINDY BURKES, third-grade teacher, Las Vegas, Nevada

USING CLICKERS FOR DAILY REVIEW

We use a classroom performance system (CPS) for a variety of purposes, including daily review. This system enables me to enter a series of questions into a Power-Point presentation, and it includes a handheld "clicker" (like a remote control) for each student to record their answers to these questions. On my computer screen, I can immediately see the results for each question and each student.

I begin each day with "The Daily Four," which are two review questions and two preview questions that students answer using their clickers. The instant feedback on student performance provided by the clickers helps me determine if remediation is needed or if future lessons can be pared down, thereby eliminating the need for in-depth lessons when a quick overview will be sufficient.

URBAN EDUCATION

Establishing Set. **Set induction** is the initial activity at the beginning of the lesson that is used to induce students to a state of wanting to learn. This activity helps establish the context for the learning that is to follow and helps students engage in the learning. Typically, the set is brief, lasting only long enough to develop student readiness to accomplish the lesson's objective. Set induction helps students see what the topic of the lesson is in a way that is related to their own interests and their own lives. Madeline Hunter (1994) used the term **anticipatory set** to describe this concept, pointing out that the activity is intended to develop a mental readiness (or "set") for the lesson.

For example, a health lesson on the topic of first aid might begin with the reading of a newspaper report about a recent fire or accident. After reading the article, you could ask the students what they would do if they were the first ones to arrive after the accident. A number of ideas are likely to be generated in this discussion. Then you could bring that opening discussion to a close by saying that today's lesson will be about that exact topic— what type of first aid to administer for various conditions. Then you would move into the first part of the lesson. This set induction activity helps create interest in the lesson in a way that students can relate to their own lives.

Effective set induction activities should meet several criteria:

1. *Get the student interested in what is to be taught during the lesson.* This is referred to as an *initiating activity.* For example, you might begin a lesson on creative writing by turning off the lights in the room and explaining to the students that you will take them on an adventure to a distant planet. As the room remains dark, they are to imagine their trip into outer space.

2. *The set induction activity must be connected to the lesson.* An activity that is designed to get the students' attention but is not connected to the lesson does not meet this criterion.

3. *Students must understand the material and/or activity.* The information contained in the initiating activity must be stated in a clear manner so students will not only understand the activity but also know how it is connected to later content. Later, the set induction activity can be referred to while teaching the lesson.

4. *The set induction and the content of the lesson should be related to the students' lives or a previous lesson.* Students will be more interested in a lesson if they can relate the material to their own lives. For example, a lesson at the secondary level in measurement can include measuring ingredients to bake a cake or some other practical application. At the elementary level, a lesson in division can be related to determining baseball batting averages. Also, you can reduce anxiety by relating the lesson to material already learned by the students.

Introducing Lesson Objectives. At the start of a lesson, you should clearly describe its purpose. In addition, it is helpful to discuss the activities and evaluation process; these procedures help reduce student anxiety about the lesson. At the beginning, some teachers will clearly explain the objectives, the activities, and evaluation procedures to be used; others will write these elements on the board for the students or wait for an appropriate point in the lesson, such as after the set induction.

By using set-induction activities and introducing lesson objectives, you provide students with an **advance organizer** that supplies a framework for the new content and helps the students relate it to content they already know. Advance organizers, discussed more fully in Chapter 7, help students by focusing their attention on the subject being considered, informing them where the lesson is going, relating new material to content already understood, and providing structure for the subsequent lesson.

Distributing and Collecting Materials. Teachers often need to distribute materials to students. Students' maturity should be considered when determining the most appropriate time and way to distribute materials. Handouts, maps, and student guides can be distributed at the beginning of class to focus student attention on important material and to avoid disruptions during the lesson. Materials can be handed to students as they enter the room to save time during the lesson. You may prefer to distribute materials at the point in the lesson when they are actually needed.

Materials should be strategically located in the classroom to provide easy distribution and to minimize disruptions. For example, resource books that are used often should be located where there is sufficient room when they are needed. Procedures should be established for their distribution. You may have one row of students at a time get the resource books, have one student in each row get enough copies for that row, have students pick up a copy as soon as they enter the room, or give students copies as they enter the room.

VOICES from the Classroom

JOANN SNOOK, high school English/language arts teacher, Allentown, New Jersey

WEEKLY REVIEWS INVOLVING TEAM COMPETITION

Teachers sometimes disagree about whether cooperation or competition is most appropriate for the classroom. I think both can be used successfully. For example, offering team games is a way to foster cooperation among teammates as well as friendly competition between teams.

In my classroom, one of the vocabulary review activities each week is a team competition. We play Vocabulary Poker, Vocabulary Scrabble, Vocabulary Jenga, Synonym Smack-Down, Vocabulary Taboo, and a host of others. The games add interest, build unity, and encourage everyone to come prepared for hard team play. Sections of the weekly vocabulary quiz are modeled after the SAT, but other sections are modeled after the game we used that week for review.

Some materials that are distributed need to be collected later in the lesson, and appropriate ways to collect these materials should be selected. The manner of collecting the materials may be the same as or different from the way they were distributed.

Giving Clear, Focused Directions. To give clear and focused directions, you first must carefully plan them. Directions are often given at the beginning of a lesson; of course, directions may also be needed for activities throughout a lesson.

When planning for directions, you should (1) have no more than three student actions that are required for the activity to be described; (2) describe the directions in the order that students will be required to complete the tasks; (3) clarify what type and quality of product is expected; (4) make the description of each step specific and fairly brief; (5) provide written (on a whiteboard, a projection screen, or a handout) and oral directions; (6) give the directions just before the activity; and (7) make provisions for assisting students who have difficulty.

When actually giving directions, you need to (1) get student attention, (2) give the directions, (3) check to see if students understand the directions ("Do you have any questions about what you need to do?"), (4) have the students begin the tasks, and (5) remediate if necessary when one or more students are not following directions. Clearly state what books and materials are needed.

It is often helpful to demonstrate the actions expected of the students by doing one problem or activity together. Students then see what is expected of them before they begin to work independently. Once students begin work, you should walk around to observe them to see if they are following the directions and to be available to answer student questions. If many questions arise, it may be useful to gain everyone's attention for further explanation.

MIDDLE OF A LESSON

A number of teacher behaviors during lesson delivery contribute to effective group management. These include pacing the lesson, providing smooth transitions, having a task orientation, ensuring academic learning time, being clear, and exhibiting enthusiasm.

Pacing the Lesson. Pacing is the speed at which a lesson proceeds. It is the rhythm, the ebb and flow, of a lesson. Effective pacing is neither too slow nor too fast. Adjustments in the pace of the lesson are made as needed. To effectively pace a lesson, you should give directions without dwelling on them, distribute papers in a timely and efficient manner, and move from one activity to another smoothly and without interruption. Classrooms that lack effective pacing will drag at times or will move along at a pace where the students are unable to grasp the material. However, you should recognize it takes more time for students to mentally and physically transition from one activity to another than it does the teacher.

The following guidelines can be followed to effectively pace a lesson (Good & Brophy, 2008; Jones & Jones, 2010):

1. *Develop awareness of your own teaching tempo.* As you gain more experience in the classroom, you will become more aware of your own personal pace in the classroom. A good means of determining your pace is to audio or videotape your performance. In this way, you will be able to determine how fast you talk, how you move around the classroom, or how much wait time you provide your students.

2. *Watch for nonverbal cues indicating that students are becoming puzzled or bored.* Monitor student attentiveness, and then modify the pacing of the lesson as needed. If high-achieving students are looking puzzled, they and perhaps most of the class may be lost. The content may be too complex or being covered too quickly. A good indication that your pacing is too slow is if students are becoming restless and inattentive—looking out the window or fiddling with materials on their desks.

3. *Break activities up into short segments.* Many teachers go through an entire activity before beginning discussion or review. However, it is more effective to break the activities up into shorter segments and to ask questions or review these shorter segments rather than the entire activity.

4. *Provide short breaks for lessons that last longer than 30 minutes.* Long lessons can cause inattentiveness and disruptive behavior. A three- to five-minute break can allow the students to return fresh to the activity. These breaks can be short games related to the activity or a stand-up-and-stretch break. A brief activity that allows students to get up to mingle can also provide this break.

5. *Vary the style as well as the content of the instruction.* Students often become restless with only a single instructional approach. A lesson plan that incorporates several instructional strategies will result in better attentiveness.

6. *Avoid interrupting the flow of the lesson with numerous stops and starts.* **Jerkiness** is a term that refers to behaviors that interfere with the smooth flow of the lesson. This occurs when the teacher (a) interrupts an ongoing activity without warning and gives directions to begin another activity, (b) leaves one activity dangling in midair and begins another, only to return to the first, or (c) leaves one activity for another and never returns to the first activity.

7. *Avoid slowdowns that interfere with the pace of the lesson.* **Slowdowns**, or delays in the momentum or pace of a class, can occur due to overdwelling or fragmentation. **Overdwelling** occurs when teachers spend too much time on directions or explanations. Overdwelling also occurs when the teacher becomes so enthralled with the details of the lesson or a prop being used for a demonstration that students lose sight of the main idea. For example, an English teacher may get so carried away describing the details of an author's life that the students barely have time to read the author's works. Another example is the science teacher who gets carried away describing the laboratory equipment so that the students have little time to conduct any experiments.

Fragmentation is another form of slowdown in which the teacher divides the lesson into such minute fragments that some of the students are left waiting and become bored. For example, the directions for an experiment may be broken down into such minute, simple parts that the students feel belittled by the teacher, or an activity may be done by one row of students at a time, leaving many students waiting.

8. *Provide a summary at the end of a lesson segment.* Rather than plan for a single summary at the end of a lesson, it might help the pacing of the lesson to summarize after each main point or activity. For example, students might be asked to write a one-sentence summary of each scene as the class reads a play orally.

Providing Smooth Transitions. **Transitions** are movements from one activity to another. A smooth transition allows one activity to flow into another without any breaks in the delivery of the lesson. Transitions that are not smooth create gaps in the delivery of the lesson.

Transition times can occur when (1) students remain at their seats and change from one subject to another, (2) students move from their seats to an activity in another part of the classroom, (3) students move from somewhere else in the classroom back to their seats, (4) students leave the classroom to go outside or to another part of the school building, or (5) students come back into the classroom from outside or another part of the building.

To reduce the potential for disorder during transitions, you should prepare students for upcoming transitions, establish efficient transition routines, and clearly define the boundaries of lessons. Jones and Jones (2010) offer several suggestions for effective transitions:

1. *Arrange the classroom for efficient movement.* Arrange the classroom so you and the students can move freely without disturbing those who are working.

2. *Create and post a daily schedule, and discuss any changes each morning.* Posting a daily schedule will aid in the elimination of confusion in the students.

CARLA ROMAN, kindergarten teacher (National Board Certified Teacher), Miami, Florida

TRANSITIONS BETWEEN ACTIVITIES

After providing whole-class instruction, I often ask students to work in small groups. I have found it is useful to provide a break from their small-group work when they are getting tired or having trouble staying focused on what they are doing.

Providing a break as a transition to another activity can take many forms. Sometimes, it may be just some time to rest. Other times, it may involve singing and asking the students to do certain actions. In this way, they are provided a "break" from what they are currently doing, and to them it seems like a game. Actually it provides an opportunity to listen and to follow directions, and students are more ready to get back on task for the next activity.

URBAN EDUCATION

3. *Have material ready for the next lesson.* Teachers need to prepare and gather materials for the next lesson to ensure that class time is not taken and that activities flow smoothly.

4. *Do not relinquish students' attention until you have given clear instructions for the following activity.* All too often, teachers allow the class to become disruptive while they pause between activities or lessons to prepare for the next lesson. It requires considerable time and energy to regain students' attention.

5. *Do not do tasks that can be done by students.* Have students take responsibility for their own preparations for the next class session. This will enable you to monitor student actions.

6. *Move around the room and attend to individual needs.* By moving around the room, you will be able to notice any minor disturbances that might expand into major problems.

7. *Provide students with simple, step-by-step directions.* Clearly state exactly what you want your students to do during the time given for the transition.

8. *Remind students of key procedures associated with the upcoming lesson.* Reviewing standard procedures and discussing unique procedures for an upcoming activity helps promote smooth transitions because students know what is expected of them.

9. *Develop transition activities.* After lunch or physical education, for example, students are excited and may not be ready for quieter work. Given this, you should choose structured transition activities to prepare the student for the next class session. These might include reading to students, discussing the daily schedule, having students write in a journal, or some type of activity that may not necessarily deal with the content of the next class session. After this transition time, students will likely be more ready to begin the next class session.

Being Task Oriented. **Task orientation** has to do with your concern that all relevant material be covered and learned, as opposed to your being mired in procedural matters or extraneous material. Task-oriented teachers spend an appropriate amount of time lecturing, asking questions, and engaging students in activities directly related to the material that is to be learned. Achievement is reported to be higher in classrooms of task-oriented teachers than in classrooms where teachers tend to be off task.

Task-oriented teachers are goal oriented, and they plan instructional strategies and activities that support these goals. In addition, task-oriented teachers have a high but realistic set of expectations for their students. To be task oriented in the classroom, you should (1) develop unit and lesson plans that reflect the curriculum; (2) handle administrative and clerical interruptions efficiently; (3) stop or prevent misbehavior with a minimum of class disruption; (4) select the most appropriate instructional model for objectives being taught; and (5) establish cycles of review, feedback, and testing.

Ensuring Academic Learning Time.

Academic learning time is the amount of time students are successfully engaged in learning activities. However, the amount of time that students are actively engaged, or on task, can vary greatly across and within classrooms. Low-achieving students often go off task due to frustrations about not understanding class material. High-achieving students, on the other hand, tend to go off task after they have completed their assigned work. Therefore, you should ensure that all students are able to successfully engage in classroom tasks while also ensuring that high-achieving students are engaged throughout the lesson. Provide feedback and correctives to students who need assistance, and at the same time, monitor the rate of students' progress through the lesson.

For new material that students have not yet mastered, expect a lower success rate initially but set a goal of higher success rates as students receive feedback on their performance and gain confidence. As a general rule, students should have a success rate of approximately 80 percent on most initial tasks. The rate of success should be somewhat higher when students are engaged in independent work, such as homework and independent seatwork. The goal is to ensure that students are given meaningful tasks to complete, are given feedback and correctives when needed, and are ultimately able to successfully complete all assigned tasks.

Being Clear.

Clarity refers to the precision of your communication to your students regarding the desired behavior. Clarity in teaching helps students understand better, work more accurately, and be more successful. Effective teachers exhibit a high degree of clarity by providing very clear and explicit directions, instructions, questions, and expectations. If you are constantly asked to repeat questions, directions, and explanations or if your students do not understand your expectations, you are not exhibiting clarity in your instructional behavior.

Clear directions, instructions, and expectations ensure that students know what is expected of them and can act accordingly as they work on classroom activities, assignments, and other tasks. If you are not very clear when giving directions, for example, students may not complete the assignment in the way you intended, may become confused, and may need additional time and attention to later complete the assignment in the manner intended.

To be clear in the classroom, (1) inform the learners of the objective; (2) provide learners with advance organizers; (3) check for task-relevant prior learning and reteach, if necessary; (4) give directions slowly and distinctly; (5) know the ability levels of students and teach to those levels; (6) use examples, illustrations, and demonstrations to explain and clarify; and (7) provide a review or summary at the end of each lesson (Borich, 2011).

Exhibiting Enthusiasm.

Enthusiasm is an expression of excitement and intensity. It is quite obvious that a teacher who is enthusiastic and vibrant is more entertaining to observe than an unenthusiastic teacher. In addition, teacher enthusiasm has been related to higher student achievement (Good & Brophy, 2008). Enthusiasm has two important dimensions: (1) interest and involvement with the subject matter and (2) vigor and physical dynamism. Enthusiastic teachers are often described as stimulating, dynamic, expressive, and energetic. Their behavior suggests that they are committed to the students and to the subject matter. While teachers often expect students to be interested in *what* they say, students more often react to *how* enthusiastically it is said.

Enthusiasm can be conveyed in a variety of ways. These include the use of animated gestures, eye contact, voice inflection, and movement around the room. A teacher who is enthusiastic in the classroom often manages to develop enthusiastic students. Constant, highly enthusiastic actions are not necessary and in fact may be counterproductive. Instead, a variety of enthusiastic actions, ranging from low to high degrees of enthusiasm, is appropriate.

ENDING OF A LESSON

As stated earlier, an effective lesson has three important sections: a beginning, a middle, and an end. All three sections must be planned and implemented effectively if a lesson is to be successful. Simply ending a lesson when the bell rings or when you have covered the planned material is not appropriate. In such cases, students are not given the opportunity to place the lesson in a context with other related lessons or are not permitted to ask questions that might clarify a misunderstood point from the lesson. Providing a summary is imperative for a successful lesson. Furthermore, students need time at the end of the lesson to get ready to leave the classroom.

Providing Closure to Part of a Lesson. Closure refers to actions or statements that are designed to bring a lesson presentation to an appropriate conclusion (Shostak, 2011). There are three major purposes for closure:

1. *Draw attention to the end of a lesson segment or the lesson itself.* Often students need to be cued that they have arrived at an important segment of the lesson or that it is time to wrap things up. They might be cued with a statement that it is time to summarize key concepts.

2. *Help organize student learning.* It is the teacher's responsibility to relate the many pieces of the lesson to the whole. Some students are able to do this by themselves while others need the teacher's assistance. To accomplish this purpose, you might provide a diagram, illustration, outline, or other type of summary that indicates how all the content of the lesson is related.

3. *Consolidate or reinforce the major points.* You might emphasize or highlight certain concepts at this point. The major objective is to help the student retain the information presented in the lesson for future use.

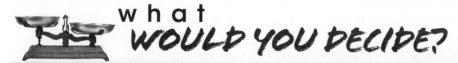

what WOULD YOU DECIDE?

PROVIDING CLOSURE

Let's assume that you are teaching a history lesson in which a series of significant dates has been identified and related events have been discussed.

1. How might you bring closure to this part of the lesson in a way that helps students see how all the dates and events are related?

2. How might you involve students in this closure?

3. How might you take into account students' varied learning styles?

Closure is important because students instinctively structure information into patterns that make sense to them. If a learning experience is left with some uncertainties, students may draw inaccurate conclusions as they create their own patterns of understanding from the material, thus detracting from future learning. The second and third purposes involve summarizing, which is addressed later. The time at the end of a lesson segment or the lesson itself can be used to make homework assignments. Between lesson segments, students may be given 5 to 10 minutes to start the homework assignment while you move around the room to answer questions that might arise.

Summarizing the Lesson. Providing a **summary** of the main points of a lesson can help students to gain a better idea of the content or to clarify any misunderstandings. You should plan to stop the lesson several minutes before the bell rings to begin the summation. Make sure that you have the attention of all students before the summary begins. You should avoid merely reiterating the content covered during the lesson. Ask several questions that encourage the students to relate key aspects of the lesson or to evaluate key points. Also, you can ask students for their opinions about what they believe are the key points of the lesson.

To add interest and variety, vary the way that you conduct lesson summaries. Some days you might pose a simple series of questions for students. On other days, you might want to ask several students to go to the whiteboard to solve a problem and discuss the thought process involved. A game format can be used as a means of summary, such as questions out of a hat or a Trivial Pursuit type of approach. Several creative approaches could offer the desired variety of lesson summaries.

The summary should be used to determine whether the students have grasped the main ideas of the lesson. For example, your summary might discover that several students do not understand the key concepts of a math lesson. It would be foolish to teach the next math lesson as though students understood the concept. Therefore, you can use the information gathered during the summary to adjust the next day's lesson plan.

Getting Ready to Leave. At the end of the lesson, middle, junior high, or senior high school students usually need to leave the classroom and go to their next class. The bell will ring at the end of the class period, and students will have just a few minutes to get to their next class in another room in the building.

You should plan to complete all instruction and lesson summary by the end of the class period so students are not delayed in moving to the next class. You should not teach right up to the bell, because time needs to be allowed for several other events. First, you must allow time for students to return any books, supplies, or materials to the appropriate locations. Also, students need time to throw away any scrap paper and to straighten up the classroom. They need time to put away their own books, papers, pencils, or other materials before leaving. You may plan to reserve from one to four minutes at the end of a lesson to allow sufficient time for these final actions to be completed before the bell rings. Students then should be dismissed on time. You need to schedule this time when planning lessons.

Managing Student Work

Students prepare homework and seatwork as a regular part of their instruction. To effectively manage this student work, guidelines are offered here for managing seatwork effectively, collecting assignments and monitoring their completion, maintaining records of student work, managing paperwork, and giving students feedback. It is helpful to develop a plan to organize your instructional records, grading and assessment records, classroom management records, parental contact records, and special needs and accommodation records (Mierzwik, 2005).

EFFECTIVELY MANAGING SEATWORK

Seatwork involves students working on assignments during class that provide practice or review of previously presented material. Students spend hundreds of hours during a school year doing seatwork privately at their desks. It is imperative that you structure seatwork so that it is done effectively while enabling students to experience a high rate of success.

Guidelines for successfully implementing seatwork in the classroom come from a variety of sources (Jones & Jones, 2010; Rosenshine & Stevens, 1986; Weinstein, 2011; Weinstein & Mignano, 2011). The following 12 recommendations represent a synthesis from these sources:

1. Recognize that seatwork is intended to practice or review previously presented material. It is not suited for students to learn new material.

2. Devote no more time to seatwork than is allocated to content development activities.

3. Give clear instruction—explanations, questions, and feedback—and sufficient practice before the students begin their seatwork. Having to provide lengthy explanations during seatwork is troublesome for both you and the students. In addition to procedural directions, explain why the activities are being done and how to do the seatwork.

4. Work through the first few problems of the seatwork together with the students before having them continue independently. This provides a model for completing the work and provides an opportunity for the students to ask questions for clarification about the content or procedures.

5. Decide if you will allow talking during seatwork. It is often desirable to start out with no talking during seatwork and to have students work alone. After a month or two, teachers sometimes allow students to talk quietly with others to seek or provide help. Clarify when quiet talking is allowed.

6. Circulate from student to student during seatwork, actively explaining, observing, asking questions, and giving feedback. Monitoring students to provide this positive and corrective feedback is very important.

7. Determine how students will seek your help. When students are working at their seats and need help, ask them to raise their hands. You can then go to them or signal them to come to you at an appropriate time.

8. Determine when students can get out of their seats. To eliminate unnecessary wandering around the room during seatwork, decide when and for what purpose students may get out of their seats. For example, students may get supplies, sharpen pencils, or turn in papers only when necessary.

9. Have short contacts with individual students (i.e., 30 seconds or less).

10. Break seatwork into short segments, rather than plan one long time slot. Rather than having one lengthy presentation of content followed by an extended period of seatwork, break up instruction into a number of segments followed by brief seatwork after each segment.

11. Arrange seats to facilitate monitoring the students (e.g., face both small groups and independently working students).

12. Establish a routine to use during seatwork activity that prescribes what students will do when they have completed the exercises. Students may complete an additional enrichment assignment for extra credit, or they may use the time for free reading or to work on assignments from other classes.

MANAGING LESSON DELIVERY

Logan Reynolds's 12th-grade English class just finished reading George Orwell's *1984*, one of his favorite books to teach. The students participated in panel discussions and debates, and the desks were arranged in a circle to promote discussion. Mr. Reynolds encouraged lively conversations by asking probing questions and engaged his students in role-playing and simulation activities. His animated nature during class discussions motivated the students to become actively involved. Students also responded to a number of journal prompts at the beginning of each class session just prior to discussion. These prompts required students to reflect on the underlying ideas presented in their readings and to make connections to present-day concerns.

The class next moved to a unit on Shakespeare. Although Mr. Reynolds was not particularly interested in the works of Shakespeare, he understood the importance of introducing his class to classics such as *Macbeth*. Since Mr. Reynolds was concerned about the complexity of Shakespeare's works, he decided that lecturing about the material was the best way to promote student learn-

ing, and the desks were put into rows for this approach. As a result, student interactions were minimal, with no room for debate, role playing, and simulation games. Mr. Reynolds felt those activities would only complicate study of an already obscure literary subject. Mr. Reynolds conducted all of his class meetings in a similar fashion, asking students to read a certain number of pages for homework and be prepared for the lectures, with only brief opportunities for discussion. Mr. Reynolds became concerned when his students were not very engaged in the brief class discussions and seemed to lose focus and interest.

FOCUS QUESTIONS

1. What factors contributed to the high level of student involvement in the unit on *1984*? To the low level of student involvement in the unit on Shakespeare?

2. Based on what you know about managing lesson delivery and other instructional factors, what suggestions do you have for Mr. Reynolds when teaching the unit on Shakespeare?

COLLECTING ASSIGNMENTS AND MONITORING THEIR COMPLETION

Whether it is homework or seatwork, you need to establish a process for collecting assignments and monitoring their completion:

- *Institute a regular procedure for collecting assignments.* Papers can be collected during class by asking students to pass them in a given direction until you have all papers in your hands. As an alternative, students may be asked to place their completed assignments in certain basket, tray, or drop box at a designated time during class. Once students know this collection procedure, assignments can be gathered quickly and efficiently.

- *Have a procedure for grouping papers by subject or class session.* In an elementary classroom, assignments on a variety of subjects may be submitted during the day. It is useful to have a separate drop box for each subject. In this way, only papers of a certain subject are in a drop box, and you do not need to spend time sorting through all the papers to pick out just the math papers or just the social studies papers. Similarly, middle and secondary classrooms should have a different drop box for each class period. Thus, students in the fourth hour would place their assignments in the box for their class period.

- *Keep a record of whose papers have been turned in.* If you evaluate the papers quickly, you will know who has or has not submitted the assignments when you record the grades in your grade book. If there is a delay in grading, you may have a checklist to record who has submitted the assignments. In this way, you can follow up with students who did not submit the materials. Some teachers also have students keep an assignment notebook for homework and seatwork to record the items that were due and what was turned in.

MAINTAINING RECORDS OF STUDENT WORK

Records of student progress and completion are entered in your grade book. For elementary classes, you may organize your grade book by having a separate section for each subject area. The date and description of the assignment can be entered at the top as a subject heading, and each student's scores can be placed in the appropriate column on the line for his or her name. Similarly, middle-level and secondary teachers can have separate sections of the grade book for each of their class sections. It is useful to establish a coding system to indicate a student absence or other information related to the assignment. Grade book software can be used to record the submission of assignments and the scores students receive. Progress reports for individual students can be easily prepared, and these are useful to show the students and parents.

MANAGING PAPERWORK

Homework and seatwork involve a lot of paperwork, and it is easy to become overwhelmed by the volume of papers you deal with on a regular basis. Here are some guidelines to effectively manage your handling of the papers:

- *Assess, record, and return assignments quickly.* Make a commitment to assess and return all assignments in a day or two. Delays in your return of assignments often lead to a backlog of assignments to be graded. That situation puts a lot of pressure on you, and it is not fair to the students because they need to receive feedback as quickly as possible.

- *Be realistic about your grading capabilities.* Plan sufficient time in your schedule to assess and record the assignments. If you are making frequent assignments and getting behind in the grading, it is time to reassess your use of assignments. Strategically space out the assignments that are to be graded. Long assignments take time to assess. The use of short and specific assignments may be effective in monitoring student learning, and they take less time to assess.

- *Recognize that every seatwork assignment does not need to have a grade.* Every subject or every class period does not need an assignment that must be graded by you every day. Therefore, you do not need to receive papers each day. Students can be assessed in class and given feedback in various ways without asking them to submit the paperwork to you to be assessed. For example, you can assign seatwork and then check each student's work and give feedback during class.

- *Institute a system for coding the papers for each subject or class section.* As mentioned previously, have a system for collecting assignments from your students. Using color-coded folders for each subject or class period can be a helpful technique for organizing the paperwork.

- *Have a predetermined way to return papers to the students.* When returning papers to students, keep them in labeled folders by the subject or class period. You could organize the papers by rows or groups to facilitate the return. Plan a certain way to return the papers each time. You may choose to use student helpers in returning the papers.

GIVING STUDENTS FEEDBACK

You will assign seatwork and homework to help students learn, and it is important that students receive feedback about this work. Follow these guidelines for giving students feedback:

- *Provide frequent and regular feedback.* Students need fairly immediate feedback about their performance so they have an opportunity to correct any errors in their knowledge or skills before moving ahead to new material. Thus, plan for ways for students to demonstrate their learning and for ways that you can provide frequent and regular feedback about their learning.

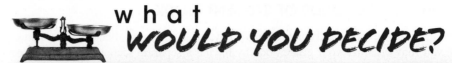

GIVING STUDENTS FEEDBACK

You regularly use seatwork in your classroom, and you provide prompt feedback. However, three students often have difficulty with the seatwork and need more feedback and guidance.

1. What are some ways that you can provide these students with the extra feedback that they need?

2. How might you use other students in the class to provide this needed guidance and feedback?

■ *Develop ways to provide feedback to students in class.* To provide prompt feedback and to avoid assigning homework every day, develop ways to provide feedback to students after instruction and practice have taken place in class. For example, you could have students work on problems at the board and give feedback, show answers on an overhead screen, or have students help review each other's work.

■ *Take prompt corrective actions with students who do not perform well.* Don't wait until several poor assignments have been turned in or until it is time to submit the report card grade before meeting with a student who is not performing well. Some students may need more assistance to learn the content, and this feedback and assistance should come early and without delay.

Managing Whole-Group Instruction

In his widely respected book *Discipline and Group Management in Classrooms* (1970), Jacob Kounin reported how instructional techniques contribute to classroom management. The implications from his research can be organized into three areas: preventing misbehavior, managing movement through the lesson, and maintaining group focus. Suggestions are also provided for ways to maintain student attention and involvement.

PREVENTING MISBEHAVIOR

When approaching whole-group instruction, teachers can take a number of actions, based on Kounin's work, to prevent misbehavior:

1. *Exhibit withitness.* Jacob Kounin (1970) is considered the first researcher to systematically study the characteristics of effective classroom managers. He coined the term *withitness* to describe a teacher's disposition (or mental set) to look at all parts of the classroom at all times, notice who is misbehaving, and respond to the misbehavior in an appropriate and prompt manner (see Chapter 1). Systematic and periodic monitoring of each student in the class is a key part of withitness, because it will help prevent misbehavior from occurring.

2. *Use overlapping.* **Overlapping** refers to teachers supervising or handling more than one group or activity at a time. For example, a teacher working with one group of students can notice and simultaneously address a behavior incident in another part of the classroom.

Teachers who are skilled at overlapping are more aware of what is going on; thus, they have good withitness as well. As a result, teachers who overlap can effectively monitor classroom behavior and intervene when needed to keep students on task. When students know their teacher has withitness and is able to overlap, they are less inclined to get off task.

3. *Use desists.* **Desists** are statements by teachers to stop an inappropriate action or a misbehavior by asking or telling a student what to do. To be effective, desist statements should be specific and spoken clearly. A desist might be in the form of an appeal, such as "Shanae, please put away the comb and continue with the class assignment." Or it could be in the form of a command, such as "Wayne, stop talking with your friends and continue with your calculations in the lab activity." Effective use of desists helps keep students on task and minimizes disorder and misbehavior.

4. *Avoid satiation.* **Satiation** occurs when a teacher asks the students to stay on a learning task too long and the students begin to lose interest and get off task. For example, students may enjoy seeing a DVD, writing a creative story, or working in pairs on a project. When these activities are used too often or for too much time, however, students will start to lose interest, become bored, and likely get off task. Satiation can be minimized by (a) highlighting progress toward a learning goal and providing students with feedback; (b) providing variety in the content, group structure, level of difficulty, and instructional materials and activities; and (c) offering a challenging activity to promote a greater sense of purpose and accomplishment.

MANAGING MOVEMENT THROUGH THE LESSON

To minimize misbehavior and to promote learning, teachers need to have the lesson progress at a reasonable pace and avoid letting the lesson go astray with abrupt changes or shifts. Kounin (1970) described the movement of the lesson in terms of momentum and smoothness, as described here:

1. *Momentum.* **Momentum** refers to teachers starting lessons with dispatch, keeping lessons moving ahead, making transitions among activities efficiently, and bringing lessons to a satisfactory close. Momentum deals primarily with the pacing of the lesson, and the teacher needs to avoid slowdowns in the progression through the lesson. For example, one problem in momentum is jerkiness, when the teacher fails to develop a consistent flow of instruction, going too fast at some times and too slow at others.

2. *Smoothness.* **Smoothness** refers to staying on task in the lesson without abrupt changes, digressions, or divergences. Kounin described several problems when trying to maintain a smooth, continuous flow of activities throughout a lesson. Some of these problems include shifting from one topic to another, shifting back to earlier activities or content, and injecting unrelated information into a lesson.

what WOULD YOU DECIDE?

HAVING SMOOTH TRANSITIONS

Assume that you have planned a lesson in which your students viewed a videotape, then had small-group discussions about the videotape, and finally individually outlined some content and answered some questions from the textbook.

1. What arrangements would you need to make to ensure smooth transitions throughout the lesson?

2. How might the directions that you select for the lesson promote smooth transitions?

MAINTAINING A GROUP FOCUS

Group focus occurs when a teacher makes a conscious effort to keep the attention of all students at all times. When this occurs, the teacher maintains efficient classroom control and reduces student misbehavior (Kounin, 1970). Group focus includes group alerting, group accountability, and high-participation formats:

1. *Use group alerting.* **Group alerting** refers to taking actions to engage the attention of the whole class when only individuals are responding. This includes a teacher's attempts to involve all students in learning tasks, maintain their attention, and keep them "on their toes." With group alerting, teachers create suspense before calling on a student to answer a question, keep students in suspense regarding who will be called on next, call on different students to answer questions, and alert nonperformers that they might be called upon next.

2. *Maintain group accountability.* **Group accountability** takes place when a teacher lets students know that their performance in class will be observed and evaluated in some manner. This assessment does not necessarily mean a grade will be recorded, only that the students' performance will be gauged. For example, the teacher might use record-keeping devices such as checklists and task cards. Other strategies include asking students to raise their hands in response to certain questions, asking students to take notes and then checking them, and asking students to write answers and then use various techniques to check them during the class session. Student misbehavior decreases when students know that they are held accountable for their learning and behavior and the teacher knows each student's progress.

3. *Use high-participation formats.* **High-participation formats** are lessons that have all students performing in some way, even though they may not be involved in answering a teacher's question. High-participation formats occur when each student is expected to manipulate materials, solve problems, read along, write answers, or perform a concurrent task. In this way, students do not simply sit when others are answering questions; they are actively engaged as well.

MAINTAINING STUDENT ATTENTION AND INVOLVEMENT

To manage a group of students effectively, you need to capture and hold student attention and encourage ongoing involvement. **Attention** means focusing certain stimuli while screening out others. General guidelines and specific techniques for maintaining student attention and involvement are offered here (Eggen & Kauchak, 2010; Good & Brophy, 2008; Jones & Jones, 2010):

1. *Use attention-getting strategies.* You can use certain strategies to capture students' attention at the start of a lesson and throughout the lesson. Overuse of any one approach, however, reduces its ability to arouse and maintain attention. These strategies include the use of stories, physical products, activities, and statements.

2. *Monitor attention during lessons and provide situational assistance as necessary.* Students are much more likely to pay attention if they know you regularly watch them, both to see if they are paying attention and to note signs of confusion or difficulty. Regularly scan the class or group throughout the lesson. When students show signs of losing interest or getting frustrated, you should provide **situational assistance**, which are teacher actions designed to help students cope with the instructional situation and to keep students on task. Situational assistance is discussed more fully in Chapter 10.

3. *Stimulate attention periodically.* Student attention wanders when instruction becomes predictable and repetitive. You can promote continual attention as a lesson or an activity progresses. You can stimulate attention by cueing students through transitional signals that a new section of the lesson is coming up. For example, you might say "We have

just spent the last 15 minutes considering what running water erosion is. Now let's look at the ways that farmers and other people try to stop this erosion." Or you can use challenging statements, such as "Now, here's a really difficult (or tricky or interesting) question. Let's see if you can figure it out."

4. *Vary instructional media and methods.* Repeated use of one approach to instruction will soon result in a classroom of bored students. Moreover, student achievement is increased when a variety of instructional materials and techniques are used (Good & Brophy, 2008). Use a variety of media such as PowerPoint presentations, whiteboards, DVDs, and a computer. Also use various teaching methods to solicit students' attention through the use of demonstrations, small and large groups, lectures, discussions, field trips, and the like. Not only does variability decrease boredom in students, but it also appeals to the different student learning styles.

5. *Use humor.* Students appreciate a certain amount of humor in the classroom, and it can help maintain students' attention. You may enjoy making silly statements or sharing funny experiences with your students. Be cautious that jokes are not used to tease or demean any student, even if expressed in a funny way, because the student may interpret these statements as being serious.

6. *Maintain individual accountability.* Students should be accountable for being involved in lessons and learning all of the material. It is helpful to ask a question or require the student periodically to make some kind of response. An unpredictable pattern in the way you handle questions or responses helps maintain individual accountability and causes students to be mentally engaged in the lesson and to be more attentive.

7. *Pay close attention when students* talk and answer questions. The use of active-listening skills often entails using nonverbal techniques that indicate that you are interested in what students are saying. If you do not give attention and show interest when students answer questions, you communicate to them that what they have to say is not very important, which in turn will discourage involvement. Nonverbal expressions of your interest include nodding, moving toward the student, leaning forward, maintaining eye contact with the student, and showing interest in your facial expression. Verbal expressions of interest include statements such as "Uh-huh," "I see," "That's a thoughtful answer," and "I appreciate your thorough, insightful answer."

8. *Reinforce students' efforts and maintain a high ratio of positive to negative verbal statements.* Students attend more fully if a positive learning environment has been created. One of the best means for accomplishing this is to respond positively to their efforts. Positive and encouraging statements are very important for all students. Make many

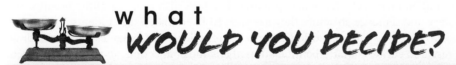

HOLDING STUDENTS ACCOUNTABLE

Let's assume that you are teaching a math lesson and that you are having five students complete sample problems at the whiteboard while the rest of the students remain in their seats.

1. For those who are still in their seats, how might you hold them academically accountable for the material?

2. How could you provide feedback to the students at the board as well as to those still in their seats?

3. How might the lack of a procedure for academic accountability in this setting contribute to a loss of order in the classroom?

more positive and encouraging statements than negative statements. Think about it from the students' point of view: Would you like to be in a classroom where you hear mostly negative statements or positive statements?

9. *Terminate lessons that have gone on too long.* When the group is having difficulty maintaining attention, it is better to end the lesson than to struggle through it. This is especially important for younger students whose attention spans are limited. Nevertheless, some teachers continue lessons to maintain a certain schedule. This can be counterproductive since students may not learn under certain conditions and in any case will have to be taught again. It is always helpful to give advance thought to a backup activity for each lesson. For example, you may select a different instructional technique for covering the same lesson objectives.

Applying the SIOP Model to Lesson Delivery

Meeting the needs of English language learners can be facilitated by the use of the SIOP model to provide more flexibility in the design and delivery of instruction. As outlined in Chapter 1, there are eight components of that model, and four components are related to lesson delivery: (1) comprehensible input, (2) interaction, (3) lesson delivery, and (4) review and assessment (Echevarria, Vogt, & Short, 2008). While these strategies were originally designed for use with ELLs, they are also helpful in meeting the needs of all learners in the classroom. The excellent content from Echevarria, Vogt, and Short (2008) serves as the foundation for much of the information in this section.

COMPREHENSIBLE INPUT

Information that is understandable to students is referred to as **comprehensible input** (Krashen, 1985). When working with ELLs, teachers need to make verbal communication more understandable by consciously attending to students' linguistic needs and consistently incorporating input techniques into their daily teaching routines:

1. *Speak appropriately for students' proficiency levels.* Students who are at the beginning level of English proficiency benefit when teachers slow down their rate of speech, use pauses, and enunciate clearly while speaking. Teachers also must carefully monitor the vocabulary and sentence structure they use with ELLs to match the students' proficiency levels. Paraphrasing and repetition are useful practices that enhance understanding. Brain research suggests that repetition strengthens the connections in the brain (Jensen, 2005, 2008). Teacher should use simple sentences with beginning students and reduce or eliminate embedded clauses.

2. *Provide clear explanations of academic tasks.* All learners perform better when the teacher gives clear instructions for assignments and activities. For ELLs, it is critical to have instructions presented in a step-by-step manner, preferably modeled or demonstrated. Sample completed projects can be shown to provide further clarity and guidance. Oral directions should be accompanied by written directions so learners can refer back to them.

3. *Use a variety of techniques to make concepts clear and understandable.* High-quality lessons offer students a variety of ways to access the content. With deliberate planning, teachers can incorporate many techniques and activities throughout the week's lessons. A variety of techniques can be achieved through modeling, visuals, hands-on activities, demonstrations, gestures, body language, graphic organizers, and many other approaches that match students' learning styles.

VOICES from the Classroom

CLAIRE LOVE, first-grade teacher, Virginia Beach, Virginia

COMPREHENSIBLE INPUT IN THE SIOP MODEL

I teach first grade in an inclusion setting with students from France, Mexico, and the Philippines. Since many of my students are English language learners, I deliberately attend to their linguistic needs and incorporate input techniques into my daily plans. Here are a few things I have done to help make the language more accessible to my students:

■ I have labeled the entire classroom with English words so that these students can familiarize themselves with how words look compared to how they sound.

■ I keep in contact with a Peace Corp volunteer in the Philippines who teaches us about life in the Philippines. We have sent each other PowerPoint presentations to share what our lives are like, and I use that information in class.

■ I use picture and vocabulary books with my ESL students' native language.

■ I have people who speak my ESL students' native language volunteer about once a week to help during independent center time. These volunteers are able to explain stories that we have read in class, or they can help with students' daily tasks.

URBAN EDUCATION

INTERACTION

Teachers must provide opportunities for students to actively engage with the subject matter. Teachers must avoid the tendency to dominate talk in the classroom and permit only limited time for discussion and interaction. The following strategies can be used to plan more deliberate opportunities for student interaction:

1. *Provide frequent opportunities for interaction and discussion.* Reading comprehension skills and writing skills are positively correlated with oral language proficiency in English (Geva, 2006). Thus, teachers need to offer students opportunities to develop these important oral language skills. Effective teachers structure their lessons in ways that promote student discussion, and they strive to provide a balanced exchange with students, rather than dominate talk. Effective teachers also encourage elaborated responses from students when discussing concepts, going beyond simple yes–no answers and short phrases. This can be done by using prompts such as "Tell me more about that" and "Why is that important?"

2. *Group students to support language and content objectives of the lesson.* All students, including ELLs, benefit from instruction that includes a variety of grouping configurations. Effective classrooms use a variety of grouping structures, including individual work, partners, triads, small groups of four or five, cooperative learning groups, and the whole group. Groups also may vary by being homogeneous or heterogeneous by gender, language proficiency, language background, and/or ability. Using a variety of grouping configurations also helps maintain student interest and increases the chance that a student's preferred mode of instruction will be matched.

3. *Consistently provide sufficient wait time for student responses.* Wait time refers to the length of time the teacher waits for students to respond before answering a question himself or herself or calling on someone else to participate. Effective teachers consciously allow students time to reply and to express their thoughts fully, without interruption. Providing sufficient wait time is especially pertinent with ELLs, who need extra time to process questions in English, think of an answer in their second language, and formulate their responses in English.

4. *Give ample opportunities for students to clarify key concepts in their first language.* The National Literacy Panel on Language-Minority Children and Youth found that teaching academic skills such as reading in the first language transfers to the second language (August & Shanahan, 2006). Some ELLs may need a concept or assignment explained or clarified in their first language. This may be accomplished with the assistance of a bilingual instructional aide or peer or by using materials written in the student's first language.

LESSON DELIVERY

Although a lesson may be well planned, lesson delivery can go astray if the activities take longer than expected, students do not participate in the expected manner, or a host of other factors occur. The following guidelines will help teachers stay on track in a lesson by identifying and supporting lesson objectives, engaging students in the lesson, and proceeding at an appropriate pace:

1. *Clearly support content objectives by lesson delivery.* Lesson objectives must be stated orally and displayed for students to see. Lesson objectives from professional standards, written in student-friendly terms, convey the purpose and direction for the lesson, provide a structure for classroom procedures, and help students stay on task.

2. *Clearly support language objectives by lesson delivery.* Language objectives are an important part of effective sheltered lessons, in which language development is supported. Teachers and students benefit from having a clear language objective written for them to see and review during the lesson. The language objective may relate to an aspect of reading, writing, speaking, or listening.

3. *Engage students during 90 to 100 percent of the lesson.* This means students are paying attention and on task 90 to 100 percent of the class period. This does not mean they need to be highly active in reading, writing, and moving the entire time. Rather, it means they are following the lesson, responding to teacher directions, and performing the activities as expected.

4. *Appropriately pace the lesson to the students' ability levels.* Pacing refers to the rate at which information is presented during a lesson. The pace depends on the nature of the lesson's content and the level of the students' background knowledge. Once teachers become familiar with their students, it becomes easier to determine an appropriate pace—one that does not present information too quickly yet is brisk enough to maintain students' interest.

REVIEW AND ASSESSMENT OF LESSON OBJECTIVES

Effective sheltered instruction involves reviewing important concepts, providing constructive feedback through clarification, and making instructional decisions based on students' responses. Reviewing and assessing take place throughout each lesson and again when the lesson is concluded. It is especially important for ELLs to receive this review and assessment to find out what is important and where they stand in their comprehension of the lesson:

1. *Provide comprehensive review of key vocabulary.* Language objectives should be identified in lesson plans, introduced to students at the beginning of the lesson, and reviewed throughout the lesson. Multiple exposures to new words also build familiarity, confidence, and English proficiency. The more times students encounter new words, the more likely they are to remember and use them. Key vocabulary words are reinforced if introduced and reviewed through multiple modalities.

2. *Supply comprehensive review of key content concepts.* Just as with key vocabulary, key content concepts must be reviewed for ELLs during and at the end of a lesson. Student learning is supported when teachers stop and briefly summarize, along with students' help, the key content covered to that point. This type of review is informal, but it must be carefully planned. It is important to link the review to the content objectives of the lesson so you and the students stay focused on essential content concepts.

3. *Provide regular feedback to students on their output.* By periodically reviewing language, vocabulary, and content, teachers can provide specific academic feedback to students that clarifies and corrects any misunderstandings. Proficiency in English can be reinforced during these feedback sessions. Teacher can provide feedback verbally, orally, or even nonverbally through facial expressions and body language. Students can also provide feedback to each other through various techniques.

4. *Assess student comprehension and learning for all lesson objectives throughout the lesson.* Assessment must be conducted throughout the lesson to gather and synthesize information about student learning. Assessment must be linked to the instruction and the lesson objectives. Toward the end of the lesson, student progress should be assessed to determine whether it is appropriate to move on or whether it is necessary to review and reteach. As a general rule, multiple assessments should be conducted.

Key Terms

Ability grouping	Cooperative learning	Motivation to	Small-group instruction
Academic accountability	Desists	learn	Smoothness
Academic learning time	Enthusiasm	Overdwelling	Student-centered
Advance organizer	Fragmentation	Overlapping	approaches
Anticipatory set	Group accountability	Pacing	Summary
Attention	Group alerting	Peer tutoring	Task orientation
Between-class	High-participation	Satiation	Teacher-centered
grouping	formats	Seatwork	approaches
Clarity	Independent work	Set induction	Transitions
Closure	Jerkiness	Situational assistance	Whole-group instruction
Comprehensible input	Momentum	Slowdowns	Within-class grouping

Major Concepts

1. The degree of structure in a lesson and the manner in which students are grouped for instruction need to be taken into account when managing instruction and promoting appropriate behavior.

2. Students are more likely to stay on task when they are held academically accountable for their work.

3. When beginning a lesson, teachers need to take attendance, get attention, provide daily review, provide a set induction, introduce lesson objectives, distribute and collect materials, and give clear, focused directions.

4. When conducting the body of a lesson, effective teachers are clear, pace the lesson, provide smooth transitions, have a task orientation, ensure academic learning time, and exhibit enthusiasm.

5. An effective teacher ends a lesson with a summary of important concepts and allows students time to get ready to leave the room after the lesson.

6. Managing student work involves effectively managing seatwork, collecting assignments and monitoring their completion, maintaining records of student work, managing paperwork, and giving students feedback.

7. Successful management of whole-group instruction can be achieved by deliberate actions to prevent misbehavior, manage movement through the lesson, maintain a group focus, and maintain student attention and involvement.

8. Several components of the **SIOP** model can be used to enhance lesson delivery.

Discussion/Reflective Questions

1. What are some merits of whole-group, small-group, and independent work? What might teachers do to minimize misbehavior with each strategy?

2. In what ways might the selection of the various accountability procedures be affected by differences in grade level and subject areas?

3. From your own school experiences, what approaches to review did you find the most successful? What are the merits of using different approaches for review?

4. Recall several examples when your teachers were not clear in providing directions, instructions, or expectations. What effect did this lack of clarity have on you as a student?

5. Why would attention-getting strategies promote student involvement? What precautions could you identify for their use?

Suggested Activities

FOR CLINICAL SETTINGS

1. List several ways to conduct daily and weekly reviews.

2. Using Figure 8.1 as a guide, describe how you will monitor progress of your students and their completion of assignments.

3. Reflect on your schooling experiences and identify some strategies that your teachers used to capture and maintain students' interest successfully.

FOR FIELD EXPERIENCES

1. Talk to teachers about how they hold students academically accountable for each area in Figure 8.1.

2. Talk with several teachers about the procedures they use to manage seatwork, collect and monitor assignments, maintain records, and manage paperwork. Then outline the ways that you will handle these responsibilities

3. Ask several teachers how they try to meet the needs of ELLs during lesson delivery.

Further Reading

Good, T., & Brophy, J. (2008). *Looking in classrooms* (10th ed.). Boston: Allyn & Bacon.

Includes a thorough review of many aspects of teaching including classroom life, expectations, management, motivation, groupings, and instructional approaches.

Marzano, R. J. (2007). *The art and science of teaching: A comprehensive framework for effective instruction.* Alexandria, VA: Association for Supervision and Curriculum Development.

Provides research-based guidelines for many aspects of lesson delivery, planning, management, student involvement, and assessment.

Thompson, J. G. (2009). *The first-year teacher's checklist.* San Francisco: Jossey-Bass.

Offers concise recommendations about many aspects of lesson delivery and related issues such as planning, instruction, classroom climate, management, and behavior. Based on her 2007 book, *The First-Year Teacher's Survival Guide.*

Technology Resources

THREE TYPES OF LEARNING GROUPS

http://www.adprima.com/grouping.htm

Provides a comparison of problem-solving groups, cooperative teams, and collaborative groups, as well as links to additional resources.

TIME-SAVING TIPS FOR TEACHERS FOR SEATWORK AND OTHER DUTIES

http://www.educationoasis.com/resources/Articles/time_saving_tips.htm

Offers suggestions for organization and strategies.

TEACHING ENGLISH LANGUAGE LEARNERS THE SIOP WAY—LESSON IMPLICATIONS

http://www.prel.org/products/paced/fall06/siop.pdf

Thoroughly describes the components of the SIOP model, and then explores implications for lesson design and delivery.

MyEducationLab™

Go to the **MyEducationLab** (www.myeducationlab.com) for General Methods and familiarize yourself with the content:

- Topically organized Assignments and Activities, tied to learning outcomes for the course, that can help you more deeply understand course content

- Topically organized Building Teaching Skills and Dispositions learning units allow you to apply and develop understanding of teaching methods.

- A chapter-specific pretest that assesses your understanding of the content offers hints and feedback for

each question and generates a study plan including links to Review, Practice, and Enrichment activities that will enhance your understanding of the concepts. A Study Plan posttest with hints and feedback ensures you understood concepts from the chapter after having completed the enrichment activities.

A Correlation Guide may be downloaded by instructors to show how MyEducationLab content aligns to this book.

Classroom Management

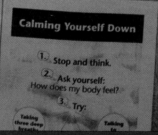

CLASSROOM RULES

1. follow directions

2. work quietly

3. use indoor voices

4. respect others

How to Solve Problems

1. What is the problem?

2. What are some solutions?

3. For each solution, ask yourself:
Is it safe?
How might people feel about it?
Is it fair?
Will it work?

4. Choose a solution and us

5. Is it working? → Yes
If not, what can I do now?

Calming Yourself Down

1. Stop and think.

2. Ask yourself:
How does my body feel?

3. Try:

Taking three deep breaths

Talking to

THIS CHAPTER PROVIDES INFORMATION THAT WILL HELP YOU TO

1. Describe the role of classroom management in creating a learning community.

2. Describe the areas of responsibility for classroom management and discipline.

3. Apply the strategies to prepare for the school year.

4. Organize your classroom and materials.

5. Select and teach classroom rules and procedures.

6. Describe ways to maintain appropriate student behavior.

CLASSROOM
RULES

1. follow directions
2. work quietly
3. use indoor voices
4. respect others

What do award-winning teachers do that makes them so popular and successful? Do they jazz up the curriculum in some way? Do they use especially creative instructional approaches? Do they warm up to the students as if they were their own children? Do they add some magic or sparkle to the classroom experience? The answer is they probably do a little of each of those things. But it likely goes deeper than that.

Successful teachers are often very effective managers of the classroom environment. They create a positive learning community in which students are actively involved in their own learning and the management of the classroom. Successful teachers organize the physical environment, manage student behavior, create a respectful environment, facilitate instruction, promote safety and wellness, and interact with others when needed. All these actions relate to classroom management. The main objective is to create a positive learning community and then to take steps to maintain this positive environment by guiding and correcting student behavior.

Problems with student misbehavior are minimized in a learning community in which students are actively involved in their classroom and instruction. A learning community is designed to help all students to feel safe, respected, and valued in order to learn new skills. Successful classrooms are those in which students feel supported in their learning, are willing to take risks, and are open to new possibilities. Many aspects of classroom management help to promote learning communities.

Classroom Management

Classroom management involves teacher actions to create a learning environment that encourages positive social interaction, active engagement in learning, and self-motivation. Several key questions come to mind about classroom management: How can the physical environment be organized? How can the school year begin effectively? What rules and procedures are appropriate? How can students be held academically accountable? How can appropriate behavior be encouraged and supported? How might order be restored if there are disruptions? How can class time and instruction be managed effectively? How can the safety of students be ensured? All these issues are part of classroom management.

AREAS OF RESPONSIBILITY

A learning community needs to have order for students to be successful. **Order** means that students are following the actions necessary for a particular classroom event to be successful; students are focused on instructional tasks and are not misbehaving. Establishing and maintaining order are important parts of classroom management.

FIGURE 9.1

AREAS OF RESPONSIBILITY FOR CLASSROOM MANAGEMENT AND DISCIPLINE

1. Select a philosophical model of classroom management and discipline.
2. Organize the physical environment.
3. Manage student behavior.
4. Create a respectful, supportive learning environment.
5. Manage and facilitate instruction.
6. Promote classroom safety and wellness.
7. Interact with colleagues, families, and others to achieve classroom management objectives.

It is useful to distinguish between off-task behavior and misbehavior. **Off-task behavior** includes student actions that are not focused on instructional activities yet would not be considered to be disruptive or be defined as misbehavior. Off-task behavior includes daydreaming, writing notes or doodling, or not paying attention. **Misbehavior** includes behavior that interferes with your teaching, interferes with the rights of others to learn, is psychologically or physically unsafe, or destroys property (Levin & Nolan, 2010). Classroom order is threatened by misbehavior. **Discipline** is the act of responding to misbehaving students in an effort to restore order.

There are several areas of responsibility for classroom management and discipline (see Figure 9.1). An effective classroom manager handles the following seven areas of responsibility (Burden, 2013):

1. *Select a philosophical model of classroom management and discipline.* A number of educators have proposed certain models of classroom management and discipline, such as teaching with love and logic, cooperative discipline, discipline with dignity, and assertive discipline. These models reflect various philosophical views of student development, teaching and learning, and classroom management. Viewing these proposed models on a continuum, they range from low teacher control to high teacher control.

These theoretical models are useful to teachers because they offer a basis for analyzing, understanding, and managing student and teacher behavior. With an understanding of these varied theoretical approaches, you can assess your position on these issues and then

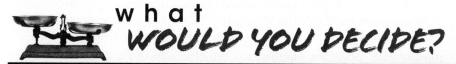

what WOULD YOU DECIDE?

YOUR PHILOSOPHICAL PERSPECTIVE

Some teachers are very teacher centered and prefer to make most of the decisions and direct what goes on in the classroom. Other teachers are student centered and prefer to give some decision-making responsibility to the students and have more student–student interaction. There is a range of these perspectives.

1. Where do you fall on that continuum of teacher-centered to student-centered perspectives? Why do you place yourself at that point?
2. What are the implications of your philosophical perspective on the selection of rules and procedures, course content, instructional approaches, and assessments?

select a philosophical model that is consistent with your beliefs. The techniques that you use to manage student behavior should be consistent with your beliefs about how students learn and develop.

2. *Organize the physical environment.* The way the desks, tables, and other classroom materials are arranged affects instruction and influences order in the classroom. To create an effective learning environment, you will need to organize several aspects of the physical space, which are discussed later in this chapter.

3. *Manage student behavior.* Guidelines are needed to promote order in the classroom and to provide a conducive learning environment. Rules and procedures support teaching and learning and provide students with clear expectations and well-defined norms. This, in turn, helps to create a safe, secure atmosphere for learning.

4. *Create a respectful, supportive learning environment.* There are many facets to creating a favorable learning environment, but it is vital for a positive learning community:

■ Teachers can take a number of actions to establish a cooperative, responsible classroom by developing positive teacher–student relationships, promoting students' self-esteem, and building group cohesiveness. These actions will help to create an environment in which students feel valued and comfortable, thus setting the stage for teaching and learning.

■ Teachers can focus student attention on appropriate classroom behavior by helping students to assume responsibility for their behavior, maintaining student attention and involvement, and reinforcing desired behaviors.

■ Teachers can develop a comprehensive plan to motivate students to learn, involving decisions about instructional tasks, feedback and evaluation, and academic and behavioral expectations.

■ Teachers can be most effective in creating a respectful, supportive learning environment when they have an understanding of the diverse learners in their classroom.

5. *Manage and facilitate instruction.* Certain factors in a lesson have a bearing on classroom order, and teachers need to take these factors into account when planning lessons. These include decisions about the degree of structure of the lesson, the type of instructional groups to use, and the means of holding the students academically accountable.

6. *Promote classroom safety and wellness.* Students need to feel physically and emotionally safe before they can give their full attention to the instructional tasks. Strategies used to manage student behavior, create a supportive classroom, and manage and facilitate instruction all contribute to classroom safety and wellness. In addition, teachers sometimes need to take actions to solve problems and conflicts that threaten classroom order and the learning environment. For this reason, it is helpful to have a set of tools, such as dealing with conflict resolution and anger management, to solve problems.

7. *Interact with colleagues, families,* and others to achieve classroom management *objectives.* Working with families is another means to help maintain order in the classroom. When the family and teacher communicate and get along together, students will more likely receive the needed guidance and support and will likely have more self-control in the classroom. In addition, teachers may need to consult and interact with colleagues and others when difficulties occur with classroom management and student behavior.

PRINCIPLES FOR WORKING WITH STUDENTS AND PREVENTING MISBEHAVIOR

Problem behaviors have a variety of causes, and evidence suggests that some factors are within the school and classroom environment (California Department of Education, 2000; Charles, 2011). To promote classrooms that are conducive to learning and to help prevent problem behaviors, teachers must address certain contextual factors within the classroom. Here are some basic principles for working with students in a manner that establishes a positive, productive classroom in which students learn and have a satisfying educational experience:

1. *Maintain focus on your major tasks in teaching.* Your major tasks are to help students be successful in achieving educational objectives, to promote student learning, and to help students develop the knowledge and skills to be successful in your classroom and beyond.

2. *Understand your students' needs and how to meet them.* Know your students' likes and dislikes, what motivates them, their needs and desires, and what influences their lives. Use that information to create an appropriate learning environment.

3. *Understand and respect ethnic/cultural differences.* Teachers are more prepared to facilitate learning and guide behavior when they understand the ethnic or cultural background of their students.

4. *Know what causes misbehavior and how to deal with those causes.* Take steps to reduce or remove the causes of misbehavior.

5. *Provide clear rules and procedures to guide student conduct.* Rules and procedures need to be clearly identified and taught so students understand the behavioral expectations.

6. *Have a specific plan for responding to misbehavior with a hierarchy of interventions.* Have a specific set of strategies to stop the misbehavior, keep students positively on track, and preserve good relations.

7. *Reduce the use of punitive methods of control.* Coercive or punitive environments may promote antisocial behavior. Other techniques that involve the students in creating a positive learning environment are more desirable.

VOICES
from the Classroom

CLAUDIA ARGUELLO COCA, fifth-grade teacher, Las Cruces, New Mexico

WHAT IS CLASSROOM MANAGEMENT?

When I began teaching 10 years ago, I thought classroom management meant being the one in control of my class. Control was the number one objective for me because then I knew that my students would be safe, would receive the best instruction, and would be well behaved (thus making me look good). But every approach I used to control the environment did not work.

Gradually, I learned that children will follow you if you encourage them and take the time to catch them doing great things. Some flexibility is also needed. Students want to impress you and will do anything you ask if you manage your class by focusing on hardworking students and positive behaviors. These lessons have allowed me to have great success with my students.

I always keep in mind that my students are little children. I make a huge effort to treat them like little children, offer them kind words, create a safe and predictable environment, and provide a fun learning stage. I have one rule for myself—always talk to my students as if their parents were standing behind them. When I work with my students, I want us to work together cooperatively, this only happens when my students feel safe and comfortable with me.

URBAN EDUCATION

8. *Take actions to establish a cooperative, responsible classroom.* Use techniques to maintain attention and involvement, reinforce desired behaviors, promote student accountability and responsibility, and create a positive learning community.

9. *Involve students meaningfully in making decisions.* Decisions can involve things such as the selection of classroom rules and procedures, instructional activities and assessments, and curriculum materials. Their involvement generates commitment to the learning process and to the classroom environment.

10. *Teach critical social skills.* Many students lack the social skills necessary to relate positively to peers and to do well academically. Teachers who help students develop these social skills help promote learning and successful classroom discipline.

11. *Involve families to a reasonable degree.* Communicate regularly with families about what you are doing in the classroom and about the progress of their children. Make it clear that you want and need their support.

Preparing for the School Year

Imagine that you are going to take a two-week vacation to see the numerous state and national parks in southern Utah and northern Arizona. You gather information about the parks and attractions from a variety of sources, and then you start to plan your itinerary. Next, you make motel reservations and list all the things that you need to take with you, such as hiking shoes, water bottles, sunscreen, sunglasses, camera, and clothing. Before you leave on the trip, you stop your newspaper and mail delivery and make arrangements for your pets for the days that you are gone. All these arrangements, and probably more, are needed to have a fun, trouble-free vacation.

Starting the school year also requires this type of planning. Even before school starts, you can make a number of decisions about instructional and management preparations; plans to promote a positive learning climate; plans for the first day of school; and arrangements for floor space, storage, and other aspects of classroom space. Early planning and decision making on these issues will help to ensure a positive start to the school year. Studies on classroom management have verified that the first few days of the school year set the tone for the entire year (Emmer & Evertson, 2009; Evertson & Emmer, 2009).

To begin, you can make management preparations and instructional preparations, establish a plan for misbehavior, and also plan for the first day of school. When the school year finally begins, there are certain actions that are appropriate during the first day and over the following few days. A number of these issues are addressed in this section.

A number of resources provide more details than can be discussed in this chapter. Resources are available for the elementary grades (Bosch, 2010; Jonson, 2010; Moran, Stobbe, Baron, Miller, & Moir, 2009; Roberts, 2001), secondary grades (Wyatt & White, 2007), and K–12 grades (Guillaume, 2012; Marzano, Gaddy, Foseid, Foseid, & Marzano, 2009; McEwan, 2006; J. G. Thompson, 2007; Wong & Wong, 2009).

MAKING MANAGEMENT PREPARATIONS

It is important to carefully consider a variety of management issues, such as your school environment, room arrangement, materials, rules and procedures, communication with parents, seating arrangements, and other issues. Based on a study of experienced teachers (Schell & Burden, 2006), you could direct your attention to the following classroom management issues:

1. *The school environment.* The first step is to become thoroughly familiar with the total environment before school starts: the room, school, facilities, personnel, services, resources, policies and procedures, other teachers, children, and the community. You will then have more information with which to make decisions, will probably feel more confident about your job, and will not need to devote time in the first few weeks to gather this information.

2. *Gather support materials.* After examining the curriculum guide and textbooks, you might have ideas about activities for a certain unit or lesson. Supplementary materials may be needed when the time comes to teach that lesson. This is the time to gather any additional support materials, such as games and devices, pictures, CDs, ideas for activities, charts, maps, and graphs. The school may have discretionary funds for their purchase. They may be obtained from school supply catalogs, a local teacher store, or even at garage sales.

3. *Organize materials.* It is useful to set up a filing system for storing district and school communications and other important documents. Papers that should be kept in a filing cabinet include the district's policy handbook; correspondence from the principal, superintendent, or other supervisors; correspondence from professional organizations; lesson plans; and items on curricular content. Some teachers use file folders. A separate file folder may be created for each course unit to hold pertinent notes and resource materials. Textbooks, resource books, manipulative materials, and other types of instructional supplies and materials also need to be organized and stored.

4. *Classroom procedures.* You can follow various procedures to accomplish specific tasks. Procedures may be identified regarding handing in completed work, sharpening a pencil, using the restroom, or putting away supplies. Before school starts, identify actions or activities requiring procedures that will contribute to a smoothly running classroom, and then decide what those procedures should be.

5. *Classroom helpers.* Teachers call on students at all grade levels as helpers to perform various classroom tasks. Make a list of tasks that need to be done, and then decide which ones students can perform. Give attention to how task assignment will be rotated to give every student an opportunity to help. Roles are often held for one or two weeks before the assignments are rotated. Depending on the grade level and circumstances, some tasks

sample STANDARDS

CLASSROOM MANAGEMENT

There are 10 InTASC standards (see pages xx–xxi), and each standard in the original document includes a list of performances, essential knowledge, and critical dispositions to indicate more clearly what is intended in the standard.

Since this chapter deals with classroom management, some representative statements from InTASC Standard #3, Learning Environments, are listed here concerning topics in this chapter.

PERFORMANCES

■ The teacher manages the learning environment to actively and equitably engage learners by organizing, allocating, and coordinating the resources of time, space, and learners' attention.

■ The teacher intentionally builds learner capacity to collaborate in face-to-face and virtual environments through applying effective interpersonal communication skills.

ESSENTIAL KNOWLEDGE

■ The teacher knows how to help learners work productively and cooperatively with each other to achieve learning goals.

■ The teacher knows how to collaborate with learners to establish and monitor elements of a safe and productive learning environment including norms, expectations, routines, and organizational structures.

CRITICAL DISPOSITIONS

■ The teacher is committed to working with learners, colleagues, families, and communities to establish positive and supportive learning environments.

■ The teacher values the role of learners in promoting each other's learning and recognizes the importance of peer relationships in establishing a climate of learning.

for students may include line leader, light switcher, pencil sharpener, paper collector, plant waterer, whiteboard eraser, window and blind opener, and supply manager.

6. *Class lists and rosters.* It is useful to plan a means to record whether students have returned their book orders, picture money, field-trip permission forms, and so on. You can prepare a generic class roster listing the students' names in alphabetical order in the left column, with blank columns on the right to check off the action. It is helpful to input the list on a computer program so that an updated sheet can be easily generated when the roster changes.

7. *School/home communication.* Open communication with families is vital. Before school starts, many teachers prepare an introductory letter to families to welcome them and to inform them about the teacher, the curriculum, grading practices and standards, the homework policy, rules and procedures, and so on. This letter can be sent home with the students on the first day of school. Teachers can also make plans for other types of communication with families, such as phone calls, progress reports, or a back-to-school night.

8. *Birthdays and other celebrations.* Depending on your grade level, you may want to recognize student birthdays. Most schools have very specific policies for celebrating major holidays, such as Halloween, Christmas, Hanukkah, Martin Luther King Jr. Day, and Easter. Inquire about these policies so you will understand what is expected.

9. *Distributing textbooks.* Sometime in the first few days of school, you will need to distribute textbooks. You need to obtain the textbooks and prepare an inventory form on which to record each book number, with a space in which to write the student's name.

Think about when and how the textbooks will be distributed. Since the first day of school often necessitates many announcements and activities, you might want to wait until the second or third day before distributing textbooks, or distribute them just before they are needed for the first time. Attention might be given to the specific means of distribution. One way is to have students line up one row at a time and go to the table where the books are stacked. When giving the book to the student, you can record the student's name on the inventory form.

10. *Room identification.* On the first day of school, students need to locate your classroom. Especially for students new to the building, it is important to have the room clearly labeled. A poster on the outside doorway should include the room number, the teacher's name, the grade level and/or subject (Room 211, Mr. Rodriguez, World History). This information should also be written on the whiteboard so students see that they are in the correct classroom. Some type of welcoming statement should also be placed on the whiteboard, such as "Welcome! I'm glad you're here."

11. *Room arrangement.* Room arrangement is an issue that can be decided before school starts. Take into account the fixed features in the room, instructional materials and supplies, traffic areas, work areas, boundaries for activity areas, visibility (being able to see all students), and the purposes of various seating arrangements. Determine the arrangement in the classroom for your desk, the students' desks, tables, bookshelves, filing cabinets, and other furniture. The room arrangement that you select should be consistent with your instructional goals and activities. Teacher-led instructional approaches such as presentations and demonstrations require one type of room arrangement, whereas small-group work requires a different type of arrangement.

12. *Seat selections and arrangements.* One teacher may prefer to assign each student's seat, while another may let students select their seats. This decision should be made before school starts. In either case, be sure that there are enough seats for the number of students you expect. You might take the age level and maturity of the students into account as you select the manner of assigning seats. You might change the seating arrangements during the school year to accommodate work groups, to move students who need close supervision to more accessible seats, or simply to provide a change.

13. *Room decoration.* It is important to make your classroom an attractive, comfortable place. Consider having some plants in the classroom or even an aquarium. Displays of pictures, posters, charts, and maps also help cover the walls with informative and appealing materials. Attractive bulletin boards add color. You might prepare one bulletin board listing classroom information and use another one to display seasonal items. After school starts, you can have students prepare bulletin boards.

MAKING INSTRUCTIONAL PREPARATIONS

Prior to the start of the school year, carefully consider a variety of instructional issues, such as long-range plans, supplementary materials, student assessment, a folder for substitute teachers, a syllabus, and so on. Based on a study of experienced teachers (Schell & Burden, 2006), you should direct your attention to the following instructional issues:

1. *Long-range plans.* It is helpful to peruse the curriculum guides and other related materials so you can appreciate what should be covered by the end of the school year. Some tentative decisions need to be made for the amount of time to spend on each particular unit. Some curriculum guides include recommendations for the number of weeks to spend on each unit.

You may want to solicit advice from other teachers, particularly from those who teach your same subject or grade level. To the extent possible, make these rough schedules conform to the school calendar by taking into account grading periods and holidays. Be careful not to overschedule yourself. Leave some time for review near the end of each unit or chapter, for reteaching as the situation warrants, and for unexpected occurrences, such as school closings due to inclement weather.

2. *Supplementary materials.* For each major curricular topic in your rough long-range plans, start an ongoing list of related supplementary materials or activities. It may include field trip locations, resource people, media, games, assignments, bulletin boards, and additional books. Inquire about library or media center resources, such as films or videotapes, and order and reserve them. You might prepare other supplementary materials to use during the first few weeks of school.

3. *Skeleton plans.* A **skeleton plan** is a brief overview of intended accomplishments. It often includes a weekly list of expected accomplishments. Skeleton plans include more details than the long-range yearly plans but not the detail needed for daily lesson plans. Skeleton plans for the first three or four weeks serve as a guide for preparing the more detailed lesson plans.

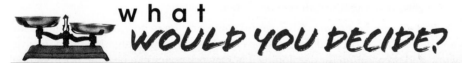

what WOULD YOU DECIDE?

PLANS FOR THE YEAR AND THE FIRST MARKING TERM

Even before school starts, you need to begin making plans for the year and for the first marking term. By looking at the school year, you can tentatively set a time frame for each section or unit of the course (e.g., unit 3 will run from mid-October to mid-November). You also can begin detailed planning for the first marking period.

1. When considering yearly plans before school starts, what else can you put into your tentative plans or schedule of activities?

2. What information would you put into your plans for the first marking term? How will this help in your unit and lesson planning?

4. *Weekly time schedules.* You should establish your weekly schedule before school starts and include a copy in a handy place, such as in your lesson plan book. The weekly schedule is often displayed in a chart, with the weekdays listed at the top and the hours listed on the left-hand column. The class schedule for middle and secondary teachers probably will be determined by the principal or others in the school building, and it will show what grade level and subject are taught during each class period.

5. *Daily lesson plans.* After you have completed the skeleton plans for the first three or four weeks, it is time to prepare the daily lesson plans for the first week of school. Lesson plan formats vary. One that is often used includes boxes for the days of the week and the subjects taught. In these boxes, you might include notes about objectives, a list of topics to be covered or activities to be conducted, materials, and means of assessment. Beginning and probationary teachers are often required to show the principal or assistant principal their weekly lesson plans for the coming week.

6. *Preparing a syllabus.* You need to give students information about each course at the start of the year. You could plan and prepare this information as well as any related materials before school starts. At the middle and secondary levels, teachers often give each student a course syllabus that outlines this introductory information (see Chapter 3). The **course syllabus** includes the course title, the title of the textbook and any other primary resource materials, a brief course description, a list of course objectives, a content outline, course requirements (e.g., tests, homework, projects), how grades will be calculated (e.g., the points for each requirement and the point total needed for certain grades), a description of the homework policy, the attendance and tardiness policy, and a listing of classroom rules and procedures. Some teachers also include a description of the instructional methods and activities that students are to engage in.

7. *Preparing policy sheets.* The syllabus might include all related classroom policies and procedures, although some teachers do not include these items. (Depending on the grade level and circumstances, some teachers do not provide a course syllabus.) As a result, a teacher might prepare a separate policy sheet for the students. The sheet may state the classroom rules and procedures, the policy for attendance and tardiness, and the like. If a course syllabus is not used, this policy sheet might also state the grading policy.

8. *Tentative student assessment.* It is useful to make an initial assessment of the students' understanding and skills at the start of the school year so you can better recognize the abilities and differences within the class. These assessments could be conducted sometime during the first week of school, but you should think about how to plan for the assessment and then make any necessary arrangements before school starts. Assessment procedures might include worksheets, oral activities, observation checklists, pretests, or review lessons. After conducting these early assessments, you should then record the results on a class roster that was drawn up earlier.

9. *Planning for homework.* Give careful consideration to how you will evaluate students and determine report card grades. One element of student evaluation often involves homework, and preparation for developing a homework policy can be done before school starts. Prepare a homework policy in the form of a letter that is sent home to families at the start of the school year (see Chapter 13).

10. *Backup materials.* It is useful to have some backup materials available when instruction takes less time than anticipated, when a change of plans is necessary, or when students finish their activities early. These backup materials may be related to the particular topics being covered at the time. Many teachers have a collection of puzzles, educational games, discussion questions, brain teasers, creative writing, word searches, and riddles. You can gather these materials before school starts.

11. *Opening class routine.* Students often perform better when they know that a particular routine will be regularly followed at the start of class. You can decide on the particular actions to be taken. You may need to take attendance, make announcements, and attend to other tasks at the start of the class period. The purpose of having a routine is to provide an orderly transition as students enter the room and get ready for instruction.

Some teachers have students review vocabulary words or other problems related to the curriculum while other tasks are performed.

12. *Folder for substitute teachers.* A substitute teacher will take your place when you are absent. It is important to prepare materials for substitute teachers to help support what they do, maximize the learning, and minimize any off-task behavior. Many teachers keep a folder for substitute teachers that includes important information. It can be kept on your desk with the plan book.

The type of material you might keep for substitute teachers varies, but the following information would be useful to include: a copy of the daily schedule, times for recess and lunch, a list of the classroom rules, a list of classroom procedures (e.g., morning opening, taking attendance, lunch count, lunch, dismissal, fire drills), a list of reliable students in each class period, hall-pass procedures (to go to the restroom, library, or office), information on where to find certain items (e.g., lesson plans, audiovisual equipment, supplies), others to contact for information or help (e.g., a nearby teacher with room number), and a list and description of students with special needs. Much of this information can be collected before school starts, and additional information can be added as needed.

MANAGING ASSESSMENTS, RECORD KEEPING, AND REPORTING

It is vital to give advance thought to how you will assess student achievement, record student progress and scores, and report the assessment information. Assessment always has been important in teaching, but the No Child Left Behind Act (2002) and additional state and local accountability demands for ensuring student learning have elevated the level of attention on assessment and reporting. Even before the school year starts, you should decide how you will assess student learning, keep records of student performance, and report the assessment data.

Electronic grade books are provided in many districts, or they can be purchased by individual teachers. These have a spreadsheet design in which scores for each type of assessment can be entered for each student. Electronic grade books facilitate record keeping and reporting of grades.

Assessments. While there are many aspects to assessment, you will need to select the means of assessment. Teacher-made tests and quizzes are common. In addition, you may choose to have students demonstrate their learning through the use of performance-based measures with (1) products (e.g., portfolios, work samples, projects, laboratory reports) or (2) performances (e.g., oral presentation, presentation with media, demonstration, debate, athletic demonstration). For each of these assessment approaches, you will also need to determine how you will evaluate the level of student proficiency. This could be done through an answer key for a test or with the use of rubrics or other rating forms for performance-based measures.

Record Keeping. Once students have been assessed and you have scored their work, you must keep records in a grade book. Grade books typically have a section for the daily attendance log, achievement scores, and conduct scores. All student assessment scores are placed in the grade book, so prior thinking about your overall assessment plan will help you design the columns and labels in a useful manner. In addition to scores for performance on test items, portfolios, and other measuring techniques, some teachers have separate charts to record student proficiency for particular knowledge and skills related to the curriculum standards.

Entering the assessment scores in the grade book is only part of your task. You must also have a plan to translate all of the performance measures into a grade at the end of the report card period. For example, in a given subject, will you have a weight of 20 percent for homework, 40 percent for tests, 20 percent for a portfolio, and 20 percent for cooperative group projects? Furthermore, what performance level constitutes an A or a B? You need to think about your grading system before the start of the school year and establish your plan.

Reporting. Your school district will likely determine a number of aspects of what will be recorded on report cards and how the information will be reported. First, the district determines what achievement and nonachievement (e.g., conduct) progress will be reported. Also, it determines what grading system will be used (e.g., letter grades, pass–fail, checklists). There may be additional ways the district determines how grades are reported.

In addition to report cards, you can communicate students' progress to their families in various ways, such as through parent–teacher conferences, newsletters, and open houses. During a parent–teacher conference, you may want to have a portfolio for each student ready to show representative work. For a newsletter, you may want to share information about the activities and the performance of the entire class. Give advance thought to what information you will be reporting, and develop a plan for the kinds of data and materials you need to gather and report.

ESTABLISHING A PLAN TO DEAL WITH MISBEHAVIOR

With an understanding of classroom management and discipline, you will need to develop a plan for dealing with misbehavior in the classroom. A seven-step plan is presented here that begins with establishment of a system of rules and procedures. You need to provide a supportive environment during instruction and also provide situational assistance when students get off task. If a student does not get back on task, you need to move through advancing levels of punishment. If none of these actions works, you may need to involve other personnel.

You should deal with misbehavior in a way that is effective while also avoiding unnecessary disruptions. Researchers and educators have also proposed movement from low to high intervention when developing a plan to address misbehavior (e.g., Charles, 2011; Levin & Nolan, 2010; Wolfgang, 2009). Once the rules and procedures and a supportive classroom environment are in place, the teacher moves from low to high interventions, as follows:

1. *Establish your system of rules and procedures.* Establish an appropriate system of rules and procedures as a foundation for dealing with discipline issues. It is vital that you select a system of rules and procedures appropriate to the situation. This system should incorporate reward or reinforcement for desirable behavior and consequences for misbehavior.

No single approach is best for all teachers and all teaching situations. For instance, rules and procedures for a 10th-grade English class would not be appropriate for a 3rd-grade class. Furthermore, the system needs to be consistent with established school and district policies and with your own educational philosophy, personality, and preferences.

2. *Provide a supportive environment during class sessions.* Once the system of rules and procedures has been established at the start of the school year, you need to maintain a supportive environment. Actions taken in the normal course of instruction are for the purpose of guiding and reinforcing students for positive behavior.

Providing a supportive environment is accomplished primarily through cueing and reinforcing appropriate behavior and through getting and holding attention. Cueing and reinforcing involves stressing positive, desirable behaviors; recognizing and reinforcing desired behaviors; and praising effectively. Getting and holding attention necessitates focusing students' attention at the start of lessons; keeping lessons moving at a good pace; monitoring attention during lessons; periodically stimulating attention; maintaining accountability; and terminating lessons that have gone on too long. Treat students with dignity and respect, and offer challenging, interesting, and exciting classes.

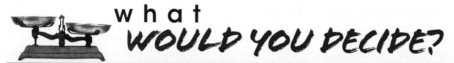

PROVIDING SITUATIONAL ASSISTANCE

Before using mild responses for off-task behavior, teachers often provide situational assistance to get students back on task.

1. What are the benefits of using situational assistance?

2. How might situational assistance differ for students in the 1st, 7th, and 11th grades?

3. How might cultural differences of students affect your decisions about the ways to provide situational assistance?

3. *Provide situational assistance during class sessions.* Students may get off task during a lesson. This off-task behavior may be in the form of misbehavior or a lapse in attention. Either way, you need to promptly provide situational assistance. **Situational assistance** denotes actions you take to get a student back on task with the least amount of intervention and disruption possible. Situational assistance can be provided by removing distracting objects, reinforcing appropriate behaviors, boosting student interest, providing cues, helping students over hurdles, redirecting the behavior, altering the lesson, and other approaches (discussed more fully in Chapter 10).

Some inappropriate behaviors are of such short duration and are so insignificant that they can be safely ignored. Your use of situational assistance might be considered a "forgiveness step" for the student by recognizing that the off-task behavior is minor or fleeting and by allowing the student to get back on task without penalty.

4. *Use mild responses.* If a student continues to be off task after situational assistance is provided, then you need to use mild responses that are intended to correct the student's behavior. These are not intended to be punitive. Mild responses may be nonverbal or verbal (see Chapter 10). Nonverbal responses include ignoring the behavior, using signal interference, using proximity control, and using touch control. Verbal responses include reinforcing peers, calling on the student during the lesson, using humor, giving a direct appeal or command, reminding the student of the rules, and several other approaches.

5. *Use moderate responses.* If students do not respond favorably to mild responses and continue to exhibit off-task behavior, then you need to deliver moderate responses (see Chapter 10). These punitive responses deal with misbehavior by removing desired stimuli so as to minimize the inappropriate behavior. Moderate responses include the use of logical consequences and various behavior modification techniques, such as time-out and loss of privileges.

6. *Use stronger responses.* If moderate responses are insufficient, then you need to move to a more intrusive type of intervention (see Chapter 10). These stronger responses are intended to be punitive by adding aversive stimuli such as reprimands and overcorrection. The purpose of aversive stimuli is to decrease unwanted behavior.

7. *Involve others when necessary.* If all efforts have failed to get the student to behave properly, then you need to involve other persons in the process. This occurs most commonly with chronic or severe behaviors. You may consult or involve counselors, psychologists, principals and assistant principals, teaching colleagues, college personnel, mental health centers, school social workers, school nurses, supervisors and department heads, and families. Their assistance and involvement will vary, depending on their expertise.

PLANNING FOR THE FIRST DAY

Starting the school year effectively is vitally important when implementing a system of classroom management. Marzano and colleagues (2009) report that a strong first day and an emphasis on classroom management in the first few days make a big difference in getting off to a good start. Several principles should guide your decisions about planning the start of the school year and your actions in the first few days of school (Burden, 2013; Emmer & Evertson, 2009; Evertson & Emmer, 2009; Good & Brophy, 2008; Wong & Wong, 2009).

1. Plan to clearly state your rules, procedures, and academic expectations.
2. Plan uncomplicated lessons to help students be successful.
3. Keep a whole-class focus.
4. Be available, visible, and in charge.
5. Plan strategies to deal with potential problems.
6. Closely monitor student compliance with rules and procedures.
7. Stop inappropriate behavior quickly.
8. Organize instruction on the basis of ability levels.
9. Hold students academically accountable.
10. Be clear when communicating information.
11. Maintain students' attention.
12. Organize the flow of lesson activities.

Organizing Your Classroom and Materials

Decisions about room arrangement must be made before students arrive on the first day of school. Before arranging the classroom, you should consider (1) the movement patterns of students throughout the classroom; (2) the need for students to obtain a variety of materials, texts, reference books, equipment, and supplies; and (3) the need for students to see the instructional presentations and display materials.

Arrange and decorate your classroom in a manner that supports effective classroom management (Marzano et al., 2009). Good room arrangement can help teachers cope with the complex demands of teaching by minimizing interruptions, delays, and dead times. Based on studies of effective classroom managers, there are five keys to good room arrangement (Emmer & Evertson, 2009; Evertson & Emmer, 2009):

1. *Use a room arrangement consistent with your instructional goals and activities.* You will need to think about the main types of instructional activities that will be used in your classes and then organize the seating, materials, and equipment compatibly. Teacher-led presentations, demonstrations, and recitations require students to be seated so that they can see the instructional area. In contrast, small-group work requires a very different room arrangement.

2. *Keep high-traffic areas free of congestion.* High-traffic areas include the space around doorways, the pencil sharpener and trash can, group work areas, certain bookshelves and supply areas, the teacher's desk, and student desks. High-traffic areas should be separated from the primary instructional area, have plenty of space, and be easily accessible. For example, try not to seat a student next to the pencil sharpener because of the traffic in that area and the possibility for inappropriate behavior.

3. *Be sure students are easily seen by the teacher.* It is important that teachers clearly see students to identify when a student needs assistance or to prevent task avoidance or disruption. Clear lines of sight must be maintained between student work areas and areas of the room that the teacher will frequent.

4. *Keep frequently used teaching materials and student supplies readily accessible.* By having easy access and efficient storage of these materials, activities are more likely to begin and end promptly, and time spent on getting ready and cleaning up will be minimized. Establishing regulated storage areas can help to reduce the occurrence of students leaving materials in their desks or taking them out of the room.

5. *Be certain students can easily see instructional presentations and displays.* The seating arrangement should allow all students to see the whiteboard or projector screen without moving their chairs, turning their desks around, or craning their necks. Place the primary instructional area in a prominent location to help students pay attention and to facilitate note taking.

FLOOR SPACE

A classroom typically contains many materials that take up floor space, such as student desks, the teacher's desk, bookcases, tables, and activity centers. Consider the functions of your classroom space and the five keys to good room arrangement to facilitate learning and to minimize interruptions and delays.

A good starting point in creating the floor plan is to decide where you will conduct whole-group instruction. Examine the room and identify where you will stand or work when you address the entire class to conduct lessons or to give directions. This area should have a whiteboard, a projector screen, a table for the projector unit, a small table to hold items needed during instruction, and an electrical outlet. Consider the following items:

- *Student desks.* Even if other arrangements are to be used later in the year, you might start the year with student desks in rows facing the major instructional area, since it is easier to manage students with this pattern. Be sure all students can see the major instructional area without having their backs to it and without having to get out of their seats. It is important to keep student desks away from high-traffic areas. Avoid placing their desks near the door, pencil sharpener, trash can, and supply areas. Leave ample room for aisles between the desks to enable easy movement of students and yourself when monitoring seatwork.

- *The teacher's desk.* Your desk should be situated so that you can see the students, but it is not essential that the desk be at the front of the room. Placement of your desk at the rear of the room, in fact, may help when monitoring students during independent work. Students facing away from you cannot tell when you are looking at them unless they turn around. This tends to encourage students to stay at their assigned tasks. Instead of sitting at their desks during independent work, many teachers prefer to move around the room to monitor and assist students.

- *Bookcases and filing cabinets.* These should be placed so students' visibility of whiteboards and relevant displays is not obstructed. These items should also not interfere with your monitoring of students. If a bookcase contains frequently used items such as resource books, dictionaries, or supplies, then it should be conveniently located and monitored. Seldom-used items are best stored in an out-of-the-way place. If there is only one bookcase, it is helpful to use it for frequently used items.

- *Activity centers or work areas.* An **activity center** is an area where one or more students come to work on a special activity. It may be in the form of a learning center or a computer work area. One or more tables are commonly used as the work surfaces in these areas. When selecting the placement of tables for an activity

VOICES
from the Classroom

LEILA POST, fourth-grade teacher, Reno, Nevada

ORGANIZING YOUR MATERIALS AND SPACE

I find that good organization makes me a better teacher. I organize my daily lessons and activities in five plastic trays lined across a counter, and they are labeled by the day of the week. On top of each tray is another tray for a second week. This allows me to plan and collect related materials for two weeks at a time. This organization also makes it easier for a substitute teacher to locate all the needed materials.

I have student supplies easily accessible on shelves, and I have labeled trays for turning in daily seatwork, homework, and center work. At each cluster of student desks, I have a plastic basket containing glue, erasers, pencils, and crayons. Each student is assigned a number at the start of the school year, and this number is used to identify all folders, mailboxes, scissors, and other items.

I find classroom organization of teacher and student materials reduces wasted time, increases productivity, and teaches organizational skills to the students.

center, be sure that you can see all students in the work area, keep traffic lanes clear, and avoid congested areas. A center often will have special equipment, such as a computer, and other instructional materials and supplies. Enough table and work space must be provided for students to work efficiently. It is useful to place a work area at the side or the back of the room and to the backs of other students.

STORAGE SPACE

Teachers and students use a wide variety of instructional materials. Materials that are not used every day must be stored when not in use. Therefore, storage space must be provided for textbooks and resource books, frequently used instructional materials, teacher's supplies and instructional materials, equipment, and infrequently used materials. Here are some guidelines:

1. *Textbooks and resource books.* Some textbooks are not kept by students and thus must be stored in the classroom for easy access when needed. In addition, resource books obtained from the school library, public library, or other sources may be available for student use. All of these books should be stored in a bookcase that enables easy access.

2. *Instructional materials.* Materials that students need will vary with the subject area that you teach. These may include rulers, scissors, special paper, pencils, staplers, tape, glue, and other supplies. As with textbooks and resource books, a storage location should be selected to enable easy access to the materials. Clearly labeled containers for each of the supply items are often very helpful in maintaining an orderly supply area. These materials may be stored on shelves of a bookcase or cabinet or on a counter.

3. *Teacher supplies.* Supplies that only you would use should be kept in your desk or in storage areas used only by you. These supplies include items such as hall passes, attendance and lunch count forms, lesson plan book, tablets, file folders, and whiteboard markers. These items should be placed in secure places so students do not have access to them.

4. *Equipment.* The type of equipment needing to be stored will vary considerably depending on a teacher's grade level and subject area. A physical education teacher, for example, may need to store many types of equipment and supplies when not needed for a class session. Teachers in self-contained classrooms may need to store computers or other instructional media that are not used every day.

5. *Infrequently used items.* Some instructional materials are used only once a year. These include seasonal decorations (e.g., Halloween, Thanksgiving), bulletin board displays, and special project materials. Certain instructional materials may be used for only one unit, as in the case of a model of the human eye for a science class. Some teachers prefer to keep seasonal decorations and other infrequently used materials at their homes.

BULLETIN BOARDS AND WALL SPACE

Constructive use of bulletin boards and wall space can contribute to a positive classroom environment. This can be achieved by displaying relevant instructional material, assignments, rules, schedules, student work, and other items of interest. Many teachers involve students in the selection of content and the preparation of bulletin boards and the use of wall space. One approach is to select a different group of students to plan and prepare a bulletin board each month.

Some teachers prefer to dedicate a certain purpose for each bulletin board. For example, one bulletin board can be used to post classroom rules, a daily or weekly schedule, classroom helpers, lunch menus, a school map, emergency information, or any other procedural information. Another bulletin board can be used to display student work. A third type of bulletin board can be simply for decoration, with seasonal, motivational, or artistic items. Other bulletin boards can be used to post information and news articles about school or community events. In addition, bulletin boards can also be used to post content-related news articles, posters, or information.

Some of this material, such as a listing of classroom rules, can be placed on posters and displayed on the walls of the classroom if the content is not likely to change during the school year. Designated areas of the whiteboard can also be used to display student assignments or special announcements, because this information is likely to change daily.

Selecting and Teaching Rules and Procedures

Think about all the traffic laws that govern the use of motor vehicles. Guidelines are set for ways to signal, turn, yield the right of way, pass other vehicles, and numerous other aspects of driving. These laws have been established in each state to ensure the safety of the drivers and others. In a similar way, guidelines are also needed in the classroom to govern how the teacher and the students conduct themselves so that learning objectives are achieved and everyone is successful.

Rules and procedures are used to guide and govern student behavior in classrooms. Even in positive learning communities, where students are actively involved in arranging their learning environment, rules and procedures are necessary to guide behavior. Teachers need to carefully consider what rules and procedures are needed to effectively manage the class.

Your philosophical perspective about teaching, classroom management, and discipline will greatly influence how you select rules and procedures. Teachers who prefer to take more control of the classroom decision making will likely select rules and procedures without consulting students. Teachers who prefer to involve students to some degree in the decision making will likely have a discussion with the students and then collaboratively decide on the rules and procedures. Teachers who are very student oriented may turn the discussion over to the students and let them determine the rules and procedures.

As you consider the information on rules and procedures, reflect on your philosophical perspective concerning discipline and classroom management. One model may represent your beliefs about child development and management of student behavior. This, in turn, will give you a perspective about the degree of control that you would want to take when determining rules and procedures.

RULES

Rules refer to general behavioral standards or expectations that are to be followed in the classroom. They are general codes of conduct that are intended to regulate individual behavior in an attempt to avoid disruptive behavior. Rules may be identified to guide the way students interact with each other, prepare for class, and conduct themselves during class. They are commonly stated in positive terms to guide student behavior. In addition to general rules, teachers sometime state rules for specific situations (e.g., gum chewing is not allowed).

Consider these guidelines about creating and enforcing rules:

1. *Examine the need for rules.* Rules provide guidelines for appropriate behaviors so that teaching and learning can take place. They should be directed at organizing the learning environment to ensure the continuity and quality of teaching and learning and not simply focused on exerting control over students.

Rules are necessary for teaching and learning to take place, and they need to be realistic, fair, and reasonable. Rules that are selected should meet the following purposes: (a) the teacher's right to teach is protected; (b) the students' rights to learn are protected; (c) the students' psychological and physical safety are protected; and (d) property is protected (Levin & Nolan, 2010).

You need to examine the way you teach and the type of classroom environment you would like to maintain when considering rules. A number of factors should be considered, including your educational philosophy, the age and maturity of the students, school rules and expectations, the type of classroom climate to be developed, and the rationale for a particular rule.

2. *Select the rules.* After considering the need for classroom rules, you are ready to select rules that are appropriate for your classroom. Sample rules include (a) follow the teacher's directions; (b) obey all school rules; (c) speak politely to all people; and (d) keep your hands, feet, and objects to yourself. These rules are probably appropriate for all grade levels (K–12).

Due to differences in student maturity and developmental levels, some rules may be needed only for certain grade levels. For example, students in the primary grades (K–3) often need direct guidance on many matters. Some additional rules that would be appropriate for these grades may include (a) follow directions the first time they are given, (b) raise your hand and wait to be called on, (c) stay in your seat unless you have permission to get up, and (d) do not leave the room without permission. For departmentalized settings and grade levels, some rules about materials and starting class are often used, such as bring all needed materials to class and be in your seat and ready to work when the bell rings at the start of the period. A number of guidelines for selecting classroom rules are displayed in Figure 9.2.

Consider the degree to which students will be involved in identifying classroom rules. Among other things, student involvement is affected by the teacher's philosophical perspective. Many teachers do not provide for student choice in rule setting; these teachers clearly present the rules and discuss the rationale for them. Other teachers find that students have more commitment and adhere to the rules if they helped set the rules and

FIGURE 9.2

GUIDELINES FOR SELECTING CLASSROOM RULES

1. Make sure classroom rules are consistent with school rules.

2. Involve students in making rules to the degree that you are comfortable and to the degree that the students' age level and sophistication permit.

3. Identify appropriate behaviors, and translate them into positively stated classroom rules.

4. Focus on important behavior.

5. Keep the number of rules to a minimum (four to six).

6. Keep the wording of each rule simple and short.

7. Have rules address behaviors that can be observed.

8. Identify rewards for when students follow the rules and consequences for when they break the rules.

VOICES
from the Classroom

TERESA KRELL, fourth-grade teacher, Corpus Christi, Texas

SELECTING AND REINFORCING RULES

On the very first day of a school year, I make sure that the students understand the guiding rule in my classroom—that no one in the class is allowed to do anything to keep them from learning. Students love the sound of this. They immediately get that they have rights in this new class. Through serious class discussions throughout the first week of school, we really nail down the implications and meanings of this rule. We talk about the hopes of their parents, grandparents, and guardians for their school year, and how none of these people would want anyone to hurt the students' feelings, hurt them physically, or keep them from learning what they need to learn on any given day of school.

After two or three days, the students write what they think the "small rules" should be for our classroom. I read these aloud and students vote on a set of rules that will help the one big rule work. I type these up and make a poster for the room. All the students sign the poster showing that they agree, and we are off to a very problem-free year.

LISA ZEBLEY, first-grade teacher, Virginia Beach, Virginia

On the first day of school, I talk to my first-graders about how children are expected to behave at school. We make a list of the ideas that are brainstormed and then sort these into categories (looks like/sounds like). I then propose one agreement: "I will behave in a way that allows my teachers to teach, lets others learn, and makes my teachers and parents proud!" We then go back to the list and see if all of the ideas fit into our agreement. It always amazes me that children as young as six years old get this concept.

URBAN EDUCATION

FIGURE 9.3

GUIDELINES FOR TEACHING AND REVIEWING CLASSROOM RULES

1. Discuss the rules in the first class session.
2. Discuss the reasons for the rules.
3. Identify specific expectations relevant to each rule. Provide examples and emphasize the positive side of the rules.
4. Inform students of consequences when rules are followed and also when they are broken.
5. Verify students' understanding of the rules.
6. Send a copy of your discipline policy home to families and to the principal.
7. Post the rules in a prominent location.
8. Remind the class of the rules at times other than when someone has just broken a rule.
9. Review the rules regularly.

consequences in the first place. Teachers can be effective managers whether or not they involve students in identifying classroom rules.

3. *Select rewards and consequences.* As previously mentioned, both rewards and penalties need to be identified for the classroom rules. Rewards may include a variety of reinforcers, such as social reinforcers, activities and privileges, tangible reinforcers, and token reinforcers. Students need to be told that these reinforcers will be delivered if they follow the rules. Similarly, students need to be told what consequences will be delivered if they choose to break a rule. When a student gets off task, first provide situational assistance in an effort to get the student back to work. If the student stays off task, then you should deliver mild responses such as nonverbal and verbal actions. If that does not work, you can move to logical consequences and other actions.

4. *Teach and review the rules.* After the classroom rules have been identified, teach them in the first class session as if they were subject-matter content. This discussion should include an explanation of the rules, rehearsal, feedback, and reteaching. It is important that the students recognize the rationale for the rules and are provided with specific expectations for each rule. Specific guidelines for teaching and reviewing classroom rules are displayed in Figure 9.3.

5. *Obtain commitments.* After teaching the rules to the students, have them express their understanding of the rules and indicate their intention to follow the rules. This can be done in a variety of ways. One of the most effective is to have each student sign a copy of the paper that lists the rules and includes a statement such as "I am aware of these rules and understand them." In this way, each student makes an affirmation of the rules. You can keep these signed sheets. An extra copy of the rules could be given to students for placement in their desks or in a notebook.

As discussed earlier, sending the discipline policy home to the families is another means of obtaining a commitment to the policy. In this way, they are informed of the policy at the start of the school year. Parents can contact you if they have any concerns or questions about the discipline policy. If not, they are asked to sign and return a form that states that they are aware of the rules and understand them (similar to the form their child could sign at school).

PROCEDURES

Procedures are approved ways to achieve specific tasks in the classroom. They are intended to help students accomplish a particular task, rather than prevent inappropriate behavior, as in the case of rules. Procedures may be identified to direct activities such as handing in completed work, sharpening a pencil, using the restroom, and putting away supplies. The use of procedures, or routines, has several advantages: they increase the shared understanding for an activity between you and students, reduce the complexity of the classroom environment to a predictable structure, and allow for efficient use of time.

As with rules, it is important to clearly state the procedures, discuss the rationale for them, and provide opportunities for practice and feedback, where appropriate:

■ *Examine the need for procedures.* As a first step, you must examine the need for procedures in your classroom. What activities or actions would benefit from having a procedure that would regularize student conduct in the performance of that action? To answer this key question, you might think about all the actions that take place in the classroom and identify those that would benefit from having an associated procedure.

Fortunately, you do not need to start from scratch in doing this assessment, because research studies of classroom management in K–12 classrooms have produced a framework that can be used to examine and identify typical classroom procedures. A number of the specific areas that might need classroom procedures are displayed in Figure 9.4, some of which are adapted from Emmer and Evertson (2009), Evertson and Emmer (2009), Jones and Jones (2010), and Weinstein and Mignano (2011).

■ *Select the procedures.* When examining the items in Figure 9.4, you need to consider the unique circumstances in your classroom. The grade level, maturity of the students, your preference for order and regularity, and other factors may be taken into account when deciding which items will need a procedure. It may turn out that you will select many items from the table, because these items involve fairly standard actions in many classrooms. After selecting the items needing a procedure, decide specifically what each procedure will be.

FIGURE 9.4

AREAS NEEDING CLASSROOM PROCEDURES

1. **Room Use Procedures**
   a. Teacher's desk and storage areas
   b. Student desks and storage for belongings
   c. Storage for class materials used by all students
   d. Pencil sharpener, wastebasket, sink, drinking fountain
   e. Bathroom
   f. Learning stations, computer areas, equipment areas, centers, and display areas

2. **Transitions in and out of the Classroom**
   a. Beginning the school day
   b. Leaving the room
   c. Returning to the room
   d. Ending the school day

3. **Out-of-Room Procedures**
   a. Bathroom, drinking fountain
   b. Library, resource room
   c. School office
   d. Playground or school grounds
   e. Cafeteria
   f. Lockers
   g. Fire or disaster drills

FIGURE 9.4 (continued)

AREAS NEEDING CLASSROOM PROCEDURES

4. Procedures for Whole-Class Activities and Instruction and Seatwork

   a. Student participation
   b. Signals for student attention
   c. Talk among students
   d. Making assignments
   e. Distributing books, supplies, and materials
   f. Obtaining help
   g. Handing back assignments
   h. Tasks after work is completed
   i. Makeup work
   j. Out-of-seat procedures

5. Procedures during Small-Group Work

   a. Getting the class ready
   b. Taking materials to groups
   c. Student movement in and out of groups
   d. Expected behavior in groups
   e. Expected behavior out of groups

6. Other General Procedures for Secondary Classrooms

   a. Beginning the class period
   - Attendance check
   - Previously absent students
   - Late students
   - Expected student behavior

   b. Out-of-room policies

   c. Materials and equipment
   - What to bring to class
   - Pencil sharpener
   - Other room equipment
   - Student contact with teacher's desk, storage, and other materials

   d. Movement of student desks

   e. Split lunch period

   f. Ending the class period

7. Other Procedures

   a. Classroom helpers
   b. Behavior during delays or interruptions

■ *Teach and review the procedures.* Students should not have to guess if they need to raise their hands during a discussion or interpret subtle signals from you to determine what you want them to do. From the very first day of school, teach and review the various procedures that are needed. Effective teachers spend more time during the first four days of school on management tasks than on academic tasks.

There are several steps that serve as guides when teaching and reviewing classroom procedures with the students:

1. Explain the procedure immediately prior to the first time the activity will take place.

2. Demonstrate the procedure.

3. Practice and check for understanding.

4. Give feedback.

5. Reteach as needed.

6. Review the procedures with the students prior to each situation for the first few weeks.

7. Review the procedures after long holidays.

Maintaining Appropriate Student Behavior

When you walk into a classroom where students are actively engaged in learning and cooperating with the teacher and others, you can almost feel the good vibrations given off by the class. Students want to be involved and productive, and they enjoy working together. This type of classroom, however, does not happen by chance. Teachers take deliberate actions to establish a cooperative, responsible classroom where students will choose to cooperate and make efforts to be academically successful. Students need to feel that they are expected to be orderly, cooperative, and responsible. Developing a positive classroom climate is one of the most important ways to establish and maintain student cooperation and responsibility (Burke, 2008).

There are several factors in maintaining appropriate student behavior. These include having a mental set for management, building positive teacher–student relationships, and reinforcing desired behaviors.

HAVING A MENTAL SET FOR MANAGEMENT

A review of research studies on classroom management has verified the importance and effectiveness of having a mental set about managing student behavior (Marzano et al., 2009). In relation to classroom management, a **mental set** is a teacher's heightened awareness of his or her surroundings and involves a conscious effort to control his or her thoughts and behaviors in that setting. That translates into the following actions that you can take in the classroom when attending to student behavior.

Withitness. Use specific techniques to be aware of the actions of students in your classroom (withitness). Jacob Kounin (1970) is considered the first researcher to systematically study the characteristics of effective classroom managers. He coined the term *withitness* to describe a teacher's disposition (or mental set) to look at all parts of the classroom at all times in order to be aware of what is happening and then to demonstrate this withitness to students by quickly and accurately intervening when there is inappropriate behavior. Reflecting on the old adage, teachers who are "with it" seem to have "eyes in the back of their heads."

Such teachers do these things:

1. *Monitor regularly and react immediately*. To exhibit withitness, you should periodically and systematically scan your classroom, note the behaviors of individual students or groups of students, and respond quickly to inappropriate actions.

2. *Foresee problems.* Another aspect of withitness is the ability to foresee potential problems and make needed adjustments to minimize behavior problems. You should mentally review what might go wrong with specific students in specific classes and consider how you might address these potential problems. When planning certain classroom activities, for example, you might recognize possible confusion or disruption when supplies are being distributed. With this advance thought, you can either modify the way you distribute the materials or take certain precautions when the materials are passed out.

CLASSROOM MANAGEMENT

Jasmine Nichols is an experienced fourth-grade teacher in an urban school district. Misbehavior is rare in her classroom, because she creates a secure environment that fosters mutual respect. Ms. Nichols and her students generate the classroom rules and their consequences during the first class session of the school year. Each student is asked to sign a copy of the rules and consequences, verifying his or her commitment to them and assuming responsibility for his or her own behavior. The rules and expectations are then posted in the classroom.

Ms. Nichols also gives thought to the classroom arrangement to eliminate distractions for her students. Students' desks are located at a reasonable distance from pencil sharpeners, trash cans, and other such distractions. Infrequently used items are out of the way in a nearby supply closet. Ms. Nichols often moves around the room and monitors her students to be sure they are on task.

Ms. Nichols also implements a token reward system to reinforce desired behaviors. If a student is seen exhibiting positive behavior, he or she is rewarded with a Nichols Nickel. Students know that Nichols Nickels can be used to purchase larger rewards, such as homework passes, colored pencil sets, and other classroom necessities. When Ms. Nichols noticed that one of her students helped a fellow classmate organize his notebook, the student was rewarded with a Nickel. In another instance, when Ms. Nichols had a substitute teacher fill in for the day, she rewarded all of her students with Nickels after the substitute left a note mentioning how well the students behaved.

FOCUS QUESTIONS

1. Identify the classroom management techniques that Ms. Nichols uses to promote and maintain appropriate behavior.

2. What are some additional ways to establish a cooperative, responsible classroom?

Emotional Objectivity. Use specific techniques to be emotionally objective with your students. When students misbehave, you may get upset and emotional to some degree. It is important that your disciplinary actions are not seen as an attack on the students involved. You should try to be as objective as possible. **Emotional objectivity** is the ability to interact with students in a businesslike, matter-of-fact manner even though you might be experiencing strong emotions. This is particularly important when you are carrying out negative consequences for inappropriate behavior. Your feelings of anger and frustration are only natural when dealing with misbehavior, but it is not useful to display these emotions when delivering consequences. Look for reasons for the misbehavior, and monitor your own thoughts and attitudes.

BUILDING POSITIVE TEACHER–STUDENT RELATIONSHIPS

Research studies on classroom management highlight the importance of having positive teacher–student relationships in promoting appropriate student behavior (Marzano et al., 2009). The level of dominance and cooperation established by the teacher is an important factor in forming good relationships. An optimal teacher–student relationship consists of equal parts of dominance and cooperation.

Level of Dominance. Effective classroom managers use specific techniques to establish an appropriate level of dominance in the classroom. High dominance is characterized by clarity of purpose and strong guidance in both academic and behavioral aspects of the classroom. Thus, the teacher provides guidance about the content to be addressed and the behavior to be expected in the class. A moderate to high level of dominance and a moderate to high level of cooperation (addressed next) provide the optimal teacher–student relationship for learning (Marzano et al., 2009).

You can express dominance in the following ways:

1. *Establish rules and procedures.* The rules and procedures that you determine will clearly help establish your dominance in the classroom.

2. *Use disciplinary interventions.* When misbehavior occurs, follow it with interventions to stop the inappropriate behavior. Your use of interventions is another expression of your dominance in the classroom.

3. *Exhibit assertive behavior.* One of the best ways to communicate a proper level of dominance is to exhibit assertive behavior. **Assertive behavior** involves standing up for one's legitimate rights in ways that make it less likely that others will ignore or circumvent them. To express assertive behavior, you can use assertive body language, speak in an appropriate tone of voice, and persist until the appropriate behavior is displayed.

4. *Establish clear learning goals.* Another way to express a proper level of dominance is to be very clear about the learning goals to be addressed in a unit, a quarter, or a semester. Clear learning goals can be communicated by establishing learning goals at the beginning of a unit of instruction, providing feedback on those goals, continuously and systematically revisiting the goals, and providing summative feedback regarding the goals.

Level of Cooperation. Effective classroom managers use specific behaviors that communicate an appropriate level of cooperation. High cooperation is characterized by a concern for the needs and opinions of others and a desire to function as a member of a team as opposed to an individual. A moderate to high level of dominance and a moderate to high level of cooperation provide the optimal teacher–student relationship for learning (Marzano et al., 2009).

You can promote cooperation in the following ways:

1. *Provide flexible learning goals.* While you will determine the learning goals for each lesson and unit, you may provide some flexibility by allowing students to set some of their own learning goals at the beginning of a unit or by asking students what they would like to learn. This conveys a sense of cooperation.

VOICES from the Classroom

MARJORIE MARKS, middle school communication arts teacher, Wixom, Michigan

SELECTING AND DISCUSSING RULES

My rules and procedures do not vary among the three grade levels I teach, and my students are told on the first day (through verbal discussion and succinct handouts) that respect is the critical aspect of our learning environment. I emphasize that each detail of behavior, work ethic, and project outcomes are directly influenced by the level of respect we show one another and ourselves. I talk to my classes openly and warmly about this, as I do not believe that being harsh or threatening elicits a respectful, unified classroom environment.

Together, we offer examples that illustrate respectful behavior, such as being on time to class, showing kindness to your peers, sticking to a project with effort, exhibiting energy and open-mindedness, and doing what you say you're going to do. All of these represent self-respect and respect toward others. My classroom quickly becomes a Safe Zone where we do our individual best and support one another.

2. *Take a personal interest in students.* All students appreciate the personal attention of the teacher, and anything that you do to show interest in students as individuals has an impact on their learning. For example, you could talk informally with students before, during, and after class about their interests. Or you could compliment students on important achievements in and outside of school, single out a few students each day in the lunchroom and talk with them, or comment on important events in their lives.

3. *Use equitable and positive classroom behaviors.* Teachers should ensure that their behaviors are equal and equitable for all students, thus creating an atmosphere in which all students feel accepted. These behaviors also foster positive teacher–student relationships. This can be done in many ways, such as making eye contact with each student in the room, deliberately moving toward and being close to each student, allowing and encouraging all students to be part of class discussions and interactions, and providing appropriate wait time for all students.

4. *Respond appropriately to students' incorrect responses.* When students respond incorrectly or make no response at all to a question you have posed, they are particularly vulnerable. Your appropriate actions at these critical points go a long way toward establishing a positive teacher–student relationship. You can emphasize what was right, encourage collaboration, restate the question, rephrase the question, give hints or cues, provide the answer and then ask for elaboration, and respect the student's option to pass, when appropriate.

Interacting with Students. A significant body of research indicates that academic achievement and student behavior are influenced by the quality of the teacher–student relationship (Jones & Jones, 2010). Students prefer teachers who are warm and friendly. Students who feel liked by their teachers are reported to have higher academic achievement and more productive classroom behavior than students who feel their teachers hold them in low regard.

This research suggests that you need to learn and conscientiously apply skills in relating more positively to students. The guidelines listed here will help you build positive relationships (Charles, 2011; Good & Brophy, 2008; Jones & Jones, 2010):

1. *Use human relations skills.* When managing the classroom climate, appropriate **human relations skills** are needed. There are four general human relations skills that apply to almost everyone in all situations: friendliness, positive attitude, the ability to listen, and the ability to compliment genuinely (Charles, 2011). When working with students, also give regular attention, use reinforcement, show continual willingness to help, and model courtesy and good manners.

2. *Enable success.* Students need to experience success. Successful experiences are instrumental in developing feelings of self-worth and confidence toward new activities. Students need to be provided with opportunities to achieve true accomplishments and to realize significant improvements (Charles, 2011). Learning is increased when students experience high rates of success in completing tasks (Jones & Jones, 2010). Students tend to raise their expectations and set higher goals. Failure, however, is met with lowered aspirations.

To establish moderate to high rates of success, (a) establish unit and lesson content that reflects prior learning; (b) correct partially correct, correct but hesitant, and incorrect answers; (c) divide instructional stimuli into small segments at the learners' current level of functioning; (d) change instructional stimuli gradually; and (e) vary the instructional pace or tempo to create momentum.

3. *Communicate basic attitudes and expectations to students, and model them in your behavior.* Students tend to conform not so much to what teachers say as to what they actually expect. You must think through what you really expect from your students and then see that your own behavior is consistent with those expectations. If you expect students to be polite to each other, for example, you should treat your students in the same manner.

4. *Communicate high expectations.* Teacher behaviors that create positive expectations almost always enhance the teacher–student relationship, and behaviors that create negative expectations result in poor relationships and poor student self-concepts and thus reduce learning. For example, students often put forth a solid effort when you say that work may be hard but also express confidence that they will be able to do it.

5. *Be fair and consistent.* Students want to be treated fairly, not preferentially. Your credibility is established largely by making sure that your words and actions coincide and by pointing this out to the class when necessary. If students can depend on what you say, they will be less likely to test you constantly.

6. *Show respect and affection to students.* You must like your students and respect them as individuals. Your enjoyment of students and concern for their welfare will come through in tone of voice, facial expressions, and other routine behaviors. Middle and secondary teachers should make efforts to get to know students personally. Students who like and respect their teachers will want to please them and will be more likely to imitate their behavior and attitudes.

7. *Create opportunities for personal discussions.* Beyond day-to-day activities, teachers often find it helpful to set time aside to get to know their students. Some possible activities include (a) talking with students before and after class; (b) demonstrating your interest in students' activities; (c) arranging for interviews with students; (d) sending letters and notes to students; (e) using a suggestion box; and (f) joining in school and community events (Jones & Jones, 2010).

REINFORCING DESIRED BEHAVIORS

A **reinforcer** is an event or consequence that increases the strength or future probability of the behavior it follows. Reinforcement is used to strengthen behaviors that are valued and to motivate students to do things that will benefit them.

It is important to recognize the general principle of reinforcement: *Behaviors that are reinforced will be retained; behaviors that are not reinforced will be extinguished.* You need to carefully consider whom to reinforce, under what conditions, and with what kinds of reinforcement. Reinforcement is likely to be effective only to the extent that (1) the consequences used for reinforcers are experienced as reinforcers by the student; (2) reinforcers are contingent on the student achieving specific performance objectives; and (3) reinforcers are awarded in a way that complements rather than undermines the development of intrinsic motivation and other natural outcomes of behavior (Good & Brophy, 2008).

Several techniques of reinforcement are available, including recognition, activities and privileges, tangible reinforcers, and token reinforcers. Many of these reinforcers can be used with both individual students and the entire class.

Recognition. **Recognition** is a **social reinforcer** serving as a positive consequence to appropriate behavior. Social reinforcers may be expressed as verbal or written expressions, nonverbal facial or bodily expressions, nonverbal proximity, and nonverbal physical contact. Social reinforcers are especially valued by students when given by people important to them. Social forms of approval are especially useful when reinforcing student behavior if you and the students have a good relationship.

Praise is an expression of approval by the teacher after the student has attained something, and social reinforcers are often used to express this praise. Recognition should always be contingent on performance of appropriate behavior. You should be specific about the behavior that resulted in the praise and the reasons for giving it.

Most social reinforcement should be done privately with the student, but some may be done publicly. You need to carefully consider student characteristics when deciding how to deliver praise. A seventh-grader, for example, might be somewhat embarrassed being praised in front of the class.

TABLE 9.1

Examples of Activity and Privilege Reinforcers

PRIVILEGES	CLASSROOM JOBS
Playing a game	Distributing or collecting papers and materials
Helping the teacher	Taking attendance
Going to the library	Adjusting the window shades
Decorating a bulletin board	Taking a note to the office
Working or studying with a friend	Watering the plants
Reading for pleasure	Stapling papers together
Using the computer	Erasing the whiteboard
Writing on the whiteboard	Operating a computer or projector
Earning extra recess time	Cleaning the erasers

Activities and Privileges. **Activity reinforcers** include privileges and preferred activities. After students complete desired activities or behave in appropriate ways, you can then reinforce them with various activities and privileges. Some of these reinforcers can be various jobs as a classroom helper. Activity reinforcers are often very effective for reinforcing the entire class. A list of sample activities and privileges that can be used as reinforcers is provided in Table 9.1.

It is important to verify that certain behaviors are desirable. When you and students are on good terms, students just performing certain tasks such as straightening the room and cleaning the whiteboards with you can be rewarding. Many other activities and privileges have an intrinsic value that does not depend on a student's relationship to you. Running errands, studying with a friend, going to the library, being first in line, or choosing an activity are likely to be positive incentives that produce satisfaction in their own right. You may have students fill out a sheet at the beginning of the school year to identify activities and reinforcers that they would appreciate.

Tangible Reinforcers. **Tangible,** or **material, reinforcers** are objects valued in and of themselves: certificates, awards, stars, buttons, bookmarkers, book covers, posters, ribbons, plaques, and report cards. Food also may serve as a tangible reinforcer: cookies, sugarless gum, popcorn, jelly beans, peanuts, candy, or raisins.

If you are interested in using food (M & Ms, cookies, etc.), recognize some cautions. Some families may object to certain foods (such as those high in sugar), and there may be cultural differences related to food. Students may be allergic to certain foods, and health and state regulations may govern dispensing food in schools.

Since tangible reinforcers serve as external or extrinsic reinforcement, their use should be limited. Other types of reinforcers are generally more available and more reinforcing in natural settings than tangible reinforcers. When you give awards, it is a good idea to distribute them so as to include a good number of the students. Don't give awards only for outstanding achievement; award for improvement, excellent effort, good conduct, creativity, and so on.

Token Reinforcers. A **token reinforcer** is a tangible item that can be exchanged for a desired object, activity, or social reinforcer at a later time. Tokens may be chips, points, stars, tickets, buttons, play money, metal washers, happy faces, or stickers. The backup reinforcer is the reward for which tokens can be exchanged. Token reinforcement is useful when praise and attention have not worked. Tokens are accumulated and cashed in for the reinforcer.

Key Terms

Activity center	Emotional objectivity	Order	Situational assistance
Activity reinforcers	Human relations	Praise	Skeleton plan
Assertive behavior	skills	Procedures	Social reinforcers
Classroom management	Mental set	Recognition	Tangible or material
Course syllabus	Misbehavior	Reinforcer	reinforcers
Discipline	Off-task behavior	Rules	Token reinforcers

Major Concepts

1. Classroom management involves teacher actions to create a learning environment that encourages positive social interaction, active engagement in learning, and self-motivation.

2. Maintaining order means that students are performing within acceptable limits the actions necessary for a particular classroom event to be successful.

3. Establishing order begins by preparing for the start of the school year, organizing the classroom and materials, and selecting and teaching rules and procedures.

4. Organizing your classroom and materials involves decisions about floor space, storage space, and bulletin boards and wall space.

5. Rules refer to general behavioral guidelines or expectations that are to be followed in the classroom. Procedures are approved ways to achieve specific tasks in the classroom.

6. Effective classroom managers have a mental set for management, in which they consciously have a high awareness for the actions in the classroom and respond quickly when misbehavior occurs.

7. Recognition, activities and privileges, tangible reinforcers, and token reinforcers can be used to reinforce desired student behavior.

Discussion/Reflective Questions

1. What are the benefits of planning uncomplicated lessons at the start of the school year? What might happen if the lessons are too challenging?

2. What are the merits of having a plan for systematically dealing with misbehavior?

3. What are the advantages and disadvantages of involving students in the selection of rules and procedures?

4. What can you do to exhibit withitness in your classroom so that you monitor regularly, react immediately, and foresee problems?

5. How might your selection and use of reinforcers be affected by subject area or grade level?

Suggested Activities

FOR CLINICAL SETTINGS

1. For your grade level or subject area, select the classroom rules that you prefer to use. Next, develop a plan for teaching these rules to the students on the first day of class.

2. For your grade level or subject area, select the classroom procedures you prefer to use for the areas identified in Figure 9.4.

3. List some guidelines for yourself as you take actions to create an appropriate level of dominance and cooperation in your classroom.

FOR FIELD EXPERIENCES

1. Find out what policies exist in the school district and the school for student conduct and academic expectations (e.g., homework).

2. Talk to two or more teachers to determine what rules and specific procedures they use.

3. Talk to teachers to identify specifically how they begin the school year and establish their classroom management system.

Further Reading

Burden, P. R. (2013). *Classroom management: Creating a successful K–12 learning community* (5th ed.). New York: Wiley.

Provides a comprehensive K–12 review of ways to create a learning community. It carries a practical, realistic view of decisions teachers make about getting organized for management, planning for management, managing when conducting the class, and restoring order after misbehavior.

Burke, K. (2008). *What to do with the kid who . . . : Developing cooperation, self-discipline, and responsibility in the classroom* (3rd ed.). Thousand Oaks, CA: Corwin Press.

Offers guidelines for setting a positive classroom climate, teaching students appropriate social skills, and helping students who won't accept responsibility or who cause class disruptions.

Wong, H. K., & Wong R. T. (2009). *The first days of school: How to be an effective teacher* (4th ed.). Mountain View, CA: Harry K. Wong.

Includes a number of practical suggestions to prepare for the school year and to conduct the opening days of school. Covers characteristics of effective teachers, positive expectations, classroom management, lesson mastery, and professional development.

Technology Resources

CLASSROOM MANAGEMENT STRATEGIES

http://www.theteachersguide.com/
ClassManagement.htm

Includes many links to sites with recommendations about classroom management and discipline. Also has links to other teacher-related topics.

PREPARING FOR THE FIRST DAY OF CLASS

http://backtoschool.about.com/od/forteachers/
Preparing_for_the_First_Day_of_Class.htm

Includes many articles and links offering specific suggestions to start the school year successfully.

BLOGGER

http://www.blogger.com

Blogger is a Google tool and offers lots of tools for easy blogging. You will need a Google account (free), but it works well with all the other Google tools. You can search for classroom management topics in this blog.

NOODLE TOOLS

http://www.noodletools.com/debbie/literacies/information/5locate/adviceengine.html

Noodle Tools provides a range of free and subscription-based Web search and annotations tools. The free "Choose the Best Search for Your Information Need" tool helps you define topics, select search tools, and search effectively.

MyEducationLab™

Go to the **MyEducationLab** (www.myeducationlab.com) for General Methods and familiarize yourself with the content:

- Topically organized Assignments and Activities, tied to learning outcomes for the course, that can help you more deeply understand course content
- Topically organized Building Teaching Skills and Dispositions learning units allow you to apply and develop understanding of teaching methods.
- A chapter-specific pretest that assesses your understanding of the content offers hints and feedback for

each question and generates a study plan including links to Review, Practice, and Enrichment activities that will enhance your understanding of the concepts. A Study Plan posttest with hints and feedback ensures you understood concepts from the chapter after having completed the enrichment activities.

A Correlation Guide may be downloaded by instructors to show how MyEducationLab content aligns to this book.

Even when teachers have an effective management system in place, students may lose interest in a lesson and get off task. You must be prepared to respond with appropriate strategies to restore order. To provide a context for your decision making in this area, you should first understand misbehavior in context and the types and causes of misbehavior. A three-step response plan for misbehavior is described. Next, chronic misbehaviors are discussed, and ways to address them are identified. Finally, many aspects of bullying are addressed.

Misbehavior

Misbehavior is any student behavior that is perceived by the teacher to compete with or threaten the academic actions at a particular moment. Misbehavior creates disruptions in the academic flow of classroom activities, but not every infraction of a rule is necessarily misbehavior. Therefore, misbehavior needs to be seen as an action in context and requires a considerable amount of interpretation when decisions are made about addressing it.

First, it is important to recognize that the best way to deal with discipline problems is to avoid them in the first place. Teachers should develop challenging, interesting, and exciting lessons and treat students with dignity and respect. You should also establish an effective classroom management system, as described in other chapters. If misbehavior then occurs, teachers can consider the guidelines and principles presented in this chapter.

MISBEHAVIOR IN CONTEXT

Students who are off task are not performing the planned instructional activity. They may be pausing to think about an issue, daydreaming, or doing other things that are nondisruptive but prohibit them from being engaged in the instructional activities. Students who are off task need to be addressed differently than students who are purposely misbehaving and interfering with the academic activities. In such cases, you may need to intervene to stop the misbehavior.

Recognize that your decisions about interventions are complex judgments about the act, the student, and the circumstances at a particular moment in the classroom. Some student actions are clearly misbehavior and require teacher intervention. In many cases, however, the situation is not quite as simple. The key to understanding misbehavior is to view what students do in the context of the classroom structure. Not every infraction of a rule is necessarily misbehavior. For instance, inattention in the last few minutes of a class session will often be tolerated because the lesson is coming to an end. However, you would most likely intervene when inattention is evident earlier in the class.

TYPES OF MISBEHAVIOR

Misbehavior includes behavior that interferes with your teaching, interferes with the rights of others to learn, is psychologically or

There are 10 InTASC standards (see pages xx–xxi), and each standard in the original document includes a list of performances, essential knowledge, and critical dispositions to indicate more clearly what is intended in the standard.

Since this chapter deals with classroom discipline, some representative statements from InTASC Standard #1, Learner Development; Standard #3, Learning Environments; and Standard #8, Instructional Strategies, are listed here concerning topics in this chapter.

PERFORMANCES

■ The teacher collaborates with learners and colleagues to develop shared values and expectations for respectful interactions, rigorous academic discussions, and individual and group responsibility for quality work. (InTASC #3)

■ The teacher communicates verbally and nonverbally in ways that demonstrate respect for and responsiveness to the cultural backgrounds and differing perspectives learners bring to the learning environment. (InTASC # 3)

ESSENTIAL KNOWLEDGE

■ The teacher identifies readiness for learning, and understands how development in any one area may affect performance in others. (InTASC #1)

■ The teacher understands how multiple forms of communication (oral, nonverbal, digital, visual) convey ideas, foster self expression, and build relationships. (InTASC #8)

CRITICAL DISPOSITIONS

■ The teacher takes responsibility for promoting learners' growth and development. (InTASC #1)

■ The teacher seeks to foster respectful communications among all members of the learning community. (InTASC #3)

physically unsafe, or destroys property. This misbehavior may show up in the classroom in a number of ways, as indicated in the following categories:

■ *Needless talk.* Talks during instructional time about topics unrelated to the lesson or talks when should be silent.

■ *Annoying others.* Teases, calls names, or bothers others.

■ *Moving around the room.* Moves around the room without permission or goes to areas that are not permitted.

■ *Noncompliance.* Does not do what is requested, breaks rules, argues, makes excuses, delays, does the opposite of what is asked.

■ *Disruption.* Talks or laughs inappropriately, hums or makes noises, gets into things, causes "accidents."

■ *Aggressive actions.* Shows hostility toward others, pushes or fights, verbally abuses, is cruel to others, damages property, steals others' property.

■ *Defiance of authority.* Is hostile to comply with the teacher's requests, talks back to the teacher.

CAUSES OF MISBEHAVIOR

One way to understand classroom control is to determine why students misbehave. In some cases, the reasons are complex and personal and perhaps beyond your comprehension or control. But some misbehavior comes from common, general causes that can be anticipated:

1. *Health factors.* Student behavior problems may be related to health factors. Lack of sleep, an allergy, illness, or an inadequate diet can greatly affect a student's ability to complete assignments or interact with others. For some children, sugar has an effect on their

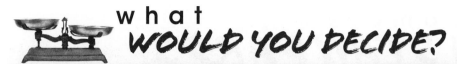

what WOULD YOU DECIDE?

DEALING WITH A SLEEPY STUDENT

You have a student in your classroom who has difficulty paying attention in class and appears to be sleepy much of the time. One day during a classroom film, the student fell asleep. Many other days, she does not complete her class work or homework.

1. What might be some reasons for the student's sleepiness and lack of attention in class?

2. What might you do to identify the actual cause of the sleepiness and inattention?

behavior and may result in hyperactivity. Physical impairments—such as a vision or hearing loss, paralysis, or a severe physiological disorder—may also contribute to behavior problems.

2. *Neurological conditions.* Some students may have a mental disorder that affects their behavior. For example, attention-deficit disorder is a mental condition in which the area of the brain that controls motor activity does not work like it should. This is one of the most common childhood mental disorders and affects between 3 and 5 percent of school-aged children, according to the National Institute of Mental Health (2008). Such students may be inattentive (are easily distracted, don't follow directions well, shift from one unfinished task to another, and seem not to be listening), hyperactive (talkative, fidgety, and squirmy), or impulsive (don't wait their turn, blurt out answers, and engage in dangerous activities without considering the consequences). Children born with fetal alcohol syndrome may be hyperactive or impulsive, and children born to women who used crack cocaine during pregnancy may exhibit similar behaviors.

3. *Medication or drugs.* Medication or drugs, whether legal or illegal, may also be a factor. Over-the-counter medicine for nasal congestion, for example, may cause a student to be less alert than usual. Alcohol or drug abuse also may contribute to unusual behavior at school.

4. *Influences from the home or society.* Conditions in the student's home may be related to behavior problems. Student behavior problems may be associated with a lack of adequate clothing or housing, parental supervision and types of discipline, or home routines or by significant events such as divorce or the death of a friend or relative. Factors in the community or in society also may contribute to student behavior problems. There has been considerable concern and debate over the effects of television on the beliefs and conduct of children. Violence on television is seen by some to influence students to be more aggressive.

5. *The physical environment.* The physical arrangement of the classroom, temperature, noise, and lighting may affect student behavior. Student crowding may also be involved. These factors may contribute to a student's lack of commitment to a lesson and may lead to inattention and misbehavior.

6. *Poor behavior decisions by students.* The classroom is a complex environment for students as well as for teachers. Students are confronted with challenges, temptations, and circumstances that will cause them to make decisions about their own behavior. Their own personalities and habits come into play here. Given all of these factors, students will sometimes make poor decisions that lead to misbehavior.

7. *Other students in the classroom.* Some misbehavior results from students being provoked by other students in the classroom. A student may be drawn into an incident of misbehavior when another student does something inappropriate. In addition, peer pressure from other students may cause individual students to misbehave in ways they would not consider by themselves.

VOICES
from the Classroom

KURT GRABER, high school science teacher, Dallas, Texas

HIDDEN CAUSES OF MISBEHAVIOR

Some of our students have challenging and even turbulent lives. It can be both emotionally and physiologically difficult for them to achieve a state of readiness to learn when they arrive in our classrooms. We may see the negative classroom behaviors, but we sometimes do not see the causes of their misbehavior. When we are able to identify the cause of the misbehavior, we are sometimes more able to help them.

For example, Johnny was provoking a fight with nearly everyone in class one morning. We didn't know until later that, once again, Johnny had been slapped around in the school parking lot by his stepfather. In class, we only saw his fighting and didn't realize he was in pain and distress.

Sharona came to class nearly every day with a wide array of new and highly fashionable cosmetics—lip gloss, foundation, makeup, eyeliner, and even some lotion for the boys. She had it all. Her show-and-tell in the opening minutes of each day led to some disruption. We later learned that she hails from a small Latin American country and that she is somewhat insecure about herself. She used the cosmetics as a way to gain approval from her peers. For our science fair, I fortunately was able to guide her to do a project about making lipstick, and this earned her quite a bit of admiration and popularity in a constructive way.

URBAN EDUCATION

8. *Teacher factors when managing the class.* Teachers sometimes needlessly create disciplinary problems by the way they manage and conduct their classes. Inappropriate teacher behaviors include being overly negative, maintaining an authoritarian climate, overreacting to situations, using mass punishment for all students, blaming students, lacking a clear instructional goal, repeating or reviewing already learned material, pausing too long during instruction, dealing with one student at length, and lacking recognition of student ability levels. While few teachers can avoid all of these behaviors all of the time, effective teachers recognize the potentially damaging effects on classroom order and discipline. Being aware of these characteristics is the first step to avoiding them. It is useful periodically to reflect on your own teaching behavior to determine whether you are taking actions that are contributing to inattention or misbehavior.

9. *Teacher factors concerning instruction.* Teachers make many decisions about the content and delivery of instruction. Students may lose interest in a lesson if the teacher presents uninteresting lessons, does not plan meaningful activities or engage students in the lessons, is ineffective in instructional delivery, or does not deliberately plan to incorporate motivational elements into the instruction. When students lose interest in a lesson, they are more likely to get off task and misbehave.

Three-Step Response Plan

The teacher must decide when and how to intervene when students are off task or misbehaving. An **intervention** is an action taken by the teacher that is intended to stop the disruptive actions and return the student to the academic activities.

Intervention decisions are typically based on the teacher's knowledge of who is misbehaving, what the misbehavior is, and when it occurs. Decisions about the intensity of the intervention may depend on the student's history of inappropriate behavior. However, you should not automatically jump to conclusions if an incident involves a student with a history of behavior problems. It is helpful to discuss the problem with the student to clarify the problem from both your perspective and the student's before considering possible interventions.

The **principle of least intervention** states that when routine classroom behavior is being handled, misbehaviors should be corrected with the simplest, least intrusive intervention that will work (Slavin, 2012). If the least intrusive intervention does not work, then you move up to a more intrusive approach. The main goal is to handle the misbehavior in an effective manner that avoids unnecessarily disrupting the lesson. To the extent possible, the lesson should continue while the misbehavior is handled.

How do you apply this principle of least intervention? You can use a three-step response plan to address off-task behavior and misbehavior. When you notice students starting to lose interest in the lesson or beginning to get off task, you can provide situational assistance—these are actions to help the student cope with the situation and stay on task. If the student then is still off task, you can select mild responses to get the student back on task. If mild responses are not effective, you can use moderate responses. If misbehavior continues after moderate responses are applied, other interventions may be needed. In these cases, it is useful to discuss the situation with the principal and school counselor. Based on the principle of least intervention, this three-step response plan is displayed in Table 10.1.

TABLE 10.1

Three-Step Response Plan to Misbehavior Using the Principle of Least Intervention			
TEACHER RESPONSE	**STEP 1: PROVIDE SITUATIONAL ASSISTANCE**	**STEP 2: USE MILD RESPONSES**	**STEP 3: USE MODERATE RESPONSES**
Purpose	To help the student to cope with the instructional situation and keep the student on task	To take nonpunitive actions to get the student back on task	To remove specific stimuli to decrease unwanted behavior
Sample actions	■ Remove distracting objects. ■ Provide support with routines. ■ Reinforce appropriate behaviors. ■ Boost student interest. ■ Provide cues. ■ Help students over hurdles. ■ Redirect the behavior. ■ Provide nonpunitive time-out. ■ Modify the classroom environment.	**Nonverbal responses:** ■ Ignore the behavior. ■ Use nonverbal signals. ■ Stand near the student. ■ Touch the student. **Verbal responses:** ■ Call on the student during the lesson. ■ Use humor. ■ Send an I-message. ■ Use positive phrasing. ■ Remind students of the rules. ■ Give students choices. ■ Ask "What should you be doing?" ■ Give a verbal reprimand.	**Logical consequences:** ■ Withdraw privileges. ■ Change the seat assignment. ■ Have the student write reflections on the problem. ■ Place the student in a time-out. ■ Hold the student for detention. ■ Contact the family. ■ Have the student visit the principal.

SITUATIONAL ASSISTANCE

Students sometimes pause from the instructional task to look out the window, daydream, fiddle with a comb or other object, or simply take a brief mental break from the work. In these examples, the students are not misbehaving; they are simply off task for a short time. You should take steps to draw the student back into the lesson and to keep the student on task.

To communicate to students that you have noticed off-task behavior, you should first provide **situational assistance**—actions designed to help the students cope with the instructional situation and to keep them on task or to get them back on task before problems worsen. Problem behaviors thus can be stopped early before they escalate or involve other students.

If students remain off task after situational assistance has been provided, move on to mild responses. These nonverbal and verbal nonpunitive responses are designed to get the student back on task. The continuum of responses to misbehavior (see Table 10.1) illustrates that situational assistance is the starting point when dealing with off-task behavior. The following techniques can be used to provide situational assistance to help get the students back on task:

1. *Remove distracting objects.* Students sometimes bring objects to school that may be distracting, such as combs, keys, or magazines. When you see that such an object is keeping a student from the assigned tasks, simply walk over to him or her and collect the object. The student should be quietly informed that the object can be picked up after class. Be kind and firm; no discussion is necessary. Inform students that they should store such objects in an appropriate place before school.

2. *Provide support with routines.* Students appreciate and often find comfort in knowing what is going to happen during the class period or during the day. They like to know where, when, why, and with whom they will be at various times. It is helpful to announce and post the daily schedule. Changes in the schedule should be announced in advance, if possible. Even for a single lesson, students often appreciate knowing at the start what activities are planned for the lesson. Knowing the schedule provides students with a sense of security and direction. Routines for entering and leaving the classroom, distributing classroom papers and materials, and participating in group work contribute to this sense of security.

3. *Reinforce appropriate behaviors.* Students who have followed the directions can be praised. This communicates to the student who is off task what is expected. A statement such as "I'm pleased to see that Juan has his notebook ready for today's lesson" communicates to others what is expected. Appropriate behavior is reinforced while simultaneously a signal is given to students who are off task. This approach is more commonly used in elementary classrooms; middle and secondary students may consider it to be a little juvenile.

4. *Boost student interest.* Student interest may wane in time as the lesson proceeds. You should express interest in the student's work when he or she shows signs of losing interest or being bored. Offer to help, noting how much work has been completed, noting how well done the completed part of the task is, or discussing the task. These actions can help bring the student back on task. Interest boosting is often needed when students do individual or small-group class work.

5. *Provide cues.* Sometimes all the students are asked to do one thing, such as to prepare their materials or to clean up at the end of class, and cues can be given in these cases. **Cues** are signals that it is time for a selected behavior. For example, you may close the door at the start of class as a cue that instruction is about to begin and that everyone is expected to have all materials ready. The lights could be flipped or a bell sounded to signal time to begin cleanup or to finish small-group work. You can select an appropriate cue and explain its use to the students. This conveys behavioral expectations and encourages constructive, on-task behavior.

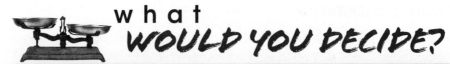

USING CUES OR SIGNALS

Imagine that your students are working in cooperative learning groups on a seven-day project. When they come into the room, they immediately go to their groups and start work. On some days and during some of the class sessions, you need to give some information to all students.

1. How can you use a cue as a signal for students to stop work at that point and pay attention to you?

2. How can you give a cue that it is time to prepare to leave the class at the end of the class period?

6. *Help students over hurdles.* Students who are experiencing difficulty with a specific task need help in overcoming the problem—helping them over a hurdle—to keep them on task. **Hurdle helping** may consist of encouraging words from you, offering to assist with a specific task, or making available additional materials or equipment. For example, in a seatwork activity in which students need to draw several elements, including some straight lines, you might notice that one student is becoming upset that his or her lines are not straight. You could help by handing the student a ruler. In this way, you help before the student gives up on the assignment or becomes disruptive.

7. *Redirect the behavior.* When students show signs of losing interest, you can ask them to answer a question, do a problem, or read as a means of drawing them back into the lesson. Students should be treated as if they were paying attention and should be reinforced if they respond appropriately. It is important not to embarrass or ridicule students by saying that they would have been able to answer the question if they had been paying attention. Simply by asking a content-related question, you will show students that you are trying to draw them back into the lesson. Redirecting student behavior back into the lesson discourages off-task behavior.

8. *Alter the lesson.* Lessons sometimes do not go as well as you would like, and students may lose interest in them for a variety of reasons. The lesson needs to be altered in some way when students are seen daydreaming, writing notes to friends, yawning, stretching, or moving around in their seats. When altering the lesson, select a different type of activity than the one that has proven unsuccessful. For example, if a whole-class discussion proves to be unsuccessful, you might have students work in pairs on a related issue that still deals with the lesson's objectives.

9. *Provide a nonpunitive time-out.* Students who become frustrated, agitated, or fatigued may get off task and disruptive. When you notice this happening, provide a nonpunitive time-out. A **time-out** is a period of time that the student is away from the instructional situation to calm down and reorganize his or her thoughts. The student then returns to the task with a fresh perspective. This time-out is not intended to be punishment for the off-task behavior. When a time-out is needed, you can ask the student to run an errand, help you with something, go get a drink, or do some other task not related to the instructional activity. Be alert to students showing signs of frustration and agitation and be ready to respond quickly.

10. *Modify the classroom environment.* The classroom environment itself may contribute to off-task behavior. The arrangement of the desks, tables, instructional materials, and other items in the classroom may give rise to inefficient traffic patterns or limited views of the instructional areas. Other factors include the boundaries between areas for quiet student and group projects and access to supplies. In addition, both your actions and those of your students may affect their behavior. Once misbehavior develops, you may need to separate the students or change the setting in some way. Examine the disturbance and identify the element that contributes to it. Modification in the classroom arrangement may include moving tables, student desks, or the storage area.

MILD RESPONSES

Students may misbehave even after you have developed a system of rules and procedures, provided a supportive instructional environment, and given situational assistance to get misbehaving students back on task. In that case, mild responses should be used to correct the student's behavior. **Mild responses** are nonpunitive ways to deal with misbehavior while providing guidance for appropriate behavior. Nonverbal and verbal mild responses are meant to stop the off-task behavior and to restore order. The three-step response plan shown in Table 10.1 illustrates the movement to more directive responses if situational assistance is not successful.

Nonverbal Responses. Even with situational assistance, students may get off task. Nonverbal responses are taken as a nonpunitive means to get the student back on task. **Nonverbal responses** may include planned ignoring, signal interference, proximity control, and touch control. These approaches are taken in increasing order of teacher involvement and control.

   1. *Ignore the behavior.* Intentionally ignoring minor misbehavior is sometimes the best course of action as a means to weaken the behavior. This is based on the reinforcement principle called **extinction**; that is, if you ignore a behavior and withhold reinforcement, the behavior will lessen and ultimately disappear. Minor misbehaviors that might be ignored are pencil tapping, body movements, hand waving, book dropping, calling out an answer instead of raising a hand, interrupting the teacher, whispering, and so on. Student behaviors designed to get your attention or that of their classmates are likely candidates for extinction, or ignoring the behavior.

   Ignoring the behavior is best used to control only behaviors that cause little interference to teaching/learning, and it should be combined with praise for appropriate behavior. Extinction is inappropriate for behaviors (e.g., talking out, aggression) reinforced by consequences that you do not control and behaviors (violence) that cannot be tolerated during the time required for extinction to work (Kerr & Nelson, 2010). If the behavior continues after a reasonable period of planned ignoring, you should be more directive.

   There are limitations to ignoring the behavior. One risk is that students may conclude that you are not aware of what is happening and may continue the behavior. While you may ignore the behavior and not give the student the desired attention, other students may give such attention. Furthermore, the student may continue the behavior for a while after you ignore it, and thus the time taken for correcting the problem will be too long. Aggressive or hostile behaviors may be too dangerous to ignore.

   2. *Use nonverbal signals.* A nonverbal signal can be used to communicate to the disrupting student that the behavior is not appropriate. Signals must be directed at the student. They let the student know that the behavior is inappropriate and that it is time to get back to work.

   Nonverbal signal interference may include making eye contact with the student who is writing a note, shaking a hand or finger to indicate not to do some inappropriate action, holding a hand up to stop a student's calling out, or giving the "teacher look." These actions should be done in a businesslike manner. You need to move to the next level of intervention if these disruptive behaviors persist.

   3. *Stand near the student.* Using your physical presence near the disruptive student to help him or her get back on task is **proximity control**. This is warranted at times when you cannot get the student's attention to send a signal because he or she is so engrossed in an inappropriate action. For example, a student may be reading something other than

VOICES
from the Classroom

LYNNE HAGAR, high school history and English teacher, Mesquite, Texas

USING BODY LANGUAGE AND THE "TEACHER LOOK"

I am a small woman, but I can effectively control 30 senior students just by using my voice and my body language. When I want a certain behavior to stop, the first thing I do is to look at the student. Even if that student is not looking at me, he or she eventually becomes aware that I am staring. Then I point at the student and nonverbally indicate that the behavior is to stop. A finger placed on my lips indicates that talking needs to stop.

Often, a questioning or disapproving look or gesture can stop undesirable behaviors right there. I may have to move into a student's personal space or comfort zone to stop a behavior, but a combination of a look and physical proximity are effective about 90 percent of the time. I might even casually rest my hand on the student's desk, never stopping teaching, and stay put for a minute or so until I'm sure the student is back on task.

My advice is to practice "the look" in the mirror until you get it right. It shouldn't be a friendly look, but it doesn't have to be angry either. Learn to say in your manner, "I am in charge here."

Also, move around the classroom. Getting close to your students is essential, not only when you are correcting them but also when you want to reassure them or reinforce their positive feelings about you and your classroom. A friendly touch on the shoulder as you are helping a student with a problem or a hug when a student has a big success can go miles toward cementing your positive relationship with that student.

URBAN EDUCATION

class-related material or may be writing a note. While doing this, the student may not even look up at you. As a result, signals will not work. While conducting the lesson, walk around the room and approach the student's desk. The student will then likely notice your presence and put the material away without a word being spoken.

Some proximity-control techniques are somewhat subtle, such as walking toward the student, while other approaches, such as standing near the student's desk, are more direct. If students do not respond to proximity control, you need to move to a more directive level of intervention.

4. *Touch the student.* Without any verbal exchange, you may place a hand on a student's shoulder in an effort to achieve calm or take a student's hand and escort the student back to his or her seat. **Touch control** involves mild, nonaggressive physical contact that is used to get the student on task. It communicates that you disapprove of the action. Talk to your principal to be certain that you understand the guidelines and legal considerations of appropriate touching.

When deciding whether and how to use touch control, you should take into account the circumstances of the behavior and the characteristics of the students. Students who are angry or visibly upset sometimes do not want to be touched, and some do not want to be touched at any time. How well touch will be received depends on where it occurs and how long it lasts. A touch on the back, hand, arm, or shoulder is acceptable to many students, whereas a touch to the face, neck, leg, chest, or other more personal area is often not acceptable. Brief touch is considered acceptable; the longer the touch, the more it becomes unacceptable.

Verbal Responses. Although nonverbal mild responses may be effective, verbal responses can be used as nonpunitive, mild responses to misbehavior. Their purpose is

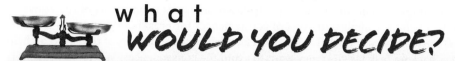

w h a t
WOULD YOU DECIDE?

USING NONVERBAL RESPONSES

Students are working in small groups on an activity, and you notice that in one group, two students are off task. They are not misbehaving or causing disruption, they just are not working on the activity.

1. How can you respond nonverbally to get these two students back on task? What factors might affect your decision about the particular method?

2. Later, you are making a presentation to the whole class when you notice two other students off task. What nonverbal responses might you make in that situation?

to get the student back on task with limited disruption and intervention. Various verbal responses are described here:

1. *Call on the student during the lesson.* You can recapture a misbehaving student's attention by using his or her name in the lesson, such as "Now, in this next example, suppose that John had three polygons that he. . . ." You can then ask a question of the student to recapture his or her attention. Calling on the student in these ways allows you to communicate that you know what is going on and to capture his or her attention without citing the misbehavior.

Be cautious: students' dignity should be preserved. If you call on students in these ways only when they misbehave, they will sense that you are just waiting to catch them misbehaving, and this strategy will backfire by creating resentment (Good & Brophy, 2008).

2. *Use humor.* Humor can be used as a gentle reminder to students to correct their behavior. Humor directed at the situation or even at yourself can defuse tension that might be created due to the misbehavior. It can depersonalize the situation and thus help resolve the problem. You must be careful that the humor is not sarcastic. **Sarcasm** includes statements that are directed at correcting or making fun of the student; these statements are intended to criticize or embarrass the student. Instead, humor is directed at or makes fun of the situation or the teacher. The student may then reconsider his or her actions and then get back on task.

3. *Send an I-message.* An I-message verbally prompts appropriate behavior without giving a direct command (Gordon, 1991). An **I-message** has three parts: (a) a brief description of the misbehavior; (b) a description of its effects on you or the other students; and (c) a description of your feelings about the effects. For example, you might say, "When you tap your pen on the desk during the test, it makes a lot of noise, and I am concerned that it might distract other students."

I-messages are intended to help students recognize that their behavior has consequences for other students and that you have genuine feelings about the actions. Since I-messages leave the decision about changing the behavior up to the student, they are likely to promote a sense of responsibility.

4. *Use positive phrasing.* **Positive phrasing** is used when inappropriate off-task behavior allows you to highlight positive outcomes for appropriate behavior. This usually takes the form of "When you do X [behave in a particular appropriate way], then you can do Y [a positive outcome]." For example, when a student is out of her seat, you might say, "Renee, it will be your turn to pick up supplies when you return to your seat." Through the use of positive phrasing, you redirect students from disruptive to appropriate behavior by simply stating the positive outcomes. In the long run, students begin to believe that proper behavior does lead to positive outcomes.

5. *Remind students of the rules.* Each classroom needs to have a set of rules governing student behavior, along with a set of consequences for breaking them. When students see that consequences of misbehavior are in fact delivered, reminders of the rules can help them get back on task because they want to avoid the consequences. When one student is poking another student, for example, you might say, "Delores, the classroom rules state that students must keep their hands and feet to themselves." This reminder often ends the misbehavior because the student does not want the consequence. If the inappropriate behavior continues, you must deliver the consequence or the reminder will be of little value, because students will recognize that there is no follow-through.

6. *Give students choices.* Some students feel defensive when confronted about their misbehavior. As a result, you can give them choices about resolving the problem. This allows the student to feel that he or she settled the problem without appearing to back down. All the choices that you give to the student should lead to resolution of the problem. If a student is talking to another nearby student, you might say, "Harvey, you can turn back in your seat and get back to your project, or you can take the empty seat at the end of the row." In this way, Harvey has a choice, but the result is that he gets back to work in his seat or in the seat at the end of the row.

7. *Ask "What should you be doing?"* Glasser (1998) proposes that teachers ask disruptive students questions in an effort to direct them back to appropriate behavior. When a student is disruptive, you might ask, "What should you be doing?" This question can have a positive effect because it helps redirect the student back to appropriate behavior.

Of course, some students may not answer this question honestly or may refuse to reply at all. In that case, you should make statements related to the question. For example, "Keith, you were swearing and name calling. That is against our classroom rules. You should not swear or call others names." If the student continues to break the rule, then appropriate consequences should be delivered.

8. *Give a verbal reprimand.* A straightforward way to have the students stop misbehaving is simply to ask or direct them to do so. This is sometimes called a **desist order** or a **reprimand**, and it is given to decrease unwanted behavior. Verbal reprimands are effective with many mild and moderate behavior problems but by themselves are less successful with severe behavior disorders (Kerr & Nelson, 2010).

A **direct appeal** involves a courteous request for the student to stop the misbehavior and to get back on task. You might say, "Martina, please put away the comb and continue with the class assignment." A direct appeal often gives the student a sense of ownership

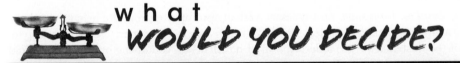

THE EFFECT OF CULTURAL DIFFERENCES

The cultural background of students will likely affect the way that they interact with teachers and others students, respond to authority, use language, and conduct themselves in formal or informal settings. A student action that you view as disruptive or disrespectful might not be viewed that way by the student. The cultural differences between a teacher and students have the potential to create difficulties when dealing with off-task behavior or misbehavior.

1. What can you do as a first-year teacher to better understand the cultural characteristics of your students? How can your students help? How can other teachers, administrators, or parents help?

2. How might this cultural understanding of your students cause you to modify what you do as a teacher?

for deciding to get back on task and to do as you requested. The student feels a sense of responsibility.

As an alternative, you could use a **direct command**, in which you take the responsibility and give a direction in a straightforward manner, such as "Wayne, stop talking with your friends and get to work on the lab activity." With the direct appeal and the direct command, the student is expected to comply with your directions. If the student defies your request or command, you must be prepared to deliver an appropriate consequence.

Soft reprimands, audible only to the misbehaving student, are more effective than loud reprimands in reducing disruptive classroom behavior (Kerr & Nelson, 2010). Soft, private reprimands do not call the attention of the entire class to the misbehaving student and also may be less likely to trigger emotional reactions.

MODERATE RESPONSES

Following situational assistance and mild nonverbal and verbal responses, some students might continue to misbehave. In that case, moderate responses should be used to correct the problem. The three-step response plan shown in Table 10.1 illustrates the movement to more directive responses if mild responses are not successful.

Moderate responses are intended to be **punitive responses** to deal with misbehavior by removing desired stimuli to decrease the occurrence of the inappropriate behavior. Moderate responses include logical consequences and behavior modification techniques. Since student behaviors that warrant moderate responses are more problematic than mild misbehaviors, it is often useful to discuss specific problems with the principal, other teachers, or the school counselor. The family can be contacted at any point to inform them of their child's actions and to solicit their help.

A **logical consequence** is an event arranged by the teacher that is directly and logically related to the misbehavior (Dreikurs, Grunwald, & Pepper, 1998). The consequence should be reasonable, respectful, and related to the student action. For instance, if a student leaves paper on the classroom floor, then he or she must pick it up off the floor. If a student breaks the rule of speaking out without raising his or her hand, you will ignore the response and call on a student whose hand is up. If a student marks on the desk, then he or she will be required to clean the marks off. Students are more likely to respond favorably to logical consequences because they do not consider the consequences mean or unfair.

You may tell the student what the consequence is right after the behavior occurs. For example, "Milton, you left the study area a mess. You need to clean it up at the end of class." As an alternative, you may give the student a choice when inappropriate behavior is noticed. This tells the student that the inappropriate behavior must be changed or, if it is not changed, that a particular consequence will occur. For example, you may say, "Joellen, you have a choice of not bothering students near you or having your seat changed."

When given a choice, students will often stop the inappropriate behavior. This approach can be very effective because the student feels a sense of ownership in solving the problem, and the issue is over quickly. Of course, if the problem behavior continues, you must deliver the consequence that you stated to the student.

At the start of the school year, you should think of two or three logical consequences for each of the classroom rules and inform students of them. When logical, reasonable consequences are preplanned, you are not under the pressure of thinking up something appropriate at the time misbehavior occurs. Some examples of logical consequences include the following:

- *Withdraw privileges.* As a regular part of the classroom activities, you may provide your students with a number of special privileges such as a trip to the library, use of a computer, use of special equipment or a game, service as a classroom helper, or other valued privileges. If the misbehavior relates to the type of privilege offered, a logical consequence would be to withdraw the privilege. For example, if a student mishandles some special equipment, then the student would lose the privilege of using the equipment.

USING AN OOPS SHEET FOR REFLECTIONS

When my students misbehave, I sometimes ask them to fill out an OOPS Sheet to have them reflect on their behavior. OOPS stands for an Outstanding Opportunity for a Personal Stretch. The sheet has a place for their name and date at the top. Then there are several other areas that the student needs to fill in: (1) Describe the problem. (2) What other choices did you have to settle the situation without difficulty? (3) How might you handle this differently if it happens again?

After the student fills out the OOPS Sheet, I meet with the student privately to briefly discuss the situation and to review the options and solutions that the student wrote. This reflection and discussion with me helps students to understand my expectations and to recognize that they have a responsibility to consider reasonable options when they meet a challenging situation.

I sign the OOPS Sheet and make a copy for my files. The original is then sent home with the student to obtain the parent's signature. All the student's privileges are suspended until the signed sheet is returned. If the sheet is not returned the next day, I call the parents and another copy is sent home, if necessary. I have found that students show more self-control after completing the OOPS Sheet.

- *Change the seat assignment.* Students may talk, poke, or interact with other students in nearby seats. Sometimes, a problem occurs because certain students are seated near each other. Other times, just the placement of the seats enables easy interaction. If inappropriate interaction occurs, a logical consequence would be to relocate the student's seat.

- *Have the student write reflections on the problem.* It is often useful to ask the student to reflect on the situation to help him or her recognize the logical connection between the behavior and the consequences. You may ask the student to provide written responses to certain questions; this might be done during a time-out. These questions include: What is the problem? What did I do to create the problem? What should happen to me? What should I do next time to avoid a problem? Other questions may require the student to describe the rule that was broken, why he or she chose to misbehave, who was bothered by the misbehavior, what more appropriate behavior could be chosen next time, and what should happen to him or her the next time the misbehavior occurs.

- *Place the student in a time-out.* Sometimes a student is talking or disrupting the class in such a way that interferes with the progress of the lesson. As noted earlier, such a student can be excluded from the group; this is called a time-out. Removing the student from the group is a logical consequence of interfering with the group. An area of the room should be established as the time-out area, such as a desk in a corner or partially behind a filing cabinet. As a general rule, a time-out should last no longer than 10 minutes.

- *Hold the student for detention.* **Detention** means detaining or holding back a student when he or she normally would be free to go and do other things. The student is deprived of free time and perhaps the opportunity to socialize with other students. Detention may include remaining after class or staying after school. Detention can be a logical consequence for student behaviors that waste class time. A student might be asked to work on the social studies paper that was not completed during class due to inappropriate behavior. Students will soon see the logic that time wasted in class will have to be made up later, on their own time in detention.

Make sure the student understands the reasons for the detention. It should logically fit the offense, and the time should not be excessive. A reasonable amount of time is 20 to 30 minutes after school. Confer with the student and work out a plan to help him or her avoid detention in the future and move toward self-control.

■ *Contact the family.* If a student shows a pattern of repeated misbehavior, then you may need to contact the family. The logic here is that if all earlier attempts to extinguish the misbehavior do not work, it is appropriate to go to a higher authority. The parents, guardians, or other family members may be notified by a note or a letter to inform them of the problem and to solicit their involvement or support. You may choose to call them instead. If the situation is fairly serious, a conference may be warranted.

■ *Have the student visit the principal.* In cases of repeated misbehavior or serious misbehavior such as fighting, students may be sent to the school office to see the principal. The principal may talk with the student in an effort to use his or her legitimate authority to influence the student to behave properly. Some schools have specific procedures to be followed when students are sent to the principal. When the behavior problems reach this point, additional personnel, including the school counselor or psychologist, and the family need to be consulted to help the student.

Cautions and Guidelines

Before school starts, it is best to have a plan to address off-task behavior and misbehavior when it occurs. However, teachers may make decisions in the heat of the moment when responding to misbehavior, and these responses may not be appropriate. You should be aware of some disciplinary practices to avoid and some guidelines for using punishment.

SOME PRACTICES TO AVOID

Research and practice suggest that some strategies are inappropriate or unsuccessful when trying to restore order. The disadvantages outweigh the advantages for the use of harsh reprimands, threats, and physical punishment. Furthermore, practitioners have identified additional approaches that have questionable effectiveness. Teachers should avoid the following practices:

1. *Harsh and humiliating reprimands.* A harsh reprimand is very negative verbal feedback. Teachers may get carried away with this verbal thrashing and humiliate the student. Research reports suggest that the use of harsh reprimands is an ineffective, inefficient, and costly strategy. Harsh reprimands include speaking to the student in an exceptionally stern manner, yelling, and screaming, especially if done to the point that the student is humiliated.

2. *Threats.* A **threat** is a statement that expresses the intent to punish the student if he or she does not comply with the teacher's wishes. Most practitioners and researchers believe the disadvantages of using threats outweigh any possible benefits. Teachers may warn students to alert them to potential consequences, but a threat often expresses more severe consequences than would normally be expected and is stated when the teacher has lost emotional control.

3. *Nagging.* Continual or unnecessary scolding of a student only upsets the student and arouses the resentment of other students. The teacher may consider these scoldings to be minilectures, but they are seen as nagging from the students' point of view.

4. *Forced apologies.* Forcing a student to express an apology that is not felt is a way of forcing him or her to lie. This approach solves nothing.

5. *Sarcastic remarks.* Sarcastic remarks are statements that the teacher uses to deride, taunt, or ridicule a student. While the teacher may consider such remarks as a means of punishment, they create resentment, may lower the student's self-esteem, and in fact may lower the esteem of the teacher in the eyes of the students.

6. *Group punishment.* **Group punishment** occurs when the entire class or group is punished because of the misbehavior of an individual. The intent is for peer pressure to help modify the behavior of the individual. Group punishment is difficult to use effectively, however, and the undesirable side effects are likely to outweigh the advantages. It forces students to choose between the teacher and one of their classmates. Many students will unite in sullen defiance of the teacher and refuse to blame the classmate if group punishment is used. Even if the students go along with the teacher, the technique engenders unhealthy attitudes.

7. *Assigning extra academic work.* When assigning extra academic work as a punishment, the teacher implies that the work is unpleasant. This extra work is often in the form of homework that is not normally required. The student then associates schoolwork with punishment. This is not a message teachers should convey.

8. *Reducing grades.* Penalizing a student academically for misbehavior again creates an undesirable association. Students who are penalized for misbehaving may develop an attitude of "What's the use?" toward academic work. Furthermore, reducing grades for misbehavior confounds the grade, which is intended to report only the student's academic progress.

9. *Writing as punishment.* After students misbehave, teachers may have them copy pages out of a dictionary, encyclopedia, or other book or have them write a certain statement ("I will not do such and such again.") a number of times. Unfortunately, this approach leads to hostility by the students, gives the impression that writing is a bad thing (English teachers will get upset about the message being conveyed here), and is not logically linked to what the students may have done.

10. *Physical labor or exercise.* A teacher may use push-ups or some other physical action as punishment. However, the teacher may not be familiar with a student's physical abilities, and the student could get hurt. In addition to concerns about student safety, having students do extra exercises in physical education in response to misbehavior may cause the students to lose interest in the physical activities when the teacher assigns them as punishment.

11. *Corporal punishment.* **Corporal punishment** is a strategy in which the teacher inflicts physical pain on the student in an attempt to punish him or her for misbehaving. Paddling, spanking, slapping, and pinching are examples. There are many disadvantages to using physical consequences (Hyman, 1997). Other negative behaviors often emerge, such as escape (running away from the punisher), avoidance (lying, stealing, cheating), anxiety, fear, tension, stress, withdrawal, poor self-concept, resistance, and counteraggression. Because of these disadvantages, *physical consequences should not be used.* Many districts have a policy either prohibiting the use of corporal punishment or establishing specific guidelines for its limited use.

GUIDELINES FOR PUNISHMENT

The later steps of the principle of least intervention may involve punishment. **Punishment** is the act of imposing a penalty with the intention of suppressing undesirable behavior. You should express confidence in the students' ability to improve, and punish only as a last resort when students repeatedly fail to respond to more positive treatment. Apply punishment as part of a planned response, not as a means to release your anger or frustration.

The following factors are important to consider when effectively using punishment:

1. *Discuss and reward acceptable behaviors.* Acceptable behaviors should be emphasized when classroom rules are first discussed. Make it clear to students why the rules exist. Discuss the reasons for not engaging in behavior considered to be inappropriate. Most students will behave appropriately if they know what is expected.

2. *Clearly specify the behaviors that will lead to punishment.* Clarifying acceptable behaviors for the students may not be enough. To help the students to understand, identify and discuss examples of behaviors that break the rules and lead to punishment.

3. *Use punishment only when rewards or nonpunitive interventions have not worked or if the behavior must be decreased quickly because it is dangerous.* Punishment should be used as a last resort when other techniques have failed.

4. *Administer punishment in a calm, unemotional manner.* If you deliver punishment while still emotionally upset, you may select an overly harsh punishment and may also provoke the student into further inappropriate reactions. Punishment should not be an involuntary emotional response, a way to get revenge, or a spontaneous response to provocation.

5. *Deliver a warning before punishment is applied to any behavior.* The warning itself could reduce the need for the punishment. If the student does not correct the behavior after the warning, punishment should be delivered at the next occurrence.

6. *Apply punishment fairly with everyone who exhibits the targeted behaviors.* You should treat students from both genders the same way and low-achieving and high-achieving students the same way.

7. *Apply punishment consistently after every occurrence of the targeted misbehavior.* Behaviors that reliably receive punishment are less likely to be tried by students than behaviors that occasionally go uncorrected.

8. *Use punishment of sufficient intensity to suppress the unwanted behaviors.* Generally, the greater the intensity, the longer lasting the effect. But this does not mean that you need to resort to extreme measures. For example, the loss of positive reinforcement because of inappropriate behavior is better than shouting "Don't do that" with increasing intensity.

9. *Select a punishment that is effective, that is not associated with a positive or rewarding experience, and that fits the situation.* Not all aversive consequences that you select may be seen as punishment. Some students, for instance, might think that it is a reward to be placed in a time-out area in the classroom. In this case, a different consequence should be used that is not seen by the student as being positive or rewarding. Also, don't overreact to mild misbehavior or underreact to serious misbehavior. The seriousness of the misbehavior, the student, and the context of the situation need to be taken into account.

10. *Avoid extended periods of punishment.* Lengthy, mild punishment, such as missing open study time for a week, may have a boomerang effect. Punishment with a short duration is more effective.

Dealing with Chronic Misbehaviors

Chronic misbehaviors are troublesome behaviors that students repeatedly or compulsively perform. They include tattling, clowning, cheating, lying, stealing, profanity, rudeness toward the teacher, defiance or hostility, and failure to do schoolwork. This behavior is recurring and inappropriate, and teachers can take actions to minimize its presence in the classroom (Gootman, 2008). Strategies to address a number of common chronic misbehaviors are presented here:

1. *Tattling.* Tattling occurs when students report minor infractions or perceived injustices to the teacher. Tattling is not disruptive, but it can become a problem when students commonly report minor, petty complaints. To prevent tattling from occurring in the first place, let students know what kinds of information they should and should not report to you. You need to know about an incident where a student got hurt, for example, but not when some other student is not doing the schoolwork.

Many teachers, especially in the primary grades, have an explicit lesson about tattling. They describe the difference between reporting important information to the teacher and reports that are tattling about minor infractions. Numerous examples can be provided and discussed for each category. Students can offer examples, as well. It is important to convey to students that you will be available to help them with important matters but that you are not interested in minor complaints.

2. *Clowning.* Students who clown behave in silly or funny ways or may play practical jokes. This clowning is disruptive to the class. Figuring out the source of the student's clowning can help determine what to do about it (Gootman, 2008). Some students may use clowning to cover up a deficiency; they may clown during a math lesson because they are weak in math. Clowning also may be a vehicle for a student to achieve success—to gain some recognition, fame, and popularity among other students. For other students, clowning may be a way of venting frustrations and pressures that they experience from school, home, or other factors.

Keeping a record of who, what, when, where, and how clowning incidents occur can help pinpoint the source. Then you can meet privately with the student to discuss the pattern of the clowning behavior and why it is disruptive. Help the student figure out ways to meet his or her needs without being disruptive.

3. *Cheating.* Cheating involves students getting answers or projects from someone else and turning it in as their own work. Students cheat for several reasons. They may cheat if teachers' expectations are too high and they are not capable of mastering the material. Students then may see cheating as a way out. Other students are simply not prepared, or they have test anxiety.

It is best to minimize the temptation to cheat by discussing the difference between helping and cheating, demonstrating expected behaviors for various activities, and having students identify appropriate and inappropriate actions. In addition, it is important to minimize the opportunity to cheat by determining desk placement during tests and by giving attention to policies, procedures, and submission guidelines for other types of student products.

If you catch a student cheating, you can talk to the student privately, present your reasons for suspecting cheating, express concern and try to find out why the student cheated, explain the consequences, and then discuss the consequences for subsequent cheating (Weinstein & Mignano, 2011). Rather than give the student a zero on the assignment, you may ask him or her to complete the test or assignment again under

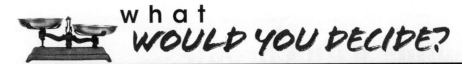

what WOULD YOU DECIDE?

ADDRESSING CHEATING

On three successive quizzes in your class, you notice that four students have received the same score. You are suspicious that this is more than a coincidence.

1. Under what circumstances would you talk with these four students about their scores?
2. What could you do about the questions and the formatting of the quiz to minimize cheating?
3. What could you do about room arrangement and your monitoring of students during a quiz to minimize cheating?

controlled conditions where cheating cannot occur. Some schools have predetermined consequences for cheating, such as parental notification.

4. *Lying.* Lying involves saying something that is not true in a conscious effort to deceive somebody. Students have many reasons for lying, such as trying to protect their self-image, to mask their vulnerable points, or to inflate their image in front of others. They may feel afraid, feel insecure, or fear rejection. Students may lie to protect themselves from punishment or if teachers are too strict with them.

The best response is to express concern about the student's need to lie by saying, "I wonder why you couldn't tell me what really happened." This approach makes it easier for the student to talk about the reason he or she felt compelled to lie. Stay calm and encourage the student to discuss his or her reason for telling a lie. In doing so, try not to overreact or get angry with the student. Focus on the student's reasons and feelings that led to the lie. You might encourage the private conversation with a statement such as "If you tell me what really happened, we can figure out what to do about this situation and perhaps I can help you not let this happen again." Encourage students to be honest about their feelings, and use a calm problem-solving approach to help students address the problems that caused them to lie in the first place.

5. *Stealing.* Stealing involves taking something that belongs to somebody else without the owner's permission. Students in early grades may still be learning the difference between sharing and taking what does not belong to them. Students may impulsively steal because they want something, or they may take something from another student because they are angry with him or her.

If an incident of stealing takes place and you know the culprit, you can have a private conversation with the student about what happened. Describe what you saw and have the student return the item, replace it, or make restitution. Help the student figure out options other than stealing. You may need to respond forcefully depending on the value of the property and the frequency of stealing. In such cases, you may need to contact the principal and the family. Because of legal implications, it is wise to discuss an incident with the principal before conducting a search of backpacks, lockers, or a student's clothing.

6. *Profanity.* Profanity occurs when students use abusive, vulgar, or irreverent language. Age plays a role in the use of profanity. Young children may simply be restating language they heard on television, from family, or from friends with little or no understanding of the meaning. An instructional response is appropriate here, rather than a disciplinary one (e.g., "We don't use words like that in school."). For older students, such language may have become a regular part of their vocabulary, or they may use profanity when they are angry with another person. In such cases, students need to see what is acceptable and unacceptable in school. Stress that using language to hurt others will not be permitted and that there are other acceptable ways to express anger.

7. *Rudeness toward the teacher.* Students may be rude to the teacher by using disagreeable or discourteous words or actions that are outside acceptable standards. Rudeness may be expressed in talking back, arguing, making crude remarks, or showing inappropriate gestures. It is best to avoid overreacting, arguing, or getting into a power struggle. A low-key, respectful response is more suitable. When rude behavior is first evident, you should inform the student that the behavior is inappropriate, and you might also refer to a classroom rule that relates to respectful behaviors. If the actions continue, you should meet with the student privately to identify the reason for the behavior and possibly to deliver consequences. If the rude behavior continues, you may need to consult with the principal or counselors about additional responses.

8. *Defiance or hostility toward the teacher.* Defiance occurs when a student refuses to obey or conform to teacher directions. These actions may be open, bold, or even hostile, and defiance may be in the form of a confrontation with the teacher during a class session. The best way to deal with defiance is to try to defuse it by keeping it in private and handling it individually with the student. Put the student off by saying that you will discuss the situation in a few minutes when you have time. Avoid a power struggle and remain objective. Listen to the student's point of view, but don't engage in an argument. State the consequence clearly and implement it.

Here are some guidelines when students become defiant:

- Stay in control of yourself.

- Direct the rest of the class to work on something while you speak to the student in a private area away from the rest of the students.

- Stand a few feet away from the defiant student (i.e., don't get in his or her face).

- Acknowledge the student's feelings by saying something like "I can see that you are really angry."

- Avoid a power struggle in the conversation (e.g., "I am the boss here, and I am telling you what to do.").

- As a means to defuse the situation, offer the student a choice of actions for what the student needs to do next (Weinstein & Mignano, 2011).

9. *Failure to do work in class or homework.* You may have some students who regularly do not complete seatwork or homework. You should first examine how you hold students academically accountable in your class and make any needed adjustments to ensure accountability. Next, you should plan to maintain accurate records of the schoolwork and respond early when you recognize students who are regularly not completing their class work.

CLASSROOM CASE STUDY

CLASSROOM DISCIPLINE

Marilyn Schmidt is an experienced middle school music teacher who recently started teaching at a new school after her family relocated. She found the first month at her new school very stressful. On the first day of school, she wanted to show her students how friendly she was by giving them some time to socialize before starting class. As the students came into her classroom, she greeted them and allowed them to move desks around to talk to one another. But when she tried to start class a few minutes later, the students kept talking.

Finally, Ms. Schmidt stood up and yelled for everyone to "Shut up!" The class all looked at one another in shock and then began laughing. Humiliated, Ms. Schmidt made all the students put their heads down for the rest of the period and allowed no talking. One student asked if she could use the bathroom, and Ms. Schmidt explained the class had lost that privilege. The girl began arguing and said that "she really had to go," so Ms. Schmidt gave her a detention. Ms. Schmidt did not like doing that, but she knew she had to demonstrate her authority.

Since that day, the students have not cooperated with Ms. Schmidt. They come into the classroom and immediately begin talking, even after the bell rings for class to begin. Ms. Schmidt thinks the students are intentionally ignoring her. They do not quiet down until she yells several times that class has begun. Throughout the class, students ask to go to the bathroom. The angrier Ms. Schmidt becomes, the more the students laugh. She feels that she has no choice but to hand out more detentions, and now she is also staying after school every day because of it. Ms. Schmidt wishes she were back at her old school, where she had control over the students.

FOCUS QUESTIONS

1. What decisions and procedures did Ms. Schmidt make and use that contributed to the student disorder?

2. What decisions and procedures would have been more appropriate and successful for establishing and maintaining order?

You also should examine the nature of the assignments and homework. Is the material too difficult to be completed independently? Is it too boring? Is it too long? Could the material be mastered with a shorter assignment? Was there sufficient preparation in class before students were to do the seatwork or homework? Are there other ways to provide practice and to assess student progress without having seatwork and homework every day? Your reflection on these questions may lead you to adjust your assignments and expectations.

Bullying

Bullying is when a person, or group of persons, uses power to harass or intimidate one or more people who have less power. Bullying takes the form of belittling weaker students, calling them names, and threatening or harassing them. For elementary students, the bully may be the student who pushed them out of the cafeteria line or bothers them on the school bus. For older students, bullying may even be in the form of harassment on the Internet though photographs or text messages.

CHARACTERISTICS OF BULLYING

Regardless of the type of bullying, three characteristics that are apparent:

1. *Imbalance of power.* People who bully use their power to control or harm, and the people being bullied may have a hard time defending themselves.

2. *Intent to cause harm.* The person bullying has a goal to cause harm. Actions done by accident are not bullying.

3. *Repetition.* Incidents of bullying happen to the same person over and over by the same person or group.

Bullies may do many things to harass or dominate others, such as make verbal threats, boss people around, take people's money, put people down, make obscene gestures, attack people physically, intimidate people, gossip, leave people out, spread rumors, tease, hit, or hurt others in many possible ways.

There are no differences in rates of bullying for urban, suburban, or rural communities. The overall percentage of students being bullied does not vary based on school size, although bullying does happen more often in larger schools. Boys and girls are just as likely to be involved in bullying. However, forms of bullying vary by gender. Some research has found girls are more likely to bully others socially (U.S. Department of Education, 2011b).

Bullies tend to be average students academically. Bullies have an inflated self-concept but usually have low self-esteem or feel inferior to others, which reflects a strong need to dominate with threats. Bullies lack empathy for their victims and feel justified in their actions. Reciprocal aggressive behavior by the victim usually does not stop the bully (Khalsa, 2007).

Bullying is most commonly learned, with modeling and reinforcement by parents and peers playing major roles and influences (W. B. Roberts, 2006). Bullies tend to come from homes whose parents are authoritarian, hostile, and rejecting. The parents may have poor problem-solving skills and use fighting as a solution to conflicts; their children then imitate these behaviors. Bullies are often emotionally underdeveloped, and they are unable to understand or empathize with others' perspectives or regulate their own behavior (Berk, 2009, 2012).

People who bully take advantage of imbalances in power, such as greater size or strength, higher status, or the support of a peer group. Surveys indicate that nearly

75 percent of 8- to 11-year olds and more than 85 percent of 12- to 15-year olds report bullying at their school (W. B. Roberts, 2006). In other studies, nearly one third of students reported that they had bullied, been a victim of bullying, or both within the last month (Viadero, 2003). Bullying is most prevalent at the middle school level, with more than 40 percent of students reporting at least one incident of bullying a week, compared to slightly more than 20 percent at both the elementary and high school levels (National Center for Educational Statistics, 2007). Incidents of bullying may actually be higher than reported because it most commonly occurs in areas where students interact informally, such as playgrounds, school buses, hallways, cafeterias, and places where they have little adult supervision (Siris & Osterman, 2004). Students are often hesitant to report bullying because they fear reprisals or don't want to appear weak or unable to solve their own social problems (Newman, 2008).

EFFECTS OF BULLYING

Bullying has serious and long-lasting effects for both bullies and their victims. Students who are bullied have a higher risk of depression and anxiety that may persist into adulthood, including feelings of sadness and loneliness, changes in sleep and eating patterns, and loss of interest in activities. They are more likely to have health complaints, decreased academic achievement and school participation, and increased thoughts about suicide that may persist into adulthood; they are also more likely to skip or drop out of school, and to retaliate through extremely violent measures (Hoglund, 2007; U.S. Department of Education, 2011a).

People who bully others are more likely to get into fights, vandalize property, and drop out of school; have a higher risk of abusing alcohol and other drugs in adolescence and as adults; are more likely to engage in early sexual activity; are more likely to be abusive toward their romantic partners, spouses, or children as adults; and are more likely to have criminal convictions and traffic citations as adults (U.S. Department of Education, 2011a).

Bullying is linked to a number of antisocial and aggressive behaviors that can have negative consequences for bullies and their victims (Raskauskas & Stoltz, 2007). Studies suggest bullying is a major factor in many school shooting incidents (Fast, 2008). Another study found that both bullies and victims were more likely to carry a weapon to school and become involved in serious fights (Viadero, 2003).

TYPES OF BULLYING

There are several types of bullying (Breakstone, Dreiblatt, & Dreiblatt, 2009; Khalsa, 2007):

1. **Physical bullying** is action oriented. It includes hitting, shoving, kicking, pushing, spitting, or taking or damaging a person's property.

2. **Verbal bullying** involves the use of words to hurt or humiliate another person. It includes teasing, name-calling, insulting, put-downs, and making threats or rude comments.

3. **Relational bullying**, also known as social aggression, is the use of relationships to hurt others. It includes preventing people from playing with others, using the silent treatment, and spreading rumors and lies.

4. **Sexual bullying** involves hurtful teasing and comments about sexuality, sexual preference, physical development, and sexual experiences as a way to undermine an individual's self-esteem and self-confidence. Victims may even be physically threatened or injured. Some experts would not consider these actions sexual bullying; they would call them sexual harassment. Harassment of girls and young women ranges from name-calling, to touching, and even rape. Lesbian, gay, bisexual, or transgender (LGBT) youth report verbal, sexual, and physical harassment that ends in physical assaults for one in five LGBT students. The most common harassment experienced by LGBT students is in the form of verbal abuse, with sexist and homophobic name-calling such as "faggot" or "dyke." These homophobic remarks are applied to both LGBT and non-LGBT students as derogatory terms meant to call into question a student's masculinity or femininity (Greytak, Kosciw, & Diaz, 2009).

VOICES from the Classroom

KEN JACKSON, high school counselor, Atlanta, Georgia

BULLYING STUDENTS WHO ARE LGBTQ

Students who are lesbian, gay, bisexual, transgender, or queer/questioning (LGBTQ) are often the targets of bullies. Since these characteristics are not typically exhibited until adolescence, bullying of LGBTQ students occurs more often in middle school and high school.

I am a high school counselor, and I recently needed to address an incident with two students. Claudia is a self-identified lesbian, rather small in stature, and a relatively successful student taking advanced placement courses. One day, she approached me relatively timidly but very upset. She explained that she was experiencing harassment in one of her classes from a varsity football player. He was talking to her in class telling her to have sex with him, using explicit language to describe what he wanted them to do. He spoke softly so the teacher could not hear, and he had a female varsity athlete giving him support for his taunting. After Claudia kept

refusing, the other student then began making statements about her being a lesbian and continued to mess with her.

As the school counselor, I gave Claudia some options and strategies. With her permission, I met with the classroom teacher to discuss how to help Claudia without making things more difficult since the teacher had not heard any of the remarks. The teacher decided to rearrange some classroom groupings to separate the students, place Claudia closer to the teacher's desk, and make the commitment to monitor students more closely. With these adjustments, Claudia felt that she could trust the teacher and go to the teacher for support should there be a recurrence.

URBAN EDUCATION

5. Cyberbullying involves the use of technology to hurt or humiliate others. It includes using computers and the Internet, e-mails, cell phones, text messaging, Facebook, Weblogs, and digital photography to embarrass or exclude others. The anonymity of the Internet distinguishes cyberbullying from other types of bullying. This anonymity can make bullies even more insensitive to the hurtful nature of the bullying incidents (Willard, 2006). While cyberbullying is hard to measure, experts estimate that between 10 and 30 percent of students are victims of online harassment (Stobbe, 2007).

TECHNOLOGY

CONFRONTING BULLYING

Adult intervention is one of the best defenses against bullying. Teachers need to recognize the warning signs of bullying and intervene when it happens, sending the message that bullying is not acceptable. While there is no set formula for how teachers should respond to bullying incidents, here are some actions to consider:

- *Intervene immediately*. Separate the students involved. Do not immediately ask about or discuss the reason for the bullying.

- *Get the facts*. Speak to the students involved, both participants and observers, and ask what happened. Request more information. Get all sides of the story before taking any action.

- *Tell the students you are aware of their behavior*. Talk to the students involved separately. Make it a teachable moment. Helping the students and bystanders understand what happened and why it happened may help prevent future incidents.

- *Consider an appropriate intervention*. Base your decision on the circumstances, the severity and history of the incident, and the students involved.

- *Follow up with the students.* Follow up on the incident and monitor the students involved to ensure the bullying does not continue.

- *Report the incident to the right person.* The school may have a reporting policy about bullying incidents, and a report may need to be submitted to the school administrator, a counselor, or a member of the school safety committee. This report will help the school track the incidents and the responses. Some states have laws that require incidences to be reported.

Teachers can take steps to deal with aggression and to encourage cooperation. Teachers can present themselves as a nonaggressive model. They can ensure that their classroom has enough space and appropriate materials for all students, thus minimizing the source of some conflicts. They can make sure students do not profit from aggressive behaviors by delivering appropriate consequences. They can teach directly about positive social behaviors. Teachers also can provide opportunities for learning tolerance and cooperation. Furthermore, states and school districts are developing safe school laws and policies that promote changing the behaviors of bullies. They include procedures for reporting and investigating incidents.

A number of books are available for teachers with information along with classroom activities and discussions to address bullying. These include *How to Stop Bullying and Social Aggression* (Breakstone et al., 2009), *No Kidding about Bullying* (Drew, 2010), *Break the Bully Cycle* (Khalsa, 2007), and *Bully Prevention* (Barton, 2006). A search of the Internet will reveal a number of sources to address bullying.

Key Terms

Bullying	Extinction	Nonverbal responses	Reprimand
Chronic misbehaviors	Group punishment	Physical bullying	Sarcasm
Corporal punishment	Hurdle helping	Positive phrasing	Sexual bullying
Cues	I-message	Principle of least	Situational
Cyberbullying	Intervention	intervention	assistance
Desist order	Logical	Proximity control	Threat
Detention	consequence	Punishment	Time-out
Direct appeal	Mild responses	Punitive response	Touch control
Direct command	Misbehavior	Relational bullying	Verbal bullying

Major Concepts

1. Misbehavior is any student behavior that is perceived by the teacher to compete with or threaten the academic actions at a particular moment.

2. The principle of least intervention states that when dealing with routine classroom behavior, misbehavior should be corrected with the simplest, least intrusive intervention that will work. If that does not work, then move up to a more intrusive approach.

3. Due to inherent problems in the use of punishment, teachers should follow certain guidelines when using punitive responses.

4. A three-step response plan is recommended to address off-task behavior and misbehavior.

5. The first step, situational assistance, is designed to help students cope with the instructional situation and to keep them on task.

6. Next, mild responses are nonpunitive ways to deal with misbehavior while providing guidance for appropriate behavior. Nonverbal and verbal approaches can be used.

7. Moderate responses, the final step, deliver punishment as a means to restore order.

8. Chronic misbehaviors are troublesome behaviors that students repeatedly or compulsively perform. They include tattling, clowning, cheating, lying, stealing, profanity, rudeness toward the teacher, defiance or hostility, and failure to do schoolwork.

9. Bullying is when a person, or group of persons, uses power to harass or intimidate one or more people who have less power. Bullying may be physical, verbal, relational, sexual, or cyber.

Discussion/Reflective Questions

1. How might the cause of a misbehavior affect the teacher's choice of an appropriate response?

2. In the three-step response plan for misbehavior, what are the merits and disadvantages of moving from situational assistance to mild responses to moderate responses?

3. What are the benefits of providing situational assistance?

4. What justification can teachers offer for the use of punishment?

5. What are examples of chronic misbehaviors you have witnessed? How were these behaviors addressed by the teacher?

6. What difficulties might teachers experience when trying to identify and address problems with cyberbullying done by their students?

Suggested Activities

FOR CLINICAL SETTINGS

1. Review Table 10.1, and identify examples of student behavior at each step that would warrant teacher actions in the three-step response plan.

2. Identify examples of punishments that teachers might deliver. Determine where those actions fall in the three-step response plan, and judge whether the punishments are appropriate.

3. Search the topic of bullying on the Internet. From the many resources and the many topics, identify 10 significant guidelines that teachers might follow in addressing bullying.

FOR FIELD EXPERIENCES

1. Find out if there are printed school or district policies about any aspect of classroom discipline (e.g., types of punishments, detention, corporal punishment, suspensions). Read and critique the printed policies.

2. Talk to teachers to identify ways they use situational assistance and mild and moderate responses to misbehavior.

3. Ask teachers what types of chronic misbehavior they encounter, and discuss how they address these misbehaviors.

Further Reading

Burden, P. R. (2013). *Classroom management: Creating a successful K–12 learning community* (5th ed.). New York: Wiley.

Provides a comprehensive K–12 review of ways to establish, maintain, and restore order in the classroom. It takes a practical, realistic view of decisions teachers make about getting organized for management, planning for management, managing when conducting the class, and restoring order after misbehavior.

Burke, K. (2008). *What to do with the kid who . . . : Developing cooperation, self-discipline, and responsibility in the classroom* (3rd ed.). Thousand Oaks, CA: Corwin Press.

VOICES from the Classroom

CLAUDIA ARGUELLO COCA, fifth-grade teacher, Las Cruces, New Mexico

DATA-DRIVEN DECISION MAKING

In my classroom, data drives my instruction in every subject area. In order to serve my students at the highest level possible, I need to know what they know, what they don't know, and what their misconceptions are about core content areas.

I use homogenous student grouping when providing direct-guided reading instruction so that I can offer very specific strategies to those students who are struggling. I create my groups by ongoing assessments that are teacher created, by New Mexico's standards-based assessment (NMSBA) scores, and by our district measures of academic progress (MAPS) scores. All of these scores are used to create a picture of each of my students as a learner.

I use ongoing assessments to make decisions about student progress during unit studies. I use formal assessments and language objectives to measure students' proficiency. By using all of these tools, I am able to create fluid groups for instruction, reteaching, and enrichment. Using these assessments also helps when grouping students for daily response to intervention (RTI) instruction.

URBAN EDUCATION

TYPES OF ASSESSMENTS FOR DECISION MAKING

There are three types of assessment, each serving a different purpose and each being conducted at different times (McMillan, 2011). Each type of assessment is linked to a stage of instruction—before instruction, during instruction, and after instruction.

Pre-Assessment. Pre-assessment is done by the teacher before instruction to determine students' knowledge, attitudes, and interests. This information is then used as a starting point to make decisions about instruction. Having information about the students' prior knowledge about a topic can help the teacher determine what content to cover and to what depth. It will also provide information about the strengths and weaknesses of individual students in relation to the content.

Teachers may consider questions such as: How much do my students know? Are my students motivated to learn? Are there any students with special learning needs? What instructional activities should I plan?

Formative Assessment. Formative assessment occurs during instruction and is a way to assess students' progress, provide students with feedback, and assist the teacher in making decisions about further instruction. Teachers make ongoing changes during instruction based on how a lesson is going and on whether the students are learning the material.

Teachers check for understanding during the lesson as one way to assess student progress. In *Checking for Understanding*, Fisher and Frey (2007) state that student understanding can be determined by many formative assessment approaches, such as through oral language, questions, writing, projects and performances, and tests.

Summative Assessment. Summative assessment occurs after instruction and it serves as a means to document what students know, understand, and can do. Summative assessment takes place at the end of a unit, marking period, or course and is intended to (1)

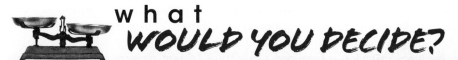

what WOULD YOU DECIDE?

YOUR STUDENTS' PRIOR KNOWLEDGE

Students in your class will likely have a wide range of prior knowledge about the content in the next unit you will teach. Most students may know a lot about the topic, or only a little. A few students may have considerable information due to their own life experiences and investigations. It is helpful to identify what they know.

1. To more effectively plan content and experiences in the unit, how can you determine the students' prior knowledge?

2. How might you enable students to contribute to the planning of the unit?

3. How might the grade level that you teach affect your responses to these questions?

determine the extent of the students' achievement and competence, (2) provide a basis for assigning grades, and (3) provide the data from which reports to families and transcripts can be prepared. Summative assessment typically examines the student's broad ability as compared to the detailed examination of each component in formative assessment.

NORM-REFERENCED AND CRITERION-REFERENCED EVALUATION

Norm-referenced evaluation is used to interpret a score of an individual by comparing it with the scores of other individuals. Ranking students is the primary issue. For example, a teacher would use a norm-referenced test to compare the reading abilities of students

VOICES from the Classroom

DANIEL HRDINA, middle school math teacher, Union, New Jersey

ANALYZING TEST RESULTS TO GUIDE PLANNING AND INSTRUCTION

Students are assessed frequently throughout the school year. Oftentimes the assessments are graded, recorded, quickly reviewed, and placed into a portfolio never to be seen again. Most schools use quarterly benchmarks to track their students' progress through the school year. This process can be beneficial if each skill is examined independently.

For example, this past school year every seventh-grade student in my middle school took part in a midyear proficiency assessment. When the test was completed, teachers sat down and looked at each question on their students' exams. They categorized each question under one of the core curriculum content areas. Teachers then looked at each question that every student answered incorrectly and determined if there was a pattern of student mistakes. This enabled teachers to create lesson plans for the following year that would address these weak areas. They also used this information to address areas of concern with their current students for the remainder of the school year.

before forming reading groups. A norm-referenced test finds a student's performance level in relation to the levels of other students on the same test. Many standardized achievement and aptitude tests are norm-referenced instruments.

In contrast, **criterion-referenced evaluation** is used to interpret an individual's performance by comparing it to some specified criterion, such as a performance standard. Individual mastery is the primary issue. The object is to determine whether the student can or cannot perform at a certain standard. How well others perform on the same standard is not considered.

CHARACTERISTICS OF GOOD ASSESSMENT INSTRUMENTS

The effectiveness of any measuring device depends on its validity, reliability, and practicality (Russell & Airasian, 2012):

1. Validity deals with the extent to which a measuring device measures what it purports to measure. While there are several types of validity, teachers are usually most concerned with content validity. *Content validity* refers to the degree to which an instrument samples the subject matter in the area to be measured or the degree to which it coincides with the instructional objectives to be measured. This is typically the only type of validity used in teacher-made tests and other measures. To determine content validity, you examine the outline of instructional objectives and check the congruence with the test questions. High content validity means that there is a good match between test questions and instructional objectives covered in class. Low content validity means that there is a poor match.

2. Reliability deals with the consistency of results. The more consistent the results, the higher the reliability of the test. If you administer a reliable test and shortly after readminister an equivalent form of the same test, students should score roughly the same as they did on the first test.

All measuring devices have some type of error. **Measurement error** may come from errors in the instrument, errors in the use of the instrument, and errors emanating from the subject's response. The more objective the scoring of a test, the more reliable the score. Factors that may act to make a test less reliable are the length of a test (i.e., very short tests are not very reliable), the ambiguity of directions and questions, and an overload of questions that are too difficult or too easy. Variability in the students' responses can be affected by temporal factors such as poor motivation, lack of interest, improper test environment, poor emotional set, and illness.

3. Practicality refers to the ease of administering the measuring device, the time required, the energy expended to collect the data, and the ease with which the data can be interpreted. For instance, an essay test may be easily prepared by the teacher, but the time required to grade it can make such a test impractical. Conversely, an objective test can be graded relatively quickly but may take much longer to prepare.

ADAPTING ASSESSMENTS FOR ENGLISH LANGUAGE LEARNERS

English language learners (ELLs) may know the content on which they are being assessed but have difficulty demonstrating their knowledge with standard assessments. These challenges stem from the vocabulary, reading, and writing that are part of a typical assessment. Given this, teachers must adapt assessments to accurately determine the content knowledge of ELLs.

Echevarria, Vogt, and Short (2008) offer the following six suggestions when adapting assessments for ELLs:

1. *Range.* Adapt the number of items that ELLs are expected to complete, such as only the odd or even questions.

sample
STANDARDS

There are 10 InTASC standards (see pages xx–xxi), and each standard in the original document includes a list of performances, essential knowledge, and critical dispositions to indicate more clearly what is intended in the standard.

Since this chapter deals with assessment, some representative statements from InTASC Standard #6, Assessment, are listed here concerning topics in this chapter.

PERFORMANCES

■ The teacher balances the use of formative and summative assessment as appropriate to support, verify, and document learning.

■ The teacher designs assessments that match learning objectives with assessment methods and minimize sources of bias that can distort assessment results.

ESSENTIAL KNOWLEDGE

■ The teacher understands the range of types and multiples purposes of assessment and how to design, adapt, or select appropriate assessments to address specific learning goals and individual differences, and to minimize sources of bias.

■ The teacher knows when and how to engage learners in analyzing their own assessment results and in helping to set goals for their own learning.

CRITICAL DISPOSITIONS

■ The teacher takes responsibility for aligning instruction and assessment with learning goals.

■ The teacher is committed to making accommodations in assessments and testing conditions, especially for learners with disabilities and language learning needs.

2. *Time.* Adapt the amount of time that ELLs have for completing a task, such as providing more processing time or breaking tasks down into manageable chunks. Unless taking a timed test is required, allowing additional time should not affect a student's score.

3. *Level of support.* Adapt the amount of scaffolding provided to ELLs during assessments by asking an aide, peer assistant, or parent volunteer to read or explain the task or even to read the test items aloud. If you are assessing for content knowledge, then it is acceptable to have someone help with reading or clarifying what is expected in the task.

4. *Difficulty.* Adapt the skill level, the type of problem or task, and the process for how ELLs can approach the task, such as allowing use of a calculator, dictionary, or simplified directions. None of these adaptations reduces the expectation of what the student should know; it only makes it easier for him or her to demonstrate understanding.

5. *Product.* Adapt the type of response ELLs are allowed to provide, such as permitting a drawing, a hands-on demonstration, a verbal response, or a translated response, if necessary. These alternatives do not rely on sophisticated English usage.

6. *Participation.* Adapt ELLs' degree of active involvement in assessment, such as encouraging individual or cooperative group self-assessment and assistance in creating rubrics. Content learning is enhanced for all students but especially for ELLs through interaction and group work. English language learners, particularly those in the upper grades, can be involved in assessing their own progress.

ADAPTING ASSESSMENTS FOR STUDENTS WITH SPECIAL NEEDS

Students with special needs or disabilities may have difficulty with standard assessment and test-taking procedures. As a result, teachers often need to make accommodations or changes in formative and summative assessments for these students.

Depending on the type of special need or disability, students may encounter problems in testing situations (McMillan, 2011). These problems include comprehension difficulties, auditory difficulties, visual difficulties, time constraint difficulties, anxiety, embarrassment, and variability in behavior from one day to the next. When considering summative tests, accommodations for these problems can be grouped into the following categories (J. W. Wood, 2006):

1. *Test construction.* Attention needs to be given to test directions and the test format. When modifying *test directions*, take the following suggestions into account (Mastropieri & Scruggs, 2010); some of these guidelines can be used for all students. Read written directions aloud, slowly, and give students opportunities to ask questions about directions. Keep directions short and simple. Give examples of how to answer questions. Focus attention by underlining verbs. Provide separate directions for each section of the test. Check students' understanding of the directions. During the test, observe students' answers to be sure that the students understand the directions. Adjust the reading level of the items or provide assistance with reading if necessary.

The general *test format* should be designed to simplify the amount of information that is processed at one time. Leave plenty of white space so students don't feel overwhelmed. Use large printing with adequate space between items. Create clearly distinguished short sections. For multiple choice questions, list the alternatives vertically. Number each page of the test. If possible, design the test format of an adapted test to look as much like the test for other students as possible (Salend, 2009). Other accommodations to the test format may be needed depending on the needs of the learner.

2. *Test administration.* Adaptations during test administration involve changes in procedures that lessen the negative effect of disabilities while the student is taking the test. Most of these procedural accommodations depend on the nature of the disability or difficulty mentioned earlier (e.g., comprehension difficulties, time constraint difficulties). A good rule of thumb is to provide students with disabilities 50 percent additional time to complete a test (Reynolds, Livingston, & Willson, 2009).

3. *Testing site.* It may be necessary to allow students with special needs to take the test in a different location than the regular classroom. The alternative site is often a resource room in the school or another room that is quiet with few distractions. As long as someone can monitor the test, the student will have more opportunities to ask questions and feel less embarrassed when asking questions for clarification or further explanation.

Establishing a Framework for Assessment

Even before instruction begins, you need to establish a framework for student assessment by addressing the following issues:

1. *Identify the reasons for assessing student performance.* A classroom test, for instance, can serve a variety of purposes, such as judging student mastery, measuring growth over time, ranking pupils in terms of their achievement, and diagnosing student difficulties. Different purposes lend themselves to various assessment measures. Therefore, it is essential that you know the major use of the assessment results.

2. *Plan to gather information for both formative and summative assessment.* Formative assessment should be conducted frequently to provide feedback about the student's developing knowledge and skills. In fact, all scores for formative assessment may not need to be recorded for the report card grade. Summative assessment is more comprehensive and is conducted at selected concluding points, such as at the end of a chapter or unit. Scores from summative assessments are tallied as part of the report card grade.

3. *Identify course content that is to be assessed.* This content is often included in a course curriculum guide. It will be translated into instructional objectives for daily lesson plans. These objectives will likely be written for the cognitive, psychomotor, and affective learning domains.

4. *Relate the assessment to the prestated objectives.* Each objective should be evaluated, but the means for gathering assessment information will vary depending on the stated objectives and the purpose of the assessment.

5. *Include assessment measures in all three learning domains.* Instructional objectives should be written for each of the three learning domains, and each objective should be assessed. Different types of assessment instruments are often used to measure student performance in each domain. The cognitive domain is often assessed through the use of (a) tests developed by teachers themselves; (b) achievement tests developed by local, regional, or state agencies, which may or may not be normed; and (c) nationally standardized tests and scales. Skills in the psychomotor domain are evaluated through performance and product tests.

Objectives in the affective learning domain are more difficult to assess than objectives in the other domains. Techniques often used include attitude scales, opinion polls, questionnaires, open-ended questions, checklists, observation, group discussion, anecdotal records, interviews, and role playing. Observation of students in the process of performing a particular task can also provide useful information concerning their attitudes toward the task.

6. *Use multiple approaches when gathering assessment information.* Do not rely only on teacher-made tests. Also use performance-based assessments when appropriate.

7. *Devise an assessment plan before instruction.* This will guide your planning and preparation for the class sessions. Then communicate the objectives and assessment criteria to the students.

Performance-Based Assessment

As an alternative to teacher-made tests, teachers can measure student learning by assessing products that students prepare reflecting their learning or by assessing actual student performances designed to demonstrate their learning. This is **performance-based assessment**. Once the student produces the product or conducts the performance, the teacher then needs to use various types of rating scales or checklists to translate the student performance into some type of score.

Since performance-based assessments are seen as alternatives to teacher-made tests, terms such as *alternative assessment*, *authentic assessment*, and *direct assessment* have been used to describe performance-based assessments. There are two types of performance-based assessments: product assessment and performance assessment (see Table 11.1).

PRODUCT ASSESSMENTS

Instead of completing a traditional paper-and-pencil test, students are asked to prepare a product reflecting their learning, and the teacher then completes a rating scale or composes written comments to assess student learning as reflected in the product. Product assessments include (1) directions that outline the nature of the products that students will develop; (2) the product itself, which students prepare; and (3) a rating scale of some

TABLE 11.1

Performance-Based Assessments	
PRODUCTS	**PERFORMANCES**
Portfolio	Oral presentation
Work sample	Presentation with media
Project or report	Science lab demonstration
Research paper	Athletic demonstration
Science lab report	Musical, dance, or dramatic presentation
Log or journal	Debate
Model	Demonstration of specific tasks
Media products (computer presentation file, audio- or videotape)	Participation in an event Interview with the student

kind that assesses the nature of the student product. There are many types of products that students might be asked to prepare. Some of the more common types of student products are discussed here.

Portfolios. A **portfolio** is a collection of a student's work over time that demonstrates mastery of specific performance criteria against which the tasks in the portfolio can be judged. The student systematically chooses and compiles work products that go into the portfolio. Work products can be items such as reports, letters, drawings, journals, and other documents. Portfolios are intended to actively involve students in learning, develop self-assessment skills, and provide insights to students and teachers on progress and accomplishment (Burke, K., 2009; Popham, 2011).

You can guide students through portfolio development by identifying the characteristics of good academic work, applying criteria for good work to their own work, using peer-revision groups to refine and assess their work, and selecting work so that the portfolio creates a portrait of the student as a learner. Teachers who have implemented portfolios report that (1) students have a richer, more positive, and expanded sense of their progress; (2) assessment becomes collaborative rather than competitive; (3) teachers obtain a richer, clearer view of their students over time; and (4) records of what students are actually doing are available to teachers.

Some teachers think portfolios are only appropriate for use in the elementary grades, but teachers at the middle and secondary levels have also used portfolios successfully. Geometry portfolios, for example, might include work that displays problem solving, communication, or other skills. Language arts and social studies portfolios might include writings and other projects that offer evidence of progress and goal setting.

Work Samples. Gathering work samples provides a longitudinal record of student progress. Work samples might include (1) written work such as a report, test, or story; (2) artwork; (3) tape recordings; (4) a construction project done in art, industrial arts, or an appropriate subject; or (5) other types of finished products, depending on the subject area. Using work samples probably occurs more often in the elementary grades, but teachers in certain secondary subject areas may use work samples as well.

Experience Summaries. In so-called experience summaries, students record what they have learned from a particular experience. Teachers and students may do this

VOICES from the Classroom

KAYE LYNN MAZUREK, high school German teacher, Commerce, Michigan

STUDENTS REFLECT ON THEIR ASSESSMENTS

I believe that all assessments can be formative assessments in my high school German classes. We have one major summative assessment each marking period with five sections—listening, reading, writing, speaking, and culture. I use the summative assessment from one unit as a stepping-stone for the next marking period.

When I return the summative assessment from the unit, I have a score sheet that accompanies it. Following the score sheet is a section that asks students to rewrite the sentences where they had the most mistakes, to summarize one of their consistent errors, or to reflect on strongest and weakest sections of their test. The task is very brief. Sometimes students don't even realize they're making a consistent error until they actually have to identify it. Thus, this process helps students reflect on their assessments by identifying their strengths, weakness, and areas where they need to give attention for improvement.

URBAN EDUCATION

cooperatively. For instance, after going on a field trip to an art gallery, the class could identify facts and concepts that they learned. This listing would be useful for you to determine the extent of student learning.

Logs or Journals. While experience summaries are used for one event, logs or journals are kept on a continuing basis. Students might keep a journal to record their insights, conclusions, and feelings about their classroom experiences. The class can log daily progress concerning learning activities in a notebook or on a chart. This provides a running account of work in the unit and can be used to review and check on previous plans and decisions as the unit progresses.

Projects, Reports, or Papers. Students might prepare various types of projects, reports, or papers that reflect their learning. These products often involve a number of skills and are developed over more than one class period.

Models. Students can prepare models concerning people, places, or topics being addressed in class. The models may contain information and represent certain aspects of their learning.

Media Products. Working individually or in groups, students are asked in many classrooms to prepare an audiotape, videotape, or computer-assisted presentation concerning some aspect of the curriculum. The final media product will represent certain aspects of student learning.

PERFORMANCE ASSESSMENTS

As with product assessments, teachers complete a rating scale or compose written comments to assess student learning reflected in a performance that students are asked to conduct. Performance assessments include (1) directions that outline the nature of the products that students will develop; (2) the product itself, which students prepare; and

(3) a rating scale of some kind that assesses the nature of the student product. There are many types of performances that students can be asked to conduct. Some of the more common ones are discussed here.

Oral or Mediated Presentations. Students can be asked to prepare a report on a selected topic and then present it to the rest of the class. Sometimes these reports include instructional media (e.g., computer-assisted presentations). The teacher may choose to rate the actual presentation as a way to gauge student learning.

Actual Demonstrations. Students can be asked to demonstrate their skill in some type of athletic, musical, dance, or dramatic performance. Skills might also be demonstrated in a science lab, a computer class, or any other class where the student's learning is best reflected in actual performance.

Participation in an Event. Sometimes a group of students or the entire class is involved in an activity in which students exhibit certain knowledge and skills through their participation. A student's knowledge and skill in forensics or debate, for instance, can be seen through participation.

Interviews. Interviews and individual conferences can be used to evaluate cognitive skills as well as attitudes and values. Students sometimes express ideas and feelings during interviews that they might not otherwise state.

WAYS TO RATE STUDENT PRODUCTS OR PERFORMANCES

It is easy to say that it is a great idea to gather student products or to ask students to perform in certain ways as a means to demonstrate their learning. However, teachers may find it challenging to specify the actual observable criteria that demonstrate student learning and to determine what the actual rating approaches will be. Some guidelines are provided in this section.

Selecting Rating Criteria. The following guidelines can be used when selecting observable criteria for products or performances (Russell & Airasian, 2012):

1. *Select the performance or product to be assessed and then either perform it yourself or imagine yourself performing it.* This step will help you to understand the actual student actions that will need to be completed.

2. *List the important aspects of the performance or product.* The most important behaviors or attributes should be reflected in the rating criteria.

3. *Try to limit the number of performance criteria that can reasonably be observed and assessed.* Each item needs to be assessed, so limit the number of performance criteria to 10 to 15.

4. *If possible, have a group of teachers think through the criteria as a group.* This step will save time and will help to produce a more complete set of criteria than that produced by any single teacher.

5. *Express the criteria in terms of observable student behaviors or product characteristics.* Be specific when stating the criteria.

6. *Avoid vague and ambiguous words.* Avoid wording such as *correctly*, *appropriately*, or *good* that can result in multiple interpretations.

7. *Arrange the performance criteria in the order in which they are likely to be observed.* This will save time when observing and maintain focus on the performance.

8. *Check for existing performance criteria before constructing your own.* Preexisting criteria might be available for your use.

Rating Approaches. Various approaches can be used to rate student products or performances. The most commonly used approaches are reviewed here:

1. *Rating scales.* A **rating scale** allows a teacher to judge student performance along a continuum, rather than as a dichotomy (present/not present). The rating scale may be numerical (e.g., 1 through 4), descriptive (using a range of words to reflect the criteria), or a combination of the two. Instead of merely indicating the presence or absence of a trait, as in a checklist, a rating scale enables you to indicate the status or quality of what is being rated.

A **rubric** is a type of rating scale used to judge student performance on a continuum. Rubrics can be created in many ways to describe the levels of student performance based on the performance criteria. Rubrics often have more thorough ways of describing each performance level than simple rating scales. The thorough descriptions of performance criteria in rubrics provide considerable guidance for the students as they prepare their products or performances. See Table 11.2 and Table 11.3 for examples.

2. *Checklists.* A **checklist** is a written list of performance criteria. A teacher reviews the student product or performance to determine which criteria are met. A check mark indicates that the criterion was met; if it is not, the item is left blank. A checklist enables you to note quickly and effectively whether a trait or characteristic is present, but it does not permit you to rate the quality or frequency of a particular behavior. When that additional information is needed, you may want to use a rating scale or an anecdotal record.

TABLE 11.2

A Sample Rubric Assessing a Research Report

	EXCELLENT	SATISFACTORY	NEEDS IMPROVEMENT
COMPREHENSION OF THE SUBJECT	Writing indicates an excellent understanding of the topic. Reflects use of a range of resources.	Writing indicates satisfactory understanding of the topic. Reflects use of one or more resources.	Writing indicates a limited understanding of the topic. Contains factual errors and may miss critical information.
IDEA DEVELOPMENT	Develops relevant ideas clearly and fully. Details and examples explain and clarify the information.	Develops ideas satisfactorily with details and examples.	Develops ideas incompletely with few or no supporting details.
ORGANIZATION	Organizes information logically in the paragraphs. Includes an effective introduction and ending.	Organizes information in an acceptable order that is easy to understand.	Presents ideas with little or no organization.
LANGUAGE USAGE	Uses lively and descriptive language. Details and examples explain and clarify the information. Varies sentence structure.	Uses some descriptive language. Demonstrates some sense of sentence variety.	Uses limited vocabulary. Uses respective, simple sentences.
MECHANICS	Writing shows few errors in basic language conventions.	Limited errors in basic language conventions do not interfere with meaning.	Shows many errors in conventions, but still conveys some meaning.

TABLE 11.3

Sample Rubric Rating Scales

4	3	2	1
Excellent	Good	Fair	Poor
Excellent	Above average	Average	Needs Work
Advanced	Proficient	Apprentice	Novice
Superior	Advanced	Intermediate	Novice
Consistently	Usually	Sometimes	Rarely
Fully developed	Adequate	Developing	Absent
Exemplary	Mastery	Approaching	Emerging

3. *Anecdotal records.* An **anecdotal record** is a written account of events and behaviors that a teacher has observed concerning a student's product or performance. Only those observations that have special significance and cannot be obtained from other assessment methods should be included in an anecdotal record. Anecdotal records should contain factual descriptions of what happened, when it happened, and under what circumstances it happened. The interpretation of the behavior and the recommended action should be noted separately. Each anecdotal record should contain a record of a single incident.

4. *Participation charts.* A **participation chart** is intended only to indicate the degree of involvement and the type of involvement in classroom discussion or activities. A typical form has students' names on one axis and the degree and frequency of involvement on the other axis. The charts are not intended to indicate why students participate.

Teacher-Made Tests

To achieve the purpose of teacher-made tests, you need to carefully plan the test and then select and prepare test questions. Next, you need to assemble, administer, and score the test.

PLANNING THE CLASSROOM TEST

The preparation of a classroom test involves many decisions. Advance attention to the following decision areas will likely result in an improved test (McMillan, 2011):

1. *Decide the purpose of the test.* To be helpful, classroom tests must relate to the teacher's instructional objectives and procedures. Classroom achievement tests serve a variety of purposes, such as (a) judging students' mastery of certain knowledge and skills, (b) measuring growth over time, (c) ranking students in terms of their achievement, (d) diagnosing student difficulties, (e) determining the effectiveness of the curriculum, (f) encouraging good study habits, and (g) motivating students. These purposes are not mutually exclusive.

2. *Decide what is to be tested.* What should be tested? The answer depends on the instructional objectives and what has been stressed in class. As noted below, the table of specifications should be determined prior to instruction, and this should serve as the basis for preparing a test. The table of specifications includes instructional objectives and content. The relative emphasis on the three domains of learning should be reflected in the table of specifications. Furthermore, an effective test should include only questions that address important outcomes of instruction.

3. *Prepare a table of specifications showing the content and objectives to be tested.* A **table of specifications**, sometimes referred to as a test blueprint, identifies the intended outcomes of instruction; it specifies objectives or behaviors that students should attain by the end of the instruction and the content related to these objectives. These statements should be precisely stated to clearly convey intentions. Summative evaluation, then, is intended to examine the degree of success with which the objectives were achieved by the students.

When making a test, the table of specifications is intended to identify the scope and emphasis of the test, to relate the objectives to the content, and to construct a balanced test. The table of specifications should be prepared before instruction. Some teachers prepare a one-way table of specifications that includes a list of the objectives to be addressed on the test and a notation for the percent of test questions for each objective. Objectives that are more important or more involved may require a higher percentage of the test questions.

A two-way table of specifications is more descriptive. First, teachers need to prepare a list of the instructional objectives with the level of the learning domain being identified for each. Next, teachers need to outline the course content. Then a two-way chart is prepared that relates the instructional objectives to the instructional content. The table of specifications displayed in Table 11.4 indicates the number of test questions in each learning domain for each content area in a sample unit in science.

4. *Decide when to test.* The use of the test results will determine the frequency of testing. If used in formative evaluation, students should be given short, criterion-referenced tests frequently to keep you apprised of their performance and identify those in need of additional or remedial instruction. Summative evaluation will be conducted less often.

TABLE 11.4

Table of Specifications for a U.S. Constitution Unit in a Middle School Class

CONTENT OUTLINE	OBJECTIVES IN THE LEVELS OF THE COGNITIVE DOMAIN						Total Number of Items	Percent of Items
	1. Remembering	2. Understanding	3. Applying	4. Analyzing	5. Evaluating	6. Creating		
Executive branch	1	2	4	4	1		12	24
Legislative branch		1	1	4	2	1	9	18
Judicial branch		2	2	2	2	1	9	18
States rights	1	1	2	1	1	1	7	14
Amendments	1	2	5	3	1	1	13	26
Total number of items	3	8	14	14	7	4	50	
Percent of items	6	16	28	28	14	8		100

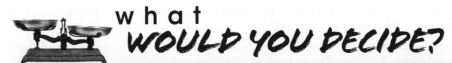

USING A TABLE OF SPECIFICATIONS

When planning a unit, your preparation of a table of specifications can help you identify instructional objectives in all appropriate learning domains for each content area within the unit.

1. When you prepare a test, how might you use the table of specifications to ensure that there are test questions covering all the learning domains in all the content areas in the unit?

2. How might this table help you distribute points for the various sections of the test?

To some extent, the frequency of testing is affected by institutional regulations on marking and reporting grades to parents. More frequent evaluation is superior to less frequent evaluation. Teachers in secondary schools sometimes communicate with each other in an effort to stagger the days when students are tested, so several tests are not scheduled for the same day.

5. *Decide what kinds of questions to use.* There basically are two item formats: essay and objective (multiple choice, matching, true–false). Some item formats are less appropriate than others for measuring certain objectives. Therefore, carefully consider the advantages and disadvantages of each item format. These will be discussed in greater detail in a later section.

6. *Decide how many questions to include in the test.* The length of a test will vary according to its purpose, the kinds of items used, the reliability desired, the length of testing time available, and the age and ability of the students. Formative tests are more in-depth and frequent than summative tests. As explained later, the time needed to complete different item formats varies. The longer the test, the more reliable it tends to be, but only so many items can be completed within a 50-minute class period. The age and ability of the students also must be considered.

7. *Decide the level of difficulty for questions included in the test.* The difficulty of a test should depend to a large extent on its purpose. Item difficulty will not be a factor in the selection of test items if the test results are to be used to describe the status of individual students. However, test difficulty is a consideration when the test results will be used to differentiate among students in terms of their achievement.

8. *Decide the format of the test.* You need to decide about the mechanical and formatting features of the test, such as grouping and arranging test items, directions for answering questions, distribution of correct responses, the layout of items, and other aspects. These will be discussed in a later section.

SELECTING AND PREPARING TEST QUESTIONS

There are two categories of test questions: essay and objective. **Essay questions** include short-answer or restricted responses (about a half page), discussion or extended responses (about two to three pages), or oral responses. **Objective questions** include multiple choice, matching, true–false, and short answer (a single word or several words). Since some item formats are less appropriate than others for measuring certain objectives, teachers should carefully consider the advantages of each type of item format.

Test questions are sometimes included in the teacher's edition of a textbook, and you might consider using them. Carefully examine test items included in the teacher's edition to be sure they are worded effectively, are at the proper levels of the learning domains being tested, are directed at content that was covered during instruction, and are at the appropriate reading level for your students.

Essay Questions. Two common types of essay questions are the restricted response and the extended response. **Restricted response essay questions** establish limits for the form and scope of the students' answers. Students are often asked to discuss one specific aspect of an issue and to limit their answers to perhaps half a page. Restricted essay questions are useful for measuring comprehension, application, and analysis (Stiggins & Chappuis, 2012).

Extended response essay questions, by contrast, place no limits on the student concerning the points to discuss or the organization used in the answer. Extended response questions require students to call on factual knowledge, evaluate this knowledge, organize the ideas, and present these ideas in a logical, coherent way. Skills in synthesis and evaluation are effectively tested with this type of question.

A variety of mental processes can be evaluated through the use of essay tests. From simple to higher-order skills, these include (1) what, who, when, which, and where; (2) list; (3) outline; (4) describe; (5) contrast; (6) compare; (7) explain; (8) discuss; (9) develop; (10) summarize; and (11) evaluate.

There are advantages and disadvantages to the use of essay questions. Advantages include the fact that they are comparatively easier and less time consuming to prepare than objective tests, require that students supply the answer rather than simply select the answer, measure higher-order thinking, and stimulate creativity and freedom of expression.

But essay questions also have several disadvantages. First, they generally sample content in a limited way. Three essay questions may not sample unit content as thoroughly as 50 multiple-choice questions. Therefore, essay tests that have several questions requiring short answers are preferable to a test that has few questions requiring lengthy answers. Second, essay questions are vulnerable to unreliable scoring. This problem of reader reliability can be minimized by careful construction of the test question and by setting up specified scoring procedures. Third, a student may not always understand the question and therefore may be unsure of how to respond, or he or she may be unable to put all appropriate ideas on paper in the given time. Fourth, essay questions require a great deal of time to read and score.

Writing Essay Questions. To minimize the associated problems, it is important to carefully prepare essay questions using the following guidelines:

1. *Reserve adequate time to prepare test questions.* Allow sufficient time to thoughtfully prepare each question and to be certain that each measures the intended objective, is worded in a simple and clear manner, and is reasonable and can be answered by the students.

2. *Precisely define the direction and scope of the desired response.* This can be done by (a) delimiting the area covered by the question; (b) using descriptive, precise words in the question, such as *outline, illustrate, define,* and *summarize* (as compared to the term *discuss*); (c) guiding the student into a certain direction by indicating what should be considered and presented in the answer; and (d) indicating the length of the answer (typically one-half page to two pages per question).

3. *Indicate the point value of each question.* Students need to know the point value of each question to be able to decide how much time to spend on it.

4. *Use essay questions to measure objectives that cannot be measured as well with other item formats.* As compared to other item formats, essay questions are especially useful in assessing students' understanding in the upper levels of the cognitive domain, such as application, analysis, synthesis, and evaluation.

5. *Use many questions requiring relatively brief answers, as compared to just a few questions involving long answers.* Brief answers (about one-half page) provide for a broader sampling of content, tend to discourage bias when some teachers grade for quantity rather than quality, enable the teacher to read the answers more rapidly and reliably, and also enable the teacher to direct the student to the desired response area.

6. *Take into consideration the time needed for an adequate response and the time available for the testing period.* Students need to have an appropriate amount of time to write out their responses to all questions.

7. *Adapt the length of response and the complexity of the answer to the maturity of the students.* The depth and breadth of the responses from 5th-graders certainly would be different from responses expected from 10th-graders.

8. *Do not provide optional questions on an essay test.* Providing options for students undermines the basic function of summative tests (e.g., comparing the performance of students in a common area). Furthermore, it is difficult to construct questions of equal difficulty.

9. *Decide in advance how the essay questions will be scored.* In addition to the substance of student answers, decide how grammar, spelling, punctuation, handwriting, composition, and clarity of expression will be scored.

10. *Prepare a scoring key.* When preparing test questions, also identify what topics should be included in student responses to each essay question, and then determine relative points for weak, average, and strong answers.

Evaluating Essay Questions. The usefulness of a carefully constructed essay test can be undermined by improper grading procedures and standards. Essay tests must be reliably graded with either the analytical method or the rating method. In the *analytical method*, the teacher identifies all the specific points or topics that should be included in an appropriate answer. The student's score is determined by the number of points or topics he or she includes in the response to the essay question.

The *rating method* also involves the teacher identifying the points to be included in the answer, but the wholeness of the response is emphasized. Several student papers are selected to reflect the range of responses on a given question. These papers serve as anchor points as the other papers are read and rated. Papers may be read using a 2-point scale (acceptable–unacceptable) up to a 5-point scale (with steps going from superior to inferior). With the 5-point scale, the teacher will place students' papers in one of these five piles upon reading the students' responses. It is preferable that each paper be read and rated twice. The rating method is effective when a large number of essays are to be read.

When evaluating essay questions, consider the following guidelines.

1. *Check the scoring key against actual responses.* Before scoring actually begins, read a few randomly selected papers to determine the appropriateness of the scoring key. Adjustments might be made in the key based on actual responses. The key should not be changed once actual scoring begins.

2. *If spelling, penmanship, grammar, and writing style of the responses are to be scored, it should be done independently of the subject matter content in the responses.*

3. *Score the students' responses anonymously.* If possible, conceal the student's name as each paper is evaluated in an effort to reduce biases.

4. *Evaluate one question at one time for all students.* This is designed to eliminate the so-called halo effect, a general impression of high, medium, or low quality that might carry over from one response to another for each student. This practice also enables the teacher to more easily keep in mind the standards that are being applied for a particular question.

5. *Shuffle test papers before grading each question.* The ratings given to preceding papers sometimes affect the way teachers rate the next paper to be evaluated. Therefore, shuffle test papers before grading the next test question to try to minimize the effects of the preceding grades.

6. *Try to score all responses to a particular question without interruption.* To keep the standards clearly in mind, the papers should be read without excessive interruption or delay.

7. *Whenever possible, conduct two readings of the test and use the average as the final score.* Two independent readings simply help improve the reliability of the test score. Of

w h a t
WOULD YOU DECIDE?

ESSAY QUESTIONS

For middle school and high school teachers who have many students, including essay questions on a test can be very time consuming to prepare the questions and to assess the student responses. Similarly, elementary teachers have many subjects to address and including essay questions in most subject areas may not be practical. Yet essay questions can assess certain knowledge and skills.

1. What are the benefits of essay questions over other types of questions?
2. What could you do to be more time efficient in your evaluating of essay questions that you prepare?

course, this may not be realistic at the secondary level if you have 125 student papers to evaluate.

8. *Provide comments and indications of correct answers.* By providing comments, you give students more information about their progress, motivate them, indirectly teach them, and also help to explain the system of grading and determining scores.

9. *Set realistic standards.* Avoid being overly generous or overly demanding as you review student responses.

Objective Questions. The most common types of objective test items are multiple choice, matching, true–false, and short answer.

Multiple Choice. A multiple-choice question has two parts: (1) a *stem*, which contains the problem, and (2) a list of suggested answers, or *responses*. The stem is typically in the form of a question or an incomplete statement. The incorrect responses are often called *distracters*. Generally, four or five responses are listed and all but one is a distracter.

From the list of responses provided, the student selects the one that is correct or best. Some questions have only one possible answer that is correct. In other questions, students are asked to identify the most appropriate, or best, answer from the choices given.

The *direct question format* has several advantages. It forces the teacher to state the problem clearly in the stem, it reduces the possibility of giving the student grammatical clues, and it may be more easily handled by younger and less able students because less demand is placed on good reading skills. The *incomplete statement format* can also be effective. In this case, the stem must be clear and meaningful and not lead into a series of unrelated true–false statements. A reverse (or negative) version of the direct question format and the incomplete statement format asks the student to select the one incorrect choice from a list of correct choices.

There are several advantages of multiple-choice questions. They (1) can test students in several levels of the cognitive domain, (2) can be scored quickly and accurately, (3) are relatively efficient in terms of the number of questions that can be asked in a given amount of time and the space needed to present the answers, (4) can test a wide range of topics in a short time, and (5) are not significantly affected by guessing.

Multiple-choice questions also have several disadvantages. First, they are very difficult to construct and plausible-sounding distracters are hard to find. Second, there is a tendency by teachers to write only factual recall questions. Of all the selection-type objective tests, multiple-choice items require the most time for the student to respond. Finally, testwise students perform better than do non-testwise students.

Consider the following guidelines when writing multiple-choice questions:

1. Use either a direct question or an incomplete statement as the item stem. A direct question is often preferable.

PERFORMANCE-BASED ASSESSMENTS

Nadine Espinoza, a sixth-grade teacher, has been introducing her students to a number of algebraic topics in math class. Recently, the students have been studying single-variable equations.

This year, instead of her usual end-of-unit written test, Ms. Espinoza has decided to substitute a performance-based project. She wants to show her students where the concepts they are learning in class can be found in real-life situations. For their end-of-unit project, the students will be asked to collect information about how a family's cutting energy and fuel costs can help them save for a fantasy vacation. Specifically, students will collect data about their families' electricity and automotive fuel consumption and costs for a month.

Using these data, each student will develop an equation to determine the average amount of electricity and fuel his or her family uses on a daily basis. Each student will decide on a reasonable dollar amount that his or her family

can put aside each month toward their fantasy vacation. The student will then create an equation to show how much needs to be cut from his or her family's daily electricity and fuel consumption to save that amount. Students will be asked to graph the information they have gathered and to incorporate the graphs and data into a brochure that can be used to persuade their families to reduce electricity and fuel consumption to save for the fantasy vacation.

FOCUS QUESTIONS

1. What advantages do performance assessments have over traditional paper-and-pencil exams? What disadvantages do they have, if any?

2. Think of some examples of performance assessments that might be used in the following content areas: science, language arts, social studies, and/or foreign language.

---

2. Write items in clear and simple language.

3. Make the response choices as brief as possible.

4. Include only one correct or best answer to every item.

5. With an incomplete statement, place the choices at the end of the statement.

6. Include four to five response choices.

7. State only plausible response choices.

8. List the response choices below the stem in a vertical, easy-to-read format.

9. Use letters for the response choices.

10. Avoid patterns of answers.

Matching. Matching questions consist of a set of directions, a list of stems or numbered items (e.g., statements, phrases, words, incomplete sentences), and a list of choices (e.g., words, phrases, numbers). Students are required to make an association between each premise and the choices.

Matching questions are well suited to test knowledge in terms of definitions, dates, names, events, and other matters involving simple relationships. Since they require relatively little reading time, many questions can be asked in a limited amount of testing time. Matching questions are also easy to score. The range of test material can be broad, and guessing is limited.

There are some disadvantages to matching questions. They may encourage serial memorization rather than association. It can also be difficult to get clusters of questions which are sufficiently alike that a common set of responses can be used. It is sometimes difficult to avoid giving clues, and too many items may be confusing to the students. Furthermore, matching questions are not well adapted to measure students' understanding of concepts or their ability to organize and apply knowledge.

The following guidelines will assist you in preparing matching questions:

1. List the homogeneous premises on the left and the options to be matched on the right.

2. List the premises and choices in some logical or systematic order (e.g., alphabetically, chronologically).

3. Keep the list of premises and responses relatively short; the optimum is five to eight items to be matched.

4. Provide extra responses to reduce guessing.

5. Be sure the stem includes the longer and more involved statements, and the response choices are short and simple.

6. Number each stem and use capital letters for each response choice.

True-False. A true–false item is simply a declarative statement to which the student responds by indicating whether it is true or false. One variation asks the student to correct false statements to make them true; these are often called modified true–false.

True–false questions have a number of advantages including the fact that they are good for students who are poor readers; can cover a large amount of content in a given testing period; generally provide high reliability; can be scored quickly and reliably; are adaptable to most subject areas; and can be constructed to measure the higher mental processes of understanding, application, and interpretation.

There are several disadvantages in the use of true–false questions. Scores may be unduly influenced by guessing. True–false items are often susceptible to ambiguity and misinterpretation, resulting in low reliability. The questions lend themselves to cheating more often than do some other types of questions. Some statements are not entirely true or false, and thus specific determiners are often added to the questions.

To help overcome some of the disadvantages, the following guidelines should be used when writing true–false items:

1. Be certain that the item is absolutely true or false, without any qualifications or exceptions.

2. Avoid loosely worded and ambiguous statements.

3. Highlight the central point of the question by placing it in a prominent position in the statement.

4. Avoid negative statements whenever possible.

5. Avoid making true statements consistently longer than false statements.

6. Avoid a disproportionate number of either true or false statements.

Short Answer. Short-answer or completion questions require students to provide a word or phrase. They are typically in the form of a direct question or a completion statement.

Short-answer questions reduce the chance that students will guess the correct answer, and test items are relatively easy to construct. On the other hand, short-answer items are more difficult to score than other types of objective tests. There is also an emphasis on vocabulary and recall of information.

Use the following guidelines when constructing short-answer questions:

1. Generally, it is better to use a direct question rather than a completion statement.

2. Use short-answer questions to measure only the recall of important information.

3. Have the statement lead to one or two specific words or phrases.

4. For completion statements, in general, place the blanks near or at the end of the sentence.

5. For completion statements, do not require more than one or two completions to be made in any one test item.

6. When omitting words to make an incomplete statement, leave enough clues so students know that the answer selected is correct.

INCLUDING A VARIETY OF TEST QUESTIONS

When writing a teacher-made test, I try to include questions of all types. There will be short sections of each of the following: multiple choice, true–false, short answer (a sentence or two), an activity (such as a graph or data table), and a short essay question.

I believe this variety helps test all aspects of a student's learning. I also think it puts students at ease to see at least one type of test question that they are comfortable with. These tests take time to prepare, but they seem more like a true measure of student learning in your classroom.

ASSEMBLING THE TEST

The mechanical features of a test—how the questions are grouped and arranged, what directions are given, and how the test is formatted—are no less important than the test items themselves. Careful attention to these aspects will enhance the value of the test as an evaluation tool and will also help save you time and effort.

Grouping and Arranging Test Items. For most classroom purposes, test items can be arranged by a systematic consideration of the type of items used, the learning outcomes measured, the difficulty of the items, and the subject matter measured. First, all questions of an item format should be grouped because doing so requires the fewest sets of directions, is the easiest for the students because they retain the same mental set throughout each section, and greatly facilitates scoring. Second, when two or more item formats are used in a test, they should be sequenced in the following order (Miller, Linn, & Gronlund, 2009):

1. true–false or alternative response items
2. matching items
3. short-answer items
4. multiple-choice items
5. interpretive exercises
6. essay questions

Arranging the sections of a test in this order produces a sequence that roughly approximates the complexity of the learning outcomes measured, ranging from simple to complex.

Third, within each item format, questions related to the same instructional objective should be grouped. Fourth, items within each item format should be arranged in order of ascending difficulty. Therefore, both the sections and the items within the sections are arranged in an ascending order of difficulty throughout the test.

Writing Test Directions. Directions should indicate what the students need to do, how they are to do it, and where they should record their answers. Furthermore, the directions should indicate the time to be allocated to the test, the value of each test item, and whether students should guess at any answers they are unsure of. When determining test directions, teachers can use the following guidelines:

1. Provide a specific set of written directions for each item format.
2. Indicate the basis for the student answering the question.
3. Indicate how the student is to record the answers.
4. Indicate the point value of each question in an item format.
5. Indicate the purpose of the test, the length of time available, and whether students should guess. These issues can be announced verbally as compared to being written on the test paper.

Formatting and Reproducing the Test. The visual display of test items on the paper can affect the time and effort the students expend taking the test and also the teacher's time during scoring. Use the following guidelines when formatting, typing, and reproducing a test:

1. Space items so they can be easily read, answered, and scored.
2. Number items consecutively throughout the test.
3. Make sure all items have generous borders.
4. Keep all stems and options on one page.
5. For matching questions, be sure the list of premises and choices are on the same page.
6. The most convenient method of response in true–false, matching, and multiple-choice questions is circling the correct answer.
7. Avoid a definite response pattern to the correct answer.
8. If no answer sheet is used, one side of the page should be used for responses to all objective questions, regardless of the item format.
9. Use a typewriter or a letter-quality printer to make the most legible-quality print.

ADMINISTERING THE TEST

The physical and psychological environment should be conducive for students to demonstrate their achievement of learning outcomes. Bearing this in mind, consider the following guidelines when administering a test:

1. Provide comfortable testing conditions, paying attention to such factors as adequate light, ventilation, temperature, noise level, and work space.
2. Do not promote test anxiety by giving warnings about the importance of the test or by threatening the students.
3. Avoid giving a test just before or after a long vacation or some other important school event.
4. During the test, provide reminders about the time remaining.
5. Discourage cheating through careful proctoring and other means.
6. Do not talk unnecessarily before the test.
7. Keep interruptions to a minimum during the test.
8. Avoid giving students hints about any test item.
9. At the start of the test, indicate what the students should do once they complete the test.

SCORING THE TEST

Guidelines were presented earlier for evaluating essay tests. Scoring objective tests can be done by machine or by hand. Some schools have facilities to score tests by machines that read students' responses off computer cards.

When scoring tests by hand, you have a few options. If the students write their answers on the test sheets themselves, you can simply create an answer key by using a blank test to write the correct answers. It is extremely helpful, as noted earlier, to have all the answers in one column, such as on the left side of the page. In this way, you can hold the answer key next to the student's test and mark the errors. If the student is asked to write the letter of the correct answer, you should draw a line through the incorrect answer and then add the letter of the correct answer. But if all letter choices are given at the left of the question and students are expected to circle the correct answer, you can easily see an incorrect answer and then indicate the error by circling the correct answer. In this way, in one stroke of the pen, the student knows the choice was incorrect and is also given the correct answer.

A scoring stencil can also be used in a similar way to cover all choices except the correct answer. You then can see which items were correctly marked by the students and place a mark on the correct choice when the students have chosen another response.

You can have students place their answers to objective questions (multiple choice, true–false, matching) on computer cards and use scanning systems to score the tests. This can save considerable time, especially when you have many tests to score, such as at the middle and secondary levels. The cards that the students complete are run through a scanning machine and each card is scored. Most scanning systems can generate an item analysis of the questions and a class roster with the score. Some scanning systems allow entering the scores from performance-based assignments (essays, special projects, oral exams, homework) with the machine-scored questions to obtain a combined score. The most sophisticated systems include software to scan, score, handle surveys, and develop a gradebook.

Regardless of the scoring method selected, the scoring key or answer key should be prepared and checked well in advance of the administration of the test. Generally, each item should have equal weight.

Achievement Tests

Standardized tests are those that are prepared by testing agencies with standard items, directions, testing conditions, and scoring procedures. The tests are typically created by test-preparing agencies, such as the Educational Testing Service. The test items are of high technical quality (thoroughly developed, pretested, and selected by the testing agencies). The directions for administering and scoring are so precisely stated that the procedures are standard for different users of the test. Test manuals and other accessory materials are also included as guides for administering and scoring the test, evaluating its technical qualities, and interpreting and using the results (Miller at al., 2009).

Standardized achievement batteries are used in elementary and secondary schools. The term **test battery** in this context means a coordinated series of tests covering different content areas and multiple grade levels (e.g., a series of tests in science in each elementary grade, or a series in mathematics in each grade). Widely used standardized achievement tests include the Iowa Tests of Basic Skills, Stanford Achievement Test Series, Metropolitan Achievement Tests, TerraNova, and California Achievement Tests.

It has been common practice for state departments of education, with the authority of state and federal legislation, to use standardized tests to diagnose and evaluate students' academic progress on a yearly basis. The results of these tests are given to schools and teachers. In many states, test scores are summarized by the school and by subgroups within schools. Each school is compared to other schools in the state. These comparisons are sometimes published in newspapers. Test results are often used to make high-stakes decisions about students, teachers, and schools. Thus, standardized achievement tests are often referred to as **high-stakes tests**.

Beginning teachers will be expected to understand and administer standardized tests that have been selected by the district for use. Further, they will be expected to use the test results to improve teaching and learning, and to communicate the results to students and their parents. Some school districts hold teachers accountable for their students' success on these tests.

TYPES OF ACHIEVEMENT TEST SCORES

Since teachers are expected to use the test results, it is important to understand the types of scores that are reported from achievement tests. There are five different types of scores that may be reported on norm-referenced tests (Popham, 2011; Stiggins & Chappuis, 2012).

- *Raw Score*. When the students take the test, the number of items that they answer correctly is called the **raw score**.

- *Percent Correct*. **Percent correct** refers to the percent of the test items that the students answered correctly. This score is used to determine mastery over the objectives. Students are judged to have mastered the objectives if they answer correctly a certain percentage of the items covered on the test. The cutoff for mastery on a given test, for example, may be 75 percent of the answers correct.

- *Percentile Score*. The **percentile score** (sometimes called the percentile rank) tells us what percent of the norm group a student with a given raw score outperformed. A student with a percentile score of 56 percent, for example, outscored 56 percent of the other test takers in the test's norm group. Thus, the percentile score gives a straightforward comparison of student-to-student performance.

- *Stanine*. This is a less precise score scale that is based on percentile rank. The percentile scale is divided into nine segments, each of which represents a "standard nine" or abbreviated, a **stanine**. Students scoring with the lowest percentile scores would be in the first stanine (well below average), while students scoring with the highest percentile scores would be in the ninth stanine (well above average).

- *Grade Equivalent Scores*. The basis of the **grade equivalent score** is the performance of the students in the norm group at specified grade levels. For example, a student with a grade equivalent score of 6.4 in reading is said to have scored about the same as students in the norm group who were in their fourth month of sixth grade.

THE TEACHER'S ROLE IN STANDARDIZED TESTING

Teachers play several important roles concerning standardized testing. These include preparing the students for the test, administering the test, and then using test scores in various ways (Hogan, 2007; McMillan, 2011; Miller et al., 2009).

Preparing the Students. A number of actions can be taken before test day to adequately prepare students for the standardized test. Students will perform better if they understand the reasons for the test, know about the test format and characteristics, know how they can prepare, and are prepared to use effective test-taking skills.

- *Discuss the reasons for taking the test and communicate a positive attitude toward standardized tests*. If you convey negative comments to students about the test, then students will also adopt such an attitude and may not try their best. Instead, discuss the reasons for the test and for the ways the test results will help improve teaching and learning. Convey an attitude of challenge and opportunity. Emphasize that it is important for students to try to do their best, not just to obtain a high score.

- *Familiarize students with the test format and provide practice opportunities*. Acquaint students with the test format, number of sections and questions, time limits, directions, types of test items, and other factors. Make sure students know what the test covers. Whenever possible, let them practice on previously released tests so they become familiar with all aspects of the test. Let them see the blank answer sheet that will be used.

■ *Talk to students about the test*. Motivate students to put forth their best effort. Reassure students that some test anxiety is normal and can provide energy to help them perform better. Emphasize that a good night's sleep and a healthy breakfast or lunch will help students stay alert and at their best for the test.

■ *Help students learn effective test-taking skills*. Most experts agree that students who have good test-taking skills do better on standardized tests than do those students with poor skills (Russell & Airasian, 2012; McMillan, 2011). Many districts have designed programs specifically to improve test-taking skills, and these materials may be available to classroom teachers when working with their students. Some test-taking skills include strategies for using test time, avoiding errors, guessing at answers, and using deductive reasoning (Nitko & Brookhart, 2011).

Administering the Test. Administering a standardized test is more formal than administering a teacher-made test. Standardized tests have very specific instructions for teachers when administering the tests, and the stakes for student performance are higher than for teacher-made tests. For these reasons, it is important to pay attention to the following issues when administering the standardized test (Hogan, 2007; McMillan, 2011):

■ *Establish a suitable environment for the test*. Just before administering the test, make sure the lighting is adequate, students have acceptable working space, desks are cleared, and distracting objects are removed. Put a "Do Not Disturb" sign on the classroom door when the test is being conducted.

■ *Follow the test administration directions precisely*. Standardized tests have been developed with directions designed to standardize the conditions under which students in different classes and schools take the test. Teachers must follow the instructions developed by the publisher. The directions indicate what to say, how to respond to student questions, and what to do as students are working on the test. Read the directions to the students word for word as specified. During the test, teachers may answer questions about the directions or procedures about answering items, but they may not give clues or hints.

■ *Time the test accurately*. Most standardized tests have time limits, and it is important to adhere to the time. Mark down the starting time when you say "Go" and also make a note of the ending time. When saying "Stop," make sure students really do stop.

■ *Monitor the situation*. After students have started the test, teachers should circulate around the room. Notice if students are working on the correct sections of the test and are recording answers appropriately. Circulating should also discourage cheating. Be prepared for students who finish early because their actions may be a source of distraction for other students who have not yet completed the test.

■ *Make notes of any unusual circumstance or event*. While observing students as they take the test, teachers may see some unusual behavior or events that could affect the students' performance, such as construction noise outside or several interruptions at the classroom door. Or individual students may have some difficulty, such as a contact lens causing a vision problem. It is best to record these behaviors or events for use in subsequent interpretation of the results. Interruptions should also be recorded.

■ *Take actions after the test has been completed*. Retrieve all test materials once the test has been completed and store them securely until you submit them to the school's central office. File any notes you made during the test administration about any unusual behaviors or events. Submit all materials to the school's central office.

Using the Test Scores. Published tests of achievement and ability can play an important role in the school's evaluation program. The test results also can be useful for individual classroom teachers in the following ways (Miller et al., 2009; Nitko & Brookhart, 2011).

Guiding Instructional Planning. The test results provide a data source for instructional planning and help teachers meet students' learning needs.

- *Identifying the level and range of ability among students in the classroom.* Instructional plans take into account the students' learning abilities and their present levels of achievement. Test results provide evidence for the students' level of achievement and can serve as the basis for future instructional planning.

- *Identifying areas of instruction needing greater emphasis.* If the published tests were selected in accordance with the school's curricular objectives, weaknesses will be revealed by those areas of the test in which students perform poorly. Published tests are especially helpful in appraising strengths and weaknesses in learning. Based on the test results, teachers may need to make adjustments in their selection of content to address any weak areas.

- *Identifying discrepancies between learning ability and achievement.* Large discrepancies in a student's perceived learning ability and the achievement test score may be a sign that a student is underachieving. However, a number of factors may contribute to a student's low test performance, and teachers may seek additional information before modifying instructional plans.

- *Clarifying and selecting instructional objectives.* The results of published tests provide evidence that can help in the selection of objectives at a particular grade level

VOICES
from the Classroom

PATRICIA SMITH, sixth-grade teacher, Monroe Township, New Jersey

USING STANDARDIZED
TEST DATA TO INFORM INSTRUCTION

At the beginning of the school year, the district provides us with student assessment data from standardized testing. The students also take a computerized benchmark test in language arts and math during the first month of school and complete a writing prompt that is scored using a holistic rubric. Classroom teachers are required to keep a spreadsheet of all of the data to be used to inform instruction. With this data collected in one resource for the entire class, it is easy to identify areas by student or class that are in need of instruction.

I identify students who show areas of weakness in language arts and wherever possible match the deficiencies to our curriculum and the state standards. I keep a separate section in a binder where these students' data are highlighted, and I document what I have done to address their needs. Through differentiated instruction, I can provide these students with reteaching or practice on a skill while other students work on enrichment activities. I keep folder activities for this purpose, and each student will have specific folders assigned for him or her to work on. I can also post assignments online through various programs, and all of the students will be working on laptops but on different assignments. This is also a time for small-group or individualized instruction. I also use the information to group students heterogeneously so that group work supports struggling students.

I constantly update my spreadsheet and binder to reflect the most recent data and mark each student's progress. This information also helps me to conference with parents. Having accurate and meaningful data is a valuable tool for informing classroom instruction.

or in a particular course. Sixth-grade test results on the Iowa Tests of Basic Skills in science, for example, may provide information that fifth-grade teachers can use when selecting instructional objectives. Low performance in sections of that science test may suggest changes in instructional objectives in fifth grade to provide better preparation, and changes in the school's science curriculum also may be changed.

Identifying the Needs of Exceptional Children. For exceptional students, published tests can be helpful in identifying problems of learning and development so that special provisions can be made for meeting specific needs. This information can be useful when preparing an individualized educational plan for each student.

Providing Parents with an Independent Source of Information. By means of report cards, parent–teacher conferences, and other means of parental contact, teachers inform parents about the educational progress of their children. Standardized test results are a useful supplement to report card grades and other measures that are reported. They have the added advantage of being independent of teacher opinions.

Key Terms

Anecdotal records	Extended response essay	Participation chart	Reliability
Checklist	questions	Percent correct	Restricted response essay
Classroom	Formative assessment	Percentile score	questions
assessment	Grade equivalent score	Performance-based	Rubric
Criterion-referenced	High-stakes tests	assessment	Standardized tests
evaluation	Measurement	Portfolio	Stanine
Data-driven decision	Measurement error	Practicality	Summative assessment
making	Norm-referenced	Pre-assessment	Table of specifications
Essay questions	evaluation	Rating scale	Test battery
Evaluation	Objective questions	Raw score	Validity

Major Concepts

1. Classroom assessment is the collection, evaluation, and use of information to help teachers make decisions that improve student learning.

2. Measurement is the process used to obtain data concerning student learning. Evaluation is the process of making a value judgment about student learning based on the data.

3. Data-driven decision making means that teachers use information from many sources to make decisions about planning, teaching, and assessing.

4. There are three types of assessment: pre-assessment, formative, and summative. Each serves a different purpose, and each is conducted at different times.

5. Even before beginning instruction, teachers need to establish a framework for classroom assessment.

6. When using performance-based assessment, teachers must specify the criteria by which the student products or performances will be rated, and then they must prepare the actual rating forms.

7. A table of specifications identifies objectives in all three learning domains that students should attain by the end of instruction and also the content related to these objectives.

8. Student assessment should be related to instructional objectives that are included in the table of specifications.

9. Guidelines for planning the classroom test, selecting and preparing test items, assembling the test, and administering and scoring the test can aid in effective measurement.

10. Standardized tests are those that are prepared by testing agencies with standard items, directions, testing conditions, and scoring procedures. Teachers have responsibilities to prepare students for the tests, administer the tests, and then use the test scores in various ways.

Discussion/Reflective Questions

1. During a class session, what are some ways that teachers could check for student understanding with formative assessment?

2. Why is it useful to have a variety of assessment measures when evaluating student learning?

3. To what extent should assessments be adjusted for students with special needs? Is there a limit to how many adjustments should be made for a student?

4. What are the advantages and disadvantages of using products and performances to assess student learning?

5. What are the advantages of using a table of specifications when preparing a test?

Suggested Activities

FOR CLINICAL SETTINGS

1. Prepare a table of specifications for this chapter that includes learning objectives and content.

2. For a test on this chapter, prepare three questions for each of the following types of questions: true–false, short answer, multiple choice, and essay questions.

3. Construct a rubric that could be used in assessing students' understanding of a short story.

FOR FIELD EXPERIENCES

1. Ask one or more teachers to discuss the way they evaluate students. Analyze their responses in relation to the framework for assessment discussed in this chapter.

2. Talk with several teachers about the ways that they conduct product or performance assessments. Ask specifically about rating criteria and rating forms.

3. Obtain one or more teacher-made tests, and critique them based on the guidelines discussed in this chapter for planning the test, selecting and preparing test items, and assembling the test.

Further Reading

Butler, S. M., & McMunn, N. D. (2006). *A teacher's guide to classroom assessment: Understanding and using assessment to improve student learning.* San Francisco: Jossey-Bass.

A comprehensive guide that shows step-by-step ways to integrate assessment in the classroom. Considers meeting standards, setting expectations, gathering assessment evidence, making sense of the data, and linking assessment to instruction.

Gareis, C. R., & Grant, L. W. (2008). *Teacher-made assessments: How to connect curriculum, instruction, and student learning.* Larchmont, NY: Eye on Education.

It is not sufficient to simply gather information about student performance through teacher-made tests, portfolios, work samples, and other approaches. You must also determine the grade for the student's work, place that grade within a grading system, and then report the grade to the student's family.

Marks or **grades** are summative, numerical, or quasi-numerical symbols that represent a student's performance in a marking period or a course and become a part of the student's permanent records. The terms *mark* and *grade* are frequently used interchangeably.

It is important to differentiate a mark or a grade from a score. A **score** is assigned for a specific report, homework assignment, or test that is done while instruction is still taking place; this is formative assessment. *Grades* are used in summative assessment to represent the extent of the student's achievement and competence after instruction has occurred.

You will decide the type of information to gather to assess students, how heavily to weigh each source of information, and which frame of reference (i.e., criterion-referenced, norm-referenced, or potential standards) to use in assigning the grades. This information may come from homework, tests, quizzes, written or oral reports, or other measures. The choice of the grading system is often made by the school district and is reflected in the format used on the report cards.

When addressing the issue of grading student performance, you will need to make decisions about a number of factors: What are the purposes of grading? What types of grading systems can be used? How are grades to be assigned? How are nonachievement outcomes reported? How can a grade book be formatted, and how can information be recorded in it? How is student progress to be reported? These factors will be examined in this chapter, along with some general principles about grading and reporting.

Purposes of Grading

Grades convey information concisely, without needless detail. They also must be able to communicate information to a number of diverse audiences who use the grades for different purposes. The major audiences include students, parents, school administrators, counselors, other schools, college admission officers, and prospective employers. Each of these audiences uses grades in a somewhat different manner.

FUNCTIONS OF GRADES

Grades and other reports of student progress serve several functions (Russell & Airasian, 2012; Carey, 2006). The two major purposes of grades are to provide information and to aid in making administrative decisions within the school, but there are other purposes as well:

1. *Informational functions.* Grades are used to inform students and families about the student's academic progress. This feedback should enable students to judge their performance, lead to modification of their behavior, differentiate strong and weak areas of their performance, and serve as reinforcement for jobs well done. Grades inform families about their children's performance and also may provide the basis for questions to ask the children's teachers. This information enables families to give their children needed emotional support and encouragement. These summary reports also give families the basis for helping their children make sound educational plans.

2. *Administrative functions.* Grades are used for a variety of internal administrative purposes by the institution where they are assigned. They are used for determining promotion and graduation, awarding honors, deciding on admission to special courses and programs, and determining eligibility for scholarships and extracurricular activities, including athletic competition.

3. *Guidance functions.* By looking at a student's entire record, the student and a counselor may determine strengths, weaknesses, and interests. Counselors use this information to help students develop better self-understanding and make more realistic educational and vocational plans. This information could be used to make decisions about enrollment in certain courses or programs and about potential careers.

4. *Sorting and selecting functions.* Grades are often used when choosing individuals for academic honors, fellowships and awards, employment, advanced education in colleges and universities, and participation in various professional institutional activities. These decisions are competitive, and the decision makers are typically from an institution other than the one where the grades were assigned. Employers and admission officers from colleges and universities use grades to determine whether an individual will be hired or admitted.

5. *Motivational functions.* Periodic progress reports can contribute to student motivation by providing short-term goals and knowledge of results. How motivating the reports are likely to be, however, depends on the nature of the report and how it is used. If a single letter grade is used and students are threatened with low grades unless they study harder, the results are likely to be negative. However, when the reports are viewed as opportunities to check on learning progress, they are likely to have positive motivational effects.

6. *Research functions.* An often overlooked function of grades is the role they play in educational research. In research on student selection, grades are used as the criterion

from the VOICES Classroom

JEANNE POHLMAN, high school mathematics teacher, Wichita, Kansas

INFORMING STUDENTS ABOUT GRADING PROCEDURES

At the start of the school year, I give my students a handout that describes my grading procedures and expectations. The handout outlines the weight for tests, quizzes, and homework. Procedures are described for obtaining extra help and for using a three-ring notebook. I also include information about materials needed in class and the procedures that we will use when beginning class. The policies on tardiness and cheating are also included. I think it is important to clearly state all these guidelines and expectations.

URBAN EDUCATION

against which a predictor variable is validated (e.g., using high school grades as a predictor of success in college). Grades are also sometimes used in curriculum research and evaluation by using student success as an index of student performance.

Students know that assessment has to take place, but you can build understanding and commitment to assessment by discussing the reasons for it and how it can benefit students. For example, formative assessment measures student learning as you proceed through a unit and provides feedback about areas of strength and weakness in student performance prior to the final, summative assessment. Formative assessment performance is recorded but may not be used to calculate the report card grade. Once students know the reasons for formative assessment and realize that it will not be used for the report card score, they will feel less pressured and more willing to participate. In addition, there may be various ways to involve students in the development of assessments in an effort to build their understanding and commitment to assessment in a learning community.

CONFOUNDING THE ACHIEVEMENT GRADE

When trying to create a comprehensive index of student progress, some teachers might combine scores on conduct and achievement, thinking that improves the accuracy of students' grades, but the exact opposite occurs. The combining of these variables *confounds*, or mixes up, the meaning of the grade. Therefore, the meaning of the grade for achievement is compromised, and valid interpretation becomes difficult.

There are four common ways that teachers confound achievement grades (Carey, 2006). You should avoid the following practices:

1. *Treating practice tests and homework as summative assessment.* As discussed in Chapter 11, pre-assessment, formative assessment, and summative assessment serve different purposes. You would not consider using pre-assessment data as the basis of a report card grade, since that information is used to make placement and planning decisions. In a similar way, formative assessment data are intended to give the students and teacher feedback about student performance while instruction is still taking place. Unfortunately, teachers often combine formative assessment data with summative assessment data to determine the grade for the marking period or course. This combination of formative and summative assessment data confounds the meaning of the grade.

Since the purpose of practice tests, homework, and related assignments used in formative assessment is rehearsal, they are premature measures of achievement. Consequently, students' scores on practice tests tend to be lower than their scores on legitimate posttests. Teachers who confound practice and achievement in this way usually attempt to minimize this negative influence by reducing the percentage that practice tests or homework contribute to the composite score, eliminating the lowest practice test score, providing opportunities for extra credit, or a combination of these three strategies.

2. *Administering unannounced posttests.* Some teachers use unannounced posttests, called *pop quizzes*, as a means to keep students studying on a regular basis rather than cramming before a scheduled test. Unfortunately, this practice confounds actual achievement and study habits. Student scores tend to be lower on unannounced tests as compared to their performance on scheduled tests. Teachers who use unannounced tests generally need to develop strategies to counter their negative influence.

3. *Reducing posttest scores due to misbehavior.* This practice confounds achievement with conduct. Unacceptable student behavior may include cheating on a test, talking or being disruptive during a test, or submitting assignments late. Teachers usually alter the earned score to teach the student that such misbehaviors will not be tolerated. Instead of reducing earned scores, alternative strategies should be used for encouraging honesty, consideration, and promptness. Many districts have a separate area of the report card to record behavior and citizenship.

ASSESSMENT

There are 10 InTASC standards (see pages xx–xxi), and each standard in the original document includes a list of performances, essential knowledge, and critical dispositions to indicate more clearly what is intended in the standard.

Since this chapter deals with assessment, some representative statements from InTASC Standard #6, Assessment, are listed here concerning topics in this chapter.

PERFORMANCES

■ The teacher works independently and collaboratively to examine test and other performance data to understand each learner's progress and to guide planning.

■ The teacher continually seeks appropriate ways to employ technology to support assessment practice both to engage learners more fully and to assess and address learner needs.

ESSENTIAL KNOWLEDGE

■ The teacher knows how to analyze assessment data to understand patterns and gaps in learning, to guide planning and instruction and to provide meaningful feedback to all learners.

■ The teacher knows when and how to evaluate and report learner progress against standards.

CRITICAL DISPOSITIONS

■ The teacher is committed to engaging learners actively in assessment processes and to developing each learner's capacity to review and communicate about his or her own progress and learning.

■ The teacher is committed to using multiple types of assessment processes to support, verify, and document learning.

---

4. *Using extra-credit assignments to alter grades.* Extra-credit assignments are those not required of all students in the regular conduct of the classroom, and these assignments may be used as the basis for altering the student's grade. This practice, however, confounds student achievement and effort. A higher grade that a student would earn through the use of extra-credit assignments actually masks the student's actual mastery level. Some teachers view extra-credit assignments as opportunities for the student to show added mastery or special skills.

Grading Systems

Effective grading and reporting should provide the type of information needed by the reports' users and present it in an understandable form. Depending on the purpose of the grade, as described earlier, some users of grades prefer comprehensive and detailed reports, while other users prefer a single mark. As a consequence, most grading systems represent a compromise between detailed information and a concise report.

A **grading system** is the manner in which the students' achievement is reported (McMillan, 2011). There are several commonly used grading systems, as discussed in the following sections (Miller, Linn, & Gronlund, 2009). Regardless of the procedure used, you should inform your students of the grading system that you will be using and clearly describe what your grading procedures and requirements will be.

PERCENTAGE GRADES

In a percentage grading system, the teacher assigns a number between 0 and 100; often this number is supposed to correspond to the percentage of the material that the student has learned. A disadvantage of this approach is the difficulty in making distinctions of less than 4 to 7 points out of the 100. Consequently, during the 1930s and 1940s, many school districts switched from numerical to letter grades.

LETTER GRADES

Letter grades have become the most commonly used grading system to represent students' achievement. In this system, a single letter (e.g., A, B, C, D, F) is used to represent a student's achievement. There are at least two variations of the A-to-F grading system. One involves the use of a single number (e.g., 5, 4, 3, 2, 1) to represent the same meaning as the A-to-F system. Another variation is the use of only two letters such as S (satisfactory) and U (unsatisfactory). This approach is most commonly used in elementary schools.

While concise and convenient, the letter grade system has shortcomings: (1) the meaning of the grades is often unclear because they are a collection of such factors as achievement, effort, and good behavior; (2) interpretation is difficult; and (3) letter grades have resulted in an undesirable emphasis on grades as ends in themselves (Miller et al., 2009).

But the letter grade system does have a number of benefits. First, it is relatively easy to translate from letter grading to percentage grading and back. This conversion is convenient for the teacher who is able to record all student information on a numerical basis, weigh and average this information, and then assign letter grades accordingly. Second, the plus (+) and minus (−) symbols may be used to represent more specificity in the grade. Third, letter grades can easily be averaged to form a summary index called a *grade point average (GPA)*.

DESCRIPTIVE ASSESSMENTS

Descriptive assessments are qualitative descriptions of learning, skills, and abilities that characterize a student's work. These may be in the form of written reports that are sent to families or are included in the student's cumulative record folder. These reports enable greater flexibility in reporting student progress to families by indicating strengths, weaknesses, learning needs, and suggestions for improvement.

Criticisms of this grading system center on (1) the need to wade through extensive documentation in an effort to differentiate students, (2) the validity of the descriptions being affected by the style and personality of the student, and (3) the time and effort involved in writing the descriptions. Some grade cards, including computerized versions, provide a space for brief comments.

PASS–FAIL GRADING

Some high schools have permitted students to take courses on a pass–fail basis, rather than on the traditional A-to-F system. Because the pass–fail grade is not included in students' grade point average, this system encourages them to explore new areas of study without the fear of lowering their grade point average. As a grade reporting system, this approach offers less information than the A-to-F system.

CHECKLISTS OF OBJECTIVES

For more informative progress reports, some schools have replaced or supplemented the letter or percentage grading systems with a list of major objectives to be checked or rated. This approach is most commonly used at the elementary level. For instance, five major objectives might be listed for each subject area, with a checklist for each objective indicating the level of performance (e.g., outstanding, satisfactory, needs improvement).

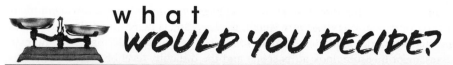

what WOULD YOU DECIDE?

WHICH GRADING SYSTEM FOR FORMATIVE ASSESSMENT?

Let's say that you are teaching your students how to write position papers on a particular topic. You want students to use and build on the needed skills, but you also want to provide each student with feedback about other language arts issues such as spelling, punctuation, grammar, and the like. You want to have formative assessment during the unit, before the unit's summative assessment.

1. Which type of grading system would you like to use for this formative assessment to give each student feedback?

2. Why would you select that grading system? For these purposes, why did you not select the other types of grading systems?

Assigning Letter Grades

Since most schools use the A-to-F grading system, you will need to determine what will be included in a grade and then establish a way to determine a composite score for each student. Next, you will need to select the frame of reference that is used in grading and then determine a method of distributing the grades for all the students in the class. Finally, you will need to calculate semester and annual grades.

DETERMINING WHAT TO INCLUDE IN A GRADE

Letter grades are most meaningful and useful when they represent achievement only. The interpretation of grades becomes confused when extraneous factors such as effort, conduct, study habits, and practice are included with achievement. Descriptions of student learning and development will be more precise if achievement alone is used in determining the grade.

Grades should be valid measures of achievement. An **assessment measure** is the means by which a teacher gathers information about the students' achievement. Assessment measures include tests, quizzes, reports, homework, and other approaches. Tests and other assessment measures should actually measure student learning outcomes of the course objectives. Letter grades should reflect the extent to which students have achieved the learning objectives specified in the course objectives, and these should be weighted according to their relative importance.

CREATING A COMPOSITE SCORE

At the end of a marking term, you will need to combine assessment measure scores into a score that reflects each student's achievement throughout the term. This summative assessment score for the marking term is called a **composite score**. A composite score is created by combining two or more scores obtained from the assessment measures.

Teachers need to consider the following four steps as they develop a procedure that works best for them when creating a composite score (Carey, 2006; Miller et al., 2009):

1. *Select assessment measures that will be used in determining the student's grade.* Measures of student achievement can be obtained through a variety of means, such as tests, written or oral reports, homework, ratings, laboratory performance, and projects.

2. *Analyze the relationship between the assessment measures.* Some assessment measures may be worthy of carrying more weight as the grade is determined. Therefore, first examine characteristics of the assessment measures. When considering the complexity of an assessment measure, look at its scope and the difficulty level of goals it measures. The scope can be compared using the number of goals measured and the length of time between instruction and testing. Difficulty can be compared using the relative complexity of the goals measured by each assessment measure.

When considering scope, quizzes administered immediately following instruction that measure only one instructional goal are the least complex. Unit tests measuring more goals and spanning more time are more complex. Based on differences in complexity, a teacher might decide that a comprehensive final should contribute more to the composite score than any midterm exam; a midterm exam should contribute more than any unit test; and a unit test should contribute more than any quiz (Carey, 2006).

The difficulty of the goals being measured also has to be taken into account. Based on differences in skill level, you might decide to assign more weight to tests that measure more difficult goals. One test that measures several less difficult goals may be considered comparable in overall complexity to another test that measures fewer but more difficult goals.

3. *Determine the percentage to be contributed to the composite score by each assessment measure.* You need to calculate the percentage that each individual assessment measure will contribute to the composite score. For example, if there are six unit tests and the teacher has identified that unit tests would contribute a total of 33.3 percent to the composite score, then you would divide the percent of contribution by the number of unit tests. In this case, each of the six tests would contribute 5.55 percent to the composite score (6 tests × 5.55 percent = 33.3 percent). In a similar way, each of two midterm exams would be worth 16.65 percent if the total weight of midterm exams were to total 33.3 percent. Then, the final exam would be worth 33.3 percent. Figure 12.1 displays a sample for the way these percentages would be allocated for each assessment measure. The example shown in Figure 12.1 includes only tests; teachers may want to include other measures, such as homework and projects, as part of the composite score.

Usually, it is a matter of professional judgment when deciding on the percentage to allocate to each of the assessment measures that are part of the composite score. Some districts, however, have grading policies that prescribe the percentage to be allocated to final exams.

4. *Combine scores from assessment measures into a composite score.* Although teachers may calculate a composite score in various ways, the objective is to combine the scores from each assessment measure into a composite score. The complicated part is to devise a system to have the scores from each assessment measure reflect the appropriate relative weight when calculating the composite score. This composite-score calculation can be done in several ways.

One way is to use a commercially prepared computer program to make these calculations. Grade analysis software such as this can automatically calculate composite scores using the relative weights that teachers specify for each assessment measure. Such software can analyze and report data in a variety of ways. Second, you may calculate the average score for each type of assessment measure and then calculate the composite score from these averages.

Third, at the start of the marking term, you may assign points for each individual assessment measure that reflects the appropriate weight of the composite score. In this way, you need only to add up the total points at the end of the term to calculate the composite score. A drawback of this approach is that you will need to predetermine the exact type and number of assessment measures to be used throughout the term. Fourth, you may identify a weight factor for each assessment measure, calculate weighted scores for each measure, and combine weighted scores into a composite score. Fifth, you may devise a number of variations to these approaches or use completely different approaches in an effort to calculate a composite score.

FIGURE 12.1

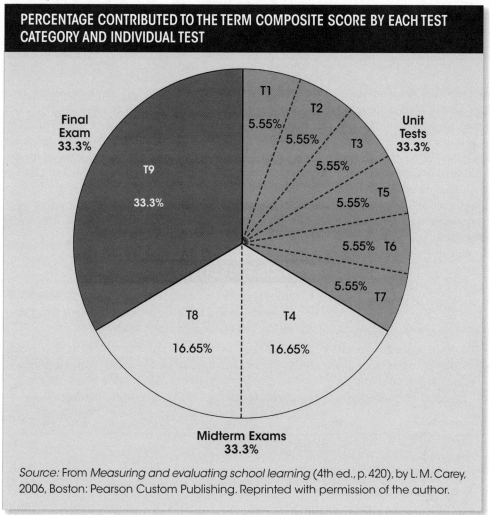

PERCENTAGE CONTRIBUTED TO THE TERM COMPOSITE SCORE BY EACH TEST CATEGORY AND INDIVIDUAL TEST

Source: From *Measuring and evaluating school learning* (4th ed., p. 420), by L. M. Carey, 2006, Boston: Pearson Custom Publishing. Reprinted with permission of the author.

SELECTING A FRAME OF REFERENCE FOR GRADING

Teachers should consider three frames of reference when determining students' grades (Miller et al., 2009):

1. *Criterion-referenced standards.* Assigning grades based on **criterion-referenced standards** involves comparing a student's performance to prespecified standards set by the teacher, usually indicated in percentages of material learned. Setting criterion-referenced standards for grading is a matter of professional judgment. With this approach, you would select score ranges for A to F that reflect outstanding, very good, satisfactory, very weak, and unsatisfactory achievement.

To some extent, this approach does involve comparisons with other individuals because standards have to be realistically set; they should be based on previous evidence of student performance. If the standards are set too high, many students will fail; if they are too low, students will achieve invalidly high grades. However, when preset standards are used, students do not compete with one another as they may when peer comparisons are made.

The criterion-referenced system of grading is more complex than it first appears. To use an absolute level of achievement as a basis for grading requires that (a) the domain of learning tasks be clearly defined, (b) the standards of performance be clearly specified and justified, and (c) the measures of student achievement be criterion referenced (Miller et al., 2009).

CREATING A COMPOSITE SCORE FOR THE REPORT CARD

David DeFranco, an 11th-grade chemistry teacher, was in his first year of teaching, and he started his first semester out with considerable enthusiasm. He was committed to planning interesting yet rigorous lessons for his students. When differentiating his instruction, Mr. DeFranco included some presentations, demonstrations, small-group work, and problem-solving sessions. He tried to build in lesson objectives at several levels of the cognitive domain to promote higher-order thinking. Lab activities were conducted on a regular basis to engage the students in the content. He used various types of instructional media, including a classroom response system, Web searches, PowerPoint presentations, and various types of computer software applications. He was applying what he had learned in his college methods courses.

To assess student learning throughout the report card period, Mr. DeFranco had several small quizzes, two lab reports, two unit tests, and a report on vocations applying chemistry information. The weeks passed by and then in four days, he needed to submit a report card grade for each student.

He then came to a startling realization—he had scores for each student for each assessment item, but he had not determined any way to process all of those scores into a report card grade. He had never determined the relative weight, for example, for the quizzes or for the lab reports. Were the combined quiz scores equal in value to a test? Was the vocational report more important than the lab reports? All he had was 14 scores for each student from various assessments. What a mess. What was he to do?

FOCUS QUESTIONS

1. What should Mr. DeFranco have done differently to avoid having this problem when determining a report card grade for each student?

2. What are the advantages of determining your plan for preparing the composite score for the report card at the beginning of the term? What are the advantages for the students if you tell them early how their composite score will be determined?

2. *Norm-referenced standards.* Assigning grades based on **norm-referenced standards** involves comparing a student's performance with that of a reference group, typically one's classmates. Therefore, the grade is determined by the student's relative ranking in the total group, rather than by some absolute standard of achievement. Because grading is based on relative performance, the grade is influenced by both the student's performance and the performance of the group.

3. *Potential standards.* Grading students with respect to their potential involves several considerations: their apparent ability levels, their past performances, and the efforts they have made. Under the **potential standards** system, students receive high marks if they perform well relative to their apparent abilities, improve considerably, or appear to be making extensive efforts.

Teachers often have difficulty in grading effectively using the potential standards method. Making reliable estimates of learning potential, with or without tests, is a challenging task because judgments of potential are likely to be contaminated by achievement to some unknown degree. It is also difficult to estimate improvement over a short span of time. Consequently, grades based on potential are not dependable due to the lack of reliability in judging achievement in relation to potential and due to problems in judging the degree of improvement.

DETERMINING THE DISTRIBUTION OF GRADES

Once the frame of reference has been selected, teachers need to decide how to distribute grades within that frame of reference. A number of guidelines exist for this task.

Criterion-Referenced Grading. When criterion-referenced grading is used, conditions for grading on an absolute basis must be met. These conditions include identifying the domain of learning tasks to be achieved, defining the instructional objectives in performance terms, specifying the standards of performance to be attained, and measuring the intended outcomes with criterion-referenced measurements.

The letter grades in a criterion-referenced system may be defined as the degree to which the objectives have been attained as illustrated here:

A = Outstanding. The student has mastered all of the course's major and minor instructional objectives.

B = Very Good. The student has mastered all of the course's major instructional objectives and most of the minor objectives.

C = Satisfactory. The student has mastered all of the major instructional objectives but just a few of the minor objectives.

D = Very Weak. The student has mastered just a few of the course's major and minor instructional objectives and barely has the essentials needed for the next highest level of instruction. Remedial work is desirable.

F = Unsatisfactory. The student has not mastered any of the course's major instructional objectives and lacks the essentials needed for the next highest level of instruction. Remedial work is needed.

Using these definitions as a guide, a point range must be determined for each letter grade. Some school districts have identified the point range for each letter grade. Often, however, this decision is left up to the professional judgment of the teacher.

There are a number of possibilities when determining the point range for each letter grade. For instance, you might determine the lowest passing score and then have an equal range of points for each letter grade, as illustrated in the samples in Table 12.1. The three samples show the lowest passing score of 60, 65, and 70, and each sample illustrates a fairly even number of points for each letter grade. Sometimes teachers prefer to have fewer points for an A or have a decreasing range of points as the grade gets higher. Again, the range of points that a teacher selects is a matter of professional judgment.

With criterion-referenced grading, the distribution of grades is not predetermined. If all students perform well, all will receive high grades. If some students demonstrate

TABLE 12.1

Sample Grading Standards

	COMPOSITE SCORE AND THE RANGE OF POINTS		
Grade	Sample 1	Sample 2	Sample 3
A	90–100 (11 pts.)	92–100 (9 pts.)	93–100 (8 pts.)
B	80–89 (10 pts.)	83–91 (9 pts.)	85–92 (8 pts.)
C	70–79 (10 pts.)	74–82 (9 pts.)	77–84 (8 pts.)
D	60–69 (10 pts.)	65–73 (9 pts.)	70–76 (7 pts.)
F	Below 60	Below 65	Below 70

Source: Adapted from *Measuring and evaluating school learning* (4th ed., p. 424), by L. M. Carey, 2006, Boston: Pearson Custom Publishing. Reprinted with permission of the author.

low levels of performance, they will receive lower grades. Therefore, the distribution of grades is not determined by the student's relative position in the group but rather by each student's level of performance.

Norm-Referenced Grading. Norm-referenced grading involves the ranking of students in order of their overall achievement and assigning letter grades on the basis of each student's rank in the group. A common method for assigning norm-referenced grades has two steps:

1. *Determine what proportion of the class will receive each letter grade.* This task is not as simple as it first might appear, because the teacher needs to take a number of factors into account as the selection of the proportions is made. As the starting point of these decisions, the normal bell-shaped curve can be used. Grading on the normal curve results in an equal number of As and Fs, and Bs and Ds.

In a classroom of 20 to 30 students, the use of norm-referenced grading may not be desirable because (a) the groups are usually too small to yield a normal distribution, (b) classroom assessment instruments are usually not designed to yield normally distributed scores, and (c) the student population becomes more select as it moves through the grades and less-able students fail or drop out of school (Miller et al., 2009). Consequently, teachers who use norm-referenced grading consider additional factors such as the type of class (e.g., introductory or advanced), the type of student (e.g., gifted, average, or slow learning), and others. After considering these factors, teachers may use their professional judgment to adjust the percentages for each letter grade.

Recognizing that a variety of factors need to be considered, you can use the following as a guide when selecting the proportion of students to receive each letter grade (Miller et al., 2009).

A	=	10–20 percent of the students
B	=	20–30 percent of the students
C	=	30–50 percent of the students
D	=	10–20 percent of the students
F	=	0–10 percent of the students

These percentage ranges are for illustration only. There are no simple ways for determining the ranges for a given situation.

2. *Make grade assignments based on the students' ranked scores.* There are three steps to this process. First, using the percentage of students that you selected in the first step, determine the number of students who are to receive each letter grade. Second, rank students in the order of their achievement. This can be done by listing the scores in descending order and indicating a frequency tally by each score. And finally, assign the grade for each student based on his or her score and on the letter grade designation for that score based on the previous steps.

CALCULATING SEMESTER AND ANNUAL GRADES

At the end of two or more marking terms, term grades are combined into a semester grade. At the end of the year, semester grades are then combined into an annual grade. Teachers often calculate semester and annual grades in a way similar to that which they used to calculate the composite scores for each marking term. As noted previously, there is a great deal of variability among teachers in the way this is done.

One way to calculate semester and annual grades is to use a computer program to aid in grade analysis and record keeping. Second, you can take the average of the marking term grades to calculate the semester grade or take the average of the marking term grades and the final exam to calculate the annual grade. Third, you can identify a weight factor for the marking terms, semester grades, and final exam; calculate weighted scores for each measure; and combine weighted scores into a composite score. Fourth, you can

devise a number of variations to these approaches or use completely different approaches in an effort to calculate semester or annual grades.

Nonachievement Outcomes

In addition to reporting achievement, teachers are often expected to measure and report student conduct. **Nonachievement outcomes** involve student conduct in areas such as effort, study habits, attitude toward learning, and citizenship. Most commonly, the report card used by a school district will indicate the categories to be reported along with the manner in which the report will be made. Nonachievement outcomes typically reported include rating scales, checklists, and special reports; these same approaches may be used for recording achievement outcomes.

RATING SCALES

Probably the most popular method of reporting judgments of effort, work habits, character traits, and other nonachievement information is a rating scale (see Chapter 11). For example, work habits, effort, and initiative can be rated as superior, average, or unsatisfactory. Other items such as the respect for rights, property, and feelings of others can be rated on a three-step scale with shows great respect, shows proper respect, and shows little respect. Rating scales on report cards may include three to five intervals for such traits as honesty, dependability, and leadership.

There are some disadvantages to the use of rating scales. First, ratings require considerable teacher time. Second, ratings are subject to the halo effect, which is the tendency of raters to consistently rate certain individuals positively and other individuals negatively regardless of the trait or characteristic being rated. This is a special danger when a teacher does not know a student well and consequently relies on general impressions of the student in making ratings of specific traits or when a teacher lacks objectivity.

CHECKLISTS

A second procedure for reporting nonachievement outcomes is the checklist (see Chapter 11). A listing of specific behaviors or behavior patterns related to the traits to be judged is typically

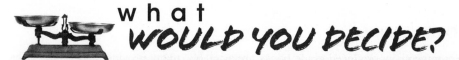

what WOULD YOU DECIDE?

NONACHIEVEMENT OUTCOMES

Nonachievement outcomes include items such as effort, study habits, attitude toward learning, and citizenship. It is helpful to record student performance for these items and to report that information to students and families. Teachers can promote the development of these outcomes.

1. What additional nonachievement outcomes might be related to particular subject areas (e.g., physical education, social studies, science, art)?

2. What kind of information will you need to gather for each nonachievement outcome, and how will you record it in your grade book?

3. What might you do to promote the development of effort and study habits?

presented. While the checklist may include both desired and undesirable behaviors, it is more common for items to be stated all positively or all negatively.

For example, items listed under the heading of work habits might include positive statements such as "Uses time effectively," "Organizes work well," "Follows directions," "Uses resource materials appropriately," and "Demonstrates the capacity for independent study." In contrast, a list of negative statements for work habits might include "Makes poor use of time," "Does not organize work well," "Distracts others," "Does not follow directions," "Fails to use resource materials appropriately," and "Lacks the capacity for independent study." Positive statements have the advantage of praising desired behavior. On the other hand, it is probably more informative to students and their families to know what weaknesses in study habits a teacher perceives so that steps can be taken to remedy them.

SPECIAL REPORTS

An alternative to rating scales and checklists is the use of special report forms to communicate with families and for use in cumulative student records. These are used when a teacher considers a student's behavior to (1) merit special commendation or (2) warrant a formal reprimand or warning. Special reports take less teacher time and energy than do ratings forms or checklists. To be used fairly and consistently, it is helpful to have a guide prepared by the district to assist teachers in making such reports. It is important that the reports not be viewed by students simply as a system for recording disciplinary problems.

Using a Grade Book

A **grade book** includes three types of student behavior that teachers are usually expected to monitor and report: achievement, attendance, and conduct. Consequently, a grade book documents students' progress throughout the school year. While teaching assignments and information requirements vary, most teachers need a daily record of students' attendance and other information related to classroom management, a record of achievement scores, and a record of conduct scores.

Your grade book design should reflect the nature of your teaching assignment. A teacher who is assigned five different groups needs a grade book that contains a daily log, a record of achievement scores, and a conduct record for each class. On the other hand, an elementary teacher who teaches five different subjects to the same group needs to create one daily log, one conduct record, and then a different achievement record for each subject.

RECORD KEEPING

While commercially produced grade books are available, many provide inadequate space for good documentation and are not formatted in ways that are the most efficient for the teacher. Consequently, you may be more satisfied with a grade book that you construct using a large loose-leaf notebook; large block, two-sided graph paper; and divider pages with tabs. After students' names are recorded on the first page, subsequent pages can be trimmed so the names remain visible as new pages are added. With this design, you can add new pages as needed, remove and store information from previous semesters, and insert records you might generate using the various computer programs available for grade books.

However, electronic grade books are also available. Most electronic grade books can store many types of student information, including test scores, homework grades, project grades, attendance, and even teacher comments. Some schools provide an electronic grade book program for teachers. These programs typically provide great assistance in determining a composite score which is recorded on a report card. Teachers simply identify the types of assessment measures and the proportion of the report card grade for each type of measure, then the software program calculates the grade. Teachers choosing to purchase a grade book program can find abundant choices by an Internet search.

SECTIONS IN A GRADE BOOK

While there will be some variation due to the nature of the your teaching assignment, an efficiently designed grade book should have three sections to record (1) the daily record, (2) achievement scores, and (3) summary charts for the semester and the school year.

Daily Record. The **daily record** is used to document information about attendance, homework and classroom assignments, particular instances of conduct that you want to record, and other school matters (Carey, 2006). To prepare this section, select the information you will document, choose symbols that represent each type of information, create a legend for the symbols, list the class dates, and record the selected behaviors. A sample list of symbols for recording behaviors is shown in Table 12.2, along with an illustration of how to record these symbols in the daily log. The sample shown in Table 12.2 includes only symbols for negative behavior; teachers often include symbols for positive behavior as well.

You will also need a summary section for the marking term in which you record the frequency of each behavior over the term. A sample summary section of the daily record is displayed in Table 12.3.

Achievement Scores. The grade book should also contain a section to record and summarize students' achievement scores on posttests (e.g., tests conducted after instruction). Again, the amount and type of information that needs to be recorded will vary with the teacher's assignment. In general, the more complete the information recorded, the

TABLE 12.2

Sample Symbols and Format for Recording Behaviors			
SAMPLE SYMBOLS FOR RECORDING BEHAVIORS			
ATTENDANCE	**STUDY HABITS**	**PARTICIPATION**	**CONDUCT**
/ = Absent	H = Homework	M = Materials not present	A = Aggressive
⊘ = Unexcused absence	Ⓗ = Homework accurate	C = Clothing inadequate	D = Disruptive
X = Tardy	XH = No homework	P = Did not participate	CT = Cheating on test
⊗ = Unexcused tardy	IH = Inaccurate homework	T = Time wasted	
	CH = Homework not complete		
	LH = Late homework		

SAMPLE DAILY RECORD OF CONDUCT											
Dates	9–1	2	3	4	5	8	9	10	11		12
Students						H				Trip	
Allen, B.					⊘	X	IH	X	P	ok	
Baker, J.						H	/			ok	

Source: Adapted from *Measuring and evaluating school learning* (4th ed., pp. 435–436), by L. M. Carey, 2006, Boston: Pearson Custom Publishing. Reprinted with permission of the author.

TABLE 12.3

Sample Summary Section of the Daily Record																
	ATTENDANCE				**STUDY HABITS**					**PARTICIPATION**				**CONDUCT**		
Students	/	Ⓘ	X	Ⓧ	Ⓗ	XH	IH	CH	LH	M	C	P	T	A	D	CT
Allen, B.	0	1	1	0	12	2	1	0	0	1	0	0	0	0	0	1
Baker, J.	3	0	1	0	2	4	6	1	2	7	0	2	0	0	1	0

Source: Adapted from *Measuring and evaluating school learning* (4th ed., p. 437), by L. M. Carey, 2006, Boston: Pearson Custom Publishing. Reprinted with permission of the author.

easier it is to determine the student's grade for the marking term, semester, and school year. A format is needed in the grade book to systematically record necessary information.

Summary Charts. Another section of the grade book is needed to record summary information for the semester and the school year. Selected information and summaries from the sections for daily records and for achievement scores will be transferred to this summary section. The summary section, therefore, will include summary information on the daily record, on the semester summary of achievement scores, and on the annual summary of achievement scores.

Reporting Grades

Families need to know how their children are progressing in school. In addition to reporting information about achievement and nonachievement outcomes, families often want information about course content, instructional activities, grading procedures and student requirements, and special activities. By properly communicating with families, you (1) fulfill your responsibility in telling them of their children's progress, (2) explain the academic program to them and solicit their understanding and assistance, and (3) enlist their help in educating their children.

Achievement and nonachievement outcomes are communicated through report cards. A cumulative record file for each student is also maintained in the school as a source of information for the teacher and families. Ways to communicate with families about grades and other issues are discussed in Chapter 13.

REPORT CARDS

Report cards serve as the primary means to report to families about their children's achievement and nonachievement progress (Stiggins & Chappuis, 2012). The school district determines a number of aspects that will be reported on report cards and how the information will be reported:

1. The district determines what achievement and nonachievement progress will be reported.

2. It determines what grading system will be used to report achievement progress. This may be in the form of letter grades, percentage grades, pass–fail, description evaluations, checklists of objectives, or other approaches.

3. It may determine the frame of reference (criterion-referenced or norm-referenced grading) to be used when assigning grades.

VOICES from the Classroom

ALICE DWYER, third-grade teacher, Guthrie, Oklahoma

EACH STUDENT HAS A GRADE BOOK

Each student in my class keeps a grade book, which is a folder where they record their own scores for the assessments they take. There is a simple line graph for the students to record the scores for their addition, subtraction, and multiplication facts. There are also several blank laminated sheets for students to place the stickers that they got on returned papers. It also contains a log where students write their scores from computerized reading tests. Students record their scores immediately after receiving their returned papers.

The purpose of this student grade book is to instill ownership in their own learning, provide immediate and regular feedback, and promote motivation. I want my students to compete with themselves instead of their peers. Students are also able to communicate better with their parents since their grades are accessible and not a mystery.

4. It may determine guidelines when calculating term or annual grades; for example, requiring that a semester exam count as 25 percent of the semester grade.

5. It may determine the percentages that should be used for each letter grade.

All of these decisions are beyond your control, and you need to be prepared at the end of the marking term to record information on the report card in the manner the district dictates. Some districts send progress reports to families halfway through the marking period. Beginning teachers, in particular, should examine the district's report card for their grade level to see what information they are expected to report at the end of the marking term. Take this into account as you devise the assessment system for your classroom.

Report cards differ in the way that nonachievement progress is reported. These reports vary considerably among districts and also by grade level. Report cards for the elementary grades, especially the primary grades of K–3, often have a number of non-achievement measures such as social development, work habits, effort, citizenship, academic readiness, and other areas. Report cards for the intermediate grades (4–6) place less emphasis on these items and have fewer items for teachers to report. Likewise, report cards for middle school, junior high school, and high school students have fewer items for reporting nonachievement information.

CUMULATIVE RECORD FILES

The school maintains a **cumulative record file** for each student as a source of information for the teacher and families. The file for each student commonly contains one or more cumulative record cards recording the following information: (1) personal information (home address and telephone number, parents' names, parents' work addresses and phone numbers, the name of a person to contact in an emergency, and other useful background information); (2) information for each school year and in each subject area concerning the student's attendance, achievement (often including grades for each marking term, each semester, final exams, and final annual grades), nonachievement areas (often related to work habits, citizenship, and conduct); (3) the student's scores on various achievement tests and other standardized tests taken over the years he or she has been in school; (4) health; and (5) honors or participation in special activities. In addition, the cumulative record

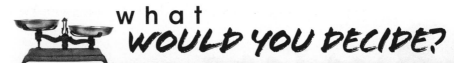

CUMULATIVE RECORD FILES

The cumulative record file for each student contains a great deal of information about the student, such as personal information, academic performance in previous years, achievement test scores, health information, honors, and even records of previous problems in school. Some teachers like to look at the cumulative record files for their students prior to the school year or in the opening weeks. Yet other teachers deliberately do not look at these files at the start of the year.

1. Why would some teachers choose to delay looking at the cumulative record files?

2. What benefits do you see in looking at these files, early or later on?

file often includes information about specially scheduled parent–teacher conferences and other anecdotal information.

The responsibility for updating the cumulative files for each student for each year varies among districts. For certain types of information, the school's secretarial staff sometimes enters the information. For other information, it is the classroom teacher's responsibility to have the file completely updated at the end of the school year. The balance of responsibility often depends on the situation in each individual school.

Cumulative record files serve several important purposes. First, the file provides the official record of a student's attendance, achievement, promotions, and graduation. It constitutes the basis for the student's transcript when transferring to another school. Second, the academic information can assist in determining each student's appropriate assignment to grade level or to specific classes. For instance, reading levels indicated for a student during second grade can help the classroom teacher make the appropriate reading group assignment when the student starts third grade.

Third, the data recorded in these records can help teachers understand the student's academic and social behavior. By examining these records, you may be able to identify special needs, distinguish between transient and permanent behavior tendencies, find out when a problem started, and discover clues concerning causal factors underlying a student's difficulties. And fourth, this record can help families and teachers achieve a more objective and accurate picture of the student's achievements, special abilities, and special problems. Cumulative record files are also accessible to families.

General Principles in Grading and Reporting

The following general principles can serve as the basis of your system of grading and reporting:

1. Describe the grading requirements to the students. This includes providing information about the type of assessment measures that will be used, the proportion of the marking term grade that each measure will carry, and the percentages required for each letter grade.

2. Grades should represent academic achievement only. Do not alter grades due to student misbehavior.

3. Assess students at all levels of the cognitive domain.

4. Assess frequently throughout the marking term so that sufficient data concerning student achievement are obtained to determine the grades.

5. Communicate clearly to students what they will be assessed on each time an assessment is to occur.

6. Use many different assessment measures. There should be a good balance of homework, class work, quizzes, major tests, projects, and other appropriate assessment measures.

7. Keep students informed about their progress throughout the marking term.

8. Devise an efficient format for the grade book to accurately record all assessment data and to simplify the task of calculating marking term, semester, and annual grades.

Key Terms

Assessment measure	Cumulative record file	Grading system	Norm-referenced
Composite score	Daily record	Marks	standards
Criterion-referenced	Grade book	Nonachievement	Potential standards
standards	Grades	outcomes	Score

Major Concepts

1. Grades convey information about a student's progress to students, families, school administrators, counselors, other schools, college admission officers, and prospective employers. They serve informational, administrative, guidance, and sorting and selecting functions.

2. A grading system is the manner in which grades are reported. Grading systems include percentage grades, letter grades, descriptive assessments, parent–teacher conferences, pass–fail grading, and checklists of objectives.

3. To assign grades, teachers must determine what to include in a grade, create a composite score, select the proper frame of reference for grading, and determine the distribution of grades.

4. Assigning grades on a criterion-referenced basis involves comparing a student's performance to prespecified standards set by the teacher. Norm-referenced grading involves comparing the student's performance with that of a reference group, typically one's classmates.

5. Teachers are often expected to measure and report on students' conduct in such areas as effort, study habits, attitude toward learning, and citizenship. These areas are often reported in rating scales, checklists, and special reports.

6. A grade book should be designed and formatted for efficient recording and use of the daily record (e.g., attendance, homework and classroom assignments, conduct), a record of achievement scores, and summary charts for the semester and the school year.

7. A student's cumulative record file can also serve as a source of information.

8. Teachers should describe the grading requirements to their students. This includes providing information about the types of assessment measures that will be used, the proportion of the marking term grade that each measure will carry, and the percentages required for each letter grade.

Discussion/Reflective Questions

1. What are the benefits of discussing your assessment system with your students and informing them of the types of assessments and their value in determining a report card grade?

2. How does awarding extra-credit points confound the meaning of a student's summative grade on a report card?

3. What benefits might letter grades offer over a pass–fail grading system?

4. What are some of the challenges teachers face when setting up a system for determining a composite score?

5. For the grade level and/or subject area that you intend to teach, what type of nonachievement outcomes (e.g., conduct, effort, citizenship) would be appropriate to report? How would you measure these outcomes and report them?

Suggested Activities

FOR CLINICAL SETTINGS

1. Select the types of conduct (e.g., effort, study habits, attitude toward learning, citizenship, or others) that you would want to measure and report on the report card for the grade level you intend to teach. Design a grade book format to record information about this conduct. This should include a key for the information, a way to record the daily log, and a way to provide a summary of this information at the end of the marking term.

2. For your grade level and subject area, select assessment measures for achievement you would use during a marking term and identify information concerning these that you would need to record in the grade book. Next, design a grade book that would enable you to record the required information and prepare marking term summaries.

3. Identify the percentages for each letter grade that you would use in the grade level and/or subject you intend

to teach. State the rationale for the lowest passing percentage and for the range of points at each letter grade.

FOR FIELD EXPERIENCES

1. Talk with one or more teachers to determine what assessment measures they use, how they create a composite score for the marking term, what frame of reference they use when grading, and how they determine the distribution of grades within the class.

2. Examine the report card for a school district to see what achievement and nonachievement information is reported and how it is reported. Critique the report card for positive and negative aspects.

3. With the permission of the teacher, examine the cumulative record files for the students in one class. Notice the type of information recorded, and identify ways this information could be used.

Further Reading

Burke, K. (2009). *How to assess authentic learning* (5th ed.). Thousand Oaks, CA: Corwin Press.

In a practical, workbook format, this book addresses learning standards and multiple ways to assess students, including portfolios, performance tasks and rubrics, teacher-made tests, logs and journals, checklists, and conferences.

Butler, S. M., & McMunn, N. D. (2006). *A teacher's guide to classroom assessment: Understanding and using assessment to improve student learning.* San Francisco: Jossey-Bass.

A comprehensive guide that shows step-by-step ways to integrate assessment in the classroom. Considers meeting standards, setting expectations, gathering assessment evidence, making sense of the data, and linking assessment to instruction.

Guskey, T. R., & Bailey, J. M. (2001). *Developing grading and reporting systems for student learning*. Thousand Oaks, CA: Corwin Press.

Provides thorough descriptions and guidance about all aspects of establishing a grading and reporting system in the classroom.

McMillan, J. H. (2011). *Classroom assessment: Principles and practice for effective standards-based instruction* (5th ed.). Boston: Allyn & Bacon.

Shows how assessment principles apply to the full range of teacher decision making. Includes emphasis on high-quality assessments, assessing mainstreamed students, and assessments in each learning domain.

Technology Resources

ONE DISTRICT'S GRADING SCALE FOR ALL GRADE LEVELS

http://sbo.nn.k12.va.us/resources/grading.html

This website shows one school district's policy for the grading scales for the elementary school, middle school, and high school. Information available on the site also includes useful charts and descriptions.

GRADE BOOKS

http://www.savvyfrog.com/Computers/Software/ Educational/Teachers_Help/Gradebooks

This website lists and briefly describes many types of electronic grade books that are available.

REPORT CARDS: ADVICE AND SUGGESTED COMMENTS

http://www.teachervision.fen.com/school/ assessment/6964.html

This Teacher Vision site provides samples of report card comments and phrases for a variety of subjects and issues. It also has links to many other useful topics such as classroom management, lesson plans, graphic organizers, forms, and themes.

MyEducationLab™

Go to the **MyEducationLab** (www.myeducationlab.com) for General Methods and familiarize yourself with the content:

- Topically organized Assignments and Activities, tied to learning outcomes for the course, that can help you more deeply understand course content
- Topically organized Building Teaching Skills and Dispositions learning units allow you to apply and develop understanding of teaching methods.
- A chapter-specific pretest that assesses your understanding of the content offers hints and feedback for each

question and generates a study plan including links to Review, Practice, and Enrichment activities that will enhance your understanding of the concepts. A Study Plan posttest with hints and feedback ensures you understood concepts from the chapter after having completed the enrichment activities.

A Correlation Guide may be downloaded by instructors to show how MyEducationLab content aligns to this book.

Can you imagine how challenging it must have been to teach in a one-room schoolhouse? There were so many responsibilities and challenges with the curriculum, instructional materials, and student behavior, and no one to turn to for help. Fortunately, teachers today have a number of colleagues whom they can turn to for assistance concerning a variety of issues.

Families can also be contacted for assistance when working with their children. In addition, teachers must take a variety of steps to contact and communicate with families about the school program and the progress of their children. This chapter addresses ways to work with both colleagues and families.

Working with Colleagues

Teachers don't teach in isolation. They need to interact with others in various ways to meet the needs of the students in their classroom. There has been increasing recognition of collaboration in the profession. For example, when the InTASC standards for teachers were revised in 2011, a new standard was included concerning leadership and collaboration (see those standards in this book on pages xx–xxi). The number of professional education resource books on collaboration has also increased in recent years. This is happening because collaboration is needed in schools, and educators are looking for resources to be successful in their collaborative activities.

WHAT IS COLLABORATION?

Collaboration is a style of interaction between individuals engaged in shared decision making as they work toward a common goal. People who collaborate have equally valued resources to contribute, and they share decision-making authority and accountability for outcomes (CCSSO, 2011, p. 20).

Teachers often need to turn to others for assistance when dealing with student behavior problems, reading or language problems, media and instructional technology, students with special needs, curricular issues, instructional strategies, and numerous other issues. Depending on the issue, teachers may turn to one or more of these colleagues and resource people: principals, counselors or psychologists, reading specialists, special education resource teachers, librarians, media specialists, curriculum specialists, school or district committees, or district or community agencies.

Sometimes this interaction is only to obtain information from a colleague, at other times there is genuine interaction and shared decision making toward a common goal about an issue—this is collaboration. But collaboration is not only about addressing an issue concerning a certain student; there are several purposes of collaboration, as noted in the next section.

WHY COLLABORATE?

There are several reasons for going out of your own classroom to interact and collaborate with others. You might be applying your school's response to intervention (RTI) plan when addressing the learning needs of several students in your class, and you need to arrange for intensive intervention by another educator. You might have three students with disabilities, and you need to interact with the special education teacher. You might have a student who is having trouble dealing with a family problem, and you need to contact the school psychologist or counselor. You might be seeking information on how to use formative assessment, and you choose to work with another teacher on this topic. You might be asked to serve on a schoolwide committee addressing student dropouts in high school.

Many more examples could be provided, but the reasons for collaborating fall into the following categories:

1. *To meet the needs of the students.* Let's say you are dealing with a student who has significant misbehavior problems. It is wise to consult with the principal, school counselor, and/or psychologist to obtain information and advice as you work with this challenging student. Sometimes, however, students do not respond to any of your strategies, and the misbehavior may continue to be chronic and serious. Deviant and disruptive behavior warrants referrals to outside help. In such cases, you may need to refer this student to the school counselor or psychologist when you recognize that a developing problem is beyond your professional expertise. Remember that you have not been trained to be a psychologist, counselor, or social worker, and you should not view yourself as a failure when referring the student for help from someone with appropriate training.

Before students' problem behavior gets serious enough for these referrals, it is often helpful to have telephone calls and conferences with families to inform them of the student behaviors and your actions and to solicit their assistance. In addition, the principal can counsel or intervene in various ways when handling a challenging student.

In serious cases, district and community agencies might need to be contacted to work with the school and the family. Many districts or city governments have an office of substance abuse and violence prevention and intervention, and its resources may be useful. Social workers are available in various community agencies. Other types of offices and organizations within the district or community might be contacted for help.

This example of misbehaving students is one way to illustrate actions which teachers could take to meet the needs of the students. Depending on the need, teachers may interact and collaborate with many different people. These actions may involve working with other members of an instructional team, paraprofessionals, or other colleagues. Through collaboration, teachers can take responsibility for student learning and ensure learner growth.

2. *To improve professional competence by engaging in professional development activities.* Ongoing professional development is crucial when trying to meet the needs of all students. Teachers need to learn about new aspects of the curriculum, how to apply new instructional techniques, how to effectively check for student understanding, how to integrate technology into their instruction, how to provide better guidance to read in the content area, and a host of other interests and needs. Therefore, teachers seek out collaborative opportunities to increase their knowledge and skills in any number of areas. Some of these collaborative approaches to professional development include mentoring programs, co-teaching, peer coaching, teacher support groups, and teacher centers.

3. *To provide leadership when addressing a school improvement issue.* Teachers can be agents for change and for school improvement by serving on schoolwide or districtwide committees or task forces. Many types of special task forces or ongoing committees exist in schools and districts. They deal with issues such as textbook adoptions, curriculum development and revisions, improving reading ability, discipline, professional development programs, assisting English language learners, and a variety of other topics. By working in a collaborative way on these committees, teachers can address important school issues and be advocates for the students.

COLLABORATING WITH COLLEAGUES FOR DATA-DRIVEN DECISION MAKING

My third-grade team recently collaborated with our reading coach to develop a systematic approach to data-driven planning. First, our reading coach analyzes the data for the upcoming skill we are going to teach. She checks to see how our grade level did with the skill on assessments, reviews the types of questions that seemed to be a challenge for students, and then sends a list of the types of essential questions that we should have our students become familiar with.

Then our data groups meet. We divided our third-grade team into two data groups, which meet once per week. One group focuses on finding or developing skill-related activities, while the other group creates data-driven essential questions to go along with the reading materials for the skill. Finally, the information is shared through e-mail so that all of the teachers in the grade level are given input and have access to a wide variety of materials and approaches to teach the skill. This approach divides a task among many people so that all students in the grade level can receive a well-formulated plan of instruction. This collaboration to inform our decision making has made a big difference.

COLLABORATE WITH WHOM?

To serve the three reasons for collaboration mentioned above, teachers interact and collaborate with a variety of people. The particular need or circumstance will typically dictate whom the teacher may contact.

Other Teachers. When trying to meet the learning needs of the students, teachers often turn to colleagues as a source of ideas and support. This may take place in an informal manner but also may occur in grade-level or subject-area teams in more formal structures.

When trying to improve professional competence or to address a school improvement issue, teachers work with other teachers in many different ways, such as mentoring teams, peer coaching, lesson study groups, professional learning communities, action research groups, and co-teaching arrangements. Resource books are available on these approaches, as illustrated by these examples:

Teacher Collaboration for Professional Learning (Lassonde et al., 2009)

Mentoring as Collaboration (Blank & Kershaw, 2009)

Leading Lesson Study (Stepanek et al., 2007)

A Guide to Co-Teaching (Villa, Thousand, & Nevin, 2008)

Collaborative Teaching in Secondary Schools (Murawski, 2009)

The Practice of Authentic Professional Learning Communities (Venables, 2011)

Action Research (Mertler, 2011)

Other School Professionals. Teachers collaborate with many other school professionals, including counselors or psychologists, reading specialists, special education resource teachers, librarians, media specialists, and curriculum specialists. Educators in these other roles have specialized training for their particular responsibilities. Thus, they are an important source of information and expertise as teachers collaborate with them.

Teachers often interact with other school professionals when they have questions or needs related to teaching and meeting the needs of their students. These other school professionals, however, may also be involved in professional development efforts and school-wide committees.

School Administrators. Each school will have a school principal. Depending on the size of the school and the level of complexity, there may be additional school administrators such as an assistant principal or a director of the reading program. Teachers may need to consult and collaborate with one or more of these administrators concerning the students in their class, their professional development, or their involvement in school improvement opportunities.

Schoolwide Committees or Teams. There may be various types of schoolwide committees or task forces to deal with issues such as textbook adoptions, curriculum development and revisions, improving reading ability, discipline, professional development programs, assisting English language learners, and a variety of other topics. Teachers are often members of such committees. If not a member, teachers may need to consult or interact with the committees if they have a need to be addressed.

Students. While the degree of collaboration may not be the same as with other educators, teachers can collaborate with their students in various ways. If a teacher is conducting action research in her own classroom, for example, the students may be involved in the process. Collaboration can also occur with students as co-teachers in cooperative learning groups (Villa, Thousand, & Nevin, 2010).

Families. When considering the purposes of collaboration, teachers most often collaborate with families to support the learning of their children. There should be more than communication by the teacher to the families; there should be interaction and collaboration to promote the learning of the students. Parents can be partners in supporting the learning of their children.

Due to the nature of the condition and the learning needs, teachers may need to interact and collaborate more often with the parents of students with disabilities or special needs. Fortunately, there are some useful resources available to provide guidance (e.g., Cramer, 2006; Dardig, 2008). In addition, extra efforts need to be made to provide culturally responsive family involvement and collaboration (Grant & Ray, 2010).

School–Community Partnerships. Schools sometimes reach out to community agencies to capture support for student learning and to address certain problems. For example, it is becoming increasingly common for businesses to financially support certain school interests, needs, or programs. They might purchase necessary school equipment, such as computers, or support certain school programs, such as the theater department.

Common community partnerships with schools include (Sanders, 2006):

- Businesses and corporations
- Universities and other institutions of higher learning
- National and local volunteer organizations
- Social service agencies and health partners

These partnerships are often coordinated by a school administrator, but teachers are typically involved in developing the school–community partnership proposals and in conducting the actions designated in the partnership. To be successful, roles, responsibilities, and relationships between the school professionals, community agencies, and service providers need to be carefully defined (Kochhar-Bryant & Heishman, 2010).

COLLABORATION SKILLS AND DISPOSITIONS

What skills are needed to effectively collaborate with others? InTASC standard #10 on leadership and collaboration provides a perspective on what teachers might be expected to do when providing leadership and collaborating with others. Clues about necessary collaboration skills can be inferred from those performance statements. Here are some representative performances from that standard requiring collaboration:

- Take an active role on the instructional team, give and receive feedback on practice, examine learner work, analyze data from multiple sources, and share responsibility for decision making and accountability for each student's learning.

- Work with other school professionals to plan and jointly facilitate learning on how to meet diverse needs of learners.

- Work collaboratively with learners and their families to establish mutual expectations and ongoing communication to support learner development and achievement.

- Work with school colleagues to build ongoing connections with community resources to enhance student learning and well-being.

- Engage in professional learning, contribute to the knowledge and skill of others, and work collaboratively to advance professional practice.

When examining these representative performances, some broader skills necessary for effective collaboration become apparent. These collaboration skills include the following:

Communication Skills. Effective verbal and nonverbal communication skills are needed. How a person uses these skills also makes a difference in collaboration. Active listening, providing information, and asking questions are part of good interpersonal relations that are based on communication skills.

Problem-Solving Skills. There are several steps in problem solving: identify the problem, generate potential solutions, evaluate potential solutions, select the solution, implement the solution, and evaluate the outcome. Collaboration often involves addressing problems, and problem-solving skills are needed for effective collaboration.

Conflict Resolution Skills. Collaboration with others may be needed to address a conflict situation with students or others. Also, conflicts might arise with your collaborative partners when addressing issues of attention or concern. Mediation and negotiations skills may be need to resolve the conflict.

Administrative and Management Skills. Skills are needed to coordinate and implement the actions identified from the collaborative discussions. This may involve practical matters such as scheduling and coordinating services. When interacting with other school professionals on an ongoing basis, additional skills may be needed. When working with a paraprofessional, for example, a teacher will need skills related to training, planning, assigning responsibilities, communicating, supervising, and evaluating the work of the paraprofessional (Ashbaker & Morgan, 2006; Friend & Cook, 2010).

In addition to the skills just reviewed, certain dispositions are needed for effective collaboration. Some representative dispositions include:

- Takes the initiative to grow and develop with colleagues through interactions that enhance practice and support student learning.

- Respects families' beliefs, norms, and expectations and seeks to work collaboratively with learners and families in setting and meeting challenging goals.

- Willing to be helpful in making necessary compromises to accomplish a common goal. Willing to assume shared responsibility for collaborate work.

sample
STANDARDS

PARENTS AND PARTNERSHIPS

There are 10 InTASC standards (see pages xx–xxi), and each standard in the original document includes a list of performances, essential knowledge, and critical dispositions to indicate more clearly what is intended in the standard.

Since this chapter deals with colleagues and parents, some representative statements from InTASC Standard #7, Planning for Instruction, and Standard #10, Leadership and Collaboration, are listed here concerning topics in this chapter.

ESSENTIAL KNOWLEDGE

■ The teacher knows when and how to access resources and collaborate with others (e.g., special educators, related service providers, language learner specialists, librarians, media specialists, community organizations) to support student learning. (InTASC #7)

■ The teacher knows how to work with other adults and has developed skills in collaborative interaction appropriate for both face-to-face and virtual contexts. (InTASC #10)

PERFORMANCES

■ The teacher works with other school professionals to plan and jointly facilitate learning on how to meet diverse needs of learners. (InTASC #10)

■ The teacher works collaboratively with learners and their families to establish mutual expectations and ongoing communication to support learner development and achievement. (InTASC #10)

CRITICAL DISPOSITIONS

■ The teacher values planning as a collegial activity that takes into consideration the input of learners, colleagues, families, and the larger community. (InTASC #7)

■ The teacher respects families' beliefs, norms, and expectations and seeks to work collaboratively with learners and families in setting and meeting challenging goals. (InTASC #10)

■ Values the individual contributions made by each team member.

■ Willing to participate in respectful and reciprocal communication.

Many schools have various types of committees and task forces, and collaboration takes place in those venues. These groups may meet in an ongoing basis, and certain skills are needed to conduct these committees in an effective manner (Glaser, 2005). The responsibility for conducting these committees falls to the group leader. The skills of effective group processing are also needed for collaboration in this context.

Working with Families

Imagine that you are a parent and you and your family have just moved into the community during the summer. You have one child in third grade and another in seventh grade. Because you moved from another state, you are concerned that the curriculum might be quite different in this new district, and you wonder how your children will adjust to the new community and their new school and teacher. Wouldn't you want to talk to the teachers to share some of these issues? Wouldn't you like to hear about the curriculum and how the teachers will handle instruction? Wouldn't you like to maintain ongoing contact throughout the school year? Of course you would!

Good communication with families should be a priority, because it keeps teachers and families informed about what is happening. It also builds trust so that there can be a working partnership in the event that there are difficulties with a student. Although a teacher's primary responsibility is to work with students, it is important to communicate and interact with the students' families throughout the school year. The reason for the communication will often determine the timing of the contact and the means by which the contact will be made.

At the start, we must recognize that children come from many types of family settings. While some students come from traditional or nuclear families (47 percent), others come from single-parent families (27 percent), blended families (16 percent), extended or multigenerational families (6 percent), or other types of families, such as gay and lesbian families, families headed by grandparents, families with adopted or foster children, and even homeless families (Barbour, Barbour, & Scully, 2011; Olsen & Fuller, 2012). Some children are cared for by a combination of community caregivers, not in a traditional home.

As a result of these various family settings, the term **parent** is used throughout this book to represent the adult or adults who have parental responsibility. Thus, this definition of a parent could include the biological parents, foster or stepparents, a grandparent, an aunt or uncle, an older sibling, or a guardian.

Families want their children to succeed in school and generally appreciate teachers' efforts to keep them informed and involved about academic and behavioral issues (Berger & Riojas-Cortez, 2012). Families' reactions to problems vary widely. Reactions are largely determined by individual experiences, life experiences, education and training, expectations, socioeconomic circumstances, and other factors. The reactions of the child, the teacher, and others also have a bearing on how the problem will be handled (Shae & Bauer, 2012).

It is important to listen carefully to families to identify their concerns and suggestions. Trust is developed when they know that their ideas are recognized and understood. The full benefits of parent–school relationships are not realized without this interaction and collaboration. Fortunately, a number of useful resources provide guidance when working with families (e.g., Canter & Canter, 2001; National PTA, 2000; Olender, Elias, & Mastroleo, 2010).

What are the reasons for working with families? Why is it important to understand them and their point of view? When should families be contacted? What are the ways that teachers might communicate with families? We will examine these questions in this chapter.

REASONS FOR WORKING WITH FAMILIES

Students ultimately benefit from good communication and effective working relationships between the school and home. Families' involvement in their children's schooling has been associated with better attendance, more positive student attitudes and behavior, greater willingness to do homework, and higher academic achievement.

You should communicate with families for several reasons:

1. *To create open, two-way communication and to establish friendly relations.* Positive contacts with families early in the year help families establish constructive, friendly relations. In this way, families and teachers do not see each other as adversaries but as allies in helping students to be successful. Fostering two-way communication will result in appropriate school–community relations that benefit everyone involved.

2. *To understand the student's home condition.* Information about a student's home condition can help you decide on an appropriate course of action with the student. You may learn the parents are having marital problems, have limited ability to read or speak English, exert excessive pressure for the child to excel academically, or tend to be abusive to the student when there are problems at school. Such factors can be important as you decide how best to help each student academically and behaviorally.

3. *To inform families of academic expectations and events as well as student performance.* Families appreciate knowing your policy concerning homework, late papers, and grading guidelines. They also like to know what content will be covered, when the quizzes or tests are scheduled, and what special events are scheduled. Introductory letters or a Back-to-School Night are helpful, as are newsletters devoted to special events, units to be covered, or the academic schedule. Finally, families want to know how their children are doing. Report cards and conferences provide information periodically, but many families appreciate learning about early indications of academic difficulties.

4. *To enlist help from families about academic issues.* Teachers often seek help from families at the start of the year. They may send a list of needed classroom and instructional supplies home to the families to supplement purchases made by the school district. You may want to identify family members who might be available to serve as classroom aides or chaperones for regular or special events. This assistance may include preparing materials for bulletin boards, assisting during a field trip, and the like.

5. *To inform families of disciplinary expectations and actions.* At the start of the year, teachers often inform families of their disciplinary policy and their expectations for student conduct. As with the academic information at the start of the year, this communication is often accomplished through an introductory letter or a newsletter, or at the Back-to-School Night. If a student misbehaves, you may need to inform the family of the situation without having to seek additional support and assistance from them.

6. *To enlist help from families about dealing with their children.* When a student has difficulties, the family should be contacted to identify ways they might help. When a student has misbehaved, the family should be contacted so that you can work together to help the student stay on task and be successful. Families exert a great deal of influence on their children, and they can cooperate and support your actions.

You and the family may both agree on strategies to help the child and to build the child's cooperation and commitment to address any problems. A behavior-modification program may be agreed on; as part of the plan, the family may withhold privileges or offer rewards at home. The family has access to more attractive rewards than does the school,

VOICES
from the **Classroom**

LYDIA DIGIOVANNI, middle school science teacher, Union, New Jersey

GETTING TO KNOW YOUR STUDENTS FROM THEIR PARENTS

During the first days of school, I have a homework assignment which the students' parents are asked to complete. I ask the parents to describe their child in a letter to me in any way they choose, with the goals of helping me better understand their child and giving me information that will assist me when creating unique and meaningful lessons which match their needs and interests. This also opens the line of communication with the families in a positive way.

I explain to the students that this parent homework helps me get to know them to the core, and this information helps me educate them to the best of my ability. I further explain that I do not want to let any of their earlier school activities or behaviors influence me; the parent homework allows students to start with a fresh slate, and I quickly gain their respect for that. They also realize that I genuinely care about them as individuals and that I take their education seriously.

I express to students the potential I see in them and how I hope to see those great qualities which their family member had written about them. I hold high expectations for my students; after this activity, every student tries to live up to those expectations. I have been told time after time, "Mrs. DiGiovanni, you are different, you care about us . . . you know us," and this makes them want to work hard in my class.

such as a videotape rental, a trip to the pool, or the purchase of an item of clothing. Establishing a plan of action with the student as an active participant and with the support of the family is crucial for successful progress.

WHY SOME FAMILIES RESIST INVOLVEMENT

As much as you would like the cooperation and support of families when dealing with a student who is experiencing academic or behavioral difficulties, you may find some families apathetic or resistant to involvement. There also may be circumstances in the lives of the families that create barriers to good communication and involvement, such as work schedules or English language limitations. There are several possible barriers or reasons for family resistance to involvement (Appelbaum, 2009; McEwan, 2005):

- Some adults may have had unhappy experiences when they were students. They may view school as being oppressive and not a place of hope for their children. These families may consider it unlikely that school personnel can solve problems.

- Families of children who have a history of misbehavior may adopt coping mechanisms in an effort to deal emotionally with the problems (Shae & Bauer, 2012). Their responses may point to self-doubt, denial, withdrawal, hostility, and frustration. These families may resist involvement with all school personnel.

- Some families view teachers, principals, counselors, and other school personnel as the experts in addressing issues such as misbehavior (Turnbull, Turnbull, Erwin, Soodak, & Shogren, 2011). Consequently, they may resist involvement because they do not want to interfere with the actions taken by the teacher or other officials.

- Some families are threatened by the school itself and the bureaucracy. They may be intimidated by the size of the school, the need to report to the school office when visiting the school, the busy nature of the school, the lack of private areas for discussion, and other physical aspects of the school. As a result, these families may resist involvement because they have a sense of discomfort about the school.

- Diversity among the population and the sense of being different from school personnel may make families uncomfortable in seeking contact with teachers or administrators. For example, Asian immigrant parents may think that communication with teachers is considered to be "checking up on them" and an expression of disrespect. Members of other ethnic groups may likewise feel out of place.

- Some families do not know what is expected of them or how they might contribute to their child's education. They may withdraw or become angry or frustrated when the school seems to be failing to meet their child's needs. They do not realize that the school would value their involvement.

- Some families do not become involved with the school for practical reasons. They may not speak English or have limited competency in English. They may not drive a car or have limited access to transportation. They may not have access to a babysitter or cannot afford one. Or they simply may be too tired after long days at work themselves.

- Teachers or administrators may have done things in the past to upset family members, and now they may not want to get involved or may participate in an angry manner. In previous interactions, educators may have failed to communicate with the family, held stereotypes, broken promises, or been rude, condescending, dishonest, or unprofessional in various ways (McEwan, 2005).

- Schools may have not met a family's expectations for various reasons, and this may influence their involvement. Some families' concerns may be about a lack of student learning in the school, poor behavior in the school, a lack of competent teachers, erosion of values, a lack of safety, or even a feeling of having to settle for financially poor schools (McEwan, 2005).

what WOULD YOU DECIDE?

FAMILIES NOT ATTENDING

Let's assume that you teach in a school that has much ethnic diversity and that some families do not attend the Back-to-School Night or the parent–teacher conferences at the end of the report card periods.

1. How can you find out why the families do not attend?

2. How can you communicate to these families that it is acceptable to attend such sessions and that their child will ultimately benefit from their attendance?

3. What support might you seek from the principal in communicating with families?

■ Some families have personal problems themselves, and these factors may interfere with good communication and involvement with the school. There may be separated or divorced parents or problems such as abuse, addiction, dysfunction, and mental illness. There are also some parents who simply must complain (McEwan, 2005).

WORKING THROUGH CULTURAL AND LANGUAGE DIFFERENCES

An increasing number of students are from culturally and linguistically diverse families. It is imperative that you make adjustments in how you approach and interact with the families to develop successful home–school communication and partnerships (Grant & Ray, 2010):

1. *Learn about the cultures of the families of students.* Information is available about families of different cultures. For example, Lynch and Hanson (2011) provide detailed cultural descriptions on families with Anglo American, American Indian, African American, Latino, Asian, Filipino, and Middle Eastern roots. *Involving Latino Families in Schools* (Gaitan, 2005), *Teaching Hispanic Children* (Jones & Fuller, 2003), and *Educating Immigrant Students in the Twenty-First Century* (Rong & Preissle, 2009) are examples of books addressing specialized cultures.

2. *Use school resources and interpreters to communicate with families who have limited English language proficiency.* With increasing student diversity, many schools have forms, letters, policies, and other types of communication translated into one or more languages beyond English to facilitate communication with families. In addition, schools sometimes have interpreters available for one or more other languages. Classroom teachers need to use these school resources to effectively communicate with the families of students in their classrooms.

3. *Acknowledge and adapt to cultural differences in social etiquette and ways of communicating and expressing respect.* If you do not speak the same language as the family, your nonverbal messages become more important. Use positive body language when you meet family members at an open house or other school event. Greeting families at the door, for example, expresses respect. Any notes, letters, or newsletters sent home should be translated into the home language.

4. *Have early and frequent teacher–family contacts.* Initiate positive home–school contact and dialogue by chatting, making phone calls and home visits, talking with community workers, and arranging for afternoon homework help or tutoring to promote student success.

5. *Provide families with information about the school.* Keep families informed (in the home language, if possible) about important classroom, school, and community events, help available in the school or from community-based organizations, and sources of academic support. Communicate through student-produced newsletters, telephone calls, and other notices. Provide materials in the home language.

6. *Encourage family participation at the school and in the home.* Encourage and welcome families to come to school meetings and social events and even to come to the classroom. Encourage family members to come to class to share skills or to discuss their culture. Provide suggestions for ways families can enable their students' learning by supporting homework and creating a positive learning environment at home.

7. *Adjust how you conduct family–teacher conferences.* Schedule a time for the conference that is convenient for family members, and show them a portfolio of the student's successes. Including the student in a three-way conference can promote a dialogue about schooling. The use of an interpreter is sometimes necessary, and this shows respect for the home language of the family. Watch for any facial expressions, voice intonations, and body movements to extend communication (Diaz-Rico, 2008).

Contacting and Communicating with Families

As discussed previously, there are several reasons for working with families. The timing of the contact will depend on the reason for it. There are three points to consider when contacting families:

1. *Initial contact with all families* should occur at the start of the year. This contact should be designed to inform families about the academic program, grading guidelines, the homework policy, rules and procedures, and other academic and behavioral expectations. Requests for additional classroom supplies and for volunteers for activities are generally made at this time. You can make these contacts through an introductory letter, a newsletter, Back-to-School Night, or other means.

2. *Ongoing contact with all families* occurs throughout the year to provide information about content being covered in class, the schedule for tests or other evaluation requirements, field trips, the progress of the students, and so on. You may need additional volunteers throughout the year and may contact family members at various times as the need arises. These ongoing contacts can be made through a newsletter or information sheet, an open house, report cards, or other means.

3. *Contact with selected families* needs to occur to inform them about concerns unique to their child's progress. These contacts may occur when there is either positive or negative news to report. You will often contact families when there is a problem, yet it is easy to overlook contacting them when there is good news to report. Families especially appreciate reports of good news. If a problem arises later, they are often more willing to support and cooperate with the teacher. Guidebooks are available for advice on working with parents of students with special needs (e.g., Dardig, 2008) and even for working with parents of bullies and victims (e.g., W. B. Roberts, 2008).

WAYS TO COMMUNICATE WITH FAMILIES

There are many ways to communicate with families, and the method chosen is often determined by its purpose. To discuss a serious act of misbehavior, for example, you would probably not wait for a parent–teacher conference scheduled at the end of a report card period to contact the family but would likely call them immediately.

Much communication with families occurs at the start of the year in the form of an introductory letter, a letter about classroom management and discipline, a Back-to-School Night, and information sheets. Ongoing communication can occur through an open house, newsletters, notes and letters, phone calls, special events and informal contacts, sending home student work, report cards, home visits, and parent–teacher conferences.

KAYE LYNN MAZUREK, high school German teacher, Commerce, Michigan

COMMUNICATING WITH PARENTS

When a parent contacts me for any reason, my first response is to say, "Thanks for your e-mail, for your phone call, for coming to conferences. . . ." If the parent expresses a concern, my second response is to say, "What can I do to help?" I've found that these two responses to parents have been the key to setting a positive tone for a discussion which will lead to a productive outcome. The last question I ask is, "What suggestions do you have for me to help your child be successful in my class?"

Of course, I have to be willing to listen to and accept the parent's suggestions. In nearly all cases, I've found that the parent request ends up being as simple as wanting the student to retake a quiz, hand in a late assignment, stay after school, or have a seat moved. I firmly believe that a teacher who is interested in the academic success of a student should be willing to make any of these adjustments in order to establish a foundation of trust. It's important for both the parent and the student to realize that the teacher is invested in the student's academic success instead of focusing on a particular rule such as "no late work" that may result in the student's academic failure.

URBAN EDUCATION

To contact a family about their child's academic work or behavior, you could call them or arrange for a special conference.

Figure 13.1 is a summary of the ways to communicate with families that are discussed in the following sections.

FIGURE 13.1

WAYS TO COMMUNICATE WITH FAMILIES

1. Introductory letter
2. Newsletters
3. Letter about classroom management and discipline
4. Back-to-School Night
5. Information sheets
6. Open houses
7. Assignment sheets
8. Individual notes and letters
9. Phone calls
10. Websites and e-mail
11. Special events and informal contacts
12. Sending home student work
13. Report cards
14. Parent–teacher conferences

Introductory Letter. Teachers sometimes send an **introductory letter** home with the students to give to their parents during the first week of school prior to the Back-to-School Night. This letter is intended to serve as a brief welcome to the new year, include some basic information about the class, and invite family members to the Back-to-School Night that will soon follow.

The letter may include some information about the schedule, homework, absences, and the curriculum. You may mention in the letter that more will be said about these and other issues at the Back-to-School Night. A sample introductory letter to families is displayed in Figure 13.2. You can adapt this letter for your particular situation.

Newsletters. At the start of the school year or a new course, teachers sometimes prepare a newsletter that will go to the families of all the students in the class. An initial

FIGURE 13.2

SAMPLE INTRODUCTORY LETTER TO FAMILIES

September 4

Dear Parents:

Now that the schoolyear has begun, I'd like to introduce myself. I am Melissa Riley, and I am your child's ninth-grade algebra teacher this year. I have taught in this school district for 14 years, and have taught pre-algebra, algebra, geometry, and trigonometry. I completed my undergraduate work at the University of Illinois and my master's degree at Kansas State University.

I want this to be a successful schoolyear for you and your child. To ensure this success, it is important that we maintain open communication. Please do not hesitate to contact me if you have any questions or concerns. You can call me at school after dismissal between 3:30–4:30 p.m. at 555-7308. Or you can call anytime during the day and leave a message for me to call you back. My e-mail address is mriley@hotmail.com.

At various times throughout the schoolyear, I will be sending a newsletter home with your child to provide information about classroom activities and special events. On a regular basis, your child will bring home graded assignments for you to look at. I also look forward to seeing you at the conference session, which we schedule at the end of each report-card period.

The annual Back-to-School Night for this school is scheduled for next Thursday, September 12, from 7:30–9:15 p.m. On that evening, you will have the opportunity to go through your child's schedule of classes in shortened 10-minute class periods. When you meet me during algebra class, I will share information about the curriculum, my approach to instruction, my academic expectations and procedures, my policy on discipline, and other issues. The books and materials that we will be using this year will also be on display. I encourage you to attend the Back-to-School Night because it will give you an opportunity to understand the mathematics program and become better acquainted with me.

Working together and keeping in good contact, I'm confident that this will be an exciting and successful schoolyear. I look forward to meeting you at the Back-to-School Night.

Sincerely,

Melissa Riley

Melissa Riley

newsletter may be sent instead of an introductory letter to the families. This newsletter often includes information about the course content, instructional activities, and grading procedures and student requirements. Of course, the nature of the initial newsletter will vary with the grade level and the type of teaching assignment. As a guide, though, the initial newsletter may include a description of the following:

1. Course title or subject area(s).

2. Brief course or subject area description.

3. Course objectives.

4. A brief content outline.

5. Typical learning activities.

6. Grading procedures. This could include a listing of the types of evaluation measures to be used and the proportion of the marking term grade that each measure will carry. For example, tests (40 percent), homework (20 percent), projects (20 percent), and quizzes (20 percent). In addition, the grading scale could be included indicating the percentages for each letter grade.

7. Materials that the student will need.

8. Behavioral guidelines and expectations.

9. The school telephone number. This is included as a convenience for the parents in the event they need to contact you.

It is important that you convey this initial information to the students as well. Students especially need to know grading procedures and guidelines and also behavioral expectations. During the school year, additional newsletters might be sent to all families with information about special events, programs, content to be covered in the curriculum, tests or quizzes that are coming up, student projects, and other issues. Newsletters can be as brief as one page or longer, according to need. You can report accomplishments of the class and of individual students. Computers can be used to prepare the newsletters. Students can prepare the newsletter as a group or class project, under suitable circumstances.

Letter on Classroom Management and Discipline. You need to share your plan for classroom management and discipline with families and the principal. If you expect them to be involved when you need them, they need to know that you have a plan and to be aware of your rationale for rules, positive recognition, and consequences.

At the start of the school year, you need to discuss rules, consequences, and other aspects of management with students. A copy of this information sheet should be given to the students to take home to their parents. The letter should provide details of the classroom management and discipline plan and explain why it is important. Ask the parents to discuss the plan with their children, sign the plan, and return the signature portion to you. A sample letter to parents on classroom management and discipline is displayed in Figure 13.3. You may adapt that letter for your particular situation.

If the Back-to-School Night is scheduled early in the year, you may ask the families to return the signature portion at that time. Or you may prefer to wait and present the letter to the families at the Back-to-School Night and get the signatures at that time. Letters can then be sent home to families who did not attend that evening.

Back-to-School Night. Many schools schedule a **Back-to-School Night** or Family Night during the first or second week so families can receive information about the academic program, grading guidelines, the homework policy, rules and procedures, and other expectations. Requests for additional classroom supplies and for volunteers for activities are generally made at this time.

Some schools do not schedule a Back-to-School Night, or if they do, it comes later than the first or second week of school. Given this, you may find other ways to communicate

FIGURE 13.3

SAMPLE LETTER TO FAMILIES ON CLASSROOM MANAGEMENT AND DISCIPLINE

Dear Parents:

Now that the school year has begun, I'd like to introduce myself and give you some information about how I conduct my classes. My name is Keith McKinsey, and I am your child's fifth-grade teacher. I have taught in this school district for eight years. I completed my undergraduate work at Florida State University and my master's degree at Kansas State University.

To maintain an appropriate learning environment, I have established the following class-room rules, which all students are expected to follow:

1. Follow the teacher's directions.
2. Keep your hands, feet, and objects to yourself.
3. Do not swear or tease.

To encourage students to follow the rules, I will recognize appropriate behavior with praise, various types of reinforcement, and notes or calls home to you. If students choose to break the rules, I have established an escalating series of responses ranging from gentle prompts and reminders, to the use of logical consequences, and to detention. In class, we have discussed these rules, the reinforcement for following the rules, and the consequences if the students choose to break the rules. My goal is to ensure success for your child. Working together, I'm confident that it will be an enjoyable and productive school year.

Please indicate that you understand this discipline plan by signing your name below and indicating the phone numbers where you can be reached during the day and evening. You might also discuss the rules to make sure your child understands them.

Please do not hesitate to contact me if you have any questions or concerns. You can call me at school after dismissal between 3:30–4:30 p.m. at 555-6188. Or you can call anytime during the day and leave a message for me to call you back. My e-mail address is kkeith@hotmail.com.

Sincerely,

Keith McKinsey

Keith McKinsey

(Tear off and return the part below to Mr. McKinsey)

- -

I have read and understand Mr. McKinsey's classroom management plan, and I have dis-cussed it with my child.

Parent/Guardian Signature _____   Date _____

Comments:

with families, since it is important to establish contact as early as possible. For example, a letter about classroom management and discipline might be expanded to include information that is commonly covered at a Back-to-School Night.

The scheduling of the Back-to-School Night is handled in different ways. For middle, junior high, and senior high schools, families are often given their child's schedule, and they follow it just as the student would but in shortened class sessions of 10 to 15 minutes. In this way, the family sees every teacher in the way that their child would during the school day. Teachers often use this time to present information to families about academic and behavioral guidelines and expectations.

Preparing for Back-to-School Night. Back-to-School Night is often your first contact with families, so thorough preparation is necessary. There are many ways to prepare for this evening:

■ *Prepare your own introductory letter to families about the Back-to-School Night in your classroom.* (See the sample introductory letter that mentions Back-to-School Night in Figure 13.2.) Do not rely only on notices that the school sends home. Some teachers like to have their students prepare special invitations for their own families.

■ *Make sure that the classroom looks attractive and neat.* Post your name and room number prominently on the door and the front chalkboard. Display samples of work by all students. Display copies of the textbooks and other instructional materials.

■ *Prepare a list of any instructional supplies or materials that families might be able to provide.* This list will vary depending on the subject and grade level. It may include items such as rulers, buttons, a box of facial tissue, or other supplies. Have enough copies of the list to give to all families.

■ *Prepare separate sign-up sheets for families.* These may concern the need for a private follow-up conference about their child, volunteers to help at special events such as field trips, volunteers such as guest speakers in class, or volunteers to provide various instructional supplies requested by the teacher.

■ *Plan a well-organized, succinct presentation.* Families want to hear about your background and experience, behavioral and academic expectations, procedures for issues such as homework and absences, and other policies. Be sure to plan for time at the end of the presentation for questions.

■ *Prepare handouts for your presentation.* Families will receive these handouts at the Back-to-School Night. Have enough copies of this material to give to all of them. A sample content outline of the presentation is shown in Figure 13.4. Your handout should include details about issues such as those listed in that figure. On the front page of the handout, include your name, the school phone number, and the times that you can be reached at the school at that phone number. Attach other related materials to this handout; these materials may include a sheet showing the daily or weekly class schedule, a sheet of needed instructional materials and supplies, or a sheet concerning the classroom management and discipline policy. To simplify distribution, staple all the handouts together as one set of materials sequenced in the order that you will cover the material during the presentation.

Conducting the Back-to-School Night. Take several guidelines into account when conducting the Back-to-School Night. Since your presentation is usually limited, possibly to only 10 to 15 minutes, it is important to plan how to conduct yourself.

Greet families at the door, introduce yourself, and ask them to be seated. Begin your presentation using the handout that you previously prepared concerning your background, the daily and weekly schedule, the curriculum, academic goals and activities, academic expectations and procedures, discipline, and other issues. At the start, hand a copy of the handout to each family member.

Have parents sign up for individual follow-up conferences if they want to talk with you at length about their child. Back-to-School Night is not intended to deal with concerns about individual students. Allow time for family members to ask questions. This will be an opportunity for you to provide clarification about issues and to hear families' concerns.

Information Sheets. Not all schools schedule a Back-to-School Night, and not all families attend a scheduled night. In both cases, you can prepare a packet to send home that provides information about the curriculum, grading expectations and requirements, rules and procedures, the discipline plan, and other matters. The sheets may be the same as those given to families who attend the Back-to-School Night or shortened versions.

Open Houses. Once or twice a year, most schools schedule an open house for families to visit the classrooms during a particular evening to see their child's teacher, observe the classroom and samples of student work, and learn about books and materials being used. Some districts do not have a Back-to-School Night but instead schedule the first open house in mid- to late September. At open house, teachers may give a formal presentation

FIGURE 13.4

SAMPLE CONTENT OUTLINE FOR THE BACK-TO-SCHOOL NIGHT PRESENTATION

1. Background about yourself
   a. College training and degrees earned
   b. Professional experience, including length of teaching service, grade levels taught, where taught
   c. Personal information (e.g., family, hobbies, special interests or experiences)

2. The curriculum, academic goals, and activities
   a. Overview of the curriculum and the topics to be covered (refer to the textbooks and related instructional materials on display in the room)
   b. Your approach to instruction
   c. Instructional activities and any special events, such as field trips or unique programs

3. Academic expectations and procedures
   a. Grading guidelines and procedures (how grades are determined)
   b. Grading requirements (e.g., tests, quizzes, homework, projects)
   c. Homework (purposes, how often, makeup policy, absences)
   d. When report cards are delivered
   e. Parent–teacher conferences

4. Discipline
   a. Classroom rules
   b. Positive rewards
   c. Consequences for breaking the rules
   d. Incremental steps taken when misbehavior continues
   e. When parents will be contacted
   f. Parents need to sign the sheet concerning the classroom management and discipline policy

5. Ask families to sign up for selected issues
   a. For a private follow-up conference about their child
   b. For parent volunteers for providing instructional materials and supplies
   c. For parent volunteers to help at special events such as field trips
   d. For parent volunteers such as guest speakers in class

6. Express an interest to hear any ideas and concerns from families at any time

7. Allow time for questions at the end of the session (save several minutes if possible)

about the program, or schools may allow families to drop in at any time during open house to informally discuss issues with the teacher.

Since open houses are conducted well into the school year, materials and projects that students have prepared can be displayed. A science fair, for example, may be scheduled at the same time as an open house to provide an opportunity for families to see students' science displays. Since some of the families attending the open house may not have attended the Back-to-School Night, it is often useful to have extra copies of the handout provided at the Back-to-School Night to describe your policies. The open house is typically not a time when teachers meet with individual families about their child's progress.

Assignment Sheets. Another way to communicate with families is through an assignment sheet, which describes the assignments for the next week or two. Students are asked to show it to their parents. Some teachers prefer that parents sign the sheet and return it to school. The assignment sheet also helps students recognize the assignments that are due in the next week or two and enables the students to make plans to complete the assignments on time. Especially when students have many school-related activities or other outside-school activities, they can plan which day or days they will work on school-related assignments while still participating in their other activities.

Individual Notes and Letters. Notes and letters are written to individual parents to discuss some particular issue about their child. You can use them to request that a conference be arranged with you, to invite family members to class functions, to inform them about their child's work, or to offer suggestions.

Notes should be carefully written. They should be free of errors in spelling, grammar, and sentence structure. Furthermore, they should be brief, clear, honest, and factual. Educational jargon should be avoided. Notes and letters are especially useful for contacting families who are hard to reach by telephone.

Make sure that you address the letter with the correct names, since the parent and child may not have the same last name. If the family does not read English, try to take steps to write the letter or note in their native language. Avoid writing a letter when you are upset about a classroom event; calm down first. Try to end with a positive statement about working together for the benefit of the child.

Be cautious about sending notes home to families only when there is bad news to deliver. Certainly, there are times when such notes need to be sent. You should also send notes home to families with good news about the child's academic work or behavior. Brief, positive notes take only a few minutes to write to express pleasure about the child's performance. By systematically writing one or two notes to different parents each day, you will provide good news and help build positive relationships with them. Parents will usually talk with their child about the note, and the child may come to school the next day with a more positive attitude.

Phone Calls. Like notes and letters, telephone calls are made to families to discuss a particular issue. The phone call could request that a conference be arranged with you, invite the family to class functions, inform them about their child's work, or offer suggestions. As with notes and letters, be cautious about calling families only when you have bad news. Also call them when there is good news to report.

Phone calls can be quite brief, because you need to have only two or three positive statements to share. They are not intended to be lengthy discussions about students. The parents should be asked to tell the child about the phone call.

There are times when you need to contact the family about the child's misbehavior. You need to plan ahead before making the call. The call should begin with a statement of concern, such as "Mrs. Erickson, I care about Kristina and I feel that her behavior in the

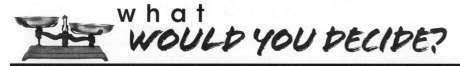

COMMUNICATING WITH FAMILIES

Sending notes or letters home to families is one way to communicate with them. To communicate effectively, you need to consider the purpose of your communications, the content, and the mode of your communications.

1. What types of information might you convey in the notes or letters?

2. What guidelines will you establish for yourself about the content, the writing form, the frequency, and other factors?

3. How might you modify your procedures if a number of parents have limited English proficiency or several ethnic groups are represented?

classroom is not in her best interest." You then should describe the specific problem and present any pertinent documentation. You should go on to describe what you are doing and have done to deal with the misbehavior. At this point, it is helpful to invite the family's input by asking questions such as "Has Kristina had similar problems in the past? Why do you think she is having these problems at school? Is there something going on at home that could be affecting her behavior?"

It is then useful to get input about how to solve the problem. State what you will do to help solve the problem, and explain what you want the parent to do. Before ending the telephone conversation, you should let the family know that you are confident that the problem can be worked out and tell them that there will be follow-up contact from you. Then recap the conversation.

Websites and E-Mail. Increasingly, schools are using computer technology and webpages to make information available to parents, students, and the public. Webpage information about the school might include the school calendar; directories for teachers, administrators, and the staff; school policies; special events; and other information.

Some schools make provisions so that each teacher has a webpage for his or her classroom. In these cases, teachers can place information on their classroom website to communicate to students and families about their syllabus, rules and procedures, notices about special events, listing of assignments or homework, Web links to useful resources, and much more. These classroom websites can be prepared, developed, and tailored by each teacher, and they can be a fine source of information for the students and families. Since these classroom websites are on the Internet, they typically are not blocked by firewalls and thus are easily accessible for good communication.

As computer use has become more common, many families have e-mail capability. Teachers can provide students and families with their e-mail addresses to open this type of communication. Families can contact the teacher with questions or comments through e-mail, and teachers can report student progress and other information to parents through e-mail. Some schools and districts, however, have firewalls or other protections to limit e-mails. In these cases, teachers need to maintain communication through other approaches.

Special Events and Informal Contacts. Throughout the year, teachers and families attend many special events. These include sporting events, concerts, plays, carnivals, craft displays, and others. Contacts with family members at these events can provide

VOICES from the Classroom

BERNADETTE HAMPTON, high school mathematics teacher, Beaufort, South Carolina

MAKING "GOOD NEWS" PHONE CALLS TO FAMILIES

To build positive relationships with parents and students, I call home for the top three students after a quiz or a test. I do this to encourage and motivate the student to excel. You can also select other criteria for the phone calls, such as most improved, most creative, or others to include most students over time.

Parents are often surprised to receive this phone call, especially when they usually receive phone calls with negative news. Students return to school with much appreciation for the good news call. The student's self-esteem is increased, and support is gained from the parent. If I need to call the parent about difficult behavior or another troublesome issue, I then have the support of the parent. The "good news" phone calls help me develop a positive relationship with the parents as well as the students.

what WOULD YOU DECIDE?

CREATING YOUR OWN CLASSROOM WEBSITE

Many schools make provisions so that each teacher has a webpage for his or her classroom. Teachers may post their syllabi, rules and procedures, notices about special events, listing of assignments or homework, web links to useful resources, and much more.

1. If you had a webpage available for your use for your classroom, how might you use it? What information might you post?

2. Would you want to only post information or would you want the webpage to have interactive capability (like a blog)? What advantages or problems might there be with a classroom blog?

brief opportunities to share a few words about their children's work. These contacts are especially useful as progress reports and as a means of discussing a particular issue.

Sending Home Student Work. You can inform families about their child's academic progress by sending home completed and graded student work. They can see what you have covered, the child's work, and any notes or remarks you have made.

Sending home only completed worksheets may not be very enlightening for families. It is useful to send home a variety of materials, including worksheets, tests, quizzes, homework, projects, lab reports, writing samples, artwork, and other types of student products. Be sensitive about notes or remarks you place on the papers. These notes are evaluative statements, but they should also include comments about good points and improvement as well as about areas still needing attention.

Papers that are sent home with students to show their parents may not actually get there, and those that do get home may not be shown to the parents. To overcome these problems, you can devise various ways to have parents sign a sheet to indicate that they have seen the material. For example, a parent response sheet might list the material being sent home, with a blank space for parents to sign and date. The student then returns the response sheet to you.

Report Cards. Families are informed of their child's academic performance when report cards are distributed. Most report cards have an area where you can either write a statement or indicate a code for a statement concerning effort and citizenship. As with notes, letters, and phone calls, you should be cautious about making only negative notes on report cards. Deserving students should receive positive notes.

When warranted, include notes on the report card to indicate the need to improve. Families may call teachers shortly after report cards have been delivered if they have any question about them. Have documentation ready to justify what you have noted.

Grade book software often provides the capability to print out reports for individual students, which display each assessment measure, points earned, and point tallies. These individual student printouts can be useful if family members inquire about their child's grade. The printouts can also be generated for individual students for parent–teacher conferences, which are considered in the next section.

PARENT–TEACHER CONFERENCES

Another important way of communicating with families is through **parent–teacher conferences** to report information about progress, academic performance, or behavior.

VOICES from the Classroom

ANA BERMUDEZ, second-grade teacher (National Board Certified Teacher), Miami, Florida

WAYS TO COMMUNICATE WITH PARENTS

I believe that most parents want to be involved in their children's education. Due to different circumstances, however, they may not be able to fully engage in the process. As a teacher, I understand the importance of parent–teacher communication and how it benefits the students. Therefore, I make it a priority to communicate with parents constantly. I keep all my contact records in Microsoft Outlook; it is a great way to keep track of everything and to have it readily available.

There are many different ways I reach out to parents. I send *weekly notes* reminding them of events and activities. Every time there is a new concept introduced in math, I send them a *letter* with family activities that deal with the new skill. I *e*-mail parents back and forth, which I find is the fastest and best way to reach many of them. I make *good news phone calls* to share positive information about student behavior or performance. I *meet with parents* before the report cards go home so they have an opportunity to help their child. I also *send tests home* so parents can see the mistakes and then better guide their children.

I basically have constant contact with parents, and they are so appreciative of this. By keeping them informed, I start a blossoming relationship with many of the parents that ultimately affects their children in a positive way. Parents need to see how much a teacher cares for their child.

URBAN EDUCATION

Many school districts schedule a day or two at the end of each report card period for parent–teacher conferences so parents can meet individually with teachers. Conference days are typically scheduled only for elementary grades; all parents are invited to attend these individually scheduled conferences.

Many middle schools, junior high schools, and high schools do not schedule parent–teacher conferences but instead arrange for a block of time on one day at the end of the report card period for families to visit with each teacher on a drop-in basis. The ways to prepare for and conduct this session will be somewhat different than that used at the elementary level, but the general principles discussed here for preparing for this contact still apply.

In addition to the conferences conducted at the end of report card periods, parent–teacher conferences are held with particular parents as the need warrants. When a student persistently misbehaves or has academic problems, you may ask the family of that child to come to the school for a conference. Prior to having such a conference, you may want to meet with the student to work out a plan to address the problem. If this meeting with the student does not lead to resolution, then a meeting with the family is warranted, and the student may be asked to also attend.

To have effective parent–teacher conferences, teachers should thoroughly prepare for the meeting, take certain actions when conducting the conference, and provide appropriate follow-up. Guidelines discussed in the following sections center primarily on parent–teacher conferences to address academic issues. These guidelines would need to be adapted somewhat to address individually scheduled parent–teacher conferences concerning academic or disciplinary issues.

Preparing for the Conference. Preparation for a drop-in conference with the family at the end of the report card period will be different from preparation for an individually scheduled parent–teacher conference. Administrators in middle schools, junior

Hui Chen is an eighth-grade mathematics teacher at a middle school. At a grade-level team meeting about six months into the school year, Ms. Chen and her colleagues discussed issues of concern. They noted that one of their students, Miranda, had been struggling in all of her classes all year. Miranda was on the verge of failing three of these classes, and she would likely have to repeat the eighth grade unless her performance improved. Even when the teachers had discussed Miranda in previous team meetings, they had agreed that her poor organizational and study skills contributed to her current academic standing.

Ms. Chen and her colleagues scheduled a student–teacher meeting with Miranda, where they discussed ways to improve her organizational and study skills. Miranda was given a booklet to record her homework assignments, and she was encouraged to attend after-school homework sessions. Despite these efforts, Miranda continued to struggle in all of her classes, and her grades worsened. After determining that Miranda was on the verge of being held back, Ms. Chen and her colleagues decided to contact Miranda's family.

When Ms. Chen telephoned Miranda's family, the conversation was tension filled and awkward. Miranda's parents were frustrated that they had not been contacted sooner. They stated that Miranda had never performed at the top of her class but that she always earned passing marks. Even though Ms. Chen attempted to address the issues and schedule a meeting about the concerns, Miranda's parents refused and declared that they would go straight to the school administration to discuss their daughter's situation.

FOCUS QUESTIONS

1. What errors did the teachers make in handling the situation with Miranda?

2. How could the teachers have handled the situation differently to establish better communication and collaboration with Miranda's parents from the start?

high schools, and high schools commonly take steps to inform families about the day and time for the drop-in conferences at the end of the report card periods. Since these teachers are responsible for many students, it is usually not feasible to have sample materials available for all of them. Instead, teachers often have the grade book on hand along with sample tests, quizzes, homework, and projects that students have completed throughout the marking period.

If an individual parent–teacher conference is needed, the teacher often calls the family to schedule a day and time to meet. Before the conference, the teacher may gather pertinent materials about the student and the situation. If it is an academic issue, the teacher may collect the grade book and a sample of work done by the student, including tests, projects, and homework to be shown to the family during the conference. If it is a behavioral issue, anecdotal record sheets and other documentation may be gathered.

Whether for a drop-in conference at the end of the report card period or for an individually scheduled conference, the physical environment needs to be prepared for the session. You should arrange for (1) a table for the conference, (2) three or four adult-sized chairs for the table, and (3) a clean, tidy room. Be sure to allow enough time for the conference, and do not overwhelm parents with the presence of other school personnel or irrelevant materials.

Conducting the Conference. Discussion and questions in the conference should be sequenced to develop rapport, obtain information from the family, provide information to them, and summarize follow-up. The following guidelines include a technique to sandwich your main messages between good news or positive statements at the start and at the end of the conference. The parents who hear good comments at the start will be in a comfortable frame of mind. As the conference comes to a close, it is useful to summarize your main points and then conclude with additional positive statements.

of middle school students at-risk for failure in mathematics. *Journal of Instructional Psychology, 34,* 84–94.

Fogarty, R. J., & Stoehr, J. (2008). *Integrating curricula with multiple intelligences* (2nd ed.). Thousand Oaks, CA: Corwin Press.

Freeman, D., & Freeman, Y. (2007). *English language learners: The essential guide.* New York: Scholastic.

Freiberg, H. J., & Driscoll, A. (2005). *Universal teaching strategies* (4th ed.). Boston: Pearson/Allyn & Bacon.

Friend, M., & Cook, L. (2010). *Interactions: Collaboration skills for school professionals* (6th ed.). Boston: Pearson/Merrill.

Gagné, R. M. (1985). *The conditions of learning and theory of instruction* (4th ed.). New York: Holt, Rinehart & Winston.

Gagnon, G. W., & Collay, M. (2006). *Constructivist learning design: Key questions for teaching to standards.* Thousand Oaks, CA: Corwin Press.

Gaitan, C. D. (2005). *Involving Latino families in schools: Raising student achievement through home-school partnerships.* Thousand Oaks, CA: Corwin Press.

Gaitan, C. D. (2006). *Building culturally responsive classrooms: A guide for K–6 teachers.* Thousand Oaks, CA: Corwin Press.

Gardner, H. (1983). *Frames of mind: The theory of multiple intelligences.* New York: Basic Books.

Gardner, H. (1995). Reflections on multiple intelligences: Myths and messages. *Phi Delta Kappan, 77*(3), 202–209.

Gardner, H. (1999). *The disciplined mind: What all students should understand.* New York: Simon & Schuster.

Gareis, C. R., & Grant, L. W. (2008). *Teacher-made assessments: How to connect curriculum, instruction, and student learning.* Larchmont, NY: Eye on Education.

Gay, G. (2000). *Culturally responsive teaching.* New York: Teachers College Press.

Gay, G. (2005). Politics of multicultural teacher education. *Journal of Teacher Education, 56*(3), 221–228.

Geva, E. (2006). Second-language oral proficiency and second-language literacy. In D. August & T. Shanahan (Eds.), *Developing literacy in second-language learners: Report of the National Literacy Panel on Language Minority Children and Youth.* Mahwah, NJ: Erlbaum.

Gillies, R. M. (2007). *Cooperative learning: Integrating theory into practice.* Thousand Oaks, CA: Sage.

Glaser, J. (2005). *Leading through collaboration: Guiding groups to productive solutions.* Thousand Oaks, CA: Corwin Press.

Glasser, W. (1998). *The quality school: Managing students without coercion* (Rev. ed.). New York: HarperPerennial.

Goeke, J. L. (2009). *Explicit instruction: A framework for meaningful direct instruction.* Upper Saddle River, NJ: Pearson/Merrill.

Goldenberg, C. (2008, Summer). Teaching English language learners: What the research does—and does not—say. *American Educator, 32*(2), 8–23,42–44. Retrieved June 1, 2011, from http://www.aft.org/pdfs/americaneducator/summer2008/goldenberg.pdf

Gollnick, D. M., & Chinn, P. C. (2009). *Multicultural education in a pluralistic society* (8th ed.). Boston: Allyn & Bacon.

Good, T. L., & Brophy, J. E. (2008). *Looking in classrooms* (10th ed.). Boston: Pearson/Allyn & Bacon.

Gootman, M. E. (2008). *The caring teacher's guide to discipline: Helping students learn self-control, responsibility, and respect, K–6* (3rd ed.). Thousand Oaks, CA: Corwin Press.

Gordon, T. (1991). *Discipline that works: Promoting self-discipline in children.* New York: Plume.

Gorski, P. (2008). The myth of the "culture of poverty." *Educational Leadership, 65*(7), 32–36.

Grant, K. B., & Ray, J. A. (2010). *Home, school, and community collaboration: Culturally responsive family involvement.* Thousand Oaks, CA: Sage.

Gregory, G. H. (2005). *Differentiating instruction with style: Aligning teacher and learner intelligences for maximum achievement.* Thousand Oaks, CA: Corwin Press.

Gregory, G. H., & Chapman, C. (2006). *Differentiated instructional strategies: One size doesn't fit all* (2nd ed.). Thousand Oaks, CA: Corwin Press.

Gregory, G. H., & Parry, T. (2006). *Designing brain-compatible learning* (3rd ed.). Thousand Oaks, CA: Corwin Press.

Greytak, E. A., Kosciw, F. G., & Diaz, E. M. (2009). *Harsh realities: The experiences of transgender youth in our nation's schools.* New York: Gay, Lesbian and Straight Education Network.

Grigg, W., Daane, M., Jin, Y., & Campbell, J. (2002). *The nation's report card: Reading 2002.* Washington, DC: U.S. Department of Education.

Gronlund, N. E., & Brookhart, S. M. (2009). *Gronlund's writing instructional objectives* (8th ed.). Upper Saddle River, NJ: Pearson/Prentice-Hall.

Gronlund, N. E., & Waugh, C. K. (2009). *Assessment of student achievement* (8th ed.). Boston: Allyn & Bacon.

Guillaume, A. M. (2012). *K–12 classroom teaching: A primer for the new professional* (4th ed.). Upper Saddle River, NJ: Pearson/Prentice-Hall.

Gurian, M., & Henley, P. (2010). *Boys and girls learn differently: A guide for teachers and parents* (Rev. ed.). San Francisco: Jossey-Bass.

Gurian, M., & Stevens, K. (2007). *The minds of boys: Saving our sons from falling behind in school and life.* San Francisco: Jossey-Bass.

Gurian, M., Stevens, K., & King, K. (2008). *Strategies for teaching boys and girls: Elementary level.* San Francisco: Jossey-Bass.

Guskey, T. R., & Bailey, J. M. (2001). *Developing grading and reporting systems for student learning.* Thousand Oaks, CA: Corwin Press.

Haager, D., & Klingner, J. K. (2005). *Differentiating instruction in inclusive classrooms: The special educator's guide.* Boston: Pearson/Allyn & Bacon.

Hale, M. S., & City, E. A. (2006). *The teacher's guide to leading student-centered discussions.* Thousand Oaks, CA: Corwin Press.

Harrow, A. J. (1972). *A taxonomy of the psychomotor domain: A guide for developing behavioral objectives.* New York: Longman.

Hill, J. D., & Flynn, K. M. (2006). *Classroom instruction that works with English language learners.* Alexandria, VA: Association for Supervision and Curriculum Development.

Hogan, T. P. (2007). *Educational assessment: A practical introduction.* New York: Wiley.

Hoglund, W. L. G. (2007). School functioning in early adolescence: Gender-linked responses to peer victimization. *Journal of Educational Psychology, 99,* 683–699.

Hole, S., & McEntee, G. (1999). Reflection is at the heart of practice. *Educational Leadership, 56*(8), 34–37.

Hollingsworth, J., & Ybarra, S. (2009). *Explicit direct instruction: The power of the well-crafted, well-taught lesson.* Thousand Oaks, CA: Corwin Press.

Howard, M. (2009). *RTI from all sides: What every teacher needs to know.* Portsmouth, NH: Heinemann.

Hunter, M. (1994). *Enhancing teaching.* New York: Macmillan.

Hyman, I. A. (1997). *School discipline and school violence.* Boston: Pearson/Allyn & Bacon.

Irvine, J. J., & Armento, B. J. (2001). *Culturally responsive teaching: Lesson planning for elementary and middle grades.* New York: McGraw-Hill.

Jackson, R. R., & Lambert, C. (2010). *How to support struggling students.* Alexandria, VA: Association for Supervision and Curriculum Development.

Jacobsen, D. A., Eggen, P. D., & Kauchak, D. P. (2009). *Methods for teaching* (8th ed.). Upper Saddle River, NJ: Merrill/Prentice-Hall.

James, A. N. (2007). *Teaching the male brain: How boys think, feel, and learn in school.* Thousand Oaks, CA: Corwin Press.

Jensen, E. (2005). *Teaching with the brain in mind* (2nd ed.). Alexandria, VA: Association for Supervision and Curriculum Development.

Jensen, E. (2008). *Brain-based learning: The new paradigm of teaching* (2nd ed.). Thousand Oaks, CA: Corwin Press.

Jensen, E. (2009). *Teaching with poverty in mind.* Alexandria, VA: Association for Supervision and Curriculum Development.

Jensen, R. A., & Kiley, T. J. (2005). *Teaching, leading, and learning in pre K–8 settings: Strategies for success* (2nd ed.). Boston: Houghton Mifflin.

Johnson, D. W., & Johnson, R. T. (1999). *Learning together and alone: Cooperative, competitive, and individualistic learning* (5th ed.). Boston: Pearson/Allyn & Bacon.

Jolliffe, W. (2007). *Cooperative learning in the classroom: Putting it into practice.* Thousand Oaks, CA: Sage.

Jones, T. G., & Fuller, M. L. (2003). *Teaching Hispanic children.* Boston: Pearson/Allyn & Bacon.

Jones, V. F., & Jones, L. S. (2010). *Comprehensive classroom management: Creating communities of support and solving problems* (9th ed.). Boston: Pearson/Allyn & Bacon.

Jonson, K. F. (2010). *The new elementary teacher's handbook* (3rd ed.). Thousand Oaks, CA: Corwin Press.

Joyce, B., & Weil, M. (2009). *Models of teaching* (8th ed.). Boston: Pearson/Allyn & Bacon.

Karnes, F. A., & Stephens, K. R. (2008). *Achieving excellence: Educating the gifted and talented.* Upper Saddle River, NJ: Pearson/Prentice-Hall.

Kellough, R. D., & Carjuzaa, J. (2009). *Teaching in the middle and secondary schools* (9th ed.). Upper Saddle River, NJ: Merrill/Prentice-Hall.

Kellough, R. D., & Kellough, N. G. (2008). *Teaching young adolescents: A guide to methods and resources* (5th ed.). Upper Saddle River, NJ: Merrill/ Prentice-Hall.

Kerr, M., & Nelson, C. (2010). *Strategies for addressing behavior problems in the classroom* (6th ed.). Upper Saddle River, NJ: Merrill/Prentice-Hall.

Khalsa, S. (2007). *Break the bully cycle: Intervention techniques and activities to create a respectful school community.* Tucson, AZ: Good Year Books.

Kindler, A. (2002). *Survey of the states' limited English proficient students and available education programs and services. 2000–01 summary report.* Washington, DC: National Clearinghouse for English Language Acquisition.

Kober, N. (2006). *A public education primer: Basic (and sometimes surprising) facts about the U.S. education system.* Washington, DC: Center on Education Policy.

Kochhar-Bryant, C. A., & Heishman, A. (2010). *Effective collaboration for educating the whole child.* Thousand Oaks, CA: Corwin Press.

Kounin, J. S. (1970). *Discipline and group management in classrooms.* New York: Holt, Rinehart & Winston.

Kralovec, E., & Buell, J. (2000). *The end of homework: How homework disrupts families, overburdens children, and limits learning.* Boston: Beacon Press.

Krashen, S. (1985). *The input hypothesis: Issues and implications.* New York: Longman.

Krathwohl, D. R., Bloom, B. S., & Masia, B. B. (1964). *Taxonomy of educational objectives: Handbook II: Affective domain.* New York: David McKay.

Ladson-Billings, G. (2009). *The dreamkeepers: Successful teachers of African American children* (2nd ed.). San Francisco: Jossey-Bass.

Lassonde, C. A., Israel, S. E., & Almasi, J. F. (2009). *Teacher collaboration for professional learning: Facilitating study, research, and inquiry communities.* San Francisco: Jossey-Bass.

Lazear, D. (2003). *Eight ways of teaching: The artistry of teaching with multiple intelligences* (4th ed.). Thousand Oaks, CA: Corwin Press.

Lee, J. S., & Bowen, N. K. (2006). Parent involvement, cultural capital, and the achievement gap among elementary school children. *American Educational Research Journal, 43,* 193–218.

Leno, L. C., & Dougherty, L. A. (2007). Using direct instruction to teach content vocabulary. *Science Scope, 31,* 63–66.

Levin, J., & Nolan, J. F. (2010). *Principles of classroom management: A professional decision-making model* (6th ed.). Boston: Allyn & Bacon.

Levin, B. B., & Rock, T. C. (2003). The effects of collaborative action research on preservice and experienced teacher partners in professional development schools. *Journal of Teacher Education, 54*(2), 135–149.

Lou, Y., Abrami, P. C., Spence, J. C., Paulsen, C., Chanvers, B., & d'Apollonio, S. (1996). Within-class grouping: A meta-analysis. *Review of Educational Research, 66*(40), 423–458.

Lynch, E. W., & Hanson, M. J. (Eds.). (2011). *Developing cross-cultural competence: A guide for working with children and their families* (4th ed.). Baltimore: Paul H. Brookes.

Macionis, J. J. (2011). *Society: The basics* (11th ed.). Upper Saddle River, NJ: Pearson.

Mager, R. F. (1997). *Preparing instructional objectives* (3rd ed.). Atlanta, GA: Center for Effective Performance.

Marlowe, B. A., & Page, M. L. (2005). *Creating and sustaining the constructivist classroom* (2nd ed.). Thousand Oaks, CA: Corwin Press.

Martin-Kniep, G., & Picone-Zocchia, J. (2009). *Changing the way you teach: Improving the way students learn.* Alexandria, VA: Association for Supervision and Curriculum Development.

Marzano, R. J. (2007). *The art and science of teaching: A comprehensive framework for effective instruction.* Alexandria, VA: Association for Supervision and Curriculum Development.

Marzano, R. J. (2011). Objectives that students understand. *Educational Leadership, 68*(8), 86–87.

Marzano, R. J., Gaddy, B. B., Foseid, M. C., Foseid, M. P., & Marzano, J. S. (2009). *A handbook for classroom management that works.* Upper Saddle River, NJ: Pearson/Prentice-Hall.

Marzano, R. J., Norford, J. S., Paynter, D. E., Pickering, D. J., & Gaddy, B. B. (2005). *A handbook for classroom instruction that works.* Upper Saddle River, NJ: Merrill/Prentice-Hall.

Marzano, R. J., & Pickering, D. J. (2005). *Building academic vocabulary.* Alexandria, VA: Association for Supervision and Curriculum Development.

Marzano, R. J., & Pickering, D. J. (2007). The case for and against homework. *Educational Leadership, 64*(6), 74–79.

Marzano, R. J., Pickering, D. J., & Heflebower, T. (2011). *The highly engaged classroom.* Bloomington, IN: Marzano Research Laboratory, Solution Tree.

Marzano, R. J., Pickering, D. J., & Pollock, J. E. (2005). *Classroom instruction that works: Research-based strategies for increasing student achievement.* Upper Saddle River, NJ: Merrill/Prentice-Hall.

Marzano, R. J., Pickering, D. J., & Heflebower, T. (2011). *The highly engaged classroom.* Bloomington, IN: Marzano Research Laboratory, powered by Solution Tree.

Mastropieri, M. A., & Scruggs, T. E. (2010). *The inclusive classroom: Strategies for effective instruction* (4th ed.). Boston: Pearson/Merrill.

McCombs, B. L. (2003, April). *Defining tools for teacher reflection: The assessment of learner-centered practices.* Paper presented at the annual meeting of the American Educational Research Association, Chicago.

McEwan, E. K. (2005). *How to deal with parents who are angry, troubled, afraid, or just plain crazy* (2nd ed.). Thousand Oaks, CA: Corwin Press.

McEwan, E. K. (2006). *How to survive and thrive in the first three weeks of school.* Thousand Oaks, CA: Corwin Press.

McEwan, E. K. (2007). *40 ways to support struggling readers in content classrooms, grades 6–12.* Thousand Oaks, CA: Corwin Press.

McKnight, K. S. (2010). *The teacher's big book of graphic organizers.* San Francisco: Jossey-Bass.

McMillan, J. H. (2011). *Classroom assessment: Principles and practice for effective standards-based instruction* (5th ed.). Boston: Pearson/Allyn & Bacon.

Mertler, C. A. (2011). *Action research: Improving schools and empowering educators* (3rd ed.). Thousand Oaks, CA: Sage.

Mierzwik, N. D. (2005). *Classroom record keeping made simple.* Thousand Oaks, CA: Corwin Press.

Miller, M. D., Linn, R. L., & Gronlund, N. E. (2009). *Measurement and assessment in teaching* (10th ed.). Upper Saddle River, NJ: Pearson/Prentice-Hall.

Minott, M. (2007). *The extent to which seasoned teachers in the Cayman Islands use elements of reflective teaching in their lesson planning, implementing, and evaluation: Implication for teacher education and training globally and locally.* Report from the International University of the Caribbean. (ERIC Digest Document Reproduction Service ED495112)

Moje, E. B., Collazo, T., Carrillo, R., & Marx, R. W. (2001). "Maestro, what is quality?": Language, literacy, and discourse in project-based science. *Journal of Research in Science Teaching, 38*(4), 469–496.

Moore, K. D. (2011). *Effective instructional strategies* (3rd ed.). Thousand Oaks, CA: Sage.

Moran, C., Stobbe, J., Baron, W., Miller, J., & Moir, E. (2009). *Keys to the elementary classroom: A teacher's guide to the first month of school* (3rd ed.). Thousand Oaks, CA: Corwin Press.

Morgan, N., & Saxton, J. (2006). *Asking better questions.* (2nd ed.). Markham, Ontario, Canada: Pembroke.

Morrison, G. R., Ross, S. M., Kemp, J. E., & Kalman, H. (2010). *Designing effective instruction* (6th ed.). New York: Wiley.

Murawski, W. W. (2009). *Collaborative teaching in secondary schools.* Thousand Oaks, CA: Corwin Press.

Murnane, R. J., & Steele, J. L. (2007). What is the problem? The challenge of providing effective teachers for all children. *Future of Children, 17*(1), 15–43.

National Board for Professional Teacher Standards (NBPTS). (2005). *What teachers should know and be able to do: The five core propositions of the National Board.* Arlington, VA: Author. Retrieved May 26, 2011, from http://www.nbpts.org/about/coreprops.cfm

National Center for Education Statistics (NCES). (2005). *Dropout rates in the United States: 2005.* Washington, DC: Author. Retrieved June 1, 2011, from http://nces.ed.gov/pubs/dropout05

National Center for Educational Statistics (NCES). (2007). *Crime, violence, discipline, and safety in U.S. public schools: Findings from the School Survey on Crime and Safety: 2005–2006.* Washington, DC: Author. Retrieved April 2, 2011, from http://nces.ed.gov/pubsearch/pubsinfo.asp?pubid=2007361

National Clearinghouse for English Language Acquisition (NCELA). (2004). *Data on languages spoken by U.S. students.* Washington, DC: Author and Language Instruction Educational Programs. Retrieved June 2, 2011, from http://www.ncela.gwu.edu/stats/4_toplanguages

National Clearinghouse for English Language Acquisition (NCELA). (2005). *ELL demographics by state, 2000–2005.* Washington, DC: Author and Language Instruction Educational Programs. Retrieved June 2, 2011, from http://www.ncela.gwu.edu/stats/3_bystate.htm

National Clearinghouse for English Language Acquisition (NCELA). (2006). *How has the English language learner population changed in recent years?* Washington, DC: Author and Language Instruction Educational Programs. Retrieved June 2, 2011, from http://www.ncela.gwu.edu/expert/faq/08leps.html

National Clearinghouse for English Language Acquisition (NCELA). (2008). *Title III Biennial Report 2004–2006.* Washington, DC: Author. Retrieved Sept. 17, 2011, from http://www.ncela.gwu.edu/accountability

National Clearinghouse for English Language Acquisition (NCELA). (2011). *The growing numbers of English language learners.* Washington, DC: Author. Retrieved Sept. 17, 2011, from http://www.ncela.gwu.edu/files/uploads/9/growingLEP_0809.pdf

National Council for Accreditation of Teacher Education. (2008). *Professional standards for the accreditation of teacher preparation institutions.* Washington, DC: Author.

National Council of Teachers of Mathematics. (2000). *Principles and standards for school mathematics.* Reston, VA: Author.

National Institute of Mental Health. (2008). *Attention deficit hyperactivity disorder.* Washington, DC: Author. Retrieved May 26, 2011, from http://www.nimh.nih.gov/healthpublications/attention-deficit-hyperactivity-disorder/adhd_booklet.pdf

National Parent Teachers Association (NPTA). (2000). *Building successful partnerships: A guide for developing parent and family involvement programs.* Bloomington, IN: Solution Tree.

Newman, R. (2008). Adaptive and nonadaptive help seeking with peer harassment: An integrative perspective of coping and self-regulation. *Educational Psychologist, 42*(1), 1–15.

Newmann, F. (1990). Qualities of thoughtful social studies classes: An empirical profile. *Journal of Curriculum Studies, 22*, 253–275.

Nitko, A. J., & Brookhart, S. M. (2011). *Educational assessment of students* (6th ed.). Boston: Pearson/Allyn & Bacon.

No Child Left Behind (NCLB). (2002). U.S. Department of Education. Available online at http://www.ed.gov/nclb/landing.jhtml

Norris, S. P., & Ennis, R. H. (1989). *Evaluating critical thinking.* Pacific Grove, CA: Critical Thinking Press & Software.

Oakes, J. (2005). *Keeping track: How schools structure inequality* (2nd ed.). New Haven, CT: Yale University Press.

Olender, R. A., Elias, J., & Mastroleo, R. D. (2010). *The school-home connection: Forging positive relationships with parents.* Thousand Oaks, CA: Corwin Press.

Olsen, G. W., & Fuller, M. L. (2012). *Home–school relations: Teachers and parents working together* (4th ed.). Upper Saddle River, NJ: Pearson/Merrill.

Orlich, D. C., Harder, R. J., Callahan, R. C., Trevisan, M. S., & Brown, A. H. (2010). *Teaching strategies: A guide to effective instruction* (9th ed.). Boston: Houghton Mifflin.

Ormrod, J. E. (2011). *Educational psychology: Developing learners* (7th ed.). Upper Saddle River, NJ: Pearson/Prentice-Hall.

Ost, L., & Gates, G. J. (2004). *The gay and lesbian atlas*. Washington, DC: Urban Institute.

Osterman, K. F., & Kottkamp, R. B. (2004). *Reflective practice for educators: Professional development to improve student learning* (2nd ed.). Thousand Oaks, CA: Corwin Press.

Partnership for 21st Century Skills. (2006). *Partnership for 21st Century Skills urges states to implement 21st century skills initiatives*. Washington, DC: Author. Retrieved from http://www.p21.org/index.php?option=com_content&task=view&id=220&Itemid=64

Partnership for 21st Century Skills. (2009). *P21 framework definitions*. Washington, DC: Author. Retrieved from http://www.p21.org/documents/P21_Framework_Definitions.pdf

Payne, R. K. (2005). *A framework for understanding poverty* (Rev. ed.). Highlands, TX: aha! Process.

Payne, R. K. (2008). Nine powerful practices. *Educational Leadership, 65*(7), 48–52.

Pearson, P. D., & Gallagher, G. (1983). The gradual release of responsibility model of instruction. *Contemporary Educational Psychology, 8*, 112–123.

Piaget, J. (1952). *The origins of intelligence in children*. New York: Norton.

Pintrich, P. R. (2003). A motivational science perspective on the role of student motivation in learning and teaching contexts. *Journal of Educational Psychology, 95*(4), 667–686.

Popham, W. J. (2011). *Classroom assessment: What teachers need to know* (6th ed.). Boston: Allyn & Bacon.

Price, K. M., & Nelson, K. L. (2011). *Planning effective instruction: Diversity responsive methods and management* (4th ed.). Belmont, CA: Thomson Wadsworth.

Public Agenda. (2008). *Lessons learned: New teachers talk about their jobs, challenges and long-range plans* (Issue No. 3: Report from the National Comprehensive Center for Teacher Quality and Public Agenda). New York: Author.

Pultorak, E., & Barnes, D. G. (2009). Reflectivity and teaching performance of novice teachers: Three years of investigation. *Action in Teacher Education, 31*(2), 33–46.

Quate, S., & McDermott, J. (2009). *Clock watchers: Six steps to motivating and engaging disengaged students across the content areas*. Portsmouth, NH: Heinemann.

Raskauskas, J., & Stoltz, A. (2007). Involvement in traditional and electronic bullying among adolescents, *Developmental Psychology, 43*(3) 564–575.

Renaissance Teacher Work Sample Consortium. (2011). *Teacher work samples*. Retrieved May 17, 2011, from http://edtech.wku.edu/rtwsc/index.htm

Reynolds, C. R., Livingston, R. B., & Willson, V. (2009). *Measurement and assessment in education* (2nd ed.). Boston: Pearson/Allyn & Bacon.

Roberts, M. P. (2001). *Your mentor: A practical guide for first-year teachers in grades 1–3*. Thousand Oaks, CA: Corwin Press.

Roberts, P. L., & Kellough, R. D. (2008). *A guide for developing interdisciplinary thematic units* (4th ed.). Upper Saddle River, NJ: Pearson/Prentice-Hall.

Roberts, W. B. (2006). *Bullying from both sides*. Thousand Oaks, CA: Corwin Press.

Roberts, W. B. (2008). *Working with parents of bullies and victims*. Thousand Oaks, CA: Corwin Press.

Robins, K. N., Lindsey, R. B., Lindsey, D. B., & Terrell, R. D. (2011). *Culturally proficient instruction: A guide for people who teach* (3rd ed.). Thousand Oaks, CA: Corwin Press.

Rong, S. L., & Preissle, J. (2009). *Educating immigrant students in the twenty-first century: What educators need to know* (2nd ed.). Thousand Oaks, CA: Corwin Press.

Rosenshine, B. (1987). Explicit teaching. In D. C. Berliner & B. V. Rosenshine (Eds.), *Talks to teachers* (pp. 75–92). New York: Random House.

Rosenshine, B. (1995). Advances in research on instruction. In E. J. Lloyd, E. J. Kameanui, & D. Chard (Eds.), *Issues in educating students with disabilities* (pp. 197–221). Mahwah, NJ: Erlbaum.

Rosenshine, B., & Stevens, R. (1986). Teacher functions. In M. C. Wittrock (Ed.), *Handbook of research on teaching* (3rd ed., pp. 376–391). New York: Macmillan.

Rothenberg, C., & Fisher, D. (2007). *Teaching English language learners: A differentiated approach*. Upper Saddle River, NJ: Pearson/Prentice-Hall.

Ruiz-de-Velasco, J., & Fix, M. (2000). *Overlooked and underserved: Immigrant students in U.S. secondary schools*. Washington, DC: Urban Institute.

Russell, M., & Airasian, P. W. (2012). *Classroom assessment* (7th ed.). New York: McGraw-Hill.

Sadker, D. M., & Silber, E. S. (2007). *Gender in the classroom: Foundations, skills, methods, and strategies across the curriculum*. Mahwah, NJ: Erlbaum.

Salend, S. J. (2009). *Classroom testing and assessment for ALL students: Beyond standardization*. Thousand Oaks, CA: Corwin Press.

Sanders, M. G. (2006). *Building school-community partnerships: Collaboration for student success*. Thousand Oaks, CA: Corwin Press.

Schell, L. M., & Burden, P. R. (2006). *Countdown to the first day of school* (3rd ed.). Washington, DC: National Education Association.

Schoenfeldt, M. K., & Salsbury, D. E. (2009). *Lesson planning: A research-based model for K–12 classrooms.* Upper Saddle River, NJ: Pearson/Prentice-Hall.

Serdyukov, P., & Ryan, M. (2008). *Writing effective lesson plans: A five-star approach.* Boston: Allyn & Bacon.

Shae, T. M., & Bauer, A. (2012). *Behavior management: A practical approach for educators* (10th ed.). Upper Saddle River, NJ: Merrill/Prentice-Hall.

Shostak, R. (2011). Involving students in learning. In J. M. Cooper (Ed.), *Classroom teaching skills* (9th ed., pp. 77–99). Boston: Houghton Mifflin.

Silver, H. F. (2010). *Compare and contrast: Teaching comparative thinking to strengthen student thinking.* Alexandria, VA: Association for Supervision and Curriculum Development.

Silver, H. F., Strong, R. W., & Perini, M. J. (2000). *So each may learn: Integrating learning styles and multiple intelligences.* Alexandria, VA: Association for Supervision and Curriculum Development.

Simpson, E. J. (1972). The classification of educational objectives in the psychomotor domain. *The psychomotor domain* (Vol. 3). Washington, DC: Gryphon House.

Siris, K., & Osterman, K. (2004). Interrupting the cycle of bullying and victimization in the elementary classroom. *Phi Delta Kappan, 86*(4), 288–291.

Skinner, E. A., Kindermann, T. A., Connell, J. P., & Wellborn, J. G. (2009). Engagement and disaffection as organizational constructs in the dynamics of motivational development. In K. R Wentzel & A. Wigfield (Eds.), *Handbook of motivation at school* (pp. 223–246). New York: Routledge.

Skowron, J. (2006). *Powerful lesson planning: Every teacher's guide to effective instruction* (2nd ed.). Thousand Oaks, CA: Corwin Press.

Slavin, R. E. (1995). *Cooperative learning* (2nd ed.). Boston: Pearson/Allyn & Bacon.

Slavin, R. E. (2012). *Educational psychology* (10th ed.). Boston: Pearson/Allyn & Bacon.

Slavin, R. E., Cheung, A., Groff, C., & Lake, C. (2004). Effective reading programs for middle and high schools: A best evidence synthesis. *Reading Research Quarterly, 43*(3), 290–322.

Smutny, J. F., & von Fremd, S. (2009). *Igniting creativity in gifted learners, K–6.* Thousand Oaks, CA: Corwin Press.

Sousa, D. A. (2011). *How the brain learns* (4th ed.). Thousand Oaks, CA: Corwin Press.

Spaulding, E., & Wilson, A. (2002). Demystifying reflection: A study of pedagogical strategies that encourage reflective journal writing. *Teachers College Record, 104*(7), 1303–1421.

Sprick, R. S. (2008). *Discipline in the secondary school: A positive approach to behavior management* (2nd ed.). San Francisco: Jossey-Bass.

Steffy, B. E., Wolfe, M. P., Pasch, S. H., & Enz, B. J. (Eds.). (2000). *Life cycle of the career teacher.* Thousand Oaks, CA: Corwin Press.

Stein, J., Meltzer, L., Krishnan, K., Pollica, L. S., Papadopoulos, I., & Roditi, B. (2007). *Parent guide to hassle-free homework.* New York: Scholastic.

Steinberg, A., & Almeida, C. (2004). *The dropout crisis: Promising approaches in prevention and recovery.* Boston: Jobs for the Future.

Steinberg, L. (2011). *Adolescence* (9th ed.). New York: McGraw-Hill.

Stepanek, J., Appel, G., Leong, M., Mangan, M. T., & Mitchell, M. (2007). *Leading lesson study: A practical guide for teachers and facilitators.* Thousand Oaks, CA: Corwin Press.

Stiggins, R. J., & Chappuis, J. (2012). *An introduction to student-involved assessment for learning* (6th ed.). Boston: Pearson/Allyn & Bacon.

Stobbe, M. (2007, December 4). Studies suggest online harassment of children is on the rise. *Salt Lake Tribune,* p. E4.

Taggart, G. L., & Wilson, A. P. (2005). *Promoting reflective thinking in teachers: Fifty action strategies* (2nd ed.). Thousand Oaks, CA: Corwin Press.

Teaching Commission. (2004). *Teaching at risk: A call to action.* New York: Author. Retrieved December 22, 2005, from http://www.theteachingcommission.org/press/FINAL_Report.pdf

Thompson, G. L. (2004). *Through ebony eyes: What teachers need to know but are afraid to ask about African American students.* San Francisco: Jossey-Bass.

Thompson, G. L. (2007). *Up where we belong: Helping African American and Latino students rise in school and life.* San Francisco: Jossey-Bass.

Thompson, J. G. (2007). *The first-year teacher's survival guide* (2nd ed.). San Francisco: Jossey-Bass.

Thompson, J. G. (2009). *The first-year teacher's checklist.* San Francisco: Jossey-Bass.

Thompson, J. G. (2010). *Discipline survival guide for the secondary teacher* (2nd ed.). San Francisco: Jossey-Bass.

Tileston, D. W., & Darling, S. K. (2008). *Why culture counts: Teaching children of poverty.* Bloomington, IN: Solution Tree.

Tomlinson, C. A. (2005a). *How to differentiate in mixed-ability classrooms* (2nd ed.). River, NJ: Pearson/Prentice-Hall

Tomlinson, C. A. (2005b). *The differe, Responding to the needs of all learn.* River, NJ: Pearson/Prentice-Hall.

Tomlinson, C. A., & Allan, S. D. (2000). *Leadership for differentiating schools and classrooms.* Alexandria, VA: Association for Supervision and Curriculum Development.

Tomlinson, C. A., & Imbeau, M. B. (2010). *Leading and managing a differentiated classroom.* Alexandria, VA: Association for Supervision and Curriculum Development.

Tomlinson, C. A., & McTighe, J. (2006). *Integrating differentiated instruction and understanding by design.* Alexandria, VA: Association for Supervision and Curriculum Development.

Trilling, B., & Fadel, C. (2009). *21st century skills: Learning for life in our times.* San Francisco: Jossey-Bass.

Tsui, M. (2007). Gender and mathematics achievement in China and the United States. *Gender Issues, 24*(3), 1–11.

Turnbull, A. P., & Turnbull, H. R. (2010). *Exceptional lives: Special education in today's schools* (6th ed.). Upper Saddle River, NJ: Merrill/Prentice-Hall.

Turnbull, A. P., Turnbull, H. R., Erwin, E., Soodak, L., & Shogren, K. (2011). *Families, professionals, and exceptionality: Positive outcomes through partnership and trust* (6th ed.). Upper Saddle River, NJ: Merrill/Prentice-Hall.

U.S. Department of Education. (2011a). *Effects of bullying.* Retrieved April 3, 2011, from http://www.stopbullying.gov/topics/risk_factors.html

U.S. Department of Education. (2011b). *Know the risk factors before bullying begins.* Retrieved April 3, 2011, from http://www.stopbullying.gov/topics/risk_factors.html

Valli, L. (1997). Listening to other voices: A description of teacher reflection in the United States. *Peabody Journal of Education, 72*(1), 67–88.

VanDeWeghe, R. (2009). *Engaged learning.* Thousand Oaks, CA: Corwin Press.

Vatterott, C. (2009). *Rethinking homework: Best practices that support diverse needs.* Alexandria, VA: Association for Supervision and Curriculum Development.

Venables, D. R. (2011). *The practice of authentic PLCs: A guide to effective teacher teams.* Thousand Oaks, CA: Corwin Press.

Viadero, D. (2003). Two studies highlight links between violence, bullying by student. *Education Week, 22*(36), 6.

Villa, R. A., Thousand, J. S., & Nevin, A. I. (2008). *A guide to co-teaching: Practical tips for facilitating student learning* (2nd ed.). Thousand Oaks, CA: Corwin Press.

Villa, R. A., Thousand, J. S., & Nevin, A. I. (2010). *Collaborating with students in instruction and decision making.* Thousand Oaks, CA: Corwin Press.

Vygotsky, L. S. (1962). *Thought and language.* Cambridge, MA: MIT Press.

Vygotsky, L. S. (1978). *Mind in society.* (M. Cole, trans.) Cambridge, MA: Harvard University Press.

Walsh, J. A., & Sattes, B. D. (2005). *Quality questioning: A research-based practice to engage every learner.* Thousand Oaks, CA: Corwin Press.

Walsh, J. A., & Sattes, B. D. (2011). *Thinking through quality questioning: Deepening student engagement.* Thousand Oaks, CA: Corwin Press.

Weinstein, C. S. (2011). *Middle and secondary classroom management: Lessons from research and practice* (4th ed.). New York: McGraw-Hill.

Weinstein, C. S., & Mignano, A. J., Jr. (2011). *Elementary classroom management: Lessons from research and practice* (5th ed.). New York: McGraw-Hill.

Wiggins, G., & McTighe, J. (2006). *Understanding by design* (Exp. 2nd ed.). Upper Saddle River, NJ: Pearson/Prentice-Hall.

Willard, N. (2006). *Cyberbullying and cyberthreats: Responding to the challenge of online social cruelty, threats, and distress.* Eugene, OR: Center for Safe and Responsible Internet Use.

Wolfgang, C. H. (2009). *Solving discipline and classroom management problems* (7th ed.). New York: Wiley.

Wong, H. K., & Wong, R. T. (2009). *The first days of school: How to be an effective teacher* (4th ed.). Mountain View, CA: Harry K. Wong.

Wood, C. (2007). *Yardsticks: Children in the classroom, ages 4–14* (3rd ed.). Turner Falls, MA: Northeast Foundation for Children.

Wood, D., Bruner, J. S., & Ross, G. (1976). The role of tutoring and problem solving. *Journal of Child Psychology and Psychiatry, 17,* 89–100.

Wood, J. W. (2006). *Teaching students in inclusive settings: Adapting and accommodating instruction* (5th ed.). Boston: Pearson/Merrill.

Woolfolk, A. (2010). *Educational psychology* (11th ed.). Boston: Pearson/Allyn & Bacon.

Wormeli, R. (2005). *Summarization on any subject: Fifty techniques to improve student learning.* Alexandria, VA: Association for Supervision and Curriculum Development.

Wormeli, R. (2007). *Differentiation: From planning to practice, grades 6–12.* Portland, ME: Stenhouse.

Wyatt, R. L., & White, J. E. (2007). *Making your first year a success: A classroom survival guide for middle and high school teachers* (2nd ed.). Thousand Oaks, CA: Corwin Press.

Yarhouse, M. A. (2001). Sexual identity development: The influence of valuative frameworks on identity synthesis. *Psychotherapy, 38*(3), 331–341.

York-Barr, J., Sommers, W. A., Ghere, G. S., & Montie, J. K. (2006). *Reflective practice to improve schools: An action guide for educators* (2nd ed.). Thousand Oaks, CA: Corwin Press.

SUBJECT INDEX

socioeconomic status (SES), 32, 38–39
students at risk, 38
Individualized assistance, 42–43
Individualized educational plans (IEPs), 43
Individualized study, 42
Individual notes and letters, 351
Individuals with Disabilities Education Act (IDEA),
18, 37
Individuals with Disabilities Improvement Act of 2004, 86
Inductive approaches, to promote student understanding,
181–182
Inductive instructional approaches, 123, 126, 148–157
concept attainment approaches, 148–153
inquiry and discovery learning, 153–154
problem-based strategies, 154–155
projects, reports, problems, 156–157
Inductive strategies, 126
Inferring, 101
Informal contacts, 352–353
Informal groups, 161
Information functions of grades, 313
Information on students
sources of information, 50–51
types of information, 50
using, 51
Information sheets, 349
Inquiry, 147, 148–157
defined, 153
inductive approaches based on, 153–154
Inspiration (software), 188
Instruction
differentiating, 29, 31, 43–49, 101, 147
factors related to instructional activities, 59–61
in Framework for Teaching, 8
preparations for, 231–233
sheltered instruction, 20–21
translating curriculum standards into, 65–66
varying, 41–42
Instructional decision making, 13
Instructional design. *See* Linear-rational approach to
planning
Instructional objectives, 79, 94–105
converting standards into, 94–95
defined, 94
within learning domains, 99–105
types of, 95–97
writing, 97–99
Instructional strategies, 60, 80–81, 122
InTASC Model Core Teaching Standards, 7, 10–11, 16, 62–63
application of content, 184, 189
assessment of students, 185, 287, 315
classroom discipline, 257
classroom management, 229
content knowledge, 184
curriculum influence from, 63
decision making and reflection, 5, 10–11
differentiating instruction for diverse learners, 29
instructional strategies, 129, 158
leadership and collaboration, 338
lesson delivery, 195
parents and partnerships, 339
planning, 59, 97
to promote thinking, 184–185

revision of, 334
strategies to promote understanding, thinking,
and engagement, 174
Intelligence, 27–28
Interaction
concerning essential questions, 156
in SIOP model, 217–218
Interdisciplinary planning, 84–85
Interest, 47
boosting student, 261
of teachers in students, 248
Interpreting, 101
Interstate New Teacher Assessment and Support
Consortium (InTASC), 7. *See also* InTASC Model
Core Teaching Standards
Intervention
for misbehavior, 259–269
three-step response plan for, 259–269
Interviews, 292
Introductory activities, 105
Introductory lessons, 113–114
Introductory letters, 346
Invention, 182
Iowa Tests of Basic Skills, 304

Jerkiness, 204
Jigsaw, 161
Journal writing
student, 17, 291
teacher, 16–17

Kidspiration (software), 188
Kinesthetic activities, as graphic organizers, 179
Knowledge
as essential teacher characteristic, 3–4
types of, 3–4, 6
Knowledge dimension, 100
K-W-L chart, 130

Language differences, 34–36
in collaboration with families, 343–344
English language learners (ELLs), 19–21, 34–36
Learning activities, 80–81
Learning centers, 165
Learning contracts, 165–166
Learning domains, 99–105, 134
Learning environment, 60
creating supportive, 226, 234
Learning plans, 71
Learning profiles, 47
Learning styles, 30–32
brain-compatible learning, 31–32
cognitive style, 30–31
defined, 30
knowing students', 33
sensory modality, 32
student inventory sheets, 31
student selection of test format, 45
Learning together, 161–162
Least restrictive environment, 37
Lecture, 147
Lesbian, gay, bisexual, or transgender (LGBT) students,
33–34, 276–277

in professional standards, 10–11
sample teacher reflection, 14–15
standards for, 5, 10–11
student, 268
tools for becoming more reflective, 15–17
Reflective practice, 9–10
Reflex movement, 104
Reinforcers, 249–251
activity, 250
for appropriate behavior, 261
defined, 249
social, 249
tangible, 250
token, 250–251
Reinforcing effort, to promote understanding, 173–174
Relational bullying, 276
Reliability, of good assessment instruments, 286
Remembering, 100, 101
Renaissance Teacher Work Sample Consortium, 52
Report cards, 320, 327, 353
Reporting
general principles, 328–329
grades, 326–328, 353
managing reports, 234
Reports, 291
special reports, 324
Representation, multiple means of, 48
Reprimands, 266
Research functions of grades, 313–314
Respect, 249
Responding, 102–103
Response to intervention (RTI), 86–87, 335
Restricted response essay questions, 297
Reviews, 138–139, 218–219
Rewards, 242, 270–271
Role playing, 147, 163–164
Room arrangement, 230, 236–237
bulletin boards and wall space, 239
floor space, 237–238
storage space, 238–239
Room decoration, 231
Room identification, 230
Routines, providing support for, 261
Rubrics, 180, 181
nature of, 293
sample, 293–294
Rudeness, 273
Rule-based summarizing strategy, 172
Rules
defined, 240
establishing, 234
examining need for, 240
guidelines for creating and enforcing, 240–242
obtaining commitments, 242
reminding students of, 266
rewards and consequences, 242
selecting, 240–242
teaching and reviewing, 242

Safety, classroom, 226
Sarcasm, 265, 270
Satiation, 213
Scaffolding techniques, 188–189

School administrators, collaboration with, 337
School-community partnerships, 337
School environment, management preparations and, 228–229
School/home communication, 230, 344–353
School improvement, 335
School Lunch program, 62
Schoolwide committees, collaboration with, 337
Schoolwide teams, collaboration with, 337
Scores, 312
Scoring tests, 303–304
Seat selections and arrangements, 230, 268
Seatwork, 139
managing, 209, 211
Self-assessment, 180, 181
Self-regulation, 49, 184
Semester grades, 322–323
Sensory modality, 32
Set induction, 129, 201–202
Sexual bullying, 276–277
Sexual orientation, 33–34, 276–277
Sheltered instruction, 20–21
Sheltered instruction observation protocol (SIOP)
model. See SIOP (sheltered instruction observation protocol) model
Short-answer questions, 301
Similarities, identifying, 171–172
Simulations, 164
Simulations/games, 147
SIOP (sheltered instruction observation protocol) model
addressing language objectives, 117
applying to lesson delivery, 216–219
applying to planning, 115–117
applying to practice/application, 189
applying to strategies, 188–189
building background, 116–117
components of, 21
comprehensible input, 216–217
described, 20–21
interaction, 217–218
lesson delivery, 218
lesson preparation, 115–116
review and assessment of lesson objectives, 218–219
Situational assistance, 214, 235, 260, 261–263
defined, 261
techniques use in, 261–263
Skeleton plans, 231
Skilled movements, 104
Skills
collaboration, 338–339
as essential teacher characteristic, 4
practicing, 176
Slowdowns, 204
Small-group discussions, 159
Small-group instruction, 195–197
SMARTER Balanced Assessment Consortium (SBAC), 67
Smoothness, 213
Social instructional approaches, 123, 157–164
cooperative learning, 147, 159–162, 196
discussions, 147, 157–159, 217–218
games, 147, 164
panels and debates, 147, 162–163
role playing, 147, 163–164
simulations, 147, 164

What's the Big Idea? (Burke), 113

Whole-class discussion, 157–158

Whole-group instruction, 195, 212–216

    maintaining group focus, 214

    maintaining student attention and involvement, 214–216

    managing movement through the lesson, 213

    preventing misbehavior, 212–213

Why Culture Counts (Tileston & Darling), 39

Withdrawing privileges, 267

Within-class grouping, 197

Withitness, 13, 212, 245

Work samples, 290

Writing. *See also* Reflection

    essay questions, 297–298

    instructional objectives, 97–99

    journal, 16–17, 291

    as punishment, 270

    student reflections on behavior, 268

    test directions, 302–303

Yardsticks (Wood), 27

Zones of proximal development, 124